Java™ Foundations

Introduction to Program Design & Data Structures

John Lewis
Radford University

Peter J. DePasquale
The College of New Jersey

Joseph Chase
Radford University

Java™ Foundations

Introduction to Program Design & Data Structures

Boston San Francisco New York
London Toronto Sydney Tokyo Singapore Madrid
Mexico City Munich Paris Cape Town Hong Kong Montreal

Publisher	Greg Tobin
Executive Editor	Michael Hirsch
Assistant Editor	Lindsey Triebel
Associate Managing Editor	Jeffrey Holcomb
Senior Production Supervisor	Marilyn Lloyd
Senior Marketing Manager	Michelle Brown
Marketing Assistant	Sarah Milmore
Cover Designer	Joyce Cosentino Wells
Cover Image	©Creativ Studio Heinemann/Getty Images
Senior Manufacturing Buyer	Carol Melville
Senior Media Producer	Bethany Tidd
Project Manager	Megan Schwenke/Scott Harris/Argosy Publishing, Inc.
Composition	Argosy Publishing, Inc.
Senior Media Buyer	Ginny Michaud

Library of Congress Cataloging-in-Publication Data

Lewis, John, 1963-

Java foundations / John Lewis, Peter DePasquale, Joseph Chase. -- 1st ed.

p. cm.

ISBN 0-321-42972-9 (pbk.)

1. Java (Computer program language) I. DePasquale, Peter J. (Peter Joseph) II. Chase, Joseph, 1964- III. Title.

QA76.73.J38L48845 2007

005.13'3--dc22

2007000627

ISBN-13: 978-0-321-42972-8

ISBN-10: 0-321-42972-9

2 3 4 5 6 7 8 9 10—QWT—10 09 08

To Justin, Kayla, Nathan, and Samantha. And to Sharon, for her encouragement during the great transition.

– John

To Lisa, my wife, whose belief in me and support of my work gives me great strength. All my love.

– Pete

To my loving and supportive wife Melissa and to both our families for their enduring support.

– Joe

Preface

Welcome to *Java Foundations*. This book is designed to serve as the primary resource for a two- or three-term introductory course sequence, ranging from the most basic programming concepts to the design and implementation of complex data structures. This unified approach makes the important introductory sequence more cohesive and accessible for students.

We've borrowed the best elements from the industry-leading text *Java Software Solutions* for the introductory material, reworked to complement the design and vision of the overall text. For example, instead of having graphics sections spread throughout many chapters, the coverage of graphical user interfaces is accomplished in a well-organized chapter of its own.

In the later chapters, the exploration of collections and data structures is modeled somewhat after the coverage in *Java Software Structures*, but has been thoroughly retooled to flow cleanly from the introductory material. The result is a comprehensive, cohesive, and seamless exploration of programming concepts.

Regarding Objects

Phrases like *objects-first*, *objects-early*, and *objects-late* continue to be bandied about by computing educators, despite the fact that the nuances of the pedagogy of the introductory sequence cannot be summed up so easily. We'll take this opportunity to discuss our approach.

First, this book is **purely object-oriented**, presented in a gradual, natural manner. Concepts that overlap with procedural programming, such as methods and their invocation, are discussed in terms of an object-oriented approach. Thus, no example is ever made up of a single class with multiple methods. In fact, in our examples the class that contains the `main` method never contains another.

We **use objects** right from the start, and discuss everything in object-oriented terms at all times. An overview of object-oriented concepts is given in Chapter 1, then reinforced and fleshed out throughout the book. Classes from the Java standard class library are introduced immediately, and objects from these classes are instantiated and used for the various services they provide. In the first four chapters, students explore and write programs made up of a single class with a single `main` method, but these programs actively *use* predefined classes and objects from the standard library in addition to exploring fundamental programming concepts such as expressions and conditionals.

We **never introduce third-party classes** simply as fodder to create examples. That approach can confuse students by blurring the distinction between classes that are part of the standard library (and thus always available) and "extras" thrown in by textbook authors as a convenience. Every non-library class used in an example is fully explored in this book. There's no "magic" behind the scenes.

The debate continues: should coverage of control structures come before the details of writing classes, or vice versa? The truth is there are advantages either way, and a knowledgeable instructor can capitalize on either approach. If class composition comes first, it exposes the underlying essence of objects earlier and demystifies their use. However, without the ability to use basic control structures, the examples at that point are often uninteresting and unrealistic. This book **explores control structures before writing classes**. Chapter 4 uses small, single-method examples to examine the details of conditionals and loops, providing a strong foundation for the multiclass examples in Chapter 5.

Chapter Breakdown

Chapter 1 (Introduction) introduces the Java programming language and the basics of program development. It contains an introduction to object-oriented development, including an overview of concepts and terminology. This chapter contains broad introductory material that can be covered while students become familiar with their development environment.

Chapter 2 (Data and Expressions) explores some of the basic types of data used in a Java program and the use of expressions to perform calculations. It discusses the conversion of data from one type to another, and how to read input interactively from the user with the help of the `Scanner` class.

Chapter 3 (Using Classes and Objects) explores the use of predefined classes and the objects that can be created from them. Classes and objects are used to manipulate character strings, produce random numbers, perform complex calculations, and format output. Packages, enumerated types, and wrapper classes are also discussed.

Chapter 4 (Conditionals and Loops) covers the use of boolean expressions to make decisions. All related statements for conditionals and loops are discussed, including the enhanced version of the `for` loop. The `Scanner` class is revisited for iterative input parsing and reading text files.

Chapter 5 (Writing Classes) explores the basic issues related to writing classes and methods. Topics include instance data, visibility, scope, method parameters, and return types. Constructors, method design, static data, and method overloading are covered as well.

Chapter 6 (Graphical User Interfaces) is a thorough exploration of Java GUI processing, focusing on components, events, and listeners. Many types of components and events are discussed using numerous GUI examples. Additionally, layout mangers, containment hierarchies, borders, tooltips, and mnemonics are introduced.

Chapter 7 (Arrays) contains extensive coverage of arrays and array processing. Topics include bounds checking, initializer lists, command-line arguments, variable-length parameter lists, and multidimensional arrays.

Chapter 8 (Inheritance) covers class derivations and associated concepts such as class hierarchies, overriding, and visibility. Strong emphasis is put on the proper use of inheritance and its role in software design.

Chapter 9 (Polymorphism) explores the concept of binding and how it relates to polymorphism. Then we examine how polymorphic references can be accomplished using either inheritance or interfaces. Design issues related to polymorphism are examined as well.

Chapter 10 (Exceptions) covers exception handling and the effects of uncaught exceptions. The `try-catch` statement is examined, as well as a discussion of exception propagation. The chapter also explores the use of exceptions when dealing with input and output, and examines an example that writes a text file.

Chapter 11 (Building, Testing, and Debugging) explores the details of Java packaging and introduces the use of a build file to assist in the development of medium and large-scale programs. Additionally, the chapter discusses the concepts behind testing, test case development, and unit testing via JUnit. An introduction to debugging is also presented. The examples in this chapter are built around a custom email client that the students can extend.

Chapter 12 (Recursion) covers the concept, implementation, and proper use of recursion. Several examples are used to elaborate on the discussion, including a maze traversal and the classic Towers of Hanoi problem.

Chapter 13 (Searching and Sorting) explores the linear and binary searching algorithms, as well as five sorting algorithms. This chapter also discusses the techniques for analyzing the complexity of algorithms, including recursive algorithms.

Chapter 14 (Collections and Linked Lists) discusses the purpose of collections and establishes the importance of separating the interface from the implementation. Generic types are introduced in this chapter, detailing their use in supporting the collection classes. Dynamic and fixed implementations are covered, and dynamically linked lists are explored.

Chapter 15 (Stacks and Queues) introduces two classic collections and discusses options for their implementation. In both cases, the collections are explored first conceptually, then as tools to help us solve problems, and finally by examining their underlying data structures. Both array-based and dynamic link implementations are discussed.

Chapter 16 (Trees) introduces the terms and concepts behind trees. Various implementation strategies are discussed, and a recursive, linked approach is examined in detail. An example of a binary decision tree is explored as well.

Chapter 17 (Search Trees and Heaps) covers binary search trees and a linked implementation. Tree rotation algorithms are also discussed. Then the chapter explores heaps and their implementation.

Chapter 18 (Graphs) discusses both directed and undirected graphs. Additionally, weighted graphs are explored, and the differences between breadth-first and depth-first graph traversals are covered. Minimal spanning trees are introduced, and implementation strategies are discussed.

Student CD

The CD included with each textbook contains:

- Source code for all of the programs in the text.
- The Java Software Development Kit (SDK).
- Various Java development environments, including NetBeans™, Eclipse™, Dr. Java, jGRASP™, JCreator®, and TextPad™.

Instructor Resources

The following supplements are available to qualified instructors only. Visit Addison-Wesley's Instructor Resource Center (www.aw.com/irc) or send email to computing@aw.com for information on how to access these resources.

- Presentation Slides for each chapter in Microsoft PowerPoint® format.
- Full solutions to the exercises and programming projects.
- Test Bank with powerful test generator software—includes a wealth of free-response, multiple-choice, and true/false questions.
- Lab Activities to accompany the topic progression in the text.

Acknowledgments

Educators and students from around the world have provided feedback on previous work that has allowed us to mold this book into a fresh, valuable resource. Your comments and questions are always welcome.

The talent and commitment of the team at Addison-Wesley continues to amaze us. Michael Hirsch, our editor, has keen insight into the nuances of publishing, and we greatly appreciate his collaborative approach. His assistant, Lindsey Triebel, is a source of consistent and helpful support. Marketing Manager Michelle Brown makes sure that instructors understand the pedagogical advantages of the text. Joyce Wells created the cover and interior design. Marilyn Lloyd led the production effort. The Addison-Wesley folks were supported by a talented team at Argosy Publishing, led by Megan Schwenke. Our copy editor, Bill McManus, amazed us with his eye for detail and his technical savvy. We thank all of these people for ensuring that this book meets the highest quality standards.

We'd like to acknowledge the collective input from hundreds of professors and students around the world in the development of the material upon which this book is based. There are too many of you to individually name, but your influence on *Java Software Solutions* and *Java Software Structures* is evident in *Java Foundations*.

Special thanks go to Jason Snyder at The College of New Jersey for his assistance testing code and many other contributions. Jason is starting his graduate work soon, with an eye toward computing pedagogy. His future colleagues will be lucky to have him, unless they play poker with him.

Groups like the ACM Special Interest Group on Computer Science Education (SIGCSE), the Consortium for Computing Sciences in Colleges (CCSC), and the Computer Science Teachers Association (CSTA) are phenomenal resources. Their conferences and online activities provide opportunities for educators from all levels and all types of schools to share ideas and materials. If you are a computing educator and are not involved with these groups, you're missing out.

Finally, we thank our families for their support and patience during the busy process of writing.

Feature Walkthrough

Key Concepts. Throughout the text, the Key Concept boxes highlight fundamental ideas and important guidelines. These concepts are summarized at the end of each chapter.

after another. Programs are sometimes called *applications*. *Software* consists of programs and the data those programs use. Software is the intangible counterpart to the physical hardware components. Together, they form a tool that we can use to solve problems.

A computer system consists of hardware and software that work in concert to help us solve problems.

A program is written in a particular *programming language* that uses specific words and symbols to express the problem solution. A programming language defines a set of rules that determines exactly how a programmer can combine the words and symbols of the language into *programming statements*, which are the instructions that are carried out when the program is executed.

Since the inception of computers, many programming languages have been created. We use the Java language in this book to demonstrate various programming

Listing **2.2**

```
//********************************************************************
//  Facts.java        Java Foundations
//
//  Demonstrates the use of the string concatenation operator and the
//  automatic conversion of an integer to a string.
//********************************************************************

public class Facts
{
   //-----------------------------------------------------------------
   //  Prints various facts.
   //-----------------------------------------------------------------
   public static void main (String[] args)
   {
      // Strings can be concatenated into one long string
      System.out.println ("We present the following facts for your "
                          + "extracurricular edification:");

      System.out.println ();

      // A string can contain numeric digits
      System.out.println ("Letters in the Hawaiian alphabet: 12");

      // A numeric value can be concatenated to a string
      System.out.println ("Dialing code for Antarctica: " + 672);

      System.out.println ("Year in which Leonardo da Vinci invented "
                          + "the parachute: " + 1515);

      System.out.println ("Speed of ketchup: " + 40 + " km per year");
   }
}
```

Output

```
We present the following facts for your extracurricular edification:

Letters in the Hawaiian alphabet: 12
Dialing code for Antarctica: 672
Year in which Leonardo da Vinci invented the parachute: 1515
Speed of ketchup: 40 km per year
```

Listings. All programming examples are presented in clearly labeled listings, followed by the program output, a sample run, or screen shot display as appropriate. The code is colored to visually distinguish comments and reserved words.

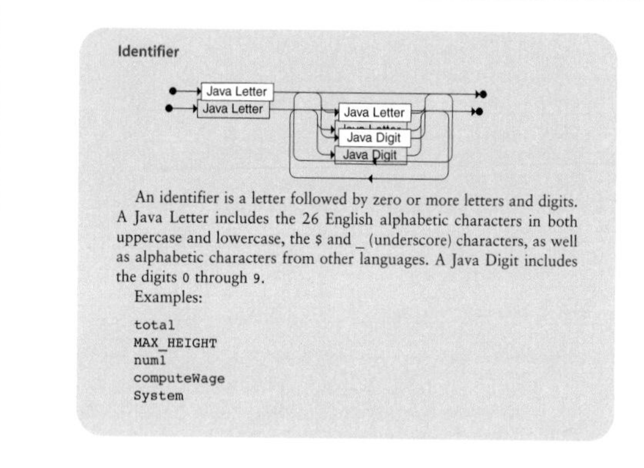

Identifier

An identifier is a letter followed by zero or more letters and digits. A Java Letter includes the 26 English alphabetic characters in both uppercase and lowercase, the $ and _ (underscore) characters, as well as alphabetic characters from other languages. A Java Digit includes the digits 0 through 9.

Examples:

```
total
MAX_HEIGHT
num1
computeWage
System
```

Syntax Diagrams. At appropriate points in the text, syntactic elements of the Java language are discussed in special highlighted sections with diagrams that clearly identify the valid forms for a statement or construct. Syntax diagrams for the entire Java language are presented in Appendix J.

Summary of Key Concepts. The Key Concepts presented throughout a chapter are summarized at the end of the chapter.

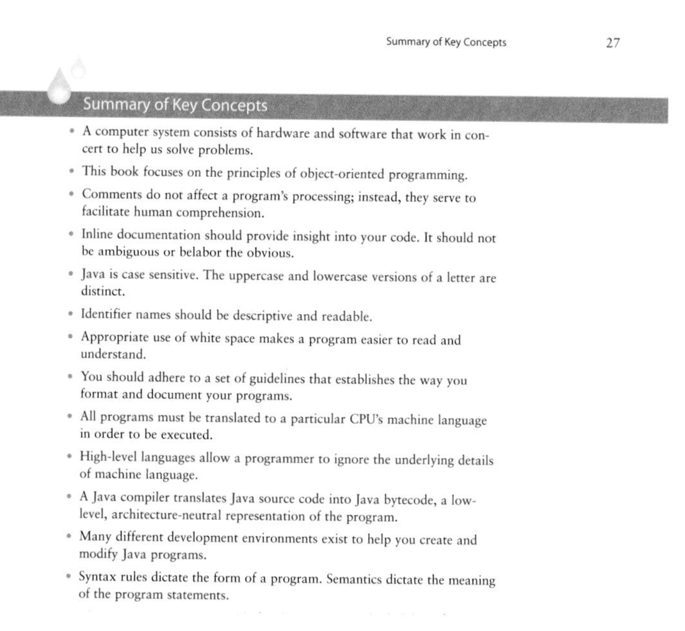

Summary of Key Concepts 27

Summary of Key Concepts

- A computer system consists of hardware and software that work in concert to help us solve problems.
- This book focuses on the principles of object-oriented programming.
- Comments do not affect a program's processing; instead, they serve to facilitate human comprehension.
- Inline documentation should provide insight into your code. It should not be ambiguous or belabor the obvious.
- Java is case sensitive. The uppercase and lowercase versions of a letter are distinct.
- Identifier names should be descriptive and readable.
- Appropriate use of white space makes a program easier to read and understand.
- You should adhere to a set of guidelines that establishes the way you format and document your programs.
- All programs must be translated to a particular CPU's machine language in order to be executed.
- High-level languages allow a programmer to ignore the underlying details of machine language.
- A Java compiler translates Java source code into Java bytecode, a low-level, architecture-neutral representation of the program.
- Many different development environments exist to help you create and modify Java programs.
- Syntax rules dictate the form of a program. Semantics dictate the meaning of the program statements.

Self-Review Questions and Answers. These short-answer questions review the fundamental ideas and terms established in the chapter. They are designed to allow students to assess their own basic grasp of the material. The answers to these questions can be found at the end of the problem sets.

Self-Review Questions

SR 1.1 What is hardware? What is software?

SR 1.2 What is the relationship between a high-level language and machine language?

SR 1.3 What is Java bytecode?

SR 1.4 What is white space? How does it affect program execution? How does it affect program readability?

SR 1.5 Which of the following are not valid Java identifiers? Why?

a. `RESULT`

b. `result`

c. `12345`

d. `x12345y`

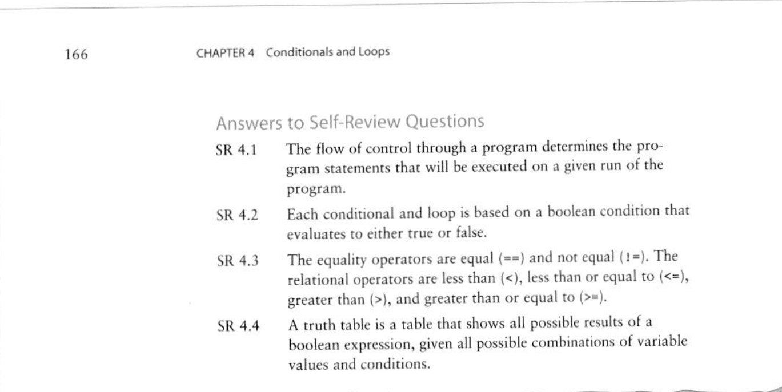

166 CHAPTER 4 Conditionals and Loops

Answers to Self-Review Questions

SR 4.1 The flow of control through a program determines the program statements that will be executed on a given run of the program.

SR 4.2 Each conditional and loop is based on a boolean condition that evaluates to either true or false.

SR 4.3 The equality operators are equal (==) and not equal (!=). The relational operators are less than (<), less than or equal to (<=), greater than (>), and greater than or equal to (>=).

SR 4.4 A truth table is a table that shows all possible results of a boolean expression, given all possible combinations of variable values and conditions.

Exercises

EX 4.1 What happens in the `MinOfThree` program if two or more of the values are equal? If exactly two of the values are equal, does it matter whether the equal values are lower or higher than the third?

EX 4.2 What is wrong with the following code fragment? Rewrite it so that it produces correct output.

```
if (total == MAX)
   if (total < sum)
      System.out.println ("total == MAX and < sum");
else
   System.out.println ("total is not equal to MAX");
```

EX 4.3 What is wrong with the following code fragment? Will this code compile if it is part of an otherwise valid program? Explain.

```
if (length = MIN_LENGTH)
   System.out.println ("The length is minimal.");
```

Exercises. These intermediate problems require computations, the analysis or writing of code fragments, and probing questions about the chapter content. While the exercises may deal with code, they generally do not require any online activity.

Programming Projects. These problems require the design and implementation of Java programs. They vary widely in level of difficulty.

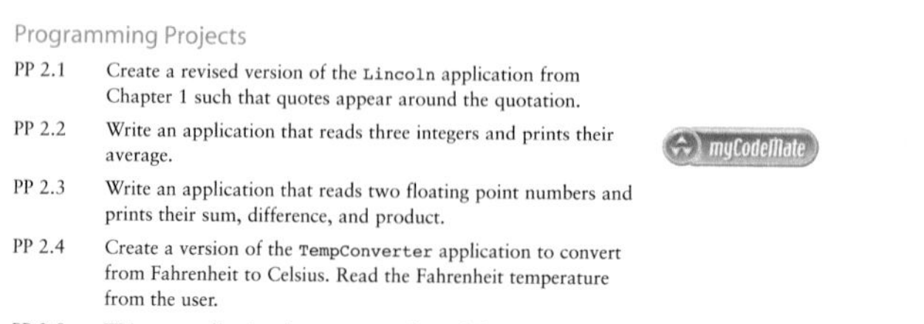

Programming Projects

PP 2.1 Create a revised version of the `Lincoln` application from Chapter 1 such that quotes appear around the quotation.

PP 2.2 Write an application that reads three integers and prints their average. myCodeMate

PP 2.3 Write an application that reads two floating point numbers and prints their sum, difference, and product.

PP 2.4 Create a version of the `TempConverter` application to convert from Fahrenheit to Celsius. Read the Fahrenheit temperature from the user.

PP 2.5 Write an application that converts miles to kilometers. (One mile equals 1.60935 kilometers.) Read the miles value from the user as a floating point value. myCodeMate

PP 4.15 Design and implement an application that simulates a simple slot machine in which three numbers between 0 and 9 are randomly selected and printed side by side. Print an appropriate statement if all three of the numbers are the same, or if any two of the numbers are the same. Continue playing until the user chooses to stop. myCodeMate

PP 4.16 Design and implement a program that counts the number of integer values in a text input file. Produce a table listing the values you identify as integers from the input file. myCodeMate

PP 4.17 Design and implement a program to process golf scores. The scores of four golfers are stored in a text file. Each line represents one hole, and the file contains 18 lines. Each line contains five values: par for the hole followed by the number of strokes each golfer used on that hole. Determine the winner and produce a table showing how well each golfer did (compared to par). myCodeMate

PP 4.18 Design and implement a program that compares two text input files, line by line, for equality. Print any lines that are not equivalent.

Addison-Wesley's MyCodeMate. Working online, students can view, compile, run, and edit select programming problems and all code listings from the textbook. Look for this MyCodeMate icon to see which Programming Projects are available with your included online subscription to MyCodeMate.

Contents

Chapter Objectives

- Introduce the Java programming language.
- Describe the steps involved in program compilation and execution.
- Explore the issues related to problem solving in general.
- Discuss the activities involved in the software development process.
- Present an overview of object-oriented principles.

Introduction

This book is about writing well-designed software. We begin by examining a very basic Java program and using it to explore some initial programming concepts. We then lay the groundwork for software development on a larger scale, exploring the foundations of problem solving, the activities involved in software development, and the principles of object-oriented programming.

1.1 The Java Programming Language

A computer is made up of hardware and software. The *hardware* components of a computer system are the physical, tangible pieces that support the computing effort. They include chips, boxes, wires, keyboards, speakers, disks, cables, printers, and so on. The hardware is essentially useless without instructions to tell it what to do. A *program* is a series of instructions that the hardware executes one after another. Programs are sometimes called *applications*. *Software* consists of programs and the data those programs use. Software is the intangible counterpart to the physical hardware components. Together, they form a tool that we can use to solve problems.

A computer system consists of hardware and software that work in concert to help us solve problems.

A program is written in a particular *programming language* that uses specific words and symbols to express the problem solution. A programming language defines a set of rules that determines exactly how a programmer can combine the words and symbols of the language into *programming statements*, which are the instructions that are carried out when the program is executed.

Since the inception of computers, many programming languages have been created. We use the Java language in this book to demonstrate various programming concepts and techniques. Although our main goal is to learn these underlying software development concepts, an important side effect will be to become proficient in the development of Java programs.

Java is a relatively new programming language compared to many others. It was developed in the early 1990s by James Gosling at Sun Microsystems. Java was introduced to the public in 1995 and has gained tremendous popularity since.

Java has undergone various changes since its creation. The most recent Java technology is generally referred to as the *Java 2 Platform*, which is organized into three major groups:

- Java 2 Platform, Standard Edition (J2SE)
- Java 2 Platform, Enterprise Edition (J2EE)
- Java 2 Platform, Micro Edition (J2ME)

This book focuses on the Standard Edition, which, as the name implies, is the mainstream version of the language and associated tools. Furthermore, this book is based on the most recent version of the Standard Edition, which is J2SE 6.0.

Some parts of early Java technologies have been *deprecated*, which means they are considered old-fashioned and should not be used. When it is important, we point out deprecated elements and discuss their preferred alternatives.

Java is an *object-oriented programming language*. Objects are the fundamental elements that make up a program. The principles of object-oriented software development are the cornerstone of this book. We explore object-oriented programming concepts later in this chapter and throughout the rest of the book.

This book focuses on the principles of object-oriented programming.

The Java language is accompanied by a library of extra software that we can use when developing programs. This software, referred to as the Java *standard class library*, provides the ability to create graphics, communicate over networks, and interact with databases, among many other features. The standard library that supports Java programming is huge and quite versatile. Although we won't be able to cover all aspects of the library, we will explore many of them.

Java is used in commercial environments all over the world. It is one of the fastest growing programming technologies of all time. So not only is it a good language in which to learn programming concepts, it is also a practical language that will serve you well in the future.

A Java Program

Let's look at a simple but complete Java program. The program in Listing 1.1 prints two sentences to the screen. This particular program prints a quote by Abraham Lincoln. The output is shown below the program listing.

All Java applications have a similar basic structure. Despite its small size and simple purpose, this program contains several important features. Let's carefully dissect it and examine its pieces.

The first few lines of the program are *comments*, which start with the `//` symbols and continue to the end of the line. Comments don't affect what the program does but are included to make the program easier to understand by humans. Programmers can and should include comments as needed throughout a program to clearly identify the purpose of the program and describe any special processing. Any written comments or documents, including a user's guide and technical references, are called *documentation*. Comments included in a program are called *inline documentation*.

Comments do not affect a program's processing; instead, they serve to facilitate human comprehension.

The rest of the program is a *class definition*. This class is called `Lincoln`, though we could have named it just about anything we wished. The class definition runs

Listing 1.1

```
//********************************************************************
//  Lincoln.java       Java Foundations
//
//  Demonstrates the basic structure of a Java application.
//********************************************************************

public class Lincoln
{
   //-----------------------------------------------------------------
   //  Prints a presidential quote.
   //-----------------------------------------------------------------
   public static void main (String[] args)
   {
      System.out.println ("A quote by Abraham Lincoln:");

      System.out.println ("Whatever you are, be a good one.");
   }
}
```

Output

```
A quote by Abraham Lincoln:
Whatever you are, be a good one.
```

from the first opening brace (`{`) to the final closing brace (`}`) on the last line of the program. All Java programs are defined using class definitions.

Inside the class definition are some more comments describing the purpose of the `main` method, which is defined directly below the comments. A *method* is a group of programming statements that is given a name. In this case, the name of the method is `main` and it contains only two programming statements. Like a class definition, a method is also delimited by braces.

All Java applications have a `main` method, which is where processing begins. Each programming statement in the `main` method is executed, one at a time in order, until the end of the method is reached. Then the program ends, or *terminates*. The `main` method definition in a Java program is always preceded by the words `public`, `static`, and `void`, which we examine later in the text. The use of `String` and `args` does not come into play in this particular program. We describe these later also.

The two lines of code in the `main` method invoke another method called `println` (pronounced print line). We *invoke*, or *call*, a method when we want it to execute. The `println` method prints the specified characters to the screen. The characters to be printed are represented as a *character string*, enclosed in double quote characters ("). When the program is executed, it calls the `println` method to print the first statement, calls it again to print the second statement, and then, because that is the last line in the `main` method, the program terminates.

The code executed when the `println` method is invoked is not defined in this program. The `println` method is part of the `System.out` object, which is part of the Java standard class library. It's not technically part of the Java language, but is always available for use in any Java program. We explore the `println` method in more detail in Chapter 2.

Comments

Let's examine comments in more detail. Comments are the only language feature that allows programmers to compose and communicate their thoughts independent of the code. Comments should provide insight into the programmer's original intent. A program is often used for many years, and often many modifications are made to it over time. The original programmer often will not remember the details of a particular program when, at some point in the future, modifications are required. Furthermore, the original programmer is not always available to make the changes; thus, someone completely unfamiliar with the program will need to understand it. Good documentation is therefore essential.

As far as the Java programming language is concerned, the content of comments can be any text whatsoever. Comments are ignored by the computer; they do not affect how the program executes.

The comments in the `Lincoln` program represent one of two types of comments allowed in Java. The comments in `Lincoln` take the following form:

```
//  This is a comment.
```

This type of comment begins with a double slash (//) and continues to the end of the line. You cannot have any characters between the two slashes. The computer ignores any text after the double slash to the end of the line. A comment can follow code on the same line to document that particular line, as in the following example:

```
System.out.println ("Monthly Report"); // always use this title
```

The second form a Java comment may have is the following:

```
/*  This is another comment.  */
```

This comment type does not use the end of a line to indicate the end of the comment. Anything between the initiating slash-asterisk (`/*`) and the terminating asterisk-slash (`*/`) is part of the comment, including the invisible *newline* character that represents the end of a line. Therefore, this type of comment can extend over multiple lines. No space can be between the slash and the asterisk.

If there is a second asterisk following the `/*` at the beginning of a comment, the content of the comment can be used to automatically generate external documentation about your program by using a tool called *javadoc*. More information about javadoc is given in Appendix I.

The two basic comment types can be used to create various documentation styles, such as:

```
// This is a comment on a single line.

//– – – – – – – – – – – – – – – – – – – – – – – – – – – – – – –
// Some comments such as those above methods or classes
// deserve to be blocked off to focus special attention
// on a particular aspect of your code. Note that each of
// these lines is technically a separate comment.
//– – – – – – – – – – – – – – – – – – – – – – – – – – – – – – –

/*
  This is one comment
  that spans several lines.
*/
```

Inline documentation should provide insight into your code. It should not be ambiguous or belabor the obvious.

Programmers often concentrate so much on writing code that they focus too little on documentation. You should develop good commenting practices and follow them habitually. Comments should be well written, often in complete sentences. They should not belabor the obvious but should provide appropriate insight into the intent of the code. The following examples are *not* good comments:

```
System.out.println ("hello");  // prints hello
System.out.println ("test");   // change this later
```

The first comment paraphrases the obvious purpose of the line and does not add any value to the statement. It is better to have no comment than a useless one.

The second comment is ambiguous. What should be changed later? When is later? Why should it be changed?

Identifiers and Reserved Words

The various words used when writing programs are called *identifiers*. The identifiers in the `Lincoln` program are `class`, `Lincoln`, `public`, `static`, `void`, `main`, `String`, `args`, `System`, `out`, and `println`. These fall into three categories:

- words that we make up when writing a program (`Lincoln` and `args`)
- words that another programmer chose (`String`, `System`, `out`, `println`, and `main`)
- words that are reserved for special purposes in the language (`class`, `public`, `static`, and `void`)

While writing the program, we simply chose to name the class `Lincoln`, but we could have used one of many other possibilities. For example, we could have called it `Quote`, or `Abe`, or `GoodOne`. The identifier `args` (which is short for arguments) is often used in the way we use it in `Lincoln`, but we could have used just about any other identifier in its place.

The identifiers `String`, `System`, `out`, and `println` were chosen by other programmers. These words are not part of the Java language. They are part of the Java standard library of predefined code, a set of classes and methods that someone has already written for us. The authors of that code chose the identifiers in that code—we're just making use of them.

Reserved words are identifiers that have a special meaning in a programming language and can only be used in predefined ways. A reserved word cannot be used for any other purpose, such as naming a class or method. In the `Lincoln` program, the reserved words used are `class`, `public`, `static`, and `void`. Throughout the book, we show Java reserved words in `blue` type. Figure 1.1 lists all of the Java reserved words in alphabetical order. The words marked with an asterisk are reserved for possible future use in later versions of the language but currently have no meaning in Java.

An identifier that we make up for use in a program can be composed of any combination of letters, digits, the underscore character (_), and the dollar sign ($), but it cannot begin with a digit. Identifiers may be of any length. Therefore, `total`, `label7`, `nextStockItem`, `NUM_BOXES`, and `$amount` are all valid identifiers, but `4th_word` and `coin#value` are not valid.

abstract	default	goto*	package	this
assert	do	if	private	throw
boolean	double	implements	protected	throws
break	else	import	public	transient
byte	enum	instanceof	return	true
case	extends	int	short	try
catch	false	interface	static	void
char	final	long	strictfp	volatile
class	finally	native	super	while
const*	float	new	switch	
continue	for	null	synchronized	

FIGURE 1.1 Java reserved words

Identifier

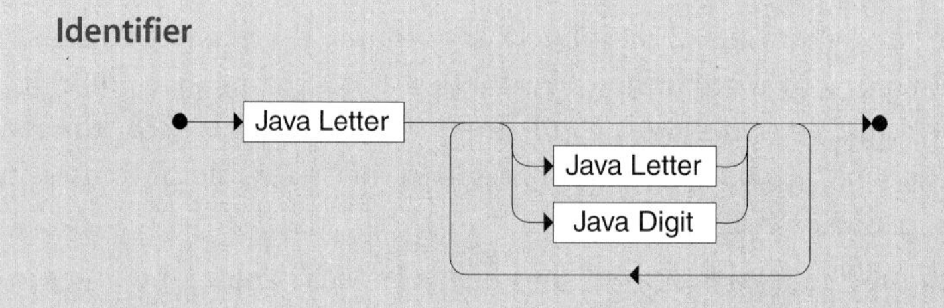

An identifier is a letter followed by zero or more letters and digits. A Java Letter includes the 26 English alphabetic characters in both uppercase and lowercase, the `$` and _ (underscore) characters, as well as alphabetic characters from other languages. A Java Digit includes the digits `0` through `9`.

Examples:

```
total
MAX_HEIGHT
num1
computeWage
System
```

Both uppercase and lowercase letters can be used in an identifier, and the difference is important. Java is *case sensitive*, which means that two identifier names that differ only in the case of their letters are considered to be different identifiers. Therefore, `total`, `Total`, `ToTaL`, and `TOTAL` are all different identifiers. As you can imagine, it is not a good idea to use multiple identifiers that differ only in their case, because they can be easily confused.

Java is case sensitive. The uppercase and lowercase versions of a letter are distinct.

Although the Java language doesn't require it, using a consistent case format for each kind of identifier makes your identifiers easier to understand. There are various Java conventions regarding identifiers that should be followed, though technically they don't have to be. For example, we use *title case* (uppercase for the first letter of each word) for class names. Throughout the text, we describe the preferred case style for each type of identifier when it is first encountered.

While an identifier can be of any length, you should choose your names carefully. They should be descriptive but not verbose. You should avoid meaningless names such as `a` or `x`. An exception to this rule can be made if the short name is actually descriptive, such as using `x` and `y` to represent (x, y) coordinates on a two-dimensional grid. Likewise, you should not use unnecessarily long names, such as the identifier `theCurrentItemBeingProcessed`. The name `currentItem` would serve just as well. As you might imagine, the use of identifiers that are verbose is a much less prevalent problem than the use of names that are not descriptive.

You should always strive to make your programs as readable as possible. Therefore, you should always be careful when abbreviating words. You might think `curStVal` is a good name to represent the current stock value, but another person trying to understand the code may have trouble figuring out what you meant. It might not even be clear to you two months after writing it.

Identifier names should be descriptive and readable.

A *name* in Java is a series of identifiers separated by the dot (period) character. The name `System.out` is the way we designate the object through which we invoked the `println` method. Names appear quite regularly in Java programs.

White Space

All Java programs use *white space* to separate the words and symbols used in a program. White space consists of blanks, tabs, and newline characters. The phrase white space refers to the fact that, on a white sheet of paper with black printing, the space between the words and symbols is white. The way a programmer uses white space is important because it can be used to emphasize parts of the code and can make a program easier to read.

Appropriate use of white space makes a program easier to read and understand.

Except when it's used to separate words, the computer ignores white space. It does not affect the execution of a program. This fact gives programmers a great deal of flexibility in how they format a program. The lines of a program should be divided in logical places and certain lines should be indented and aligned so that the program's underlying structure is clear.

Because white space is ignored, we can write a program in many different ways. For example, taking white space to one extreme, we could put as many words as possible on each line. The code in Listing 1.2, the `Lincoln2` program, is formatted quite differently from `Lincoln` but prints the same message.

Taking white space to the other extreme, we could write almost every word and symbol on a different line with varying amounts of spaces, such as `Lincoln3`, shown in Listing 1.3.

Listing **1.2**

```
//********************************************************************
//  Lincoln2.java       Java Foundations
//
//  Demonstrates a poorly formatted, though valid, program.
//********************************************************************

public class Lincoln2{public static void main(String[]args){
System.out.println("A quote by Abraham Lincoln:");
System.out.println("Whatever you are, be a good one.");}}
```

Output

```
A quote by Abraham Lincoln:
Whatever you are, be a good one.
```

Listing 1.3

```
//********************************************************************
//  Lincoln3.java       Java Foundations
//
//  Demonstrates another valid program that is poorly formatted.
//********************************************************************

           public        class
      Lincoln3
   {
                   public
   static
         void
  main
         (
String
              []
    args                              )
  {
  System.out.println         (
"A quote by Abraham Lincoln:"             )
  ;         System.out.println
              (
        "Whatever you are, be a good one."
       )
  ;
}
           }
```

Output

```
A quote by Abraham Lincoln:
Whatever you are, be a good one.
```

All three versions of `Lincoln` are technically valid and will execute in the same way, but they are radically different from a reader's point of view. Both of the latter examples show poor style and make the program difficult to understand. You may be asked to adhere to particular guidelines when you write your programs. A software development company often has a programming style policy that it requires its programmers to follow. In any case, you

You should adhere to a set of guidelines that establishes the way you format and document your programs.

should adopt and consistently use a set of style guidelines that increases the readability of your code.

1.2 Program Development

The process of getting a program running involves various activities. The program has to be written in the appropriate programming language, such as Java. That program has to be translated into a form that the computer can execute. Errors can occur at various stages of this process and must be fixed. Various software tools can be used to help with all parts of the development process as well. Let's explore these issues in more detail.

Programming Language Levels

Suppose a particular person is giving travel directions to a friend. That person might explain those directions in any one of several languages, such as English, Russian, or Italian. The directions are the same no matter which language is used to explain them, but the manner in which the directions are expressed is different. The friend must be able to understand the language being used in order to follow the directions.

Similarly, a problem can be solved by writing a program in one of many programming languages, such as Java, Ada, C, C++, C#, Pascal, and Smalltalk. The purpose of the program is essentially the same no matter which language is used, but the particular statements used to express the instructions, and the overall organization of those instructions, vary with each language. A computer must be able to understand the instructions in order to carry them out.

Programming languages can be categorized into the following four groups. These groups basically reflect the historical development of computer languages.

- machine language
- assembly language
- high-level languages
- fourth-generation languages

In order for a program to run on a computer, it must be expressed in that computer's *machine language*. Each type of CPU has its own language. For that reason, we can't run a program specifically written for a Sun Workstation, with its Sparc processor, on a Dell PC, with its Intel processor.

Each machine language instruction can accomplish only a simple task. For example, a single machine language instruction might copy a value into a register or compare a value to zero. It might take four separate machine language instructions to add two numbers together and to store the result. However, a computer can do millions of these instructions in a second, and therefore many simple commands can be executed quickly to accomplish complex tasks.

All programs must be translated to a particular CPU's machine language in order to be executed.

Machine language code is expressed as a series of binary digits and is extremely difficult for humans to read and write. Originally, programs were entered into the computer by using switches or some similarly tedious method. Early programmers found these techniques to be time consuming and error prone.

These problems gave rise to the use of *assembly language*, which replaced binary digits with *mnemonics*, short English-like words that represent commands or data. It is much easier for programmers to deal with words than with binary digits. However, an assembly language program cannot be executed directly on a computer. It must first be translated into machine language.

Generally, each assembly language instruction corresponds to an equivalent machine language instruction. Therefore, similar to machine language, each assembly language instruction accomplishes only a simple operation. Although assembly language is an improvement over machine code from a programmer's perspective, it is still tedious to use. Both assembly language and machine language are considered *low-level languages*.

Today, most programmers use a *high-level language* to write software. A high-level language is expressed in English-like phrases, and thus is easier for programmers to read and write. A single high-level language programming statement can accomplish the equivalent of many—perhaps hundreds—of machine language instructions. The term *high-level* refers to the fact that the programming statements are expressed in a way that is far removed from the machine language that is ultimately executed. Java is a high-level language, as are Ada, C++, Smalltalk, and many others.

High-level languages allow a programmer to ignore the underlying details of machine language.

Figure 1.2 shows equivalent expressions in a high-level language, assembly language, and machine language. The expressions add two numbers together. The assembly language and machine language in this example are specific to a Sparc processor.

The high-level language expression in Figure 1.2 is readable and intuitive for programmers. It is similar to an algebraic expression. The equivalent assembly

High-Level Language	Assembly Language	Machine Language
<a + b>	ld [%fp-20], %o0	...
	ld [%fp-24], %o1	1101 0000 0000 0111
	add %o0, %o1, %o0	1011 1111 1110 1000
		1101 0010 0000 0111
		1011 1111 1110 1000
		1001 0000 0000 0000
		...

FIGURE 1.2 A high-level expression and its assembly language and machine language equivalent

language code is somewhat readable, but it is more verbose and less intuitive. The machine language is basically unreadable and much longer. In fact, only a small portion of the binary machine code to add two numbers together is shown in Figure 1.2. The complete machine language code for this particular expression is over 400 bits long.

A high-level language insulates programmers from needing to know the underlying machine language for the processor on which they are working. But high-level language code must be translated into machine language in order to be executed.

Some programming languages are considered to operate at an even higher level than high-level languages. They might include special facilities for automatic report generation or interaction with a database. These languages are called *fourth-generation languages*, or simply 4GLs, because they followed the first three generations of computer programming: machine, assembly, and high-level.

Editors, Compilers, and Interpreters

Several special-purpose programs are needed to help with the process of developing new programs. They are sometimes called *software tools* because they are used to build programs. Examples of basic software tools include an editor, a compiler, and an interpreter.

Initially, you use an *editor* as you type a program into a computer and store it in a file. There are many different editors with many different features. You should become familiar with the editor you will use regularly because it can dramatically affect the speed at which you enter and modify your programs.

Figure 1.3 shows a very basic view of the program development process. After editing and saving your program, you attempt to translate it from high-level code into a form that can be executed. That translation may result in errors, in which case you return to the editor to make changes to the code to fix the problems. Once the translation occurs successfully, you can execute the program and evaluate the results. If the results are not what you want, or if you want to enhance your existing program, you again return to the editor to make changes.

The translation of source code into (ultimately) machine language for a particular type of CPU can occur in a variety of ways. A *compiler* is a program that translates code in one language to equivalent code in another language. The original code is called *source code*, and the language into which it is translated is called the *target language*. For many traditional compilers, the source code is translated directly into a particular machine language. In that case, the translation process occurs once (for a given version of the program), and the resulting executable program can be run whenever needed.

An *interpreter* is similar to a compiler but has an important difference. An interpreter interweaves the translation and execution activities. A small part of the source code, such as one statement, is translated and executed. Then another statement is translated and executed, and so on. One advantage of this technique is that it eliminates the need for a separate compilation phase. However, the program generally runs more slowly because the translation process occurs during each execution.

The process generally used to translate and execute Java programs combines the use of a compiler and an interpreter. This process is pictured in Figure 1.4. The Java compiler translates Java source code into Java *bytecode*, which is a representation of the program in a low-level form similar to machine language code. The Java interpreter reads Java bytecode and executes it on a specific machine. Another compiler could translate the bytecode into a particular machine language for efficient execution on that machine.

A Java compiler translates Java source code into Java bytecode, a low-level, architecture-neutral representation of the program.

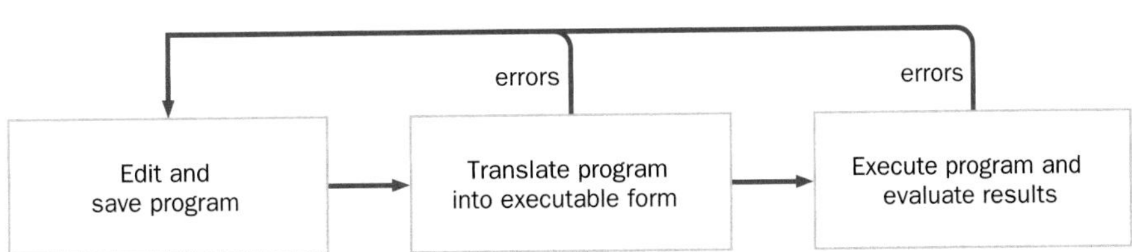

FIGURE 1.3 Editing and running a program

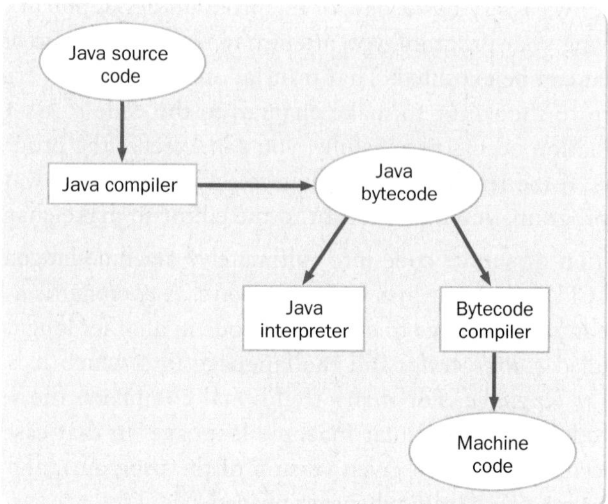

FIGURE 1.4 The Java translation and execution process

The difference between Java bytecode and true machine language code is that Java bytecode is not tied to any particular processor type. This approach has the distinct advantage of making Java *architecture neutral*, and therefore easily portable from one machine type to another. The only restriction is that there must be a Java interpreter or a bytecode compiler for each processor type on which the Java bytecode is to be executed.

Since the compilation process translates the high-level Java source code into a low-level representation, the interpretation process is more efficient than interpreting high-level code directly. Executing a program by interpreting its bytecode is still slower than executing machine code directly, but it is fast enough for most applications. Note that for efficiency, Java bytecode could be compiled into machine code.

Development Environments

A software *development environment* is the set of tools used to create, test, and modify a program. Some development environments are available for free while others, which may have advanced features, must be purchased. Some environments are referred to as *integrated development environments* (IDEs) because they integrate various tools into one software program.

Any development environment will contain certain key tools, such as a Java compiler and interpreter. Some will include a *debugger*, which helps you find errors in a program. Other tools that may be included are documentation generators, archiving tools, and tools that help you visualize your program structure.

Sun Microsystems, the creator of the Java programming language, provides the Java *Software Development Kit* (SDK), which is sometimes referred to simply as the *Java Development Kit* (JDK). The SDK can be downloaded free of charge for various hardware platforms from Sun's Java Web site, java.sun.com, and is also included on the CD that accompanies this book.

The SDK tools are not an integrated environment. The commands for compilation and interpretation are executed on the command line. That is, the SDK does not have a *graphical user interface* (GUI), with windows, menus, buttons, etc. It also does not include an editor, although any editor that can save a document as simple text can be used.

Sun also has a Java IDE called NetBeans (www.netbeans.org) that incorporates the development tools of the SDK into one convenient GUI-based program. IBM promotes a similar IDE called Eclipse (www.eclipse.org). Both NetBeans and Eclipse are *open source* projects, meaning that they are developed by a wide collection of programmers and are available for free.

Many different development environments exist to help you create and modify Java programs.

A research group at Auburn University has developed jGRASP, a free Java IDE that is included on the CD that accompanies this book. It can also be downloaded from www.jgrasp.org. In addition to fundamental development tools, jGRASP contains tools that graphically display program elements.

Various other Java development environments are available, and several are provided on this book's CD. The choice of which development environment to use is important. The more you know about the capabilities of your environment, the more productive you can be during program development.

Syntax and Semantics

Each programming language has its own unique *syntax*. The syntax rules of a language dictate exactly how the vocabulary elements of the language can be combined to form statements. These rules must be followed in order to create a program. We've already discussed several Java syntax rules. For instance, the fact that an identifier cannot begin with a digit is a syntax rule. The fact that braces are used to begin and end classes and methods is also a syntax rule. Appendix J formally defines the basic syntax rules for the Java programming language, and specific rules are highlighted throughout the text.

During compilation, all syntax rules are checked. If a program is not syntactically correct, the compiler will issue error messages and will not produce bytecode. Java has a similar syntax to the programming languages C and C++, and therefore the look and feel of the code is familiar to people with a background in those languages.

The *semantics* of a statement in a programming language define what will happen when that statement is executed. Programming languages are generally unambiguous, which means the semantics of a program are well defined. That is, there is one and only one interpretation for each statement. On the other hand, the *natural languages* that humans use to communicate, such as English and Italian, are full of ambiguities. A sentence can often have two or more different meanings. For example, consider the following sentence:

Time flies like an arrow.

The average human is likely to interpret this sentence as a general observation: that time moves quickly in the same way that an arrow moves quickly. However, if we interpret the word *time* as a verb (as in "run the 50-yard dash and I'll time you") and the word *flies* as a noun (the plural of fly), the interpretation changes completely. We know that arrows don't time things, so we wouldn't normally interpret the sentence that way, but it is a valid interpretation of the words in the sentence. A computer would have a difficult time trying to determine which meaning is intended. Moreover, this sentence could describe the preferences of an unusual insect known as a "time fly," which might be found near an archery range. After all, fruit flies like a banana.

Syntax rules dictate the form of a program. Semantics dictate the meaning of the program statements.

The point is that one specific English sentence can have multiple valid meanings. A computer language cannot allow such ambiguities to exist. If a programming language instruction could have two different meanings, a computer would not be able to determine which one should be carried out.

Errors

Several different kinds of problems can occur in software, particularly during program development. The term *computer error* is often misused and varies in meaning depending on the situation. From a user's point of view, anything that goes awry when interacting with a machine can be called a computer error. For example, suppose you charged a $23 item to your credit card, but when you received the bill, the item was listed at $230. After you have the problem fixed, the credit card company apologizes for the "computer error." Did the computer arbitrarily add a zero to the end of the number, or did it perhaps multiply the value by 10? Of course not. A computer follows the commands we give it and operates on the data we provide. If our programs are wrong or our data inaccurate, then we cannot expect the results to be correct. A common phrase used to describe this situation is "garbage in, garbage out."

The programmer is responsible for the accuracy and reliability of a program.

You will encounter three kinds of errors as you develop programs:

- compile-time error
- run-time error
- logical error

The compiler checks to make sure you are using the correct syntax. If you have any statements that do not conform to the syntactic rules of the language, the compiler will produce a *syntax error*. The compiler also tries to find other problems, such as the use of incompatible types of data. The syntax might be technically correct, but you may be attempting to do something that the language doesn't semantically allow. Any error identified by the compiler is called a *compile-time error*. If a compile-time error occurs, an executable version of the program is not created.

A Java program must be syntactically correct or the compiler will not produce bytecode.

The second kind of problem occurs during program execution. It is called a *run-time error* and causes the program to terminate abnormally. For example, if we attempt to divide by zero, the program will "crash" and halt execution at that point. Because the requested operation is undefined, the system simply abandons its attempt to continue processing your program. The best programs are *robust*; that is, they avoid as many run-time errors as possible. For example, the program code could guard against the possibility of dividing by zero and handle the situation appropriately if it arises. In Java, many run-time problems are called *exceptions* that can be caught and dealt with accordingly.

The third kind of software problem is a *logical error*. In this case, the software compiles and executes without complaint, but it produces incorrect results. For example, a logical error occurs when a value is calculated incorrectly or when a graphical button does not appear in the correct place. A programmer must test the program thoroughly, comparing the expected results to those that actually occur. When defects are found, they must be traced back to the source of the problem in the code and corrected. The process of finding and correcting defects in a program is called *debugging*. Logical errors can manifest themselves in many ways, and the actual root cause might be difficult to discover.

1.3 Problem Solving

Creating software involves much more than just writing code. The mechanics of editing and running a program are necessary steps, but the heart of software development is *problem solving*. We write a program to solve a particular problem.

In general, problem solving consists of multiple steps:

1. Understanding the problem.
2. Designing a solution.
3. Considering alternatives to the solution and refining the solution.
4. Implementing the solution.
5. Testing the solution and fixing any problems that exist.

Although this approach applies to any kind of problem solving, it works particularly well when developing software. These steps aren't purely linear. That is, some of the activities will overlap others. But at some point, all of these steps should be carefully addressed.

The first step, understanding the problem, may sound obvious, but a lack of attention to this step has been the cause of many misguided software development efforts. If we attempt to solve a problem we don't completely understand, we often end up solving the wrong problem or at least going off on improper tangents. Each problem has a *problem domain*, the real-world issues that are key to our solution. For example, if we are going to write a program to score a bowling match, then the problem domain includes the rules of bowling. To develop a good solution, we must thoroughly understand the problem domain.

Problem solving involves breaking a solution down into manageable pieces.

The key to designing a problem solution is breaking it down into manageable pieces. A solution to any problem can rarely be expressed as one big task. Instead, it is a series of small cooperating tasks that interact to perform a larger task. When developing software, we don't write one big program. We design separate pieces that are responsible for certain parts of the solution, and then we integrate them with the other parts.

Our first inclination toward a solution may not be the best one. We must always consider alternatives and refine the solution as necessary. The earlier we consider alternatives, the easier it is to modify our approach.

Implementing the solution is the act of taking the design and putting it in a usable form. When developing a software solution to a problem, the implementation stage is the process of actually writing the program. Too often programming is thought of as writing code. But in most cases, the act of designing the program should be far more interesting and creative than the process of implementing the design in a particular programming language.

At many points in the development process, we should test our solution to find any errors that exist so that we can fix them. Testing cannot guarantee that there aren't still problems yet to be discovered, but it can raise our confidence that we have a viable solution.

Throughout this text we explore techniques that allow us to design and implement elegant programs. Although we will often get immersed in these details, we should never forget that our primary goal is to solve problems.

1.4 Software Development Activities

Given that the goal of software development is to solve problems, it shouldn't surprise you that the activities involved in the software development process mirror the general problem solving steps we discussed in the previous section. In particular, any proper software development effort consists of four basic *development activities*:

- Establishing the requirements.
- Creating a design.
- Implementing the design.
- Testing.

It would be nice if these activities, in this order, defined a step-by-step approach for developing software. However, although they may seem to be sequential, they are almost never completely linear in reality. They overlap and interact. Let's discuss each development activity briefly.

Software requirements specify *what* a program must accomplish. They indicate the tasks that a program should perform, not how it performs them. Often, requirements are expressed in a document called a *functional specification*.

Requirements are a clear expression of the problem to be solved. Until we truly know what problem we are trying to solve, we can't actually solve it.

In a classroom setting, students are generally provided the software requirements in the form of the problem assignment. However, even when they are provided, such requirements need to be discussed and clarified. In professional development, the person or group who wants a software product developed (the *client*) will often provide an initial set of requirements. However, these initial requirements are often incomplete, ambiguous, and perhaps even contradictory. The software developer must work with the client to refine the requirements until all key decisions about what the system will do have been addressed.

Requirements often address user interface issues such as output format, screen layouts, and graphical interface components. Essentially, the requirements establish the characteristics that make the program useful for the end user. They may also apply constraints to your program, such as how fast a task must be performed.

A *software design* indicates *how* a program will accomplish its requirements. The design specifies the classes and objects needed in a program and defines how they interact. It also specifies the relationships among the classes. Low-level design issues deal with how individual methods accomplish their tasks.

A civil engineer would never consider building a bridge without designing it first. The design of software is no less essential. Many problems that occur in software are directly attributable to a lack of good design effort. It has been shown time and again that the effort spent on the design of a program is well worth it, saving both time and money in the long run.

The effort put into design is both crucial and cost-effective.

During software design, alternatives need to be considered and explored. Often, the first attempt at a design is not the best solution. Fortunately, changes are relatively easy to make during the design stage.

Implementation is the process of writing the source code that will solve the problem. More precisely, implementation is the act of translating the design into a particular programming language. Too many programmers focus on implementation exclusively when actually it should be the least creative of all development activities. The important decisions should be made when establishing the requirements and creating the design.

Testing is the act of ensuring that a program will solve the intended problem given all of the constraints under which it must perform. Testing includes running a program multiple times with various inputs and carefully scrutinizing the results. But it means far more than that. Testing in one form or another should be a part of every stage of development. The accuracy of the requirements, for instance, should be tested by reviewing them with the client. We revisit the issues related to testing in Chapter 11.

1.5 Object-Oriented Programming

As we stated earlier in this chapter, Java is an object-oriented language. As the name implies, an *object* is a fundamental entity in a Java program. This book is focused on the idea of developing software by defining objects that interact with each other.

The principles of object-oriented software development have been around for many years, essentially as long as high-level programming languages have been used. The programming language Simula, developed in the 1960s, had many characteristics that define the modern object-oriented approach to software development. In the 1980s and 1990s, object-oriented programming became wildly popular, due in large part to the development of programming languages like C++ and Java. It is now the dominant approach used in commercial software development.

One of the most attractive characteristics of the object-oriented approach is the fact that objects can be used quite effectively to represent real-world entities. We can use a software object to represent an employee in a company, for instance. We'd create one object per employee, each with behaviors and characteristics that we need to represent. In this way, object-oriented programming allows us to map our programs to the real situations that the programs represent. That is, the object-oriented approach makes it easier to solve problems, which is the point of writing a program in the first place.

Let's explore the specific characteristics of the object-oriented approach that help us solve those problems.

Object-Oriented Software Principles

Object-oriented programming ultimately requires a solid understanding of the following terms:

- object
- attribute
- method
- class

- encapsulation
- inheritance
- polymorphism

In addition to these terms, there are many associated concepts that allow us to tailor our solutions in innumerable ways. This book is designed to help you evolve your understanding of these concepts gradually and naturally. This section provides an overview of these ideas at a high level to establish some terminology and provide the big picture.

We mentioned earlier that an *object* is a fundamental element in a program. A software object often represents a real object in our problem domain, such as a bank account. Every object has a *state* and a set of *behaviors*. By "state" we mean state of being—fundamental characteristics that currently define the object. For example, part of a bank account's state is its current balance. The behaviors of an object are the activities associated with the object. Behaviors associated with a bank account probably include the ability to make deposits and withdrawals.

In addition to objects, a Java program also manages primitive data. *Primitive data* includes fundamental values such as numbers and characters. Objects usually represent more interesting or complex entities.

An object's *attributes* are the values it stores internally, which may be represented as primitive data or as other objects. For example, a bank account object may store a floating point number (a primitive value) that represents the balance of the account. It may contain other attributes, such as the name of the account owner. Collectively, the values of an object's attributes define its current state.

As mentioned earlier in this chapter, a *method* is a group of programming statements that is given a name. When a method is invoked, its statements are executed. A set of methods is associated with an object. The methods of an object define its potential behaviors. To define the ability to make a deposit into a bank account, we define a method containing programming statements that will update the account balance accordingly.

Each object has a state, defined by its attributes, and a set of behaviors, defined by its methods.

An object is defined by a *class*. A class is the model or blueprint from which an object is created. Consider the blueprint created by an architect when designing a house. The blueprint defines the important characteristics of the house—its walls, windows, doors, electrical outlets, and so on. Once the blueprint is created, several houses can be built using it, as depicted in Figure 1.5.

In one sense, the houses built from the blueprint are different. They are in different locations, have different addresses, contain different furniture, and are

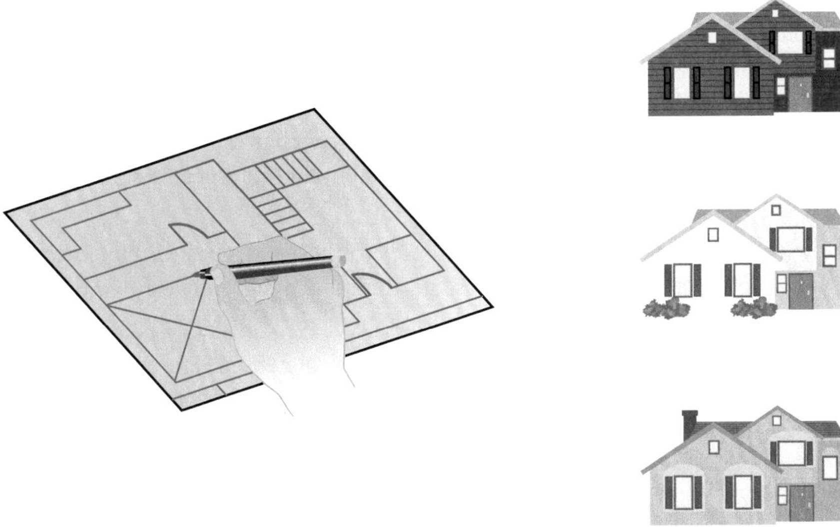

FIGURE 1.5 A house blueprint and three houses created from it

inhabited by different people. Yet in many ways they are the "same" house. The layout of the rooms and other crucial characteristics are the same in each. To create a different house, we would need a different blueprint.

A class is a blueprint of an object. It establishes the kind of data an object of that type will hold and defines the methods that represent the behavior of such objects. However, a class is not an object any more than a blueprint is a house. In general, a class contains no space to store data. Each object has space for its own data, which is why each object can have its own state.

A class is a blueprint of an object. Multiple objects can be created from one class definition.

Once a class has been defined, multiple objects can be created from that class. For example, once we define a class to represent the concept of a bank account, we can create multiple objects that represent specific, individual bank accounts. Each bank account object would keep track of its own balance.

An object should be *encapsulated*, which means it protects and manages its own information. That is, an object should be self-governing. The only changes made to the state of the object should be accomplished by that object's methods. We should design an object so that other objects cannot "reach in" and change its state.

Classes can be created from other classes by using *inheritance*. That is, the definition of one class can be based on another class that already exists. Inheritance is a form of *software reuse*, capitalizing on the similarities between various kinds of classes that we may want to create. One class can be used to derive several new classes. Derived classes can then be used to derive even more classes. This creates a hierarchy of classes, where the attributes and methods defined in one class are inherited by its children, which in turn pass them on to their children, and so on. For example, we might create a hierarchy of classes that represent various types of accounts. Common characteristics are defined in high-level classes, and specific differences are defined in derived classes.

Polymorphism is the idea that we can refer to multiple types of related objects over time in consistent ways. It gives us the ability to design powerful and elegant solutions to problems that deal with multiple objects.

Some of the core object-oriented concepts are depicted in Figure 1.6. We don't expect you to understand these ideas fully at this point. Most of this book is designed to flesh out these ideas. This overview is intended only to set the stage.

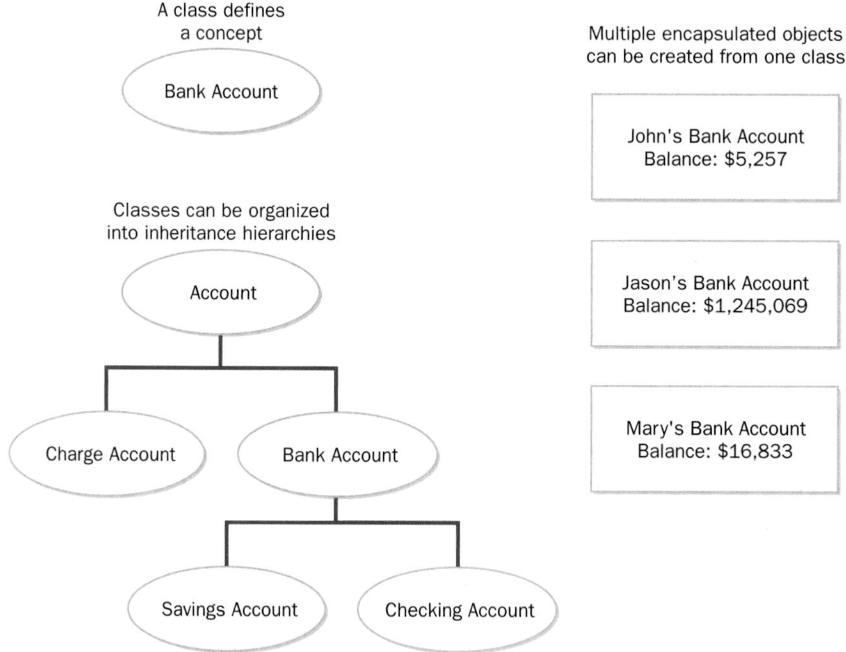

FIGURE 1.6 Various aspects of object-oriented software

Summary of Key Concepts

- A computer system consists of hardware and software that work in concert to help us solve problems.
- This book focuses on the principles of object-oriented programming.
- Comments do not affect a program's processing; instead, they serve to facilitate human comprehension.
- Inline documentation should provide insight into your code. It should not be ambiguous or belabor the obvious.
- Java is case sensitive. The uppercase and lowercase versions of a letter are distinct.
- Identifier names should be descriptive and readable.
- Appropriate use of white space makes a program easier to read and understand.
- You should adhere to a set of guidelines that establishes the way you format and document your programs.
- All programs must be translated to a particular CPU's machine language in order to be executed.
- High-level languages allow a programmer to ignore the underlying details of machine language.
- A Java compiler translates Java source code into Java bytecode, a low-level, architecture-neutral representation of the program.
- Many different development environments exist to help you create and modify Java programs.
- Syntax rules dictate the form of a program. Semantics dictate the meaning of the program statements.
- The programmer is responsible for the accuracy and reliability of a program.
- A Java program must be syntactically correct or the compiler will not produce bytecode.
- Problem solving involves breaking a solution down into manageable pieces.
- The effort put into design is both crucial and cost-effective.

- Each object has a state, defined by its attributes, and a set of behaviors, defined by its methods.
- A class is a blueprint of an object. Multiple objects can be created from one class definition.

Self-Review Questions

SR 1.1 What is hardware? What is software?

SR 1.2 What is the relationship between a high-level language and machine language?

SR 1.3 What is Java bytecode?

SR 1.4 What is white space? How does it affect program execution? How does it affect program readability?

SR 1.5 Which of the following are not valid Java identifiers? Why?

a. `RESULT`

b. `result`

c. `12345`

d. `x12345y`

e. `black&white`

f. `answer_7`

SR 1.6 What do we mean by the syntax and semantics of a programming language?

SR 1.7 Name the four basic activities that are involved in a software development process.

SR 1.8 What are the primary concepts that support object-oriented programming?

Exercises

EX 1.1 Give examples of the two types of Java comments and explain the differences between them.

EX 1.2 Which of the following are not valid Java identifiers? Why?

a. `Factorial`

b. `anExtremelyLongIdentifierIfYouAskMe`

c. `2ndLevel`

d. `level2`

e. `MAX_SIZE`

f. `highest$`

g. `hook&ladder`

EX 1.3 Why are the following valid Java identifiers not considered good identifiers?

a. `q`

b. `totVal`

c. `theNextValueInTheList`

EX 1.4 Java is case sensitive. What does that mean?

EX 1.5 What do we mean when we say that the English language is ambiguous? Give two examples of English ambiguity (other than the example used in this chapter) and explain the ambiguity. Why is ambiguity a problem for programming languages?

EX 1.6 Categorize each of the following situations as a compile-time error, run-time error, or logical error:

a. multiplying two numbers when you meant to add them

b. dividing by zero

c. forgetting a semicolon at the end of a programming statement

d. spelling a word wrong in the output

e. producing inaccurate results

f. typing a `{` when you should have typed `(`

Programming Projects

PP 1.1 Enter, compile, and run the following application:

```
public class Test
{
   public static void main (String[] args)
   {
      System.out.println ("An Emergency Broadcast");
   }
}
```

PP 1.2 Introduce the following errors, one at a time, to the program from the programming project 1.1. Record any error messages that the compiler produces. Fix the previous error each time before you introduce a new one. If no error messages are produced, explain why. Try to predict what will happen before you make each change.

a. change `Test` to `test`

b. change `Emergency` to `emergency`

c. remove the first quotation mark in the string

d. remove the last quotation mark in the string

e. change `main` to `man`

f. change `println` to `bogus`

g. remove the semicolon at the end of the `println` statement

h. remove the last brace in the program

PP 1.3 Write an application that prints, on separate lines, your name, your birthday, your hobbies, your favorite book, and your favorite movie. Label each piece of information in the output.

PP 1.4 Write an application that prints the phrase `Knowledge is Power`:

a. on one line

b. on three lines, one word per line, with the words centered relative to each other

c. inside a box made up of the characters = and |

PP 1.5 Write an application that prints a list of four or five Web sites that you enjoy. Print both the site name and the URL.

PP 1.6 Write an application that prints the first few verses of a song (your choice). Label the chorus.

PP 1.7 Write an application that prints the following diamond shape. Don't print any unneeded characters. (That is, don't make any character string longer than it has to be.)

```
    *
   ***
  *****
 *******
*********
 *******
  *****
   ***
    *
```

PP 1.8 Write an application that displays your initials in large block letters. Make each large letter out of the corresponding regular character. For example:

```
JJJJJJJJJJJJJJJ     AAAAAAAAA     LLLL
JJJJJJJJJJJJJJJ    AAAAAAAAAAA    LLLL
       JJJJ        AAA     AAA    LLLL
       JJJJ        AAA     AAA    LLLL
       JJJJ        AAAAAAAAAAA    LLLL
J       JJJJ       AAAAAAAAAAA    LLLL
JJ      JJJJ       AAA     AAA    LLLL
 JJJJJJJJJJJ       AAA     AAA    LLLLLLLLLLLLLL
  JJJJJJJJJ        AAA     AAA    LLLLLLLLLLLLLL
```

Answers to Self-Review Questions

SR 1.1 The hardware of a computer system consists of its physical components such as a circuit board, monitor, and keyboard. Software is the programs that are executed by the hardware and the data that those programs use. Hardware is tangible, whereas software is intangible.

SR 1.2 High-level languages allow a programmer to express a series of program instructions in English-like terms that are relatively easy to read and use. However, in order to execute, a program must be expressed in a particular computer's machine language, which consists of a series of bits that is basically unreadable by humans. A high-level language program must be translated into machine language before it can be run.

SR 1.3 Java bytecode is a low-level representation of a Java source code program. The Java compiler translates the source code into bytecode, which can then be executed using the Java interpreter. The bytecode might be transported across the Web before being executed by a Java interpreter that is part of a Web browser.

SR 1.4 *White space* is a term that refers to the spaces, tabs, and newline characters that separate words and symbols in a program. The compiler ignores extra white space; therefore, it doesn't affect execution. However, it is crucial to use white space appropriately to make a program readable to humans.

SR 1.5 All of the identifiers shown are valid except `12345` (since an identifier cannot begin with a digit) and `black&white` (since an identifier cannot contain the character `&`). The identifiers `RESULT` and `result` are both valid, but should not be used together in a program because they differ only by case. The underscore character (as in `answer_7`) is a valid part of an identifier.

SR 1.6 Syntax rules define how the symbols and words of a programming language can be put together. The semantics of a programming language instruction determine what will happen when that instruction is executed.

SR 1.7 The four basic activities in software development are requirements analysis (deciding what the program should do), design (deciding how to do it), implementation (writing the solution in source code), and testing (validating the implementation).

SR 1.8 The primary elements that support object-oriented programming are objects, classes, encapsulation, and inheritance. An object is defined by a class, which contains methods that define the operations on those objects (the services that they perform). Objects are encapsulated such that they store and manage their own data. Inheritance is a reuse technique in which one class can be derived from another.

2 Data and Expressions

Chapter Objectives

- Discuss the use of character strings, concatenation, and escape sequences.
- Explore the declaration and use of variables.
- Describe the Java primitive data types.
- Discuss the syntax and processing of expressions.
- Define the types of data conversions and the mechanisms for accomplishing them.
- Introduce the `Scanner` class to create interactive programs.

This chapter explores some of the basic types of data used in a Java program and the use of expressions to perform calculations. It discusses the conversion of data from one type to another, and how to read input interactively from the user running a program.

2.1 Character Strings

In Chapter 1 we discussed the basic structure of a Java program, including the use of comments, identifiers, and white space, using the `Lincoln` program as an example. Chapter 1 also included an overview of the various concepts involved in object-oriented programming, such as objects, classes, and methods. Take a moment to review these ideas if necessary.

A character string is an object in Java, defined by the class `String`. Because strings are so fundamental to computer programming, Java provides the ability to use a *string literal*, delimited by double quotation characters, as we've seen in previous examples. We explore the `String` class and its methods in more detail in Chapter 3. For now, let's explore the use of string literals further.

The following are all examples of valid string literals:

```
"The quick brown fox jumped over the lazy dog."
"2201 Birch Leaf Lane, Blacksburg, VA 24060"
"x"
""
```

A string literal can contain any valid characters, including numeric digits, punctuation, and other special characters. The last example in the list above contains no characters at all.

The `print` and `println` Methods

In the `Lincoln` program in Chapter 1, we invoked the `println` method as follows:

```
System.out.println ("Whatever you are, be a good one.");
```

This statement demonstrates the use of objects. The `System.out` object represents an output device or file, which by default is the monitor screen. To be more precise, the object's name is `out` and it is stored in the `System` class. We explore that relationship in more detail at the appropriate point in the text.

The `println` method is a service that the `System.out` object performs for us. Whenever we request it, the object will print a character string to the screen. We can say that we send the `println` message to the `System.out` object to request that some text be printed.

Each piece of data that we send to a method is called a *parameter*. In this case, the `println` method takes only one parameter: the string of characters to be printed.

The `System.out` object also provides another service we can use: the `print` method. The difference between `print` and `println` is small but important. The `println` method prints the information sent to it, then moves to the beginning of the next line. The `print` method is similar to `println`, but does not advance to the next line when completed.

The `print` and `println` methods represent two services provided by the `System.out` object.

The program shown in Listing 2.1 is called `Countdown`, and it invokes both the `print` and `println` methods.

Listing 2.1

```
//********************************************************************
//  Countdown.java       Java Foundations
//
//  Demonstrates the difference between print and println.
//********************************************************************

public class Countdown
{
   //-----------------------------------------------------------------
   //  Prints two lines of output representing a rocket countdown.
   //-----------------------------------------------------------------
   public static void main (String[] args)
   {
      System.out.print ("Three... ");
      System.out.print ("Two... ");
      System.out.print ("One... ");
      System.out.print ("Zero... ");

      System.out.println ("Liftoff!"); // appears on first output line

      System.out.println ("Houston, we have a problem.");
   }
}
```

Output

```
Three... Two... One... Zero... Liftoff!
Houston, we have a problem.
```

Carefully compare the output of the `Countdown` program, shown at the bottom of the program listing, to the program code. Note that the word `Liftoff` is printed on the same line as the first few words, even though it is printed using the `println` method. Remember that the `println` method moves to the beginning of the next line *after* the information passed to it is printed.

String Concatenation

A string literal cannot span multiple lines in a program. The following program statement is improper syntax and would produce an error when attempting to compile:

```
// The following statement will not compile
System.out.println ("The only stupid question is
the one that's not asked.");
```

When we want to print a string that is too long to fit on one line in a program, we can rely on *string concatenation* to append one string to the end of another. The string concatenation operator is the plus sign (+). The following expression concatenates one character string to another, producing one long string:

```
"The only stupid question is " + "the one that's not asked."
```

The program called `Facts` shown in Listing 2.2 contains several `println` statements. The first one prints a sentence that is somewhat long and will not fit on one line of the program. Since a character literal cannot span two lines in a program, we split the string into two and use string concatenation to append them. Therefore, the string concatenation operation in the first `println` statement results in one large string that is passed to the method to be printed.

Note that we don't have to pass any information to the `println` method, as shown in the second line of the `Facts` program. This call does not print any visible characters, but it does move to the next line of output. So in this case calling `println` with no parameters has the effect of printing a blank line.

The last three calls to `println` in the `Facts` program demonstrate another interesting thing about string concatenation: Strings can be concatenated with numbers. Note that the numbers in those lines are not enclosed in double quotes and are therefore not character strings. In these cases, the number is automatically converted to a string, and then the two strings are concatenated.

Listing **2.2**

```
//********************************************************************
//  Facts.java       Java Foundations
//
//  Demonstrates the use of the string concatenation operator and the
//  automatic conversion of an integer to a string.
//********************************************************************

public class Facts
{
   //-----------------------------------------------------------------
   //  Prints various facts.
   //-----------------------------------------------------------------
   public static void main (String[] args)
   {
      // Strings can be concatenated into one long string
      System.out.println ("We present the following facts for your "
                          + "extracurricular edification:");

      System.out.println ();

      // A string can contain numeric digits
      System.out.println ("Letters in the Hawaiian alphabet: 12");

      // A numeric value can be concatenated to a string
      System.out.println ("Dialing code for Antarctica: " + 672);

      System.out.println ("Year in which Leonardo da Vinci invented "
                          + "the parachute: " + 1515);

      System.out.println ("Speed of ketchup: " + 40 + " km per year");
   }
}
```

Output

```
We present the following facts for your extracurricular edification:

Letters in the Hawaiian alphabet: 12
Dialing code for Antarctica: 672
Year in which Leonardo da Vinci invented the parachute: 1515
Speed of ketchup: 40 km per year
```

Because we are printing particular values, we simply could have included the numeric value as part of the string literal, such as:

```
"Speed of ketchup: 40 km per year"
```

Digits are characters and can be included in strings as needed. We separate them in the `Facts` program to demonstrate the ability to concatenate a string and a number. This technique will be useful in upcoming examples.

As you might think, the + operator is also used for arithmetic addition. Therefore, what the + operator does depends on the types of data on which it operates. If either or both of the operands of the + operator are strings, then string concatenation is performed.

In Java, the + operator is used both for addition and for string concatenation.

The `Addition` program shown in Listing 2.3 demonstrates the distinction between string concatenation and arithmetic addition. The `Addition` program uses the + operator four times. In the first

Listing **2.3**

```
//********************************************************************
//  Addition.java        Java Foundations
//
//  Demonstrates the difference between the addition and string
//  concatenation operators.
//********************************************************************

public class Addition
{
   //-----------------------------------------------------------------
   //  Concatenates and adds two numbers and prints the results.
   //-----------------------------------------------------------------
   public static void main (String[] args)
   {
      System.out.println ("24 and 45 concatenated: " + 24 + 45);

      System.out.println ("24 and 45 added: " + (24 + 45));
   }
}
```

Output

```
24 and 45 concatenated: 2445
24 and 45 added: 69
```

call to `println`, both + operations perform string concatenation, because the operators are executed left to right. The first operator concatenates the string with the first number (`24`), creating a larger string. Then that string is concatenated with the second number (`45`), creating an even larger string, which gets printed.

In the second call to `println`, we use parentheses to group the + operation with the two numeric operands. This forces that operation to happen first. Because both operands are numbers, the numbers are added in the arithmetic sense, producing the result `69`. That number is then concatenated with the string, producing a larger string that gets printed.

We revisit this type of situation later in this chapter when we formalize the precedence rules that define the order in which operators get evaluated.

Escape Sequences

Because the double quotation character (`"`) is used in the Java language to indicate the beginning and end of a string, we must use a special technique to print the quotation character. If we simply put it in a string (`"""`), the compiler gets confused because it thinks the second quotation character is the end of the string and doesn't know what to do with the third one. This results in a compile-time error.

To overcome this problem, Java defines several *escape sequences* to represent special characters. An escape sequence begins with the backslash character (`\`), which indicates that the character or characters that follow should be interpreted in a special way. Figure 2.1 lists the Java escape sequences.

An escape sequence can be used to represent a character that would otherwise cause compilation problems.

The program in Listing 2.4, called `Roses`, prints some text resembling a poem. It uses only one `println` statement to do so, despite the fact that the poem is several lines long. Note the escape sequences used throughout the string. The `\n` escape sequence forces the output to a new line, and the `\t` escape sequence represents a tab character. (Note that you may see a different amount of indentation when you run this program—tab stops depend on the system settings.) The `\"` escape sequence ensures that the quote character is treated as part of the string, not the termination of it, which enables it to be printed as part of the output.

Escape Sequence	Meaning
\b	backspace
\t	tab
\n	newline
\r	carriage return
\"	double quote
\'	single quote
\\	backslash

FIGURE 2.1 Java escape sequences

Listing **2.4**

```
//********************************************************************
//  Roses.java       Java Foundations
//
//  Demonstrates the use of escape sequences.
//********************************************************************

public class Roses
{
   //-----------------------------------------------------------------
   //  Prints a poem (of sorts) on multiple lines.
   //-----------------------------------------------------------------
   public static void main (String[] args)
   {
      System.out.println ("Roses are red,\n\tViolets are blue,\n" +
         "Sugar is sweet,\n\tBut I have \"commitment issues\",\n\t" +
         "So I'd rather just be friends\n\tAt this point in our " +
         "relationship.");
   }
}
```

Output

```
Roses are red,
        Violets are blue,
Sugar is sweet,
        But I have "commitment issues",
        So I'd rather just be friends
        At this point in our relationship.
```

2.2 Variables and Assignment

Most of the information we manage in a program is represented by variables. Let's examine how we declare and use them in a program.

Variables

A *variable* is a name for a location in memory used to hold a data value. A variable declaration instructs the compiler to reserve a portion of main memory space large enough to hold a particular type of value and indicates the name by which we refer to that location.

A variable is a name for a memory location used to hold a value of a particular data type.

Consider the program `PianoKeys`, shown in Listing 2.5. The first line of the `main` method is the declaration of a variable named `keys` that holds an integer (`int`) value. The declaration also gives `keys` an initial value of 88. If an initial value is not specified for a variable, the value is undefined. Most Java compilers

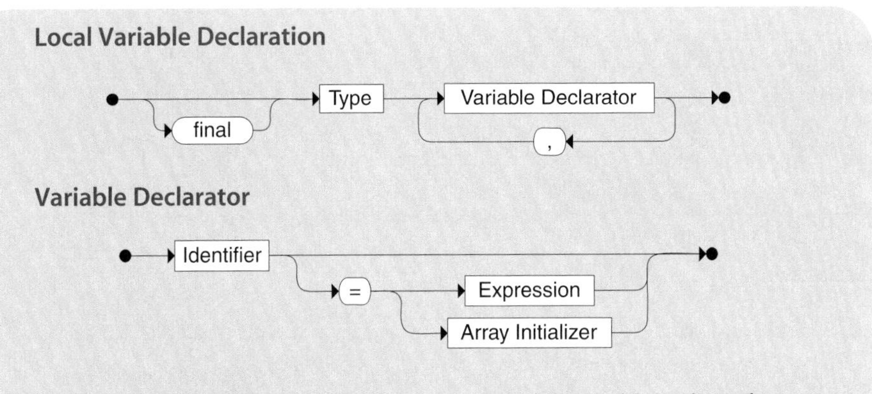

A variable declaration consists of a Type followed by a list of variables. Each variable can be initialized in the declaration to the value of the specified Expression. If the `final` modifier precedes the declaration, the identifiers are declared as named constants whose values cannot be changed once set.

Examples:

```
int total;
double num1, num2 = 4.356, num3;
char letter = 'A', digit = '7';
final int MAX = 45;
```

give errors or warnings if you attempt to use a variable before you've explicitly given it a value.

The `keys` variable, with its value, could be pictured as follows:

```
keys  [ 88 ]
```

In the `PianoKeys` program, two pieces of information are used in the call to the `println` method. The first is a string, and the second is the variable `keys`. When a variable is referenced, the value currently stored in it is used. Therefore, when the call to `println` is executed, the value of `keys`, which is 88, is obtained. Because that value is an integer, it is automatically converted to a string and concatenated with the initial string. The concatenated string is passed to `println` and printed.

A variable declaration can have multiple variables of the same type declared on one line. Each variable on the line can be declared with or without an initializing value. For example:

```
int count, minimum = 0, result;
```

Listing 2.5

```
//********************************************************************
//  PianoKeys.java        Java Foundations
//
//  Demonstrates the declaration, initialization, and use of an
//  integer variable.
//********************************************************************

public class PianoKeys
{
   //-----------------------------------------------------------------
   //  Prints the number of keys on a piano.
   //-----------------------------------------------------------------
   public static void main (String[] args)
   {
      int keys = 88;

      System.out.println ("A piano has " + keys + " keys.");
   }
}
```

Output

```
A piano has 88 keys.
```

The Assignment Statement

Let's examine a program that changes the value of a variable. Listing 2.6 shows a program called `Geometry`. This program first declares an integer variable called `sides` and initializes it to `7`. It then prints out the current value of `sides`.

The next line in `main` changes the value stored in the variable `sides`:

```
sides = 10;
```

This is called an *assignment statement* because it assigns a value to a variable. When executed, the expression on the right-hand side of the assignment operator

Listing 2.6

```
//********************************************************************
//  Geometry.java        Java Foundations
//
//  Demonstrates the use of an assignment statement to change the
//  value stored in a variable.
//********************************************************************

public class Geometry
{
   //-----------------------------------------------------------------
   //  Prints the number of sides of several geometric shapes.
   //-----------------------------------------------------------------
   public static void main (String[] args)
   {
      int sides = 7;  // declaration with initialization
      System.out.println ("A heptagon has " + sides + " sides.");

      sides = 10;  // assignment statement
      System.out.println ("A decagon has " + sides + " sides.");

      sides = 12;
      System.out.println ("A dodecagon has " + sides + " sides.");
   }
}
```

Output

```
A heptagon has 7 sides.
A decagon has 10 sides.
A dodecagon has 12 sides.
```

Basic Assignment

The basic assignment statement uses the assignment operator (=) to store the result of the Expression into the specified Identifier, usually a variable.

Examples:

```
total = 57;
count = count + 1;
value = (min / 2) * lastValue;
```

(=) is evaluated, and the result is stored in the memory location indicated by the variable on the left-hand side. In this example, the expression is simply a number, `10`. We discuss expressions that are more involved than this in the next section.

Accessing data leaves it intact in memory, but an assignment statement overwrites the old data.

A variable can store only one value of its declared type. A new value overwrites the old one. In this case, when the value `10` is assigned to `sides`, the original value `7` is overwritten and lost forever, as follows:

After initialization:	sides	7
After first assignment:	sides	10

When a reference is made to a variable, such as when it is printed, the value of the variable is not changed. This is the nature of computer memory: Accessing (reading) data leaves the values in memory intact, but writing data replaces the old data with the new.

We cannot assign a value of one type to a variable of an incompatible type.

The Java language is *strongly typed*, meaning that we are not allowed to assign a value to a variable that is inconsistent with its declared type. Trying to combine incompatible types will generate an error when you attempt to compile the program. Therefore, the expression on the right-hand side of an assignment statement must evaluate to a value compatible with the type of the variable on the left-hand side.

Constants

Sometimes we use data that is constant throughout a program. For instance, we might write a program that deals with a theater that can hold no more than 427 people. It is often helpful to give a constant value a name, such as `MAX_OCCUPANCY`, instead of using a literal value, such as `427`, throughout the code. The purpose and meaning of literal values such as `427` is often confusing to someone reading the code. By giving the value a name, you help explain its role in the program.

Constants are identifiers and are similar to variables except that they hold a particular value for the duration of their existence. Constants are, to use the English meaning of the words, not variable. Their value doesn't change.

Constants hold a particular value for the duration of their existence.

In Java, if you precede a declaration with the reserved word `final`, the identifier is made a constant. By convention, uppercase letters are used when naming constants to distinguish them from regular variables, and individual words are separated using the underscore character. For example, the constant describing the maximum occupancy of a theater could be declared as follows:

```
final int MAX_OCCUPANCY = 427;
```

The compiler will produce an error message if you attempt to change the value of a constant once it has been given its initial value. This is another good reason to use constants. Constants prevent inadvertent coding errors because the only valid place to change their value is in the initial assignment.

There is a third good reason to use constants. If a constant is used throughout a program and its value needs to be modified, then you have to change it in only one place. For example, if the capacity of the theater changes (because of a renovation) from 427 to 535, then you have to change only one declaration, and all uses of `MAX_OCCUPANCY` automatically reflect the change. If the literal `427` had been used throughout the code, each use would have to be found and changed. If you were to miss any uses of the literal value, problems would surely arise.

2.3 Primitive Data Types

There are eight *primitive data types* in Java: four subsets of integers, two subsets of floating point numbers, a character data type, and a boolean data type. Everything else is represented using objects. Let's examine these eight primitive data types in some detail.

Integers and Floating Points

Java has two basic kinds of numeric values: integers, which have no fractional part, and floating points, which do. There are four integer data types (`byte`, `short`, `int`, and `long`) and two floating point data types (`float` and `double`). All of the numeric types differ by the amount of memory space used to store a value of that type, which determines the range of values that can be represented. The size of each data type is the same for all hardware platforms. All numeric types are *signed*, meaning that both positive and negative values can be stored in them. Figure 2.2 summarizes the numeric primitive types.

Java has two kinds of numeric values: integer and floating point. There are four integer data types and two floating point data types.

A *bit*, or binary digit, can be either a 1 or a 0. Because each bit can represent two different states, a string of N bits can be used to represent 2^N different values. Appendix B describes number systems and these kinds of relationships in more detail.

When designing programs, we sometimes need to be careful about picking variables of appropriate size so that memory space is not wasted. This occurs in situations where memory space is particularly restricted, such as a program that runs on a personal data assistant (PDA). In such cases, we can choose a variable's data type accordingly. For example, if the value of a particular variable will not vary outside of a range of 1 to 1000, then a two-byte integer (`short`) is large enough to accommodate it. On the other hand, when it's not clear what the range of a particular variable will be, we should provide a reasonable, even generous, amount of space. In most situations memory space is not a serious restriction, and we can usually afford generous assumptions.

Note that even though a `float` value supports very large (and very small) numbers, it only has seven significant digits. Therefore, if it is important to accurately maintain a value such as 50341.2077, we need to use a `double`.

Type	Storage	Min Value	Max Value
`byte`	8 bits	–128	127
`short`	16 bits	–32,768	32,767
`int`	32 bits	–2,147,483,648	2,147,483,647
`long`	64 bits	–9,223,372,036,854,775,808	9,223,372,036,854,775,807
`float`	32 bits	Approximately –3.4E+38 with 7 significant digits	Approximately 3.4E+38 with 7 significant digits
`double`	64 bits	Approximately –1.7E+308 with 15 significant digits	Approximately 1.7E+308 with 15 significant digits

FIGURE 2.2 The Java numeric primitive types

As we've already discussed, a *literal* is an explicit data value used in a program. The various numbers used in programs such as `Facts` and `Addition` and `PianoKeys` are all *integer literals*. Java assumes all integer literals are of type `int`, unless an `L` or `l` is appended to the end of the value to indicate that it should be considered a literal of type `long`, such as `45L`.

Likewise, Java assumes that all *floating point literals* are of type `double`. If we need to treat a floating point literal as a `float`, we append an `F` or `f` to the end of the value, as in `2.718F` or `123.45f`. Numeric literals of type `double` can be followed by a `D` or `d` if desired.

The following are examples of numeric variable declarations in Java:

```
int answer = 42;
byte smallNumber1, smallNumber2;
long countedStars = 86827263927L;
float ratio = 0.2363F;
double delta = 453.523311903;
```

Characters

Characters are another fundamental type of data used and managed on a computer. Individual characters can be treated as separate data items, and, as we've seen in several examples, they can be combined to form character strings.

A *character literal* is expressed in a Java program with single quotes, such as `'b'` or `'J'` or `';'`. You will recall that *string literals* are delineated using double

Decimal Integer Literal

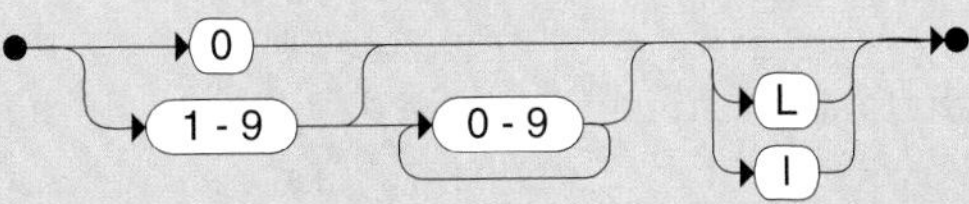

An integer literal is composed of a series of digits followed by an optional suffix to indicate that it should be considered a `long` integer. Negation of a literal is considered a separate operation.

Examples:

```
5
2594
4920328L
```

quotation marks, and that the `String` type is not a primitive data type in Java, it is a class name. We discuss the `String` class in detail in the next chapter.

Note the difference between a digit as a character (or part of a string) and a digit as a number (or part of a larger number). The number `602` is a numeric value that can be used in an arithmetic calculation. But in the string `"602 Greenbriar Court"` the `6`, `0`, and `2` are characters, just like the rest of the characters that make up the string.

The characters we can manage are defined by a *character set*, which is simply a list of characters in a particular order. Each programming language supports a particular character set that defines the valid values for a character variable in that language. Several character sets have been proposed, but only a few have been used regularly over the years. The *ASCII character set* is a popular choice. ASCII stands for the American Standard Code for Information Interchange. The basic ASCII set uses 7 bits per character, providing room to support 128 different characters, including:

- uppercase letters, such as `'A'`, `'B'`, and `'C'`
- lowercase letters, such as `'a'`, `'b'`, and `'c'`
- punctuation, such as the period (`'.'`), semicolon (`';'`), and comma (`','`)
- the digits `'0'` through `'9'`
- the space character, `' '`
- special symbols, such as the ampersand (`'&'`), vertical bar (`'|'`), and backslash (`'\'`)
- control characters, such as the carriage return, null, and end-of-text marks

The *control characters* are sometimes called nonprinting or invisible characters because they do not have a specific symbol that represents them. Yet they are as valid as any other character and can be stored and used in the same ways. Many control characters have special meaning to certain software applications.

As computing became a worldwide endeavor, users demanded a more flexible character set containing other language alphabets. ASCII was extended to use 8 bits per character, and the number of characters in the set doubled to 256. The extended ASCII contains many accented and diacritical characters used in languages other than English.

However, even with 256 characters, the ASCII character set cannot represent the world's alphabets, especially given the various Asian alphabets and their many thousands of ideograms. Therefore, the developers of the Java programming language chose the *Unicode character set*, which uses 16 bits per character, supporting 65,536 unique characters. The characters and symbols from many languages are included in the Unicode definition. ASCII is a subset of the Unicode character set. Appendix C discusses the Unicode character set in more detail.

Java uses the 16-bit Unicode character set to represent character data.

A character set assigns a particular number to each character, so by definition the characters are in a particular order. This is referred to as lexicographic order. In the ASCII and Unicode ordering, the digit characters `'0'` through `'9'` are continuous (no other characters intervene) and in order. Similarly, the lowercase alphabetic characters `'a'` through `'z'` are continuous and in order, as are the uppercase alphabetic characters `'A'` through `'Z'`. These characteristics make it relatively easy to sort data, such as a list of names, in alphabetical order. Sorting is discussed in Chapter 13.

In Java, the data type `char` represents a single character. The following are some examples of character variable declarations in Java:

```
char topGrade = 'A';
char symbol1, symbol2, symbol3;
char terminator = ';', separator = ' ';
```

Booleans

A boolean value, defined in Java using the reserved word `boolean`, has only two valid values: `true` and `false`. A boolean variable is usually used to indicate whether a particular condition is true, but it can also be used to represent any situation that has two states, such as a light bulb being on or off. The term boolean is named in honor of English mathematician George Boole, who developed a form of algebra (Boolean algebra) in which variables take on only one of two values.

A boolean value cannot be converted to any other data type, nor can any other data type be converted to a boolean value. The words `true` and `false` are reserved in Java as *boolean literals* and cannot be used outside of this context.

The following are some examples of boolean variable declarations in Java:

```
boolean flag = true;
boolean tooHigh, tooSmall, tooRough;
boolean done = false;
```

2.4 Expressions

An *expression* is a combination of one or more operators and operands that usually performs a calculation. The value calculated does not have to be a number, but often is. The operands used in the operations might be literals, constants, variables, or other sources of data. The manner in which expressions are evaluated and used is fundamental to programming. For now we will focus on arithmetic expressions that use numeric operands and produce numeric results.

Expressions are combinations of operators and operands used to perform a calculation.

Arithmetic Operators

The usual arithmetic operations are defined for both integer and floating point numeric types, including addition (+), subtraction (–), multiplication (*), and division (/). Java also has another arithmetic operation: The remainder operator (%) returns the remainder after dividing the second operand into the first. The remainder operator is sometimes called the modulus operator. The sign of the result of a remainder operation is the sign of the numerator. This table shows some examples:

Operation	Result
17 % 4	1
-20 % 3	-2
10 % -5	0
3 % 8	3

As you might expect, if either or both operands to any numeric operator are floating point values, the result is a floating point value. However, the division operator (/) produces results that are less intuitive, depending on the types of the operands. If both operands are integers, the / operator performs *integer division*, meaning that any fractional part of the result is discarded. If one or the other or both operands are floating point values, the / operator performs *floating point division*, and the fractional part of the result is kept. For example, the result of `10/4` is `2`, but the results of `10.0/4` and `10/4.0` and `10.0/4.0` are all `2.5`.

The type of result produced by arithmetic division depends on the types of the operands.

A *unary operator* has only one operand, while a *binary operator* has two. The + and – arithmetic operators can be either unary or binary. The binary versions accomplish addition and subtraction, and the unary versions represent positive and negative numbers. For example, –1 is an example of using the unary negation operator to make the value negative. The unary + operator is rarely used.

Java does not have a built-in operator for raising a value to an exponent. However, the `Math` class provides methods that perform exponentiation and many other mathematical functions. The `Math` class is discussed in Chapter 3.

Operator Precedence

Operators can be combined to create more complex expressions. For example, consider the following assignment statement:

```
result = 14 + 8 / 2;
```

The entire right-hand side of the assignment is evaluated, and then the result is stored in the variable. But what is the result? If the addition is performed first, the result is `11`; if the division operation is performed first, the result is `18`. The order of operator evaluation makes a big difference. In this case, the division is performed before the addition, yielding a result of `18`.

Note that in this and subsequent examples, we use literal values rather than variables to simplify the expression. The order of operator evaluation is the same if the operands are variables or any other source of data.

All expressions are evaluated according to an *operator precedence hierarchy* that establishes the rules that govern the order in which operations are evaluated. The arithmetic operators generally follow the same rules you learned in algebra. Multiplication, division, and the remainder operator all have equal precedence and are performed before (have higher precedence than) addition and subtraction. Addition and subtraction have equal precedence.

Java follows a well-defined set of precedence rules that governs the order in which operators will be evaluated in an expression.

Any arithmetic operators at the same level of precedence are performed left to right. Therefore we say the arithmetic operators have a *left-to-right association*.

Precedence, however, can be forced in an expression by using parentheses. For instance, if we really wanted the addition to be performed first in the previous example, we could write the expression as follows:

```
result = (14 + 8) / 2;
```

Any expression in parentheses is evaluated first. In complicated expressions, it is good practice to use parentheses even when it is not strictly necessary, to make it clear how the expression is evaluated.

Parentheses can be nested, and the innermost nested expressions are evaluated first. Consider the following expression:

```
result = 3 * ((18 – 4) / 2);
```

In this example, the result is 21. First, the subtraction is performed, forced by the inner parentheses. Then, even though multiplication and division are at the same level of precedence and usually would be evaluated left to right, the division is performed first because of the outer parentheses. Finally, the multiplication is performed.

After the arithmetic operations are complete, the computed result is stored in the variable on the left-hand side of the assignment operator (=). In other words, the assignment operator has a lower precedence than any of the arithmetic operators.

The evaluation of a particular expression can be shown using an *expression tree*, such as the one in Figure 2.3. The operators are executed from the bottom up, creating values that are used in the rest of the expression. Therefore, the operations lower in the tree have a higher precedence than those above, or they are forced to be executed earlier using parentheses.

The parentheses used in expressions are actually operators themselves. Parentheses have a higher precedence than almost any other operator. Figure 2.4 shows a precedence table with the relationships between the arithmetic operators, parentheses, and the assignment operator. Appendix D includes a full precedence table showing all Java operators.

For an expression to be syntactically correct, the number of left parentheses must match the number of right parentheses and they must be properly nested. The following examples are *not* valid expressions:

```
result = ((19 + 8) % 3) – 4);    // not valid
result = (19 (+ 8 %) 3 – 4);    // not valid
```

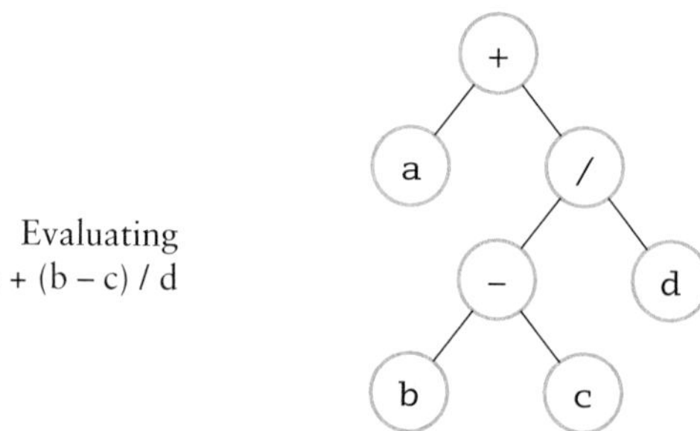

FIGURE 2.3 An expression tree

Precedence Level	Operator	Operation	Associates
1	+	unary plus	R to L
	–	unary minus	
2	*	multiplication	L to R
	/	division	
	%	remainder	
3	+	addition	L to R
	–	subtraction	
	+	string concatenation	
4	=	assignment	R to L

FIGURE 2.4 Precedence among some of the Java operators

Keep in mind that when a variable is referenced in an expression, its current value is used to perform the calculation. In the following assignment statement, the current value of the variable `count` is added to the current value of the variable `total`, and the result is stored in the variable `sum`:

```
sum = count + total;
```

The original value contained in `sum` before this assignment is overwritten by the calculated value. The values stored in `count` and `total` are not changed.

The same variable can appear on both the left-hand side and the right-hand side of an assignment statement. Suppose the current value of a variable called `count` is `15` when the following assignment statement is executed:

```
count = count + 1;
```

Because the right-hand expression is evaluated first, the original value of `count` is obtained and the value `1` is added to it, producing the result `16`. That result is then stored in the variable `count`, overwriting the original value of `15` with the new value of `16`. Therefore, this assignment statement *increments*, or adds one to, the variable `count`.

Let's look at another example of expression processing. The program in Listing 2.7, called `TempConverter`, converts a particular Celsius temperature value to its equivalent Fahrenheit value using an expression that computes the following formula:

$$\text{Fahrenheit} = \frac{9}{5}\,\text{Celsius} + 32$$

Note that in the `TempConverter` program, the operands to the division operation are floating point literals to ensure that the fractional part of the number is kept. The precedence rules dictate that the multiplication happens before the addition in the final conversion computation.

The `TempConverter` program is not very useful because it converts only one data value that we included in the program as a constant (24 degrees Celsius). Every time the program is run it produces the same result. A far more useful

Listing **2.7**

```
//********************************************************************
//  TempConverter.java       Java Foundations
//
//  Demonstrates the use of primitive data types and arithmetic
//  expressions.
//********************************************************************

public class TempConverter
{
   //-----------------------------------------------------------------
   //  Computes the Fahrenheit equivalent of a specific Celsius
   //  value using the formula F = (9/5)C + 32.
   //-----------------------------------------------------------------
   public static void main (String[] args)
   {
      final int BASE = 32;
      final double CONVERSION_FACTOR = 9.0 / 5.0;

      double fahrenheitTemp;
      int celsiusTemp = 24;  // value to convert

      fahrenheitTemp = celsiusTemp * CONVERSION_FACTOR + BASE;

      System.out.println ("Celsius Temperature: " + celsiusTemp);
      System.out.println ("Fahrenheit Equivalent: " + fahrenheitTemp);
   }
}
```

Output

```
Celsius Temperature: 24
Fahrenheit Equivalent: 75.2
```

version of the program would obtain the value to be converted from the user each time the program is executed. Interactive programs that read user input are discussed later in this chapter.

Increment and Decrement Operators

There are two other useful arithmetic operators. The *increment operator* (++) adds 1 to any integer or floating point value. The two plus signs that make up the operator cannot be separated by white space. The *decrement operator* (--) is similar except that it subtracts 1 from the value. They are both unary operators because they operate on only one operand. The following statement causes the value of `count` to be incremented:

```
count++;
```

The result is stored back into the variable `count`. Therefore it is functionally equivalent to the following statement, which we discussed in the previous section:

```
count = count + 1;
```

The increment and decrement operators can be applied after the variable (such as `count++` or `count--`), creating what is called the *postfix form* of the operator. They can also be applied before the variable (such as `++count` or `--count`), in what is called the *prefix form*. When used alone in a statement, the prefix and postfix forms are functionally equivalent. That is, it doesn't matter if you write

```
count++;
```

or

```
++count;
```

However, when such a form is written as a statement by itself, it is usually written in its postfix form.

When the increment or decrement operator is used in a larger expression, it can yield different results depending on the form used. For example, if the variable `count` currently contains the value `15`, the following statement assigns the value `15` to `total` and the value `16` to `count`:

```
total = count++;
```

However, if count contains 15, the following statement assigns the value 16 to both total and count:

```
total = ++count;
```

The value of count is incremented in both situations, but the value used in the larger expression depends on whether a prefix or postfix form of the increment operator is used.

Because of the subtle differences between the prefix and postfix forms of the increment and decrement operators, they should be used with care. As always, favor the side of readability.

Assignment Operators

As a convenience, several *assignment operators* have been defined in Java that combine a basic operation with assignment. For example, the += operator can be used as follows:

```
total += 5;
```

This performs the same operation as the following statement:

```
total = total + 5;
```

The right-hand side of the assignment operator can be a full expression. The expression on the right-hand side of the operator is evaluated, then that result is added to the current value of the variable on the left-hand side, and that value is stored in the variable. Therefore, the following statement:

```
total += (sum - 12) / count;
```

is equivalent to:

```
total = total + ((sum - 12) / count);
```

Many similar assignment operators are defined in Java, including those that perform subtraction (-=), multiplication (*=), division (/=), and remainder (%=). The entire set of Java operators is discussed in Appendix D.

All of the assignment operators evaluate the entire expression on the right-hand side first, then use the result as the right operand of the other operation. Therefore, the following statement:

```
result *= count1 + count2;
```

is equivalent to:

```
result = result * (count1 + count2);
```

Likewise, the following statement:

```
result %= (highest - 40) / 2;
```

is equivalent to:

```
result = result % ((highest - 40) / 2);
```

Some assignment operators perform particular functions depending on the types of the operands, just as their corresponding regular operators do. For example, if the operands to the += operator are strings, then the assignment operator performs string concatenation.

2.5 Data Conversion

Because Java is a strongly typed language, each data value is associated with a particular type. It is sometimes helpful or necessary to convert a data value of one type to another type, but we must be careful that we don't lose important information in the process. For example, suppose a `short` variable that holds the number 1000 is converted to a `byte` value. Because a `byte` does not have enough bits to represent the value 1000, some bits would be lost in the conversion, and the number represented in the `byte` would not keep its original value.

A conversion between one primitive type and another falls into one of two categories: widening conversions and narrowing conversions. *Widening conversions* are the safest because they usually do not lose information. They are called widening conversions because they go from one data type to another type that uses an equal or greater amount of space to store the value. Figure 2.5 lists the Java widening conversions.

For example, it is safe to convert from a `byte` to a `short` because a `byte` is stored in 8 bits and a `short` is stored in 16 bits. There is no loss of information. All widening conversions that go from an integer type to another integer type, or from a floating point type to another floating point type, preserve the numeric value exactly.

Although widening conversions do not lose any information about the magnitude of a value, the widening conversions that result in a floating point value can

From	To
`byte`	`short`, `int`, `long`, `float`, or `double`
`short`	`int`, `long`, `float`, or `double`
`char`	`int`, `long`, `float`, or `double`
`int`	`long`, `float`, or `double`
`long`	`float` or `double`
`float`	`double`

FIGURE 2.5 Java widening conversions

lose precision. When converting from an `int` or a `long` to a `float`, or from a `long` to a `double`, some of the least significant digits may be lost. In this case, the resulting floating point value will be a rounded version of the integer value, following the rounding techniques defined in the IEEE 754 floating point standard.

Narrowing conversions should be avoided because they can lose information.

Narrowing conversions are more likely to lose information than widening conversions are. They often go from one type to a type that uses less space to store a value, and therefore some of the information may be compromised. Narrowing conversions can lose both numeric magnitude and precision. Therefore, in general, they should be avoided. Figure 2.6 lists the Java narrowing conversions.

An exception to the space-shrinking situation in narrowing conversions is when we convert a `byte` (8 bits) or `short` (16 bits) to a `char` (16 bits). These are still considered narrowing conversions because the sign bit is incorporated into the new character value. Since a character value is unsigned, a negative integer

From	To
`byte`	`char`
`short`	`byte` or `char`
`char`	`byte` or `short`
`int`	`byte`, `short`, or `char`
`long`	`byte`, `short`, `char`, or `int`
`float`	`byte`, `short`, `char`, `int`, or `long`
`double`	`byte`, `short`, `char`, `int`, `long`, or `float`

FIGURE 2.6 Java narrowing conversions

will be converted into a character that has no particular relationship to the numeric value of the original integer.

Note that `boolean` values are not mentioned in either widening or narrowing conversions. A `boolean` value cannot be converted to any other primitive type and vice versa.

Conversion Techniques

In Java, conversions can occur in three ways:

- assignment conversion
- promotion
- casting

Assignment conversion occurs when a value of one type is assigned to a variable of another type during which the value is converted to the new type. Only widening conversions can be accomplished through assignment. For example, if `money` is a `float` variable and `dollars` is an `int` variable, then the following assignment statement automatically converts the value in `dollars` to a `float`:

```
money = dollars;
```

Therefore, if `dollars` contains the value `25`, after the assignment, money contains the value `25.0`. However, if we attempt to assign `money` to `dollars`, the compiler will issue an error message alerting us to the fact that we are attempting a narrowing conversion that could lose information. If we really want to do this assignment, we have to make the conversion explicit by using a cast.

Conversion via *promotion* occurs automatically when certain operators need to modify their operands in order to perform the operation. For example, when a floating point value called `sum` is divided by an integer value called `count`, the value of `count` is promoted to a floating point value automatically, before the division takes place, producing a floating point result:

```
result = sum / count;
```

A similar conversion is taking place when a number is concatenated with a string. The number is first converted (promoted) to a string, then the two strings are concatenated.

Casting is the most general form of conversion in Java. If a conversion can be accomplished at all in a Java program, it can be accomplished using a cast. A cast is a Java operator that is specified by a type name in parentheses. It is placed in front of the value to be converted. For example, to convert money to an integer value, we could put a cast in front of it:

```
dollars = (int) money;
```

The cast returns the value in money, truncating any fractional part. If money contained the value 84.69, then after the assignment, dollars would contain the value 84. Note, however, that the cast does not change the value in money. After the assignment operation is complete, money still contains the value 84.69.

Casts are helpful in many situations where we need to treat a value temporarily as another type. For example, if we want to divide the integer value total by the integer value count and get a floating point result, we could do it as follows:

```
result = (float) total / count;
```

First, the cast operator returns a floating point version of the value in total. This operation does not change the value in total. Then, count is treated as a floating point value via arithmetic promotion. Now the division operator will perform floating point division and produce the intended result. If the cast had not been included, the operation would have performed integer division and truncated the answer before assigning it to result. Also note that because the cast operator has a higher precedence than the division operator, the cast operates on the value of total, not on the result of the division.

2.6 Reading Input Data

It is often useful to design a program to read data from the user interactively during execution. That way, new results can be computed each time the program is run, depending on the data that is entered.

The Scanner Class

The Scanner class provides methods for reading input of various types from various sources.

The Scanner class, which is part of the standard Java class library, provides convenient methods for reading input values of various types. The input could come from various sources, including data typed interactively by the user or data stored in a file. The Scanner class can also be used to parse a character string into separate pieces. Figure 2.7 lists some of the methods provided by the Scanner class.

```
Scanner (InputStream source)
Scanner (File source)
Scanner (String source)
        Constructors: sets up the new scanner to scan values from the specified source.

String next()
        Returns the next input token as a character string.

String nextLine()
        Returns all input remaining on the current line as a character string.

boolean nextBoolean()
byte nextByte()
double nextDouble()
float nextFloat()
int nextInt()
long nextLong()
short nextShort()
        Returns the next input token as the indicated type. Throws
      InputMismatchException if the next token is inconsistent with the type.

boolean hasNext()
        Returns true if the scanner has another token in its input.

Scanner useDelimiter (String pattern)
Scanner useDelimiter (Pattern pattern)
        Sets the scanner's delimiting pattern.

Pattern delimiter()
        Returns the pattern the scanner is currently using to match delimiters.

String findInLine (String pattern)
String findInLine (Pattern pattern)
        Attempts to find the next occurrence of the specified pattern, ignoring delimiters.
```

FIGURE 2.7 Some methods of the `Scanner` class

We must first create a `Scanner` object in order to invoke its methods. Objects in Java are created using the `new` operator. The following declaration creates a `Scanner` object that reads input from the keyboard:

```
Scanner scan = new Scanner(System.in);
```

This declaration creates a variable called `scan` that represents a `Scanner` object. The object itself is created by the `new` operator and a call to a special method called a *constructor* to set up the object. The `Scanner` constructor accepts a parameter that indicates the source of the input. The `System.in` object represents the *standard input stream*, which by default is the keyboard. Creating objects using the `new` operator is discussed further in the next chapter.

Unless specified otherwise, a `Scanner` object assumes that whitespace characters (space characters, tabs, and new lines) are used to separate the elements of the input, called *tokens*, from each other. These characters are called the input *delimiters*. The set of delimiters can be changed if the input tokens are separated by characters other than white space.

The `next` method of the `Scanner` class reads the next input token as a string and returns it. Therefore, if the input consisted of a series of words separated by spaces, each call to `next` would return the next word. The `nextLine` method reads all of the input until the end of the line is found, and returns it as one string.

The program `Echo`, shown in Listing 2.8, simply reads a line of text typed by the user, stores it in a variable that holds a character string, then echoes it back to the screen. User input is shown in red in the output section below the listing.

The `import` declaration above the definition of the `Echo` class tells the program that we will be using the `Scanner` class in this program. The `Scanner` class is part of the `java.util` class library. The use of the `import` declaration is discussed further in Chapter 3.

Various `Scanner` methods such as `nextInt` and `nextDouble` are provided to read data of particular types. The `GasMileage` program, shown in Listing 2.9, reads the number of miles traveled as an integer, and the number of gallons of fuel consumed as a double, then computes the gas mileage.

As you can see by the output of the `GasMileage` program, the calculation produces a floating point result that is accurate to several decimal places. In the next chapter we discuss classes that help us format our output in various ways, including rounding a floating point value to a particular number of decimal places.

A `Scanner` object processes the input one token at a time, based on the methods used to read the data and the delimiters used to separate the input values. Therefore, multiple values can be put on the same line of input or can be separated over multiple lines, as appropriate for the situation.

Listing 2.8

```
//********************************************************************
//  Echo.java       Java Foundations
//
//  Demonstrates the use of the nextLine method of the Scanner class
//  to read a string from the user.
//********************************************************************

import java.util.Scanner;

public class Echo
{
   //-----------------------------------------------------------------
   //  Reads a character string from the user and prints it.
   //-----------------------------------------------------------------
   public static void main (String[] args)
   {
      String message;
      Scanner scan = new Scanner (System.in);

      System.out.println ("Enter a line of text:");

      message = scan.nextLine();

      System.out.println ("You entered: \"" + message + "\"");
   }
}
```

Output

```
Enter a line of text:
Set your laser printer on stun!
You entered: "Set your laser printer on stun!"
```

In Chapter 5 we use the `Scanner` class to read input from a data file and modify the delimiters it uses to parse the data. Appendix H explores how to use the `Scanner` class to analyze its input using patterns called *regular expressions*.

Listing 2.9

```
//********************************************************************
//  GasMileage.java       Java Foundations
//
//  Demonstrates the use of the Scanner class to read numeric data.
//********************************************************************

import java.util.Scanner;

public class GasMileage
{
   //-----------------------------------------------------------------
   //  Calculates fuel efficiency based on values entered by the
   //  user.
   //-----------------------------------------------------------------
   public static void main (String[] args)
   {
      int miles;
      double gallons, mpg;

      Scanner scan = new Scanner (System.in);

      System.out.print ("Enter the number of miles: ");
      miles = scan.nextInt();

      System.out.print ("Enter the gallons of fuel used: ");
      gallons = scan.nextDouble();

      mpg = miles / gallons;

      System.out.println ("Miles Per Gallon: " + mpg);
   }
}
```

Output

```
Enter the number of miles: 369
Enter the gallons of fuel used: 12.4
Miles Per Gallon: 29.758064516129032
```

Summary of Key Concepts

- The `print` and `println` methods represent two services provided by the `System.out` object.
- In Java, the + operator is used both for addition and for string concatenation.
- An escape sequence can be used to represent a character that would otherwise cause compilation problems.
- A variable is a name for a memory location used to hold a value of a particular data type.
- Accessing data leaves it intact in memory, but an assignment statement overwrites the old data.
- We cannot assign a value of one type to a variable of an incompatible type.
- Constants hold a particular value for the duration of their existence.
- Java has two kinds of numeric values: integer and floating point. There are four integer data types and two floating point data types.
- Java uses the 16-bit Unicode character set to represent character data.
- Expressions are combinations of operators and operands used to perform a calculation.
- The type of result produced by arithmetic division depends on the types of the operands.
- Java follows a well-defined set of precedence rules that governs the order in which operators will be evaluated in an expression.
- Narrowing conversions should be avoided because they can lose information.
- The `Scanner` class provides methods for reading input of various types from various sources.

Self-Review Questions

SR 2.1 What is primitive data? How are primitive data types different from objects?

SR 2.2 What is a string literal?

SR 2.3 What is the difference between the `print` and `println` methods?

SR 2.4 What is a parameter?

SR 2.5 What is an escape sequence? Give some examples.

SR 2.6 What is a variable declaration?

SR 2.7 How many values can be stored in an integer variable at one time?

SR 2.8 What are the four integer data types in Java? How are they different?

SR 2.9 What is a character set?

SR 2.10 What is operator precedence?

SR 2.11 What is the result of `19%5` when evaluated in a Java expression? Explain.

SR 2.12 What is the result of `13/4` when evaluated in a Java expression? Explain.

SR 2.13 If an integer variable `diameter` currently holds the value `5`, what is its value after the following statement is executed? Explain.

```
diameter = diameter * 4;
```

SR 2.14 If an integer variable `weight` currently holds the value `100`, what is its value after the following statement is executed? Explain.

```
weight -= 17;
```

SR 2.15 Why are widening conversions safer than narrowing conversions?

Exercises

EX 2.1 Explain the following programming statement in terms of objects and the services they provide:

```
System.out.println ("I gotta be me!");
```

EX 2.2 What output is produced by the following code fragment? Explain.

```
System.out.print ("Here we go!");
System.out.println ("12345");
System.out.print ("Test this if you are not sure.");
System.out.print ("Another.");
System.out.println ();
System.out.println ("All done.");
```

EX 2.3 What is wrong with the following program statement? How can it be fixed?

```
System.out.println ("To be or not to be, that is the
question.");
```

EX 2.4 What output is produced by the following statement? Explain.

```
System.out.println ("50 plus 25 is " + 50 + 25);
```

EX 2.5 What output is produced by the following statement? Explain.

```
System.out.println ("He thrusts his fists\n\tagainst" +
" the post\nand still insists\n\the sees the \"ghost\"");
```

EX 2.6 What value is contained in the integer variable `size` after the following statements are executed?

```
size = 18;
size = size + 12;
size = size * 2;
size = size / 4;
```

EX 2.7 What value is contained in the floating point variable `depth` after the following statements are executed?

```
depth = 2.4;
depth = 20 – depth * 4;
depth = depth / 5;
```

EX 2.8 What value is contained in the integer variable `length` after the following statements are executed?

```
length = 5;
length *= 2;
length *= length;
length /= 100;
```

EX 2.9 Write four different program statements that increment the value of an integer variable `total`.

EX 2.10 Given the following declarations, what result is stored in each of the listed assignment statements?

```
int iResult, num1 = 25, num2 = 40, num3 = 17, num4 = 5;
double fResult, val1 = 17.0, val2 = 12.78;
```

a. `iResult = num1 / num4;`

b. `fResult = num1 / num4;`

c. `iResult = num3 / num4;`

d. `fResult = num3 / num4;`

e. `fResult = val1 / num4;`

f. `fResult = val1 / val2;`

g. `iResult = num1 / num2;`

h. `fResult = (double) num1 / num2;`

i. `fResult = num1 / (double) num2;`

j. `fResult = (double) (num1 / num2);`

k. `iResult = (int) (val1 / num4);`

l. `fResult = (int) (val1 / num4);`

m. `fResult = (int) ((double) num1 / num2);`

n. `iResult = num3 % num4;`

o. `iResult = num2 % num3;`

p. `iResult = num3 % num2;`

q. `iResult = num2 % num4;`

EX 2.11 For each of the following expressions, indicate the order in which the operators will be evaluated by writing a number beneath each operator.

a. `a - b - c - d`

b. `a - b + c - d`

c. `a + b / c / d`

d. `a + b / c * d`

e. `a / b * c * d`

f. `a % b / c * d`

g. `a % b % c % d`

h. `a - (b - c) - d`

i. `(a - (b - c)) - d`

j. `a - ((b - c) - d)`

k. `a % (b % c) * d * e`

l. `a + (b - c) * d - e`

m. `(a + b) * c + d * e`

n. `(a + b) * (c / d) % e`

Programming Projects

PP 2.1 Create a revised version of the `Lincoln` application from Chapter 1 such that quotes appear around the quotation.

PP 2.2 Write an application that reads three integers and prints their average.

PP 2.3 Write an application that reads two floating point numbers and prints their sum, difference, and product.

PP 2.4 Create a version of the `TempConverter` application to convert from Fahrenheit to Celsius. Read the Fahrenheit temperature from the user.

PP 2.5 Write an application that converts miles to kilometers. (One mile equals 1.60935 kilometers.) Read the miles value from the user as a floating point value.

PP 2.6 Write an application that reads values representing a time duration in hours, minutes, and seconds, and then prints the equivalent total number of seconds. (For example, 1 hour, 28 minutes, and 42 seconds is equivalent to 5322 seconds.)

PP 2.7 Create a version of the previous project that reverses the computation. That is, read a value representing a number of seconds, then print the equivalent amount of time as a combination of hours, minutes, and seconds. (For example, 9999 seconds is equivalent to 2 hours, 46 minutes, and 39 seconds.)

PP 2.8 Write an application that determines the value of the coins in a jar and prints the total in dollars and cents. Read integer values that represent the number of quarters, dimes, nickels, and pennies.

PP 2.9 Write an application that prompts for and reads a `double` value representing a monetary amount. Then determine the fewest number of each bill and coin needed to represent that amount, starting with the highest (assume that a ten-dollar bill is the maximum size needed). For example, if the value entered is 47.63 (forty-seven dollars and sixty-three cents), then the program should print the equivalent amount as:

```
4 ten dollar bills
1 five dollar bills
2 one dollar bills
2 quarters
1 dimes
0 nickles
3 pennies
```

PP 2.10 Write an application that prompts for and reads an integer representing the length of a square's side, then prints the square's perimeter and area.

PP 2.11 Write an application that prompts for and reads the numerator and denominator of a fraction as integers, then prints the decimal equivalent of the fraction.

Answers to Self-Review Questions

SR 2.1 Primitive data are basic values such as numbers or characters. Objects are more complex entities that usually contain primitive data that help define them.

SR 2.2 A string literal is a sequence of characters delimited by double quotes.

SR 2.3 Both the `print` and `println` methods of the `System.out` object write a string of characters to the monitor screen. The difference is that, after printing the characters, the `println` method performs a carriage return so that whatever is printed next appears on the next line. The `print` method allows subsequent output to appear on the same line.

SR 2.4 A parameter is data that is passed into a method when it is invoked. The method usually uses that data to accomplish the service that it provides. For example, the parameter to the `println` method indicates what characters should be printed.

SR 2.5 An escape sequence is a series of characters that begins with the backslash (\) and that implies the following characters should be treated in some special way. Examples: `\n` represents the newline character, `\t` represents the tab character, and `\"` represents the quotation character (as opposed to using it to terminate a string).

SR 2.6 A variable declaration establishes the name of a variable and the type of data that it can contain. A declaration may also have an optional initialization, which gives the variable an initial value.

SR 2.7 An integer variable can store only one value at a time. When a new value is assigned to it, the old one is overwritten and lost.

SR 2.8 The four integer data types in Java are `byte`, `short`, `int`, and `long`. They differ in how much memory space is allocated for each and therefore how large a number they can hold.

SR 2.9 A character set is a list of characters in a particular order. A character set defines the valid characters that a particular type of computer or programming language will support. Java uses the Unicode character set.

SR 2.10 Operator precedence is the set of rules that dictates the order in which operators are evaluated in an expression.

SR 2.11 The result of `19%5` in a Java expression is 4. The remainder operator `%` returns the remainder after dividing the second operand into the first. Five goes into 19 three times, with 4 left over.

SR 2.12 The result of `13/4` in a Java expression is 3 (not 3.25). The result is an integer because both operands are integers. Therefore the `/` operator performs integer division, and the fractional part of the result is truncated.

SR 2.13 After executing the statement, `diameter` holds the value `20`. First the current value of `diameter` (`5`) is multiplied by 4, and then the result is stored back in `diameter`.

SR 2.14 After executing the statement, `weight` holds the value `83`. The assignment operator `-=` modifies `weight` by first subtracting 17 from the current value (`100`), then storing the result back into `weight`.

SR 2.15 A widening conversion tends to go from a small data value, in terms of the amount of space used to store it, to a larger one. A narrowing conversion does the opposite. Information is more likely to be lost in a narrowing conversion, which is why narrowing conversions are considered to be less safe than widening ones.

3 Using Classes and Objects

Chapter Objectives

- Discuss the creation of objects and the use of object reference variables.
- Explore the services provided by the `String` class.
- Describe how the Java standard class library is organized into packages.
- Explore the services provided by the `Random` and `Math` classes.
- Discuss ways to format output using the `NumberFormat` and `DecimalFormat` classes.
- Introduce enumerated types.
- Discuss wrapper classes and the concept of autoboxing.

This chapter further explores the use of predefined classes and the objects we can create from them. Using classes and objects for the services they provide is a fundamental part of object-oriented software, and sets the stage for writing classes of our own. In this chapter, we use classes and objects to manipulate character strings, produce random numbers, perform complex calculations, and format output. This chapter also introduces the concept of an enumerated type, which is a special kind of class in Java, and discusses the concept of a wrapper class.

3.1 Creating Objects

At the end of Chapter 1 we presented an overview of object-oriented concepts, including the basic relationship between classes and objects. Then in Chapter 2, in addition to discussing primitive data, we provided some examples of using objects for the services they provide. This chapter explores these ideas further.

In previous examples, we've used the `println` method many times. As we mentioned in Chapter 2, the `println` method is a service provided by the `System.out` object, which represents the standard output stream. To be more precise, the identifier `out` is an object variable that is stored in the `System` class. It has been predefined and set up for us as part of the Java standard class library. We can simply use it.

In Chapter 2 we also used the `Scanner` class, which represents an object that allows us to read input from the keyboard or a file. We created a `Scanner` object using the `new` operator. Once the object was created, we were able to use it for the various services it provides. That is, we were able to invoke its methods.

Let's carefully examine the idea of creating an object. In Java, a variable name represents either a primitive value or an object. Like variables that hold primitive types, a variable that refers to an object must be declared. The class used to define an object can be thought of as the type of an object. The declarations of object variables have a similar structure to the declarations of primitive variables.

Consider the following two declarations:

```
int num;
String name;
```

The first declaration creates a variable that holds an integer value, as we've seen many times before. The second declaration creates a `String` variable that holds a *reference* to a `String` object. An object variable doesn't hold the object itself, it holds the address of an object.

Initially, the two variables declared above don't contain any data. We say they are *uninitialized*, which can be depicted as follows:

num	–
name	–

As we pointed out in Chapter 2, it is always important to make sure a variable is initialized before using it. For an object variable, that means we must make sure it refers to a valid object prior to using it. In most situations the compiler will issue an error if you attempt to use a variable before initializing it.

An object reference variable can also be set to `null`, which is a reserved word in Java. A null reference specifically indicates that a variable does not refer to an object.

Note that, although we've declared a `String` reference variable, no `String` object actually exists yet. The act of creating an object using the `new` operator is called *instantiation*. An object is said to be an *instance* of a particular class. To instantiate an object, we can use the `new` operator, which returns the address of the new object. The following two assignment statements give values to the two variables declared above:

```
num = 42;
name = new String("James Gosling");
```

The `new` operator returns a reference to a newly created object.

After the `new` operator creates the object, a *constructor* is invoked to help set it up initially. A constructor is a special method that has the same name as the class. In this example, the parameter to the constructor is a string literal that specifies the characters that the string object will hold. After these assignments are executed, the variables can be depicted as:

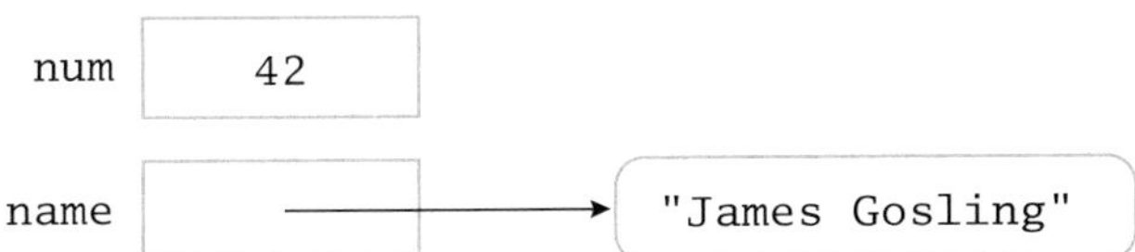

Since an object reference variable holds the address of the object, it can be thought of as a *pointer* to the location in memory where the object is held. We could show the numeric address, but the actual address value is irrelevant—what's important is that the variable refers to a particular object.

After an object has been instantiated, we use the *dot operator* to access its methods. We've used the dot operator many times already, such as in calls to `System.out.println`. The dot operator is appended directly after the object reference, followed by the method being invoked. For example, to invoke the `length` method defined in the `String` class, we can use the dot operator on the name reference variable:

```
count = name.length()
```

The `length` method does not take any parameters, but the parentheses are still necessary to indicate that a method is being invoked. Some methods produce a value that is *returned* when the method completes. The purpose of the `length` method of the `String` class is to determine and return the length of the string (the number of characters it contains). In this example, the returned value is assigned to the variable `count`. For the string `"James Gosling"`, the `length` method returns `13`, which includes the space between the first and last names. Some methods do not return a value. Other `String` methods are discussed in the next section.

The act of declaring the object reference variable and creating the object itself can be combined into one step by initializing the variable in the declaration, just as we do with primitive types:

```
String title = new String("Java Software Solutions");
```

Even though they are not primitive types, character strings are so fundamental and so often used that Java defines string literals delimited by double quotation marks, as we've seen in various examples. This is a shortcut notation. Whenever a string literal appears, a `String` object is created automatically. Therefore the following declaration is valid:

```
String city = "London";
```

That is, for `String` objects, the explicit use of the `new` operator and the call to the constructor can be eliminated. In most cases, we will use this simplified syntax.

Aliases

Because an object reference variable stores an address, a programmer must be careful when managing objects. First, let's review the effect of assignment on primitive values. Suppose we have two integer variables, `num1`, initialized to `5`, and `num2`, initialized to `12`:

num1	5
num2	12

In the following assignment statement, a copy of the value that is stored in `num1` is stored in `num2`:

```
num2 = num1;
```

The original value of `12` in `num2` is overwritten by the value `5`. The variables `num1` and `num2` still refer to different locations in memory, and both of those locations now contain the value `5`:

num1	5
num2	5

Now consider the following object declarations:

```
String name1 = "Ada, Countess of Lovelace";
String name2 = "Grace Murray Hopper";
```

Initially, the references `name1` and `name2` refer to two different `String` objects:

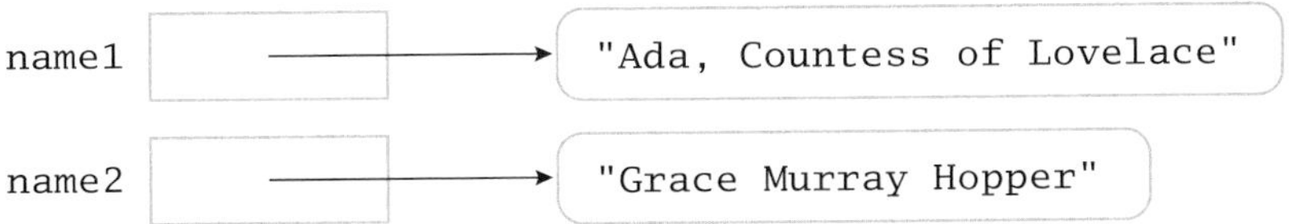

Now suppose the following assignment statement is executed, copying the value in `name1` into `name2`:

```
name2 = name1;
```

This assignment works the same as the integer assignment—a copy of the value of `name1` is stored in `name2`. But remember, object variables hold the address of an object, and it is the address that gets copied. Originally, the two references referred to different objects. After the assignment, both `name1` and `name2` contain the same address and therefore refer to the same object:

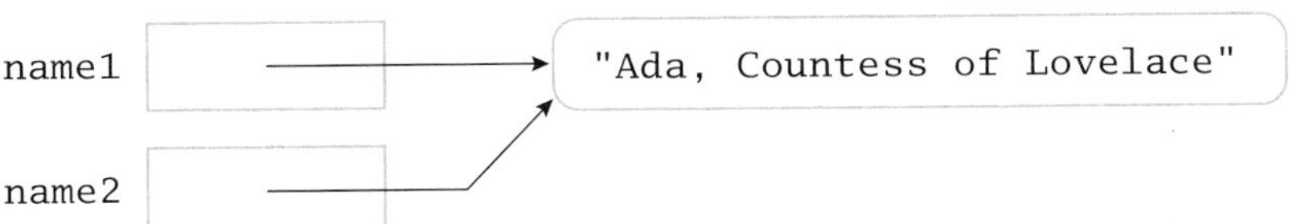

The `name1` and `name2` reference variables are now *aliases* of each other because they are two different variables that refer to the same object. All references to the object originally referenced by `name2` are now gone; that object cannot be used again in the program.

Multiple reference variables can refer to the same object.

One important implication of aliases is that when we use one reference to change an object, it is also changed for the other reference because there is really only one object. Aliases can produce undesirable effects unless they are managed carefully.

All interaction with an object occurs through a reference variable, so we can use an object only if we have a reference to it. When all references to an object are lost (perhaps by reassignment), that object can no longer contribute to the program. The program can no longer invoke its methods or use its variables. At this point the object is called *garbage* because it serves no useful purpose.

Java performs automatic *garbage collection*. When the last reference to an object is lost, the object becomes a candidate for garbage collection. Occasionally, behind the scenes, the Java environment executes a method that "collects" all the objects marked for garbage collection and returns their memory to the system for future use. The programmer does not have to worry about explicitly reclaiming memory that has become garbage.

3.2 The `String` Class

Let's examine the `String` class in more detail. Figure 3.1 lists some of the more useful methods of the `String` class.

Once a `String` object is created, its value cannot be lengthened or shortened, nor can any of its characters change. Thus we say that a `String` object is *immutable*. However, several methods in the `String` class return new `String` objects that are the result of modifying the original string's value.

Note that some of the `String` methods, such as `charAt`, refer to the *index* of a particular character. An index specifies a particular position, and therefore a particular character, in a string. The index of the first character in a string is zero, the index of the next character is one, and so on. Therefore, in the string `"Hello"`, the index of the character `'H'` is zero and the character at index four is `'o'`.

Several `String` methods are exercised in the program shown in Listing 3.1. As you examine the `StringMutation` program, keep in mind that this is not a single `String` object that changes its data; this program creates five separate `String`

`String (String str)`
Constructor: creates a new string object with the same characters as `str`.

`char charAt (int index)`
Returns the character at the specified `index`.

`int compareTo (String str)`
Returns an integer indicating if this string is lexically before (a negative return value), equal to (a zero return value), or lexically after (a positive return value), the string `str`.

`String concat (String str)`
Returns a new string consisting of this string concatenated with `str`.

`boolean equals (String str)`
Returns true if this string contains the same characters as `str` (including case) and false otherwise.

`boolean equalsIgnoreCase (String str)`
Returns true if this string contains the same characters as `str` (without regard to case) and false otherwise.

`int length ()`
Returns the number of characters in this string.

`String replace (char oldChar, char newChar)`
Returns a new string that is identical with this string except that every occurrence of `oldChar` is replaced by `newChar`.

`String substring (int offset, int endIndex)`
Returns a new string that is a subset of this string starting at index `offset` and extending through `endIndex-1`.

`String toLowerCase ()`
Returns a new string identical to this string except all uppercase letters are converted to their lowercase equivalent.

`String toUpperCase ()`
Returns a new string identical to this string except all lowercase letters are converted to their uppercase equivalent.

FIGURE 3.1 Some methods of the String class

objects using various methods of the String class. Originally, the phrase object is set up:

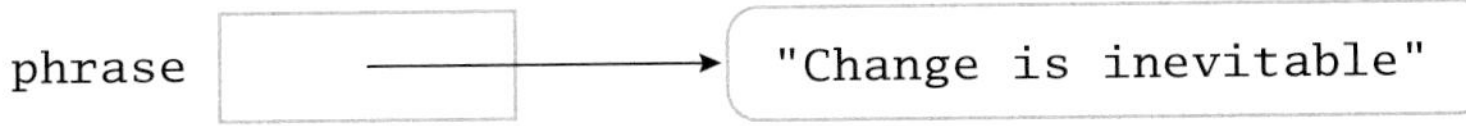

Listing 3.1

```
//********************************************************************
//  StringMutation.java       Java Foundations
//
//  Demonstrates the use of the String class and its methods.
//********************************************************************

public class StringMutation
{
   //-----------------------------------------------------------------
   //  Prints a string and various mutations of it.
   //-----------------------------------------------------------------
   public static void main (String[] args)
   {
      String phrase = "Change is inevitable";
      String mutation1, mutation2, mutation3, mutation4;

      System.out.println ("Original string: \"" + phrase + "\"");
      System.out.println ("Length of string: " + phrase.length());

      mutation1 = phrase.concat (", except from vending machines.");
      mutation2 = mutation1.toUpperCase();
      mutation3 = mutation2.replace ('E', 'X');
      mutation4 = mutation3.substring (3, 30);

      // Print each mutated string
      System.out.println ("Mutation #1: " + mutation1);
      System.out.println ("Mutation #2: " + mutation2);
      System.out.println ("Mutation #3: " + mutation3);
      System.out.println ("Mutation #4: " + mutation4);

      System.out.println ("Mutated length: " + mutation4.length());
   }
}
```

Output

```
Original string: "Change is inevitable"
Length of string: 20
Mutation #1: Change is inevitable, except from vending machines.
Mutation #2: CHANGE IS INEVITABLE, EXCEPT FROM VENDING MACHINES.
Mutation #3: CHANGX IS INXVITABLX, XXCXPT FROM VXNDING MACHINXS.
Mutation #4: NGX IS INXVITABLX, XXCXPT F
Mutated length: 27
```

After printing the original phrase and its length, the `concat` method is executed to create a new `String` object referenced by the variable `mutation1`:

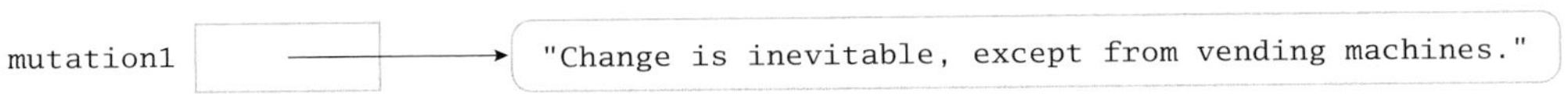

Then the `toUpperCase` method is executed on the `mutation1` object, and the resulting string is stored in `mutation2`:

mutation2 → "CHANGE IS INEVITABLE, EXCEPT FROM VENDING MACHINES."

Notice that the `length` and `concat` methods are executed on the `phrase` object, but the `toUpperCase` method is executed on the `mutation1` object. Any method of the `String` class can be executed on any `String` object, but for any given invocation, the method is executed on a particular object. The results of executing `toUpperCase` on `mutation1` would be very different than the results of executing `toUpperCase` on `phrase`. Remember, each object has its own state, which often affects the results of method calls.

Methods are often executed on a particular object, and that object's state usually affects the results.

Finally, the `String` object variables `mutation3` and `mutation4` are initialized by the calls to `mutation2.replace` and `mutation3.substring`, respectively:

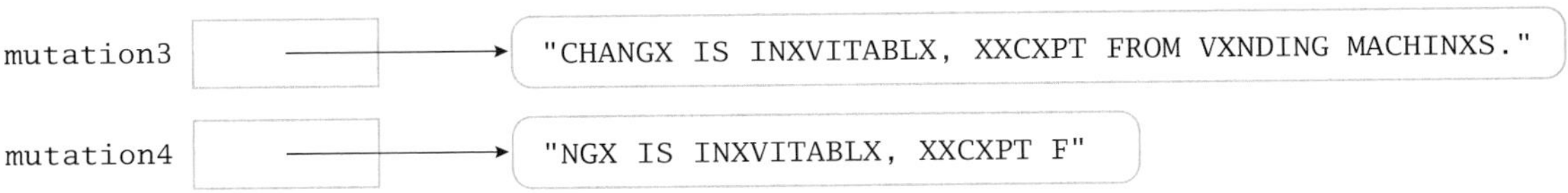

3.3 Packages

We mentioned earlier that the Java language is supported by a standard class library that we can make use of as needed. Let's examine that idea further.

A *class library* is a set of classes that supports the development of programs. A compiler or development environment often comes with a class library. Class libraries can also be obtained separately through third-party vendors. The classes in a class library contain methods that are often valuable to a programmer because of the special functionality they offer. In fact, programmers often become dependent on the methods in a class library and begin to think of them as part of the language. However, technically, they are not in the language itself.

A class library provides useful support when developing programs.

The `String` class, for instance, is not an inherent part of the Java language. It is part of the Java standard class library that can be found in any Java development environment. The classes that make up the library were created by employees at Sun Microsystems, the people who created the Java language.

The class library is made up of several clusters of related classes, which are sometimes called Java APIs, or *application programming interfaces*. For example, we may refer to the Java Database API when we're talking about the set of classes that helps us write programs that interact with a database. Another example of an API is the Java Swing API, which refers to a set of classes that defines special graphical components used in a graphical user interface. Sometimes the entire standard library is referred to generically as the Java API.

The Java standard class library is organized into packages.

The classes of the Java standard class library are also grouped into *packages*. Each class is part of a particular package. The `String` class, for example, is part of the `java.lang` package. The `System` class is part of the java.lang package as well. We mentioned in Chapter 2 that the `Scanner` class is part of the `java.util` package.

The package organization is more fundamental and language-based than the API organization. Though there is a general correspondence between package and API names, the groups of classes that make up a given API might cross packages. In this book, we primarily refer to classes in terms of their package organization.

Figure 3.2 describes some of the packages that are part of the Java standard class library. These packages are available on any platform that supports Java software development. Some of these packages support highly specific programming techniques and will not come into play in the development of basic programs.

Various classes of the Java standard class library are discussed throughout this book.

The `import` Declaration

The classes of the `java.lang` package are automatically available for use when writing a Java program. To use classes from any other package, however, we must either *fully qualify* the reference or use an *import declaration*. Let's consider these two options.

Package	Provides support to
`java.applet`	Create programs (applets) that are easily transported across the Web.
`java.awt`	Draw graphics and create graphical user interfaces; AWT stands for Abstract Windowing Toolkit.
`java.beans`	Define software components that can be easily combined into applications.
`java.io`	Perform a wide variety of input and output functions.
`java.lang`	General support; it is automatically imported into all Java programs.
`java.math`	Perform calculations with arbitrarily high precision.
`java.net`	Communicate across a network.
`java.rmi`	Create programs that can be distributed across multiple computers; RMI stands for Remote Method Invocation.
`java.security`	Enforce security restrictions.
`java.sql`	Interact with databases; SQL stands for Structured Query Language.
`java.text`	Format text for output.
`java.util`	General utilities.
`javax.swing`	Create graphical user interfaces with components that extend the AWT capabilities.
`javax.xml.parsers`	Process XML documents; XML stands for eXtensible Markup Language.

FIGURE 3.2 Some packages in the Java standard class library

When you want to use a class from a class library in a program, you could use its fully qualified name, including the package name, every time it is referenced. For example, every time you want to refer to the `Scanner` class that is defined in the `java.util` package, you could write `java.util.Scanner`. However, completely specifying the package and class name every time it is needed quickly becomes tiring. Java provides the `import` declaration to simplify these references.

The `import` declaration specifies the packages and classes that will be used in a program so that the fully qualified name is not necessary with each reference. Recall that the example programs that use the `Scanner` class in Chapter 2 include an `import` declaration like this one:

```
import java.util.Scanner;
```

This declaration asserts that the `Scanner` class of the `java.util` package may be used in the program. Once this `import` declaration is made, it is sufficient to use the simple name `Scanner` when referring to that class in the program.

If two classes from two different packages have the same name, `import` declarations will not suffice because the compiler won't be able to figure out which class is being referenced in the flow of the code. When such situations arise, which is rare, the fully qualified names should be used in the code.

Another form of the `import` declaration uses an asterisk (`*`) to indicate that any class inside the package might be used in the program. Therefore, the following declaration allows all classes in the `java.util` package to be referenced in the program without qualifying each reference:

```
import java.util.*;
```

If only one class of a particular package will be used in a program, it is usually better to name the class specifically in the `import` declaration because it provides more specific information to anyone reading the code. However, if two or more will be used, the `*` notation is usually fine.

The classes of the `java.lang` package are automatically imported because they are fundamental and can be thought of as basic extensions to the language. Therefore, any class in the `java.lang` package, such as `System` and `String`, can be used without an explicit `import` declaration. It's as if all program files automatically contain the following declaration:

All classes of the `java.lang` package are automatically imported for every program.

```
import java.lang.*;
```

3.4 The Random Class

The need for random numbers occurs frequently when writing software. Games often use random numbers to simulate the roll of a die or the shuffle of a deck of cards. A flight simulator may use random numbers to determine how often a simulated flight has engine trouble. A program designed to help high school students prepare for the SATs may use random numbers to choose the next question to ask.

The `Random` class, which is part of the `java.util` package, represents a *pseudorandom number generator*. A random number generator picks a number at random out of a range of values. Program code that serves this role is technically pseudorandom, because a program has no means to actually pick a number randomly. A pseudorandom number generator performs a series of complicated calculations, based on an initial *seed value*, and produces a number. Though they are technically not random (because they are calculated), the values produced by a pseudorandom number generator usually appear random, at least random enough for most situations.

A pseudorandom number generator performs a complex calculation to create the illusion of randomness.

Figure 3.3 lists some of the methods of the `Random` class. The `nextInt` method can be called with no parameters, or we can pass it a single integer value. If no parameter is passed in, the `nextInt` method generates a random number across the entire range of `int` values, including negative numbers. Usually, though, we need a random number within a more specific range. For instance, to simulate the roll of a die, we might want a random number in the range of 1 to 6. The `nextInt` method returns a value that's in the range from 0 to one less than its parameter. For example, if we pass 100 as a parameter to `nextInt`, we'll get a return value that is greater than or equal to 0 and less than or equal to 99.

Note that the value that we pass to the `nextInt` method is also the number of possible values we can get in return. We can shift the range as needed by adding or subtracting the proper amount. To get a random number in the range of 1 to 6, we can call `nextInt(6)` to get a value from 0 to 5, and then add 1.

The `nextFloat` method of the `Random` class returns a `float` value that is greater than or equal to 0.0 and less than 1.0. If desired, we can use multiplication to scale the result, cast it into an `int` value to truncate the fractional part, and then shift the range as we do with integers.

The program shown in Listing 3.2 produces several random numbers in various ranges.

`Random ()`
   Constructor: creates a new pseudorandom number generator.

`float nextFloat ()`
   Returns a random number between 0.0 (inclusive) and 1.0 (exclusive).

`int nextInt ()`
   Returns a random number that ranges over all possible `int` values (positive and negative).

`int nextInt (int num)`
   Returns a random number in the range 0 to `num-1`.

FIGURE 3.3 Some methods of the `Random` class

Listing **3.2**

```
//********************************************************************
//  RandomNumbers.java       Java Foundations
//
//  Demonstrates the creation of pseudo-random numbers using the
//  Random class.
//********************************************************************

import java.util.Random;

public class RandomNumbers
{
   //-----------------------------------------------------------------
   //  Generates random numbers in various ranges.
   //-----------------------------------------------------------------
   public static void main (String[] args)
   {
      Random generator = new Random();
      int num1;
      float num2;

      num1 = generator.nextInt();
      System.out.println ("A random integer: " + num1);

      num1 = generator.nextInt(10);
      System.out.println ("From 0 to 9: " + num1);

      num1 = generator.nextInt(10) + 1;
      System.out.println ("From 1 to 10: " + num1);

      num1 = generator.nextInt(15) + 20;
      System.out.println ("From 20 to 34: " + num1);

      num1 = generator.nextInt(20) - 10;
      System.out.println ("From -10 to 9: " + num1);

      num2 = generator.nextFloat();
      System.out.println ("A random float (between 0-1): " + num2);

      num2 = generator.nextFloat() * 6;  // 0.0 to 5.999999
      num1 = (int)num2 + 1;
      System.out.println ("From 1 to 6: " + num1);
   }
}
```

Listing **3.2** continued

Output

```
A random integer: 243057344
From 0 to 9: 9
From 1 to 10: 2
From 20 to 34: 33
From -10 to 9: -4
A random float (between 0-1): 0.58384484
From 1 to 6: 3
```

3.5 The Math Class

All methods of the `Math` class are static, meaning they are invoked through the class name.

The `Math` class provides a large number of basic mathematical functions that are often helpful in making calculations. The `Math` class is defined in the `java.lang` package of the Java standard class library. Figure 3.4 lists several of its methods.

All the methods in the `Math` class are *static methods* (also called *class methods*), which means they can be invoked through the name of the class in which they are defined, without having to instantiate an object of the class first. Static methods are discussed further in Chapter 5.

The methods of the `Math` class return values, which can be used in expressions as needed. For example, the following statement computes the absolute value of the number stored in `total`, adds it to the value of `count` raised to the fourth power, and stores the result in the variable `value`:

```
value = Math.abs(total) + Math.pow(count, 4);
```

Note that you can pass an integer value to a method that accepts a `double` parameter. This is a form of assignment conversion, which was discussed in Chapter 2.

It's also interesting to note that the `Math` class contains a method called `random` that returns a random floating point value in the range 0.0 to 1.0. Therefore, this method could be used as an alternative to creating a `Random` object and calling its methods, as described in the previous section. However, the `Math` class does not have a method that returns an integer, or lets you specify the range of the result, as `Random` does.

```
static int abs (int num)
```
Returns the absolute value of num.

```
static double acos (double num)
static double asin (double num)
static double atan (double num)
```
Returns the arc cosine, arc sine, or arc tangent of num.

```
static double cos (double angle)
static double sin (double angle)
static double tan (double angle)
```
Returns the angle cosine, sine, or tangent of angle, which is measured in radians.

```
static double ceil (double num)
```
Returns the ceiling of num, which is the smallest whole number greater than or equal to num.

```
static double exp (double power)
```
Returns the value e raised to the specified power.

```
static double floor (double num)
```
Returns the floor of num, which is the largest whole number less than or equal to num.

```
static double pow (double num, double power)
```
Returns the value num raised to the specified power.

```
static double random ()
```
Returns a random number between 0.0 (inclusive) and 1.0 (exclusive).

```
static double sqrt (double num)
```
Returns the square root of num, which must be positive.

FIGURE 3.4 Some methods of the `Math` class

The `Quadratic` program, shown in Listing 3.3, uses the `Math` class to compute the roots of a quadratic equation. Recall that a quadratic equation has the following general form:

$$ax^2 + bx + c$$

The `Quadratic` program reads values that represent the coefficients in a quadratic equation (`a`, `b`, and `c`), and then evaluates the quadratic formula to determine the roots of the equation. The quadratic formula is:

$$\text{roots} = \frac{-b \pm \sqrt{b^2 - 4ac}}{2a}$$

Note that this program assumes that the discriminant (the value under the square root) is positive. If it's not, the result will not be a valid number, which Java represents as `NAN`, which stands for Not A Number. In Chapter 5 we discuss how such situations can be avoided.

Listing 3.3

```
//********************************************************************
//  Quadratic.java       Java Foundations
//
//  Demonstrates the use of the Math class to perform a calculation
//  based on user input.
//********************************************************************

import java.util.Scanner;

public class Quadratic
{
   //-----------------------------------------------------------------
   //  Determines the roots of a quadratic equation.
   //-----------------------------------------------------------------
   public static void main (String[] args)
   {
      int a, b, c;  // ax^2 + bx + c
      double discriminant, root1, root2;

      Scanner scan = new Scanner (System.in);

      System.out.print ("Enter the coefficient of x squared: ");
      a = scan.nextInt();

      System.out.print ("Enter the coefficient of x: ");
      b = scan.nextInt();

      System.out.print ("Enter the constant: ");
      c = scan.nextInt();
```

Listing 3.3 continued

```
      // Use the quadratic formula to compute the roots.
      // Assumes a positive discriminant.

      discriminant = Math.pow(b, 2) - (4 * a * c);
      root1 = ((-1 * b) + Math.sqrt(discriminant)) / (2 * a);
      root2 = ((-1 * b) - Math.sqrt(discriminant)) / (2 * a);

      System.out.println ("Root #1: " + root1);
      System.out.println ("Root #2: " + root2);
   }
}
```

Output

```
Enter the coefficient of x squared: 3
Enter the coefficient of x: 8
Enter the constant: 4
Root #1: -0.6666666666666666
Root #2: -2.0
```

3.6 Formatting Output

The `NumberFormat` class and the `DecimalFormat` class are used to format information so that it looks appropriate when printed or displayed. They are both part of the Java standard class library and are defined in the `java.text` package.

The `NumberFormat` Class

The `NumberFormat` class provides generic formatting capabilities for numbers. You don't instantiate a `NumberFormat` object by using the `new` operator. Instead, you request an object from one of its static methods that you invoke through the class name itself. Figure 3.5 lists some of the methods of the `NumberFormat` class.

Two of the methods in the `NumberFormat` class, `getCurrencyInstance` and `getPercentInstance`, return an object that is used to format numbers. The `getCurrencyInstance` method returns a formatter for monetary values, and the `getPercentInstance` method returns an object that formats a percentage.

```
String format (double number)
```
Returns a string containing the specified `number` formatted according to this object's pattern.

```
static NumberFormat getCurrencyInstance()
```
Returns a NumberFormat object that represents a currency format for the current locale.

```
static NumberFormat getPercentInstance()
```
Returns a NumberFormat object that represents a percentage format for the current locale.

FIGURE 3.5 Some methods of the `NumberFormat` class

The `format` method is invoked through a formatter object and returns a `String` that contains the number formatted in the appropriate manner.

The `Purchase` program shown in Listing 3.4 uses both types of formatters. It reads in a sales transaction and computes the final price, including tax.

Listing 3.4

```
//********************************************************************
//  Purchase.java       Java Foundations
//
//  Demonstrates the use of the NumberFormat class to format output.
//********************************************************************

import java.util.Scanner;
import java.text.NumberFormat;

public class Purchase
{
   //-----------------------------------------------------------------
   //  Calculates the final price of a purchased item using values
   //  entered by the user.
   //-----------------------------------------------------------------
   public static void main (String[] args)
   {
      final double TAX_RATE = 0.06;  // 6% sales tax

      int quantity;
      double subtotal, tax, totalCost, unitPrice;
```

Listing 3.4 continued

```
      Scanner scan = new Scanner (System.in);

      NumberFormat fmt1 = NumberFormat.getCurrencyInstance();
      NumberFormat fmt2 = NumberFormat.getPercentInstance();

      System.out.print ("Enter the quantity: ");
      quantity = scan.nextInt();

      System.out.print ("Enter the unit price: ");
      unitPrice = scan.nextDouble();

      subtotal = quantity * unitPrice;
      tax = subtotal * TAX_RATE;
      totalCost = subtotal + tax;

      // Print output with appropriate formatting
      System.out.println ("Subtotal: " + fmt1.format(subtotal));
      System.out.println ("Tax: " + fmt1.format(tax) + " at "
                          + fmt2.format(TAX_RATE));
      System.out.println ("Total: " + fmt1.format(totalCost));
   }
}
```

Output

```
Enter the quantity: 6
Enter the unit price: 1.69
Subtotal: $10.14
Tax: $0.61 at 6%
Total: $10.75
```

The `getCurrencyInstance` and `getPercentInstance` methods are called *factory methods*, because they produce and return an instance of an object set up in a particular manner. So, essentially, a `NumberFormat` factory method uses the `new` operator to create a `NumberFormat` object, then sets up the object to format values in a particular way and returns it so that it can be used.

The DecimalFormat Class

Unlike the NumberFormat class, the DecimalFormat class is instantiated in the traditional way using the new operator. Its constructor takes a String parameter that represents the pattern that will guide the formatting process. We can then use the format method to format a particular value. At a later point, if we want to change the pattern that the formatter object uses, we can invoke the applyPattern method. Figure 3.6 describes these methods.

The pattern defined by the string that is passed to the DecimalFormat constructor can get fairly elaborate. Various symbols are used to represent particular formatting guidelines. The pattern defined by the string "0.###", for example, indicates that at least one digit should be printed to the left of the decimal point and should be a zero if the integer portion of the value is zero. It also indicates that the fractional portion of the value should be rounded to three digits.

This pattern is used in the CircleStats program, shown in Listing 3.5, which reads the radius of a circle from the user and computes the circle's area and circumference. Trailing zeros, such as in the circle's area of 78.540, are not printed using this pattern.

The printf Method

In addition to print and println, the System class has another output method called printf, which allows the user to print a formatted string containing data values. The first parameter to the method represents the format string, and the remaining parameters specify the values that are inserted into the format string.

```
DecimalFormat (String pattern)
   Constructor: creates a new DecimalFormat object with the specified pattern.

void applyPattern (String pattern)
   Applies the specified pattern to this DecimalFormat object.

String format (double number)
   Returns a string containing the specified number formatted according to the
   current pattern.
```

FIGURE 3.6 Some methods of the DecimalFormat class

Listing 3.5

```
//********************************************************************
//  CircleStats.java       Java Foundations
//
//  Demonstrates the formatting of decimal values using the
//  DecimalFormat class.
//********************************************************************

import java.util.Scanner;
import java.text.DecimalFormat;

public class CircleStats
{
   //-----------------------------------------------------------------
   //  Calculates the area and circumference of a circle given its
   //  radius.
   //-----------------------------------------------------------------
   public static void main (String[] args)
   {
      int radius;
      double area, circumference;

      Scanner scan = new Scanner (System.in);

      System.out.print ("Enter the circle's radius: ");
      radius = scan.nextInt();

      area = Math.PI * Math.pow(radius, 2);
      circumference = 2 * Math.PI * radius;

      // Round the output to three decimal places
      DecimalFormat fmt = new DecimalFormat ("0.###");

      System.out.println ("The circle's area: " + fmt.format(area));
      System.out.println ("The circle's circumference: "
                          + fmt.format(circumference));
   }
}
```

Output

```
Enter the circle's radius: 5
The circle's area: 78.54
The circle's circumference: 31.416
```

For example, the following line of code prints an ID number and a name:

```
System.out.printf ("ID: %5d\tName: %s", id, name);
```

The first parameter specifies the format of the output and includes literal characters that label the output values as well as escape characters such as `\t`. The pattern `%5d` indicates that the corresponding numeric value (`id`) should be printed in a field of five characters. The pattern `%s` matches the string parameter `name`. The values of `id` and `name` are inserted into the string, producing a result such as:

```
ID: 24036   Name: Larry Flagelhopper
```

The `printf` method was added to Java to mirror a similar function used in programs written in the C programming language. This makes it easier for a programmer to translate (or *migrate*) an existing C program into Java.

Older software that still has value is called a *legacy system*. Maintaining a legacy system is often a costly effort because, among other things, it is based on older technologies. But in many cases, maintaining a legacy system is still more cost-effective than migrating it to new technology, such as writing it in a newer language. Adding the `printf` method is an attempt to make such migrations easier, and therefore less costly, by providing the same kind of output statement that C programmers have come to rely on.

The `printf` method was added to Java to support the migration of legacy systems.

However, using the `printf` method is not a particularly clean object-oriented solution to the problem of formatting output, so we avoid its use in this book.

3.7 Enumerated Types

Java provides the ability to define an *enumerated type*, which can then be used as the type of a variable when it is declared. An enumerated type establishes all possible values of a variable of that type by listing, or enumerating, them. The values are identifiers, and can be anything desired.

For example, the following declaration defines an enumerated type called `Season` whose possible values are `winter`, `spring`, `summer`, and `fall`:

```
enum Season {winter, spring, summer, fall}
```

There is no limit to the number of values that you can list for an enumerated type. Once the type is defined, a variable can be declared of that type:

```
Season time;
```

The variable `time` is now restricted in the values it can take on. It can hold one of the four `Season` values, but nothing else. Java enumerated types are considered to be *type-safe*, meaning that any attempt to use a value other than one of the enumerated values will result in a compile-time error.

Enumerated types are type-safe, ensuring that invalid values will not be used.

The values are accessed through the name of the type. For example:

```
time = Season.spring;
```

Enumerated types can be quite helpful in situations in which you have a relatively small number of distinct values that a variable can assume. For example, suppose we wanted to represent the various letter grades a student could earn. We might declare the following enumerated type:

```
enum Grade {A, B, C, D, F}
```

Any initialized variable that holds a `Grade` is guaranteed to have one of those valid grades. That's better than using a simple character or `String` variable to represent the grade, which could take on any value.

Suppose we also wanted to represent plus and minus grades, such as A– and B+. We couldn't use A– or B+ as values, because they are not valid identifiers (the characters `'-'` and `'+'` cannot be part of an identifier in Java). However, the same values could be represented using the identifiers `Aminus`, `Bplus`, etc.

Internally, each value in an enumerated type is stored as an integer, which is referred to as its *ordinal value*. The first value in an enumerated type has an ordinal value of 0, the second one has an ordinal value of 1, the third one 2, and so on. The ordinal values are used internally only. You cannot assign a numeric value to an enumerated type, even if it corresponds to a valid ordinal value.

An enumerated type is a special kind of class, and the variables of an enumerated type are object variables. As such, there are a few methods associated with all enumerated types. The `ordinal` method returns the numeric value associated with a particular enumerated type value. The `name` method returns the name of the value, which is the same as the identifier that defines the value.

Listing 3.6 shows a program called `IceCream` that declares an enumerated type and exercises some of its methods. Because enumerated types are special types of classes, they are not defined within a method. They can be defined either at the class level (within the class but outside a method), as in this example, or at the outermost level.

Listing **3.6**

```
//********************************************************************
//  IceCream.java       Java Foundations
//
//  Demonstrates the use of enumerated types.
//********************************************************************

public class IceCream
{
   enum Flavor {vanilla, chocolate, strawberry, fudgeRipple, coffee,
                rockyRoad, mintChocolateChip, cookieDough}

   //-----------------------------------------------------------------
   //  Creates and uses variables of the Flavor type.
   //-----------------------------------------------------------------
   public static void main (String[] args)
   {
      Flavor cone1, cone2, cone3;

      cone1 = Flavor.rockyRoad;
      cone2 = Flavor.chocolate;

      System.out.println ("cone1 value: " + cone1);
      System.out.println ("cone1 ordinal: " + cone1.ordinal());
      System.out.println ("cone1 name: " + cone1.name());

      System.out.println ();
      System.out.println ("cone2 value: " + cone2);
      System.out.println ("cone2 ordinal: " + cone2.ordinal());
      System.out.println ("cone2 name: " + cone2.name());

      cone3 = cone1;

      System.out.println ();
      System.out.println ("cone3 value: " + cone3);
      System.out.println ("cone3 ordinal: " + cone3.ordinal());
      System.out.println ("cone3 name: " + cone3.name());
   }
}
```

Listing 3.6 continued

Output

```
cone1 value: rockyRoad
cone1 ordinal: 5
cone1 name: rockyRoad

cone2 value: chocolate
cone2 ordinal: 1
cone2 name: chocolate

cone3 value: rockyRoad
cone3 ordinal: 5
cone3 name: rockyRoad
```

3.8 Wrapper Classes

As we've discussed previously, Java represents data by using primitive types (such as `int`, `double`, `char`, and `boolean`) in addition to classes and objects. Having two categories of data to manage (primitive values and object references) can present a challenge in some circumstances. There are times when you may want to treat primitive data as if they were objects. In these cases we need to "wrap" a primitive value into an object.

A *wrapper class* represents a particular primitive type. For instance, the `Integer` class represents a simple integer value. An object created from the `Integer` class stores a single `int` value. The constructors of the wrapper classes accept the primitive value to store. For example:

```
Integer ageObj = new Integer(40);
```

A wrapper class allows a primitive value to be managed as an object.

Once this declaration and instantiation are performed, the `ageObj` object effectively represents the integer 40 as an object. It can be used wherever an object is needed in a program rather than a primitive type.

For each primitive type in Java there exists a corresponding wrapper class in the Java class library. All wrapper classes are defined in the `java.lang` package. Figure 3.7 shows the wrapper class that corresponds to each primitive type.

Primitive Type	Wrapper Class
`byte`	`Byte`
`short`	`Short`
`int`	`Integer`
`long`	`Long`
`float`	`Float`
`double`	`Double`
`char`	`Character`
`boolean`	`Boolean`
`void`	`Void`

FIGURE 3.7 Wrapper classes in the `java.lang` package

Note that there is even a wrapper class that represents the type `void`. However, unlike the other wrapper classes, the `Void` class cannot be instantiated. It simply represents the concept of a void reference.

Wrapper classes also provide various methods related to the management of the associated primitive type. For example, the `Integer` class contains methods that return the `int` value stored in the object and that convert the stored value to other primitive types. Figure 3.8 lists some of the methods found in the `Integer` class. The other wrapper classes have similar methods.

`Integer (int value)`
  Constructor: creates a new Integer object storing the specified value.

`byte byteValue ()`
`double doubleValue ()`
`float floatValue ()`
`int intValue ()`
`long longValue ()`
  Return the value of this Integer as the corresponding primitive type.

`static int parseInt (String str)`
  Returns the int corresponding to the value stored in the specified string.

`static String toBinaryString (int num)`
`static String tohexString (int num)`
`static String toOctalString (int num)`
  Returns a string representation of the specified integer value in the corresponding base.

FIGURE 3.8 Some methods of the `Integer` class

Note that the wrapper classes also contain static methods that can be invoked independent of any instantiated object. For example, the `Integer` class contains a static method called `parseInt` that converts an integer that is stored in a `String` to its corresponding `int` value. If the `String` object `str` holds the string `"987"`, the following line of code converts the string into the integer value `987` and stores that value in the `int` variable num:

```
num = Integer.parseInt(str);
```

The Java wrapper classes often contain static constants that are helpful as well. For example, the `Integer` class contains two constants, `MIN_VALUE` and `MAX_VALUE`, that hold the smallest and largest `int` values, respectively. The other wrapper classes contain similar constants for their types.

Autoboxing

Autoboxing is the automatic conversion between a primitive value and a corresponding wrapper object. For example, in the following code, an `int` value is assigned to an `Integer` object reference variable:

```
Integer obj1;
int num1 = 69;
obj1 = num1;  // automatically creates an Integer object
```

The reverse conversion, called *unboxing*, also occurs automatically when needed. For example:

```
Integer obj2 = new Integer(69);
int num2;
num2 = obj2;  // automatically extracts the int value
```

Autoboxing provides automatic conversions between primitive values and corresponding wrapper objects.

Assignments between primitive types and object types are generally incompatible. The ability to autobox occurs only between primitive types and corresponding wrapper classes. In any other case, attempting to assign a primitive value to an object reference variable, or vice versa, will cause a compile-time error.

Summary of Key Concepts

- The `new` operator returns a reference to a newly created object.
- Multiple reference variables can refer to the same object.
- Methods are often executed on a particular object, and that object's state usually affects the results.
- A class library provides useful support when developing programs.
- The Java standard class library is organized into packages.
- All classes of the `java.lang` package are automatically imported for every program.
- A pseudorandom number generator performs a complex calculation to create the illusion of randomness.
- All methods of the `Math` class are static, meaning they are invoked through the class name.
- The `printf` method was added to Java to support the migration of legacy systems.
- Enumerated types are type-safe, ensuring that invalid values will not be used.
- A wrapper class allows a primitive value to be managed as an object.
- Autoboxing provides automatic conversions between primitive values and corresponding wrapper objects.

Self-Review Questions

SR 3.1 What does the `new` operator accomplish?

SR 3.2 What is a null reference?

SR 3.3 What is an alias? How does it relate to garbage collection?

SR 3.4 Write a declaration for a `String` variable called `author` and initialize it to the string `"Fred Brooks"`. Draw a graphic representation of the variable and its value.

SR 3.5 Write a statement that prints the value of a `String` object called `title` in all uppercase letters.

SR 3.6 Write a declaration for a `String` variable called `front` and initialize it to the first 10 characters of another `String` object called `description`.

SR 3.7 What is a Java package?

SR 3.8 What does the `java.net` package contain? The `java.swing` package?

SR 3.9 What package contains the `Scanner` class? The `String` class? The `Random` class? The `Math` class?

SR 3.10 What does an `import` declaration accomplish?

SR 3.11 Why doesn't the `String` class have to be specifically imported into our programs?

SR 3.12 Given a `Random` object called `rand`, what does the call `rand.nextInt()` return?

SR 3.13 Given a `Random` object called `rand`, what does the call `rand.nextInt(20)` return?

SR 3.14 What is a class method (also called a static method)?

SR 3.15 Write a statement that prints the sine of an angle measuring 1.23 radians.

SR 3.16 Write a declaration for a `double` variable called `result` and initialize it to 5 raised to the power 2.5.

SR 3.17 What are the steps to output a floating point value as a percentage using Java's formatting classes?

SR 3.18 Write the declaration of an enumerated type that represents movie ratings.

SR 3.19 How can we represent a primitive value as an object?

Exercises

EX 3.1 Write a statement that prints the number of characters in a `String` object called `overview`.

EX 3.2 Write a statement that prints the eighth character of a `String` object called `introduction`.

EX 3.3 Write a declaration for a `String` variable called `change` and initialize it to the characters stored in another `String` object called `original` with all `'e'` characters changed to `'j'`.

EX 3.4 What output is produced by the following code fragment?

```
String m1, m2, m3;
m1 = "Quest for the Holy Grail";
m2 = m1.toLowerCase();
m3 = m1 + " " + m2;
System.out.println (m3.replace('h', 'z'));
```

EX 3.5 What is the effect of the following `import` declaration?

```
import java.awt.*;
```

EX 3.6 Assuming that a `Random` object has been created called `generator`, what is the range of the result of each of the following expressions?

a. `generator.nextInt(20)`

b. `generator.nextInt(8) + 1`

c. `generator.nextInt(45) + 10`

d. `generator.nextInt(100) – 50`

EX 3.7 Write code to declare and instantiate an object of the `Random` class (call the object reference variable `rand`). Then write a list of expressions using the `nextInt` method that generates random numbers in the following specified ranges, including the end points. Use the version of the `nextInt` method that accepts a single integer parameter.

a. 0 to 10

b. 0 to 500

c. 1 to 10

d. 1 to 500

e. 25 to 50

f. –10 to 15

EX 3.8 Write an assignment statement that computes the square root of the sum of `num1` and `num2` and assigns the result to `num3`.

EX 3.9 Write a single statement that computes and prints the absolute value of `total`.

EX 3.10 Write code statements to create a `DecimalFormat` object that will round a formatted value to four decimal places. Then write a statement that uses that object to print the value of the result, properly formatted.

EX 3.11 Write code statements that prompt for and read a `double` value from the user, and then print the result of raising that value to the fourth power. Output the results to three decimal places.

EX 3.12 Write a declaration for an enumerated type that represents the days of the week.

Programming Projects

PP 3.1 Write an application that prompts for and reads the user's first and last name (separately). Then print a string composed of the first letter of the user's first name, followed by the first five characters of the user's last name, followed by a random number in the range 10 to 99. Assume that the last name is at least five letters long. Similar algorithms are sometimes used to generate usernames for new computer accounts.

PP 3.2 Write an application that prints the sum of cubes. Prompt for and read two integer values and print the sum of each value raised to the third power.

PP 3.3 Write an application that creates and prints a random phone number of the form XXX-XXX-XXXX. Include the dashes in the output. Do not let the first three digits contain an 8 or 9 (but don't be more restrictive than that), and make sure that the second set of three digits is not greater than 742. *Hint:* Think through the easiest way to construct the phone number. Each digit does not have to be determined separately.

PP 3.4 Write an application that reads the (x,y) coordinates for two points. Compute the distance between the two points using the following formula:

$$\text{Distance} = \sqrt{(x_2 - x_1)^2 + (y_2 - y_1)^2}$$

PP 3.5 Write an application that reads the radius of a sphere and prints its volume and surface area. Use the following formulas, in which *r* represents the sphere's radius. Print the output to four decimal places.

$$\text{Volume} = \frac{4}{3}\pi r^3$$

$$\text{Surface area} = 4\pi r^2$$

PP 3.6 Write an application that reads the lengths of the sides of a triangle from the user. Compute the area of the triangle using Heron's formula (below), in which *s* represents half of the perimeter of the triangle, and *a*, *b*, and *c* represent the lengths of the three sides. Print the area to three decimal places.

myCodeMate

$$\text{Area} = \sqrt{(s(s - a)(s - b)(s - c)}$$

Answers to Self-Review Questions

SR 3.1 The `new` operator creates a new instance (an object) of the specified class. The constructor of the class is then invoked to help set up the newly created object.

SR 3.2 A null reference is a reference that does not refer to any object. The reserved word `null` can be used to check for null references to avoid following them.

SR 3.3 Two references are aliases of each other if they refer to the same object. Changing the state of the object through one reference changes it for the other because there is actually only one object. An object is marked for garbage collection only when there are no valid references to it.

SR 3.4 The following declaration creates a `String` variable called `author` and initializes it:

```
String author = new String ("Fred Brooks");
```

For strings, this declaration could have been abbreviated as follows:

```
String author = "Fred Brooks";
```

This object reference variable and its value can be depicted as follows:

SR 3.5 The following statement prints the value of a `String` object in all uppercase letters:

```
System.out.println (title.toUpperCase());
```

SR 3.6 The following declaration creates a `String` object and sets it equal to the first 10 characters of the `String` called `description`:

```
String front = description.substring(0, 10);
```

SR 3.7 A Java package is a collection of related classes. The Java standard class library is a group of packages that supports common programming tasks.

SR 3.8 Each package contains a set of classes that supports particular programming activities. The classes in the `java.net` package support network communication, and the classes in the `javax.swing` class support the development of graphical user interfaces.

SR 3.9 The `Scanner` class and the `Random` class are part of the `java.util` package. The `String` and `Math` classes are part of the `java.lang` package.

SR 3.10 An `import` delcaration establishes the fact that a program uses a particular class, specifying the package that the class is a part of. This allows the programmer to use the class name (such as `Random`) without having to fully qualify the reference (such as `java.util.Random`) every time.

SR 3.11 The `String` class is part of the `java.lang` package, which is automatically imported into any Java program. Therefore, no separate `import` declaration is needed.

SR 3.12 A call to the `nextInt` method of a `Random` object returns a random integer in the range of all possible `int` values, both positive and negative.

SR 3.13 Passing a positive integer parameter x to the `nextInt` method of a `Random` object returns a random number in the range of 0 to x–1. So a call to `nextInt(20)` will return a random number in the range 0 to 19, inclusive.

SR 3.14 A class (or static) method can be invoked through the name of the class that contains it, such as `Math.abs`. If a method is not static, it can be executed only through an instance (an object) of the class.

SR 3.15 The following statement prints the sine of 1.23 radians:

```
System.out.println (Math.sin(1.23));
```

SR 3.16 The following declaration creates a `double` variable and initializes it to 5 raised to the power 2.5:

```
double result = Math.pow(5, 2.5);
```

SR 3.17 To output a floating point value as a percentage, you first obtain a formatter object using a call to the static method `getPercentInstance` of the `NumberFormat` class. Then you pass the value to be formatted to the `format` method of the formatter object, which returns a properly formatted string. For example:

```
NumberFormat fmt = NumberFormat.getPercentageInstance();
System.out.println (fmt.format(value));
```

SR 3.18 The following is a declaration of an enumerated type for movie ratings:

```
enum Ratings {G, PG, PG13, R, NC17}
```

SR 3.19 A wrapper class is defined in the Java standard class library for each primitive type. In situations where objects are called for, an object created from a wrapper class may suffice.

4 Conditionals and Loops

Chapter Objectives

- Discuss the flow of control through a method.
- Explore boolean expressions that can be used to make decisions.
- Perform basic decision making using `if` and `switch` statements.
- Discuss issues pertaining to the comparison of certain types of data.
- Execute statements repetitively using `while`, `do`, and `for` loops.
- Discuss the concept of an iterator object and use one to read a text file.

All programming languages have statements that allow you to make decisions to determine what to do next. Some of those statements allow you to repeat a certain activity multiple times. This chapter discusses several such statements, as well as exploring some issues related to comparing data and objects. We begin with a discussion of boolean expressions, which form the basis of any decision.

4.1 Boolean Expressions

The order in which statements are executed in a running program is called the *flow of control*. Unless otherwise specified, the basic execution of a program proceeds in a linear fashion. That is, a running program starts at the first programming statement and moves down one statement at a time until the program is complete. A Java application begins executing with the first line of the `main` method and proceeds step by step until it gets to the end of the `main` method.

Invoking a method alters the flow of control. When a method is called, the flow of control jumps to the code defined for that method and it begins executing. When the method completes, control returns to the place in the calling method where the invocation was made and processing continues from there. Methods and their invocation are discussed further in the next chapter.

Conditionals and loops allow us to control the flow of execution through a method.

Within a given method, we can alter the flow of control through the code by using certain types of programming statements. Statements that control the flow of execution through a method fall into two categories: conditionals and loops.

A *conditional statement* is sometimes called a *selection statement* because it allows us to choose which statement will be executed next. The conditional statements in Java are the `if` statement, the `if-else` statement, and the `switch` statement. These statements allow us to decide which statement to execute next.

Each decision is based on a *boolean expression*, also called a *condition*, which is an expression that evaluates to either true or false. The result of the expression determines which statement is executed next.

The following is an example of an `if` statement:

```
if (count > 20)
   System.out.println ("Count exceeded");
```

An `if` statement allows a program to choose whether to execute a particular statement.

The condition in this statement is `count > 20`. That expression evaluates to a boolean (true or false) result. Either the value stored in `count` is greater than 20 or it's not. If it is, the `println` statement is executed. If it's not, the `println` statement is skipped and processing continues with whatever code follows it. The `if` statement and other conditionals are explored in detail in this chapter.

The need to make decisions like this comes up all the time in programming situations. For example, the cost of life insurance might be dependent on whether the insured person is a smoker. If the person smokes, we calculate the cost using a particular formula; if not, we calculate it using another. The role of a conditional statement is to evaluate a boolean condition (whether the person smokes) and then to execute the proper calculation accordingly.

A *loop*, or *repetition statement*, allows us to execute a programming statement over and over again. Like a conditional, a loop is based on a boolean expression that determines how many times the statement is executed.

A loop allows a program to execute a statement multiple times.

For example, suppose we wanted to calculate the grade point average of every student in a class. The calculation is the same for each student; it is just performed on different data. We would set up a loop that repeats the calculation for each student until there are no more students to process.

Java has three types of loop statements: the `while` statement, the `do` statement, and the `for` statement. Each type of loop statement has unique characteristics that distinguish it from the others.

All conditionals and loops are based on boolean expressions, which use equality operators, relational operators, and logical operators to make decisions. Before we discuss the details of conditional and loop statements, let's explore these operators.

Equality and Relational Operators

The == and != operators are called *equality operators*. They test whether two values are equal or not equal, respectively. Note that the equality operator consists of two equal signs side by side and should not be mistaken for the assignment operator that uses only one equal sign.

The following `if` statement prints a sentence only if the variables `total` and `sum` contain the same value:

```
if (total == sum)
   System.out.println ("total equals sum");
```

Likewise, the following `if` statement prints a sentence only if the variables `total` and `sum` do not contain the same value:

```
if (total != sum)
   System.out.println ("total does NOT equal sum");
```

Java also has several *relational operators* that let us decide the relative ordering between two values. Earlier in this section we used the greater than operator

(>) to decide if one value was greater than another. We can ask such questions using various operators, depending on the relationship. These include less than (<), greater than or equal to (>=), and less than or equal to (<=). Figure 4.1 lists the Java equality and relational operators.

The equality and relational operators have lower precedence than the arithmetic operators. Therefore, arithmetic operations are evaluated first, followed by equality and relational operations. As always, parentheses can be used to explicitly specify the order of evaluation.

We'll see more examples of relational operators as we examine conditional and loop statements throughout this chapter.

Logical Operators

In addition to the equality and relational operators, Java has three *logical operators* that produce boolean results. They also take boolean operands. Figure 4.2 lists and describes the logical operators.

The `!` operator is used to perform the *logical NOT* operation, which is also called the *logical complement*. The `!` operator is unary, taking only one boolean operand. The logical complement of a boolean value yields its opposite value. That is, if a `boolean` variable called `found` has the value false, then `!found` is true. Likewise, if `found` is true, then `!found` is false. Note, the logical NOT operation does not change the value stored in `found`—it creates an expression that returns a boolean result.

A logical operation can be described by a *truth table* that lists all possible combinations of values for the variables involved in an expression. Because the logical NOT operator is unary, there are only two possible values for its one operand, true or false. Figure 4.3 shows a truth table that describes the `!` operator.

Operator	Meaning
==	equal to
!=	not equal to
<	less than
<=	less than or equal to
>	greater than
>=	greater than or equal to

FIGURE 4.1 Java equality and relational operators

Operator	Description	Example	Result
!	logical NOT	`! a`	true if a is false and false if a is true
&&	logical AND	`a && b`	true if a and b are both true and false otherwise
||	logical OR	`a || b`	true if a or b or both are true and false otherwise

FIGURE 4.2 Java logical operators

a	!a
false	true
true	false

FIGURE 4.3 Truth table describing the logical NOT operator

The `&&` operator performs a *logical AND* operation. The result of an `&&` operation is true if both operands are true, but false otherwise. Compare that to the result of the *logical OR* operator (`||`), which is true if one or the other or both operands are true, but false otherwise.

The AND and OR operators are both binary operators since each uses two operands. Therefore there are four possible combinations to consider: both operands are true, both are false, one is true and the other false, and vice versa. Figure 4.4 depicts a truth table that shows both the `&&` and `||` operators.

The logical NOT has the highest precedence of the three logical operators, followed by logical AND, then logical OR.

The logical operators allow us to create complex expressions when making decisions. Consider the following `if` statement:

```
if (!done && (count > MAX))
   System.out.println ("Completed.");
```

a	b	a && b	a || b
false	false	false	false
false	true	false	true
true	false	false	true
true	true	true	true

FIGURE 4.4 Truth table describing the logical AND and OR operators

Under what conditions would the `println` statement be executed? The value of the boolean variable `done` is either true or false, and the NOT operator reverses that value. The value of `count` is either greater than `MAX` or it isn't. The truth table in Figure 4.5 breaks down all of the possibilities.

Logical operators can be used to construct sophisticated conditions.

An important characteristic of the `&&` and `||` operators is that they are "short-circuited" in Java. That is, if their left operand is sufficient to decide the boolean result of the operation, the right operand is not evaluated. This situation can occur with both operators, but for different reasons. If the left operand of the `&&` operator is false, then the result of the operation will be false no matter what the value of the right operand is. Likewise, if the left operand of the `||` operator is true, then the result of the operation is true no matter what the value of the right operand is.

Sometimes you can capitalize on the fact that an operator is short-circuited. For example, the condition in the following `if` statement will not attempt to divide by zero if the left operand is false. If `count` has the value zero, the left side of the `&&` operation is false; therefore the whole expression is false and the right side is not evaluated.

```
if (count != 0 && total/count > MAX)
   System.out.println ("Testing.");
```

You should consider carefully whether or not to rely on these kinds of subtle programming language characteristics. Not all programming languages short-circuit these operations, and such code would produce a divide-by-zero error in those languages. As we have stressed before, you should err on the side of readability. You should always strive to make the logic of your program extremely clear to anyone reading your code.

done	count > MAX	!done	!done && (count > MAX)
false	false	true	false
false	true	true	true
true	false	false	false
true	true	false	false

FIGURE 4.5 A truth table for a specific condition

4.2 The if Statement

We've used a basic if statement in earlier examples in this chapter. Let's now explore it in detail.

An *if statement* consists of the reserved word if followed by a boolean expression, followed by a statement. The condition is enclosed in parentheses and must evaluate to true or false. If the condition is true, the statement is executed and then processing continues with any statement that follows. If the condition is false, the statement controlled by the condition is skipped and processing continues immediately with any statement that follows. Figure 4.6 shows this processing.

Consider the following example of an if statement:

```
if (total > amount)
    total = total + (amount + 1);
```

In this example, if the value in total is greater than the value in amount, the assignment statement is executed; otherwise the assignment statement is skipped.

Note that the assignment statement in this example is indented under the header line of the if statement. This communicates to a human reader that the assignment statement is part of the if statement; it implies that the if statement governs whether the assignment statement will be executed. This indentation is extremely important for human readability, although it is ignored by the compiler.

Proper indentation is important for human readability; it shows the relationship between one statement and another.

The example in Listing 4.1 reads the age of the user and then makes a decision as to whether to print a particular sentence based on the age that is entered.

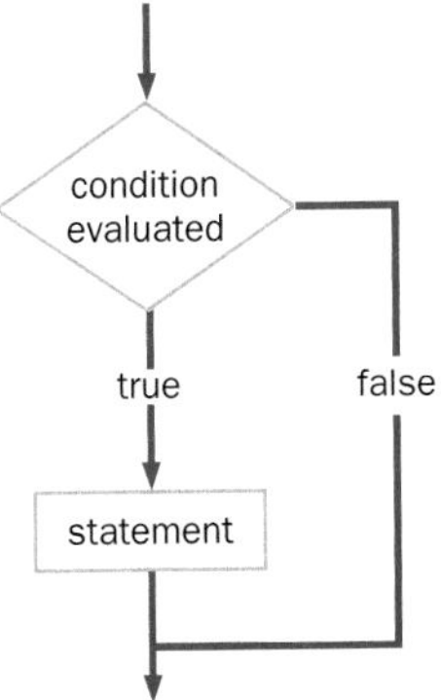

FIGURE 4.6 The logic of an if statement

Listing **4.1**

```
//********************************************************************
//  Age.java        Java Foundations
//
//  Demonstrates the use of an if statement.
//********************************************************************

import java.util.Scanner;

public class Age
{
   //-----------------------------------------------------------------
   //  Reads the user's age and prints comments accordingly.
   //-----------------------------------------------------------------
   public static void main (String[] args)
   {
      final int MINOR = 21;

      Scanner scan = new Scanner (System.in);

      System.out.print ("Enter your age: ");
      int age = scan.nextInt();

      System.out.println ("You entered: " + age);

      if (age < MINOR)
         System.out.println ("Youth is a wonderful thing. Enjoy.");

      System.out.println ("Age is a state of mind.");
   }
}
```

Output

```
Enter your age: 43
You entered: 43
Age is a state of mind.
```

The `Age` program echoes the age value that is entered in all cases. If the age is less than the value of the constant `MINOR`, the statement about youth is printed. If the age is equal to or greater than the value of `MINOR`, the `println` statement is skipped. In either case, the final sentence about age being a state of mind is printed.

Let's look at a few more examples of basic if statements. The following if statement causes the variable size to be set to zero if its current value is greater than or equal to the value in the constant MAX:

```
if (size >= MAX)
   size = 0;
```

The condition of the following if statement first adds three values together, then compares the result to the value stored in numBooks:

```
if (numBooks < stackCount + inventoryCount + duplicateCount)
   reorder = true;
```

If numBooks is less than the other three values combined, the boolean variable reorder is set to true. The addition operations are performed before the less than operator because the arithmetic operators have a higher precedence than the relational operators.

Assuming the variable generator refers to an object of the Random class, the following if statement examines the value returned from a call to nextInt to determine a random winner:

```
if (generator.nextInt(CHANCE) == 0)
   System.out.println ("You are a randomly selected winner!");
```

The odds of this code picking a winner are based on the value of the CHANCE constant. That is, if CHANCE contains 20, the odds of winning are 1 in 20. The fact that the condition is looking for a return value of 0 is arbitrary; any value between 0 and CHANCE-1 would have worked.

The if-else Statement

Sometimes we want to do one thing if a condition is true and another thing if that condition is false. We can add an *else clause* to an if statement, making it an *if-else* statement, to handle this kind of situation. The following is an example of an if-else statement:

```
if (height <= MAX)
   adjustment = 0;
else
   adjustment = MAX - height;
```

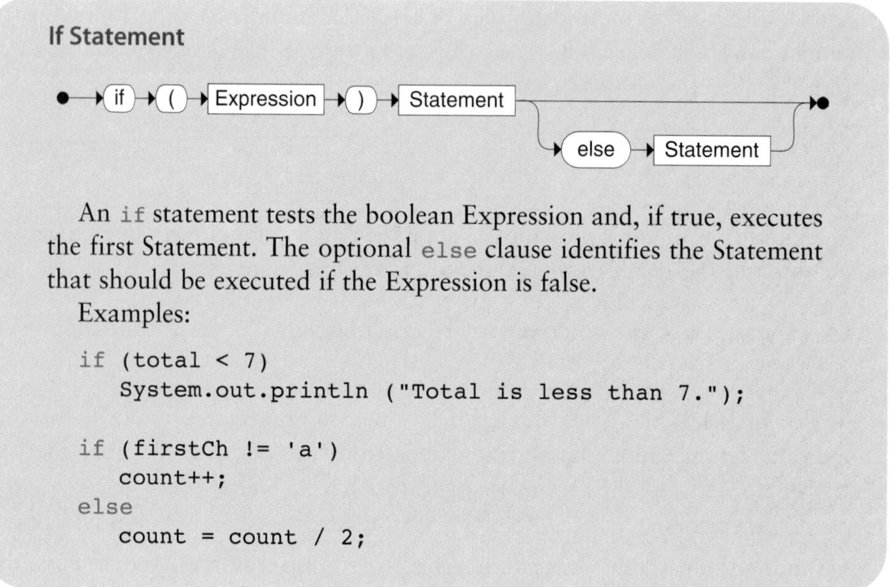

If Statement

An `if` statement tests the boolean Expression and, if true, executes the first Statement. The optional `else` clause identifies the Statement that should be executed if the Expression is false.

Examples:

```
if (total < 7)
   System.out.println ("Total is less than 7.");

if (firstCh != 'a')
   count++;
else
   count = count / 2;
```

An `if-else` statement allows a program to do one thing if a condition is true and another thing if the condition is false.

If the condition is true, the first assignment statement is executed; if the condition is false, the second assignment statement is executed. Only one or the other will be executed, because a boolean condition evaluates to either true or false. Note that proper indentation is used again to communicate that the statements are part of the governing `if` statement.

The `Wages` program shown in Listing 4.2 uses an `if-else` statement to compute the proper payment amount for an employee.

In the `Wages` program, if an employee works over 40 hours in a week, the payment amount takes into account the overtime hours. An `if-else` statement is used to determine whether the number of hours entered by the user is greater than 40. If it is, the overtime hours are paid at a rate one and a half times the normal rate. If there are no overtime hours, the total payment is based simply on the number of hours worked and the standard rate.

Let's look at another example of an `if-else` statement:

```
if (roster.getSize() == FULL)
   roster.expand();
else
   roster.addName (name);
```

Listing 4.2

```
//********************************************************************
//  Wages.java       Java Foundations
//
//  Demonstrates the use of an if-else statement.
//********************************************************************

import java.text.NumberFormat;
import java.util.Scanner;

public class Wages
{
   //-----------------------------------------------------------------
   //  Reads the number of hours worked and calculates wages.
   //-----------------------------------------------------------------
   public static void main (String[] args)
   {
      final double RATE = 8.25;  // regular pay rate
      final int STANDARD = 40;   // standard hours in a work week

      Scanner scan = new Scanner (System.in);

      double pay = 0.0;

      System.out.print ("Enter the number of hours worked: ");
      int hours = scan.nextInt();

      System.out.println ();

      // Pay overtime at "time and a half"
      if (hours > STANDARD)
         pay = STANDARD * RATE + (hours-STANDARD) * (RATE * 1.5);
      else
         pay = hours * RATE;

      NumberFormat fmt = NumberFormat.getCurrencyInstance();
      System.out.println ("Gross earnings: " + fmt.format(pay));
   }
}
```

Output

```
Enter the number of hours worked: 46

Gross earnings: $404.25
```

This example makes use of an object called roster. Even without knowing what roster represents, or from what class it was created, we can see that it has at least three methods: getSize, expand, and addName. The condition of the if statement calls getSize and compares the result to the constant FULL. If the condition is true, the expand method is invoked (apparently to expand the size of the roster). If the roster is not yet full, the variable name is passed as a parameter to the addName method.

Using Block Statements

We may want to do more than one thing as the result of evaluating a boolean condition. In Java, we can replace any single statement with a *block statement*. A block statement is a collection of statements enclosed in braces. We've used these braces many times in previous examples to delimit method and class definitions.

The program called Guessing, shown in Listing 4.3, uses an if-else statement in which the statement of the else clause is a block statement.

If the guess entered by the user equals the randomly chosen answer, an appropriate acknowledgement is printed. However, if the answer is incorrect, two sentences are printed, one that states that the guess is wrong and one that prints the actual answer. A programming project at the end of this chapter expands the basic idea in this example into the Hi-Lo game.

Note that if the block braces were not used, the sentence stating that the answer is incorrect would be printed if the answer was wrong, but the sentence revealing the correct answer would be printed in all cases. That is, only the first statement would be considered part of the else clause.

Remember that indentation means nothing except to the human reader. Statements that are not blocked properly can lead to the programmer making improper assumptions about how the code will execute. For example, the following code is misleading:

```
if (depth > 36.238)
   delta = 100;
else
   System.out.println ("WARNING: Delta is being reset to ZERO");
   delta = 0;  // not part of the else clause!
```

The indentation (not to mention the logic of the code) implies that the variable delta is reset only when depth is less than 36.238. However, without using a block, the assignment statement that resets delta to zero is not governed by the

Listing 4.3

```
//********************************************************************
//  Guessing.java       Java Foundations
//
//  Demonstrates the use of a block statement in an if-else.
//********************************************************************

import java.util.*;

public class Guessing
{
   //-----------------------------------------------------------------
   //  Plays a simple guessing game with the user.
   //-----------------------------------------------------------------
   public static void main (String[] args)
   {
      final int MAX = 10;
      int answer, guess;

      Scanner scan = new Scanner (System.in);
      Random generator = new Random();

      answer = generator.nextInt(MAX) + 1;

      System.out.print ("I'm thinking of a number between 1 and "
                        + MAX + ". Guess what it is: ");

      guess = scan.nextInt();

      if (guess == answer)
         System.out.println ("You got it! Good guessing!");
      else
      {
         System.out.println ("That is not correct, sorry.");
         System.out.println ("The number was " + answer);
      }
   }
}
```

Output

```
I'm thinking of a number between 1 and 10. Guess what it is: 4
That is not correct, sorry.
The number was 8
```

if-else statement at all. It is executed in either case, which is clearly not what is intended.

A block statement can be used anywhere a single statement is called for in Java syntax. For example, the if portion of an if-else statement could be a block, or the else portion could be a block (as we saw in the Guessing program), or both parts could be block statements. For example:

```
if (boxes != warehouse.getCount())
{
   System.out.println ("Inventory and warehouse do NOT match.");
   System.out.println ("Beginning inventory process again!");
   boxes = 0;
}
else
{
   System.out.println ("Inventory and warehouse MATCH.");
   warehouse.ship();
}
```

In this if-else statement, the value of boxes is compared to a value obtained by calling the getCount method of the warehouse object (whatever that is). If they do not match exactly, two println statements and an assignment statement are executed. If they do match, a different message is printed and the ship method of warehouse is invoked.

The Conditional Operator

The Java *conditional operator* is similar to an if-else statement in some ways. It is a *ternary operator* because it requires three operands. The symbol for the conditional operator is usually written ?:, but it is not like other operators in that the two symbols that make it up are always separated. The following is an example of an expression that contains the conditional operator:

```
(total > MAX) ? total + 1 : total * 2;
```

Preceding the ? is a boolean condition. Following the ? are two expressions separated by the : symbol. The entire conditional expression returns the value of the first expression if the condition is true, and returns the value of the second expression if the condition is false.

Keep in mind that this is an expression that returns a value, and usually we want to do something with that value, such as assign it to a variable:

```
total = (total > MAX) ? total + 1 : total * 2;
```

In many ways, the `?:` operator serves like an abbreviated `if-else` statement. The previous statement is functionally equivalent to, but sometimes more convenient than, the following:

```
if (total > MAX)
   total = total + 1;
else
   total = total * 2;
```

Now consider the following declaration:

```
int larger = (num1 > num2) ? num1 : num2;
```

If `num1` is greater than `num2`, the value of `num1` is returned and used to initialize the variable `larger`. If not, the value of `num2` is returned and used to initialize `larger`. Similarly, the following statement prints the smaller of the two values:

```
System.out.print ("Smaller: " + ((num1 < num2) ? num1 : num2));
```

As we've seen, the conditional operator is occasionally helpful. However, it is not a replacement for an `if-else` statement because the operands to the `?:` operator are expressions, not necessarily full statements. And even when the conditional operator is a viable alternative, you should use it carefully because it may be less readable than an `if-else` statement.

Nested `if` Statements

The statement executed as the result of an `if` statement could be another `if` statement. This situation is called a *nested if*. It allows us to make another decision after determining the results of a previous decision. The program in Listing 4.4, called `MinOfThree`, uses nested `if` statements to determine the smallest of three integer values entered by the user.

Listing **4.4**

```
//********************************************************************
//  MinOfThree.java       Java Foundations
//
//  Demonstrates the use of nested if statements.
//********************************************************************

import java.util.Scanner;

public class MinOfThree
{
   //-----------------------------------------------------------------
   //  Reads three integers from the user and determines the smallest
   //  value.
   //-----------------------------------------------------------------
   public static void main (String[] args)
   {
      int num1, num2, num3, min = 0;

      Scanner scan = new Scanner (System.in);

      System.out.println ("Enter three integers: ");
      num1 = scan.nextInt();
      num2 = scan.nextInt();
      num3 = scan.nextInt();

      if (num1 < num2)
         if (num1 < num3)
            min = num1;
         else
            min = num3;
      else
         if (num2 < num3)
            min = num2;
         else
            min = num3;

      System.out.println ("Minimum value: " + min);
   }
}
```

Output

```
Enter three integers:
43  26  69
Minimum value: 26
```

Carefully trace the logic of the MinOfThree program, using various input sets with the minimum value in all three positions, to see how it determines the lowest value.

An important situation arises with nested if statements. It may seem that an else clause after a nested if could apply to either if statement. For example:

```
if (code == 'R')
   if (height <= 20)
      System.out.println ("Situation Normal");
   else
      System.out.println ("Bravo!");
```

Is the else clause matched to the inner if statement or the outer if statement? The indentation in this example implies that it is part of the inner if statement, and that is correct. An else clause is always matched to the closest unmatched if that preceded it. However, if we're not careful, we can easily mismatch it in our mind and misalign the indentation. This is another reason why accurate, consistent indentation is crucial.

In a nested if statement, an else clause is matched to the closest unmatched if.

Braces can be used to specify the if statement to which an else clause belongs. For example, if the previous example should have been structured so that the string "Bravo!" is printed if code is not equal to 'R', we could force that relationship (and properly indent) as follows:

```
if (code == 'R')
{
   if (height <= 20)
      System.out.println ("Situation Normal");
}
else
   System.out.println ("Bravo!");
```

By using the block statement in the first if statement, we establish that the else clause belongs to it.

4.3 Comparing Data

When comparing data using boolean expressions, it's important to understand some nuances that arise depending on the type of data being examined. Let's look at a few key situations.

Comparing Floats

An interesting situation occurs when comparing floating point data. Two floating point values are equal, according to the == operator, only if all the binary digits of their underlying representations match. If the compared values are the results of computation, it may be unlikely that they are exactly equal even if they are close enough for the specific situation. Therefore, you should rarely use the equality operator (==) when comparing floating point values.

A better way to check for floating point equality is to compute the absolute value of the difference between the two values and compare the result to some tolerance level. For example, we may choose a tolerance level of 0.00001. If the two floating point values are so close that their difference is less than the tolerance, then we are willing to consider them equal. Comparing two floating point values, `f1` and `f2`, could be accomplished as follows:

```
if (Math.abs(f1 - f2) < TOLERANCE)
   System.out.println ("Essentially equal.");
```

The value of the constant `TOLERANCE` should be appropriate for the situation.

Comparing Characters

The relative order of characters in Java is defined by the Unicode character set.

We know what it means when we say that one number is less than another, but what does it mean to say one character is less than another? As we discussed in Chapter 2, characters in Java are based on the Unicode character set, which defines an ordering of all possible characters that can be used. Because the character `'a'` comes before the character `'b'` in the character set, we can say that `'a'` is less than `'b'`.

We can use the equality and relational operators on character data. For example, if two character variables `ch1` and `ch2` hold two characters, we might determine their relative ordering in the Unicode character set with an `if` statement as follows:

```
if (ch1 > ch2)
   System.out.println (ch1 + " is greater than " + ch2);
else
   System.out.println (ch1 + " is NOT greater than " + ch2);
```

The Unicode character set is structured so that all lowercase alphabetic characters (`'a'` through `'z'`) are contiguous and in alphabetical order. The same is true of uppercase alphabetic characters ('A' through 'Z') and characters that represent digits ('0' through '9'). The digits precede the uppercase alphabetic characters, which precede the lowercase alphabetic characters. Before, after, and in between these groups are other characters. See the chart in Appendix C for details.

Comparing Objects

The Unicode relationships among characters make it easy to sort characters and strings of characters. If you have a list of names, for instance, you can put them in alphabetical order based on the inherent relationships among characters in the character set.

However, you should not use the equality or relational operators to compare `String` objects. The `String` class contains a method called `equals` that returns a `boolean` value that is true if the two strings being compared contain exactly the same characters, and is false otherwise. For example:

```
if (name1.equals(name2))
   System.out.println ("The names are the same.");
else
   System.out.println ("The names are not the same.");
```

Assuming that `name1` and `name2` are `String` objects, this condition determines whether the characters they contain are an exact match. Because both objects were created from the `String` class, they both respond to the `equals` message. Therefore the condition could have been written as `name2.equals(name1)` and the same result would occur.

The `compareTo` method can be used to determine the relative order of strings.

It is valid to test the condition (`name1 == name2`), but that actually tests to see whether both reference variables refer to the same `String` object. For any object, the == operator tests whether both reference variables are aliases of each other (whether they contain the same address). That's different than testing to see whether two different `String` objects contain the same characters.

An interesting issue related to string comparisons is the fact that Java creates a unique object for string literals only when needed. Keep in mind that a string literal (such as `"Howdy"`) is a convenience, and is actually a shorthand technique for creating a `String` object. If the string literal `"Hi"` is used multiple times in a method, Java creates only one `String` object to represent it. Therefore, in the following code, the conditions of both `if` statements are true:

```
String str = "software";
if (str == "software")
   System.out.println ("References are the same");
if (str.equals("software"))
   System.out.println ("Characters are the same");
```

The first time the string literal `"software"` is used, a `String` object is created to represent it, and the reference variable `str` is set to its address. Each subsequent time the literal is used, the original object is referenced.

To determine the relative ordering of two strings, use the `compareTo` method of the `String` class. The `compareTo` method is more versatile than the `equals` method. Instead of returning a `boolean` value, the `compareTo` method returns an integer. The return value is negative if the `String` object through which the method is invoked precedes (is less than) the string that is passed in as a parameter. The return value is zero if the two strings contain the same characters. The return value is positive if the `String` object through which the method is invoked follows (is greater than) the string that is passed in as a parameter. For example:

```
int result = name1.compareTo(name2);
if (result < 0)
   System.out.println (name1 + " comes before " + name2);
else
   if (result == 0)
      System.out.println ("The names are equal.");
   else
      System.out.println (name1 + " follows " + name2);
```

Keep in mind that comparing characters and strings is based on the Unicode character set (see Appendix C). This is called a *lexicographic ordering*. If all alphabetic characters are in the same case (upper or lower), the lexicographic ordering will be alphabetic ordering as well. However, when comparing two strings, such as `"able"` and `"Baker"`, the `compareTo` method will conclude that `"Baker"` comes first because all of the uppercase letters come before all of the lowercase letters in the Unicode character set. If a string is the prefix of a longer string, it is considered to precede the longer string. For example, when comparing two strings such as `"horse"` and `"horsefly"`, the `compareTo` method will conclude that `"horse"` comes first.

4.4 The switch Statement

Another conditional statement in Java is called the *switch statement*, which causes the executing program to follow one of several paths based on a single value. We also discuss the *break statement* in this section because it is usually used with a switch statement.

The switch statement evaluates an expression to determine a value and then matches that value with one of several possible *cases*. Each case has statements associated with it. After evaluating the expression, control jumps to the statement associated with the first case that matches the value. Consider the following example:

```
switch (idChar)
{
   case 'A':
      aCount = aCount + 1;
      break;
   case 'B':
      bCount = bCount + 1;
      break;
   case 'C':
      cCount = cCount + 1;
      break;
   default:
      System.out.println ("Error in Identification Character.");
}
```

First, the expression is evaluated. In this example, the expression is a simple char variable. Execution then transfers to the first statement identified by the case value that matches the result of the expression. Therefore, if idChar contains an 'A', the variable aCount is incremented. If it contains a 'B', the case for 'A' is skipped and processing continues where bCount is incremented.

If no case value matches that of the expression, execution continues with the optional *default case*, indicated by the reserved word default. If no default case exists, no statements in the switch statement are executed and processing continues with the statement after the switch statement. It is often a good idea to include a default case, even if you don't expect it to be executed.

When a break statement is encountered, processing jumps to the statement following the switch statement. A break statement is usually used to break out of each case of a switch statement. Without a break statement, processing continues into the next case of the switch. Therefore if the break statement at the end of the 'A' case in the previous example were not there, both the aCount and bCount variables would be incremented when idChar contains an 'A'. Usually we want to perform only one case, so a break statement is almost always used. Occasionally, though, the "pass through" feature comes in handy.

A break statement is usually used at the end of each case alternative of a switch statement.

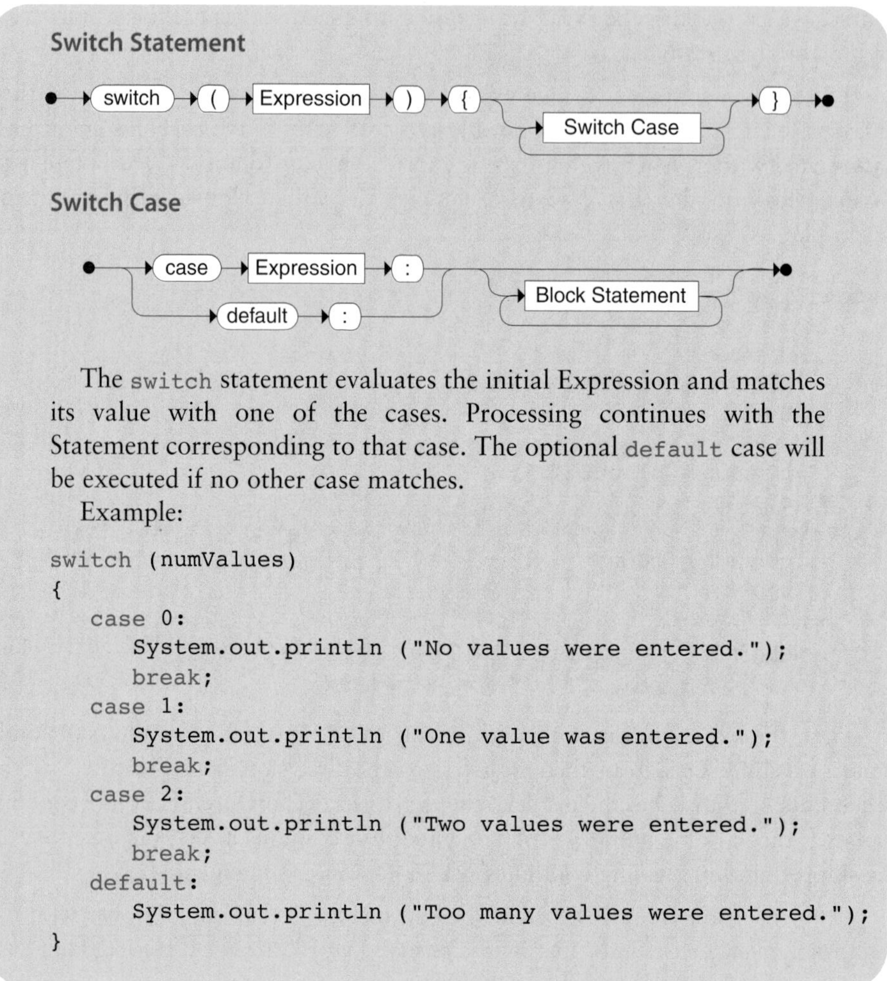

The `switch` statement evaluates the initial Expression and matches its value with one of the cases. Processing continues with the Statement corresponding to that case. The optional `default` case will be executed if no other case matches.

Example:

```
switch (numValues)
{
   case 0:
      System.out.println ("No values were entered.");
      break;
   case 1:
      System.out.println ("One value was entered.");
      break;
   case 2:
      System.out.println ("Two values were entered.");
      break;
   default:
      System.out.println ("Too many values were entered.");
}
```

The expression evaluated at the beginning of a `switch` statement must be of type `char`, `byte`, `short`, or `int`. In particular, it cannot be a `boolean`, a floating point value, or a `String`. Furthermore, the value of each case must be a constant; it cannot be a variable or other expression.

Note that the implicit boolean condition of a `switch` statement is based on equality. The expression at the beginning of the statement is compared to each case value to determine which one it equals. A `switch` statement cannot be used to determine other relational operations (such as less than), unless some preliminary processing is done. For example, the GradeReport program in Listing 4.5 prints a comment based on a numeric grade that is entered by the user.

Listing 4.5

```
//********************************************************************
//  GradeReport.java       Java Foundations
//
//  Demonstrates the use of a switch statement.
//********************************************************************

import java.util.Scanner;

public class GradeReport
{
   //-----------------------------------------------------------------
   //  Reads a grade from the user and prints comments accordingly.
   //-----------------------------------------------------------------
   public static void main (String[] args)
   {
      int grade, category;

      Scanner scan = new Scanner (System.in);

      System.out.print ("Enter a numeric grade (0 to 100): ");
      grade = scan.nextInt();

      category = grade / 10;

      System.out.print ("That grade is ");

      switch (category)
      {
         case 10:
            System.out.println ("a perfect score. Well done.");
            break;
         case 9:
            System.out.println ("well above average. Excellent.");
            break;
         case 8:
            System.out.println ("above average. Nice job.");
            break;
         case 7:
            System.out.println ("average.");
            break;
```

Listing 4.5 continued

```
            case 6:
               System.out.print ("below average. Please see the ");
               System.out.println ("instructor for assistance.");
               break;
            default:
               System.out.println ("not passing.");
         }
      }
}
```

Output

```
Enter a numeric grade (0 to 100): 87
That grade is above average. Nice job.
```

In `GradeReport`, the category of the grade is determined by dividing the grade by 10 using integer division, resulting in an integer value between 0 and 10 (assuming a valid grade is entered). This result is used as the expression of the `switch`, which prints various messages for grades 60 or higher and a default sentence for all other values.

Note that any `switch` statement could be implemented as a set of nested `if` statements. However, nested `if` statements quickly become difficult for a human reader to understand and are error prone to implement and debug. But because a `switch` can evaluate only equality, sometimes nested `if` statements are necessary. It depends on the situation.

4.5 The `while` Statement

As we discussed in the introduction of this chapter, a repetition statement (or loop) allows us to execute another statement multiple times. A *while statement* is a loop that evaluates a boolean condition just like an `if` statement does and executes a statement (called the *body* of the loop) if the condition is true. However, unlike the `if` statement, after the body is executed, the condition is evaluated again. If it is still true, the body is executed again. This repetition continues until the condition becomes false; then processing continues with the statement after the body of the `while` loop. Figure 4.7 shows this processing.

A `while` statement executes the same statement repeatedly until its condition becomes false.

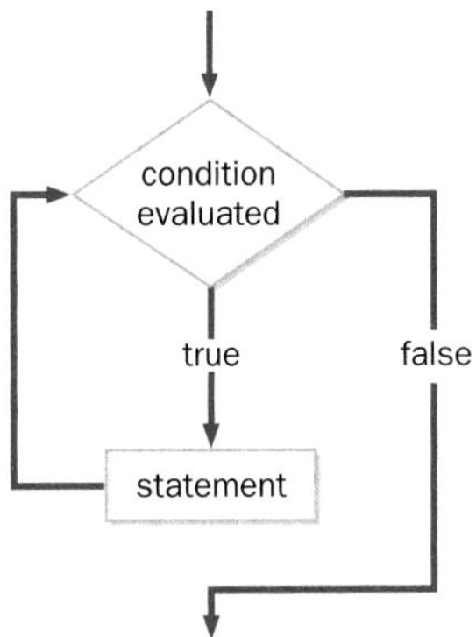

FIGURE 4.7 The logic of a `while` loop

While Statement

while (Expression) Statement

The `while` loop repeatedly executes the specified Statement as long as the boolean Expression is true. The Expression is evaluated first; therefore the Statement might not be executed at all. The Expression is evaluated again after each execution of Statement until the Expression becomes false.

Example:

```
while (total > max)
{
   total = total / 2;
   System.out.println ("Current total: " + total);
}
```

The following loop prints the values from 1 to 5. Each iteration through the loop prints one value, then increments the counter.

```
int count = 1;
while (count <= 5)
{
   System.out.println (count);
   count++;
}
```

Note that the body of the `while` loop is a block containing two statements. The entire block is repeated on each iteration of the loop.

Let's look at another program that uses a `while` loop. The `Average` program shown in Listing 4.6 reads a series of integer values from the user, sums them up, and computes their average.

Listing 4.6

```
//********************************************************************
//  Average.java        Java Foundations
//
//  Demonstrates the use of a while loop, a sentinel value, and a
//  running sum.
//********************************************************************

import java.text.DecimalFormat;
import java.util.Scanner;

public class Average
{
   //-----------------------------------------------------------------
   //  Computes the average of a set of values entered by the user.
   //  The running sum is printed as the numbers are entered.
   //-----------------------------------------------------------------
   public static void main (String[] args)
   {
      int sum = 0, value, count = 0;
      double average;

      Scanner scan = new Scanner (System.in);

      System.out.print ("Enter an integer (0 to quit): ");
      value = scan.nextInt();

      while (value != 0)   // sentinel value of 0 to terminate loop
      {
         count++;

         sum += value;
         System.out.println ("The sum so far is " + sum);

         System.out.print ("Enter an integer (0 to quit): ");
         value = scan.nextInt();
      }
```

Listing **4.6** continued

```
      System.out.println ();

      if (count == 0)
         System.out.println ("No values were entered.");
      else
      {
         average = (double)sum / count;

         DecimalFormat fmt = new DecimalFormat ("0.###");
         System.out.println ("The average is " + fmt.format(average));
      }
   }
}
```

Output

```
Enter an integer (0 to quit): 25
The sum so far is 25
Enter an integer (0 to quit): 44
The sum so far is 69
Enter an integer (0 to quit): -14
The sum so far is 55
Enter an integer (0 to quit): 83
The sum so far is 138
Enter an integer (0 to quit): 69
The sum so far is 207
Enter an integer (0 to quit): -37
The sum so far is 170
Enter an integer (0 to quit): 116
The sum so far is 286
Enter an integer (0 to quit): 0

The average is 40.857
```

We don't know how many values the user may enter, so we need to have a way to indicate that the user is done entering numbers. In this program, we designate zero to be a *sentinel value* that indicates the end of the input. The `while` loop continues to process input values until the user enters zero. This assumes that zero is not one of the valid numbers that should contribute to the average. A sentinel value must always be outside the normal range of values entered.

Note that in the `Average` program, a variable called `sum` is used to maintain a *running sum*, which means it is the sum of the values entered thus far. The variable `sum` is initialized to zero, and each value read is added to and stored back into `sum`.

We also have to count the number of values that are entered so that after the loop concludes we can divide by the appropriate value to compute the average. Note that the sentinel value is not counted. Consider the unusual situation in which the user immediately enters the sentinel value before entering any valid values. The `if` statement at the end of the program avoids a divide-by-zero error.

Let's examine yet another program that uses a `while` loop. The `WinPercentage` program shown in Listing 4.7 computes the winning percentage of a sports team based on the number of games won.

Listing **4.7**

```
//********************************************************************
//  WinPercentage.java        Java Foundations
//
//  Demonstrates the use of a while loop for input validation.
//********************************************************************

import java.text.NumberFormat;
import java.util.Scanner;

public class WinPercentage
{
   //-----------------------------------------------------------------
   //  Computes the percentage of games won by a team.
   //-----------------------------------------------------------------
   public static void main (String[] args)
   {
      final int NUM_GAMES = 12;
      int won;
      double ratio;

      Scanner scan = new Scanner (System.in);

      System.out.print ("Enter the number of games won (0 to "
                        + NUM_GAMES + "): ");
      won = scan.nextInt();

      while (won < 0 || won > NUM_GAMES)
```

Listing 4.7 continued

```
         {
            System.out.print ("Invalid input. Please reenter: ");
            won = scan.nextInt();
         }

         ratio = (double)won / NUM_GAMES;

         NumberFormat fmt = NumberFormat.getPercentInstance();

         System.out.println ();
         System.out.println ("Winning percentage: " + fmt.format(ratio));
      }
   }
```

Output

```
Enter the number of games won (0 to 12): -5
Invalid input. Please reenter: 13
Invalid input. Please reenter: 7

Winning percentage: 58%
```

We use a `while` loop in the `WinPercentage` program for *input validation*, meaning we guarantee that the user enters a value that we consider to be valid before continuing. In this example, that means that the value entered representing the number of games won must be greater than or equal to zero and less than or equal to the total number of games played. The `while` loop continues to execute, repeatedly prompting the user for valid input, until the entered number is indeed valid. The body of the `while` loop will not be executed at all if the user enters a valid value the first time.

We generally want our programs to be *robust*, which means that they handle potential problems as elegantly as possible. Validating input data and avoiding errors such as dividing by zero are situations that we should consciously address when designing a program. Loops and conditionals help us recognize and deal with such situations.

Infinite Loops

It is the programmer's responsibility to ensure that the condition of a loop will eventually become false. If it doesn't, the loop body will execute forever, or at least until the program is interrupted. This situation, referred to as an *infinite loop*, is a common mistake.

The following is an example of an infinite loop:

```
int count = 1;
while (count <= 25)   // Warning: this is an infinite loop!
{
   System.out.println (count);
   count = count - 1;
}
```

If you execute this loop, you should be prepared to interrupt it. On most systems, pressing the Control-C keyboard combination (hold down the Control key and press C) terminates a running program.

We must design our programs carefully to avoid infinite loops.

In this example, the initial value of `count` is 1 and it is decremented in the loop body. The `while` loop will continue as long as `count` is less than or equal to 25. Because `count` gets smaller with each iteration, the condition will always be true, or at least until the value of `count` gets so small that an underflow error occurs. The point is that the logic of the code is clearly wrong.

Let's look at some other examples of infinite loops:

```
int count = 1;
while (count != 50)   // infinite loop
   count += 2;
```

In this code fragment, the variable `count` is initialized to 1 and is moving in a positive direction. However, note that it is being incremented by 2 each time. This loop will never terminate because `count` will never equal 50. It begins at 1 and then changes to 3, then 5, and so on. Eventually it reaches 49, then changes to 51, then 53, and continues forever.

Now consider the following situation:

```
double num = 1.0;
while (num != 0.0)   // infinite loop
   num = num - 0.1;
```

Once again, the value of the loop control variable seems to be moving in the correct direction. And, in fact, it seems like num will eventually take on the value 0.0. However, this is an infinite loop (on most computer systems) because num will never have a value *exactly* equal to 0.0. This situation is similar to one we discussed earlier in this chapter when we explored the idea of comparing floating point values in the condition of an if statement. Because of the way the values are represented in binary, minute computational errors occur internally, making it problematic to compare two floating point values for equality.

Nested Loops

The body of a loop can contain another loop. This situation is called a *nested loop*. Keep in mind that for each iteration of the outer loop, the inner loop executes completely. Consider the following code fragment. How many times does the string "Here again" get printed?

```
int count1 = 1, count2;
while (count1 <= 10)
{
   count2 = 1;
   while (count2 <= 50)
   {
      System.out.println ("Here again");
      count2++;
   }
   count1++;
}
```

The println statement is inside the inner loop. The outer loop executes 10 times, as count1 iterates between 1 and 10. The inner loop executes 50 times, as count2 iterates between 1 and 50. For each iteration of the outer loop, the inner loop executes completely. Therefore the println statement is executed 500 times.

As with any loop situation, we must be careful to scrutinize the conditions of the loops and the initializations of variables. Let's consider some small changes to this code. What if the condition of the outer loop were (count1 < 10) instead of (count1 <= 10)? How would that change the total number of lines printed? Well, the outer loop would execute 9 times instead of 10, so the println statement would be executed 450 times. What if the outer loop were left as it was originally defined, but count2 were initialized to 10 instead of 1 before the inner loop? The inner loop would then execute 40 times instead of 50, so the total number of lines printed would be 400.

Let's look at another example that uses a nested loop. A *palindrome* is a string of characters that reads the same forward or backward. For example, the following strings are palindromes:

- radar
- drab bard
- ab cde xxxx edc ba
- kayak
- deified
- able was I ere I saw elba

Note that some palindromes have an even number of characters, whereas others have an odd number of characters. The `PalindromeTester` program shown in Listing 4.8 tests to see whether a string is a palindrome. The user may test as many strings as desired.

The code for `PalindromeTester` contains two loops, one inside the other. The outer loop controls how many strings are tested, and the inner loop scans through each string, character by character, until it determines whether the string is a palindrome.

The variables `left` and `right` store the indexes of two characters. They initially indicate the characters on either end of the string. Each iteration of the inner loop compares the two characters indicated by `left` and `right`. We fall out of the inner loop when either the characters don't match, meaning the string is not a palindrome, or when the value of `left` becomes equal to or greater than the value of `right`, which means the entire string has been tested and it is a palindrome.

Note that the following phrases would not be considered palindromes by the current version of the program:

- A man, a plan, a canal, Panama.
- Dennis and Edna sinned.
- Rise to vote, sir.
- Doom an evil deed, liven a mood.
- Go hang a salami; I'm a lasagna hog.

These strings fail our current criteria for a palindrome because of the spaces, punctuation marks, and changes in uppercase and lowercase. However, if these characteristics were removed or ignored, these strings read the same forward and backward. Consider how the program could be changed to handle these situations. These modifications are included as a programming project at the end of this chapter.

Listing 4.8

```
//********************************************************************
//  PalindromeTester.java       Java Foundations
//
//  Demonstrates the use of nested while loops.
//********************************************************************

import java.util.Scanner;

public class PalindromeTester
{
   //-----------------------------------------------------------------
   //  Tests strings to see if they are palindromes.
   //-----------------------------------------------------------------
   public static void main (String[] args)
   {
      String str, another = "y";
      int left, right;

      Scanner scan = new Scanner (System.in);

      while (another.equalsIgnoreCase("y")) // allows y or Y
      {
         System.out.println ("Enter a potential palindrome:");
         str = scan.nextLine();

         left = 0;
         right = str.length() - 1;

         while (str.charAt(left) == str.charAt(right) && left < right)
         {
            left++;
            right--;
         }

         System.out.println();
```

Listing **4.8** continued

```
         if (left < right)
            System.out.println ("That string is NOT a palindrome.");
         else
            System.out.println ("That string IS a palindrome.");

         System.out.println();
         System.out.print ("Test another palindrome (y/n)? ");
         another = scan.nextLine();
      }
   }
}
```

Output

```
Enter a potential palindrome:
radar

That string IS a palindrome.

Test another palindrome (y/n)? y
Enter a potential palindrome:
able was I ere I saw elba

That string IS a palindrome.

Test another palindrome (y/n)? y
Enter a potential palindrome:
abc6996cba

That string IS a palindrome.

Test another palindrome (y/n)? y
Enter a potential palindrome:
abracadabra

That string is NOT a palindrome.

Test another palindrome (y/n)? n
```

Other Loop Controls

We've seen how the `break` statement can be used to break out of the cases of a `switch` statement. The `break` statement can also be placed in the body of any loop, even though this is usually inappropriate. Its effect on a loop is similar to its effect on a `switch` statement. The execution of the loop is stopped, and the statement following the loop is executed.

It is never necessary to use a `break` statement in a loop. An equivalent loop can always be written without it. Because the `break` statement causes program flow to jump from one place to another, using a `break` in a loop is not good practice. Its use is tolerated in a `switch` statement because an equivalent `switch` statement cannot be written without it. However, you can and should avoid it in a loop.

A *continue statement* has a similar effect on loop processing. The `continue` statement is similar to a `break`, but the loop condition is evaluated again, and the loop body is executed again if it is still true. Like the `break` statement, the `continue` statement can always be avoided in a loop, and for the same reasons, it should be.

4.6 Iterators

An *iterator* is an object that has methods that allow you to process a collection of items one at a time. That is, an iterator lets you step through each item and interact with it as needed. For example, your goal may be to compute the dues for each member of a club, or print the distinct parts of a URL, or process a group of returned library books. An iterator provides a consistent and simple mechanism for systematically processing a group of items. This processing is inherently repetitive, and therefore ties into our discussion of loops.

An iterator is an object that helps you process a group of related items.

Technically an iterator object in Java is defined using the `Iterator` interface, which is discussed in Chapter 9. For now it is simply helpful to know that such objects exist and that they can make the processing of a collection of items easier.

Every iterator object has a method called `hasNext` that returns a `boolean` value indicating if there is at least one more item to process. Therefore the `hasNext` method can be used as a condition of a loop to control the processing of each item. An iterator also has a method called `next` to retrieve the next item in the collection to process.

There are several classes in the Java standard class library that define iterator objects. One of these is `Scanner`, a class we've used several times in previous examples to help us read data from the user. The `hasNext` method of the `Scanner` class returns true if there is another input token to process. And, as we've seen previously, it has a `next` method that returns the next input token as a string.

The `Scanner` class also has specific variations of the `hasNext` method, such as the `hasNextInt` and `hasNextDouble` methods, which allow you to determine if the next input token is a particular type. Likewise, as we've seen, there are variations of the `next` method, such as `nextInt` and `nextDouble`, that retrieve values of specific types.

When reading input interactively from the standard input stream, the `hasNext` method of the `Scanner` class will wait until there is input available, then return true. That is, interactive input read from the keyboard is always thought to have more data to process—it just hasn't arrived yet (until the user types it in). That's why in previous examples we've used special sentinel values to determine the end of interactive input.

However, the fact that a `Scanner` object is an iterator is particularly helpful when the scanner is being used to process input from a source that has a specific end point, such as processing the lines of a data file or processing the parts of a character string. Let's examine an example of this type of processing.

Reading Text Files

Suppose we have an input file called `websites.inp` that contains a list of Web page addresses (Uniform Resource Locators, or URLs) that we want to process in some way. The following are the first few lines of `websites.inp`:

```
www.google.com
newsyllabus.com/about
java.sun.com/j2se/6.0
www.linux.org/info/gnu.html
technorati.com/search/java/
www.cs.vt.edu/undergraduates/honors_degree.html
```

The program shown in Listing 4.9 reads the URLs from this file and dissects them to show the various parts of the path. It uses a `Scanner` object to process the input. In fact, the program uses multiple `Scanner` objects—one to read the lines of the data file, and another to process each URL string.

Listing 4.9

```
//********************************************************************
//  URLDissector.java       Java Foundations
//
//  Demonstrates the use of Scanner to read file input and parse it
//  using alternative delimiters.
//********************************************************************

import java.util.Scanner;
import java.io.*;

public class URLDissector
{
   //-----------------------------------------------------------------
   //  Reads urls from a file and prints their path components.
   //-----------------------------------------------------------------
   public static void main (String[] args) throws IOException
   {
      String url;
      Scanner fileScan, urlScan;

      fileScan = new Scanner (new File("websites.inp"));

      // Read and process each line of the file
      while (fileScan.hasNext())
      {
         url = fileScan.nextLine();
         System.out.println ("URL: " + url);

         urlScan = new Scanner (url);
         urlScan.useDelimiter("/");

         //  Print each part of the url
         while (urlScan.hasNext())
            System.out.println ("   " + urlScan.next());

         System.out.println();
      }
   }
}
```

Listing 4.9 continued

Output

```
URL: www.google.com
   www.google.com

URL: newsyllabus.com/about
   newsyllabus.com
   about

URL: java.sun.com/j2se/6.0
   java.sun.com
   j2se
   6.0

URL: www.linux.org/info/gnu.html
   www.linux.org
   info
   gnu.html

URL: technorati.com/search/java/
   technorati.com
   search
   java

URL: www.cs.vt.edu/undergraduates/honors_degree.html
   www.cs.vt.edu
   undergraduates
   honors_degree.html
```

There are two `while` loops in this program, one nested within the other. The outer loop processes each line in the file, and the inner loop processes each token in the current line.

The variable `fileScan` is created as a scanner that operates on the input file named `urls.inp`. Instead of passing `System.in` into the `Scanner` constructor, we instantiate a `File` object that represents the input file and pass it into the `Scanner` constructor. At that point, the `fileScan` object is ready to read and process input from the input file.

If for some reason there is a problem finding or opening the input file, the attempt to create a `File` object will throw an `IOException`, which is why we've added the `throws IOException` clause to the `main` method header. Processing exceptions is discussed further in Chapter 10.

The body of the outer `while` loop will be executed as long as the `hasNext` method of the input file scanner returns true—that is, as long as there is more input in the data file to process. Each iteration through the loop reads one line (one URL) from the input file and prints it out.

For each URL, a new `Scanner` object is set up to parse the pieces of the URL string, which is passed into the `Scanner` constructor when instantiating the `urlScan` object. The inner `while` loop prints each token of the URL on a separate line.

Recall that, by default, a `Scanner` object assumes that white space (spaces, tabs, and new lines) is used as the delimiters separating the input tokens. Using whitespace delimiters works in this example for the scanner that is reading each line of the input file. However, if the default delimiters do not suffice, as in the processing of a URL in this example, they can be changed.

The delimiters used to separate tokens in a `Scanner` object can be explicitly set as needed.

In this case, we are interested in each part of the path separated by the slash (/) character. A call to the `useDelimiter` method of the scanner sets the delimiter to a slash prior to processing the URL string.

If you want to use more than one alternate delimiter character, or if you want to parse the input in more complex ways, the `Scanner` class can process patterns called *regular expressions*, which are discussed in Appendix H.

4.7 The do Statement

The *do statement* is similar to the `while` statement in that it executes the loop body until a condition becomes false. However, unlike the `while` loop, whose condition is evaluated *before* the body is executed, the condition of a `do` loop is evaluated *after* the loop body executes. Syntactically, the condition in a `do` loop is written after the loop body to reflect this processing. The body of a `do` loop is always executed at least once, whereas with a `while` loop the body might not be executed at all (if the condition is initially false). Figure 4.8 shows the processing of a `do` loop.

A `do` statement executes its loop body at least once.

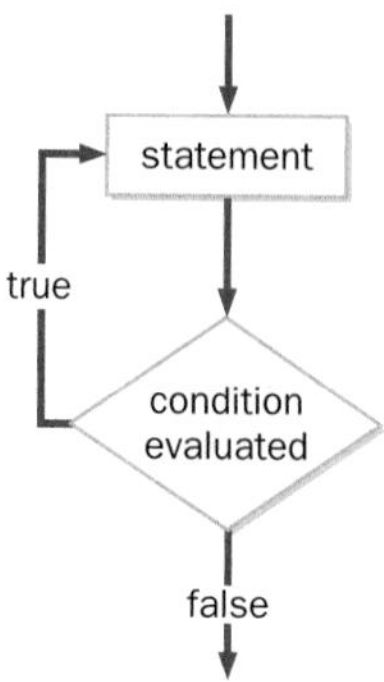

FIGURE 4.8 The logic of a do loop

The following code prints the numbers from 1 to 5 using a `do` loop. Compare this code with the similar example earlier in this chapter that uses a `while` loop to accomplish the same task.

```
int count = 0;
do
{
   count++;
   System.out.println (count);
}
while (count < 5);
```

Do Statement

The `do` loop repeatedly executes the specified Statement as long as the boolean Expression is true. The Statement is executed at least once, then the Expression is evaluated to determine whether the Statement should be executed again.

Example:

```
do
{
   System.out.print ("Enter a word:");
   word = scan.next();
   System.out.println (word);
}
while (!word.equals("quit"));
```

A do loop begins simply with the reserved word do. The body of the do loop continues until the *while clause* that contains the boolean condition that determines whether the loop body will be executed again. Sometimes it is difficult to determine whether a line of code that begins with the reserved word while is the beginning of a while loop or the end of a do loop.

Let's look at another example of the do loop. The program called ReverseNumber, shown in Listing 4.10, reads an integer from the user and reverses its digits mathematically.

The do loop in the ReverseNumber program uses the remainder operation to determine the digit in the 1's position, adds it into the reversed number, and then truncates that digit from the original number using integer division. The do loop terminates when we run out of digits to process, which corresponds to the point when the variable number reaches the value zero. Carefully trace the logic of this program with a few examples to see how it works.

If you know you want to perform the body of a loop at least once, then you probably want to use a do statement. A do loop has many of the same properties as a while statement, so it must also be checked for termination conditions to avoid infinite loops.

4.8 The for Statement

The while and the do statements are good to use when you don't initially know how many times you want to execute the loop body. The *for statement* is another repetition statement that is particularly well suited for executing the body of a loop a specific number of times that can be determined before the loop is executed.

A for statement is usually used when a loop will be executed a set number of times.

The following code prints the numbers 1 through 5 using a for loop, just as we did using a while loop and a do loop in previous examples:

```
for (int count=1; count <= 5; count++)
   System.out.println (count);
```

The header of a for loop contains three parts separated by semicolons. Before the loop begins, the first part of the header, called the *initialization*, is executed. The second part of the header is the boolean condition, which is evaluated before the loop body (like the while loop). If true, the body of the loop is executed, followed by the execution of the third part of the header, which is called the *increment*. Note that the initialization part is executed only once, but the increment part is executed after each iteration of the loop. Figure 4.9 shows this processing.

Listing 4.10

```
//********************************************************************
//  ReverseNumber.java       Java Foundations
//
//  Demonstrates the use of a do loop.
//********************************************************************

import java.util.Scanner;

public class ReverseNumber
{
   //-----------------------------------------------------------------
   //  Reverses the digits of an integer mathematically.
   //-----------------------------------------------------------------
   public static void main (String[] args)
   {
      int number, lastDigit, reverse = 0;

      Scanner scan = new Scanner (System.in);

      System.out.print ("Enter a positive integer: ");
      number = scan.nextInt();

      do
      {
         lastDigit = number % 10;
         reverse = (reverse * 10) + lastDigit;
         number = number / 10;
      }
      while (number > 0);

      System.out.println ("That number reversed is " + reverse);
   }
}
```

Output

```
Enter a positive integer: 2896
That number reversed is 6982
```

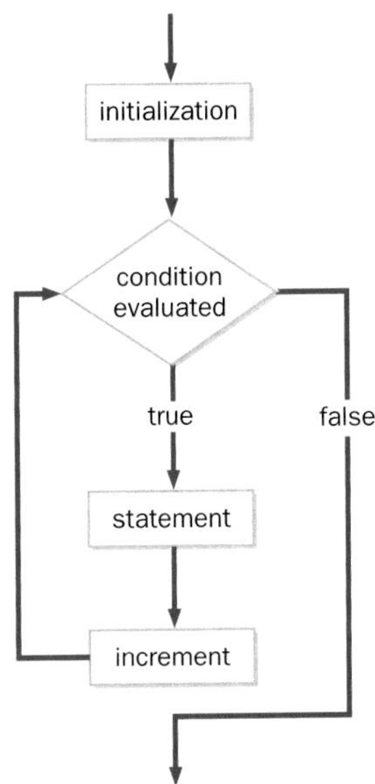

FIGURE 4.9 The logic of a `for` loop

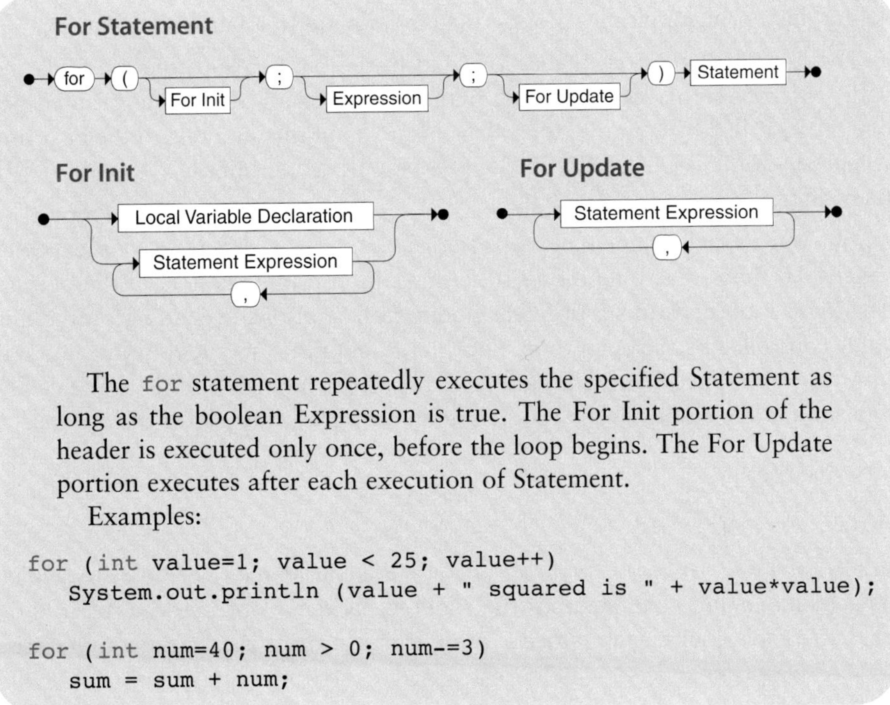

The `for` statement repeatedly executes the specified Statement as long as the boolean Expression is true. The For Init portion of the header is executed only once, before the loop begins. The For Update portion executes after each execution of Statement.

Examples:

```
for (int value=1; value < 25; value++)
   System.out.println (value + " squared is " + value*value);

for (int num=40; num > 0; num-=3)
   sum = sum + num;
```

A `for` loop can be a bit tricky to read until you get used to it. The execution of the code doesn't follow a top-to-bottom, left-to-right reading. The increment code executes after the body of the loop even though it is in the header.

In this example, the initialization portion of the `for` loop header is used to declare the variable `count` as well as to give it an initial value. We are not required to declare a variable there, but it is a common practice in situations where the variable is not needed outside of the loop. Because `count` is declared in the `for` loop header, it exists only inside the loop and cannot be referenced elsewhere. The loop control variable is set up, checked, and modified by the actions in the `for` loop header. It can be referenced inside the loop body, but it should not be modified except by the actions defined in the loop header.

Despite its name, the increment portion of the `for` loop header could actually decrement a value rather than increment it. For example, the following loop prints the integer values from 100 down to 1:

```
for (int num = 100; num > 0; num--)
   System.out.println (num);
```

In fact, the increment portion of the `for` loop could perform any calculation, not just a simple increment or decrement. Consider the program shown in Listing 4.11, which prints multiples of a particular value up to a particular limit.

The increment portion of the `for` loop in the `Multiples` program adds the value entered by the user after each iteration. The number of values printed per line is controlled by counting the values printed and then moving to the next line whenever `count` is evenly divisible by the `PER_LINE` constant.

The `Stars` program in Listing 4.12 shows the use of nested `for` loops. The output is a triangle shape made of asterisk characters. The outer loop executes exactly 10 times. Each iteration of the outer loop prints one line of the output. The inner loop performs a different number of iterations depending on the line value controlled by the outer loop. Each iteration of the inner loop prints one star on the current line. Writing programs that print variations on this triangle configuration are included in the programming projects at the end of the chapter.

Iterators and `for` Loops

In section 4.6 we discussed that some objects are considered to be iterators, which have `hasNext` and `next` methods to process each item from a group. A variation of the `for` loop, with a simplified syntax, lets us process the items in an iterator.

Listing 4.11

```
//********************************************************************
//  Multiples.java       Java Foundations
//
//  Demonstrates the use of a for loop.
//********************************************************************

import java.util.Scanner;

public class Multiples
{
   //-----------------------------------------------------------------
   //  Prints multiples of a user-specified number up to a user-
   //  specified limit.
   //-----------------------------------------------------------------
   public static void main (String[] args)
   {
      final int PER_LINE = 5;
      int value, limit, mult, count = 0;

      Scanner scan = new Scanner (System.in);

      System.out.print ("Enter a positive value: ");
      value = scan.nextInt();

      System.out.print ("Enter an upper limit: ");
      limit = scan.nextInt();

      System.out.println ();
      System.out.println ("The multiples of " + value + " between " +
                          value + " and " + limit + " (inclusive) are:");

      for (mult = value; mult <= limit; mult += value)
      {
         System.out.print (mult + "\t");

         // Print a specific number of values per line of output
         count++;
         if (count % PER_LINE == 0)
            System.out.println();
      }
   }
}
```

Listing **4.11** continued

Output

```
Enter a positive value: 7
Enter an upper limit: 400

The multiples of 7 between 7 and 400 (inclusive) are:
7       14      21      28      35
42      49      56      63      70
77      84      91      98      105
112     119     126     133     140
147     154     161     168     175
182     189     196     203     210
217     224     231     238     245
252     259     266     273     280
287     294     301     308     315
322     329     336     343     350
357     364     371     378     385
392     399
```

For example, if `bookList` is an iterator object that contains `Book` objects, we can use a `for` loop to process each `Book` object in the iterator as follows:

```
for (Book myBook : bookList)
   System.out.println (myBook);
```

This version of the `for` loop is referred to as a *foreach statement*. It processes each object in the iterator in turn. It is equivalent to the following:

```
Book myBook;
while (bookList.hasNext())
{
   myBook = bookList.next();
   System.out.println (myBook);
}
```

This version of the `for` loop can also be used on arrays, which are discussed in Chapter 7. We use the foreach loop as appropriate in various situations throughout the rest of the book.

Listing **4.12**

```
//********************************************************************
//  Stars.java       Java Foundations
//
//  Demonstrates the use of nested for loops.
//********************************************************************

public class Stars
{
   //-----------------------------------------------------------------
   //  Prints a triangle shape using asterisk (star) characters.
   //-----------------------------------------------------------------
   public static void main (String[] args)
   {
      final int MAX_ROWS = 10;

      for (int row = 1; row <= MAX_ROWS; row++)
      {
         for (int star = 1; star <= row; star++)
            System.out.print ("*");

         System.out.println();
      }
   }
}
```

Output

```
*
**
***
****
*****
******
*******
********
*********
**********
```

Comparing Loops

The three loop statements (`while`, `do`, and `for`) are functionally equivalent. Any particular loop written using one type of loop can be written using either of the other two loop types. Which type of loop we use depends on the situation.

As we mentioned earlier, the primary difference between a `while` loop and a `do` loop is when the condition is evaluated. If you know you want to execute the loop body at least once, a `do` loop is usually the better choice. The body of a `while` loop, on the other hand, might not be executed at all if the condition is initially false. Therefore we say that the body of a `while` loop is executed zero or more times, but the body of a `do` loop is executed one or more times.

A `for` loop is like a `while` loop in that the condition is evaluated before the loop body is executed. We generally use a `for` loop when the number of times we want to iterate through a loop is fixed or can be easily calculated. In many situations, it is simply more convenient to separate the code that sets up and controls the loop iterations inside the `for` loop header from the body of the loop.

Summary of Key Concepts

- Conditionals and loops allow us to control the flow of execution through a method.
- An `if` statement allows a program to choose whether to execute a particular statement.
- A loop allows a program to execute a statement multiple times.
- Logical operators are often used to construct sophisticated conditions.
- Proper indentation is important for human readability; it shows the relationship between one statement and another.
- An `if-else` statement allows a program to do one thing if a condition is true and another thing if the condition is false.
- In a nested `if` statement, an `else` clause is matched to the closest unmatched `if`.
- The relative order of characters in Java is defined by the Unicode character set.
- The `compareTo` method can be used to determine the relative order of strings.
- A `break` statement is usually used at the end of each case alternative of a `switch` statement.
- A `while` statement executes the same statement repeatedly until its condition becomes false.
- We must design our programs carefully to avoid infinite loops.
- An iterator is an object that helps you process a group of related items.
- The delimiters used to separate tokens in a `Scanner` object can be explicitly set as needed.
- A `do` statement executes its loop body at least once.
- A `for` statement is usually used when a loop will be executed a set number of times.

Self-Review Questions

SR 4.1 What is meant by the flow of control through a program?

SR 4.2 What type of conditions are conditionals and loops based on?

SR 4.3 What are the equality operators? The relational operators?

SR 4.4 What is a truth table?

SR 4.5 Why must we be careful when comparing floating point values for equality?

SR 4.6 How do we compare strings for equality?

SR 4.7 What is a nested `if` statement? A nested loop?

SR 4.8 How do block statements help us in the construction of conditionals and loops?

SR 4.9 What happens if a case in a `switch` does not end with a `break` statement?

SR 4.10 What is an infinite loop? Specifically, what causes it?

SR 4.11 Compare and contrast a `while` loop and a `do` loop.

SR 4.12 When would we use a `for` loop instead of a `while` loop?

Exercises

EX 4.1 What happens in the `MinOfThree` program if two or more of the values are equal? If exactly two of the values are equal, does it matter whether the equal values are lower or higher than the third?

EX 4.2 What is wrong with the following code fragment? Rewrite it so that it produces correct output.

```
if (total == MAX)
   if (total < sum)
      System.out.println ("total == MAX and < sum");
else
   System.out.println ("total is not equal to MAX");
```

EX 4.3 What is wrong with the following code fragment? Will this code compile if it is part of an otherwise valid program? Explain.

```
if (length = MIN_LENGTH)
   System.out.println ("The length is minimal.");
```

EX 4.4 What output is produced by the following code fragment?

```
int num = 87, max = 25;
if (num >= max*2)
   System.out.println ("apple");
   System.out.println ("orange");
System.out.println ("pear");
```

EX 4.5 What output is produced by the following code fragment?

```
int limit = 100, num1 = 15, num2 = 40;
if (limit <= limit)
{
   if (num1 == num2)
      System.out.println ("lemon");
   System.out.println ("lime");
}
System.out.println ("grape");
```

EX 4.6 Put the following list of strings in lexicographic order as if determined by the `compareTo` method of the `String` class. Consult the Unicode chart in Appendix C.

```
"fred"
"Ethel"
"?-?-?-?"
"{([])}"
"Lucy"
"ricky"
"book"
"******"
"12345"
"     "
"HEPHALUMP"
"bookkeeper"
"6789"
";+<?"
"^^^^^^^^^^"
"hephalump"
```

EX 4.7 What output is produced by the following code fragment?

```
int num = 0, max = 20;
while (num < max)
{
   System.out.println (num);
   num += 4;
}
```

EX 4.8 What output is produced by the following code fragment?

```
int num = 1, max = 20;
while (num < max)
{
   if (num%2 == 0)
      System.out.println (num);
   num++;
}
```

EX 4.9 What output is produced by the following code fragment?

```
for (int num = 0; num <= 200; num += 2)
   System.out.println (num);
```

EX 4.10 What output is produced by the following code fragment?

```
for (int val = 200; val >= 0; val -= 1)
   if (val % 4 != 0)
      System.out.println (val);
```

EX 4.11 Transform the following `while` loop into an equivalent `do` loop (make sure it produces the same output).

```
int num = 1;
while (num < 20)
{
   num++;
   System.out.println (num);
}
```

EX 4.12 Transform the `while` loop from exercise 4.11 into an equivalent `for` loop (make sure it produces the same output).

EX 4.13 What is wrong with the following code fragment? What are three distinct ways it could be changed to remove the flaw?

```
count = 50;
while (count >= 0)
{
   System.out.println (count);
   count = count + 1;
}
```

EX 4.14 Write a `while` loop that verifies that the user enters a positive integer value.

EX 4.15 Write a `do` loop that verifies that the user enters an even integer value.

EX 4.16 Write a code fragment that reads and prints integer values entered by a user until a particular sentinel value (stored in `SENTINEL`) is entered. Do not print the sentinel value.

EX 4.17 Write a `for` loop to print the odd numbers from 1 to 99 (inclusive).

EX 4.18 Write a `for` loop to print the multiples of 3 from 300 down to 3.

EX 4.19 Write a code fragment that reads 10 integer values from the user and prints the highest value entered.

EX 4.20 Write a code fragment that computes the sum of the integers from 20 to 70, inclusive, then prints the result.

EX 4.21 Write a code fragment that determines and prints the number of times the character `'z'` appears in a `String` object called `name`.

EX 4.22 Write a code fragment that prints the characters stored in a `String` object called `str` backward.

EX 4.23 Write a code fragment that prints every other character in a `String` object called `word` starting with the first character.

Programming Projects

PP 4.1 Design and implement an application that reads an integer value representing a year from the user. The purpose of the program is to determine if the year is a leap year (and therefore has 29 days in February) in the Gregorian calendar. A year is a leap year if it is divisible by 4, unless it is also divisible by 100 but not 400. For example, the year 2003 is not a leap year, but 2004 is. The year 1900 is not a leap year because it is divisible by 100, but the year 2000 is a leap year because even though it is divisible by 100, it is also divisible by 400. Produce an error message for any input value less than 1582 (the year the Gregorian calendar was adopted).

PP 4.2 Modify the solution to programming project 4.1 so that the user can evaluate multiple years. Allow the user to terminate the program using an appropriate sentinel value. Validate each input value to ensure it is greater than or equal to 1582.

PP 4.3 Design and implement an application that reads an integer value and prints the sum of all even integers between 2 and the input value, inclusive. Print an error message if the input value is less than 2. Prompt accordingly.

PP 4.4 Design and implement an application that reads a string from the user and prints it one character per line.

PP 4.5 Design and implement an application that determines and prints the number of odd, even, and zero digits in an integer value read from the keyboard.

PP 4.6 Design and implement an application that produces a multiplication table, showing the results of multiplying the integers 1 through 12 by themselves.

PP 4.7 Design and implement an application that prints the first few verses of the traveling song "One Hundred Bottles of Beer." Use a loop such that each iteration prints one verse. Read the number of verses to print from the user. Validate the input. The following are the first two verses of the song:

100 bottles of beer on the wall

100 bottles of beer

If one of those bottles should happen to fall

99 bottles of beer on the wall

99 bottles of beer on the wall

99 bottles of beer

If one of those bottles should happen to fall

98 bottles of beer on the wall

PP 4.8 Design and implement an application that plays the Hi-Lo guessing game with numbers. The program should pick a random number between 1 and 100 (inclusive), then repeatedly prompt the user to guess the number. On each guess, report to the user that he or she is correct or that the guess is high or low. Continue accepting guesses until the user guesses correctly or chooses to quit. Use a sentinel value to determine whether

the user wants to quit. Count the number of guesses and report that value when the user guesses correctly. At the end of each game (by quitting or a correct guess), prompt to determine whether the user wants to play again. Continue playing games until the user chooses to stop.

PP 4.9 Create a modified version of the `PalindromeTester` program so that the spaces, punctuation, and changes in uppercase and lowercase are not considered when determining whether a string is a palindrome. *Hint:* These issues can be handled in several ways. Think carefully about your design.

PP 4.10 Create modified versions of the `Stars` program to print the following patterns. Create a separate program to produce each pattern. *Hint:* Parts b, c, and d require several loops, some of which print a specific number of spaces.

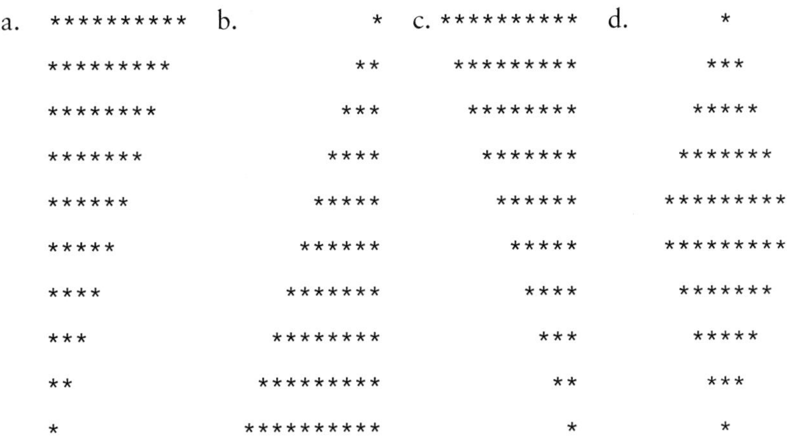

```
a. **********  b.          *  c. **********  d.     *
   *********              **      *********        ***
   ********              ***       ********       *****
   *******              ****        *******      *******
   ******              *****         ******     *********
   *****              ******          *****     *********
   ****              *******           ****      *******
   ***              ********            ***       *****
   **              *********             **        ***
   *              **********              *         *
```

PP 4.11 Design and implement an application that prints a table showing a subset of the Unicode characters and their numeric values. Print five number/character pairs per line, separated by tab characters. Print the table for numeric values from 32 (the space character) to 126 (the ~ character), which corresponds to the printable ASCII subset of the Unicode character set. Compare your output to the table in Appendix C. Unlike the table in Appendix C, the values in your table can increase as they go across a row.

PP 4.12 Design and implement an application that reads a string from the user, then determines and prints how many of each lowercase vowel (a, e, i, o, and u) appear in the entire string. Have a separate counter for each vowel. Also count and print the number of nonvowel characters.

PP 4.13 Design and implement an application that plays the Rock-Paper-Scissors game against the computer. When played between two people, each person picks one of three options (usually shown by a hand gesture) at the same time, and a winner is determined. In the game, Rock beats Scissors, Scissors beats Paper, and Paper beats Rock. The program should randomly choose one of the three options (without revealing it), then prompt for the user's selection. At that point, the program reveals both choices and prints a statement indicating whether the user won, the computer won, or it was a tie. Continue playing until the user chooses to stop, then print the number of user wins, losses, and ties.

PP 4.14 Design and implement an application that prints the verses of the song "The Twelve Days of Christmas," in which each verse adds one line. The first two verses of the song are:

On the 1st day of Christmas my true love gave to me

A partridge in a pear tree.

On the 2nd day of Christmas my true love gave to me

Two turtle doves, and

A partridge in a pear tree.

Use a `switch` statement in a loop to control which lines get printed. *Hint:* Order the cases carefully and avoid the `break` statement. Use a separate `switch` statement to put the appropriate suffix on the day number (1st, 2nd, 3rd, etc.). The final verse of the song involves all 12 days, as follows:

On the 12th day of Christmas, my true love gave to me

Twelve drummers drumming,

Eleven pipers piping,

Ten lords a leaping,

Nine ladies dancing,

Eight maids a milking,
Seven swans a swimming,
Six geese a laying,
Five golden rings,
Four calling birds,
Three French hens,
Two turtle doves, and
A partridge in a pear tree.

PP 4.15 Design and implement an application that simulates a simple slot machine in which three numbers between 0 and 9 are randomly selected and printed side by side. Print an appropriate statement if all three of the numbers are the same, or if any two of the numbers are the same. Continue playing until the user chooses to stop.

PP 4.16 Design and implement a program that counts the number of integer values in a text input file. Produce a table listing the values you identify as integers from the input file.

PP 4.17 Design and implement a program to process golf scores. The scores of four golfers are stored in a text file. Each line represents one hole, and the file contains 18 lines. Each line contains five values: par for the hole followed by the number of strokes each golfer used on that hole. Determine the winner and produce a table showing how well each golfer did (compared to par).

PP 4.18 Design and implement a program that compares two text input files, line by line, for equality. Print any lines that are not equivalent.

PP 4.19 Design and implement a program that counts the number of punctuation marks in a text input file. Produce a table that shows how many times each symbol occurred.

Answers to Self-Review Questions

SR 4.1 The flow of control through a program determines the program statements that will be executed on a given run of the program.

SR 4.2 Each conditional and loop is based on a boolean condition that evaluates to either true or false.

SR 4.3 The equality operators are equal (==) and not equal (`!=`). The relational operators are less than (`<`), less than or equal to (`<=`), greater than (`>`), and greater than or equal to (`>=`).

SR 4.4 A truth table is a table that shows all possible results of a boolean expression, given all possible combinations of variable values and conditions.

SR 4.5 Because they are stored internally as binary numbers, comparing floating point values for exact equality will be true only if they are the same bit-by-bit. Therefore it's better to use a reasonable tolerance value and consider the difference between the two values.

SR 4.6 We compare strings for equality using the `equals` method of the `String` class, which returns a boolean result. The `compareTo` method of the `String` class can also be used to compare strings. It returns a positive, 0, or negative integer result depending on the relationship between the two strings.

SR 4.7 A nested `if` occurs when the statement inside an `if` or `else` clause is itself an `if` statement. A nested `if` lets the programmer make a series of decisions. Similarly, a nested loop is a loop within a loop.

SR 4.8 A block statement groups several statements together. We use block statements to define the body of an `if` statement or loop when we want to do multiple things based on the boolean condition.

SR 4.9 If a case does not end with a `break` statement, processing continues into the statements of the next case. We usually want to use `break` statements in order to jump to the end of the `switch`.

SR 4.10 An infinite loop is a repetition statement that will not terminate because of the basic logic of the condition. Specifically, the body of the loop never causes the condition to become false.

SR 4.11 A `while` loop evaluates the condition first. If it is true, it executes the loop body. The `do` loop executes the body first and then evaluates the condition. Therefore the body of a `while` loop is executed zero or more times, and the body of a `do` loop is executed one or more times.

SR 4.12 A `for` loop is usually used when we know, or can calculate, how many times we want to iterate through the loop body. A `while` loop handles a more generic situation.

5 Writing Classes

Chapter Objectives

- Explore techniques for identifying the classes and objects needed in a program.
- Discuss the structure and content of a class definition.
- Establish the concept of object state using instance data.
- Describe the effect of visibility modifiers on methods and data.
- Explore the structure of a method definition, including parameters and return values.
- Discuss the structure and purpose of a constructor.
- Discuss the relationships among classes.
- Describe the effect of the `static` modifier on methods and data.
- Discuss issues related to the design of methods, including method decomposition and method overloading.

In previous chapters we used classes and objects for the various services they provide. We also explored several fundamental programming statements. With that experience as a foundation, we are now ready to design more complex software by creating our own classes, which is the heart of object-oriented programming. This chapter explores the basics of class definitions, including the structure of methods and the scope and encapsulation of data. It also examines the creation of static class members and overloaded methods.

5.1 Classes and Objects Revisited

In Chapter 1 we introduced basic object-oriented concepts, including a brief overview of objects and classes. In Chapters 2 and 3 we used several predefined classes from the Java standard class library to create objects and use them for the particular functionality they provide.

In this chapter we turn our attention to writing our own classes. Although existing class libraries provide many useful classes, the essence of object-oriented program development is the process of designing and implementing our own classes to suit our specific needs.

Recall the basic relationship between an object and a class: a class is a blueprint of an object. The class represents the concept of an object, and any object created from that class is a realization of that concept.

For example, from Chapter 3 we know that the `String` class represents a concept of a character string, and that each `String` object represents a particular string that contains specific characters.

Let's consider another example. Suppose a class called `Student` represents a student at a university. An object created from the `Student` class would represent a particular student. The `Student` class represents the general concept of a student, and every object created from that class represents an actual student attending the school. In a system that helps manage the business of a university, we would have one `Student` class and thousands of `Student` objects.

Recall that an object has a *state*, which is defined by the values of the *attributes* associated with that object. For example, the attributes of a student might include the student's name, address, major, and grade point average. The `Student` class establishes that each student has these attributes and each `Student` object stores the values of these attributes for a particular student. In Java, an object's attributes are defined by variables declared within a class.

An object also has *behaviors*, which are defined by the *operations* associated with that object. The operations of a student might include the ability to update that student's address and compute that student's current grade point average. The `Student` class defines the operations, such as the details of how a grade point average is computed. These operations can then be executed on (or by) a particular `Student` object. Note that the behaviors of an object may modify the state of that object. In Java, an object's operations are defined by methods declared within a class.

Figure 5.1 lists some examples of classes, with some attributes and operations that might be defined for objects of those classes. It's up to the program designer

Class	Attributes	Operations
Student	Name Address Major Grade point average	Set address Set major Compute grade point average
Rectangle	Length Width Color	Set length Set width Set color
Aquarium	Material Length Width Height	Set material Set length Set width Set height Compute volume Compute filled weight
Flight	Airline Flight number Origin city Destination city Current status	Set airline Set flight number Determine status
Employee	Name Department Title Salary	Set department Set title Set salary Compute wages Compute bonus Compute taxes

FIGURE 5.1 Examples of classes with some possible attributes and operations

to determine what attributes and operations are needed, which depends on the purpose of the program and the role a particular object plays in that purpose. Consider other attributes and operations you might include for these examples.

Identifying Classes and Objects

A fundamental part of object-oriented software design is determining which classes should be created to define the program. We have to carefully consider how we want to represent the various elements that make up the overall solution. These classes determine the objects that we will manage in the system.

One way to identify potential classes is to identify the objects discussed in the program requirements. Objects are generally nouns. You literally may want to scrutinize a problem description, or a functional specification if available, to identify the nouns found in it. For example, Figure 5.2 shows part of a problem description with the nouns circled.

```
The user must be allowed to specify each
product by its primary characteristics,
including its name and product number. If the
bar code does not match the product, then an
error should be generated to the message window
and entered into the error log. The summary
report of all transactions must be structured
as specified in section 7.A.
```

FIGURE 5.2 Finding potential objects by identifying the nouns in a problem description

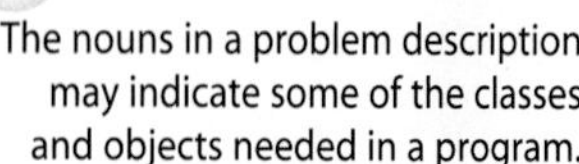

The nouns in a problem description may indicate some of the classes and objects needed in a program.

Of course, not every noun in the problem specification will correspond to a class in a program. Some nouns may be represented as attributes of other objects, and the designer may decide not to represent other nouns explicitly in the program at all. This activity is just a starting point that allows a developer to think about the types of objects a program will manage.

Remember that a class represents a group of objects with similar behavior. A plural noun in the specification, such as products, may indicate the need for a class that represents one of those items, such as `Product`. Even if there is only one of a particular kind of object needed in your system, it may best be represented as a class.

Classes that represent objects should generally be given names that are singular nouns, such as `Coin`, `Student`, and `Message`. A class represents a single item from which we are free to create as many instances as we choose.

Another key decision is whether to represent something as an object or as a primitive attribute of another object. For example, we may initially think that an employee's salary should be represented as an integer, and that may work for much of the system's processing. But upon further reflection we might realize that the salary is based on the person's rank, which has upper and lower salary bounds that must be managed with care. Therefore the final conclusion may be that we'd be better off representing all of that data and the associated behavior as a separate class.

Given the needs of a particular program, we want to strike a good balance between classes that are too general and those that are too specific. For example, it may complicate our design unnecessarily to create a separate class for each type of appliance that exists in a house. It may be sufficient to have a single `Appliance` class, with perhaps a piece of instance data that indicates what type of appliance it is. Then again, this may not be an adequate solution. It all depends on what the software is going to accomplish.

In addition to classes that represent objects from the problem domain, we likely will need classes that support the work necessary to get the job done. For example, in addition to `Member` objects, we may want a separate class to help us manage all of the members of a club.

Keep in mind that when producing a real system, some of the classes we identify during design may already exist. Even if nothing matches exactly, there may be an old class that's similar enough to serve as the basis for our new class. The existing class may be part of the Java standard class library, part of a solution to a problem we've solved previously, or part of a library that can be bought from a third party. These are all examples of software reuse.

Assigning Responsibilities

Part of the process of identifying the classes needed in a program is the process of assigning responsibilities to each class. Each class represents an object with certain behaviors that are defined by the methods of the class. Any activity that the program must accomplish must be represented somewhere in the behaviors of the classes. That is, each class is responsible for carrying out certain activities, and those responsibilities must be assigned as part of designing a program.

The behaviors of a class perform actions that make up the functionality of a program. Thus we generally use verbs for the names of behaviors and the methods that accomplish them.

Sometimes it is challenging to determine which is the best class to carry out a particular responsibility. A good designer considers multiple possibilities. Sometimes such analysis makes you realize that you could benefit from defining another class to shoulder the responsibility.

It's not necessary in the early stages of a design to identify all the methods that a class will contain. It is often sufficient to assign primary responsibilities, and consider how those responsibilities translate to particular methods.

5.2 Anatomy of a Class

Now that we've reviewed some important conceptual ideas underlying the development of classes and objects, let's dive into the programming details. In all of our previous examples, we've written a single class containing a single `main` method. Each of these classes represents a small but complete program. These programs often instantiate objects using predefined classes from the Java class library and then use those objects for the services they provide. The library classes are part of the program too, but we generally don't have to concern ourselves with their internal details. We really just need to know how to interact with them, and simply trust them to provide the services they promise.

We will continue to rely on library classes, but now we will also design and implement other classes as needed. Let's look at an example. The `SnakeEyes` class shown in Listing 5.1 contains a `main` method that instantiates two `Die` objects (as in the singular of dice). The purpose of the program is to roll the dice and count the number of times both die show a 1 on the same throw (snake eyes).

The primary difference between this example and examples we've seen in previous chapters is that the `Die` class is not a predefined part of the Java class library. For this program to compile and run, we have to write the `Die` class ourselves, defining the services we want `Die` objects to perform.

A class can contain data declarations and method declarations, as depicted in Figure 5.3. The data declarations represent the data that will be stored in each object of the class. The method declarations define the services that those objects will provide. Collectively, the data and methods of a class are called the *members* of a class.

The classes we've written in previous examples follow this model as well, but contain no data at the class level and contain only one method (the `main` method). We'll continue to define classes like this, such as the `SnakeEyes` class, to define the starting point of a program.

The heart of object-oriented programming is defining classes that represent objects with well-defined state and behavior.

True object-oriented programming, however, comes from defining classes that represent objects with well-defined state and behavior. For example, at any given moment a `Die` object is showing a particular face value, which we could refer to as the state of the die. A `Die` object also has various methods we can invoke on it, such as the ability to roll the die or get its face value. These methods represent the behavior of a die.

The `Die` class is shown in Listing 5.2. It contains two data values: an integer constant (`MAX`) that represents the maximum face value of the die, and an integer variable (`faceValue`) that represents the current face value of the die. It also contains a constructor called `Die` and four regular methods: `roll`, `setFaceValue`, `getFaceValue`, and `toString`.

You will recall from Chapters 2 and 3 that constructors are special methods that have the same name as the class. The `Die` constructor gets called when the `new` operator is used to create a new instance of the `Die` class, as we do twice in the `main` method of the `SnakeEyes` class. The rest of the methods in the `Die` class define the various services provided by `Die` objects.

Listing 5.1

```
//********************************************************************
//  SnakeEyes.java       Java Foundations
//
//  Demonstrates the use of a programmer-defined class.
//********************************************************************

public class SnakeEyes
{
   //-----------------------------------------------------------------
   //  Creates two Die objects and rolls them several times, counting
   //  the number of snake eyes that occur.
   //-----------------------------------------------------------------
   public static void main (String[] args)
   {
      final int ROLLS = 500;
      int num1, num2, count = 0;

      Die die1 = new Die();
      Die die2 = new Die();

      for (int roll=1; roll <= ROLLS; roll++)
      {
         num1 = die1.roll();
         num2 = die2.roll();

         if (num1 == 1 && num2 == 1)    // check for snake eyes
            count++;
      }

      System.out.println ("Number of rolls: " + ROLLS);
      System.out.println ("Number of snake eyes: " + count);
      System.out.println ("Ratio: " + (float)count / ROLLS);
   }
}
```

Output

```
Number of rolls: 500
Number of snake eyes: 12
Ratio: 0.024
```

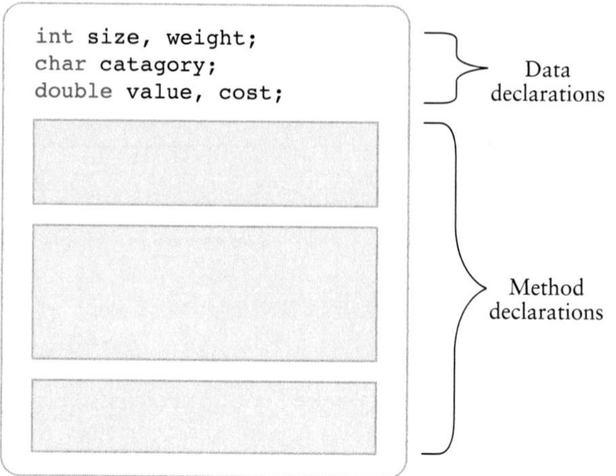
int size, weight;
char catagory;
double value, cost;
Data declarations
Method declarations

FIGURE 5.3 The members of a class: data and method declarations

Listing 5.2

```
//********************************************************************
//  Die.java       Java Foundations
//
//  Represents one die (singular of dice) with faces showing values
//  between 1 and 6.
//********************************************************************

public class Die
{
   private final int MAX = 6;  // maximum face value

   private int faceValue;  // current value showing on the die

   //-----------------------------------------------------------------
   //  Constructor: Sets the initial face value of this die.
   //-----------------------------------------------------------------
   public Die()
   {
      faceValue = 1;
   }

   //-----------------------------------------------------------------
   //  Computes a new face value for this die and returns the result.
   //-----------------------------------------------------------------
```

Listing 5.2 continued

```
   public int roll()
   {
      faceValue = (int)(Math.random() * MAX) + 1;

      return faceValue;
   }

   //-----------------------------------------------------------------
   //  Face value mutator. The face value is not modified if the
   //  specified value is not valid.
   //-----------------------------------------------------------------
   public void setFaceValue (int value)
   {
      if (value > 0 && value <= MAX)
         faceValue = value;
   }

   //-----------------------------------------------------------------
   //  Face value accessor.
   //-----------------------------------------------------------------
   public int getFaceValue()
   {
      return faceValue;
   }

   //-----------------------------------------------------------------
   //  Returns a string representation of this die.
   //-----------------------------------------------------------------
   public String toString()
   {
      String result = Integer.toString(faceValue);

      return result;
   }
}
```

We use a header block of documentation to explain the purpose of each method in the class. This practice is not only crucial for anyone trying to understand the software, it also separates the code visually so that it's easy for the eye to jump from one method to the next while reading the code.

Figure 5.4 lists the methods of the `Die` class. From this point of view, it looks no different from any other class that we've used in previous examples. The only important difference is that the `Die` class was not provided for us by the Java standard class library. We wrote it ourselves.

The methods of the `Die` class include the ability to roll the die, producing a new random face value. The `roll` method returns the new face value to the calling method, but you can also get the current face value at any time using the `getFaceValue` method. The `setFaceValue` method sets the face value explicitly, as if you had reached over and turned the die to whatever face you wanted. The `toString` method returns a representation of the die as a character string—in this case it returns the numeric value of the die face as a string. The definitions of these methods have various parts, and we'll dissect them as we proceed through this chapter.

Let's mention the importance of the `toString` method at this point. The `toString` method of any object gets called automatically whenever you pass the object to a `print` or `println` method and when you concatenate an object to a character string. There is a default version of `toString` defined for every object, but the results are not generally useful. Therefore it's usually a good idea to define a `toString` method for the classes that you create. The default version of `toString` is available because of inheritance, which we discuss in detail in Chapter 8.

For the examples in this book, we usually store each class in its own file. Java allows multiple classes to be stored in one file. But if a file contains multiple classes, only one of those classes can be declared using the reserved word `public`. Furthermore, the name of the public class must correspond to the name of the file. For instance, class `Die` is stored in a file called `Die.java`.

`Die()`
: Constructor: Sets the initial face value of the die to 1.

`int roll()`
: Rolls the die by setting the face value to a random number in the appropriate range.

`void setFaceValue (int value)`
: Sets the face value of the die to the specified value.

`int getFaceValue()`
: Returns the current face value of the die.

`String toString()`
: Returns a string representation of the die indicating its current face value.

FIGURE 5.4 Some methods of the `Die` class

Instance Data

Note that in the `Die` class, the constant `MAX` and the variable `faceValue` are declared inside the class, but not inside any method. The location at which a variable is declared defines its *scope*, which is the area within a program in which that variable can be referenced. By being declared at the class level (not within a method), these variables and constants can be referenced in any method of the class.

The scope of a variable, which determines where it can be referenced, depends on where it is declared.

Attributes such as the variable `faceValue` are called *instance data* because new memory space is reserved for that variable every time an instance of the class is created. Each `Die` object has its own `faceValue` variable with its own data space. That's how each `Die` object can have its own state. That is, one die could be showing a 5 at the same time the other die is showing a 2. That's possible only because separate memory space for the `faceValue` variable is created for each `Die` object.

We can depict this situation as follows:

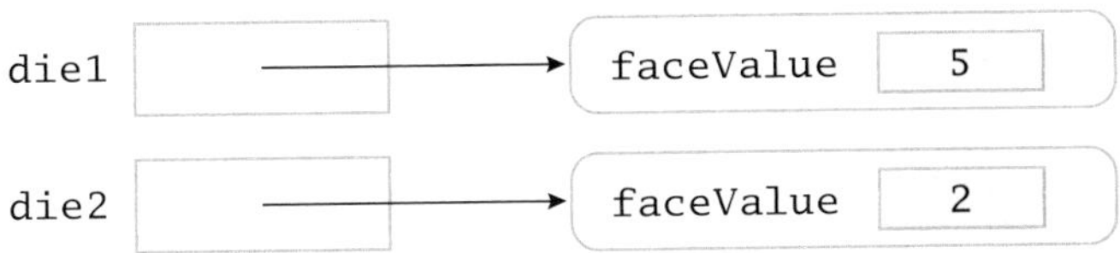

The `die1` and `die2` reference variables point to (that is, contain the address of) their respective `Die` objects. Each object contains a `faceValue` variable with its own memory space. Thus each object can store different values for its instance data.

Java automatically initializes any variables declared at the class level. For example, all variables of numeric types such as `int` and `double` are initialized to zero. However, despite the fact that the language performs this automatic initialization, it is good practice to initialize variables explicitly (usually in a constructor) so that anyone reading the code will clearly understand the intent.

UML Class Diagrams

As our programs become more complex, containing multiple classes, it's helpful to make use of a graphical notation to capture, visualize, and communicate the program design. Throughout the remainder of this book we use *UML diagrams* for this purpose. UML stands for the *Unified Modeling Language*, which has become the most popular notation for representing the design of an object-oriented program.

Several types of UML diagrams exist, each designed to show specific aspects of object-oriented programs. We focus primarily on UML *class diagrams* in this book to show the contents of classes and the relationships among them.

A UML class diagram helps us visualize the contents of and relationships among the classes of a program.

In a UML diagram, each class is represented as a rectangle, possibly containing three sections to show the class name, its attributes (data), and its operations (methods). Figure 5.5 shows a class diagram containing the classes of the `SnakeEyes` program.

UML is not designed specifically for Java programmers. It is intended to be language independent. Therefore the syntax used in a UML diagram is not necessarily the same as Java. For example, a variable's type is shown after the variable name, separated by a colon. Return types of methods are shown the same way. The initial value of an attribute can be shown in the class diagram if desired, as we do with the `MAX` constant in Figure 5.5. The + and – notations in front of variables and methods indicate their *visibility*, which is discussed in the next section.

A solid line connecting two classes in a UML diagram indicates that a relationship of one kind or another exists between the two classes. These lines are called *associations*, and indicate that one class "knows about" and uses the other in some way. For example, an association might indicate that an object of one class creates an object of the other, and/or that one class invokes a method of the other. Associations can be labeled to indicate the details of the association.

A directed association uses an arrowhead to indicate that the association is particularly one-way. For example, the arrow connecting the `SnakeEyes` and `Die` classes in Figure 5.5 indicates that the `SnakeEyes` class "knows about" and uses the `Die` class, but not vice versa.

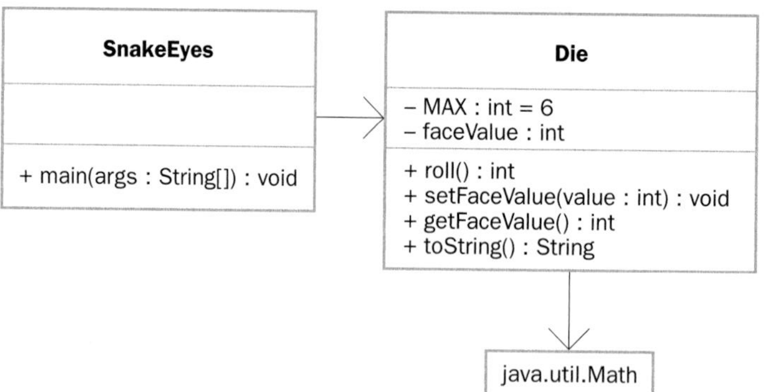

FIGURE 5.5 A UML class diagram showing the classes involved in the `SnakeEyes` program

An association can show *multiplicity* by annotating the ends of the connection with numeric values. In this case, the diagram indicates that `SnakeEyes` is associated with exactly two `Die` objects. Both ends of an association can show multiplicity values, if desired. Multiplicity also can be expressed in terms of a range of values and by using wildcards for unknown values, as we'll see in later examples.

Other types of object-oriented relationships between classes are shown with different types of connecting lines and arrows. We will explore additional aspects of UML diagrams as we discuss the corresponding object-oriented programming concepts throughout the book.

UML diagrams are versatile. We can include whatever appropriate information is desired, depending on what we are trying to convey in a particular diagram. We might leave out the data and method sections of a class, for instance, if those details aren't relevant for a particular diagram. For example, the fact that the `Die` class makes use of the `Math` class from the Java API is indicated in Figure 5.5, but the details of the `Math` class are not identified. We also could have explicitly indicated the use of the `String` class, but that is rarely done because of its ubiquity.

5.3 Encapsulation

We mentioned in our overview of object-oriented concepts in Chapter 1 that an object should be *self-governing*. That is, the instance data of an object should be modified only by that object. For example, the methods of the `Die` class should be solely responsible for changing the value of the `faceValue` variable. We should make it difficult, if not impossible, for code outside of a class to "reach in" and change the value of a variable that is declared inside that class. This characteristic is called *encapsulation*.

An object should be encapsulated, guarding its data from inappropriate access.

An object should be encapsulated from the rest of the system. It should interact with other parts of a program only through the specific set of methods that define the services that that object provides. These methods define the *interface* between that object and other objects that use it.

The nature of encapsulation is depicted graphically in Figure 5.6. The code that uses an object, sometimes called the *client* of an object, should not be allowed to access variables directly. The client should call an object's methods, and those methods then interact with the data encapsulated within the object. For example, the `main` method in the `SnakeEyes` program calls the `roll` method of

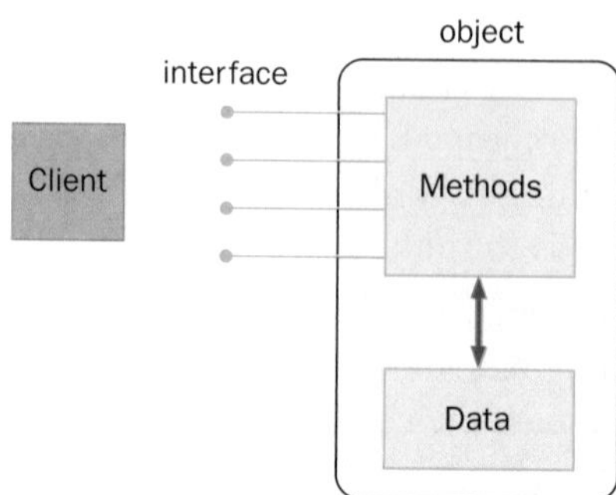

FIGURE 5.6 A client interacting with another object

the die objects. The `main` method should not (and in fact cannot) access the `faceValue` variable directly.

In Java, we accomplish object encapsulation using *modifiers*. A modifier is a Java reserved word that is used to specify particular characteristics of a programming language construct. In Chapter 2 we discussed the `final` modifier, which is used to declare a constant. Java has several modifiers that can be used in various ways. Some modifiers can be used together, but some combinations are invalid. We discuss various Java modifiers at appropriate points throughout this book, and all of them are summarized in Appendix E.

Visibility Modifiers

Some of the Java modifiers are called *visibility modifiers* because they control access to the members of a class. The reserved words `public` and `private` are visibility modifiers that can be applied to the variables and methods of a class. If a member of a class has *public visibility*, it can be directly referenced from outside of the object. If a member of a class has *private visibility*, it can be used anywhere inside the class definition but cannot be referenced externally. A third visibility modifier, `protected`, is relevant only in the context of inheritance. We discuss it in Chapter 8.

Public variables violate encapsulation. They allow code external to the class in which the data is defined to reach in and access or modify the value of the data. Therefore instance data should be defined with private visibility. Data that is declared as private can be accessed only by the methods of the class.

Instance variables should be declared with private visibility to promote encapsulation.

The visibility we apply to a method depends on the purpose of that method. Methods that provide services to the client must be declared with public visibility so that they can be invoked by the client. These methods are sometimes referred to as *service methods*. A private method cannot be invoked from outside the class. The only purpose of a private method is to help the other methods of the class do their job. Therefore they are sometimes referred to as *support methods*.

The table in Figure 5.7 summarizes the effects of public and private visibility on both variables and methods.

Giving constants public visibility is generally considered acceptable because, although their values can be accessed directly, their values cannot be changed because they were declared using the `final` modifier. Keep in mind that encapsulation means that data values should not be able to be *modified* directly by another part of the code. Because constants, by definition, cannot be changed, the encapsulation issue is largely moot.

UML class diagrams can show the visibility of a class member by preceding it with a particular character. A member with public visibility is preceded by a plus sign (+), and a member with private visibility is preceded by a minus sign (-). Review Figure 5.5 to see this notation used.

Accessors and Mutators

Because instance data is generally declared with private visibility, a class usually provides services to access and modify data values. A method such as `getFaceValue` in the `Die` class is called an *accessor method* because it provides

	public	**private**
Variables	Violate encapsulation	Enforce encapsulation
Methods	Provide services to clients	Support other methods in the class

FIGURE 5.7 The effects of public and private visibility

read-only access to a particular value. Likewise, a method such as `setFaceValue` is called a *mutator method* because it changes a particular value.

Most objects contain accessor and mutator methods to allow the client to manage data in a controlled manner.

Generally, accessor method names have the form `getX`, where `X` is the value to which it provides access. Likewise, mutator method names have the form `setX`, where `X` is the value they are setting. Therefore these types of methods are sometimes referred to as "getters" and "setters."

For example, if a class contains the instance variable `height`, it should also probably contain the methods `getHeight` and `setHeight`. Note that this naming convention capitalizes the first letter of the variable when used in the method names, which is consistent with how method names are written in general.

Some methods may provide accessor and/or mutator capabilities as a side effect of their primary purpose. For example, the `roll` method of the `Die` class changes the value of the variable `faceValue`, and returns that new value as well. Note that the code of the `roll` method is guaranteed to keep the face value of the die in the valid range (1 to `MAX`). Similarly, the `setFaceValue` method checks to see if the specified value is in the valid range, and ignores it if it is not. Service methods must be carefully designed to permit only appropriate access and valid changes. By encapsulating the data, the object can maintain this type of control.

Let's look at anther example. The program in Listing 5.3 instantiates a `Coin` object, then flips the coin multiple times, counting the number of times heads and tails come up. Notice that it uses a call to the method `isHeads` in the condition of an `if` statement to determine which result occurred.

The `Coin` class is shown in Listing 5.4. It stores an integer constant called `HEADS` that represents the face value when the coin is showing heads. An instance variable called `face` represents the current state of the coin (which side is up) and has either the value 0 or 1. The `Coin` constructor initially flips the coin by calling the `flip` method, which determines the new state of the coin by randomly choosing a number (either 0 or 1). The `isHeads` method returns a `boolean` value based on the current face value of the coin. The `toString` method returns a character string indicating the current face showing on the coin.

A `Coin` object can be in one of two states: showing heads or showing tails. We represented this state in the `Coin` class as an integer value, `0` for tails and `1` for heads, stored in the `face` variable. Of course, this representation is arbitrary—we could have used `1` to represent tails. For that matter, we could have represented the coin's state using a `boolean` value, or a character string, or an enumerated type. We chose to use an integer because the methods for choosing a random

Listing 5.3

```
//********************************************************************
//  CountFlips.java       Java Foundations
//
//  Demonstrates the use of programmer-defined class.
//********************************************************************

public class CountFlips
{
   //-----------------------------------------------------------------
   //  Flips a coin multiple times and counts the number of heads
   //  and tails that result.
   //-----------------------------------------------------------------
   public static void main (String[] args)
   {
      final int FLIPS = 1000;
      int heads = 0, tails = 0;

      Coin myCoin = new Coin();

      for (int count=1; count <= FLIPS; count++)
      {
         myCoin.flip();

         if (myCoin.isHeads())
            heads++;
         else
            tails++;
      }

      System.out.println ("Number of flips: " + FLIPS);
      System.out.println ("Number of heads: " + heads);
      System.out.println ("Number of tails: " + tails);
   }
}
```

Output

```
Number of flips: 1000
Number of heads: 486
Number of tails: 514
```

Listing 5.4

```
//********************************************************************
//  Coin.java       Java Foundations
//
//  Represents a coin with two sides that can be flipped.
//********************************************************************

public class Coin
{
   private final int HEADS = 0;  // tails is 1

   private int face;  // current side showing

   //-----------------------------------------------------------------
   //  Sets up this coin by flipping it initially.
   //-----------------------------------------------------------------
   public Coin ()
   {
      flip();
   }

   //-----------------------------------------------------------------
   //  Flips this coin by randomly choosing a face value.
   //-----------------------------------------------------------------
   public void flip ()
   {
      face = (int) (Math.random() * 2);
   }

   //-----------------------------------------------------------------
   //  Returns true if the current face of this coin is heads.
   //-----------------------------------------------------------------
   public boolean isHeads ()
   {
      return (face == HEADS);
   }

   //-----------------------------------------------------------------
   //  Returns the current face of this coin as a string.
   //-----------------------------------------------------------------
   public String toString()
   {
      return (face == HEADS) ? "Heads" : "Tails";
   }
}
```

result (`Math.random` in this case) return a numeric value, and therefore eliminated extraneous conversions.

The way the `Coin` object represents its state internally is, and should be, irrelevant to the client using the object. That is, from the perspective of the `CountFlips` program, the way the `Coin` class represents its state doesn't matter.

The way a class represents an object's state should be independent of how that object is used.

We could have made the constant `HEADS` public so that the client could access it. But as an integer variable, its value is meaningless to the client. Providing the `isHeads` method is a cleaner object-oriented solution. The internal details of the `Coin` class could be rewritten and, as long as the `isHeads` method is written appropriately, the client would not have to change.

Although many classes will have classic getter and setter methods, we chose to design the `Coin` class without them. The only way the coin's state can be changed is to flip it randomly. Unlike a `Die` object, the user cannot explicitly set the state of a coin. This is a design decision, which could be made differently if circumstances dictate.

Let's use the `Coin` class in another program. The `FlipRace` class is shown in Listing 5.5. The `main` method of `FlipRace` instantiates two `Coin` objects and flips them in tandem repeatedly until one of the coins comes up heads three times in a row.

Listing 5.5

```
//********************************************************************
//  FlipRace.java       Java Foundations
//
//  Demonstrates the reuse of programmer-defined class.
//********************************************************************

public class FlipRace
{
   //-----------------------------------------------------------------
   //  Flips two coins until one of them comes up heads three times
   //  in a row.
   //-----------------------------------------------------------------
   public static void main (String[] args)
   {
      final int GOAL = 3;
      int count1 = 0, count2 = 0;
      Coin coin1 = new Coin(), coin2 = new Coin();
```

Listing 5.5 continued

```
      while (count1 < GOAL && count2 < GOAL)
      {
         coin1.flip();
         coin2.flip();

         System.out.println ("Coin 1: " + coin1 + "\tCoin 2: " + coin2);

         // Increment or reset the counters
         count1 = (coin1.isHeads()) ? count1+1 : 0;
         count2 = (coin2.isHeads()) ? count2+1 : 0;
      }

      if (count1 < GOAL)
         System.out.println ("Coin 2 Wins!");
      else
         if (count2 < GOAL)
            System.out.println ("Coin 1 Wins!");
         else
            System.out.println ("It's a TIE!");
   }
}
```

Output

```
Coin 1: Tails   Coin 2: Heads
Coin 1: Heads   Coin 2: Heads
Coin 1: Tails   Coin 2: Tails
Coin 1: Tails   Coin 2: Tails
Coin 1: Tails   Coin 2: Heads
Coin 1: Heads   Coin 2: Tails
Coin 1: Heads   Coin 2: Tails
Coin 1: Heads   Coin 2: Heads
Coin 1 Wins!
```

The output of the `FlipRace` program shows the results of each coin flip. Note that the `coin1` and `coin2` objects are concatenated to character strings in the `println` statement. As we mentioned earlier, this situation causes the `toString` method of the object to be called, which returns a string to be printed. No explicit call to the `toString` method is needed.

The conditional operator is used in assignment statements to set the counters for the coins after they are flipped. For each coin, if the result is heads, the count is incremented. If not, the count is reset to zero. The `while` loop terminates when either or both counters reach the goal of three heads in a row.

`FlipRace` uses the `Coin` class as part of its program, just as `CountFlips` did earlier. A well-designed class often can be reused in multiple programs, just as we've gotten used to reusing the classes from the Java API over and over.

5.4 Anatomy of a Method

We've seen that a class is composed of data declarations and method declarations. Let's examine method declarations in more detail.

As we stated in Chapter 1, a method is a group of programming language statements that is given a name. A *method declaration* specifies the code that is executed when the method is invoked. Every method in a Java program is part of a particular class.

The header of a method declaration includes the type of the return value, the method name, and a list of parameters that the method accepts. The statements that make up the body of the method are defined in a block delimited by braces. We've defined the `main` method of a program many times in previous examples. Its definition follows the same syntax as any other method.

When a method is called, the flow of control transfers to that method. One by one, the statements of that method are executed. When that method is done, control returns to the location where the call was made and execution continues.

The *called method* (the one that is invoked) might be part of the same class as the *calling method* that invoked it. If the called method is part of the same class, only the method name is needed to invoke it. If it is part of a different class, it is invoked through a reference to an object of that other class, as we've seen many times. Figure 5.8 shows the flow of execution as methods are called.

Let's look at another example as we continue to explore the details of method declarations. The `Transactions` class shown in Listing 5.6 contains a `main` method that creates a few `Account` objects and invokes their services. The `Transactions` program doesn't really do anything useful except demonstrate how to interact with `Account` objects. Such programs are called *driver programs* because all they do is drive the use of other, more interesting parts of our program. They are often used for testing purposes.

The `Account` class, shown in Listing 5.7, represents a basic bank account. It contains instance data representing the name of the account's owner, the account

Method Declaration

Modifier · Type · void · Identifier · Parameters · Throws Clause · Method Body

Parameters

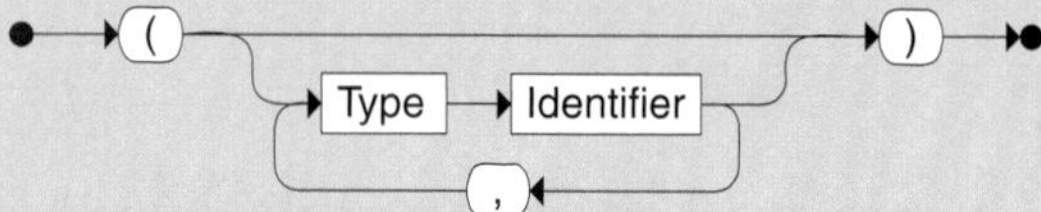

A method is defined by optional modifiers, followed by a return Type, followed by an Identifier that determines the method name, followed by a list of Parameters, followed by the Method Body. The return Type indicates the type of value that will be returned by the method, which may be `void`. The Method Body is a block of statements that executes when the method is invoked. The Throws Clause is optional and indicates the exceptions that may be thrown by this method.

Example:

```
public int computeArea (int length, int width)
{
   int area = length * width;
   return area;
}
```

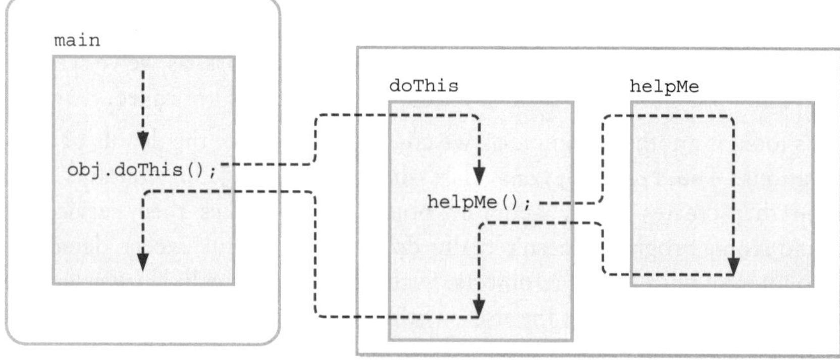

FIGURE 5.8 The flow of control following method invocations

Listing **5.6**

```
//********************************************************************
//  Transactions.java       Java Foundations
//
//  Demonstrates the creation and use of multiple Account objects.
//********************************************************************

public class Transactions
{
   //-----------------------------------------------------------------
   //  Creates some bank accounts and requests various services.
   //-----------------------------------------------------------------
   public static void main (String[] args)
   {
      Account acct1 = new Account ("Ted Murphy", 72354, 25.59);
      Account acct2 = new Account ("Angelica Adams", 69713, 500.00);
      Account acct3 = new Account ("Edward Demsey", 93757, 769.32);

      acct1.deposit (44.10);  // return value ignored

      double adamsBalance = acct2.deposit (75.25);
      System.out.println ("Adams balance after deposit: " +
                          adamsBalance);

      System.out.println ("Adams balance after withdrawal: " +
                          acct2.withdraw (480, 1.50));

      acct3.withdraw (-100.00, 1.50);  // invalid transaction

      acct1.addInterest();
      acct2.addInterest();
      acct3.addInterest();

      System.out.println ();
      System.out.println (acct1);
      System.out.println (acct2);
      System.out.println (acct3);
   }
}
```

Listing **5.6** continued

Output

```
Adams balance after deposit: 575.25
Adams balance after withdrawal: 93.75

72354   Ted Murphy       $72.13
69713   Angelica Adams   $97.03
93757   Edward Demsey    $796.25
```

number, and the account's current balance. The interest rate for the account is stored as a constant.

The constructor of the `Account` class accepts three parameters that are used to initialize the instance data when an `Account` object is instantiated. The other methods of the `Account` class perform various services on the account, such as making deposits and withdrawals. These methods examine the data passed into them to make sure the requested transaction is valid. For example, the `withdraw` method prevents the withdrawal of a negative amount (which essentially would be a deposit). There is also an `addInterest` method that updates the balance by adding in the interest earned. These methods represent the valid ways to modify the balance, so a generic mutator such as `setBalance` is not provided.

The status of the three `Account` objects just after they were created in the `Transactions` program could be depicted as follows:

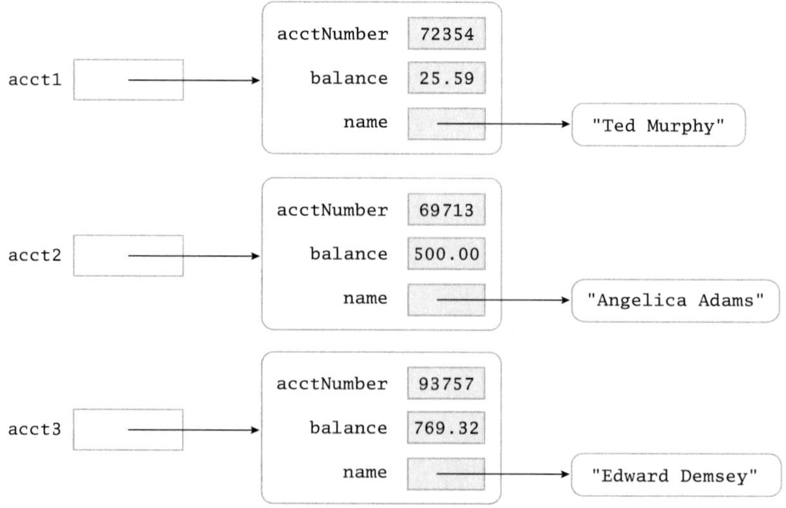

Listing **5.7**

```
//********************************************************************
//  Account.java       Java Foundations
//
//  Represents a bank account with basic services such as deposit
//  and withdraw.
//********************************************************************

import java.text.NumberFormat;

public class Account
{
   private final double RATE = 0.035;  // interest rate of 3.5%

   private String name;
   private long acctNumber;
   private double balance;

   //-----------------------------------------------------------------
   //  Sets up this account with the specified owner, account number,
   //  and initial balance.
   //-----------------------------------------------------------------
   public Account (String owner, long account, double initial)
   {
      name = owner;
      acctNumber = account;
      balance = initial;
   }

   //-----------------------------------------------------------------
   //  Deposits the specified amount into this account and returns
   //  the new balance. The balance is not modified if the deposit
   //  amount is invalid.
   //-----------------------------------------------------------------
   public double deposit (double amount)
   {
      if (amount > 0)
         balance = balance + amount;

      return balance;
   }

   //-----------------------------------------------------------------
   //  Withdraws the specified amount and fee from this account and
   //  returns the new balance. The balance is not modified if the
```

Listing 5.7 continued

```
   //  withdraw amount is invalid or the balance is insufficient.
   //-----------------------------------------------------------------
   public double withdraw (double amount, double fee)
   {
      if (amount+fee > 0 && amount+fee < balance)
         balance = balance - amount - fee;

      return balance;
   }

   //-----------------------------------------------------------------
   //  Adds interest to this account and returns the new balance.
   //-----------------------------------------------------------------
   public double addInterest ()
   {
      balance += (balance * RATE);
      return balance;
   }

   //-----------------------------------------------------------------
   //  Returns the current balance of this account.
   //-----------------------------------------------------------------
   public double getBalance ()
   {
      return balance;
   }

   //-----------------------------------------------------------------
   //  Returns a one-line description of this account as a string.
   //-----------------------------------------------------------------
   public String toString ()
   {
      NumberFormat fmt = NumberFormat.getCurrencyInstance();

      return (acctNumber + "\t" + name + "\t" + fmt.format(balance));
   }
}
```

The rest of this section discusses issues related to method declarations in more detail.

The `return` Statement

The return type specified in the method header can be a primitive type, class name, or the reserved word `void`. When a method does not return any value, `void` is used as the return type, as is always done with the `main` method of a program. The `setFaceValue` of the `Die` class and the `flip` method of the `Coin` class also have return types of `void`.

The `getFaceValue` and `roll` methods of the `Die` class return an `int` value that represents the value shown on the die. The `isHeads` method of the `Coin` class returns a `boolean` value that represents whether the coin is currently showing heads. Several of the methods of the `Account` class return a `double` representing the updated balance. The `toString` method in all of these classes returns a `String` object.

A method that returns a value must have a *return statement*. When a `return` statement is executed, control is immediately returned to the statement in the calling method, and processing continues there. A `return` statement consists of the reserved word `return` followed by an expression that dictates the value to be returned. The expression must be consistent with the return type specified in the method header.

The value returned from a method must be consistent with the return type specified in the method header.

A method that does not return a value does not usually contain a `return` statement. The method automatically returns to the calling method when the end of the method is reached. Such methods may contain a `return` statement without an expression.

Return Statement

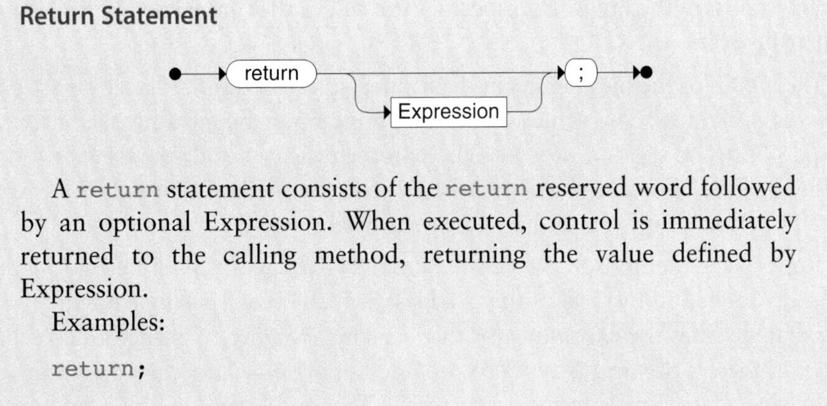

A `return` statement consists of the `return` reserved word followed by an optional Expression. When executed, control is immediately returned to the calling method, returning the value defined by Expression.

Examples:

```
return;

return distance * 4;
```

It is usually not good practice to use more than one `return` statement in a method, even though it is possible to do so. In general, a method should have one `return` statement as the last line of the method body, unless that makes the method overly complex.

The value that is returned from a method can be ignored in the calling method. Consider the following method invocation from the `Transactions` program:

```
acct1.deposit(44.10);
```

In this situation, the `deposit` method executes normally, updating the account balance accordingly, but the calling method simply makes no use of the returned value.

Constructors do not have a return type (not even `void`) and therefore cannot return a value. We discuss constructors in more detail later in this chapter.

Parameters

We introduced the concept of a parameter in Chapter 2, defining it as a value that is passed into a method when the method is invoked. Parameters provide data to a method that allows the method to do its job. Let's explore this issue in more detail.

The method declaration specifies the number and type of parameters that a method will accept. More precisely, the *parameter list* in the header of a method declaration specifies the type of each value that is passed into the method, and the name by which the called method will refer to each value. The corresponding parameter list in the invocation specifies the values that are passed in for that particular invocation.

The names of the parameters in the header of the method declaration are called *formal parameters*. The values passed into a method when it is invoked are called *actual parameters*, or *arguments*. The parameter list in both the declaration and the invocation is enclosed in parentheses after the method name. If there are no parameters, an empty set of parentheses is used.

None of the methods in the `Coin` and `Die` classes accept parameters except for the `setFaceValue` method of the `Die` class, which accepts a single integer parameter that specifies the new value for the die. The `Account` constructor accepts several parameters of various types to provide initial values for the object's instance data (this is common for constructors). The `withdraw` method in `Account` accepts two parameters of type `double`; note that the type of each formal parameter is listed separately even if the types are the same.

The formal parameters are identifiers that serve as variables inside the method and whose initial values come from the actual parameters in the invocation. When a method is called, the value in each actual parameter is copied and stored in the corresponding formal parameter. Actual parameters can be literals, variables, or full expressions. If an expression is used as an actual parameter, it is fully evaluated before the method call and the result is passed to the method.

When a method is called, the actual parameters are copied into the formal parameters.

The parameter lists in the invocation and the method declaration must match up. That is, the value of the first actual parameter is copied into the first formal parameter, the second actual parameter into the second formal parameter, and so on, as shown in Figure 5.9. The types of the actual parameters must be consistent with the specified types of the formal parameters.

In the `Transactions` program, the following call is made:

```
acct2.withdraw (480, 1.50)
```

This call passes an integer value as the first parameter of the `withdraw` method, which is defined to accept a `double`. This is valid because the actual and formal parameters must be consistent, but not necessarily match exactly. A `double` variable can be assigned an integer value because this is a widening conversion. Thus it is also allowed when passing parameters.

We explore some of the details regarding parameter passing later in this chapter.

Local Data

As we described earlier in this chapter, the scope of a variable or constant is the part of a program in which a valid reference to that variable can be made. A

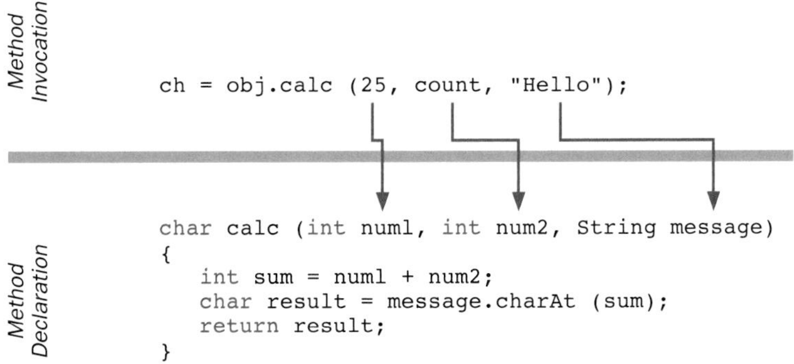

FIGURE 5.9 Passing parameters from the method invocation to the declaration

variable can be declared inside a method, making it *local data* as opposed to instance data. Recall that instance data is declared in a class but not inside any particular method.

Local data has scope limited to only the method in which it is declared. The variable `result` declared in the `toString` method of the `Die` class is local data. Any reference to `result` in any other method of the `Die` class would have caused the compiler to issue an error message. A local variable simply does not exist outside of the method in which it is declared. On the other hand, instance data, declared at the class level, has a scope of the entire class; any method of the class can refer to it.

A variable declared in a method is local to that method and cannot be used outside of it.

Because local data and instance data operate at different levels of scope, it's possible to declare a local variable inside a method with the same name as an instance variable declared at the class level. Referring to that name in the method will reference the local version of the variable. This naming practice obviously has the potential to confuse anyone reading the code, so it should be avoided.

The formal parameter names in a method header serve as local data for that method. They don't exist until the method is called, and they cease to exist when the method is exited. For example, the formal parameter `owner` in the `Account` constructor comes into existence when the constructor is called and goes out of existence when it finishes executing. To store these values in the object, the values of the parameters are copied into the instance variables of the newly created `Account` object.

Constructors Revisited

Let's discuss constructors a bit more. When we define a class, we usually define a constructor to help us set up the class. In particular, we often use a constructor to initialize the variables associated with each object.

A constructor differs from a regular method in two ways. First, the name of a constructor is the same name as the class. Therefore the name of the constructor in the `Die` class is `Die`, and the name of the constructor in the `Account` class is `Account`. Second, a constructor cannot return a value and does not have a return type specified in the method header.

A common mistake made by programmers is to put a `void` return type on a constructor. As far as the compiler is concerned, putting any return type on a constructor, even `void`, turns it into a regular method that happens to have the same name as the class.

A constructor cannot have any return type, even `void`.

As such, it cannot be invoked as a constructor. This leads to error messages that are sometimes difficult to decipher.

Generally, a constructor is used to initialize the newly instantiated object. For instance, the constructor of the `Die` class sets the face value of the die to 1 initially. The constructor of the `Coin` class calls the `flip` method to put the coin in an initial, random state. The constructor of the `Account` class sets the values of the instance variables to the values passed in as parameters to the constructor. The way you use a constructor to set up an object initially is another important design decision.

We don't have to define a constructor for every class. Each class has a *default constructor* that takes no parameters. The default constructor is used if we don't provide our own. This default constructor generally has no effect on the newly created object.

5.5 Static Class Members

We've used static methods in various situations in previous examples in the book. For example, all the methods of the `Math` class are static. Recall that a static method is one that is invoked through its class name, instead of through an object of that class.

Not only can methods be static, but variables can be static as well. We declare static class members using the `static` modifier.

Deciding whether to declare a method or variable as static is a key step in class design. Let's examine the implications of static variables and methods more closely.

Static Variables

So far, we've seen two categories of variables: local variables that are declared inside a method, and instance variables that are declared in a class but not inside a method. The term *instance variable* is used because each instance of the class has its own version of the variable. That is, each object has distinct memory space for each variable so that each object can have a distinct value for that variable.

A *static variable*, which is sometimes called a *class variable*, is shared among all instances of a class. There is only one copy of a static variable for all objects of the class. Therefore, changing the value of a static variable in one object changes it for all of the

A static variable is shared among all instances of a class.

others. The reserved word `static` is used as a modifier to declare a static variable as follows:

```
private static int count = 0;
```

Memory space for a static variable is established when the class that contains it is referenced for the first time in a program. A local variable declared within a method cannot be static.

Constants, which are declared using the `final` modifier, are often declared using the `static` modifier. Because the value of constants cannot be changed, there might as well be only one copy of the value across all objects of the class.

Static Methods

In Chapter 3 we briefly introduced the concept of a *static method* (also called a *class method*). Static methods can be invoked through the class name. We don't have to instantiate an object of the class in order to invoke the method. In Chapter 3 we noted that all the methods of the `Math` class are static methods. For example, in the following line of code the `sqrt` method is invoked through the `Math` class name:

```
System.out.println ("Square root of 27: " + Math.sqrt(27));
```

The methods in the `Math` class perform basic computations based on values passed as parameters. There is no object state to maintain in these situations; therefore there is no good reason to force us to create an object in order to request these services.

A method is made static by using the `static` modifier in the method declaration. As we've seen many times, the `main` method of a Java program is declared with the `static` modifier; this is done so that `main` can be executed by the interpreter without instantiating an object from the class that contains `main`.

Because static methods do not operate in the context of a particular object, they cannot reference instance variables, which exist only in an instance of a class. The compiler will issue an error if a static method attempts to use a nonstatic variable. A static method can, however, reference static variables because static variables exist independent of specific objects. Therefore, all static methods, including the `main` method, can access only static or local variables.

The program in Listing 5.8 instantiates several objects of the `Slogan` class, printing each one out in turn. Then it invokes a method called `getCount` through the class name, which returns the number of `Slogan` objects that were instantiated in the program.

Listing 5.8

```
//********************************************************************
//  SloganCounter.java       Java Foundations
//
//  Demonstrates the use of the static modifier.
//********************************************************************

public class SloganCounter
{
   //-----------------------------------------------------------------
   //  Creates several Slogan objects and prints the number of
   //  objects that were created.
   //-----------------------------------------------------------------
   public static void main (String[] args)
   {
      Slogan obj;

      obj = new Slogan ("Remember the Alamo.");
      System.out.println (obj);

      obj = new Slogan ("Don't Worry. Be Happy.");
      System.out.println (obj);

      obj = new Slogan ("Live Free or Die.");
      System.out.println (obj);

      obj = new Slogan ("Talk is Cheap.");
      System.out.println (obj);

      obj = new Slogan ("Write Once, Run Anywhere.");
      System.out.println (obj);

      System.out.println();
      System.out.println ("Slogans created: " + Slogan.getCount());
   }
}
```

Output

```
Remember the Alamo.
Don't Worry. Be Happy.
Live Free or Die.
Talk is Cheap.
Write Once, Run Anywhere.

Slogans created: 5
```

Listing 5.9 shows the `Slogan` class. The constructor of `Slogan` increments a static variable called `count`, which is initialized to zero when it is declared. Therefore, `count` serves to keep track of the number of instances of `Slogan` that are created.

The `getCount` method of `Slogan` is also declared as static, which allows it to be invoked through the class name in the `main` method. Note that the only data referenced in the `getCount` method is the integer variable `count`, which is static. As a static method, `getCount` cannot reference any nonstatic data.

The `getCount` method could have been declared without the `static` modifier, but then its invocation in the `main` method would have to have been done through an instance of the `Slogan` class instead of the class itself.

5.6 Class Relationships

The classes in a software system have various types of relationships to each other. Three of the more common relationships are dependency, aggregation, and inheritance.

We've seen dependency relationships in many examples in which one class "uses" another. This section revisits the dependency relationship and explores the situation where a class depends on itself. We then explore aggregation, in which the objects of one class contain objects of another, creating a "has-a" relationship. Inheritance, which we introduced in Chapter 1, creates an "is-a" relationship between classes. We defer our detailed examination of inheritance until Chapter 8.

Dependency

In many previous examples, we've seen the idea of one class being dependent on another. This means that one class relies on another in some sense. Often the methods of one class will invoke the methods of the other class. This establishes a "uses" relationship.

Generally, if class `A` uses class `B`, then one or more methods of class `A` invoke one or more methods of class `B`. If an invoked method is static, then `A` merely references `B` by name. If the invoked method is not static, then `A` must have access to a specific instance of class `B` in order to invoke the method. That is, `A` must have a reference to an object of class `B`.

Listing 5.9

```
//********************************************************************
//  Slogan.java       Java Foundations
//
//  Represents a single slogan or motto.
//********************************************************************

public class Slogan
{
   private String phrase;
   private static int count = 0;

   //-----------------------------------------------------------------
   //  Constructor: Sets up the slogan and increments the number of
   //  instances created.
   //-----------------------------------------------------------------
   public Slogan (String str)
   {
      phrase = str;
      count++;
   }

   //-----------------------------------------------------------------
   //  Returns this slogan as a string.
   //-----------------------------------------------------------------
   public String toString()
   {
      return phrase;
   }

   //-----------------------------------------------------------------
   //  Returns the number of instances of this class that have been
   //  created.
   //-----------------------------------------------------------------
   public static int getCount ()
   {
      return count;
   }
}
```

The way in which one object gains access to an object of another class is an important design decision. It occurs when one class instantiates the objects of another, but the access can also be accomplished by passing one object to another as a method parameter.

In general, we want to minimize the number of dependencies among classes. The less dependent our classes are on each other, the less impact changes and errors will have on the system.

Dependencies Among Objects of the Same Class

In some cases, a class depends on itself. That is, an object of one class interacts with another object of the same class. To accomplish this, a method of the class may accept as a parameter an object of the same class.

The `concat` method of the `String` class is an example of this situation. The method is executed through one `String` object and is passed another `String` object as a parameter. For example:

```
str3 = str1.concat(str2);
```

The `String` object executing the method (`str1`) appends its characters to those of the `String` passed as a parameter (`str2`). A new `String` object is returned as a result and stored as `str3`.

The `RationalTester` program shown in Listing 5.10 demonstrates a similar situation. A rational number is a value that can be represented as a ratio of two integers (a fraction). The `RationalTester` program creates two objects representing rational numbers and then performs various operations on them to produce new rational numbers.

The `RationalNumber` class is shown in Listing 5.11. Keep in mind as you examine this class that each object created from the `RationalNumber` class represents a single rational number. The `RationalNumber` class contains various operations on rational numbers, such as addition and subtraction.

The methods of the `RationalNumber` class, such as `add`, `subtract`, `multiply`, and `divide`, use the `RationalNumber` object that is executing the method as the first (left) operand and the `RationalNumber` object passed as a parameter as the second (right) operand.

The `isLike` method of the `RationalNumber` class is used to determine if two rational numbers are essentially equal. It's tempting, therefore, to call that

Listing **5.10**

```
//********************************************************************
//  RationalTester.java       Java Foundations
//
//  Driver to exercise the use of multiple Rational objects.
//********************************************************************

public class RationalTester
{
   //-----------------------------------------------------------------
   //  Creates some rational number objects and performs various
   //  operations on them.
   //-----------------------------------------------------------------
   public static void main (String[] args)
   {
      RationalNumber r1 = new RationalNumber (6, 8);
      RationalNumber r2 = new RationalNumber (1, 3);
      RationalNumber r3, r4, r5, r6, r7;

      System.out.println ("First rational number: " + r1);
      System.out.println ("Second rational number: " + r2);

      if (r1.isLike(r2))
         System.out.println ("r1 and r2 are equal.");
      else
         System.out.println ("r1 and r2 are NOT equal.");

      r3 = r1.reciprocal();
      System.out.println ("The reciprocal of r1 is: " + r3);

      r4 = r1.add(r2);
      r5 = r1.subtract(r2);
      r6 = r1.multiply(r2);
      r7 = r1.divide(r2);

      System.out.println ("r1 + r2: " + r4);
      System.out.println ("r1 - r2: " + r5);
      System.out.println ("r1 * r2: " + r6);
      System.out.println ("r1 / r2: " + r7);
   }
}
```

Listing **5.10** continued

Output

```
First rational number: 3/4
Second rational number: 1/3
r1 and r2 are NOT equal.
The reciprocal of r1 is: 4/3
r1 + r2: 13/12
r1 - r2: 5/12
r1 * r2: 1/4
r1 / r2: 9/4
```

method `equals`, similar to the method used to compare `String` objects (discussed in Chapter 4). However, in Chapter 8 we will discuss how the `equals` method is somewhat special due to inheritance, and that it should be implemented in a particular way. So to avoid confusion we call this method `isLike` for now.

Note that some of the methods in the `RationalNumber` class, including `reduce` and `gcd`, are declared with private visibility. These methods are private because we don't want them executed directly from outside a `RationalNumber` object. They exist only to support the other services of the object.

Aggregation

An aggregate object is composed of other objects, forming a has-a relationship.

Some objects are made up of other objects. A car, for instance, is made up of its engine, its chassis, its wheels, and several other parts. Each of these other parts could be considered a separate object. Therefore we can say that a car is an *aggregation*—it is composed, at least in part, of other objects. Aggregation is sometimes described as a *has-a relationship*. For instance, a car has a chassis.

In the software world, we define an *aggregate object* as any object that contains references to other objects as instance data. For example, an `Account` object contains, among other things, a `String` object that represents the name of the account owner. We sometimes forget that strings are objects, but technically that makes each `Account` object an aggregate object.

Listing 5.11

```
//********************************************************************
//  RationalNumber.java       Java Foundations
//
//  Represents one rational number with a numerator and denominator.
//********************************************************************

public class RationalNumber
{
   private int numerator, denominator;

   //-----------------------------------------------------------------
   //  Constructor: Sets up the rational number by ensuring a nonzero
   //  denominator and making only the numerator signed.
   //-----------------------------------------------------------------
   public RationalNumber (int numer, int denom)
   {
      if (denom == 0)
         denom = 1;

      // Make the numerator "store" the sign
      if (denom < 0)
      {
         numer = numer * -1;
         denom = denom * -1;
      }

      numerator = numer;
      denominator = denom;

      reduce();
   }

   //-----------------------------------------------------------------
   //  Returns the numerator of this rational number.
   //-----------------------------------------------------------------
   public int getNumerator ()
   {
      return numerator;
   }

   //-----------------------------------------------------------------
   //  Returns the denominator of this rational number.
   //-----------------------------------------------------------------
```

Listing 5.11 continued

```
   public int getDenominator ()
   {
      return denominator;
   }

   //-----------------------------------------------------------------
   //  Returns the reciprocal of this rational number.
   //-----------------------------------------------------------------
   public RationalNumber reciprocal ()
   {
      return new RationalNumber (denominator, numerator);
   }

   //-----------------------------------------------------------------
   //  Adds this rational number to the one passed as a parameter.
   //  A common denominator is found by multiplying the individual
   //  denominators.
   //-----------------------------------------------------------------
   public RationalNumber add (RationalNumber op2)
   {
      int commonDenominator = denominator * op2.getDenominator();
      int numerator1 = numerator * op2.getDenominator();
      int numerator2 = op2.getNumerator() * denominator;
      int sum = numerator1 + numerator2;

      return new RationalNumber (sum, commonDenominator);
   }

   //-----------------------------------------------------------------
   //  Subtracts the rational number passed as a parameter from this
   //  rational number.
   //-----------------------------------------------------------------
   public RationalNumber subtract (RationalNumber op2)
   {
      int commonDenominator = denominator * op2.getDenominator();
      int numerator1 = numerator * op2.getDenominator();
      int numerator2 = op2.getNumerator() * denominator;
      int difference = numerator1 - numerator2;

      return new RationalNumber (difference, commonDenominator);
   }
```

Listing **5.11** continued

```
   //-----------------------------------------------------------------
   //  Multiplies this rational number by the one passed as a
   //  parameter.
   //-----------------------------------------------------------------
   public RationalNumber multiply (RationalNumber op2)
   {
      int numer = numerator * op2.getNumerator();
      int denom = denominator * op2.getDenominator();

      return new RationalNumber (numer, denom);
   }

   //-----------------------------------------------------------------
   //  Divides this rational number by the one passed as a parameter
   //  by multiplying by the reciprocal of the second rational.
   //-----------------------------------------------------------------
   public RationalNumber divide (RationalNumber op2)
   {
      return multiply (op2.reciprocal());
   }

   //-----------------------------------------------------------------
   //  Determines if this rational number is equal to the one passed
   //  as a parameter.  Assumes they are both reduced.
   //-----------------------------------------------------------------
   public boolean isLike (RationalNumber op2)
   {
      return ( numerator == op2.getNumerator() &&
               denominator == op2.getDenominator() );
   }

   //-----------------------------------------------------------------
   //  Returns this rational number as a string.
   //-----------------------------------------------------------------
   public String toString ()
   {
      String result;

      if (numerator == 0)
         result = "0";
      else
         if (denominator == 1)
```

Listing 5.11 continued

```
            result = numerator + "";
         else
            result = numerator + "/" + denominator;

      return result;
   }

   //-----------------------------------------------------------------
   //  Reduces this rational number by dividing both the numerator
   //  and the denominator by their greatest common divisor.
   //-----------------------------------------------------------------
   private void reduce ()
   {
      if (numerator != 0)
      {
         int common = gcd (Math.abs(numerator), denominator);

         numerator = numerator / common;
         denominator = denominator / common;
      }
   }

   //-----------------------------------------------------------------
   //  Computes and returns the greatest common divisor of the two
   //  positive parameters. Uses Euclid's algorithm.
   //-----------------------------------------------------------------
   private int gcd (int num1, int num2)
   {
      while (num1 != num2)
         if (num1 > num2)
            num1 = num1 - num2;
         else
            num2 = num2 - num1;

      return num1;
   }
}
```

Aggregation is a special type of dependency. That is, a class that is defined in part by another class is dependent on that class. The methods of the aggregate object generally invoke the methods of the objects from which it is composed.

The more complex an object, the more likely it will need to be represented as an aggregate object. In UML, aggregation is represented by a connection between two classes, with an open diamond at the end near the class that is the aggregate. Figure 5.10 shows a UML class diagram that contains an aggregation relationship.

Note that in previous UML diagram examples, strings are not represented as separate classes with aggregation relationships, though technically they could be. Strings are so fundamental to programming that often they are represented as if they are a primitive type in a UML diagram.

The `this` Reference

Before we leave the topic of relationships among classes, we should examine another special reference used in Java programs called the `this` reference. The word `this` is a reserved word in Java. It allows an object to refer to itself. As we have discussed, a nonstatic method is invoked through (or by) a particular object or class. Inside that method, the `this` reference can be used to refer to the currently executing object.

For example, in a class called `ChessPiece` there could be a method called `move`, which could contain the following line:

```
if (this.position == piece2.position)
   result = false;
```

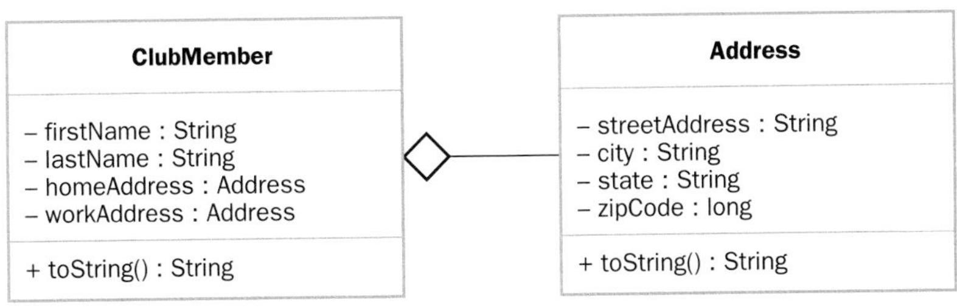

FIGURE 5.10 A UML class diagram showing an aggregation relationship

In this situation, the `this` reference is being used to clarify which position is being referenced. The `this` reference refers to the object through which the method was invoked. So when the following line is used to invoke the method, the `this` reference refers to `bishop1`:

```
bishop1.move();
```

However, when another object is used to invoke the method, the `this` reference refers to it. Therefore, when the following invocation is used, the `this` reference in the `move` method refers to `bishop2`:

```
bishop2.move();
```

Often, the `this` reference is used to distinguish the parameters of a constructor from their corresponding instance variables with the same names. For example, the constructor of the `Account` class was presented in Listing 5.7 as follows:

```
public Account (String owner, long account, double initial)
{
   name = owner;
   acctNumber = account;
   balance = initial;
}
```

When writing this constructor, we deliberately came up with different names for the parameters to distinguish them from the instance variables `name`, `acctNumber`, and `balance`. This distinction is arbitrary. The constructor could have been written as follows using the `this` reference:

```
public Account (String name, long acctNumber, double balance)
{
   this.name = name;
   this.acctNumber = acctNumber;
   this.balance = balance;
}
```

In this version of the constructor, the `this` reference specifically refers to the instance variables of the object. The variables on the right-hand side of the assignment statements refer to the formal parameters. This approach eliminates the need to come up with different yet equivalent names. This situation sometimes occurs in other methods but comes up often in constructors.

5.7 Method Design

Once you have identified classes and assigned basic responsibilities, the design of each method will determine how exactly the class will define its behaviors. Some methods are straightforward and require little thought. Others are more interesting and require careful planning.

An *algorithm* is a step-by-step process for solving a problem. A recipe is an example of an algorithm. Travel directions are another example of an algorithm. Every method implements an algorithm that determines how that method accomplishes its goals.

An algorithm is often described using *pseudocode*, which is a mixture of code statements and English phrases. Pseudocode provides enough structure to show how the code will operate, without getting bogged down in the syntactic details of a particular programming language or becoming prematurely constrained by the characteristics of particular programming constructs.

This section discusses two important aspects of program design at the method level: method decomposition and the implications of passing objects as parameters.

Method Decomposition

Occasionally, a service that an object provides is so complex that it cannot reasonably be implemented using one method. Therefore we sometimes need to decompose a method into multiple methods to create a more understandable design. As an example, let's examine a program that translates English sentences into Pig Latin.

A complex service provided by an object can be decomposed and make use of private support methods.

Pig Latin is a made-up language in which each word of a sentence is modified, in general, by moving the initial sound of the word to the end and adding an "ay" sound. For example, the word *happy* would be written and pronounced *appyhay* and the word *birthday* would become *irthdaybay*. Words that begin with vowels simply have a "yay" sound added on the end, turning the word *enough* into *enoughyay*. Consonant blends such as "ch" and "st" at the beginning of a word are moved to the end together before adding the "ay" sound. Therefore the word *grapefruit* becomes *apefruitgray*.

The `PigLatin` program shown in Listing 5.12 reads one or more sentences, translating each into Pig Latin.

Listing **5.12**

```
//********************************************************************
//  PigLatin.java       Java Foundations
//
//  Demonstrates the concept of method decomposition.
//********************************************************************

import java.util.Scanner;

public class PigLatin
{
   //-----------------------------------------------------------------
   //  Reads sentences and translates them into Pig Latin.
   //-----------------------------------------------------------------
   public static void main (String[] args)
   {
      String sentence, result, another;

      Scanner scan = new Scanner (System.in);

      do
      {
         System.out.println ();
         System.out.println ("Enter a sentence (no punctuation):");
         sentence = scan.nextLine();

         System.out.println ();
         result = PigLatinTranslator.translate (sentence);
         System.out.println ("That sentence in Pig Latin is:");
         System.out.println (result);

         System.out.println ();
         System.out.print ("Translate another sentence (y/n)? ");
         another = scan.nextLine();
      }
      while (another.equalsIgnoreCase("y"));
   }
}
```

Listing **5.12** continued

Output

```
Enter a sentence (no punctuation):
Do you speak Pig Latin

That sentence in Pig Latin is:
oday ouyay eakspay igpay atinlay

Translate another sentence (y/n)? y

Enter a sentence (no punctuation):
Play it again Sam

That sentence in Pig Latin is:
ayplay ityay againyay amsay

Translate another sentence (y/n)? n
```

The workhorse behind the `PigLatin` program is the `PigLatinTranslator` class, shown in Listing 5.13. The `PigLatinTranslator` class provides one fundamental service, a static method called `translate`, which accepts a string and translates it into Pig Latin. Note that the `PigLatinTranslator` class does not contain a constructor because none is needed.

The act of translating an entire sentence into Pig Latin is not trivial. If written in one big method, it would be very long and difficult to follow. A better solution, as implemented in the `PigLatinTranslator` class, is to decompose the `translate` method and use several other support methods to help with the task.

The `translate` method uses a `Scanner` object to separate the string into words. Recall that one role of the `Scanner` class (discussed in Chapter 3) is to separate a string into smaller elements called tokens. In this case, the tokens are separated by space characters so we can use the default whitespace delimiters. The `PigLatin` program assumes that no punctuation is included in the input.

Listing **5.13**

```
//********************************************************************
//  PigLatinTranslator.java       Java Foundations
//
//  Represents a translator from English to Pig Latin. Demonstrates
//  method decomposition.
//********************************************************************

import java.util.Scanner;

public class PigLatinTranslator
{
   //-----------------------------------------------------------------
   //  Translates a sentence of words into Pig Latin.
   //-----------------------------------------------------------------
   public static String translate (String sentence)
   {
      String result = "";

      sentence = sentence.toLowerCase();

      Scanner scan = new Scanner (sentence);

      while (scan.hasNext())
      {
         result += translateWord (scan.next());
         result += " ";
      }

      return result;
   }

   //-----------------------------------------------------------------
   //  Translates one word into Pig Latin. If the word begins with a
   //  vowel, the suffix "yay" is appended to the word.  Otherwise,
   //  the first letter or two are moved to the end of the word,
   //  and "ay" is appended.
   //-----------------------------------------------------------------
   private static String translateWord (String word)
   {
      String result = "";

      if (beginsWithVowel(word))
         result = word + "yay";
```

Listing 5.13 continued

```
      else
         if (beginsWithBlend(word))
            result = word.substring(2) + word.substring(0,2) + "ay";
         else
            result = word.substring(1) + word.charAt(0) + "ay";

      return result;
   }

   //-----------------------------------------------------------------
   //  Determines if the specified word begins with a vowel.
   //-----------------------------------------------------------------
   private static boolean beginsWithVowel (String word)
   {
      String vowels = "aeiou";

      char letter = word.charAt(0);

      return (vowels.indexOf(letter) != -1);
   }

   //-----------------------------------------------------------------
   //  Determines if the specified word begins with a particular
   //  two-character consonant blend.
   //-----------------------------------------------------------------
   private static boolean beginsWithBlend (String word)
   {
      return ( word.startsWith ("bl") || word.startsWith ("sc") ||
               word.startsWith ("br") || word.startsWith ("sh") ||
               word.startsWith ("ch") || word.startsWith ("sk") ||
               word.startsWith ("cl") || word.startsWith ("sl") ||
               word.startsWith ("cr") || word.startsWith ("sn") ||
               word.startsWith ("dr") || word.startsWith ("sm") ||
               word.startsWith ("dw") || word.startsWith ("sp") ||
               word.startsWith ("fl") || word.startsWith ("sq") ||
               word.startsWith ("fr") || word.startsWith ("st") ||
               word.startsWith ("gl") || word.startsWith ("sw") ||
               word.startsWith ("gr") || word.startsWith ("th") ||
               word.startsWith ("kl") || word.startsWith ("tr") ||
               word.startsWith ("ph") || word.startsWith ("tw") ||
               word.startsWith ("pl") || word.startsWith ("wh") ||
               word.startsWith ("pr") || word.startsWith ("wr") );
   }
}
```

The `translate` method passes each word to the private support method `translateWord`. Even the job of translating one word is somewhat involved, so the `translateWord` method makes use of two other private methods, `beginsWithVowel` and `beginsWithBlend`.

The `beginsWithVowel` method returns a `boolean` value that indicates whether the word passed as a parameter begins with a vowel. Note that instead of checking each vowel separately, the code for this method declares a string that contains all the vowels, and then invokes the `String` method `indexOf` to determine whether the first character of the word is in the vowel string. If the specified character cannot be found, the `indexOf` method returns a value of `–1`.

The `beginsWithBlend` method also returns a `boolean` value. The body of the method contains only a `return` statement with one large expression that makes several calls to the `startsWith` method of the `String` class. If any of these calls returns true, then the `beginsWithBlend` method returns true as well.

Note that the `translateWord`, `beginsWithVowel`, and `beginsWithBlend` methods are all declared with private visibility. They are not intended to provide services directly to clients outside the class. Instead, they exist to help the `translate` method, which is the only true service method in this class, to do its job. By declaring them with private visibility, they cannot be invoked from outside this class. For instance, if the `main` method of the `PigLatin` class attempted to invoke the `translateWord` method, the compiler would issue an error message.

Figure 5.11 shows a UML class diagram for the `PigLatin` program. Note the notation showing the visibility of various methods.

Whenever a method becomes large or complex, we should consider decomposing it into multiple methods to create a more understandable class design. First, however, we must consider how other classes and objects can be defined to create better overall system design. In an object-oriented design, method decomposition must be subordinate to object decomposition.

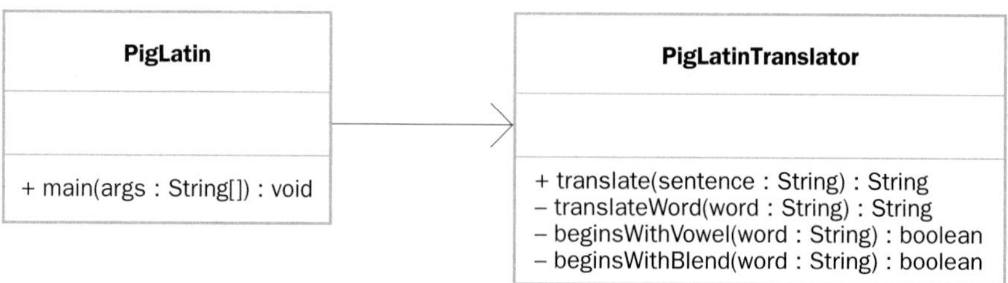

FIGURE 5.11 A UML class diagram for the `PigLatin` program

Method Parameters Revisited

Another important issue related to method design involves the way parameters are passed into a method. In Java, all parameters are passed *by value*. That is, the current value of the actual parameter (in the invocation) is copied into the formal parameter in the method header. We mentioned this issue previously in this chapter; let's examine it now in more detail.

Essentially, parameter passing is like an assignment statement, assigning to the formal parameter a copy of the value stored in the actual parameter. This issue must be considered when making changes to a formal parameter inside a method. The formal parameter is a separate copy of the value that is passed in, so any changes made to it have no effect on the actual parameter. After control returns to the calling method, the actual parameter will have the same value as it did before the method was called.

When an object is passed to a method, the actual and formal parameters become aliases.

However, when we pass an object to a method, we are actually passing a reference to that object. The value that gets copied is the address of the object. Therefore the formal parameter and the actual parameter become aliases of each other. If we change the state of the object through the formal parameter reference inside the method, we are changing the object referenced by the actual parameter, because they refer to the same object. On the other hand, if we change the formal parameter reference itself (to make it point to a new object, for instance), we have not changed the fact that the actual parameter still refers to the original object.

The program in Listing 5.14 illustrates the nuances of parameter passing. Carefully trace the processing of this program and note the values that are output. The `ParameterTester` class contains a `main` method that calls the `changeValues` method in a `ParameterModifier` object. Two of the parameters to `changeValues` are `Num` objects, each of which simply stores an integer value. The other parameter is a primitive integer value.

Listing 5.15 shows the `ParameterModifier` class, and Listing 5.16 shows the `Num` class. Inside the `changeValues` method, a modification is made to each of the three formal parameters: the integer parameter is set to a different value, the value stored in the first `Num` parameter is changed using its `setValue` method, and a new `Num` object is created and assigned to the second `Num` parameter. These changes are reflected in the output printed at the end of the `changeValues` method.

However, note the final values that are printed after returning from the method. The primitive integer was not changed from its original value because the change was made to a copy inside the method. Likewise, the last parameter still refers to its original object with its original value. This is because the new `Num` object created

Listing 5.14

```
//********************************************************************
//  ParameterTester.java       Java Foundations
//
//  Demonstrates the effects of passing various types of parameters.
//********************************************************************

public class ParameterTester
{
   //-----------------------------------------------------------------
   //  Sets up three variables (one primitive and two objects) to
   //  serve as actual parameters to the changeValues method. Prints
   //  their values before and after calling the method.
   //-----------------------------------------------------------------
   public static void main (String[] args)
   {
      ParameterModifier modifier = new ParameterModifier();

      int a1 = 111;
      Num a2 = new Num (222);
      Num a3 = new Num (333);

      System.out.println ("Before calling changeValues:");
      System.out.println ("a1\ta2\ta3");
      System.out.println (a1 + "\t" + a2 + "\t" + a3 + "\n");

      modifier.changeValues (a1, a2, a3);

      System.out.println ("After calling changeValues:");
      System.out.println ("a1\ta2\ta3");
      System.out.println (a1 + "\t" + a2 + "\t" + a3 + "\n");
   }
}
```

Output

```
Before calling changeValues:
a1      a2      a3
111     222     333

Before changing the values:
f1      f2      f3
111     222     333
```

Listing **5.14** continued

```
After changing the values:
f1      f2      f3
999     888     777

After calling changeValues:
a1      a2      a3
111     888     333
```

Listing **5.15**

```
//********************************************************************
//  ParameterModifier.java        Java Foundations
//
//  Demonstrates the effects of changing parameter values.
//********************************************************************

public class ParameterModifier
{
   //-----------------------------------------------------------------
   //  Modifies the parameters, printing their values before and
   //  after making the changes.
   //-----------------------------------------------------------------
   public void changeValues (int f1, Num f2, Num f3)
   {
      System.out.println ("Before changing the values:");
      System.out.println ("f1\tf2\tf3");
      System.out.println (f1 + "\t" + f2 + "\t" + f3 + "\n");

      f1 = 999;
      f2.setValue(888);
      f3 = new Num (777);

      System.out.println ("After changing the values:");
      System.out.println ("f1\tf2\tf3");
      System.out.println (f1 + "\t" + f2 + "\t" + f3 + "\n");
   }
}
```

Listing **5.16**

```
//********************************************************************
//  Num.java       Java Foundations
//
//  Represents a single integer as an object.
//********************************************************************

public class Num
{
   private int value;

   //-----------------------------------------------------------------
   //  Sets up the new Num object, storing an initial value.
   //-----------------------------------------------------------------
   public Num (int update)
   {
      value = update;
   }

   //-----------------------------------------------------------------
   //  Sets the stored value to the newly specified value.
   //-----------------------------------------------------------------
   public void setValue (int update)
   {
      value = update;
   }

   //-----------------------------------------------------------------
   //  Returns the stored integer value as a string.
   //-----------------------------------------------------------------
   public String toString ()
   {
      return value + "";
   }
}
```

in the method was referred to only by the formal parameter. When the method returned, that formal parameter was destroyed and the `Num` object it referred to was marked for garbage collection. The only change that is "permanent" is the change made to the state of the second parameter. Figure 5.12 shows the step-by-step processing of this program.

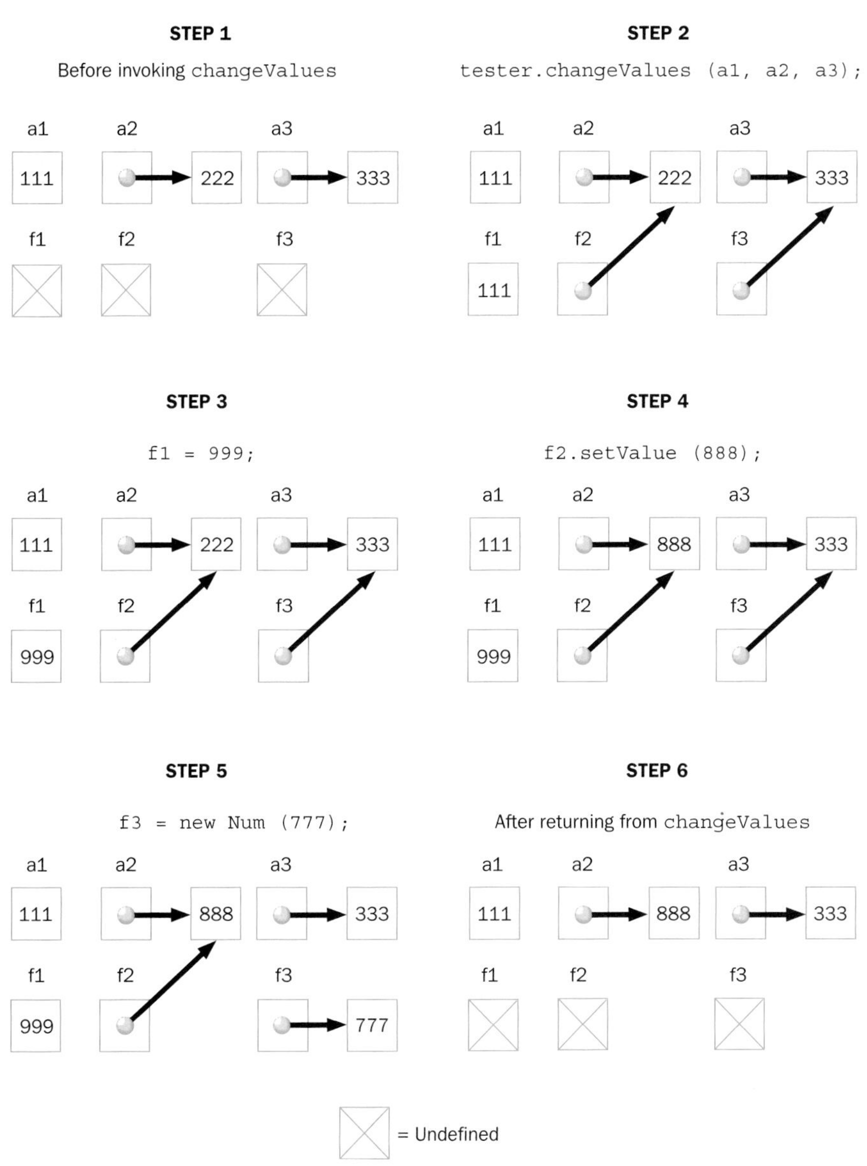

FIGURE 5.12 Tracing the parameters in the `ParameterTesting` program

5.8 Method Overloading

As we've discussed, when a method is invoked, the flow of control transfers to the code that defines the method. After the method has been executed, control returns to the location of the call, and processing continues.

Often the method name is sufficient to indicate which method is being called by a specific invocation. But in Java, as in other object-oriented languages, you can use the same method name with different parameter lists for multiple methods. This technique is called *method overloading*. It is useful when you need to perform similar methods on different types of data.

The versions of an overloaded method are distinguished by the number, type, and order of their parameters.

The compiler must still be able to associate each invocation to a specific method declaration. If the method name for two or more methods is the same, additional information is used to uniquely identify the version that is being invoked. In Java, a method name can be used for multiple methods as long as the number of parameters, the types of those parameters, and/or the order of the types of parameters is distinct.

For example, we could declare a method called sum as follows:

```
public int sum (int num1, int num2)
{
   return num1 + num2;
}
```

Then we could declare another method called sum, within the same class, as follows:

```
public int sum (int num1, int num2, int num3)
{
   return num1 + num2 + num3;
}
```

Now, when an invocation is made, the compiler looks at the number of parameters to determine which version of the sum method to call. For instance, the following invocation will call the second version of the sum method:

```
sum (25, 69, 13);
```

A method's name, along with the number, type, and order of its parameters, is called the method's *signature*. The compiler uses the complete method signature to *bind* a method invocation to the appropriate definition.

The compiler must be able to examine a method invocation to determine which specific method is being invoked. If you attempt to specify two method names with the same signature, the compiler will issue an appropriate error message and will not create an executable program. There can be no ambiguity.

Note that the return type of a method is not part of the method signature. That is, two overloaded methods cannot differ only by their return type. This is because the value returned by a method can be ignored by the invocation. The compiler would not be able to distinguish which version of an overloaded method is being referenced in such situations.

The `println` method is an example of a method that is overloaded several times, each accepting a single type. The following is a partial list of its various signatures:

- `println (String s)`
- `println (int i)`
- `println (double d)`
- `println (char c)`
- `println (boolean b)`

The following two lines of code actually invoke different methods that have the same name:

```
System.out.println ("Number of students: ");
System.out.println (count);
```

The first line invokes the version of `println` that accepts a string. The second line, assuming `count` is an integer variable, invokes the version of `println` that accepts an integer.

We often use a `println` statement that prints several distinct types, such as:

```
System.out.println ("Number of students: " + count);
```

Remember, in this case the plus sign is the string concatenation operator. First, the value in the variable `count` is converted to a string representation, then the two strings are concatenated into one longer string, and finally the definition of `println` that accepts a single string is invoked.

Constructors can be overloaded, and often are. By providing multiple versions of a constructor, we provide multiple ways to set up an object.

Summary of Key Concepts

- The nouns in a problem description may indicate some of the classes and objects needed in a program.
- The heart of object-oriented programming is defining classes that represent objects with well-defined state and behavior.
- The scope of a variable, which determines where it can be referenced, depends on where it is declared.
- A UML class diagram helps us visualize the contents of and relationships among the classes of a program.
- An object should be encapsulated, guarding its data from inappropriate access.
- Instance variables should be declared with private visibility to promote encapsulation.
- Most objects contain accessor and mutator methods to allow the client to manage data in a controlled manner.
- The way a class represents an object's state should be independent of how that object is used.
- The value returned from a method must be consistent with the return type specified in the method header.
- When a method is called, the actual parameters are copied into the formal parameters.
- A variable declared in a method is local to that method and cannot be used outside of it.
- A constructor cannot have any return type, even `void`.
- A static variable is shared among all instances of a class.
- An aggregate object is composed of other objects, forming a has-a relationship.
- A complex service provided by an object can be decomposed to make use of private support methods.
- When an object is passed to a method, the actual and formal parameters become aliases.
- The versions of an overloaded method are distinguished by the number, type, and order of their parameters.

Self-Review Questions

SR 5.1 What is an attribute?

SR 5.2 What is an operation?

SR 5.3 What is the difference between an object and a class?

SR 5.4 What is the scope of a variable?

SR 5.5 What are UML diagrams designed to do?

SR 5.6 Objects should be self-governing. Explain.

SR 5.7 What is a modifier?

SR 5.8 Why might a constant be given public visibility?

SR 5.9 Describe each of the following:

a. public method

b. private method

c. public variable

d. private variable

SR 5.10 What is the interface to an object?

SR 5.11 Why is a method invoked through (or on) a particular object? What is the exception to that rule?

SR 5.12 What does it mean for a method to return a value?

SR 5.13 What does the `return` statement do?

SR 5.14 Is a `return` statement required?

SR 5.15 Explain the difference between an actual parameter and a formal parameter.

SR 5.16 What are constructors used for? How are they defined?

SR 5.17 What is the difference between a static variable and an instance variable?

SR 5.18 What kinds of variables can the `main` method of any program reference? Why?

SR 5.19 Describe a dependency relationship between two classes.

SR 5.20 How are overloaded methods distinguished from each other?

SR 5.21 What is method decomposition?

SR 5.22 Explain how a class can have an association with itself.

SR 5.23 What is an aggregate object?

SR 5.24 What does the `this` reference refer to?

SR 5.25 How are objects passed as parameters?

Exercises

EX 5.1 For each of the following pairs, which represents a class and which represents an object of that class?

a. Superhero, Superman

b. Justin, Person

c. Rover, Pet

d. Magazine, Time

e. Christmas, Holiday

EX 5.2 List some attributes and operations that might be defined for a class called `PictureFrame` that represents a picture frame.

EX 5.3 List some attributes and operations that might be defined for a class called `Meeting` that represents a business meeting.

EX 5.4 List some attributes and operations that might be defined for a class called `Course` that represents a college course (not a particular offering of a course, just the course in general).

EX 5.5 Rewrite the `for` loop body from the `SnakeEyes` program so that the variables `num1` and `num2` are not used.

EX 5.6 Write a method called `lyrics` that prints the lyrics of a song when invoked. The method should accept no parameters and return no value.

EX 5.7 Write a method called `cube` that accepts one integer parameter and returns that value raised to the third power.

EX 5.8 Write a method called `random100` that returns a random integer in the range of 1 to 100 (inclusive).

EX 5.9 Write a method called `randomInRange` that accepts two integer parameters representing a range. The method should return a random integer in the specified range (inclusive). Assume that the first parameter is greater than the second.

EX 5.10 Write a method called `powersOfTwo` that prints the first 10 powers of 2 (starting with 2). The method takes no parameters and doesn't return anything.

EX 5.11 Write a method called `alarm` that prints the string `"Alarm!"` multiple times on separate lines. The method should accept an integer parameter that specifies how many times the string is printed. Print an error message if the parameter is less than 1.

EX 5.12 Write a method called `sum100` that returns the sum of the integers from 1 to 100, inclusive.

EX 5.13 Write a method called `maxOfTwo` that accepts two integer parameters and returns the larger of the two.

EX 5.14 Write a method called `sumRange` that accepts two integer parameters that represent a range. Issue an error message and return zero if the second parameter is less than the first. Otherwise, the method should return the sum of the integers in that range (inclusive).

EX 5.15 Write a method called `larger` that accepts two floating point parameters (of type `double`) and returns true if the first parameter is greater than the second, and false otherwise.

EX 5.16 Write a method called `countA` that accepts a `String` parameter and returns the number of times the character `'A'` is found in the string.

EX 5.17 Write a method called `evenlyDivisible` that accepts two integer parameters and returns true if the first parameter is evenly divisible by the second, or vice versa, and false otherwise. Return false if either parameter is zero.

EX 5.18 Write a method called `isAlpha` that accepts a character parameter and returns true if that character is either an uppercase or lowercase alphabetic letter.

EX 5.19 Write a method called `floatEquals` that accepts three floating point values as parameters. The method should return true if the first two parameters are equal within the tolerance of the third parameter.

EX 5.20 Write a method called `reverse` that accepts a `String` parameter and returns a string that contains the characters of the parameter in reverse order. Note: there is a method in the

String class that performs this operation, but for the sake of this exercise, you are expected to write your own.

EX 5.21 Write a method called isIsosceles that accepts three integer parameters that represent the lengths of the sides of a triangle. The method returns true if the triangle is isosceles but not equilateral (meaning that exactly two of the sides have an equal length), and false otherwise.

EX 5.22 Write a method called average that accepts two integer parameters and returns their average as a floating point value.

EX 5.23 Overload the average method of Exercise 5.22 such that if three integers are provided as parameters, the method returns the average of all three.

EX 5.24 Overload the average method of Exercise 5.22 to accept four integer parameters and return their average.

EX 5.25 Write a method called multiConcat that takes a String and an integer as parameters. Return a String that consists of the string parameter concatenated with itself count times, where count is the integer parameter. For example, if the parameter values are "hi" and 4, the return value is "hihihihi". Return the original string if the integer parameter is less than 2.

EX 5.26 Overload the multiConcat method from Exercise 5.25 such that if the integer parameter is not provided, the method returns the string concatenated with itself. For example, if the parameter is "test", the return value is "testtest".

EX 5.27 Discuss the manner in which Java passes parameters to a method. Is this technique consistent between primitive types and objects? Explain.

EX 5.28 Explain why a static method cannot refer to an instance variable.

EX 5.29 Can a class implement two interfaces that each contains the same method signature? Explain.

EX 5.30 Draw a UML class diagram for the CountFlips program.

EX 5.31 Draw a UML class diagram for the FlipRace program.

EX 5.32 Draw a UML class diagram for the Transactions program.

Programming Projects

PP 5.1 Revise the `Coin` class such that its state is represented internally using a `boolean` variable. Test the new versions of the class as part of the `CountFlips` and `FlipRace` programs.

PP 5.2 Repeat programming project 5.1, representing the state of the coin using a character string.

PP 5.3 Repeat programming project 5.1, representing the state of the coin using an enumerated type.

PP 5.4 Design and implement a class called `Sphere` that contains instance data that represents the sphere's diameter. Define the `Sphere` constructor to accept and initialize the diameter, and include getter and setter methods for the diameter. Include methods that calculate and return the volume and surface area of the sphere (see programming project 3.5 for the formulas). Include a `toString` method that returns a one-line description of the sphere. Create a driver class called `MultiSphere`, whose `main` method instantiates and updates several `Sphere` objects.

PP 5.5 Design and implement a class called `Dog` that contains instance data that represents the dog's name and age. Define the `Dog` constructor to accept and initialize instance data. Include getter and setter methods for the name and age. Include a method to compute and return the age of the dog in "person years" (seven times the dog's age). Include a `toString` method that returns a one-line description of the dog. Create a driver class called `Kennel`, whose `main` method instantiates and updates several `Dog` objects.

PP 5.6 Design and implement a class called `Box` that contains instance data that represents the height, width, and depth of the box. Also include a `boolean` variable called `full` as instance data that represents if the box is full or not. Define the `Box` constructor to accept and initialize the height, width, and depth of the box. Each newly created `Box` is empty (the constructor should initialize `full` to false). Include getter and setter methods for all instance data. Include a `toString` method that returns a one-line description of the box. Create a driver class called `BoxTest`, whose `main` method instantiates and updates several `Box` objects.

PP 5.7 Design and implement a class called `Book` that contains instance data for the title, author, publisher, and copyright date. Define the `Book` constructor to accept and initialize this data. Include setter and getter methods for all instance data. Include a `toString` method that returns a nicely formatted, multiline description of the book. Create a driver class called `Bookshelf`, whose `main` method instantiates and updates several `Book` objects.

PP 5.8 Design and implement a class called `Flight` that represents an airline flight. It should contain instance data that represents the airline name, flight number, and the flight's origin and destination cities. Define the `Flight` constructor to accept and initialize all instance data. Include getter and setter methods for all instance data. Include a `toString` method that returns a one-line description of the flight. Create a driver class called `FlightTest`, whose `main` method instantiates and updates several `Flight` objects.

PP 5.9 Design and implement a class called `Bulb` that represents a light bulb that can be turned on and off. Create a driver class called `Lights`, whose `main` method instantiates and turns on some `Bulb` objects.

PP 5.10 Using the `Die` class defined in this chapter, design and implement a class called `PairOfDice`, composed of two `Die` objects. Include methods to set and get the individual die values, a method to roll the dice, and a method that returns the current sum of the two die values. Rewrite the `SnakeEyes` program using a `PairOfDice` object.

PP 5.11 Using the `PairOfDice` class from programming project 5.10, design and implement a class to play a game called Pig. In this game, the user competes against the computer. On each turn, the current player rolls a pair of dice and accumulates points. The goal is to reach 100 points before your opponent does. If, on any turn, the player rolls a 1, all points accumulated for that round are forfeited and control of the dice moves to the other player. If the player rolls two 1's in one turn, the player loses all points accumulated thus far in the game and loses control of the dice. The player may voluntarily turn over the dice after each roll. Therefore the player must decide to either roll again (be a pig) and risk losing points or relinquish control of the dice, possibly allowing the other player to win. Implement the computer player such that it always relinquishes the dice after accumulating 20 or more points in any given round.

PP 5.12 Modify the `Account` class from this chapter so that it also permits an account to be opened with just a name and an account number, assuming an initial balance of zero. Modify the `main` method of the `Transactions` class to demonstrate this new capability.

PP 5.13 Design and implement a class called `Card` that represents a standard playing card. Each card has a suit and a face value. Create a program that deals five random cards.

Answers to Self-Review Questions

SR 5.1 An attribute is a data value stored in an object and defines a particular characteristic of that object. For example, one attribute of a `Student` object might be that student's current grade point average. Collectively, the values of an object's attributes determine that object's current state.

SR 5.2 An operation is a function that can be done to or done by an object. For example, one operation of a `Student` object might be to compute that student's current grade point average. Collectively, an object's operations are referred to as the object's behaviors.

SR 5.3 A class is the blueprint of an object. It defines the variables and methods that will be a part of every object that is instantiated from it. But a class reserves no memory space for variables. Each object has its own data space and therefore its own state.

SR 5.4 The scope of a variable is the area within a program in which the variable can be referenced. An instance variable, declared at the class level, can be referenced in any method of the class. Local variables, including the formal parameters, declared within a particular method, can be referenced only in that method.

SR 5.5 A UML diagram helps us visualize the classes used in a program as well as the relationships among them. UML diagrams are tools that help us capture the design of a program prior to writing it.

SR 5.6 A self-governing object is one that controls the values of its own data. An encapsulated object, which doesn't allow an external client to reach in and change its data, is self-governing.

SR 5.7 A modifier is a Java reserved word that can be used in the definition of a variable or method and that specifically defines certain characteristics of its use. For example, if a variable is declared with the modifier `private`, the variable cannot be directly accessed outside of the object in which it is defined.

SR 5.8 A constant might be declared with public visibility because that would not violate encapsulation. Because the value of a constant cannot be changed, it is not generally a problem for another object to access it directly.

SR 5.9 The modifiers affect the methods and variables in the following ways:

a. A public method is called a service method for an object because it defines a service that the object provides.

b. A private method is called a support method because it cannot be invoked from outside the object and is used to support the activities of other methods in the class.

c. A public variable is a variable that can be directly accessed and modified by a client. This explicitly violates the principle of encapsulation and therefore should be avoided.

d. A private variable is a variable that can be accessed and modified only from within the class. Variables almost always are declared with private visibility.

SR 5.10 An object's interface is the set of public operations (methods) defined on it. That is, the interface establishes the set of services the object will perform for the rest of the system.

SR 5.11 Although a method is defined in a class, it is invoked through a particular object to indicate which object of that class is being affected. For example, the `Student` class may define the operation that computes the grade point average of a student, but the operation is invoked through a particular `Student` object to compute the GPA for that student. The exception to this rule is the invocation of a static method, which is executed through the class name and does not affect any particular object.

SR 5.12 An invoked method may return a value, which means it computes a value and provides that value to the calling method. The calling method usually uses the invocation, and thus its return value, as part of a larger expression.

SR 5.13 An explicit `return` statement is used to specify the value that is returned from a method. The type of the return value must match the return type specified in the method definition.

SR 5.14 A `return` statement is required in methods that have a return type other than `void`. A method that does not return a value could use a `return` statement without an expression, but it is not necessary. Only one `return` statement should be used in a method.

SR 5.15 An actual parameter is a value sent to a method when it is invoked. A formal parameter is the corresponding variable in the header of the method declaration; it takes on the value of the actual parameter so that it can be used inside the method.

SR 5.16 Constructors are special methods in an object that are used to initialize the object when it is instantiated. A constructor has the same name as its class, and it does not return a value.

SR 5.17 Memory space for an instance variable is created for each object that is instantiated from a class. A static variable is shared among all objects of a class.

SR 5.18 The `main` method of any program is static, and can refer only to static or local variables. Therefore, a `main` method could not refer to instance variables declared at the class level.

SR 5.19 A dependency relationship between two classes occurs when one class relies on the functionality of the other. It is often referred to as a "uses" relationship.

SR 5.20 Overloaded methods are distinguished by having a unique signature, which includes the number, order, and type of the parameters. The return type is not part of the signature.

SR 5.21 Method decomposition is the process of dividing a complex method into several support methods to get the job done. This simplifies and facilitates the design of the program.

SR 5.22 A method executed through an object might take as a parameter another object created from the same class. For example, the `concat` method of the `String` class is executed through one `String` object and takes another `String` object as a parameter.

SR 5.23 An aggregate object is an object that has other objects as instance data. That is, an aggregate object is one that is made up of other objects.

SR 5.24 The `this` reference always refers to the currently executing object. A nonstatic method of a class is written generically for all objects of the class, but it is invoked through a particular object. The `this` reference, therefore, refers to the object through which that method is currently being executed.

SR 5.25 Objects are passed to methods by copying the reference to the object (its address). Therefore the actual and formal parameters of a method become aliases of each other.

Chapter Objectives

- Discuss the core elements needed in any Java GUI: components, events, and listeners.
- Explore the use of containers to organize components.
- Explore various types of components, including buttons, text fields, sliders, and combo boxes.
- Discuss the various types of events that components generate, and under what conditions.
- Discuss the concept of a layout manager and explore several specific ones.
- Explore various types of mouse and keyboard events.
- Discuss dialog boxes, including specialized dialog boxes for choosing files and colors.
- Explore the use of borders, tool tips, and mnemonics.

6 Graphical User Interfaces

Many programs provide a graphical user interface (GUI) through which a user interacts with the program. As the name implies, a GUI makes use of graphical screen components such as windows, buttons, check boxes, menus, and text fields. GUIs often provide a more natural and rich experience for the user compared to a simple text-based, command-line environment. This chapter explores the various issues related to developing a GUI in Java.

6.1 GUI Elements

The text-based programs we've seen in previous examples are *command-line applications*, which interact with the user through simple prompts and feedback. This type of interface is straightforward to understand, but it lacks the rich user experience possible when a true *graphical user interface* (GUI) is used. With a GUI, the user is not limited to responding to prompts in a particular order and receiving feedback in one place. Instead, the user can interact as needed with various components such as buttons and text fields. This chapter explores the many issues involved in developing a GUI in Java.

Let's start with an overview of the concepts that underlie every GUI-based program. At least three kinds of objects are needed to create a GUI in Java:

- components
- events
- listeners

A GUI *component* is an object that defines a screen element used to display information or allow the user to interact with a program in a certain way. Examples of GUI components include push buttons, text fields, labels, scroll bars, and menus. A *container* is a special type of component that is used to hold and organize other components.

An *event* is an object that represents some occurrence in which we may be interested. Often, events correspond to user actions, such as pressing a mouse button or typing a key on the keyboard. Most GUI components generate events to indicate a user action related to that component. For example, a button component will generate an event to indicate that the button has been pushed. A program that is oriented around a GUI, responding to events from the user, is called *event-driven*.

A *listener* is an object that "waits" for an event to occur and responds in some way when it does. A big part of designing a GUI-based program is establishing the relationships among the listener, the event it listens for, and the component that will generate the event.

A GUI is made up of components, events that represent user actions, and listeners that respond to those events.

For the most part, we will use components and events that are predefined by classes in the Java class library. We will tailor the behavior of the components, but their basic roles have been established already. We will, however, write our own listener classes to perform whatever actions we desire when events occur.

So, to create a Java program that uses a GUI, we must:

- instantiate and set up the necessary components,
- implement listener classes that define what happens when particular events occur, and
- establish the relationship between the listeners and the components that generate the events of interest.

Java components and other GUI-related classes are defined primarily in two packages: `java.awt` and `javax.swing`. (Note the `x` in `javax.swing`.) The *Abstract Windowing Toolkit* (AWT) was the original Java GUI package. It still contains many important classes that we will use. The *Swing* package was added later and provides components that are more versatile than those of the AWT package. Both packages are needed for GUI development, but we will use Swing components whenever there is an option.

In some respects, once you have a basic understanding of event-driven programming, the rest is just detail. There are many types of components you can use that produce many types of events that you may want to acknowledge. But they all work in the same basic way. They all have the same core relationships to one another.

Let's look at a simple example that contains all of the basic GUI elements. The `PushCounter` class shown in Listing 6.1 contains the driver of a program that presents the user with a single push button (labeled "Push Me!"). Each time the button is pushed, a counter is updated and displayed.

The components used in this program include a button, a label to display the count, a panel to hold the button and label, and a frame to display the panel. The panel is defined by the `PushCounterPanel` class, shown in Listing 6.2. Let's look at each of these pieces in more detail.

Frames and Panels

A *frame* is a container that is used to display GUI-based Java applications. A frame is displayed as a separate window with its own title bar. It can be repositioned on the screen and resized as needed by dragging it with the mouse. It contains small buttons in the corner of the frame that allow the frame to be minimized, maximized, and closed. A frame is defined by the `JFrame` class.

A *panel* is also a container. However, unlike a frame, it cannot be displayed on its own. A panel must be added to another container for it to be displayed.

Listing 6.1

```
//********************************************************************
//  PushCounter.java       Java Foundations
//
//  Demonstrates a graphical user interface and an event listener.
//********************************************************************

import javax.swing.JFrame;

public class PushCounter
{
   //-----------------------------------------------------------------
   //  Creates and displays the main program frame.
   //-----------------------------------------------------------------
   public static void main (String[] args)
   {
      JFrame frame = new JFrame ("Push Counter");
      frame.setDefaultCloseOperation (JFrame.EXIT_ON_CLOSE);

      PushCounterPanel panel = new PushCounterPanel();
      frame.getContentPane().add(panel);

      frame.pack();
      frame.setVisible(true);
   }
}
```

Display

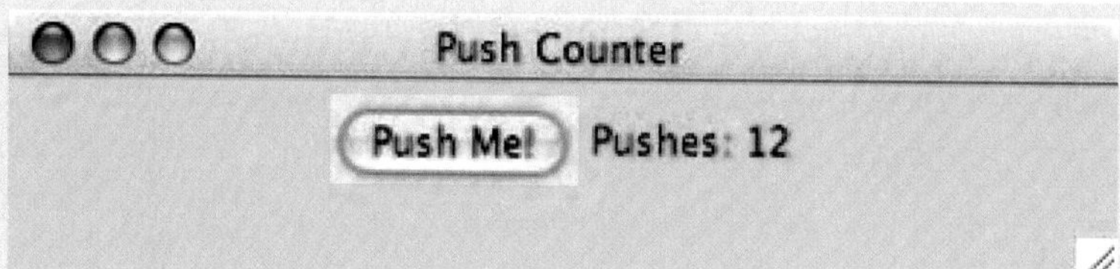

A frame is displayed as a separate window, but a panel can only be displayed as part of another container.

Generally a panel doesn't move unless you move the container that it's in. Its primary role is to help organize the other components in a GUI. A panel is defined by the `JPanel` class.

Listing 6.2

```
//********************************************************************
//  PushCounterPanel.java       Java Foundations
//
//  Demonstrates a graphical user interface and an event listener.
//********************************************************************

import java.awt.*;
import java.awt.event.*;
import javax.swing.*;

public class PushCounterPanel extends JPanel
{
   private int count;
   private JButton push;
   private JLabel label;

   //-----------------------------------------------------------------
   //  Constructor: Sets up the GUI.
   //-----------------------------------------------------------------
   public PushCounterPanel ()
   {
      count = 0;

      push = new JButton ("Push Me!");
      push.addActionListener (new ButtonListener());

      label = new JLabel ("Pushes: " + count);

      add (push);
      add (label);

      setBackground (Color.cyan);
      setPreferredSize (new Dimension(300, 40));
   }

   //*****************************************************************
   //  Represents a listener for button push (action) events.
   //*****************************************************************
   private class ButtonListener implements ActionListener
   {
      //--------------------------------------------------------------
      //  Updates the counter and label when the button is pushed.
      //--------------------------------------------------------------
      public void actionPerformed (ActionEvent event)
```

Listing 6.2 continued

```
        {
            count++;
            label.setText("Pushes: " + count);
        }
    }
}
```

We can classify containers as either heavyweight or lightweight. A *heavyweight container* is one that is managed by the underlying operating system on which the program is run, whereas a *lightweight container* is managed by the Java program itself. A frame is a heavyweight component, and a panel is a lightweight component. Another heavyweight container is an *applet,* which is used to display and execute a Java program through a Web browser. Applets are discussed in Appendix G.

Heavyweight components are more complex than lightweight components in general. A frame, for example, has multiple *panes,* which are responsible for various characteristics of the frame window. All visible elements of a Java interface are displayed in a frame's *content pane.*

Generally, we can create a Java GUI-based application by creating a frame in which the program interface is displayed. The interface is often organized onto a primary panel, which is added to the frame's content pane. The components in the primary panel are sometimes organized using other panels as needed.

In the `main` method of the `PushCounter` class, the frame for the program is constructed, set up, and displayed. The `JFrame` constructor takes a string as a parameter, which it displays in the title bar of the frame. The call to the `setDefaultCloseOperation` method determines what will happen when the close button in the corner of the frame is clicked. In most cases we'll simply let that button terminate the program, as indicated by the `EXIT_ON_CLOSE` constant.

The content pane of the frame is obtained using the `getContentPane` method, immediately after which the `add` method of the content pane is called to add the panel. The `pack` method of the frame sets its size appropriately based on its contents—in this case the frame is sized to accommodate the size of the panel it contains. This is a better approach than trying to set the size of the frame explicitly, which should change as the components within the frame change. The call to the `setVisible` method causes the frame to be displayed on the monitor screen.

You can interact with the frame itself in various ways. You can move the entire frame to another point on the desktop by grabbing the title bar of the frame and dragging it with the mouse. You can also resize the frame by dragging the bottom-right corner of the frame.

A panel is created by instantiating the `JPanel` class. In the case of the `PushCounter` program, the panel is represented by the `PushCounterPanel` class, which is derived from `JPanel`. So a `PushCounterPanel` is a `JPanel`, inheriting all of its methods and attributes. This is a common technique for creating panels.

The constructor of the `PushCounterPanel` class makes calls to several methods inherited from `JPanel`. For example, the background color of the panel is set using the `setBackground` method (the `Color` class is described in Appendix F). The `setPreferredSize` method accepts a `Dimension` object as a parameter, which is used to indicate the width and height of the component in pixels. The size of many components can be set this way, and most also have methods called `setMinimumSize` and `setMaximumSize` to help control the look of the interface.

A panel's `add` method allows a component to be added to the panel. In the `PushCounterPanel` constructor, a newly created button and label are added to the panel, and are from that point on considered part of that panel. The order in which components are added to a container often matters. In this case, it determines that the button appears before the label.

A container is governed by a *layout manager*, which determines exactly how the components added to the panel will be displayed. The default layout manager for a panel simply displays components in the order they are added, with as many components on one line as possible. Layout managers are discussed in detail later in this chapter.

Buttons and Action Events

The `PushCounter` program displays a button and a label. A *label*, created from the `JLabel` class, is a component that displays a line of text in a GUI. A label can also be used to display an image, as shown in later examples. In the `PushCounter` program, the label displays the number of times the button has been pushed.

Labels can be found in most GUI-based programs. They are very useful for displaying information or for labeling other components in the GUI. However, labels are not interactive. That is, the user does not interact with a label directly.

The component that makes the `PushCounter` program interactive is the button that the user pushes with the mouse.

A *push button* is a component that allows the user to initiate an action with a press of the mouse. There are other types of button components that we explore in later chapters. A push button is defined by the `JButton` class. A call to the `JButton` constructor takes a `String` parameter that specifies the text shown on the button.

A `JButton` generates an *action event* when it is pushed. There are several types of events defined in the Java standard class library, and we explore many of them throughout this chapter. Different components generate different types of events.

The only event of interest in this program occurs when the button is pushed. To respond to the event, we must create a listener object for that event, so we must write a class that represents the listener. In this case, we need an action event listener.

In the `PushButton` program, the `ButtonListener` class represents the action listener. We could write the `ButtonListener` class in its own file, or even in the same file but outside of the `PushCounterPanel` class. However, then we would have to set up a way to communicate between the listener and the components of the GUI that the listener updates. Instead, we define the `ButtonListener` class as an *inner class*, which is a class defined within another class. As such, it automatically has access to the members of the class that contains it. You should only create inner classes in situations in which there is an intimate relationship between the two classes and the inner class is not accessed by any other class. The relationship between a listener and its GUI is one of the few situations in which an inner class is appropriate.

Listeners are often defined as inner classes because of the intimate relationship between the listener and the GUI components.

Listener classes are written by implementing an *interface*, which is a list of methods that the implementing class must define. The Java standard class library contains interfaces for many types of events. An action listener is created by implementing the `ActionListener` interface, therefore we include the `implements` clause in the `ButtonListener` class. Interfaces are discussed in more detail in Chapter 9.

The only method listed in the `ActionListener` interface is the `actionPerformed` method, so that's the only method that the `ButtonListener` class must implement. The component that generates the action event (in this case the button) will call the `actionPerformed` method when the event occurs, passing in an `ActionEvent` object that represents the event. Sometimes we will use this event object, and other times it is simply sufficient to know that the event occurred. In this case, we have no need to interact with the event object. When the event occurs, the listener increments the count and resets the text of the label by using the `setText` method.

Remember, we not only have to create a listener for an event, we must also set up the relationship between the listener and the component that will generate the event. To do so, we add the listener to the component by calling the appropriate method. In the `PushCounterPanel` constructor, we call the `addActionListener` method, passing in a newly instantiated `ButtonListener` object.

Review this example carefully, noting how it accomplishes the three key steps to creating an interactive GUI-based program. It creates and sets up the GUI components, creates the appropriate listener for the event of interest, and sets up the relationship between the listener and the component that will generate the event.

Determining Event Sources

Let's look at an example in which one listener object is used to listen to two different components. The program represented by the `LeftRight` class, shown in Listing 6.3, displays a label and two buttons. When the Left button is pressed, the label displays the word Left and when the Right button is pressed the label displays the word Right.

The `LeftRightPanel` class, shown in Listing 6.4, creates one instance of the `ButtonListener` class, and then adds that listener to both buttons. Therefore, when either button is pressed, the `actionPerformed` method of the `ButtonListener` class is invoked.

On each invocation, the `actionPerformed` method uses an `if-else` statement to determine which button generated the event. The `getSource` method is called on the `ActionEvent` object that the button passes into the `actionPerformed` method. The `getSource` method returns a reference to the component that generated the event. The condition of the `if` statement compares the event source to the reference to the left button. If they don't match, then the event must have been generated by the right button.

We could have created two separate listener classes, one to listen to the left button and another to listen to the right. In that case the `actionPerformed` method would not have to determine the source of the event. Whether to have multiple listeners or determine the event source when it occurs is a design decision that should be made depending on the situation.

Listing 6.3

```
//********************************************************************
//  LeftRight.java       Java Foundations
//
//  Demonstrates the use of one listener for multiple buttons.
//********************************************************************

import javax.swing.JFrame;

public class LeftRight
{
   //-----------------------------------------------------------------
   //  Creates and displays the main program frame.
   //-----------------------------------------------------------------
   public static void main (String[] args)
   {
      JFrame frame = new JFrame ("Left Right");
      frame.setDefaultCloseOperation (JFrame.EXIT_ON_CLOSE);

      frame.getContentPane().add(new LeftRightPanel());

      frame.pack();
      frame.setVisible(true);
   }
}
```

Display

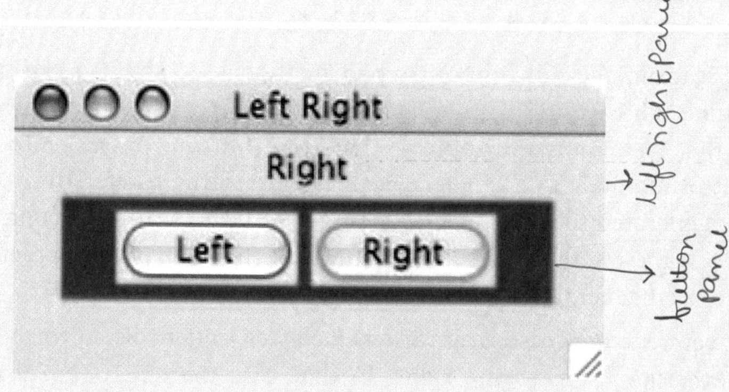

Listing **6.4**

```
//********************************************************************
//  LeftRightPanel.java       Java Foundations
//
//  Demonstrates the use of one listener for multiple buttons.
//********************************************************************

import java.awt.*;
import java.awt.event.*;
import javax.swing.*;

public class LeftRightPanel extends JPanel
{
   private JButton left, right;
   private JLabel label;
   private JPanel buttonPanel;

   //-----------------------------------------------------------------
   //  Constructor: Sets up the GUI.
   //-----------------------------------------------------------------
   public LeftRightPanel ()
   {
      left = new JButton ("Left");
      right = new JButton ("Right");

      ButtonListener listener = new ButtonListener();
      left.addActionListener (listener);
      right.addActionListener (listener);

      label = new JLabel ("Push a button");

      buttonPanel = new JPanel();
      buttonPanel.setPreferredSize (new Dimension(200, 40));
      buttonPanel.setBackground (Color.blue);
      buttonPanel.add (left);
      buttonPanel.add (right);

      setPreferredSize (new Dimension(200, 80));
      setBackground (Color.cyan);
      add (label);
      add (buttonPanel);
   }
```

Listing 6.4 continued

```
   //*****************************************************************
   //  Represents a listener for both buttons.
   //*****************************************************************
   private class ButtonListener implements ActionListener
   {
      //--------------------------------------------------------------
      //  Determines which button was pressed and sets the label
      //  text accordingly.
      //--------------------------------------------------------------
      public void actionPerformed (ActionEvent event)
      {
         if (event.getSource() == left)
            label.setText("Left");
         else
            label.setText("Right");
      }
   }
}
```

Note that the two buttons are put on the same panel called `buttonPanel`, which is separate from the panel represented by the `LeftRightPanel` class. By putting both buttons on one panel, we can guarantee their visual relationship to each other even when the frame is resized in various ways. For buttons labeled Left and Right, that is certainly important.

6.2 More Components

In addition to push buttons, there are a variety of other interactive components that can be used in a GUI, each with a particular role to play. Let's examine a few more.

Text Fields

A *text field* allows the user to enter typed input from the keyboard. The `Fahrenheit` program shown in Listing 6.5 presents a GUI that includes a text field into which the user can type a Fahrenheit temperature. When the user presses the Enter (or Return) key, the equivalent Celsius temperature is displayed.

The interface for the `Fahrenheit` program is set up in the `FahrenheitPanel` class, shown in Listing 6.6. The text field is an object of the `JTextField` class.

Listing 6.5

```
//********************************************************************
//  Fahrenheit.java       Java Foundations
//
//  Demonstrates the use of text fields.
//********************************************************************

import javax.swing.JFrame;

public class Fahrenheit
{
   //-----------------------------------------------------------------
   //  Creates and displays the temperature converter GUI.
   //-----------------------------------------------------------------
   public static void main (String[] args)
   {
      JFrame frame = new JFrame ("Fahrenheit");
      frame.setDefaultCloseOperation (JFrame.EXIT_ON_CLOSE);

      FahrenheitPanel panel = new FahrenheitPanel();
      frame.getContentPane().add(panel);

      frame.pack();
      frame.setVisible(true);
   }
}
```

Display

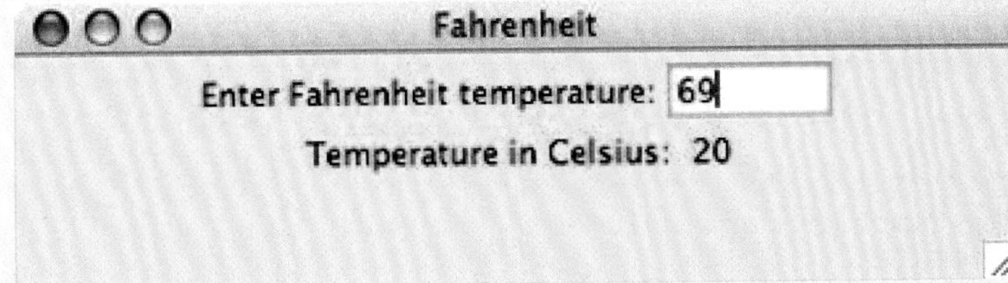

Listing **6.6**

```
//********************************************************************
//  FahrenheitPanel.java       Java Foundations
//
//  Demonstrates the use of text fields.
//********************************************************************

import java.awt.*;
import java.awt.event.*;
import javax.swing.*;

public class FahrenheitPanel extends JPanel
{
   private JLabel inputLabel, outputLabel, resultLabel;
   private JTextField fahrenheit;

   //-----------------------------------------------------------------
   //  Constructor: Sets up the main GUI components.
   //-----------------------------------------------------------------
   public FahrenheitPanel()
   {
      inputLabel = new JLabel ("Enter Fahrenheit temperature:");
      outputLabel = new JLabel ("Temperature in Celsius: ");
      resultLabel = new JLabel ("---");

      fahrenheit = new JTextField (5);
      fahrenheit.addActionListener (new TempListener());

      add (inputLabel);
      add (fahrenheit);
      add (outputLabel);
      add (resultLabel);

      setPreferredSize (new Dimension(300, 75));
      setBackground (Color.yellow);
   }

   //*****************************************************************
   //  Represents an action listener for the temperature input field.
   //*****************************************************************
   private class TempListener implements ActionListener
   {
```

Listing **6.6** continued

```
      //-----------------------------------------------------------------
      //  Performs the conversion when the enter key is pressed in
      //  the text field.
      //-----------------------------------------------------------------
      public void actionPerformed (ActionEvent event)
      {
         int fahrenheitTemp, celsiusTemp;

         String text = fahrenheit.getText();

         fahrenheitTemp = Integer.parseInt (text);
         celsiusTemp = (fahrenheitTemp-32) * 5/9;

         resultLabel.setText (Integer.toString (celsiusTemp));
      }
   }
}
```

The `JTextField` constructor takes an integer parameter that specifies the size of the field in number of characters based on the current default font.

The text field and various labels are added to the panel to be displayed. Remember that the default layout manager for a panel puts as many components on a line as it can fit. So if you resize the frame, the orientation of the labels and text field may change.

A text field generates an action event when the Enter or Return key is pressed (and the cursor is in the text field). Therefore we need to set up a listener object to respond to action events, similar to previous examples.

The text field component calls the `actionPerformed` method when the user presses the Enter key. The method first retrieves the text from the text field by calling its `getText` method, which returns a character string. The text is converted to an integer using the `parseInt` method of the `Integer` wrapper class. Then the method performs the calculation to determine the equivalent Celsius temperature and sets the text of the appropriate label with the result.

Note that a push button and a text field generate the same kind of event: an action event. So an alternative to the Fahrenheit program design is to add to the GUI a `JButton` object that causes the conversion to occur when the user uses the mouse to press the button. For that matter, the same listener object can be used to listen to multiple components at the same time. So the listener could be added to both the text field and the button, giving the user the option. Pressing either the button or the Enter key will cause the conversion to be performed. These variations are left as programming projects.

Check Boxes

A *check box* is a button that can be toggled on or off using the mouse, indicating that a particular boolean condition is set or unset. Although you might have a group of check boxes indicating a set of options, each check box operates independently. That is, each can be set to on or off and the status of one does not influence the others.

The program in Listing 6.7 displays two check boxes and a label. The check boxes determine whether the text of the label is displayed in bold, italic, both, or neither. Any combination of bold and italic is valid. For example, both check boxes could be checked (on), in which case the text is displayed in both bold and italic. If neither is checked, the text of the label is displayed in a plain style.

The GUI for the `StyleOptions` program is embodied in the `StyleOptionsPanel` class shown in Listing 6.8. A check box is represented by the `JCheckBox` class. When a check box changes state from selected (checked) to deselected (unchecked), or vice versa, it generates an *item event*. The `ItemListener` interface contains a single method called `itemStateChanged`. In this example, we use the same listener object to handle both check boxes.

This program also uses the `Font` class, which represents a particular character font. A `Font` object is defined by the font name, the font style, and the font size. The font name establishes the general visual characteristics of the characters. We are using the Helvetica font in this program. The style of a Java font can be plain, bold, italic, or bold and italic combined. The listener is set up to change the characteristics of our font style.

The style of a font is represented as an integer, and integer constants defined in the `Font` class are used to represent the various aspects of the style. The constant `PLAIN` is used to represent a plain style. The constants `BOLD` and `ITALIC` are used to represent bold and italic, respectively. The sum of the `BOLD` and `ITALIC` constants indicates a style that is both bold and italic.

The `itemStateChanged` method of the listener determines what the revised style should be now that one of the check boxes has changed state. It initially sets the style to be plain. Then each check box is consulted in turn using the

Listing **6.7**

```
//********************************************************************
//  StyleOptions.java       Java Foundations
//
//  Demonstrates the use of check boxes.
//********************************************************************

import javax.swing.JFrame;

public class StyleOptions
{
   //-----------------------------------------------------------------
   //  Creates and displays the style options frame.
   //-----------------------------------------------------------------
   public static void main (String[] args)
   {
      JFrame frame = new JFrame ("Style Options");
      frame.setDefaultCloseOperation (JFrame.EXIT_ON_CLOSE);

      frame.getContentPane().add (new StyleOptionsPanel());

      frame.pack();
      frame.setVisible(true);
   }
}
```

Display

Listing **6.8**

```
//********************************************************************
//  StyleOptionsPanel.java       Java Foundations
//
//  Demonstrates the use of check boxes.
//********************************************************************

import javax.swing.*;
import java.awt.*;
import java.awt.event.*;

public class StyleOptionsPanel extends JPanel
{
   private JLabel saying;
   private JCheckBox bold, italic;

   //-----------------------------------------------------------------
   //  Sets up a panel with a label and some check boxes that
   //  control the style of the label's font.
   //-----------------------------------------------------------------
   public StyleOptionsPanel()
   {
      saying = new JLabel ("Say it with style!");
      saying.setFont (new Font ("Helvetica", Font.PLAIN, 36));

      bold = new JCheckBox ("Bold");
      bold.setBackground (Color.cyan);
      italic = new JCheckBox ("Italic");
      italic.setBackground (Color.cyan);

      StyleListener listener = new StyleListener();
      bold.addItemListener (listener);
      italic.addItemListener (listener);

      add (saying);
      add (bold);
      add (italic);

      setBackground (Color.cyan);
      setPreferredSize (new Dimension(300, 100));
   }

   //*****************************************************************
   //  Represents the listener for both check boxes.
   //*****************************************************************
```

Listing **6.8** continued

```
   private class StyleListener implements ItemListener
   {
      //-----------------------------------------------------------------
      //  Updates the style of the label font style.
      //-----------------------------------------------------------------
      public void itemStateChanged (ItemEvent event)
      {
         int style = Font.PLAIN;

         if (bold.isSelected())
            style = Font.BOLD;

         if (italic.isSelected())
            style += Font.ITALIC;

         saying.setFont (new Font ("Helvetica", style, 36));
      }
   }
}
```

`isSelected` method, which returns a boolean value. First, if the Bold check box is selected (checked), then the style is set to bold. Then, if the Italic check box is selected, the `ITALIC` constant is added to the style variable. Finally, the font of the label is set to a new font with its revised style.

Note that, given the way the listener is written in this program, it doesn't matter which check box was clicked to generate the event. The same listener processes both check boxes. It also doesn't matter whether the changed check box was toggled from selected to unselected or vice versa. The state of both check boxes is examined if either is changed.

Radio Buttons

A *radio button* is used with other radio buttons to provide a set of mutually exclusive options. Unlike a check box, a radio button is not particularly useful by itself. It has meaning only when it is used with one or more other radio buttons. Only one option out of the group is valid. At any point in time, one and only one button of the group of radio buttons is selected (on). When a radio

Radio buttons operate as a group, providing a set of mutually exclusive options.

button from the group is pushed, the other button in the group that is currently on is automatically toggled off.

The term "radio buttons" comes from the way the buttons worked on an old-fashioned car radio. At any point, one button was pushed to specify the current choice of station; when another was pushed, the button that was in automatically popped out.

The `QuoteOptions` program, shown in Listing 6.9, displays a label and a group of radio buttons. The radio buttons determine which quote is displayed in the label. Because only one of the quotes can be displayed at a time, the use of radio buttons is appropriate. For example, if the Comedy radio button is selected, the comedy quote is displayed in the label. If the Philosophy button is then pressed, the Comedy radio button is automatically toggled off and the comedy quote is replaced by a philosophical one.

The `QuoteOptionsPanel` class, shown in Listing 6.10, sets up and displays the GUI components. A radio button is represented by the `JRadioButton` class. Because the radio buttons in a set work together, the `ButtonGroup` class is used to define a set of related radio buttons.

Note that each button is added to the button group, and also that each button is added individually to the panel. A `ButtonGroup` object is not a container to organize and display components; it is simply a way to define the group of radio buttons that work together to form a set of dependent options. The `ButtonGroup` object ensures that the currently selected radio button is turned off when another in the group is selected.

A radio button produces an action event when it is selected. The `actionPerformed` method of the listener first retrieves the source of the event using the `getSource` method, and then compares it to each of the three radio buttons in turn. Depending on which button was selected, the text of the label is set to the appropriate quote.

Note that unlike push buttons, both check boxes and radio buttons are *toggle buttons*, meaning that at any time they are either on or off. Independent options (choose any combination) are controlled with check boxes. Dependent options (choose one of a set) are controlled with radio buttons. If there is only one option to be managed, a check box can be used by itself. As we mentioned earlier, a radio button, on the other hand, makes sense only in conjunction with one or more other radio buttons.

Also note that check boxes and radio buttons produce different types of events. A check box produces an item event and a radio button produces an action event. The use of different event types is related to the differences in button

Listing **6.9**

```
//********************************************************************
//  QuoteOptions.java       Java Foundations
//
//  Demonstrates the use of radio buttons.
//********************************************************************

import javax.swing.JFrame;

public class QuoteOptions
{
   //-----------------------------------------------------------------
   //  Creates and presents the program frame.
   //-----------------------------------------------------------------
   public static void main (String[] args)
   {
      JFrame frame = new JFrame ("Quote Options");
      frame.setDefaultCloseOperation (JFrame.EXIT_ON_CLOSE);

      frame.getContentPane().add (new QuoteOptionsPanel());

      frame.pack();
      frame.setVisible(true);
   }
}
```

Display

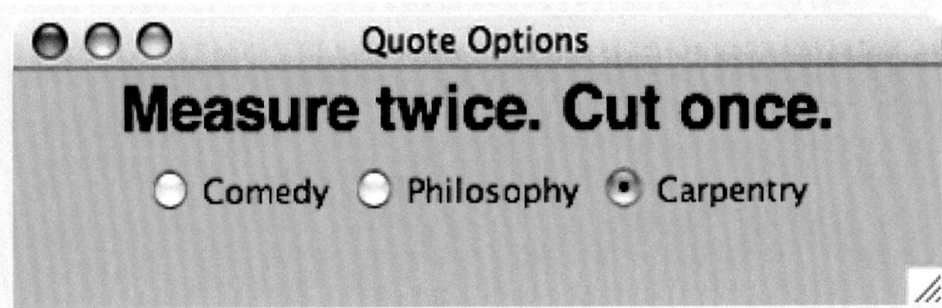

functionality. A check box produces an event when it is selected or deselected, and the listener could make the distinction if desired. A radio button, on the other hand, produces an event only when it is selected (the currently selected button from the group is deselected automatically).

Listing **6.10**

```
//********************************************************************
//  QuoteOptionsPanel.java       Java Foundations
//
//  Demonstrates the use of radio buttons.
//********************************************************************

import javax.swing.*;
import java.awt.*;
import java.awt.event.*;

public class QuoteOptionsPanel extends JPanel
{
   private JLabel quote;
   private JRadioButton comedy, philosophy, carpentry;
   private String comedyQuote, philosophyQuote, carpentryQuote;

   //-----------------------------------------------------------------
   //  Sets up a panel with a label and a set of radio buttons
   //  that control its text.
   //-----------------------------------------------------------------
   public QuoteOptionsPanel()
   {
      comedyQuote = "Take my wife, please.";
      philosophyQuote = "I think, therefore I am.";
      carpentryQuote = "Measure twice. Cut once.";

      quote = new JLabel (comedyQuote);
      quote.setFont (new Font ("Helvetica", Font.BOLD, 24));

      comedy = new JRadioButton ("Comedy", true);
      comedy.setBackground (Color.green);
      philosophy = new JRadioButton ("Philosophy");
      philosophy.setBackground (Color.green);
      carpentry = new JRadioButton ("Carpentry");
      carpentry.setBackground (Color.green);

      ButtonGroup group = new ButtonGroup();
      group.add (comedy);
      group.add (philosophy);
      group.add (carpentry);

      QuoteListener listener = new QuoteListener();
      comedy.addActionListener (listener);
```

Listing **6.10** continued

```
      philosophy.addActionListener (listener);
      carpentry.addActionListener (listener);

      add (quote);
      add (comedy);
      add (philosophy);
      add (carpentry);

      setBackground (Color.green);
      setPreferredSize (new Dimension(300, 100));
   }

   //*****************************************************************
   //  Represents the listener for all radio buttons
   //*****************************************************************
   private class QuoteListener implements ActionListener
   {
      //--------------------------------------------------------------
      //  Sets the text of the label depending on which radio
      //  button was pressed.
      //--------------------------------------------------------------
      public void actionPerformed (ActionEvent event)
      {
         Object source = event.getSource();

         if (source == comedy)
            quote.setText (comedyQuote);
         else
            if (source == philosophy)
               quote.setText (philosophyQuote);
            else
               quote.setText (carpentryQuote);
      }
   }
}
```

Sliders

A *slider* is a GUI component that allows the user to specify a numeric value within a bounded range. A slider can be presented either vertically or horizontally and can have optional tick marks and labels indicating the range of values.

A slider lets the user specify a numeric value within a bounded range.

A program called `SlideColor` is shown in Listing 6.11. This program presents three sliders that control the RGB components of a color. The color specified by the values of the sliders is shown in a square that is displayed to the right of the sliders. Using RGB values to represent color is discussed in Appendix F.

The `SlideColorPanel` class shown in Listing 6.12 is a panel used to display the three sliders and the color panel. Each slider is created from the `JSlider` class, which accepts four parameters. The first determines the orientation of the slider using one of two `JSlider` constants (`HORIZONTAL` or `VERTICAL`). The second and third parameters specify the maximum and minimum values of the slider, which are set to 0 and 255 for each of the sliders in the example. The last parameter of the `JSlider` constructor specifies the slider's initial value. In our

Listing **6.11**

```
//********************************************************************
//  SlideColor.java       Java Foundations
//
//  Demonstrates the use slider components.
//********************************************************************

import java.awt.*;
import javax.swing.*;

public class SlideColor
{
   //-----------------------------------------------------------------
   //  Presents a frame with a control panel and a panel that
   //  changes color as the sliders are adjusted.
   //-----------------------------------------------------------------
   public static void main (String[] args)
   {
      JFrame frame = new JFrame ("Slide Colors");
      frame.setDefaultCloseOperation (JFrame.EXIT_ON_CLOSE);

      frame.getContentPane().add(new SlideColorPanel());

      frame.pack();
      frame.setVisible(true);
   }
}
```

Listing **6.11** continued

Display

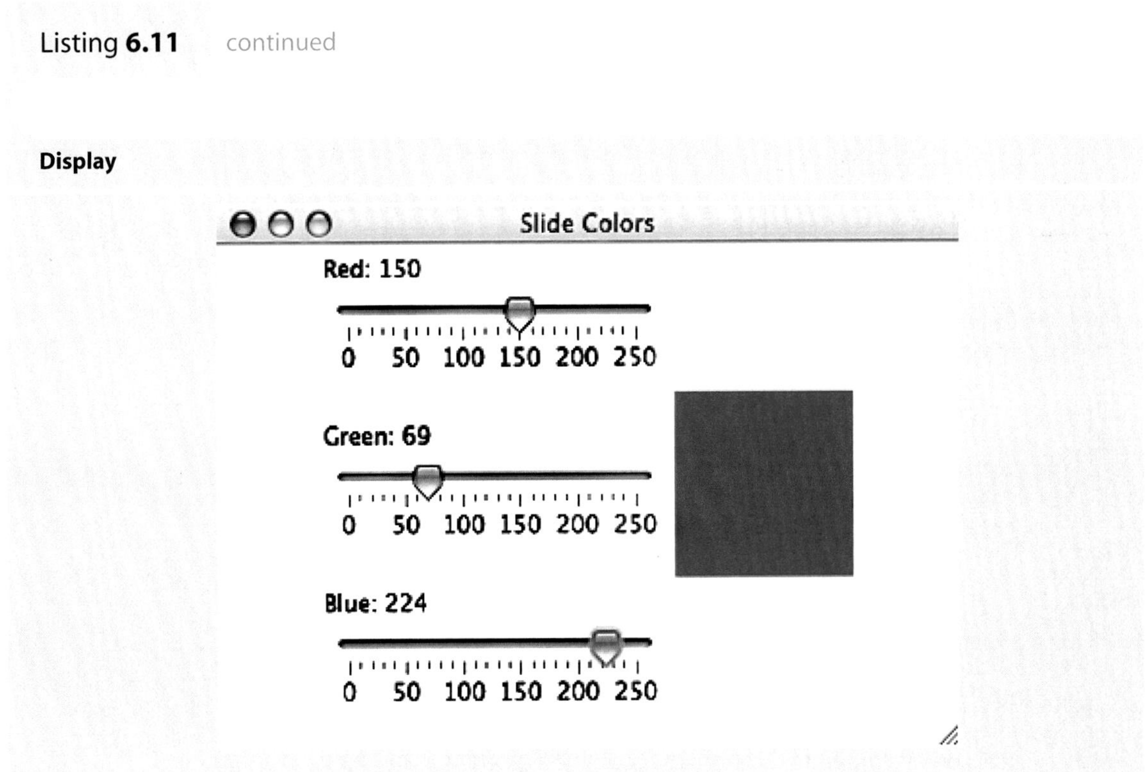

example, the initial value of each slider is 0, which puts the slider knob to the far left when the program initially executes.

The `JSlider` class has several methods that allow the programmer to tailor the look of a slider. Major tick marks can be set at specific intervals using the `setMajorTickSpacing` method. Intermediate minor tick marks can be set using the `setMinorTickSpacing` method. Neither is displayed, however, unless the `setPaintTicks` method, with a parameter of `true`, is invoked as well. Labels indicating the value of the major tick marks are displayed if indicated by a call to the `setPaintLabels` method.

Note that in this example, the major tick spacing is set to 50. Starting at 0, each increment of 50 is labeled. The last label is therefore 250, even though the slider value can reach 255.

A slider produces a *change event*, indicating that the position of the slider and the value it represents has changed. The `ChangeListener` interface contains a

Listing **6.12**

```
//********************************************************************
//  SlideColorPanel.java       Java Foundations
//
//  Represents the slider control panel for the SlideColor program.
//********************************************************************

import java.awt.*;
import javax.swing.*;
import javax.swing.event.*;

public class SlideColorPanel extends JPanel
{
   private JPanel controls, colorPanel;
   private JSlider rSlider, gSlider, bSlider;
   private JLabel rLabel, gLabel, bLabel;

   //-----------------------------------------------------------------
   //  Sets up the sliders and their labels, aligning them along
   //  their left edge using a box layout.
   //-----------------------------------------------------------------
   public SlideColorPanel()
   {
      rSlider = new JSlider (JSlider.HORIZONTAL, 0, 255, 0);
      rSlider.setMajorTickSpacing (50);
      rSlider.setMinorTickSpacing (10);
      rSlider.setPaintTicks (true);
      rSlider.setPaintLabels (true);
      rSlider.setAlignmentX (Component.LEFT_ALIGNMENT);

      gSlider = new JSlider (JSlider.HORIZONTAL, 0, 255, 0);
      gSlider.setMajorTickSpacing (50);
      gSlider.setMinorTickSpacing (10);
      gSlider.setPaintTicks (true);
      gSlider.setPaintLabels (true);
      gSlider.setAlignmentX (Component.LEFT_ALIGNMENT);

      bSlider = new JSlider (JSlider.HORIZONTAL, 0, 255, 0);
      bSlider.setMajorTickSpacing (50);
      bSlider.setMinorTickSpacing (10);
      bSlider.setPaintTicks (true);
      bSlider.setPaintLabels (true);
      bSlider.setAlignmentX (Component.LEFT_ALIGNMENT);
```

Listing **6.12** continued

```
      SliderListener listener = new SliderListener();
      rSlider.addChangeListener (listener);
      gSlider.addChangeListener (listener);
      bSlider.addChangeListener (listener);

      rLabel = new JLabel ("Red: 0");
      rLabel.setAlignmentX (Component.LEFT_ALIGNMENT);
      gLabel = new JLabel ("Green: 0");
      gLabel.setAlignmentX (Component.LEFT_ALIGNMENT);
      bLabel = new JLabel ("Blue: 0");
      bLabel.setAlignmentX (Component.LEFT_ALIGNMENT);

      controls = new JPanel();
      BoxLayout layout = new BoxLayout (controls, BoxLayout.Y_AXIS);
      controls.setLayout (layout);
      controls.add (rLabel);
      controls.add (rSlider);
      controls.add (Box.createRigidArea (new Dimension (0, 20)));
      controls.add (gLabel);
      controls.add (gSlider);
      controls.add (Box.createRigidArea (new Dimension (0, 20)));
      controls.add (bLabel);
      controls.add (bSlider);

      colorPanel = new JPanel();
      colorPanel.setPreferredSize (new Dimension (100, 100));
      colorPanel.setBackground (new Color (0, 0, 0));

      add (controls);
      add (colorPanel);
   }

   //*****************************************************************
   //  Represents the listener for all three sliders.
   //*****************************************************************
   private class SliderListener implements ChangeListener
   {
      private int red, green, blue;

      //--------------------------------------------------------------
      //  Gets the value of each slider, then updates the labels and
      //  the color panel.
      //--------------------------------------------------------------
```

Listing 6.12 continued

```
      public void stateChanged (ChangeEvent event)
      {
         red = rSlider.getValue();
         green = gSlider.getValue();
         blue = bSlider.getValue();

         rLabel.setText ("Red: " + red);
         gLabel.setText ("Green: " + green);
         bLabel.setText ("Blue: " + blue);

         colorPanel.setBackground (new Color (red, green, blue));
      }
   }
}
```

single method called `stateChanged`. In the `SlideColor` program, the same listener object is used for all three sliders. In the `stateChanged` method, which is called whenever any of the sliders is adjusted, the value of each slider is obtained, the labels of all three are updated, and the background color of the color panel is revised. It is actually only necessary to update one of the labels (the one whose corresponding slider changed). However, the effort to determine which slider was adjusted is not warranted. It's easier—and probably more efficient—to update all three labels each time. Another alternative is to have a unique listener for each slider, though that extra coding effort is not needed either.

A slider is often a good choice when a large range of values is possible but strictly bounded on both ends. Compared to alternatives such as a text field, sliders convey more information to the user and eliminate input errors.

Combo Boxes

A combo box provides a drop down menu of options.

A *combo box* allows the user to select one of several options from a "drop down" menu. When the user presses a combo box using the mouse, a list of options is displayed from which the user can choose. The current choice is displayed in the combo box. A combo box is defined by the `JComboBox` class.

A combo box can be either editable or uneditable. By default, a combo box is uneditable. Changing the value of an uneditable combo box can be accomplished only by selecting an item from the list. If the combo box is editable, however, the user can change the value by either selecting an item from the list or typing a particular value into the combo box area.

The options in a combo box list can be established in one of two ways. We can create an array of strings and pass it into the constructor of the `JComboBox` class. Alternatively, we can use the `addItem` method to add an item to the combo box after it has been created. An item in a `JComboBox` can also display an `ImageIcon` object, in addition to text or by itself.

The `JukeBox` program shown in Listing 6.13 demonstrates the use of a combo box. The user chooses a song to play using the combo box, and then presses the Play button to begin playing the song. The Stop button can be pressed at any time to stop the song. Selecting a new song while one is playing also stops the current song.

The `JukeBoxControls` class shown in Listing 6.14 is a panel that contains the components that make up the jukebox GUI. The constructor of the class also loads the audio clips that will be played. An audio clip is obtained first by creating a `URL` object that corresponds to the wav or au file that defines the clip. The first two parameters to the `URL` constructor should be `"file"` and `"localhost"`, respectively, if the audio clip is stored on the same machine on which the program is executing. Creating `URL` objects can potentially throw a checked exception; therefore they are created in a `try` block. However, this program assumes the audio clips will be loaded successfully and therefore does nothing if an exception is thrown.

Once created, the `URL` objects are used to create `AudioClip` objects using the static `newAudioClip` method of the `JApplet` class. The audio clips are stored in an array. The first entry in the array, at index 0, is set to `null`. This entry corresponds to the initial combo box option, which simply encourages the user to make a selection.

The list of songs that is displayed in the combo box is defined in an array of strings. The first entry of the array will appear in the combo box by default and is often used to direct the user. We must take care that the rest of the program does not try to use that option as a valid song.

This program also shows the ability for a push button to display an image. In this example, the Play and Stop buttons are displayed with both a text label and an image icon.

Listing **6.13**

```
//********************************************************************
//  JukeBox.java       Java Foundations
//
//  Demonstrates the use of a combo box.
//********************************************************************

import javax.swing.*;

public class JukeBox
{
   //-----------------------------------------------------------------
   //  Creates and displays the controls for a juke box.
   //-----------------------------------------------------------------
   public static void main (String[] args)
   {
      JFrame frame = new JFrame ("Java Juke Box");
      frame.setDefaultCloseOperation (JFrame.EXIT_ON_CLOSE);

      frame.getContentPane().add(new JukeBoxControls());

      frame.pack();
      frame.setVisible(true);
   }
}
```

Display

Listing **6.14**

```
//********************************************************************
//  JukeBoxControls.java       Java Foundations
//
//  Represents the control panel for the juke box.
//********************************************************************

import java.awt.*;
import java.awt.event.*;
import javax.swing.*;
import java.applet.AudioClip;
import java.net.URL;

public class JukeBoxControls extends JPanel
{
   private JComboBox musicCombo;
   private JButton stopButton, playButton;
   private AudioClip[] music;
   private AudioClip current;

   //-----------------------------------------------------------------
   //  Sets up the GUI for the juke box.
   //-----------------------------------------------------------------
   public JukeBoxControls()
   {
      URL url1, url2, url3, url4, url5, url6;
      url1 = url2 = url3 = url4 = url5 = url6 = null;

      // Obtain and store the audio clips to play
      try
      {
         url1 = new URL ("file", "localhost", "westernBeat.wav");
         url2 = new URL ("file", "localhost", "classical.wav");
         url3 = new URL ("file", "localhost", "jeopardy.au");
         url4 = new URL ("file", "localhost", "newAgeRythm.wav");
         url5 = new URL ("file", "localhost", "eightiesJam.wav");
         url6 = new URL ("file", "localhost", "hitchcock.wav");
      }
      catch (Exception exception) {}

      music = new AudioClip[7];
      music[0] = null;  // Corresponds to "Make a Selection..."
      music[1] = JApplet.newAudioClip (url1);
      music[2] = JApplet.newAudioClip (url2);
      music[3] = JApplet.newAudioClip (url3);
```

Listing 6.14 continued

```
      music[4] = JApplet.newAudioClip (url4);
      music[5] = JApplet.newAudioClip (url5);
      music[6] = JApplet.newAudioClip (url6);

      // Create the list of strings for the combo box options
      String[] musicNames = {"Make A Selection...", "Western Beat",
               "Classical Melody", "Jeopardy Theme", "New Age Rythm",
               "Eighties Jam", "Alfred Hitchcock's Theme"};

      musicCombo = new JComboBox (musicNames);
      musicCombo.setBackground (Color.cyan);

      //  Set up the buttons
      playButton = new JButton ("Play", new ImageIcon ("play.gif"));
      playButton.setBackground (Color.cyan);
      stopButton = new JButton ("Stop", new ImageIcon ("stop.gif"));
      stopButton.setBackground (Color.cyan);

      //  Set up this panel
      setPreferredSize (new Dimension (250, 100));
      setBackground (Color.cyan);
      add (musicCombo);
      add (playButton);
      add (stopButton);

      musicCombo.addActionListener (new ComboListener());
      stopButton.addActionListener (new ButtonListener());
      playButton.addActionListener (new ButtonListener());

      current = null;
   }

   //*****************************************************************
   //  Represents the action listener for the combo box.
   //*****************************************************************
   private class ComboListener implements ActionListener
   {
      //--------------------------------------------------------------
      //  Stops playing the current selection (if any) and resets
      //  the current selection to the one chosen.
      //--------------------------------------------------------------
      public void actionPerformed (ActionEvent event)
```

Listing 6.14 continued

```
      {
         if (current != null)
            current.stop();

         current = music[musicCombo.getSelectedIndex()];
      }
   }

   //*****************************************************************
   //  Represents the action listener for both control buttons.
   //*****************************************************************
   private class ButtonListener implements ActionListener
   {
      //--------------------------------------------------------------
      //  Stops the current selection (if any) in either case. If
      //  the play button was pressed, start playing it again.
      //--------------------------------------------------------------
      public void actionPerformed (ActionEvent event)
      {
         if (current != null)
            current.stop();

         if (event.getSource() == playButton)
            if (current != null)
               current.play();
      }
   }
}
```

A combo box generates an action event whenever the user makes a selection from it. The `JukeBox` program uses one action listener class for the combo box and another for both of the push buttons. They could have been combined, using code to distinguish which component fired the event.

The `actionPerformed` method of the `ComboListener` class is executed when a selection is made from the combo box. The current audio selection that is playing, if any, is stopped. The current clip is then updated to reflect the new selection. Note that the audio clip is not immediately played at that point. The way this program is designed, the user must press the Play button to hear the new selection.

The `actionPerformed` method of the `ButtonListener` class is executed when either of the buttons is pushed. The current audio selection that is playing, if any, is stopped. If the Stop button was pressed, the task is complete. If the Play button was pressed, the current audio selection is played again from the beginning.

Timers

A *timer*, created from the `Timer` class of the `javax.swing` package, can be thought of as a GUI component. However, unlike other components, it does not have a visual representation that appears on the screen. Instead, as the name implies, it helps us manage an activity over time.

A timer generates action events at regular intervals and can be used to control an animation.

A timer object generates an action event at regular intervals. To perform an animation, we can set up a timer to generate an action event periodically, and then update the animation graphics in the action listener. The methods of the `Timer` class are shown in Figure 6.1.

The program shown in Listing 6.15 displays the image of a smiling face that seems to glide across the program window at an angle, bouncing off of the window edges (though that's hard to appreciate from a screen shot).

`Timer (int delay, ActionListener listener)`
Constructor: Creates a timer that generates an action event at regular intervals, specified by the delay. The event will be handled by the specified listener.

`void addActionListener (ActionListener listener)`
Adds an action listener to the timer.

`boolean isRunning ()`
Returns true if the timer is running.

`void setDelay (int delay)`
Sets the delay of the timer.

`void start ()`
Starts the timer, causing it to generate action events.

`void stop ()`
Stops the timer, causing it to stop generating action events.

FIGURE 6.1 Some methods of the `Timer` class

Listing **6.15**

```
//********************************************************************
//  Rebound.java       Java Foundations
//
//  Demonstrates an animation and the use of the Timer class.
//********************************************************************

import java.awt.*;
import java.awt.event.*;
import javax.swing.*;

public class Rebound
{
   //-----------------------------------------------------------------
   //  Displays the main frame of the program.
   //-----------------------------------------------------------------
   public static void main (String[] args)
   {
      JFrame frame = new JFrame ("Rebound");
      frame.setDefaultCloseOperation (JFrame.EXIT_ON_CLOSE);

      frame.getContentPane().add(new ReboundPanel());

      frame.pack();
      frame.setVisible(true);
   }
}
```

Display

The constructor of the `ReboundPanel` class, shown in Listing 6.16, creates a `Timer` object. The first parameter to the `Timer` constructor is the delay in milliseconds. The second parameter to the constructor is the listener that handles the action events of the timer. The `ReboundPanel` constructor also sets up the initial position for the image and the number of pixels it will move, in both the vertical and horizontal directions, each time the image is redrawn.

Listing 6.16

```
//********************************************************************
//  ReboundPanel.java       Java Foundations
//
//  Represents the primary panel for the Rebound program.
//********************************************************************

import java.awt.*;
import java.awt.event.*;
import javax.swing.*;

public class ReboundPanel extends JPanel
{
   private final int WIDTH = 300, HEIGHT = 100;
   private final int DELAY = 20, IMAGE_SIZE = 35;

   private ImageIcon image;
   private Timer timer;
   private int x, y, moveX, moveY;

   //-----------------------------------------------------------------
   //  Sets up the panel, including the timer for the animation.
   //-----------------------------------------------------------------
   public ReboundPanel()
   {
      timer = new Timer(DELAY, new ReboundListener());

      image = new ImageIcon ("happyFace.gif");

      x = 0;
      y = 40;
      moveX = moveY = 3;

      setPreferredSize (new Dimension(WIDTH, HEIGHT));
      setBackground (Color.black);
      timer.start();
   }
```

Listing 6.16 continued

```
   //-----------------------------------------------------------------
   //  Draws the image in the current location.
   //-----------------------------------------------------------------
   public void paintComponent (Graphics page)
   {
      super.paintComponent (page);
      image.paintIcon (this, page, x, y);
   }

   //*****************************************************************
   //  Represents the action listener for the timer.
   //*****************************************************************
   private class ReboundListener implements ActionListener
   {
      //--------------------------------------------------------------
      //  Updates the position of the image and possibly the direction
      //  of movement whenever the timer fires an action event.
      //--------------------------------------------------------------
      public void actionPerformed (ActionEvent event)
      {
         x += moveX;
         y += moveY;

         if (x <= 0 || x >= WIDTH-IMAGE_SIZE)
            moveX = moveX * -1;

         if (y <= 0 || y >= HEIGHT-IMAGE_SIZE)
            moveY = moveY * -1;

         repaint();
      }
   }
}
```

The `actionPerformed` method of the listener updates the current x and y coordinate values, then checks to see if those values cause the image to "run into" the edge of the panel. If so, the movement is adjusted so that the image will make future moves in the opposite direction horizontally, vertically, or both. Note that this calculation takes the image size into account.

After updating the coordinate values, the `actionPerformed` method calls `repaint` to force the component (in this case, the panel) to repaint itself. The call to `repaint` eventually causes the `paintComponent` method to be called, which repaints the image in the new location.

The speed of the animation in this program is a function of two factors: the pause between the action events and the distance the image is shifted each time. In this example, the timer is set to generate an action event every 20 milliseconds, and the image is shifted 3 pixels each time it is updated. You can experiment with these values to change the speed of the animation. The goal should be to create the illusion of movement that is pleasing to the eye.

6.3 Layout Managers

Every container is managed by a layout manager, which determines how components are visually presented.

As we mentioned earlier in this chapter, every container is managed by an object called a *layout manager* that determines how the components in the container are arranged visually. The layout manager is consulted when needed, such as when the container is resized or when a component is added to the container.

When changes occur, the components in a container reorganize themselves according to the layout manager's policy.

A layout manager determines the size and position of each component and may take many factors into account to do so. Every container has a default layout manager, although we can replace it if we prefer another one.

The table in Figure 6.2 describes several of the predefined layout managers provided by the Java standard class library.

Every layout manager has its own particular properties and rules governing the layout of components. For some layout managers, the order in which you add the components affects their positioning, whereas others provide more specific control. Some layout managers take a component's preferred size or alignment into account, whereas others don't. To develop good GUIs in Java, it is important to become familiar with features and characteristics of various layout managers.

The layout manager for each container can be explicitly set.

We can use the `setLayout` method of a container to change its layout manager. For example, the following code sets the layout manager of a `JPanel`, which has a flow layout by default, so that it uses a border layout instead:

```
JPanel panel = new JPanel();
panel.setLayout (new BorderLayout());
```

Let's explore some of these layout managers in more detail. We'll focus on the most popular layout managers at this point: flow, border, box, and grid. The class presented in Listing 6.17 contains the `main` method of an application that demonstrates the use and effects of these layout managers.

The `LayoutDemo` program introduces the use of a *tabbed pane*, a container that allows the user to select (by clicking on a tab) which of several panes is currently visible. A tabbed pane is defined by the `JTabbedPane` class. The `addTab` method creates a tab, specifying the name that appears on the tab and the component to be displayed on that pane when it achieves focus by being "brought to the front" and made visible to the user.

Interestingly, there is an overlap in the functionality provided by tabbed panes and the card layout manager. Similar to the tabbed pane, a card layout allows several layers to be defined, and only one of those layers is displayed at any given point. However, a container managed by a card layout can be adjusted only under program control, whereas tabbed panes allow the user to indicate directly which tab should be displayed.

In this example, each tab of the tabbed pane contains a panel that is controlled by a different layout manager. The first tab simply contains a panel with an introductory message, as shown in Listing 6.18. As we explore each layout manager in more detail, we examine the class that defines the corresponding panel of this program and discuss its visual effect.

Layout Manager	Description
Border Layout	Organizes components into five areas (North, South, East, West, and Center).
Box Layout	Organizes components into a single row or column.
Card Layout	Organizes components into one area such that only one is visible at any time.
Flow Layout	Organizes components from left to right, starting new rows as necessary.
Grid Layout	Organizes components into a grid of rows and columns.
GridBag Layout	Organizes components into a grid of cells, allowing components to span more than one cell.

FIGURE 6.2 Some predefined Java layout managers

Listing 6.17

```
//********************************************************************
//  LayoutDemo.java       Java Foundations
//
//  Demonstrates the use of flow, border, grid, and box layouts.
//********************************************************************

import javax.swing.*;

public class LayoutDemo
{
   //-----------------------------------------------------------------
   //  Sets up a frame containing a tabbed pane. The panel on each
   //  tab demonstrates a different layout manager.
   //-----------------------------------------------------------------
   public static void main (String[] args)
   {
      JFrame frame = new JFrame ("Layout Manager Demo");
      frame.setDefaultCloseOperation (JFrame.EXIT_ON_CLOSE);

      JTabbedPane tp = new JTabbedPane();
      tp.addTab ("Intro", new IntroPanel());
      tp.addTab ("Flow", new FlowPanel());
      tp.addTab ("Border", new BorderPanel());
      tp.addTab ("Grid", new GridPanel());
      tp.addTab ("Box", new BoxPanel());

      frame.getContentPane().add(tp);

      frame.pack();
      frame.setVisible(true);
   }
}
```

Flow Layout

Flow layout is one of the easiest layout managers to use. As we've mentioned, the `JPanel` class uses flow layout by default. Flow layout puts as many components as possible on a row, at their preferred size. When a component cannot fit on a row, it is put on the next row. As many rows as needed are added to fit all components that have been added to the container. Figure 6.3 depicts a container governed by a flow layout manager.

Listing **6.18**

```
//********************************************************************
//  IntroPanel.java       Java Foundations
//
//  Represents the introduction panel for the LayoutDemo program.
//********************************************************************

import java.awt.*;
import javax.swing.*;

public class IntroPanel extends JPanel
{
   //-----------------------------------------------------------------
   //  Sets up this panel with two labels.
   //-----------------------------------------------------------------
   public IntroPanel()
   {
      setBackground (Color.green);

      JLabel l1 = new JLabel ("Layout Manager Demonstration");
      JLabel l2 = new JLabel ("Choose a tab to see an example of " +
                              "a layout manager.");
      add (l1);
      add (l2);
   }
}
```

Display

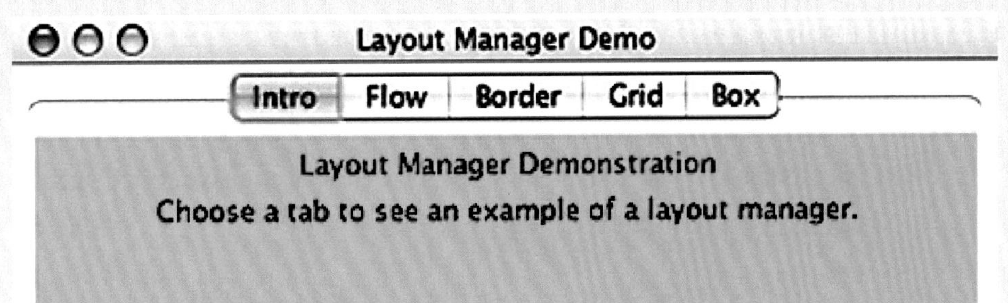

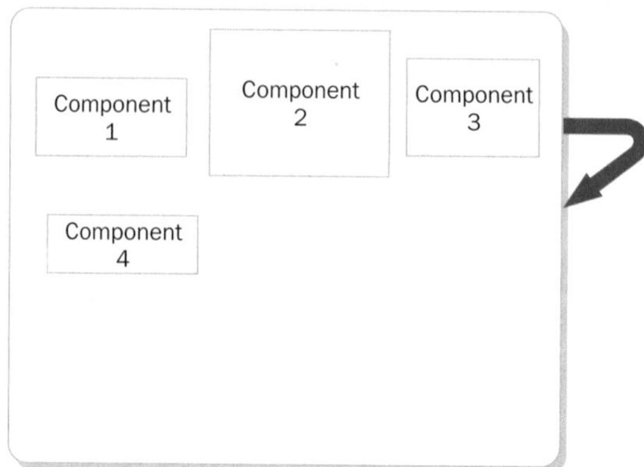

FIGURE 6.3 Flow layout puts as many components as possible on a row

The class in Listing 6.19 represents the panel that demonstrates a flow layout in the `LayoutDemo` program. It explicitly sets the layout to be a flow layout (though in this case that is unnecessary because `JPanel` defaults to flow layout). The buttons are then created and added to the panel.

The size of each button is made large enough to accommodate the size of the label that is put on it. Flow layout puts as many of these buttons as possible on one row within the panel, and then starts putting components on another row. When the size of the frame is widened (by dragging the lower-right corner with the mouse, for example), the panel grows as well, and more buttons can fit on a row. When the frame is resized, the layout manager is consulted and the components are reorganized automatically. The display in Listing 6.19 shows two screen shots of the window with different sizes.

The constructor of the `FlowLayout` class is overloaded to allow the programmer to tailor the characteristics of the layout manager. Within each row, components are either centered, left aligned, or right aligned. The alignment defaults to centered. The horizontal and vertical gap size between components also can be specified when the layout manager is created. The `FlowLayout` class also has methods to set the alignment and gap sizes after the layout manager is created.

Border Layout

A *border layout* has five areas to which components can be added: North, South, East, West, and Center. The areas have a particular positional relationship to each other, as shown in Figure 6.4.

Listing **6.19**

```
//********************************************************************
//  FlowPanel.java       Java Foundations
//
//  Represents the panel in the LayoutDemo program that demonstrates
//  the flow layout manager.
//********************************************************************

import java.awt.*;
import javax.swing.*;

public class FlowPanel extends JPanel
{
   //-----------------------------------------------------------------
   //  Sets up this panel with some buttons to show how flow layout
   //  affects their position.
   //-----------------------------------------------------------------
   public FlowPanel ()
   {
      setLayout (new FlowLayout());

      setBackground (Color.green);

      JButton b1 = new JButton ("BUTTON 1");
      JButton b2 = new JButton ("BUTTON 2");
      JButton b3 = new JButton ("BUTTON 3");
      JButton b4 = new JButton ("BUTTON 4");
      JButton b5 = new JButton ("BUTTON 5");

      add (b1);
      add (b2);
      add (b3);
      add (b4);
      add (b5);
   }
}
```

Listing 6.19 continued

Display

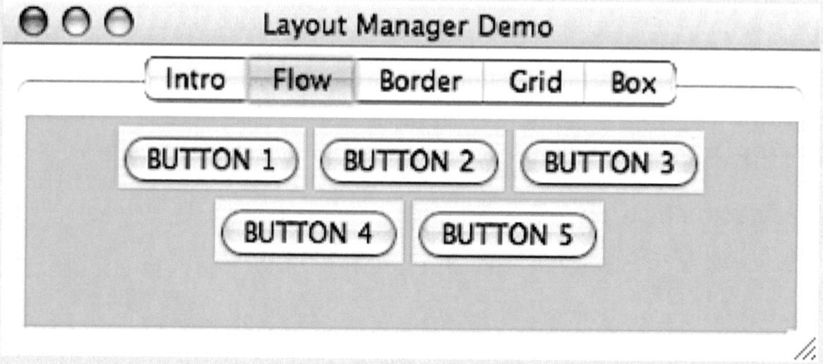

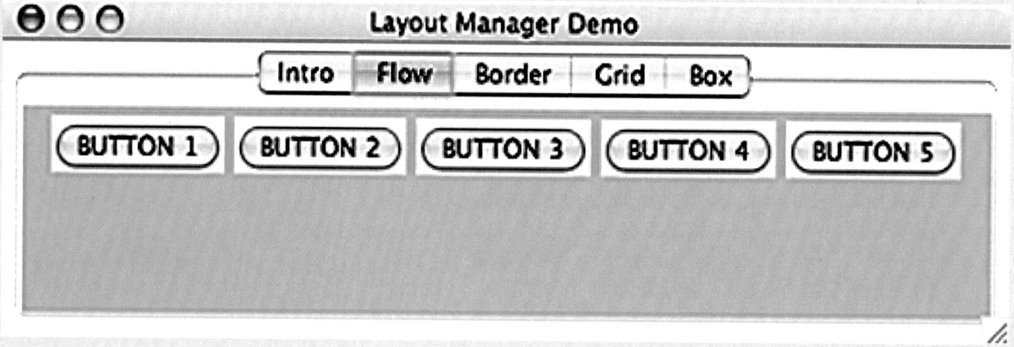

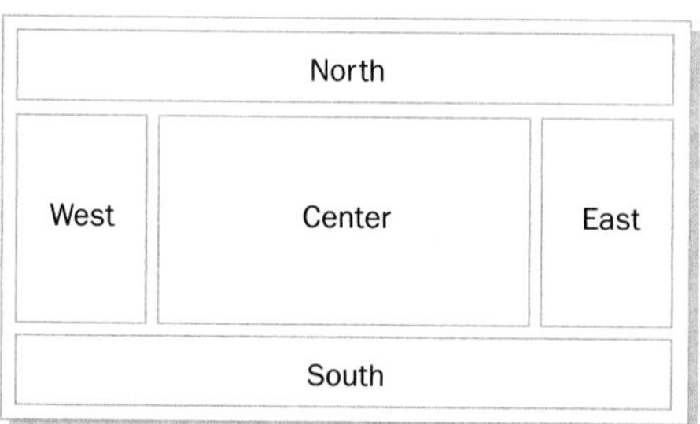

FIGURE 6.4 Border layout organizes components in five areas

The four outer areas become as big as needed in order to accommodate the component they contain. If no components are added to the North, South, East, or West areas, these areas do not take up any room in the overall layout. The Center area expands to fill any available space.

A particular container might use only a few areas, depending on the functionality of the system. For example, a program might use only the Center, South, and West areas. This versatility makes border layout a very useful layout manager.

The `add` method for a container governed by a border layout takes as its first parameter the component to be added. The second parameter indicates the area to which it is added. The area is specified using constants defined in the `BorderLayout` class. Listing 6.20 shows the panel used by the `LayoutDemo` program to demonstrate the border layout.

Listing 6.20

```
//********************************************************************
//  BorderPanel.java       Java Foundations
//
//  Represents the panel in the LayoutDemo program that demonstrates
//  the border layout manager.
//********************************************************************

import java.awt.*;
import javax.swing.*;

public class BorderPanel extends JPanel
{
   //-----------------------------------------------------------------
   //  Sets up this panel with a button in each area of a border
   //  layout to show how it affects their position, shape, and size.
   //-----------------------------------------------------------------
   public BorderPanel()
   {
      setLayout (new BorderLayout());

      setBackground (Color.green);

      JButton b1 = new JButton ("BUTTON 1");
      JButton b2 = new JButton ("BUTTON 2");
      JButton b3 = new JButton ("BUTTON 3");
      JButton b4 = new JButton ("BUTTON 4");
      JButton b5 = new JButton ("BUTTON 5");
```

Listing **6.20** continued

```
        add (b1, BorderLayout.CENTER);
        add (b2, BorderLayout.NORTH);
        add (b3, BorderLayout.SOUTH);
        add (b4, BorderLayout.EAST);
        add (b5, BorderLayout.WEST);
    }
}
```

Display

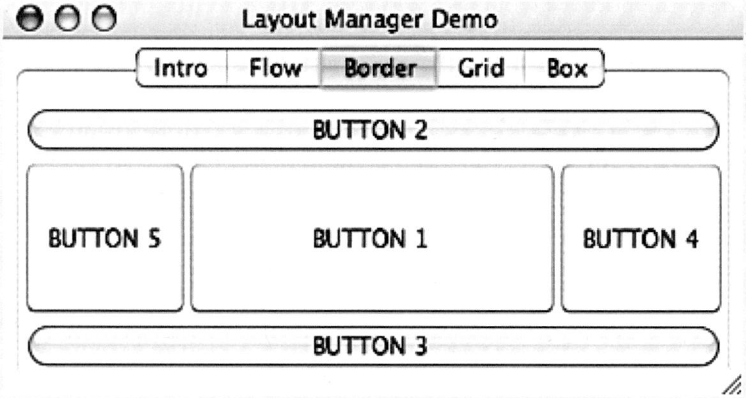

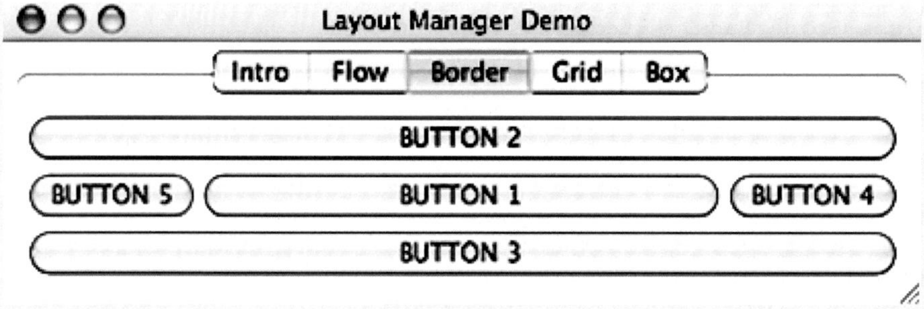

In the `BorderPanel` class constructor, the layout manager of the panel is explicitly set to be border layout. The buttons are then created and added to specific panel areas. By default, each button is made wide enough to accommodate its label and tall enough to fill the area to which it has been assigned. As the frame (and the panel) is resized, the size of each button adjusts as needed, with the button in the Center area filling any unused space.

Each area in a border layout displays only one component. That is, only one component is added to each area of a given border layout. A common error is to add two components to a particular area of a border layout, in which case the first component added is replaced by the second, and only the second is seen when the container is displayed. To add multiple components to an area within a border layout, you must first add the components to another container, such as a `JPanel`, then add the panel to the area.

Note that although the panel used to display the buttons has a green background, no green is visible in the display for Listing 6.20. By default there are no horizontal or vertical gaps between the areas of a border layout. These gaps can be set with an overloaded constructor or with explicit methods of the `BorderLayout` class. If the gaps are increased, the underlying panel will show through.

Grid Layout

A *grid layout* presents a container's components in a rectangular grid of rows and columns. One component is placed in each grid cell, and all cells are the same size. Figure 6.5 shows the general organization of a grid layout.

The number of rows and columns in a grid layout is established using parameters to the constructor when the layout manager is created. The class in Listing 6.21 shows the panel used by the `LayoutDemo` program to demonstrate a grid layout. It specifies that the panel should be managed using a grid of two rows and three columns.

Component 1	Component 2	Component 3	Component 4
Component 5	Component 6	Component 7	Component 8
Component 9	Component 10	Component 11	Component 12

FIGURE 6.5 Grid layout creates a rectangular grid of equal-size cells

Listing **6.21**

```
//********************************************************************
//  GridPanel.java       Java Foundations
//
//  Represents the panel in the LayoutDemo program that demonstrates
//  the grid layout manager.
//********************************************************************

import java.awt.*;
import javax.swing.*;

public class GridPanel extends JPanel
{
   //-----------------------------------------------------------------
   //  Sets up this panel with some buttons to show how grid
   //  layout affects their position, shape, and size.
   //-----------------------------------------------------------------
   public GridPanel()
   {
      setLayout (new GridLayout (2, 3));

      setBackground (Color.green);

      JButton b1 = new JButton ("BUTTON 1");
      JButton b2 = new JButton ("BUTTON 2");
      JButton b3 = new JButton ("BUTTON 3");
      JButton b4 = new JButton ("BUTTON 4");
      JButton b5 = new JButton ("BUTTON 5");

      add (b1);
      add (b2);
      add (b3);
      add (b4);
      add (b5);
   }
}
```

Listing **6.21** continued

Display

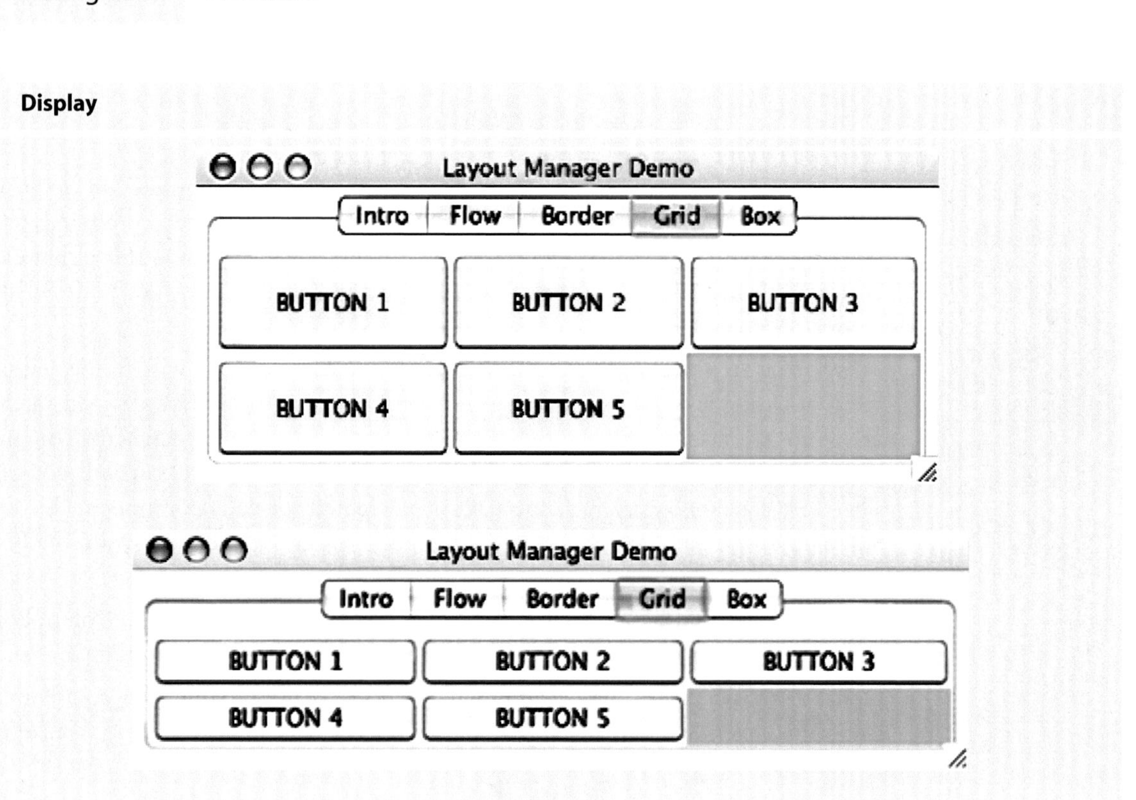

As buttons are added to the container, they fill the grid (by default) from left to right and top to bottom. There is no way to explicitly assign a component to a particular location in the grid other than the order in which they are added to the container.

The size of each cell is determined by the container's overall size. When the container is resized, all of the cells change size proportionally to fill the container.

If the value used to specify either the number of rows or the number of columns is zero, the grid expands as needed in that dimension to accommodate the number of components added to the container. The values for the number of rows and columns cannot both be zero.

By default, there are no horizontal and vertical gaps between the grid cells. The gap sizes can be specified using an overloaded constructor or with the appropriate `GridLayout` methods.

Box Layout

A *box layout* organizes components either vertically or horizontally, in one row or one column, as shown in Figure 6.6. It is easy to use, yet when combined with other box layouts, it can produce complex GUI designs similar to those that can be accomplished with a *grid bag layout*, which in general is far more difficult to master.

When a `BoxLayout` object is created, we specify that it will follow either the X axis (horizontal) or the Y axis (vertical), using constants defined in the `BoxLayout` class. Unlike other layout managers, the constructor of the `BoxLayout` class takes as its first parameter the component that it will govern. Therefore a new `BoxLayout` object must be created for each component. Listing 6.22 shows the panel used by the `LayoutDemo` program to demonstrate the box layout.

Components in containers governed by a box layout are organized (top to bottom or left to right) in the order in which they are added to the container.

There are no gaps between the components in a box layout. Unlike previous layout managers we've explored, a box layout does not have a specific vertical or

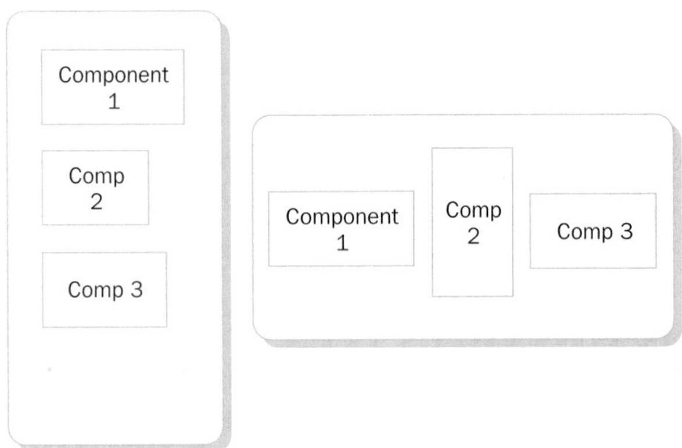

FIGURE 6.6 Box layout organizes components either vertically or horizontally

Listing 6.22

```
//********************************************************************
//  BoxPanel.java       Java Foundations
//
//  Represents the panel in the LayoutDemo program that demonstrates
//  the box layout manager.
//********************************************************************

import java.awt.*;
import javax.swing.*;

public class BoxPanel extends JPanel
{
   //-----------------------------------------------------------------
   //  Sets up this panel with some buttons to show how a vertical
   //  box layout (and invisible components) affects their position.
   //-----------------------------------------------------------------
   public BoxPanel()
   {
      setLayout (new BoxLayout (this, BoxLayout.Y_AXIS));

      setBackground (Color.green);

      JButton b1 = new JButton ("BUTTON 1");
      JButton b2 = new JButton ("BUTTON 2");
      JButton b3 = new JButton ("BUTTON 3");
      JButton b4 = new JButton ("BUTTON 4");
      JButton b5 = new JButton ("BUTTON 5");

      add (b1);
      add (Box.createRigidArea (new Dimension (0, 10)));
      add (b2);
      add (Box.createVerticalGlue());
      add (b3);
      add (b4);
      add (Box.createRigidArea (new Dimension (0, 20)));
      add (b5);
   }
}
```

Listing **6.22** continued

Display

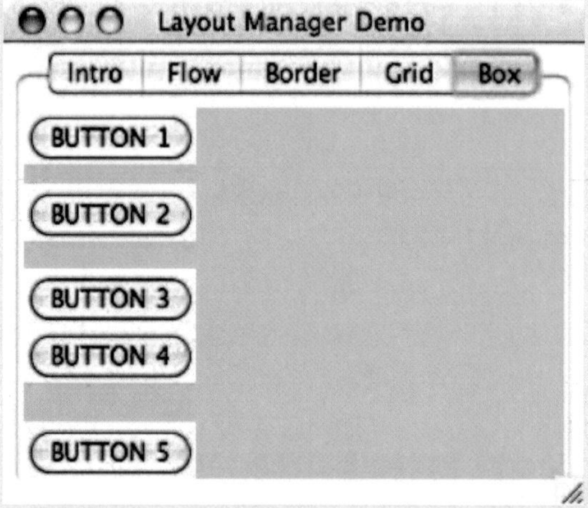

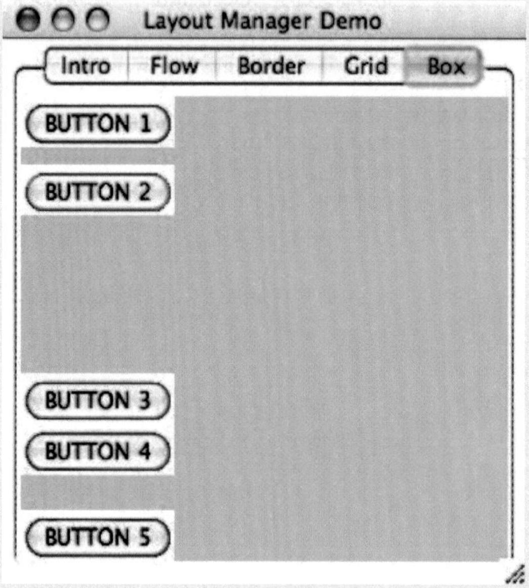

horizontal gap that can be specified for the entire container. Instead, we can add invisible components to the container that take up space between other components. The `Box` class, which is also part of the Java standard class library, contains static methods that can be used to create these invisible components.

The two types of invisible components used in the `BoxPanel` class are *rigid areas*, which have a fixed size, and *glue*, which specifies where excess space in a container should go. A rigid area is created using the `createRigidArea` method of the `Box` class, and takes a `Dimension` object as a parameter to define the size of the invisible area. Glue is created using the `createHorizontalGlue` method or `createVerticalGlue` method, as appropriate.

Note that in our example, the space between buttons separated by a rigid area remains constant even when the container is resized. Glue, on the other hand, expands or contracts as needed to fill the space.

A box layout—more than most of the other layout managers—respects the alignments and the minimum, maximum, and preferred sizes of the components it governs. Therefore, setting the characteristics of the components that go into the container is another way to tailor the visual effect.

Containment Hierarchies

The way components are grouped into containers, and the way those containers are nested within each other, establishes the *containment hierarchy* for a GUI. The interplay between the containment hierarchy and the layout managers of the containers involved dictates the overall visual effect of the GUI.

For any Java program, there is generally one primary container, called a top-level container, such as a frame or applet. The top-level container of a program often contains one or more other containers, such as panels. These panels may contain other panels to organize the other components as desired.

A GUI's appearance is a function of the containment hierarchy and the layout managers of each container.

Keep in mind that each container can have its own tailored layout manager. The final appearance of a GUI is a function of the layout managers chosen for each of the containers and the design of the containment hierarchy. Many combinations are possible, and there is rarely a single best option. We should be guided by the desired system goals and general GUI design guidelines.

When changes are made that might affect the visual layout of the components in a program, the layout managers of each container are consulted in turn. The changes in one may affect another. These changes ripple through the containment hierarchy as needed.

6.4 Mouse and Key Events

In addition to events that are generated when the user interacts with a component, there are events that are fired when the user interacts with the computer's mouse and keyboard. We can design a program to capture and respond to these as well.

Mouse Events

Java divides the events generated by the user interacting with the mouse into two categories: *mouse events* and *mouse motion events*. The tables in Figure 6.7 define these events.

When you click the mouse button over a Java GUI component, three events are generated: one when the mouse button is pushed down (*mouse pressed*) and two when it is let up (*mouse released* and *mouse clicked*). A mouse click is defined as pressing and releasing the mouse button in the same location. If you press the mouse button down, move the mouse, and then release the mouse button, a mouse clicked event is not generated.

A component will generate a *mouse entered* event when the mouse pointer passes into its graphical space. Likewise, it generates a *mouse exited* event when the mouse pointer leaves.

Moving the mouse and clicking the mouse button generate events to which a program can respond.

Mouse motion events, as the name implies, occur while the mouse is in motion. The *mouse moved* event indicates simply that the mouse is in motion. The *mouse dragged* event is generated

Mouse Event	Description
mouse pressed	The mouse button is pressed down.
mouse released	The mouse button is released.
mouse clicked	The mouse button is pressed down and released without moving the mouse in between.
mouse entered	The mouse pointer is moved onto (over) a component.
mouse exited	The mouse pointer is moved off of a component.

Mouse Motion Event	Description
mouse moved	The mouse is moved.
mouse dragged	The mouse is moved while the mouse button is pressed down.

FIGURE 6.7 Mouse events and mouse motion events

when the user has pressed the mouse button down and moved the mouse without releasing the button. Mouse motion events are generated many times, very quickly, while the mouse is in motion.

In a specific situation, we may care about only one or two mouse events. What we listen for depends on what we are trying to accomplish.

The `Coordinates` program shown in Listing 6.23 responds to one mouse event. Specifically, it draws a green dot at the location of the mouse pointer whenever the mouse button is pressed, and displays those coordinates. Keep in mind (as discussed in Appendix F) that the coordinate system in Java has the origin in the upper-left corner of a component (such as a panel), with x coordinates increasing to the right and y coordinates increasing downward.

The `CoordinatesPanel` class, shown in Listing 6.24, keeps track of the (x,y) coordinates at which the user has pressed the mouse button most recently. The

Listing **6.23**

```
//********************************************************************
//  Coordinates.java        Java Foundations
//
//  Demonstrates mouse events.
//********************************************************************

import javax.swing.JFrame;

public class Coordinates
{
   //-----------------------------------------------------------------
   //  Creates and displays the application frame.
   //-----------------------------------------------------------------
   public static void main (String[] args)
   {
      JFrame frame = new JFrame ("Coordinates");
      frame.setDefaultCloseOperation (JFrame.EXIT_ON_CLOSE);

      frame.getContentPane().add (new CoordinatesPanel());

      frame.pack();
      frame.setVisible(true);
   }
}
```

Listing **6.23** continued

Display

getX and getY methods of the MouseEvent object return the x and y coordinates of the location where the mouse event occurred.

The listener for the mouse pressed event implements the MouseListener interface. The panel invokes the mousePressed method each time the user presses down on the mouse button while it is over the panel.

A listener may have to provide empty method definitions for unheeded events to satisfy the interface.

Note that, unlike the listener interfaces that we've used in previous examples that contain one method each, the MouseListener interface contains five methods. For this program, the only event in which we are interested is the mouse pressed event. Therefore, the only method in which we have any interest is the mousePressed method. However, implementing an interface means we must provide definitions for all methods in the interface. Therefore we provide empty methods corresponding to the other events. When those events are generated, the empty methods are called, but no code is executed. At the end of this

Listing 6.24

```
//********************************************************************
//  CoordinatesPanel.java       Java Foundations
//
//  Represents the primary panel for the Coordinates program.
//********************************************************************

import javax.swing.JPanel;
import java.awt.*;
import java.awt.event.*;

public class CoordinatesPanel extends JPanel
{
   private final int SIZE = 6;  // diameter of dot

   private int x = 50, y = 50;  // coordinates of mouse press

   //-----------------------------------------------------------------
   //  Constructor: Sets up this panel to listen for mouse events.
   //-----------------------------------------------------------------
   public CoordinatesPanel()
   {
      addMouseListener (new CoordinatesListener());

      setBackground (Color.black);
      setPreferredSize (new Dimension(300, 200));
   }

   //-----------------------------------------------------------------
   //  Draws all of the dots stored in the list.
   //-----------------------------------------------------------------
   public void paintComponent (Graphics page)
   {
      super.paintComponent(page);

      page.setColor (Color.green);

      page.fillOval (x, y, SIZE, SIZE);

      page.drawString ("Coordinates: (" + x + ", " + y + ")", 5, 15);
   }

   //*****************************************************************
   //  Represents the listener for mouse events.
   //*****************************************************************
```

Listing 6.24 continued

```
   private class CoordinatesListener implements MouseListener
   {
      //-----------------------------------------------------------------
      //  Adds the current point to the list of points and redraws
      //  the panel whenever the mouse button is pressed.
      //-----------------------------------------------------------------
      public void mousePressed (MouseEvent event)
      {
         x = event.getX();
         y = event.getY();
         repaint();
      }

      //-----------------------------------------------------------------
      //  Provide empty definitions for unused event methods.
      //-----------------------------------------------------------------
      public void mouseClicked (MouseEvent event) {}
      public void mouseReleased (MouseEvent event) {}
      public void mouseEntered (MouseEvent event) {}
      public void mouseExited (MouseEvent event) {}
   }
}
```

section we discuss a technique for creating listeners that lets us avoid creating such empty methods.

Let's look at an example that responds to two mouse-oriented events. The `RubberLines` program shown in Listing 6.25 draws a line between two points. The first point is determined by the location at which the mouse is first pressed down. The second point changes as the mouse is dragged while the mouse button is held down. When the button is released, the line remains fixed between the first and second points. When the mouse button is pressed again, a new line is started.

The `RubberLinesPanel` class is shown in Listing 6.26. Because we need to listen for both a mouse pressed event and a mouse dragged event, we need a listener that responds to both mouse events and mouse motion events. Note that the listener class in this example implements both the `MouseListener` and `MouseMotionListener` interfaces. It must therefore implement all methods of both interfaces. The two methods of interest, `mousePressed` and `mouseDragged`,

Listing **6.25**

```
//********************************************************************
//  RubberLines.java       Java Foundations
//
//  Demonstrates mouse events and rubberbanding.
//********************************************************************

import javax.swing.JFrame;

public class RubberLines
{
   //-----------------------------------------------------------------
   //  Creates and displays the application frame.
   //-----------------------------------------------------------------
   public static void main (String[] args)
   {
      JFrame frame = new JFrame ("Rubber Lines");
      frame.setDefaultCloseOperation (JFrame.EXIT_ON_CLOSE);

      frame.getContentPane().add (new RubberLinesPanel());

      frame.pack();
      frame.setVisible(true);
   }
}
```

Display

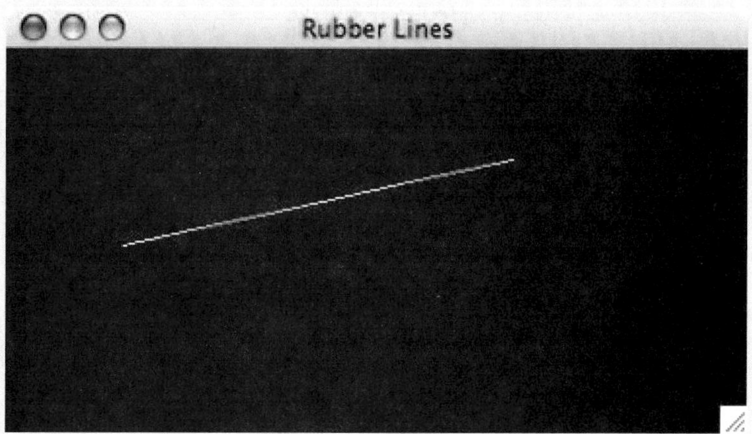

Listing 6.26

```
//********************************************************************
//  RubberLinesPanel.java       Java Foundations
//
//  Represents the primary drawing panel for the RubberLines program.
//********************************************************************

import javax.swing.JPanel;
import java.awt.*;
import java.awt.event.*;

public class RubberLinesPanel extends JPanel
{
   private Point point1 = null, point2 = null;

   //-----------------------------------------------------------------
   //  Constructor: Sets up this panel to listen for mouse events.
   //-----------------------------------------------------------------
   public RubberLinesPanel()
   {
      LineListener listener = new LineListener();
      addMouseListener (listener);
      addMouseMotionListener (listener);

      setBackground (Color.black);
      setPreferredSize (new Dimension(400, 200));
   }

   //-----------------------------------------------------------------
   //  Draws the current line from the intial mouse-pressed point to
   //  the current position of the mouse.
   //-----------------------------------------------------------------
   public void paintComponent (Graphics page)
   {
      super.paintComponent (page);

      page.setColor (Color.yellow);
      if (point1 != null && point2 != null)
         page.drawLine (point1.x, point1.y, point2.x, point2.y);
   }

   //*****************************************************************
   //  Represents the listener for all mouse events.
   //*****************************************************************
```

Listing **6.26** continued

```
   private class LineListener implements MouseListener,
                                         MouseMotionListener
   {
      //------------------------------------------------------------------
      //  Captures the initial position at which the mouse button is
      //  pressed.
      //------------------------------------------------------------------
      public void mousePressed (MouseEvent event)
      {
         point1 = event.getPoint();
      }

      //------------------------------------------------------------------
      //  Gets the current position of the mouse as it is dragged and
      //  redraws the line to create the rubberband effect.
      //------------------------------------------------------------------
      public void mouseDragged (MouseEvent event)
      {
         point2 = event.getPoint();
         repaint();
      }

      //------------------------------------------------------------------
      //  Provide empty definitions for unused event methods.
      //------------------------------------------------------------------
      public void mouseClicked (MouseEvent event) {}
      public void mouseReleased (MouseEvent event) {}
      public void mouseEntered (MouseEvent event) {}
      public void mouseExited (MouseEvent event) {}
      public void mouseMoved (MouseEvent event) {}
   }
}
```

are implemented to accomplish our goals, and the other methods are given empty definitions to satisfy the interface contract.

When the `mousePressed` method is called, the variable `point1` is set. Then, as the mouse is dragged, the variable `point2` is continually reset and the panel repainted. Therefore the line is constantly being redrawn as the mouse is dragged, giving the

Rubberbanding is the graphical effect caused when a shape seems to expand as the mouse is dragged.

appearance that one line is being stretched between a fixed point and a moving point. This effect is called *rubberbanding* and is common in graphical programs.

The starting and ending points of the line are stored as `Point` objects. The `Point` class is defined in the `java.awt` package, and encapsulates the x and y values of a two-dimensional coordinate.

Note that, in the `RubberLinesPanel` constructor, the listener object is added to the panel twice: once as a mouse listener and once as a mouse motion listener. The method called to add the listener must correspond to the object passed as the parameter. In this case, we had one object that served as a listener for both categories of events. We could have had two listener classes if desired: one listening for mouse events and one listening for mouse motion events. A component can have multiple listeners for various event categories.

Key Events

A *key event* is generated when a keyboard key is pressed. Key events allow a program to respond immediately to the user while he or she is typing or pressing other keyboard keys such as the arrow keys. If key events are being processed, the program can respond as soon as the key is pressed; there is no need to wait for the Enter key to be pressed or for some other component (like a button) to be activated.

Key events allow a program to respond immediately to the user pressing keyboard keys.

The `Direction` program shown in Listing 6.27 responds to key events. An image of an arrow is displayed and the image moves across the screen as the arrow keys are pressed. Actually, four different images are used, one for the arrow pointing in each of the primary directions (up, down, right, and left).

The `DirectionPanel` class, shown in Listing 6.28, represents the panel on which the arrow image is displayed. The constructor loads the four arrow images, one of which is always considered to be the current image (the one displayed). The current image is set based on the arrow key that was most recently pressed. For example, if the up arrow is pressed, the image with the arrow pointing up is displayed. If an arrow key is continually pressed, the appropriate image "moves" in the appropriate direction.

The arrow images are managed as `ImageIcon` objects. In this example, the image is drawn using the `paintIcon` method each time the panel is repainted. The `paintIcon` method takes four parameters: a component to serve as an image observer, the graphics context on which the image will be drawn, and the (x,y) coordinates where the image is drawn. An *image observer* is a component that

Listing 6.27

```
//********************************************************************
//  Direction.java       Java Foundations
//
//  Demonstrates key events.
//********************************************************************

import javax.swing.JFrame;

public class Direction
{
   //-----------------------------------------------------------------
   //  Creates and displays the application frame.
   //-----------------------------------------------------------------
   public static void main (String[] args)
   {
      JFrame frame = new JFrame ("Direction");
      frame.setDefaultCloseOperation (JFrame.EXIT_ON_CLOSE);

      frame.getContentPane().add (new DirectionPanel());

      frame.pack();
      frame.setVisible(true);
   }
}
```

Display

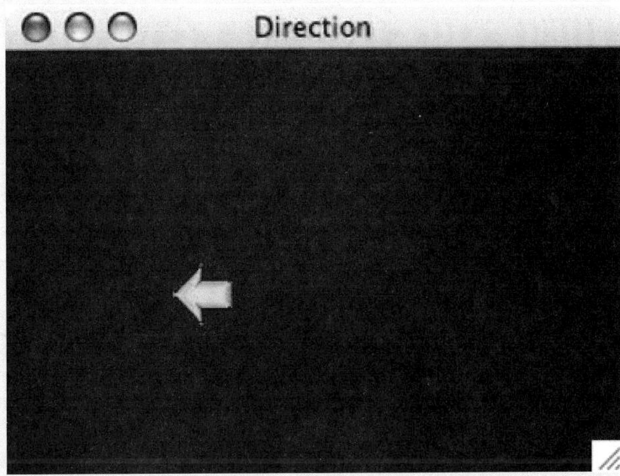

Listing 6.28

```
//********************************************************************
//  DirectionPanel.java       Java Foundations
//
//  Represents the primary display panel for the Direction program.
//********************************************************************

import javax.swing.*;
import java.awt.*;
import java.awt.event.*;

public class DirectionPanel extends JPanel
{
   private final int WIDTH = 300, HEIGHT = 200;
   private final int JUMP = 10;  // increment for image movement

   private final int IMAGE_SIZE = 31;

   private ImageIcon up, down, right, left, currentImage;
   private int x, y;

   //-----------------------------------------------------------------
   //  Constructor: Sets up this panel and loads the images.
   //-----------------------------------------------------------------
   public DirectionPanel()
   {
      addKeyListener (new DirectionListener());

      x = WIDTH / 2;
      y = HEIGHT / 2;

      up = new ImageIcon ("arrowUp.gif");
      down = new ImageIcon ("arrowDown.gif");
      left = new ImageIcon ("arrowLeft.gif");
      right = new ImageIcon ("arrowRight.gif");

      currentImage = right;

      setBackground (Color.black);
      setPreferredSize (new Dimension(WIDTH, HEIGHT));
      setFocusable(true);
   }
```

Listing 6.28 continued

```
   //-----------------------------------------------------------------
   //  Draws the image in the current location.
   //-----------------------------------------------------------------
   public void paintComponent (Graphics page)
   {
      super.paintComponent (page);
      currentImage.paintIcon (this, page, x, y);
   }

   //*****************************************************************
   //  Represents the listener for keyboard activity.
   //*****************************************************************
   private class DirectionListener implements KeyListener
   {
      //--------------------------------------------------------------
      //  Responds to the user pressing arrow keys by adjusting the
      //  image and image location accordingly.
      //--------------------------------------------------------------
      public void keyPressed (KeyEvent event)
      {
         switch (event.getKeyCode())
         {
            case KeyEvent.VK_UP:
               currentImage = up;
               y -= JUMP;
               break;
            case KeyEvent.VK_DOWN:
               currentImage = down;
               y += JUMP;
               break;
            case KeyEvent.VK_LEFT:
               currentImage = left;
               x -= JUMP;
               break;
            case KeyEvent.VK_RIGHT:
               currentImage = right;
               x += JUMP;
               break;
         }

         repaint();
      }
```

Listing **6.28** continued

```
      //-----------------------------------------------------------------
      //  Provide empty definitions for unused event methods.
      //-----------------------------------------------------------------
      public void keyTyped (KeyEvent event) {}
      public void keyReleased (KeyEvent event) {}
   }
}
```

serves to manage image loading; in this case we use the panel as the image observer.

The private inner class called `DirectionListener` is set up to respond to key events. It implements the `KeyListener` interface, which defines three methods that we can use to respond to keyboard activity. Figure 6.8 lists these methods.

Specifically, the `Direction` program responds to key pressed events. Because the listener class must implement all methods defined in the interface, we provide empty methods for the other events.

The `KeyEvent` object passed to the `keyPressed` method of the listener can be used to determine which key was pressed. In the example, we call the `getKeyCode` method of the event object to get a numeric code that represents the key that was pressed. We use a `switch` statement to determine which key was pressed and to respond accordingly. The `KeyEvent` class contains constants that correspond to the numeric code that is returned from the `getKeyCode` method. If any key other than an arrow key is pressed it is ignored.

`void keyPressed (KeyEvent event)`
Called when a key is pressed.

`void keyReleased (KeyEvent event)`
Called when a key is released.

`void keyTyped (KeyEvent event)`
Called when a pressed key or key combination produces a key character.

FIGURE 6.8 The methods of the `KeyListener` interface

Key events fire whenever a key is pressed, but most systems enable the concept of *key repetition*. That is, when a key is pressed and held down, it's as if that key is being pressed repeatedly and quickly. Key events are generated in the same way. In the `Direction` program, the user can hold down an arrow key and watch the image move across the screen quickly.

The component that generates key events is the one that currently has the keyboard focus. Usually the keyboard focus is held by the primary "active" component. A component usually gets the keyboard focus when the user clicks on it with the mouse. The call to the `setFocusable` method in the panel constructor sets the keyboard focus to the panel.

The `Direction` program sets no boundaries for the arrow image, so it can be moved out of the visible window, then moved back in if desired. You could add code to the listener to stop the image when it reaches one of the window boundaries. This modification is left as a programming project.

Extending Adapter Classes

In previous event-based examples, we've created the listener classes by implementing a particular listener interface. For instance, to create a class that listens for mouse events, we created a listener class that implements the `MouseListener` interface. As we saw in the previous examples in this section, a listener interface often contains event methods that are not important to a particular program, in which case we provided empty definitions to satisfy the interface requirement.

An alternative technique for creating a listener class is to use inheritance and extend an *event adapter class*. Each listener interface that contains more than one method has a corresponding adapter class that already contains empty definitions for all of the methods in the interface. To create a listener, we can derive a new listener class from the appropriate adapter class and override any event methods in which we are interested. Using this technique, we no longer need to provide empty definitions for unused methods.

A listener class can be created by deriving it from an event adapter class.

The `MouseAdapter` class, for instance, implements the `MouseListener` interface and provides empty method definitions for the five mouse event methods (`mousePressed`, `mouseClicked`, etc.). Therefore, you can create a mouse listener class by extending the `MouseAdaptor` class instead of implementing the `MouseListener` interface directly. The new listener class inherits the empty definitions, and therefore doesn't need to define them.

Because of inheritance, we now have a choice when it comes to creating event listeners. We can implement an event listener interface, or we can extend an event adapter class. This is a design decision that should be considered carefully. The best technique depends on the situation. Inheritance is discussed further in Chapter 8.

6.5 Dialog Boxes

A component called a *dialog box* can be helpful to assist in GUI processing. A dialog box is a graphical window that pops up on top of any currently active window so that the user can interact with it. A dialog box can serve a variety of purposes, such as conveying some information, confirming an action, or allowing the user to enter some information. Usually a dialog box has a solitary purpose, and the user's interaction with it is brief.

The Swing package of the Java class library contains a class called `JOptionPane` that simplifies the creation and use of basic dialog boxes. Figure 6.9 lists some of the methods of `JOptionPane`.

The basic formats for a `JOptionPane` dialog box fall into three categories. A *message dialog box* simply displays an output string. An *input dialog box* presents a prompt and a single input text field into which the user can enter one string of data. A *confirm dialog box* presents the user with a simple yes-or-no question.

Let's look at a program that uses each of these types of dialog boxes. Listing 6.29 shows a program that first presents the user with an input dialog box that requests the user to enter an integer. After the user presses the OK button on the input dialog box, a second dialog box (this time a message dialog box) appears,

`static String showInputDialog (Object msg)`
Displays a dialog box containing the specified message and an input text field. The contents of the text field are returned.

`static int showConfirmDialog (Component parent, Object msg)`
Displays a dialog box containing the specified message and Yes/No button options. If the parent component is null, the box is centered on the screen.

`static void showMessageDialog (Component parent, Object msg)`
Displays a dialog box containing the specified message. If the parent component is null, the box is centered on the screen.

FIGURE 6.9 Some methods of the `JOptionPane` class

informing the user whether the number entered was even or odd. After the user dismisses that box, a third dialog box appears, to determine whether the user would like to test another number. If the user presses the button labeled Yes, the series of dialog boxes repeats. Otherwise the program terminates.

Listing **6.29**

```
//********************************************************************
//  EvenOdd.java       Java Foundations
//
//  Demonstrates the use of the JOptionPane class.
//********************************************************************

import javax.swing.JOptionPane;

public class EvenOdd
{
   //-----------------------------------------------------------------
   //  Determines if the value input by the user is even or odd.
   //  Uses multiple dialog boxes for user interaction.
   //-----------------------------------------------------------------
   public static void main (String[] args)
   {
      String numStr, result;
      int num, again;

      do
      {
         numStr = JOptionPane.showInputDialog ("Enter an integer: ");

         num = Integer.parseInt(numStr);

         result = "That number is " + ((num%2 == 0) ? "even" : "odd");

         JOptionPane.showMessageDialog (null, result);

         again = JOptionPane.showConfirmDialog (null, "Do Another?");
      }
      while (again == JOptionPane.YES_OPTION);
   }
}
```

Listing **6.29** continued

Display

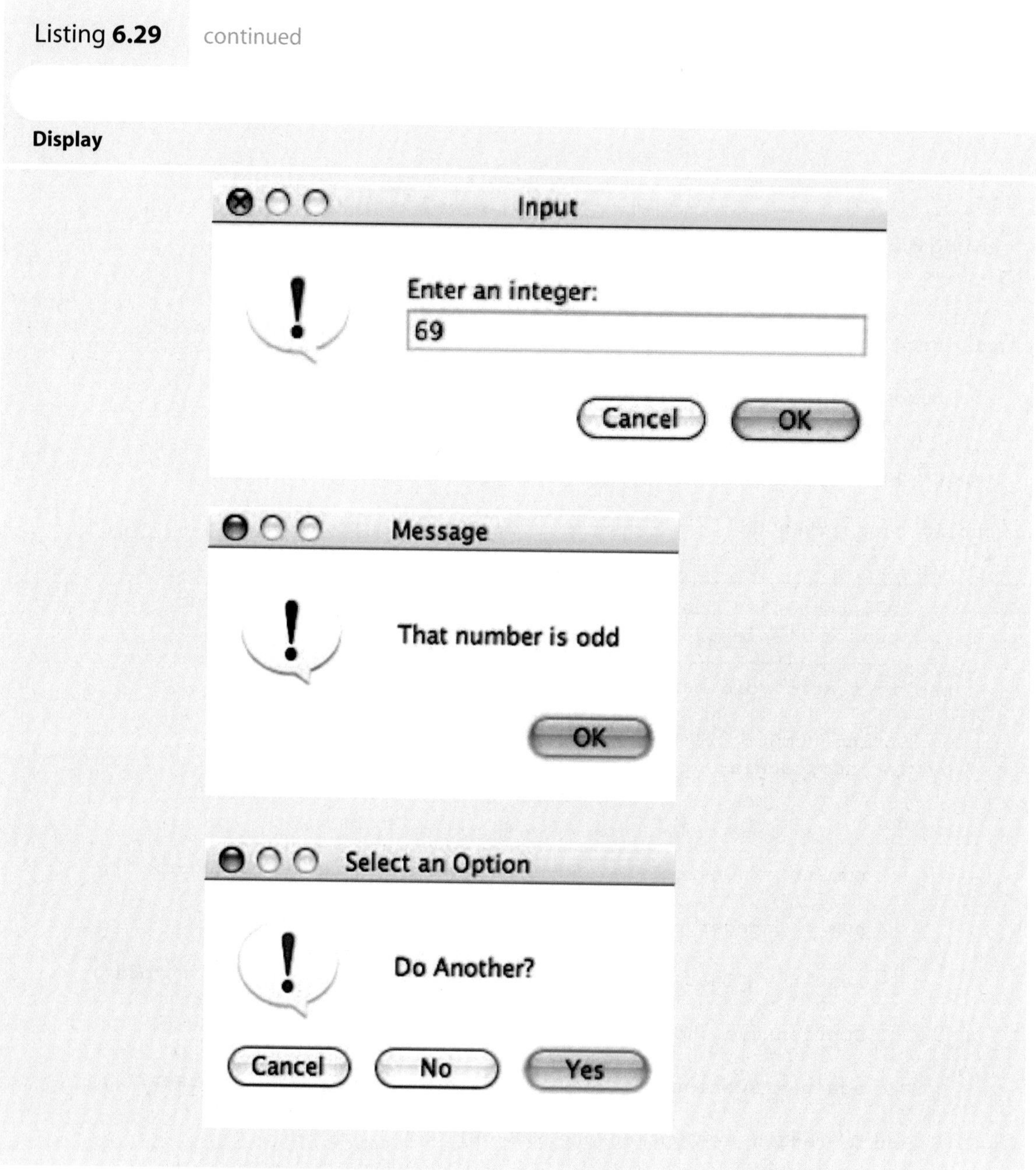

The first parameter to the `showMessageDialog` and the `showConfirmDialog` methods specifies the governing parent component for the dialog box. Using a null reference as this parameter causes the dialog box to appear centered on the screen.

Many of the `JOptionPane` methods allow the programmer to tailor the contents of the dialog box. Furthermore, the `showOptionDialog` method can be used to create dialog boxes that combine characteristics of the three basic formats for more elaborate interactions.

Dialog boxes should only be used when the immediate attention of the user is necessary. A program that constantly has new windows popping up for different interactions is annoying to the user.

File Choosers

A *file chooser* is a specialized dialog box that allows the user to select a file from a disk or other storage medium. You have probably run many programs that allow you to open a file, such as when you are specifying which file to open in a word processing program. The need to specify a file occurs so often, the `JFileChooser` class was made part of the Java standard class library for just that purpose.

A file chooser allows the user to browse a disk and select a file to be processed.

The program shown in Listing 6.30 uses a `JFileChooser` dialog box to select a file. This program also demonstrates the use of another GUI component, a *text area*, which is similar to a text field but can display multiple lines of text at one time. In this example, after the user selects a file using the file chooser dialog box, the text contained in that file is displayed in a text area.

The file chooser dialog box is displayed when the `showOpenDialog` method is invoked. It automatically presents the list of files contained in a particular directory. The user can use the controls on the dialog box to navigate to other directories, change the way the files are viewed, and specify which types of files are displayed.

The `showOpenDialog` method returns an integer representing the status of the operation, which can be checked against constants defined in the `JFileChooser` class. In this program, if a file was not selected (perhaps by pressing the Cancel button), a default message is displayed in the text area. If the user chose a file, it is opened and its contents are read using the `Scanner` class. Note that this program assumes the selected file contains text. It does not catch any exceptions, so

Listing 6.30

```
//********************************************************************
//  DisplayFile.java       Java Foundations
//
//  Demonstrates the use of a file chooser and a text area.
//********************************************************************

import java.util.Scanner;
import java.io.*;
import javax.swing.*;

public class DisplayFile
{
   //-----------------------------------------------------------------
   //  Opens a file chooser dialog, reads the selected file and
   //  loads it into a text area.
   //-----------------------------------------------------------------
   public static void main (String[] args) throws IOException
   {
      JFrame frame = new JFrame ("Display File");
      frame.setDefaultCloseOperation (JFrame.EXIT_ON_CLOSE);

      JTextArea ta = new JTextArea (20, 30);
      JFileChooser chooser = new JFileChooser();

      int status = chooser.showOpenDialog (null);

      if (status != JFileChooser.APPROVE_OPTION)
         ta.setText ("No File Chosen");
      else
      {
         File file = chooser.getSelectedFile();
         Scanner scan = new Scanner (file);

         String info = "";
         while (scan.hasNext())
            info += scan.nextLine() + "\n";

         ta.setText (info);
      }
```

Listing 6.30 continued

```
      frame.getContentPane().add (ta);
      frame.pack();
      frame.setVisible(true);
   }
}
```

Display

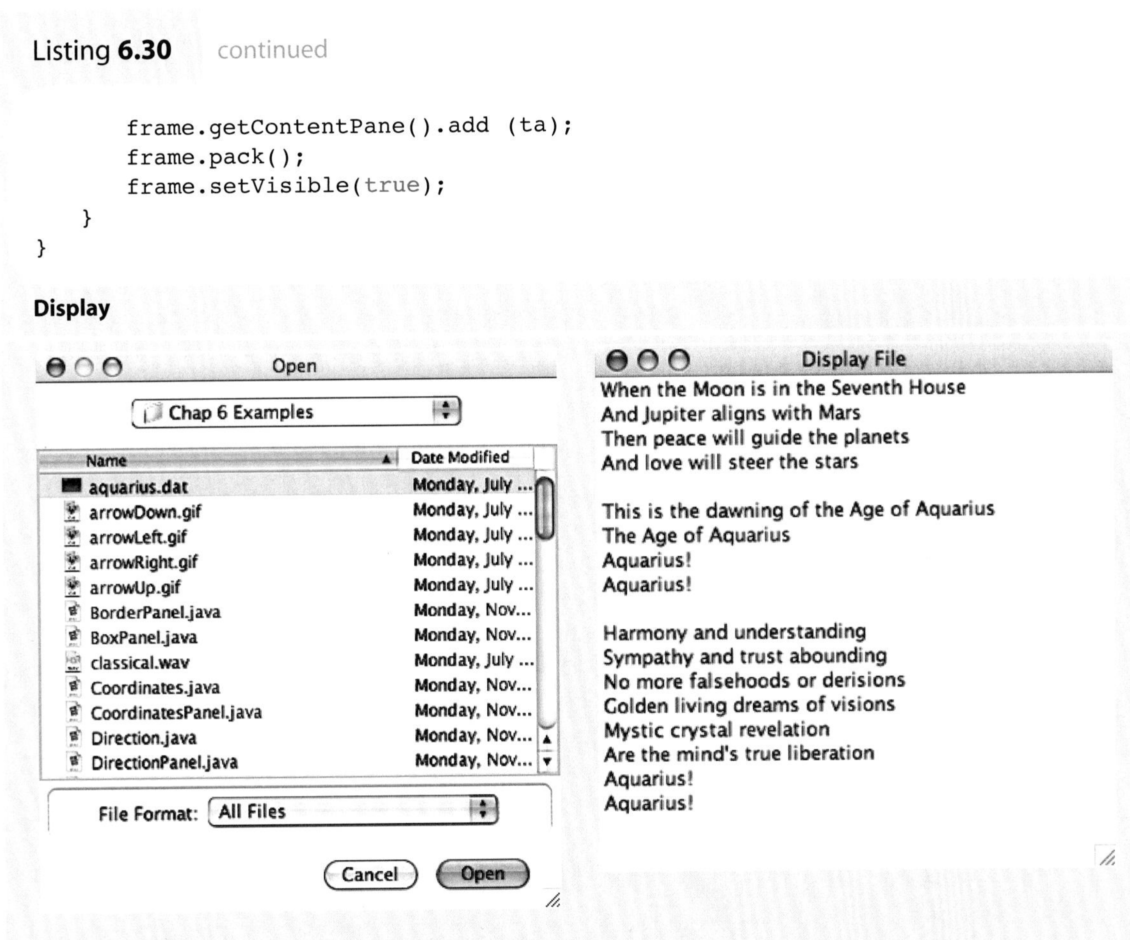

if the user selects an inappropriate file, the program will terminate when the exception is thrown.

A text area component is defined by the `JTextArea` class. In this program, we pass two parameters to its constructor, specifying the size of the text area in terms of the number of characters (rows and columns) it should display. The text to display is set using the `setText` method.

A text area component, like a text field, can be set so that it is either editable or noneditable. The user can change the contents of an editable text area by clicking on the text area and typing with the mouse. If the text area is noneditable, it is used to display text only. By default, a `JTextArea` component is editable.

A `JFileChooser` component makes it easy to allow users to specify a specific file to use. Another specialized dialog box—one that allows the user to choose a color—is discussed in the next section.

Color Choosers

A color chooser allows the user to select a color from a palette or using RGB values.

In many situations we may want to give the user of a program the ability to choose a color. We could accomplish this in various ways. For instance, we could provide a list of colors using a set of radio buttons. However, with the wide variety of colors available, it's nice to have an easier and more flexible technique to accomplish this common task. A specialized dialog box, often referred to as a *color chooser*, is a graphical component that serves this purpose.

The `JColorChooser` class represents a color chooser. It can be used to display a dialog box that lets the user click on a color of choice from a palette presented for that purpose. The user could also specify a color using RGB values or other color representation techniques. Invoking the static `showDialog` method of the `JColorChooser` class causes the color chooser dialog box to appear. The parameters to that method specify the parent component for the dialog box, the title that appears in the dialog box frame, and the initial color showing in the color chooser.

Figure 6.10 shows a color chooser dialog box.

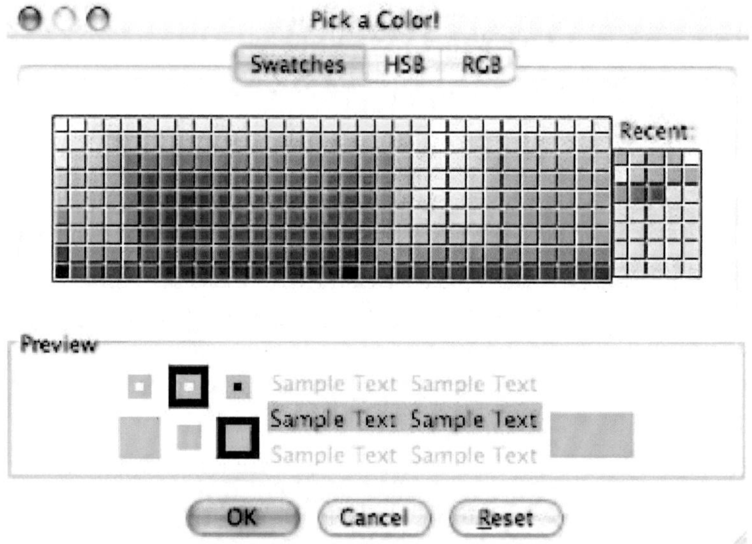

FIGURE 6.10 A color chooser dialog box

6.6 Some Important Details

There are a variety of small but important details that can add considerable value to the interface of a program. Some enhance the visual effect, while others provide shortcuts to make the user more productive. Let's examine some of them now.

Borders

Java provides the ability to put a border around any Swing component. A border is not a component itself but rather defines how the edge of any component should be drawn and has an important effect on the design of a GUI. A border provides visual cues as to how GUI components are organized, and can be used to give titles to components. Figure 6.11 lists the predefined borders in the Java standard class library.

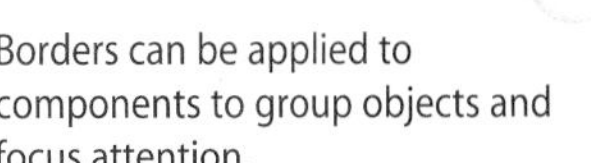
Borders can be applied to components to group objects and focus attention.

The `BorderFactory` class is useful for creating borders for components. It has many methods for creating specific types of borders. A border is applied to a component by using the component's `setBorder` method.

The program in Listing 6.31 demonstrates several types of borders. It simply creates several panels, sets a different border for each, and then displays them in a larger panel using a grid layout.

Let's look at each type of border created in this program. An *empty border* is applied to the larger panel that holds all the others, to create a buffer of space

Border	Description
Empty Border	Puts buffering space around the edge of a component, but otherwise has no visual effect.
Line Border	A simple line surrounding the component.
Etched Border	Creates the effect of an etched groove around a component.
Bevel Border	Creates the effect of a component raised above the surface or sunken below it.
Titled Border	Includes a text title on or around the border.
Matte Border	Allows the size of each edge to be specified. Uses either a soild color or an image.
Compound Border	A combination of two borders.

FIGURE 6.11 Component borders

around the outer edge of the frame. The sizes of the top, left, bottom, and right edges of the empty border are specified in pixels. The *line border* is created using a particular color and specifies the line thickness in pixels (3 in this case). The line thickness defaults to 1 pixel if left unspecified. The *etched border* created in this program uses default colors for the highlight and shadow of the etching, but both could be explicitly set if desired.

Listing **6.31**

```
//********************************************************************
//  BorderDemo.java       Java Foundations
//
//  Demonstrates the use of various types of borders.
//********************************************************************

import java.awt.*;
import javax.swing.*;
import javax.swing.border.*;

public class BorderDemo
{
   //-----------------------------------------------------------------
   //  Creates several bordered panels and displays them.
   //-----------------------------------------------------------------
   public static void main (String[] args)
   {
      JFrame frame = new JFrame ("Border Demo");
      frame.setDefaultCloseOperation (JFrame.EXIT_ON_CLOSE);

      JPanel panel = new JPanel();
      panel.setLayout (new GridLayout (0, 2, 5, 10));
      panel.setBorder (BorderFactory.createEmptyBorder (8, 8, 8, 8));

      JPanel p1 = new JPanel();
      p1.setBorder (BorderFactory.createLineBorder (Color.red, 3));
      p1.add (new JLabel ("Line Border"));
      panel.add (p1);

      JPanel p2 = new JPanel();
      p2.setBorder (BorderFactory.createEtchedBorder ());
      p2.add (new JLabel ("Etched Border"));
      panel.add (p2);
```

Listing **6.31** continued

```
        JPanel p3 = new JPanel();
        p3.setBorder (BorderFactory.createRaisedBevelBorder ());
        p3.add (new JLabel ("Raised Bevel Border"));
        panel.add (p3);

        JPanel p4 = new JPanel();
        p4.setBorder (BorderFactory.createLoweredBevelBorder ());
        p4.add (new JLabel ("Lowered Bevel Border"));
        panel.add (p4);

        JPanel p5 = new JPanel();
        p5.setBorder (BorderFactory.createTitledBorder ("Title"));
        p5.add (new JLabel ("Titled Border"));
        panel.add (p5);

        JPanel p6 = new JPanel();
        TitledBorder tb = BorderFactory.createTitledBorder ("Title");
        tb.setTitleJustification (TitledBorder.RIGHT);
        p6.setBorder (tb);
        p6.add (new JLabel ("Titled Border (right)"));
        panel.add (p6);

        JPanel p7 = new JPanel();
        Border b1 = BorderFactory.createLineBorder (Color.blue, 2);
        Border b2 = BorderFactory.createEtchedBorder ();
        p7.setBorder (BorderFactory.createCompoundBorder (b1, b2));
        p7.add (new JLabel ("Compound Border"));
        panel.add (p7);

        JPanel p8 = new JPanel();
        Border mb = BorderFactory.createMatteBorder (1, 5, 1, 1,
                                                     Color.red);
        p8.setBorder (mb);
        p8.add (new JLabel ("Matte Border"));
        panel.add (p8);

        frame.getContentPane().add (panel);
        frame.pack();
        frame.setVisible(true);
    }
}
```

Listing 6.31 continued

Display

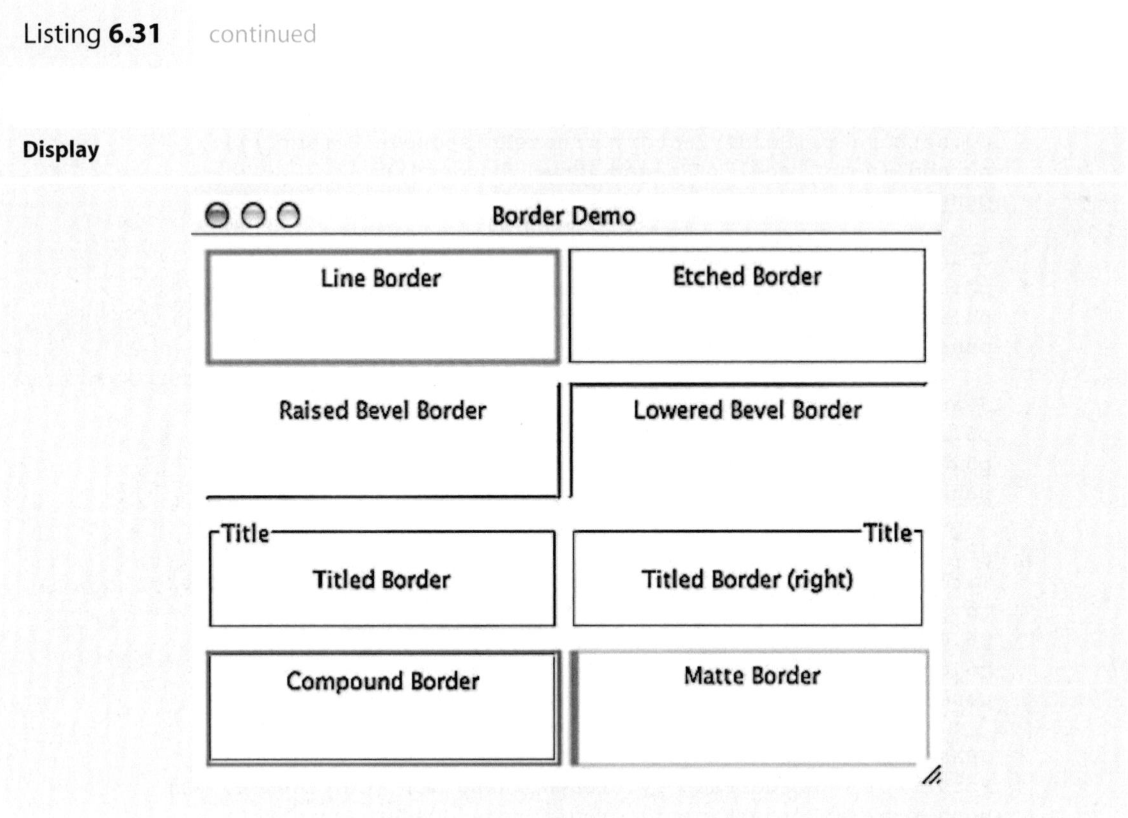

A *bevel border* can be either raised or lowered. The default coloring is used in this program, although the coloring of each aspect of the bevel can be tailored as desired, including the outer highlight, inner highlight, outer shadow, and inner shadow. Each of these aspects could be a different color if desired.

A *titled border* places a title on or around the border. The default position for the title is on the border at the top-left edge. Using the `setTitleJustification` method of the `TitledBorder` class, this position can be set to many other places above, below, on, or to the left, right, or center of the border.

A *compound border* is a combination of two or more borders. The example in this program creates a compound border using a line border and an etched border. The `createCompoundBorder` method accepts two borders as parameters and makes the first parameter the outer border and the second parameter the inner border. Combinations of three or more borders are created by first creating a compound border using two borders, then making another compound border using it and yet another one.

A *matte border* specifies the sizes, in pixels, of the top, left, bottom, and right edges of the border. Those edges can be composed of a single color, as they are in this example, or an image icon can be used.

Borders should be used carefully. They can be helpful in drawing attention to appropriate parts of your GUI and can conceptually group related items together. However, if used inappropriately, they can also detract from the elegance of the presentation. Borders should enhance the interface, not complicate or compete with it.

Tool Tips and Mnemonics

Any Swing component can be assigned a *tool tip*, which is a short line of text that will appear when the cursor is rested momentarily on top of the component. Tool tips are usually used to inform the user about the component, such as the purpose of a button.

A tool tip can be assigned using the `setToolTipText` method of a component. For example:

```
JButton button = new JButton ("Compute");
button.setToolTipText ("Calculates the area under the curve.");
```

When the button is added to a container and displayed, it appears normally. When the user rolls the mouse pointer over the button, hovering there momentarily, the tool tip text pops up. When the user moves the mouse pointer off of the button, the tool tip text disappears.

A *mnemonic* is a character that allows the user to push a button or make a menu choice using the keyboard in addition to the mouse. For example, when a mnemonic has been defined for a button, the user can hold down the Alt key and press the mnemonic character to activate the button. Using a mnemonic to activate the button causes the system to behave just as it would if the user had used the mouse to press the button.

A mnemonic character should be chosen from the label on a button or menu item. Once the mnemonic has been established using the `setMnemonic` method, the character in the label will be underlined to indicate that it can be used as a shortcut. If a letter is chosen that is not in the label, nothing will be underlined and the user won't know how to use the shortcut. You can set a mnemonic as follows:

```
JButton button = new JButton ("Calculate");
button.setMnemonic ('C');
```

When the button is displayed, the letter C in Calculate is underlined on the button label. When the user presses Alt-C, the button is activated as if the user had pressed it with the mouse.

Some components can be *disabled* if they should not be used. A disabled component will appear "grayed out," and nothing will happen if the user attempts to interact with it. To disable and enable components, we invoke the `setEnabled` method of the component, passing it a boolean value to indicate whether the component should be disabled (`false`) or enabled (`true`). For example:

```
JButton button = new JButton ("Do It");
button.setEnabled (false);
```

Disabling components is a good idea when users should not be allowed to use the functionality of a component. The grayed appearance of the disabled component is an indication that using the component is inappropriate (and, in fact, impossible) at the current time. Disabled components not only convey to the user which actions are appropriate and which aren't, they also prevent erroneous situations from occurring.

Components should be disabled when their use is inappropriate.

Let's look at an example that uses tool tips, mnemonics, and disabled components. The program in Listing 6.32 presents the image of a light bulb and provides a button to turn the light bulb on and a button to turn the light bulb off.

There are actually two images of the light bulb: one showing it turned on and one showing it turned off. These images are brought in as `ImageIcon` objects. The `setIcon` method of the label that displays the image is used to set the appropriate image, depending on the current status. This processing is controlled in the `LightBulbPanel` class shown in Listing 6.33.

The `LightBulbControls` class shown in Listing 6.34 is a panel that contains the On and Off buttons. Both of these buttons have tool tips assigned to them, and both use mnemonics. Also, when one of the buttons is enabled, the other is disabled, and vice versa. When the light bulb is on, there is no reason for the On button to be enabled. Likewise, when the light bulb is off, there is no reason for the Off button to be enabled.

Listing 6.32

```
//********************************************************************
//  LightBulb.java       Java Foundations
//
//  Demonstrates mnemonics and tool tips.
//********************************************************************

import javax.swing.*;
import java.awt.*;

public class LightBulb
{
   //-----------------------------------------------------------------
   //  Sets up a frame that displays a light bulb image that can be
   //  turned on and off.
   //-----------------------------------------------------------------
   public static void main (String[] args)
   {
      JFrame frame = new JFrame ("Light Bulb");
      frame.setDefaultCloseOperation (JFrame.EXIT_ON_CLOSE);

      LightBulbPanel bulb = new LightBulbPanel();
      LightBulbControls controls = new LightBulbControls (bulb);

      JPanel panel = new JPanel();
      panel.setBackground (Color.black);
      panel.setLayout (new BoxLayout(panel, BoxLayout.Y_AXIS));
      panel.add (Box.createRigidArea (new Dimension (0, 20)));
      panel.add (bulb);
      panel.add (Box.createRigidArea (new Dimension (0, 10)));
      panel.add (controls);
      panel.add (Box.createRigidArea (new Dimension (0, 10)));

      frame.getContentPane().add(panel);

      frame.pack();
      frame.setVisible(true);
   }
}
```

Listing **6.32** continued

Display

Listing **6.33**

```
//********************************************************************
//  LightBulbPanel.java       Java Foundations
//
//  Represents the image for the LightBulb program.
//********************************************************************

import javax.swing.*;
import java.awt.*;

public class LightBulbPanel extends JPanel
{
   private boolean on;
   private ImageIcon lightOn, lightOff;
   private JLabel imageLabel;

   //-----------------------------------------------------------------
   //  Constructor: Sets up the images and the initial state.
   //-----------------------------------------------------------------
```

Listing 6.33 continued

```
   public LightBulbPanel()
   {
      lightOn = new ImageIcon ("lightBulbOn.gif");
      lightOff = new ImageIcon ("lightBulbOff.gif");

      setBackground (Color.black);

      on = true;
      imageLabel = new JLabel (lightOff);
      add (imageLabel);
   }

   //-----------------------------------------------------------------
   //  Paints the panel using the appropriate image.
   //-----------------------------------------------------------------
   public void paintComponent (Graphics page)
   {
      super.paintComponent(page);

      if (on)
         imageLabel.setIcon (lightOn);
      else
         imageLabel.setIcon (lightOff);
   }

   //-----------------------------------------------------------------
   //  Sets the status of the light bulb.
   //-----------------------------------------------------------------
   public void setOn (boolean lightBulbOn)
   {
      on = lightBulbOn;
   }
}
```

Each button has its own listener class. The `actionPerformed` method of each sets the bulb's status, toggles the enabled state of both buttons, and causes the panel with the image to repaint itself.

Listing **6.34**

```
//********************************************************************
//  LightBulbControls.java       Java Foundations
//
//  Represents the control panel for the LightBulb program.
//********************************************************************

import javax.swing.*;
import java.awt.*;
import java.awt.event.*;

public class LightBulbControls extends JPanel
{
   private LightBulbPanel bulb;
   private JButton onButton, offButton;

   //-----------------------------------------------------------------
   //  Sets up the lightbulb control panel.
   //-----------------------------------------------------------------
   public LightBulbControls (LightBulbPanel bulbPanel)
   {
      bulb = bulbPanel;

      onButton = new JButton ("On");
      onButton.setEnabled (false);
      onButton.setMnemonic ('n');
      onButton.setToolTipText ("Turn it on!");
      onButton.addActionListener (new OnListener());

      offButton = new JButton ("Off");
      offButton.setEnabled (true);
      offButton.setMnemonic ('f');
      offButton.setToolTipText ("Turn it off!");
      offButton.addActionListener (new OffListener());

      setBackground (Color.black);
      add (onButton);
      add (offButton);
   }
```

Listing **6.34** continued

```
   //*****************************************************************
   //  Represents the listener for the On button.
   //*****************************************************************
   private class OnListener implements ActionListener
   {
      //--------------------------------------------------------------
      //  Turns the bulb on and repaints the bulb panel.
      //--------------------------------------------------------------
      public void actionPerformed (ActionEvent event)
      {
         bulb.setOn (true);
         onButton.setEnabled (false);
         offButton.setEnabled (true);
         bulb.repaint();
      }
   }

   //*****************************************************************
   //  Represents the listener for the Off button.
   //*****************************************************************
   private class OffListener implements ActionListener
   {
      //--------------------------------------------------------------
      //  Turns the bulb off and repaints the bulb panel.
      //--------------------------------------------------------------
      public void actionPerformed (ActionEvent event)
      {
         bulb.setOn (false);
         onButton.setEnabled (true);
         offButton.setEnabled (false);
         bulb.repaint();
      }
   }
}
```

Note that the mnemonic characters used for each button are underlined in the display. When you run the program, you'll see that the tool tips automatically include an indication of the mnemonic that can be used for the button.

6.7 GUI Design

As we focus on the details that allow us to create GUIs, we may sometimes lose sight of the big picture. We should always keep in mind that our goal is to solve a problem—to create software that is truly useful. Knowing the details of components, events, and other language elements gives us the tools to put GUIs together, but we must guide that knowledge with the following fundamental ideas of good GUI design:

- Know the user.
- Prevent user errors.
- Optimize user abilities.
- Be consistent.

The design of any GUI should adhere to basic guidelines regarding consistency and usability.

The software designer must understand the user's needs and potential activities in order to develop an interface that will serve that user well. Keep in mind that, to the user, the interface is the software. It is the only way the user interacts with the system. As such, the interface must satisfy the user's needs.

Whenever possible, we should design interfaces so that the user can make as few mistakes as possible. In many situations, we have the flexibility to choose one of several components to accomplish a specific task. We should always try to choose components that will prevent inappropriate actions and avoid invalid input. For example, if an input value must be one of a set of particular values, we should use components that allow the user to make only a valid choice. That is, constraining the user to a few valid choices with, for instance, a set of radio buttons is better than allowing the user to type arbitrary and possibly invalid data into a text field. We covered additional components appropriate for specific situations in this chapter.

Not all users are alike. Some are more adept than others at using a particular GUI or GUI components in general. We shouldn't design with only the lowest common denominator in mind. For example, we should provide shortcuts whenever reasonable. That is, in addition to a normal series of actions that will allow a user to accomplish a task, we should also provide redundant ways to accomplish the same task. Using keyboard shortcuts (mnemonics) is a good example. Sometimes these additional mechanisms are less intuitive, but they may be faster for the experienced user.

Finally, consistency is important when dealing with large systems or multiple systems in a common environment. Users become familiar with a particular organization or color scheme; these should not be changed arbitrarily.

Summary of Key Concepts

- A GUI is made up of components, events that represent user actions, and listeners that respond to those events.
- A frame is displayed as a separate window, but a panel can only be displayed as part of another container.
- Listeners are often defined as inner classes because of the intimate relationship between the listener and the GUI components.
- Radio buttons operate as a group, providing a set of mutually exclusive options.
- A slider lets the user specify a numeric value within a bounded range.
- A combo box provides a drop down menu of options.
- A timer generates action events at regular intervals and can be used to control an animation.
- Every container is managed by a layout manager, which determines how components are visually presented.
- When changes occur, the components in a container reorganize themselves according to the layout manager's policy.
- The layout manager for each container can be explicitly set.
- A GUI's appearance is a function of the containment hierarchy and the layout managers of each container.
- Moving the mouse and clicking the mouse button generate events to which a program can respond.
- A listener may have to provide empty method definitions for unheeded events to satisfy the interface.
- Rubberbanding is the graphical effect caused when a shape seems to expand as the mouse is dragged.
- Key events allow a program to respond immediately to the user pressing keyboard keys.
- A listener class can be created by deriving it from an event adapter class.
- A file chooser allows the user to browse a disk and select a file to be processed.
- A color chooser allows the user to select a color from a palette or using RGB values.

- Borders can be applied to components to group objects and focus attention.
- Components should be disabled when their use is inappropriate.
- The design of any GUI should adhere to basic guidelines regarding consistency and usability.

Self-Review Questions

SR 6.1 What three elements are needed in any Java GUI?

SR 6.2 What is the difference between a frame and a panel?

SR 6.3 What is the relationship between an event and a listener?

SR 6.4 Can we add any kind of listener to any component? Explain.

SR 6.5 What type of event does a push button generate? A text field? A check box?

SR 6.6 Compare and contrast check boxes and radio buttons.

SR 6.7 When would you use a slider?

SR 6.8 What does a `Timer` object do?

SR 6.9 When is a layout manager consulted?

SR 6.10 How does the flow layout manager behave?

SR 6.11 Describe the areas of a border layout.

SR 6.12 What effect does a glue component in a box layout have?

SR 6.13 What is the containment hierarchy for a GUI?

SR 6.14 What is a mouse event?

SR 6.15 What is a key event?

SR 6.16 What is an event adapter class?

SR 6.17 What is a dialog box?

SR 6.18 What is a file chooser? A color chooser?

SR 6.19 What is the role of the `BorderFactory` class?

SR 6.20 What is tool tip?

SR 6.21 When should a component be disabled?

Exercises

EX 6.1 Explain how two components can be set up to share the same listener. How can the listener tell which component generated the event?

EX 6.2 Explain how one component can use two separate listeners at the same time. Give an example.

EX 6.3 Explain what would happen if the radio buttons used in the `QuoteOptions` program were not organized into a `ButtonGroup` object. Modify the program to test your answer.

EX 6.4 Why, in the `SlideColor` program, is the value of a slider able to reach 255 but the largest labeled tick mark is 250?

EX 6.5 What are the two main factors that affect how smooth the animation is in the `Rebound` program? Explain how changing either would affect it.

EX 6.6 What visual effect would result by changing the horizontal and vertical gaps on the border layout used in the `LayoutDemo` program? Make the change to test your answer.

EX 6.7 What would happen if, in the `Coordinates` program, we did not provide empty definitions for one or more of the unused mouse events?

EX 6.8 The `Coordinates` program listens for a mouse pressed event to draw a dot. How would the program behave differently if it listened for a mouse released event instead? A mouse clicked event?

EX 6.9 What would happen if the call to `super.paintComponent` were removed from the `paintComponent` method of the `CoordinatesPanel` class? Remove it and run the program to test your answer.

EX 6.10 What would happen if the call to `super.paintComponent` were removed from the `paintComponent` method of the `RubberLinesPanel` class? Remove it and run the program to test your answer. In what ways is the answer different from the answer to exercise 6.9.

EX 6.11 Write the lines of code that will define a compound border using three borders. Use a line border on the inner edge, an etched border on the outer edge, and a raised bevel border in between.

EX 6.12 Draw a UML class diagram that shows the relationships among the classes used in the `PushCounter` program.

EX 6.13 Draw a UML class diagram that shows the relationships among the classes used in the `Fahrenheit` program.

EX 6.14 Draw a UML class diagram that shows the relationships among the classes used in the `LayoutDemo` program.

EX 6.15 Create a UML class diagram for the `Direction` program.

Programming Projects

PP 6.1 Design and implement an application that displays a button and a label. Every time the button is pushed, the label should display a random number between 1 and 100, inclusive.

PP 6.2 Design and implement an application that presents two buttons and a label to the user. Label the buttons Increment and Decrement, respectively. Display a numeric value (initially 50) using the label. Each time the Increment button is pushed, increment the value displayed. Likewise, each time the Decrement button is pressed, decrement the value displayed. Create two separate listener classes for the two buttons.

PP 6.3 Modify your solution to programming project 6.2 so that it uses only one listener for both buttons.

PP 6.4 Modify the `Fahrenheit` program so that it displays a button that, when pressed, causes the conversion calculation to take place. That is, your modification will give the user the option of pressing Enter in the text field or pressing the button. Have the listener that is already defined for the text field also listen for the button push.

PP 6.5 Modify the `Direction` program so that the image is not allowed to move out of the visible area of the panel. Ignore any key event that would cause that to happen.

PP 6.6 Modify the `Direction` program so that, in addition to responding to the arrow keys, it also responds to four other keys that cause the image to move in diagonal directions.

When the T key is pressed, move the image up and to the left. Likewise, use U to move up and right, G to move down and left, and J to move down and right. Do not move the image if it has reached a window boundary.

PP 6.7 Design and implement an application that draws a traffic light and uses a push button to change the state of the light. Derive the drawing surface from the `JPanel` class and use another panel to organize the drawing surface and the button.

PP 6.8 Develop an application that implements a prototype user interface for composing an email message. The application should have text fields for the To, CC, and Bcc address lists and subject line, and one for the message body. Include a button labeled Send. When the Send button is pushed, the program should print the contents of all fields to standard output using `println` statements.

PP 6.9 Design and implement an application that uses dialog boxes to obtain two integer values (one dialog box for each value) and display the sum and product of the values. Use another dialog box to see whether the user wants to process another pair of values.

PP 6.10 Design and implement a program whose background changes color depending on where the mouse pointer is located. If the mouse pointer is on the left half of the program window, display red; if it is on the right half, display green.

PP 6.11 Design and implement an application that serves as a mouse odometer, continually displaying how far, in pixels, the mouse has moved (while over the program window). Display the current odometer value using a label. *Hint:* Compare the current position of the mouse to the last position and use the distance formula to determine how far the mouse has traveled.

PP 6.12 Design and implement an application that draws a circle using a rubberbanding technique. The circle size is determined by a mouse drag. Use the original mouse click location as a fixed center point. *Hint:* Compute the distance between the mouse pointer and the center point to determine the current radius of the circle.

PP 6.13 Modify the `StyleOptions` program to allow the user to specify the size of the font. Use a text field to obtain the size.

PP 6.14 Modify your solution to programming project 6.13 such that it uses a slider to obtain the font size.

PP 6.15 Develop a simple tool for calculating basic statistics for a segment of text. The application should have a single window with a scrolling text box (a `JTextArea`) and a stats box. The stats box should be a panel with a titled border, containing labeled fields that display the number of words in the text box and the average word length, as well as any other statistics that you would like to add. The stats box should also contain a button that, when pressed, re-computes the statistics for the current contents of the text field.

PP 6.16 Modify the `Rebound` program from this chapter such that when the mouse button is clicked on the program window the animation stops, and when it is clicked again the animation resumes.

PP 6.17 Design and implement a program that uses a `JColorChooser` object to obtain a color from the user and display that color as the background of the primary program window. Use a dialog box to determine if the user wants to display another color, and if so, redisplay the color chooser.

PP 6.18 Modify the `JukeBox` program so that the Play and Stop button functionality can also be controlled using keyboard mnemonics.

PP 6.19 Modify the `Coordinates` program so that it creates its listener by extending an adapter class instead of implementing an interface.

PP 6.20 Design and implement an application that displays an animation of a car (side view) moving across the screen from left to right. Create a `Car` class that represents the car.

PP 6.21 Design and implement an application that plays a game called Catch-the-Creature. Use an image to represent the creature. Have the creature appear at a random location for a random duration, then disappear and reappear somewhere else. The goal is to "catch" the creature by pressing the mouse button while the mouse pointer is on the creature image. Create a separate class to represent the creature, and include in it a method that determines if the location of the mouse click corresponds to the current location of the creature. Display a count of the number of times the creature is caught.

PP 6.22 Design and implement an application that works as a stopwatch. Include a display that shows the time (in seconds) as it increments. Include buttons that allow the user to start and stop the time, and reset the display to zero. Arrange the components to present a nice interface.

Answers to Self-Review Questions

SR 6.1 A GUI in a Java program is made up of on-screen components, events that those components generate, and listeners that respond to events when they occur.

SR 6.2 Both a frame and a panel are containers that can hold GUI elements. However, a frame is displayed as a separate window with a title bar, whereas a panel cannot be displayed on its own. A panel is often displayed inside a frame.

SR 6.3 Events usually represent user actions. A listener object is set up to listen for a certain event to be generated from a particular component. The relationship between a particular component that generates an event and the listener that responds to that event is set up explicitly.

SR 6.4 No, we cannot add any listener to any component. Each component generates a certain set of events, and only listeners of those types can be added to the component.

SR 6.5 Both push buttons and text fields generate action events. A check box generates an item state changed event.

SR 6.6 Both check boxes and radio buttons show a toggled state: either on or off. However, radio buttons work as a group in which only one can be toggled on at any point in time. Check boxes, on the other hand, represent independent options. They can be used alone or in a set in which any combination of toggled states is valid.

SR 6.7 A slider is useful when the user needs to specify a numeric value within specific bounds. Using a slider to get this input, as opposed to a text field or some other component, minimizes user error.

SR 6.8 An object created from the `Timer` class produces an action event at regular intervals. It can be used to control the speed of an animation.

SR 6.9 A layout manager is consulted whenever the visual appearance of its components might be affected, such as when the container is resized or when a new component is added to the container.

SR 6.10 Flow layout attempts to put as many components on a row as possible. Multiple rows are created as needed.

SR 6.11 Border layout is divided into five areas: North, South, East, West, and Center. The North and South areas are at the top and bottom of the container, respectively, and span the entire width of the container. Sandwiched between them, from left to right, are the West, Center, and East areas. Any unused area takes up no space, and the others fill in as needed.

SR 6.12 A glue component in a box layout dictates where any extra space in the layout should go. It expands as necessary, but takes up no space if there is no extra space to distribute.

SR 6.13 The containment hierarchy of a GUI is created by nested containers. The way the containers are nested, and the layout managers that those containers employ, dictate the details of the visual presentation of the GUI.

SR 6.14 A mouse event is an event generated when the user manipulates the mouse in various ways. There are several types of mouse events that may be of interest in a particular situation, including the mouse being moved, a mouse button being pressed, the mouse entering a particular component, and the mouse being dragged.

SR 6.15 A key event is generated when a keyboard key is pressed, which allows a listening program to respond immediately to the user input. The object representing the event holds a code that specifies which key was pressed.

SR 6.16 An event adapter class is a class that implements a listener interface, providing empty definitions for all of its methods. A listener class can be created by extending the appropriate adapter class and only defining the methods of interest.

SR 6.17 A dialog box is a small window that appears for the purpose of conveying information, confirming an action, or accepting input. Generally, dialog boxes are used in specific situations for brief user interactions.

SR 6.18 A file chooser and a color chooser are specialized dialog boxes that allow the user to select a file from disk or a color, respectively.

SR 6.19 The `BorderFactory` class contains several methods used to create borders that can be applied to components.

SR 6.20 A tool tip is a small amount of text that appears when the mouse cursor is allowed to rest over a specific component. Tool tips are used to explain, briefly, the purpose of a component.

SR 6.21 GUI components should be disabled when their use is inappropriate. This helps guide the user to proper actions and minimizes error handling and special cases.

Chapter Objectives

- Define and use arrays for basic data organization.
- Discuss bounds checking and techniques for managing capacity.
- Discuss the issues related to arrays as objects and arrays of objects.
- Explore the use of command-line arguments.
- Describe the syntax and use of variable-length parameter lists.
- Discuss the creation and use of multidimensional arrays.

7

Arrays

When designing programs, we often want to organize objects or primitive data in a form that is easy to access and modify. This chapter introduces arrays, which are programming constructs that group data into lists. Arrays are a fundamental component of most high-level languages, and a useful tool in creating problem solutions.

7.1 Array Elements

An *array* is a simple but powerful programming language construct used to group and organize data. When writing a program that manages a large amount of information, such as a list of 100 names, it is not practical to declare separate variables for each piece of data. Arrays solve this problem by letting us declare one variable that can hold multiple, individually accessible values.

An array is a list of values. Each value is stored at a specific, numbered position in the array. The number corresponding to each position is called an *index* or a *subscript*. Figure 7.1 shows an array of integers and the indexes that correspond to each position. The array is called `height`; it contains integers that represent several peoples' heights in inches.

In Java, array indexes always begin at zero. Therefore the value stored at index 5 is actually the sixth value in the array. The array shown in Figure 7.1 has 11 values, indexed from 0 to 10.

An array of size *N* is indexed from 0 to *N*–1.

To access a value in an array, we use the name of the array followed by the index in square brackets. For example, the following expression refers to the ninth value in the array `height`:

```
height[8]
```

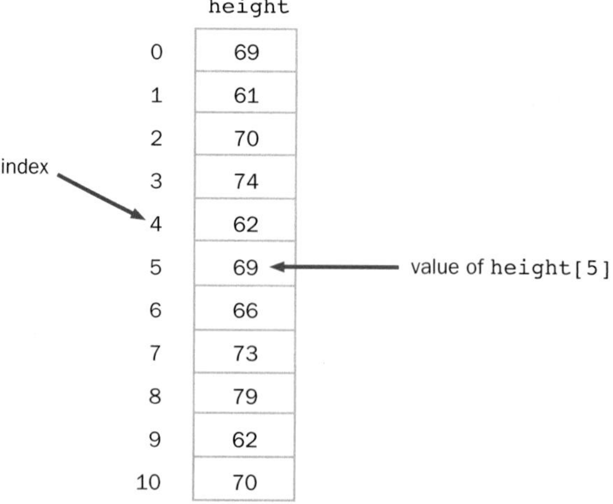

FIGURE 7.1 An array called `height` containing integer values

According to Figure 7.1, height[8] (pronounced height-sub-eight) contains the value 79. Don't confuse the value of the index, in this case 8, with the value stored in the array at that index, in this case 79.

The expression height[8] refers to a single integer stored at a particular memory location. It can be used wherever an integer variable can be used. Therefore you can assign a value to it, use it in calculations, print its value, and so on. Furthermore, because array indexes are integers, you can use integer expressions to specify the index used to access an array. These concepts are demonstrated in the following lines of code:

```
height[2] = 72;
height[count] = feet * 12;
average = (height[0] + height[1] + height[2]) / 3;
System.out.println ("The middle value is " + height[MAX/2]);
pick = height[rand.nextInt(11)];
```

7.2 Declaring and Using Arrays

In Java, arrays are objects. To create an array, the reference to the array must be declared. The array can then be instantiated using the new operator, which allocates memory space to store values. The following code represents the declaration for the array shown in Figure 7.1:

In Java, an array is an object that must be instantiated.

```
int[] height = new int[11];
```

The variable height is declared to be an array of integers whose type is written as int[]. All values stored in an array have the same type (or are at least compatible). For example, we can create an array that can hold integers or an array that can hold strings, but not an array that can hold both integers and strings. An array can be set up to hold any primitive type or any object (class) type. A value stored in an array is sometimes called an *array element*, and the type of values that an array holds is called the *element type* of the array.

Note that the type of the array variable (int[]) does not include the size of the array. The instantiation of height, using the new operator, reserves the memory space to store 11 integers indexed from 0 to 10. Once an array object is instantiated to be a certain size, the number of values it can hold cannot be changed. A reference variable such as height, declared to hold an array of integers, can refer to an array of any size. And like any other reference variable, the object (that is, the array) that height refers to can change over time.

The example shown in Listing 7.1 creates an array called `list` that can hold 15 integers, which it loads with successive increments of 10. It then changes the value of the sixth element in the array (at index 5). Finally, it prints all values stored in the array.

Figure 7.2 shows the array as it changes during the execution of the `BasicArray` program. It is often convenient to use `for` loops when handling arrays because the number of positions in the array is constant. Note that a constant called `LIMIT` is used in several places in the `BasicArray` program. This constant is used to declare the size of the array and to control the `for` loop that initializes the array values.

The iterator version of the `for` loop is used to print the values in the array. Recall from Chapter 4 that this version of the `for` loop extracts each value in the specified iterator. Every Java array is an iterator, so this type of loop can be used whenever we want to process every element stored in an array.

The square brackets used to indicate the index of an array are treated as an operator in Java. Therefore, just like the + operator or the <= operator, the *index operator* (`[ ]`) has a precedence relative to the other Java operators that determines when it is executed. It has the highest precedence of all Java operators.

Index	The array is created with 15 elements, indexed from 0 to 14	After three iterations of the first loop	After completing the first loop	After changing the value of `list[5]`
0		0	0	0
1		10	10	10
2		20	20	20
3			30	30
4			40	40
5			50	999
6			60	60
7			70	70
8			80	80
9			90	90
10			100	100
11			110	110
12			120	120
13			130	130
14			140	140

FIGURE 7.2 The array `list` as it changes in the `BasicArray` program

Listing **7.1**

```
//********************************************************************
//  BasicArray.java       Java Foundations
//
//  Demonstrates basic array declaration and use.
//********************************************************************

public class BasicArray
{
   //-----------------------------------------------------------------
   //  Creates an array, fills it with various integer values,
   //  modifies one value, then prints them out.
   //-----------------------------------------------------------------
   public static void main (String[] args)
   {
      final int LIMIT = 15, MULTIPLE = 10;

      int[] list = new int[LIMIT];

      //  Initialize the array values
      for (int index = 0; index < LIMIT; index++)
         list[index] = index * MULTIPLE;

      list[5] = 999;  // change one array value

      //  Print the array values
      for (int value : list)
         System.out.print (value + "  ");
   }
}
```

Output

```
0  10  20  30  40  999  60  70  80  90  100  110  120  130  140
```

Bounds Checking

The index operator performs automatic *bounds checking*, which ensures that the index is in range for the array being referenced. Whenever a reference to an array element is made, the index must be greater than or equal to zero and less than the size of the array. For example, suppose an array called `prices` is created with 25 elements. The valid indexes for the array are from 0 to 24. Whenever a reference is made to a particular element in the array (such as `prices[count]`), the value of the index is checked. If it is in the valid range of indexes for the array (0 to 24), the reference is carried out. If the index is not valid, an exception called `ArrayIndexOutOfBoundsException` is thrown.

Bounds checking ensures that an index used to refer to an array element is in range.

In most cases, we'll want to perform our own bounds checking. That is, we'll want to be careful to remain within the bounds of the array when making references. (The alternative is to be prepared to handle the exception when it is thrown; exception handling is discussed in Chapter 10).

Because array indexes begin at zero and go up to one less than the size of the array, it is easy to create *off-by-one errors* in a program, which are problems created by processing all but one element or by attempting to index one element too many.

One way to check for the bounds of an array is to use the `length` constant, which is an attribute of the array object and holds the size of the array. It is a public constant and therefore can be referenced directly. For example, after the array `prices` is created with 25 elements, the constant `prices.length` contains the value 25. Its value is set once when the array is first created and cannot be changed. The `length` constant, which is an integral part of each array, can be used when the array size is needed without having to create a separate constant. Remember that the length of the array is the number of elements it can hold, and thus the maximum index of an array is `length-1`.

Let's look at another example. The program shown in Listing 7.2 reads 10 integers into an array called `numbers`, and then prints them in reverse order.

Listing 7.2

```
//********************************************************************
//  ReverseOrder.java        Java Foundations
//
//  Demonstrates array index processing.
//********************************************************************

import java.util.Scanner;

public class ReverseOrder
```

Listing **7.2** continued

```
{
   //-----------------------------------------------------------------
   //  Reads a list of numbers from the user, storing them in an
   //  array, then prints them in the opposite order.
   //-----------------------------------------------------------------
   public static void main (String[] args)
   {
      Scanner scan = new Scanner (System.in);

      double[] numbers = new double[10];

      System.out.println ("The size of the array: " + numbers.length);

      for (int index = 0; index < numbers.length; index++)
      {
         System.out.print ("Enter number " + (index+1) + ": ");
         numbers[index] = scan.nextDouble();
      }

      System.out.println ("The numbers in reverse order:");

      for (int index = numbers.length-1; index >= 0; index--)
         System.out.print (numbers[index] + "  ");
   }
}
```

Output

```
The size of the array: 10
Enter number 1: 18.51
Enter number 2: 69.9
Enter number 3: 41.28
Enter number 4: 72.003
Enter number 5: 34.35
Enter number 6: 140.71
Enter number 7: 9.60
Enter number 8: 24.45
Enter number 9: 99.30
Enter number 10: 61.08
The numbers in reverse order:
61.08  99.3  24.45  9.6  140.71  34.35  72.003  41.28  69.9  18.51
```

Note that in the `ReverseOrder` program, the array `numbers` is declared to have 10 elements and therefore is indexed from 0 to 9. The index range is controlled in the `for` loops by using the `length` field of the array object. You should carefully set the initial value of loop control variables and the conditions that terminate loops to guarantee that all intended elements are processed and only valid indexes are used to reference an array element.

The `LetterCount` example, shown in Listing 7.3, uses two arrays and a `String` object. The array called `upper` is used to store the number of times each uppercase alphabetic letter is found in the string. The array called `lower` serves the same purpose for lowercase letters.

Listing 7.3

```
//********************************************************************
//  LetterCount.java       Java Foundations
//
//  Demonstrates the relationship between arrays and strings.
//********************************************************************

import java.util.Scanner;

public class LetterCount
{
   //-----------------------------------------------------------------
   //  Reads a sentence from the user and counts the number of
   //  uppercase and lowercase letters contained in it.
   //-----------------------------------------------------------------
   public static void main (String[] args)
   {
      final int NUMCHARS = 26;

      Scanner scan = new Scanner (System.in);

      int[] upper = new int[NUMCHARS];
      int[] lower = new int[NUMCHARS];

      char current;   // the current character being processed
      int other = 0;  // counter for non-alphabetics

      System.out.println ("Enter a sentence:");
      String line = scan.nextLine();
```

Listing **7.3** continued

```
      //  Count the number of each letter occurrence
      for (int ch = 0; ch < line.length(); ch++)
      {
         current = line.charAt(ch);
         if (current >= 'A' && current <= 'Z')
            upper[current-'A']++;
         else
            if (current >= 'a' && current <= 'z')
               lower[current-'a']++;
            else
               other++;
      }

      //  Print the results
      System.out.println ();
      for (int letter=0; letter < upper.length; letter++)
      {
         System.out.print ( (char) (letter + 'A') );
         System.out.print (": " + upper[letter]);
         System.out.print ("\t\t" + (char) (letter + 'a') );
         System.out.println (": " + lower[letter]);
      }

      System.out.println ();
      System.out.println ("Non-alphabetic characters: " + other);
   }
}
```

Output

```
Enter a sentence:
In Casablanca, Humphrey Bogart never says "Play it again, Sam."

A: 0          a: 10
B: 1          b: 1
C: 1          c: 1
D: 0          d: 0
E: 0          e: 3
F: 0          f: 0
G: 0          g: 2
H: 1          h: 1
I: 1          i: 2
```

Listing 7.3 continued

```
J: 0          j: 0
K: 0          k: 0
L: 0          l: 2
M: 0          m: 2
N: 0          n: 4
O: 0          o: 1
P: 1          p: 1
Q: 0          q: 0
R: 0          r: 3
S: 1          s: 3
T: 0          t: 2
U: 0          u: 1
V: 0          v: 1
W: 0          w: 0
X: 0          x: 0
Y: 0          y: 3
Z: 0          z: 0

Non-alphabetic characters: 14
```

Because there are 26 letters in the English alphabet, both the `upper` and `lower` arrays are declared with 26 elements. Each element contains an integer that is initially zero by default. These values serve as counters for each alphabetic character encountered in the input. The `for` loop scans through the string one character at a time. The appropriate counter in the appropriate array is incremented for each character found in the string.

Both of the counter arrays are indexed from 0 to 25. So we have to map each character to a counter. A logical way to do this is to use `upper[0]` to count the number of `'A'` characters found, `upper[1]` to count the number of `'B'` characters found, and so on. Likewise, `lower[0]` is used to count `'a'` characters, `lower[1]` is used to count `'b'` characters, and so on. A separate variable called `other` is used to count any nonalphabetic characters that are encountered.

Note that to determine if a character is an uppercase letter, we used the boolean expression (`current >= 'A' && current <= 'Z'`). A similar expression is used for determining the lowercase letters. We could have used the static methods `isUpperCase` and `isLowerCase` in the `Character` class to make these determinations, but we didn't in this example to drive home the point that each character has a specific numeric value and order that we can use in our programming, based on the Unicode character set.

We use the `current` character to calculate which index in the array to reference. We have to be careful when calculating an index to ensure that it remains within the bounds of the array and matches to the correct element. Remember that in the Unicode character set the uppercase and lowercase alphabetic letters are continuous and in order (see Appendix C). Therefore, taking the numeric value of an uppercase letter such as `'E'` (which is 69) and subtracting the numeric value of the character `'A'` (which is 65) yields 4, which is the correct index for the counter of the character `'E'`. Note that nowhere in the program do we actually need to know the specific numeric values for each letter.

Alternate Array Syntax

Syntactically, there are two ways to declare an array reference in Java. The first technique, which is used in the previous examples and throughout this text, is to associate the brackets with the type of values stored in the array. The second technique is to associate the brackets with the name of the array. Therefore the following two declarations are equivalent:

```
int[] grades;
int grades[];
```

Although there is no difference between these declaration techniques as far as the compiler is concerned, the first is consistent with other types of declarations. The declared type is explicit if the array brackets are associated with the element type, especially if there are multiple variables declared on the same line. Therefore we associate the brackets with the element type throughout this text.

Initializer Lists

You can use an *initializer list* to instantiate an array and provide the initial values for the elements of the array. This is essentially the same idea as initializing a variable of a primitive data type in its declaration, except that the initial value for an array contains multiple values.

The items in an initializer list are separated by commas and delimited by braces (`{}`). When an initializer list is used, the `new` operator is not used. The size of the array is determined by the number of items in the initializer list. For example, the following declaration instantiates the array `scores` as an array of eight integers, indexed from 0 to 7 with the specified initial values:

```
int[] scores = {87, 98, 69, 87, 65, 76, 99, 83};
```

An initializer list can be used to instantiate an array object instead of using the `new` operator.

An initializer list can be used only when an array is first declared.

The type of each value in an initializer list must match the type of the array elements. Let's look at another example:

```
char[] vowels = {'A', 'E', 'I', 'O', 'U'};
```

In this case, the variable `vowels` is declared to be an array of five characters, and the initializer list contains character literals.

The program shown in Listing 7.4 demonstrates the use of an initializer list to instantiate an array.

Arrays as Parameters

An entire array can be passed as a parameter to a method. Because an array is an object, when an entire array is passed as a parameter, a copy of the reference to the original array is passed. We discussed this issue as it applies to all objects in Chapter 5.

An entire array can be passed as a parameter, making the formal parameter an alias of the original.

A method that receives an array as a parameter can permanently change an element of the array because it is referring to the original element value. However, the method cannot permanently change the reference to the array itself because a copy of the original reference is sent to the method. These rules are consistent with the rules that govern any object type.

An element of an array can be passed to a method as well. If the element type is a primitive type, a copy of the value is passed. If that element is a reference to an object, a copy of the object reference is passed. As always, the impact of changes made to a parameter inside the method depends on the type of the parameter. We discuss arrays of objects further in the next section.

Listing 7.4

```
//********************************************************************
//  Primes.java       Java Foundations
//
//  Demonstrates the use of an initializer list for an array.
//********************************************************************

public class Primes
{
   //-----------------------------------------------------------------
   //  Stores some prime numbers in an array and prints them.
   //-----------------------------------------------------------------
   public static void main (String[] args)
   {
      int[] primeNums = {2, 3, 5, 7, 11, 13, 17, 19};

      System.out.println ("Array length: " + primeNums.length);

      System.out.println ("The first few prime numbers are:");

      for (int prime : primeNums)
         System.out.print (prime + "  ");
   }
}
```

Output

```
Array length: 8
The first few prime numbers are:
2  3  5  7  11  13  17  19
```

7.3 Arrays of Objects

In the previous examples in this chapter, we used arrays to store primitive types such as integers and characters. Arrays can also store references to objects as elements. Fairly complex information management structures can be created using only arrays and other objects. For example, an array could contain objects, and each of those objects could consist of several variables and the methods that use them. Those variables could themselves be arrays, and so on. The design of a program should capitalize on the ability to combine these constructs to create the most appropriate representation for the information.

Keep in mind that an array is an object. So if we have an array of `int` values called `weight`, we are actually dealing with an object reference variable that holds the address of the array, which can be depicted as follows:

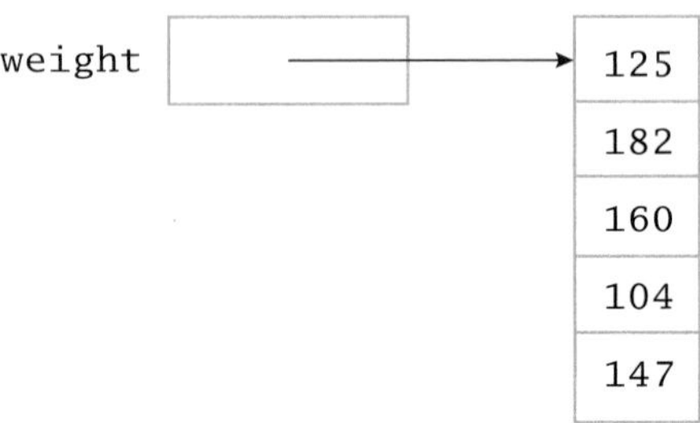

Furthermore, when we store objects in an array, each element is a separate object. That is, an array of objects is really an array of object references. Consider the following declaration:

```
String[] words = new String[5];
```

Instantiating an array of objects reserves room to store references only. The objects that are stored in each element must be instantiated separately.

The array `words` holds references to `String` objects. The `new` operator in the declaration instantiates the array object and reserves space for five `String` references. But this declaration does not create any `String` objects; it merely creates an array that holds references to `String` objects. Initially, the array looks like this:

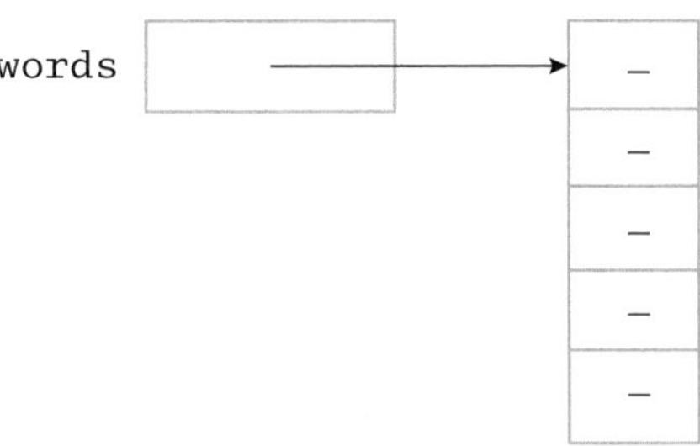

After a few String objects are created and put in the array, it might look like this:

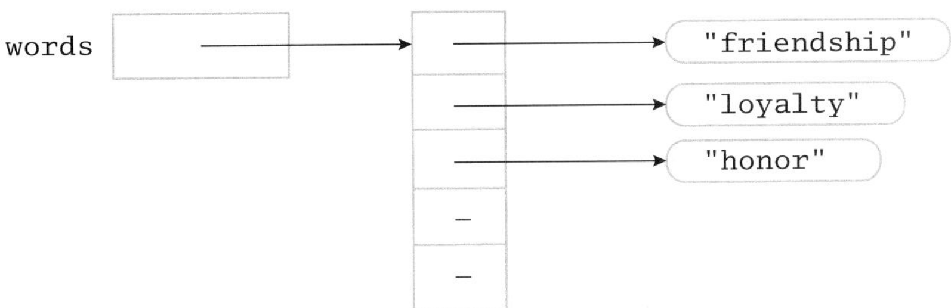

The words array is an object, and each character string it holds is its own object. Each object contained in an array has to be instantiated separately.

Keep in mind that String objects can be represented as string literals. So the following declaration creates an array called verbs and uses an initializer list to populate it with several String objects, each instantiated using a string literal:

```
String[] verbs = {"play", "work", "eat", "sleep"};
```

The program called GradeRange shown in Listing 7.5 creates an array of Grade objects, and then prints them. The Grade objects are created using several new operators in the initialization list of the array.

The Grade class is shown in Listing 7.6. Each Grade object represents a letter grade for a school course and includes a numerical lower bound. The values for the grade name and lower bound can be set using the Grade constructor, or using appropriate mutator methods. Accessor methods are also defined, as is a toString method to return a string representation of the grade. The toString method is automatically invoked when the grades are printed in the main method.

Let's look at another example. Listing 7.7 shows the Tunes class, which contains a main method that creates, modifies, and examines a compact disc (CD) collection. Each CD added to the collection is specified by its title, artist, purchase price, and number of tracks.

Listing 7.8 shows the CDCollection class. It contains an array of CD objects representing the collection. It maintains a count of the CDs in the collection and their combined value. It also keeps track of the current size of the collection array so that a larger array can be created if too many CDs are added to the collection. The CD class is shown in Listing 7.9.

Listing 7.5

```
//********************************************************************
//  GradeRange.java       Java Foundations
//
//  Demonstrates the use of an array of objects.
//********************************************************************

public class GradeRange
{
   //-----------------------------------------------------------------
   //  Creates an array of Grade objects and prints them.
   //-----------------------------------------------------------------
   public static void main (String[] args)
   {
      Grade[] grades =
      {
         new Grade("A", 95), new Grade("A-", 90),
         new Grade("B+", 87), new Grade("B", 85), new Grade("B-", 80),
         new Grade("C+", 77), new Grade("C", 75), new Grade("C-", 70),
         new Grade("D+", 67), new Grade("D", 65), new Grade("D-", 60),
         new Grade("F", 0)
      };

      for (Grade letterGrade : grades)
         System.out.println (letterGrade);
   }
}
```

Output

```
A       95
A-      90
B+      87
B       85
B-      80
C+      77
C       75
C-      70
D+      67
D       65
D-      60
F       0
```

Listing 7.6

```
//********************************************************************
//  Grade.java       Java Foundations
//
//  Represents a school grade.
//********************************************************************

public class Grade
{
   private String name;
   private int lowerBound;

   //-----------------------------------------------------------------
   //  Constructor: Sets up this Grade object with the specified
   //  grade name and numeric lower bound.
   //-----------------------------------------------------------------
   public Grade (String grade, int cutoff)
   {
      name = grade;
      lowerBound = cutoff;
   }

   //-----------------------------------------------------------------
   //  Returns a string representation of this grade.
   //-----------------------------------------------------------------
   public String toString()
   {
      return name + "\t" + lowerBound;
   }

   //-----------------------------------------------------------------
   //  Name mutator.
   //-----------------------------------------------------------------
   public void setName (String grade)
   {
      name = grade;
   }

   //-----------------------------------------------------------------
   //  Lower bound mutator.
   //-----------------------------------------------------------------
   public void setLowerBound (int cutoff)
   {
```

Listing **7.6** continued

```
      lowerBound = cutoff;
   }

   //-----------------------------------------------------------------
   //  Name accessor.
   //-----------------------------------------------------------------
   public String getName()
   {
      return name;
   }

   //-----------------------------------------------------------------
   //  Lower bound accessor.
   //-----------------------------------------------------------------
   public int getLowerBound()
   {
      return lowerBound;
   }
}
```

Listing **7.7**

```
//********************************************************************
//  Tunes.java       Java Foundations
//
//  Demonstrates the use of an array of objects.
//********************************************************************

public class Tunes
{
   //-----------------------------------------------------------------
   //  Creates a CDCollection object and adds some CDs to it. Prints
   //  reports on the status of the collection.
   //-----------------------------------------------------------------
   public static void main (String[] args)
   {
      CDCollection music = new CDCollection ();

      music.addCD ("Storm Front", "Billy Joel", 14.95, 10);
      music.addCD ("Come On Over", "Shania Twain", 14.95, 16);
```

Listing **7.7** continued

```
      music.addCD ("Soundtrack", "Les Miserables", 17.95, 33);
      music.addCD ("Graceland", "Paul Simon", 13.90, 11);

      System.out.println (music);

      music.addCD ("Double Live", "Garth Brooks", 19.99, 26);
      music.addCD ("Greatest Hits", "Jimmy Buffet", 15.95, 13);

      System.out.println (music);
   }
}
```

Output

```
~~~~~~~~~~~~~~~~~~~~~~~~~~~~~~~~~~~~~~~~~~~
My CD Collection

Number of CDs: 4
Total cost: $61.75
Average cost: $15.44

CD List:

$14.95   10      Storm Front       Billy Joel
$14.95   16      Come On Over      Shania Twain
$17.95   33      Soundtrack        Les Miserables
$13.90   11      Graceland         Paul Simon

~~~~~~~~~~~~~~~~~~~~~~~~~~~~~~~~~~~~~~~~~~~
My CD Collection

Number of CDs: 6
Total cost: $97.69
Average cost: $16.28

CD List:

$14.95   10      Storm Front       Billy Joel
$14.95   16      Come On Over      Shania Twain
$17.95   33      Soundtrack        Les Miserables
$13.90   11      Graceland         Paul Simon
$19.99   26      Double Live       Garth Brooks
$15.95   13      Greatest Hits     Jimmy Buffet
```

Listing **7.8**

```
//********************************************************************
//  CDCollection.java       Java Foundations
//
//  Represents a collection of compact discs.
//********************************************************************

import java.text.NumberFormat;

public class CDCollection
{
   private CD[] collection;
   private int count;
   private double totalCost;

   //-----------------------------------------------------------------
   //  Constructor: Creates an initially empty collection.
   //-----------------------------------------------------------------
   public CDCollection ()
   {
      collection = new CD[100];
      count = 0;
      totalCost = 0.0;
   }

   //-----------------------------------------------------------------
   //  Adds a CD to the collection, increasing the size of the
   //  collection if necessary.
   //-----------------------------------------------------------------
   public void addCD (String title, String artist, double cost,
                      int tracks)
   {
      if (count == collection.length)
         increaseSize();

      collection[count] = new CD (title, artist, cost, tracks);
      totalCost += cost;
      count++;
   }
```

Listing **7.8** continued

```
   //-----------------------------------------------------------------
   //  Returns a report describing the CD collection.
   //-----------------------------------------------------------------
   public String toString()
   {
      NumberFormat fmt = NumberFormat.getCurrencyInstance();

      String report = "~~~~~~~~~~~~~~~~~~~~~~~~~~~~~~~~~~~~~~~~~~~\n";
      report += "My CD Collection\n\n";

      report += "Number of CDs: " + count + "\n";
      report += "Total cost: " + fmt.format(totalCost) + "\n";
      report += "Average cost: " + fmt.format(totalCost/count);

      report += "\n\nCD List:\n\n";

      for (int cd = 0; cd < count; cd++)
         report += collection[cd].toString() + "\n";

      return report;
   }

   //-----------------------------------------------------------------
   //  Increases the capacity of the collection by creating a
   //  larger array and copying the existing collection into it.
   //-----------------------------------------------------------------
   private void increaseSize ()
   {
      CD[] temp = new CD[collection.length * 2];

      for (int cd = 0; cd < collection.length; cd++)
         temp[cd] = collection[cd];

      collection = temp;
   }
}
```

Listing **7.9**

```
//********************************************************************
//  CD.java       Java Foundations
//
//  Represents a compact disc.
//********************************************************************

import java.text.NumberFormat;

public class CD
{
   private String title, artist;
   private double cost;
   private int tracks;

   //-----------------------------------------------------------------
   //  Creates a new CD with the specified information.
   //-----------------------------------------------------------------
   public CD (String name, String singer, double price, int numTracks)
   {
      title = name;
      artist = singer;
      cost = price;
      tracks = numTracks;
   }

   //-----------------------------------------------------------------
   //  Returns a string description of this CD.
   //-----------------------------------------------------------------
   public String toString()
   {
      NumberFormat fmt = NumberFormat.getCurrencyInstance();

      String description;

      description = fmt.format(cost) + "\t" + tracks + "\t";
      description += title + "\t" + artist;

      return description;
   }
}
```

The `collection` array is instantiated in the `CDCollection` constructor. Every time a `CD` is added to the collection (using the `addCD` method), a new `CD` object is created and a reference to it is stored in the `collection` array.

Each time a CD is added to the collection, we check to see whether we have reached the current capacity of the `collection` array. If we didn't perform this check, an exception would eventually be thrown when we try to store a new `CD` object at an invalid index. If the current capacity has been reached, the private `increaseSize` method is invoked, which first creates an array that is twice as big as the current `collection` array. Each `CD` in the existing collection is then copied into the new array (that is, the references to the `CD` objects are copied). Finally, the `collection` reference is set to the larger array. Using this technique, we theoretically never run out of room in our `CD` collection. The user of the `CDCollection` object (the `main` method) never has to worry about running out of space because it's all handled internally.

Figure 7.3 shows a UML class diagram of the `Tunes` program. Recall that the open diamond indicates aggregation. The cardinality of the relationship is also noted: a `CDCollection` object contains zero or more `CD` objects.

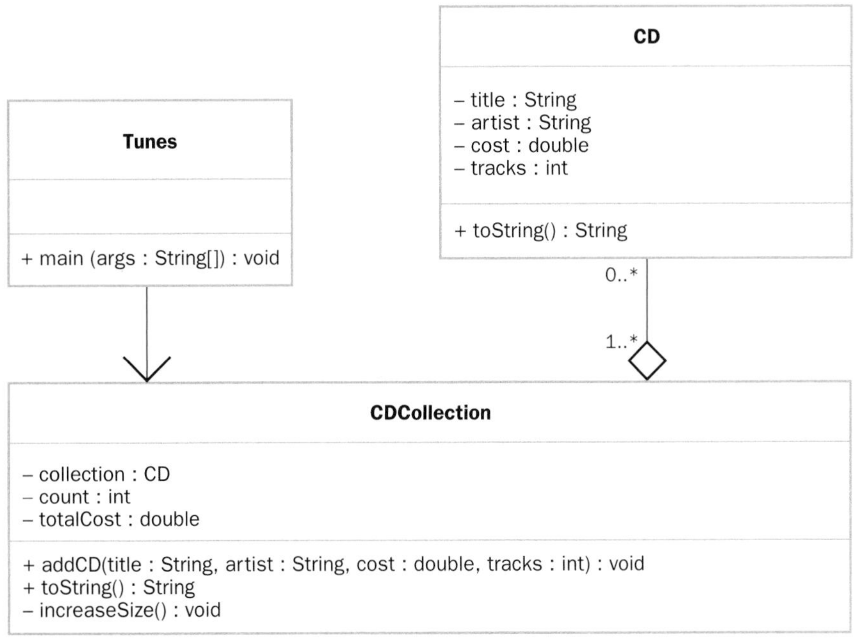

FIGURE 7.3 A UML class diagram of the `Tunes` program

The `toString` method of the `CDCollection` class returns an entire report summarizing the collection. The report is created, in part, using implicit calls to the `toString` method of each `CD` object stored in the collection.

7.4 Command-Line Arguments

The formal parameter to the `main` method of a Java application is always an array of `String` objects. We've ignored that parameter in previous examples, but now we can discuss how it might occasionally be useful.

Command-line arguments are stored in an array of `String` objects and are passed to the `main` method.

The Java run-time environment invokes the `main` method when an application is submitted to the interpreter. The `String[]` parameter, which we typically call `args`, represents *command-line arguments* that are provided when the interpreter is invoked. Any extra information on the command line when the interpreter is invoked is stored in the `args` array for use by the program. This technique is another way to provide input to a program.

The program shown in Listing 7.10 simply prints all of the command-line arguments provided when the program is submitted to the interpreter. Note that quotes can be used on the command line to delimit a multiword argument.

Remember that the parameter to the `main` method is always an array of `String` objects. If you want numeric information to be input as a command-line argument, the program has to convert it from its string representation.

When used, command-line arguments are typically reserved for information that tailors the way a program behaves. For example, you may provide the name of an input file as a command-line argument. Or perhaps you use an optional command-line argument that permits the user to specify a verbose or brief output format.

In program development environments that use a graphical user interface, a command line may not be the standard way to submit a program to the interpreter (that is, run the program). In such situations, command-line information can be specified in some other way. Consult the documentation for these specifics if necessary.

7.5 Variable-Length Parameter Lists

Suppose we wanted to design a method that processed a different amount of data from one invocation to the next. For example, let's design a method called

Listing 7.10

```
//********************************************************************
//  CommandLine.java       Java Foundations
//
//  Demonstrates the use of command line arguments.
//********************************************************************

public class CommandLine
{
   //-----------------------------------------------------------------
   //  Prints all of the command line arguments provided by the
   //  user.
   //-----------------------------------------------------------------
   public static void main (String[] args)
   {
      for (String arg : args)
         System.out.println (arg);
   }
}
```

Output

```
> java CommandLine one two "two and a half" three
one
two
two and a half
three
```

`average` that accepts a few integer values and returns their average. In one invocation of the method we might pass in three integers to average:

```
mean1 = average(42, 69, 37);
```

In another invocation of the same method we might pass in seven integers to average:

```
mean2 = average(35, 43, 93, 23, 40, 21, 75);
```

To accomplish this we could define overloaded versions of the `average` method (as we did in the exercises at the end of Chapter 5). But that solution doesn't scale to an arbitrary set of input values. It would require that we know the maximum number of parameters there might be and create a separate version of the method for each possibility.

A Java method can be defined to accept a varying number of parameters.

Alternatively, we could define the method to accept an array of integers, which could be of different sizes for each call. But that would require the calling method to package the integers into an array.

Java provides a way to define methods that accept variable-length parameter lists. By using some special syntax in the formal parameter list of the method, we can define the method to accept any number of parameters. The parameters are automatically put into an array for easy processing in the method. For example, the average method could be written as follows:

```
public double average (int ... list)
{
   double result = 0.0;

   if (list.length != 0)
   {
      int sum = 0;
      for (int num : list)
         sum += num;
      result = (double)sum / list.length;
   }

   return result;
}
```

Note the way the formal parameters are defined. The ellipsis (three periods in a row) indicates that the method accepts a variable number of parameters. In this case, the method accepts any number of int parameters, which it automatically puts into an array called list. In the method, we process the array normally.

We can now pass any number of int parameters to the average method, including none at all. That's why we check to see if the length of the array is zero before we compute the average.

The type of the multiple parameters can be any primitive or object type. For example, the following method accepts and prints multiple Grade objects (we defined the Grade class earlier in this chapter):

```
public void printGrades (Grade ... grades)
{
   for (Grade letterGrade : grades)
      System.out.println (letterGrade);
}
```

A method that accepts a variable number of parameters can also accept other parameters. For example, the following method accepts an `int`, a `String` object, and then a variable number of `double` values that will be stored in an array called `nums`:

```
public void test (int count, String name, double ... nums)
{
   // whatever
}
```

The varying parameters must come last in the formal arguments. A single method cannot accept two sets of varying parameters.

Constructors can also be set up to accept a varying number of parameters. The program shown in Listing 7.11 creates two `Family` objects, passing a varying number of strings (representing the family member names) into the `Family` constructor.

Listing 7.11

```
//********************************************************************
//  VariableParameters.java       Java Foundations
//
//  Demonstrates the use of a variable length parameter list.
//********************************************************************

public class VariableParameters
{
   //-----------------------------------------------------------------
   //  Creates two Family objects using a constructor that accepts
   //  a variable number of String objects as parameters.
   //-----------------------------------------------------------------
   public static void main (String[] args)
   {
      Family lewis = new Family ("John", "Sharon", "Justin", "Kayla",
         "Nathan", "Samantha");

      Family camden = new Family ("Stephen", "Annie", "Matt", "Mary",
         "Simon", "Lucy", "Ruthie", "Sam", "David");

      System.out.println(lewis);
      System.out.println();
      System.out.println(camden);
   }
}
```

Listing **7.11** continued

Output

```
John
Sharon
Justin
Kayla
Nathan
Samantha

Stephen
Annie
Matt
Mary
Simon
Lucy
Ruthie
Sam
David
```

The `Family` class is shown in Listing 7.12. The constructor simply stores a reference to the array parameter until it is needed. By using a variable-length parameter list for the constructor, we make it easy to create a family of any size.

7.6 Two-Dimensional Arrays

The arrays we've examined so far have all been *one-dimensional arrays* in the sense that they represent a simple list of values. As the name implies, a *two-dimensional array* has values in two dimensions, which are often thought of as the rows and columns of a table. Figure 7.4 graphically compares a one-dimensional array with a two-dimensional array. We use two indexes to refer to a value in a two-dimensional array, one specifying the row and another the column.

Brackets are used to represent each dimension in the array. Therefore the type of a two-dimensional array that stores integers is `int[][]`. Technically, Java represents a two-dimensional array as an array of arrays. So a two-dimensional integer array is really a one-dimensional array of references to one-dimensional

Listing **7.12**

```
//********************************************************************
//  Family.java        Java Foundations
//
//  Demonstrates the use of variable length parameter lists.
//********************************************************************

public class Family
{
   private String[] members;

   //-----------------------------------------------------------------
   //  Constructor: Sets up this family by storing the (possibly
   //  multiple) names that are passed in as parameters.
   //-----------------------------------------------------------------
   public Family (String ... names)
   {
      members = names;
   }

   //-----------------------------------------------------------------
   //  Returns a string representation of this family.
   //-----------------------------------------------------------------
   public String toString()
   {
      String result = "";

      for (String name : members)
         result += name + "\n";

      return result;
   }
}
```

integer arrays. In most cases it's easier to think about a two-dimensional array as a table with rows and columns.

The `TwoDArray` program shown in Listing 7.13 instantiates a two-dimensional array of integers. As with one-dimensional arrays, the size of the dimensions is specified when the array is created. The size of the dimensions can be different.

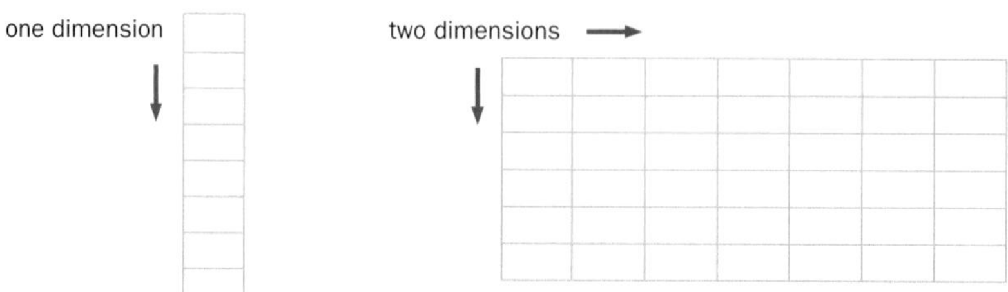

FIGURE 7.4 A one-dimensional array and a two-dimensional array

Nested `for` loops are used in the `TwoDArray` program to load the array with values and also to print those values in a table format. Carefully trace the processing of this program to see how the nested loops eventually visit each element in the two-dimensional array. Note that the outer loops are governed by `table.length`, which represents the number of rows, and the inner loops are governed by `table[row].length`, which represents the number of columns in that row.

As with one-dimensional arrays, an initializer list can be used to instantiate a two-dimensional array, where each element is itself an array initializer list. This technique is used in the `SodaSurvey` program, which is shown in Listing 7.14.

Suppose a soda manufacturer held a taste test for four new flavors to determine if people liked them. The manufacturer got 10 people to try each new flavor and give it a score from 1 to 5, where 1 equals poor and 5 equals excellent. The two-dimensional array called `scores` in the `SodaSurvey` program stores the results of that survey. Each row corresponds to a soda and each column in that row corresponds to the person who tasted it. More generally, each row holds the responses that all testers gave for one particular soda flavor, and each column holds the responses of one person for all sodas.

The `SodaSurvey` program computes and prints the average responses for each soda and for each respondent. The sums of each soda and person are first stored in one-dimensional arrays of integers. Then the averages are computed and printed.

Multidimensional Arrays

An array can have one, two, three, or even more dimensions. Any array with more than one dimension is called a *multidimensional array.*

Listing 7.13

```
//********************************************************************
//  TwoDArray.java       Java Foundations
//
//  Demonstrates the use of a two-dimensional array.
//********************************************************************

public class TwoDArray
{
   //-----------------------------------------------------------------
   //  Creates a 2D array of integers, fills it with increasing
   //  integer values, then prints them out.
   //-----------------------------------------------------------------
   public static void main (String[] args)
   {
      int[][] table = new int[5][10];

      // Load the table with values
      for (int row=0; row < table.length; row++)
         for (int col=0; col < table[row].length; col++)
            table[row][col] = row * 10 + col;

      // Print the table
      for (int row=0; row < table.length; row++)
      {
         for (int col=0; col < table[row].length; col++)
            System.out.print (table[row][col] + "\t");
         System.out.println();
      }
   }
}
```

Output

```
0	1	2	3	4	5	6	7	8	9
10	11	12	13	14	15	16	17	18	19
20	21	22	23	24	25	26	27	28	29
30	31	32	33	34	35	36	37	38	39
40	41	42	43	44	45	46	47	48	49
```

Listing **7.14**

```
//********************************************************************
//  SodaSurvey.java       Java Foundations
//
//  Demonstrates the use of a two-dimensional array.
//********************************************************************

import java.text.DecimalFormat;

public class SodaSurvey
{
   //-----------------------------------------------------------------
   //  Determines and prints the average of each row (soda) and each
   //  column (respondent) of the survey scores.
   //-----------------------------------------------------------------
   public static void main (String[] args)
   {
      int[][] scores = { {3, 4, 5, 2, 1, 4, 3, 2, 4, 4},
                         {2, 4, 3, 4, 3, 3, 2, 1, 2, 2},
                         {3, 5, 4, 5, 5, 3, 2, 5, 5, 5},
                         {1, 1, 1, 3, 1, 2, 1, 3, 2, 4} };

      final int SODAS = scores.length;
      final int PEOPLE = scores[0].length;

      int[] sodaSum = new int[SODAS];
      int[] personSum = new int[PEOPLE];

      for (int soda=0; soda < SODAS; soda++)
         for (int person=0; person < PEOPLE; person++)
         {
            sodaSum[soda] += scores[soda][person];
            personSum[person] += scores[soda][person];
         }

      DecimalFormat fmt = new DecimalFormat ("0.#");
      System.out.println ("Averages:\n");

      for (int soda=0; soda < SODAS; soda++)
         System.out.println ("Soda #" + (soda+1) + ": " +
                   fmt.format ((float)sodaSum[soda]/PEOPLE));

      System.out.println ();
      for (int person=0; person < PEOPLE; person++)
```

Listing **7.14** continued

```
            System.out.println ("Person #" + (person+1) + ": " +
                          fmt.format ((float)personSum[person]/SODAS));
      }
   }
```

Output

```
Averages:

Soda #1: 3.2
Soda #2: 2.6
Soda #3: 4.2
Soda #4: 1.9

Person #1: 2.2
Person #2: 3.5
Person #3: 3.2
Person #4: 3.5
Person #5: 2.5
Person #6: 3
Person #7: 2
Person #8: 2.8
Person #9: 3.2
Person #10: 3.8
```

It's fairly easy to picture a two-dimensional array as a table. A three-dimensional array could be drawn as a cube. However, once you are past three dimensions, multidimensional arrays might seem hard to visualize. But consider that each subsequent dimension is simply a subdivision of the previous one. It is often best to think of larger multidimensional arrays in this way.

For example, suppose we wanted to store the number of students attending universities across the United States, broken down in a meaningful way. We might represent it as a four-dimensional array of integers. The first dimension represents the state. The second dimension represents the universities in each state. The third dimension represents the colleges in each university. Finally, the fourth dimension represents departments in each college. The value stored at each location is the number of students in one particular department. Figure 7.5 shows these subdivisions.

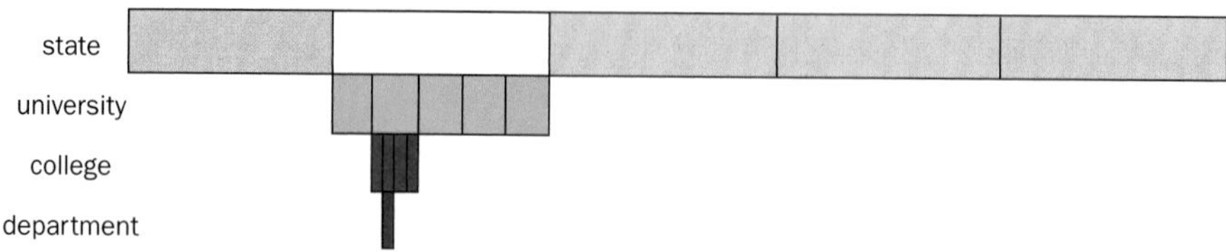

FIGURE 7.5 Visualization of a four-dimensional array

Two-dimensional arrays are fairly common and useful. However, care should be taken when deciding to create multidimensional arrays in a program. When dealing with large amounts of data that are managed at multiple levels, additional information and the methods needed to manage that information will probably be required. It is far more likely, for instance, that in the student example each state would be represented by an object, which may contain, among other things, an array to store information about each university, and so on.

Using an array with more than two dimensions is rare in an object-oriented system.

There is one other important characteristic of Java arrays to consider. As we established previously, Java does not directly support multidimensional arrays. Instead, they are represented as arrays of references to array objects. Those arrays could themselves contain references to other arrays. This layering continues for as many dimensions as required. Because of this technique for representing each dimension, the arrays in any one dimension could be of different lengths. These are sometimes called *ragged arrays*. For example, the number of elements in each row of a two-dimensional array may not be the same. In such situations, care must be taken to make sure the arrays are managed appropriately.

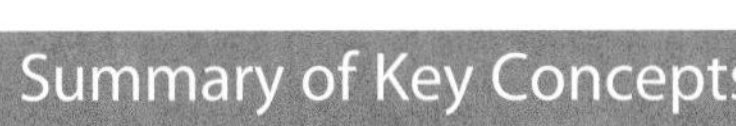

Summary of Key Concepts

- An array of size N is indexed from 0 to N–1.
- In Java, an array is an object that must be instantiated.
- Bounds checking ensures that an index used to refer to an array element is in range.
- An initializer list can be used to instantiate an array object instead of using the `new` operator.
- An entire array can be passed as a parameter, making the formal parameter an alias of the original.
- Instantiating an array of objects reserves room to store references only. The objects that are stored in each element must be instantiated separately.
- Command-line arguments are stored in an array of `String` objects and are passed to the `main` method.
- A Java method can be defined to accept a varying number of parameters.
- Using an array with more than two dimensions is rare in an object-oriented system.

Self-Review Questions

SR 7.1 What is an array?

SR 7.2 How is each element of an array referenced?

SR 7.3 What is an array's element type?

SR 7.4 Explain the concept of array bounds checking. What happens when a Java array is indexed with an invalid value?

SR 7.5 Describe the process of creating an array. When is memory allocated for the array?

SR 7.6 What is an off-by-one error? How does it relate to arrays?

SR 7.7 What does an array initializer list accomplish?

SR 7.8 Can an entire array be passed as a parameter? How is this accomplished?

SR 7.9 How is an array of objects created?

SR 7.10 What is a command-line argument?

SR 7.11 How can Java methods have variable-length parameter lists?

SR 7.12 How are multidimensional arrays implemented in Java?

Exercises

EX 7.1 Which of the following are valid declarations? Which instantiate an array object? Explain your answers.

```
int primes = {2, 3, 4, 5, 7, 11};
float elapsedTimes[] = {11.47, 12.04, 11.72, 13.88};
int[] scores = int[30];
int[] primes = new {2, 3, 5, 7, 11};
int[] scores = new int[30];
char grades[] = {'a', 'b', 'c', 'd', 'f'};
char[] grades = new char[];
```

EX 7.2 Describe five programs that would be difficult to implement without using arrays.

EX 7.3 Describe what problem occurs in the following code. What modifications should be made to it to eliminate the problem?

```
int[] numbers = {3, 2, 3, 6, 9, 10, 12, 32, 3, 12, 6};
for (int count = 1; count <= numbers.length; count++)
   System.out.println (numbers[count]);
```

EX 7.4 Write an array declaration and any necessary supporting classes to represent the following statements:

a. students' names for a class of 25 students

b. students' test grades for a class of 40 students

c. credit-card transactions that contain a transaction number, a merchant name, and a charge

d. students' names for a class and homework grades for each student

e. for each employee of the L&L International Corporation: the employee number, hire date, and the amount of the last five raises

EX 7.5 Write code that sets each element of an array called `nums` to the value of the constant `INITIAL`.

EX 7.6 Write code that prints the values stored in an array called `names` backwards.

EX 7.7 Write code that sets each element of a `boolean` array called `flags` to alternating values (`true` at index 0, `false` at index 1, etc.).

EX 7.8 Write a method called `sumArray` that accepts an array of floating point values and returns the sum of the values stored in the array.

EX 7.9 Write a method called `switchThem` that accepts two integer arrays as parameters and switches the contents of the arrays. Take into account that the arrays may be of different sizes.

Programming Projects

PP 7.1 Design and implement an application that reads an arbitrary number of integers that are in the range 0 to 50 inclusive and counts how many occurrences of each are entered. After all input has been processed, print all of the values (with the number of occurrences) that were entered one or more times.

myCodeMate

PP 7.2 Modify the program from programming project 7.1 so that it works for numbers in the range between –25 and 25.

PP 7.3 Design and implement an application that creates a histogram that allows you to visually inspect the frequency distribution of a set of values. The program should read in an arbitrary number of integers that are in the range 1 to 100 inclusive; then produce a chart similar to the one below that indicates how many input values fell in the range 1 to 10, 11 to 20, and so on. Print one asterisk for each value entered.

```
1  - 10   | *****
11 - 20   | **
21 - 30   | *******************
31 - 40   |
41 - 50   | ***
51 - 60   | ********
61 - 70   | **
71 - 80   | *****
81 - 90   | *******
91 - 100  | *********
```

PP 7.4 The lines in the histogram in programming project 7.3 will be too long if a large number of values is entered. Modify the program so that it prints an asterisk for every five values in each category. Ignore leftovers. For example, if a category had 17 values, print three asterisks in that row. If a category had 4 values, do not print any asterisks in that row.

PP 7.5 Design and implement an application that computes and prints the mean and standard deviation of a list of integers x_1 through x_n. Assume that there will be no more than 50 input values. Compute both the mean and standard deviation as floating point values, using the following formulas.

$$\text{mean} = \frac{\sum_{i=1}^{n} x_i}{n}$$

$$\text{sd} = \sqrt{\frac{\sum_{i=1}^{n} (x_i - \text{mean})^2}{n - 1}}$$

PP 7.6 The L&L Bank can handle up to 30 customers who have savings accounts. Design and implement a program that manages the accounts. Keep track of key information and allow each customer to make deposits and withdrawals. Produce appropriate error messages for invalid transactions. *Hint:* You may want to base your accounts on the `Account` class from Chapter 5. Also provide a method to add 3 percent interest to all accounts whenever the method is invoked.

PP 7.7 The programming projects of Chapter 5 discussed a `Card` class that represents a standard playing card. Create a class called `DeckOfCards` that stores 52 objects of the `Card` class. Include methods to shuffle the deck, deal a card, and report the number of cards left in the deck. The `shuffle` method should assume a full deck. Create a driver class with a `main` method that deals each card from a shuffled deck, printing each card as it is dealt.

PP 7.8 Design and implement an application that reads a sequence of up to 25 pairs of names and postal (ZIP) codes for individuals. Store the data in an object designed to store a first name (string), last name (string), and postal code (integer). Assume each line of input will contain two strings followed by an integer value, each separated by a tab character. Then, after the input has been read in, print the list in an appropriate format to the screen.

PP 7.9 Modify the program you created in programming project 7.8 to support the storing of additional user information: street address (string), city (string), state (string), and 10-digit phone number (long integer, contains area code and does not include special characters such as (,), or -).

PP 7.10 Define a class called `Quiz` that manages a set of up to 25 `Question` objects. Define the `add` method of the `Quiz` class to add a question to a quiz. Define the `giveQuiz` method of the `Quiz` class to present each question in turn to the user, accept an answer for each one, and keep track of the results. Define a class called `QuizTime` with a `main` method that populates a quiz, presents it, and prints the final results.

PP 7.11 Modify your answer to programming project 7.10 so that the complexity level of the questions given in the quiz is taken into account. Overload the `giveQuiz` method so that it accepts two integer parameters that specify the minimum and maximum complexity levels for the quiz questions and only presents questions in that complexity range. Modify the `main` method to demonstrate this feature.

Answers to Self-Review Questions

SR 7.1 An array is an object that stores a list of values. The entire list can be referenced by its name, and each element in the list can be referenced individually based on its position in the array.

SR 7.2 Each element in an array can be referenced by its numeric position, called an index, in the array. In Java, all array indexes begin at zero. Square brackets are used to specify the index. For example, `nums[5]` refers to the sixth element in the array called `nums`.

SR 7.3 An array's element type is the type of values that the array can hold. All values in a particular array have the same type, or are at least of compatible types. So we might have an array of integers, or an array of `boolean` values, or an array of `Dog` objects, etc.

SR 7.4 Whenever a reference is made to a particular array element, the index operator (the brackets that enclose the subscript) ensures that the value of the index is greater than or equal to zero and less than the size of the array. If it is not within the valid range, an `ArrayIndexOutOfBoundsException` is thrown.

SR 7.5 Arrays are objects. Therefore, as with all objects, to create an array we first create a reference to the array (its name). We then instantiate the array itself, which reserves memory space to store the array elements. The only difference between a regular object instantiation and an array instantiation is the bracket syntax.

SR 7.6 An off-by-one error occurs when a program's logic exceeds the boundary of an array (or similar structure) by one. These errors include forgetting to process a boundary element as well as attempting to process a nonexistent element. Array processing is susceptible to off-by-one errors because their indexes begin at zero and run to one less than the size of the array.

SR 7.7 An array initializer list is used in the declaration of an array to set up the initial values of its elements. An initializer list instantiates the array object, so the `new` operator is not needed.

SR 7.8 An entire array can be passed as a parameter. Specifically, because an array is an object, a reference to the array is passed to the method. Any changes made to the array elements will be reflected outside of the method.

SR 7.9 An array of objects is really an array of object references. The array itself must be instantiated, and the objects that are stored in the array must be created separately.

SR 7.10 A command-line argument is data that is included on the command line when the interpreter is invoked to execute the program. Command-line arguments are another way to provide input to a program. They are accessed using the array of strings that is passed into the `main` method as a parameter.

SR 7.11 A Java method can be defined to accept a variable number of parameters by using an ellipsis (. . .) in the formal parameter list. When several values are passed to the method, they are automatically converted into an array. This allows the method to be written in terms of array processing without forcing the calling method to create the array.

SR 7.12 A multidimensional array is implemented in Java as an array of array objects. The arrays that are elements of the outer array could also contain arrays as elements. This nesting process could continue for as many levels as needed.

Chapter Objectives

- Explore the derivation of new classes from existing ones.
- Define the concept and purpose of method overriding.
- Discuss the design of class hierarchies.
- Examine the purpose and use of abstract classes.
- Discuss the issue of visibility as it relates to inheritance.
- Discuss object-oriented design in the context of inheritance.

8

Inheritance

This chapter explains inheritance, a fundamental technique for organizing and creating classes. It is a simple but powerful idea that influences the way we design object-oriented software and enhances our ability to reuse classes in other situations and programs. In this chapter we explore the technique for creating subclasses and class hierarchies, and we discuss a technique for overriding the definition of an inherited method. We examine the `protected` modifier and discuss the effect all visibility modifiers have on inherited attributes and methods.

8.1 Creating Subclasses

In our introduction to object-oriented concepts in Chapter 1 we presented the analogy that a class is to an object what a blueprint is to a house. In subsequent chapters we've reinforced that idea, writing classes that define a set of similar objects. A class establishes the characteristics and behaviors of an object but reserves no memory space for variables (unless those variables are declared as `static`). Classes are the plan, and objects are the embodiment of that plan.

Many houses can be created from the same blueprint. They are essentially the same house in different locations with different people living in them. Now suppose you want a house that is similar to another but with some different or additional features. You want to start with the same basic blueprint but modify it to suit new, slightly different, needs. Many housing developments are created this way. The houses in the development have the same core layout, but they have unique features. For instance, they might all be split-level homes with the same basic room configuration, but some have a fireplace or full basement while others do not, or an upgraded gourmet kitchen instead of the standard version.

It's likely that the housing developer commissioned a master architect to create a single blueprint to establish the basic design of all houses in the development, then a series of new blueprints that include variations designed to appeal to different buyers. The act of creating the series of blueprints was simplified since they all begin with the same underlying structure, while the variations give them unique characteristics that may be important to the prospective owners.

Inheritance is the process of deriving a new class from an existing one.

Creating a new blueprint that is based on an existing blueprint is analogous to the object-oriented concept of *inheritance*, which is the process in which a new class is derived from an existing one. Inheritance is a powerful software development technique and a defining characteristic of object-oriented programming.

Via inheritance, the new class automatically contains the variables and methods in the original class. Then, to tailor the class as needed, the programmer can add new variables and methods to the derived class or modify the inherited ones.

One purpose of inheritance is to reuse existing software.

In general, new classes can be created via inheritance faster, easier, and cheaper than by writing them from scratch. Inheritance is one way to support the idea of *software reuse*. By using existing software components to create new ones, we capitalize on the effort that went into the design, implementation, and testing of the existing software.

Keep in mind that the word *class* comes from the idea of classifying groups of objects with similar characteristics. Classification schemes often use levels of classes that relate to each other. For example, all mammals share certain characteristics: they are warmblooded, have hair, and bear live offspring. Now consider a subset of mammals, such as horses. All horses are mammals and have all of the characteristics of mammals, but they also have unique features that make them different from other mammals such as dogs.

If we translate this idea into software terms, an existing class called `Mammal` would have certain variables and methods that describe the state and behavior of mammals. A `Horse` class could be derived from the existing `Mammal` class, automatically inheriting the variables and methods contained in `Mammal`. The `Horse` class can refer to the inherited variables and methods as if they had been declared locally in that class. New variables and methods can then be added to the derived class to distinguish a horse from other mammals.

The original class that is used to derive a new one is called the *parent class*, *superclass*, or *base class*. The derived class is called a *child class*, or *subclass*. In UML, inheritance is represented by an arrow with an open arrowhead pointing from the child class to the parent, as shown in Figure 8.1.

The process of inheritance should establish an *is-a relationship* between two classes. That is, the child class should be a more specific version of the parent. For example, a horse is a mammal. Not all mammals are horses, but all horses are mammals. For any class X that is derived from class Y, you should be able to say that "X is a Y." If such a statement doesn't make sense, then that relationship is probably not an appropriate use of inheritance.

Inheritance creates an is-a relationship between the parent and child classes.

Let's look at an example. The `Words` program shown in Listing 8.1 instantiates an object of class `Dictionary`, which is derived from a class called `Book`. In the `main` method, three methods are invoked through the `Dictionary` object: two that were declared locally in the `Dictionary` class and one that was inherited from the `Book` class.

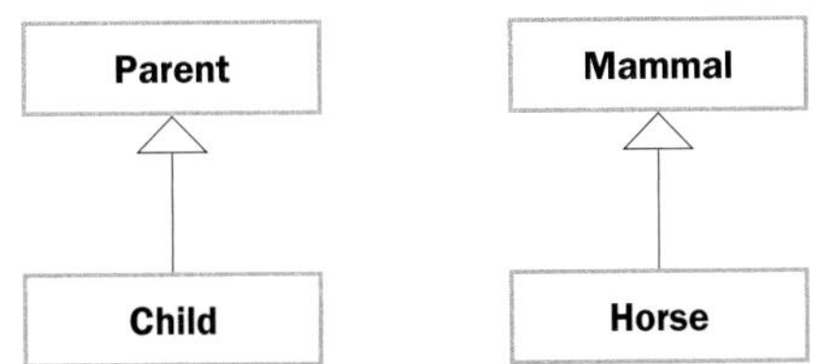

FIGURE 8.1 Inheritance relationships in UML

Listing **8.1**

```
//********************************************************************
//  Words.java       Java Foundations
//
//  Demonstrates the use of an inherited method.
//********************************************************************

public class Words
{
   //-----------------------------------------------------------------
   //  Instantiates a derived class and invokes its inherited and
   //  local methods.
   //-----------------------------------------------------------------
   public static void main (String[] args)
   {
      Dictionary webster = new Dictionary();

      System.out.println ("Number of pages: " + webster.getPages());

      System.out.println ("Number of definitions: " +
                          webster.getDefinitions());

      System.out.println ("Definitions per page: " +
                          webster.computeRatio());
   }
}
```

Output

```
Number of pages: 1500
Number of definitions: 52500
Definitions per page: 35.0
```

Java uses the reserved word `extends` to indicate that a new class is being derived from an existing class. The `Book` class (shown in Listing 8.2) is used to derive the `Dictionary` class (shown in Listing 8.3) simply by using the `extends` clause in the header of `Dictionary`. The `Dictionary` class automatically inherits the definition of the `setPages` and `getPages` methods, as well as the `pages` variable. It is as if those methods and the `pages` variable were declared inside the `Dictionary` class. Note that, in the `Dictionary` class, the `computeRatio`

Listing **8.2**

```
//********************************************************************
//  Book.java       Java Foundations
//
//  Represents a book. Used as the parent of a derived class to
//  demonstrate inheritance.
//********************************************************************

public class Book
{
   protected int pages = 1500;

   //----------------------------------------------------------------
   //  Pages mutator.
   //----------------------------------------------------------------
   public void setPages (int numPages)
   {
      pages = numPages;
   }

   //----------------------------------------------------------------
   //  Pages accessor.
   //----------------------------------------------------------------
   public int getPages ()
   {
      return pages;
   }
}
```

method explicitly references the `pages` variable, even though that variable is declared in the `Book` class.

Also note that although the `Book` class is needed to create the definition of `Dictionary`, no `Book` object is ever instantiated in the program. An instance of a child class does not rely on an instance of the parent class.

Inheritance is a one-way street. The `Book` class cannot use variables or methods that are declared explicitly in the `Dictionary` class. For instance, if we created an object from the `Book` class, it could not be used to invoke the `setDefinitions` method. This restriction makes sense because a child class is a

Listing **8.3**

```
//********************************************************************
//  Dictionary.java       Java Foundations
//
//  Represents a dictionary, which is a book. Used to demonstrate
//  inheritance.
//********************************************************************

public class Dictionary extends Book
{
   private int definitions = 52500;

   //-----------------------------------------------------------------
   //  Prints a message using both local and inherited values.
   //-----------------------------------------------------------------
   public double computeRatio ()
   {
      return definitions/pages;
   }

   //-----------------------------------------------------------------
   //  Definitions mutator.
   //-----------------------------------------------------------------
   public void setDefinitions (int numDefinitions)
   {
      definitions = numDefinitions;
   }

   //-----------------------------------------------------------------
   //  Definitions accessor.
   //-----------------------------------------------------------------
   public int getDefinitions ()
   {
      return definitions;
   }
}
```

more specific version of the parent class. A dictionary has pages because all books have pages; but although a dictionary has definitions, not all books do.

Figure 8.2 shows the inheritance relationship between the `Book` and `Dictionary` classes.

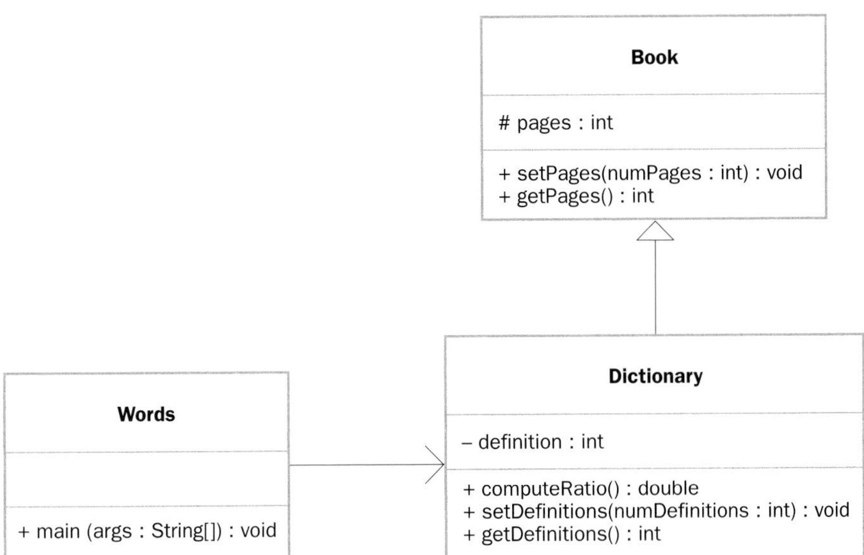

FIGURE 8.2 A UML class diagram for the `Words` program

The `protected` Modifier

As we've seen, visibility modifiers are used to control access to the members of a class. Visibility plays an important role in the process of inheritance as well. Any public method or variable in a parent class can be explicitly referenced by name in the child class, and through objects of that child class. On the other hand, private methods and variables of the parent class cannot be referenced in the child class or through an object of the child class.

Protected visibility provides the best possible encapsulation that permits inheritance.

This situation causes a dilemma. If we declare a variable with public visibility so that a derived class can reference it, we violate the principle of encapsulation. Therefore, Java provides a third visibility modifier: `protected`. Note that in the `Words` example the variable `pages` is declared with protected visibility in the `Book` class. When a variable or method is declared with protected visibility, a derived class can reference it. And protected visibility allows the class to retain some encapsulation properties. The encapsulation with protected visibility is not as tight as it would be if the variable or method were declared private, but it is better than if it were declared public. Specifically, a variable or method declared with protected visibility may be accessed by any class in the same package. The relationships among all Java modifiers are explained completely in Appendix E.

In a UML diagram, protected visibility can be indicated by preceding the protected member with a hash mark (#). The pages variable of the Book class has this annotation in Figure 8.2.

Each variable or method retains the effect of its original visibility modifier. For example, the setPages method is still considered to be public in its inherited form in the Dictionary class.

Let's be clear about our terms. All methods and variables, even those declared with private visibility, are inherited by the child class. That is, their definitions exist and memory space is reserved for the variables. It's just that they can't be referenced by name. This issue is explored in more detail in section 8.4.

Constructors are not inherited. Constructors are special methods that are used to set up a particular type of object, so it doesn't make sense for a class called Dictionary to have a constructor called Book. But you can imagine that a child class may want to refer to the constructor of the parent class, which is one of the reasons for the super reference, described next.

The super Reference

The reserved word super can be used in a class to refer to its parent class. Using the super reference, we can access a parent's members. Like the this reference, what the word super refers to depends on the class in which it is used.

A parent's constructor can be invoked using the super reference.

A common use of the super reference is to invoke a parent's constructor. Let's look at an example. Listing 8.4 shows a modified version of the Words program, in which we use a class called Book2 (shown in Listing 8.5) as the parent of the derived class Dictionary2 (shown in Listing 8.6). However, unlike earlier versions of these classes, Book2 and Dictionary2 have explicit constructors used to initialize their instance variables. The output of the Words2 program is the same as it is for the original Words program.

The Dictionary2 constructor takes two integer values as parameters, representing the number of pages and definitions in the book. Because the Book2 class already has a constructor that performs the work to set up the parts of the dictionary that were inherited, we rely on that constructor to do that work. However, since the constructor is not inherited, we cannot invoke it directly, and so we use the super reference to invoke it in the parent class. The Dictionary2 constructor then proceeds to initialize its definitions variable.

Listing **8.4**

```
//********************************************************************
//  Words2.java       Java Foundations
//
//  Demonstrates the use of the super reference.
//********************************************************************

public class Words2
{
   //-----------------------------------------------------------------
   //  Instantiates a derived class and invokes its inherited and
   //  local methods.
   //-----------------------------------------------------------------
   public static void main (String[] args)
   {
      Dictionary2 webster = new Dictionary2 (1500, 52500);

      System.out.println ("Number of pages: " + webster.getPages());

      System.out.println ("Number of definitions: " +
                          webster.getDefinitions());

      System.out.println ("Definitions per page: " +
                          webster.computeRatio());
   }
}
```

Output

```
Number of pages: 1500
Number of definitions: 52500
Definitions per page: 35.0
```

In this example, it would have been just as easy to set the `pages` variable explicitly in the `Dictionary2` constructor instead of using `super` to call the `Book2` constructor. However, it is good practice to let each class "take care of itself." If we choose to change the way that the `Book2` constructor sets up its `pages` variable, we would also have to remember to make that change in `Dictionary2`. By using the `super` reference, a change made in `Book2` is automatically reflected in `Dictionary2`.

Listing **8.5**

```
//********************************************************************
//  Book2.java       Java Foundations
//
//  Represents a book. Used as the parent of a derived class to
//  demonstrate inheritance and the use of the super reference.
//********************************************************************

public class Book2
{
   protected int pages;

   //-----------------------------------------------------------------
   //  Constructor: Sets up the book with the specified number of
   //  pages.
   //-----------------------------------------------------------------
   public Book2 (int numPages)
   {
      pages = numPages;
   }

   //-----------------------------------------------------------------
   //  Pages mutator.
   //-----------------------------------------------------------------
   public void setPages (int numPages)
   {
      pages = numPages;
   }

   //-----------------------------------------------------------------
   //  Pages accessor.
   //-----------------------------------------------------------------
   public int getPages ()
   {
      return pages;
   }
}
```

A child's constructor is responsible for calling its parent's constructor. Generally, the first line of a constructor should use the `super` reference call to a constructor of the parent class. If no such call exists, Java will automatically make

Listing **8.6**

```
//********************************************************************
//  Dictionary2.java       Java Foundations
//
//  Represents a dictionary, which is a book. Used to demonstrate
//  the use of the super reference.
//********************************************************************

public class Dictionary2 extends Book2
{
   private int definitions;

   //-----------------------------------------------------------------
   //  Constructor: Sets up the dictionary with the specified number
   //  of pages and definitions.
   //-----------------------------------------------------------------
   public Dictionary2 (int numPages, int numDefinitions)
   {
      super(numPages);

      definitions = numDefinitions;
   }

   //-----------------------------------------------------------------
   //  Prints a message using both local and inherited values.
   //-----------------------------------------------------------------
   public double computeRatio ()
   {
      return definitions/pages;
   }

   //-----------------------------------------------------------------
   //  Definitions mutator.
   //-----------------------------------------------------------------
   public void setDefinitions (int numDefinitions)
   {
      definitions = numDefinitions;
   }
```

Listing 8.6 continued

```
   //-----------------------------------------------------------------
   //  Definitions accessor.
   //-----------------------------------------------------------------
   public int getDefinitions ()
   {
      return definitions;
   }
}
```

a call to `super` with no parameters at the beginning of the constructor. This rule ensures that a parent class initializes its variables before the child class constructor begins to execute. Using the `super` reference to invoke a parent's constructor can be done only in the child's constructor, and if included it must be the first line of the constructor.

The `super` reference can also be used to reference other variables and methods defined in the parent's class. We use this technique in later sections of this chapter.

Multiple Inheritance

Java's approach to inheritance is called *single inheritance*. This term means that a derived class can have only one parent. Some object-oriented languages allow a child class to have multiple parents. This approach is called *multiple inheritance* and is occasionally useful for describing objects that could share characteristics of more than one class. For example, suppose we had a class `Car` and a class `Truck` and we wanted to create a new class called `PickupTruck`. A pickup truck is somewhat like a car and somewhat like a truck. With single inheritance, we must decide whether it is better to derive the new class from `Car` or `Truck`. With multiple inheritance, it can be derived from both, as shown in Figure 8.3.

Multiple inheritance works well in some situations, but it comes with a price. What if both `Truck` and `Car` have methods with the same name? Which method would `PickupTruck` inherit? The answer to this question is complex, and it depends on the rules of the language that supports multiple inheritance.

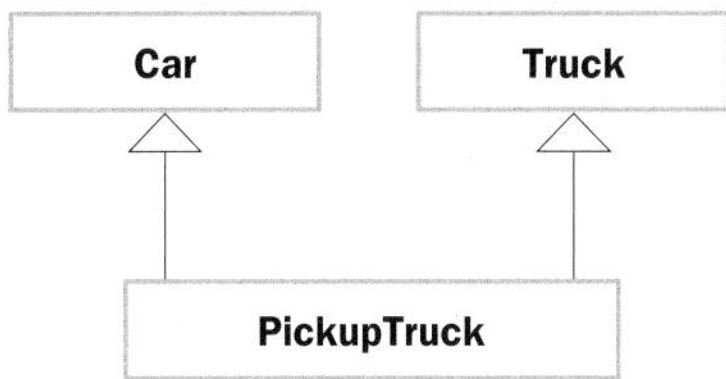

FIGURE 8.3 Multiple inheritance

The designers of the Java language explicitly decided not to support multiple inheritance. Java *interfaces*, described in Chapter 9, provide the best features of multiple inheritance, without the added complexity.

8.2 Overriding Methods

When a child class defines a method with the same name and signature as a method in the parent class, we say that the child's version *overrides* the parent's version in favor of its own. The need for overriding occurs often in inheritance situations.

A child class can override (redefine) the parent's definition of an inherited method.

The program in Listing 8.7 provides a simple demonstration of method overriding in Java. The `Messages` class contains a `main` method that instantiates two objects: one from class `Thought` and one from class `Advice`. The `Thought` class is the parent of the `Advice` class.

Both the `Thought` class (shown in Listing 8.8) and the `Advice` class (shown in Listing 8.9) contain a definition for a method called `message`. The version of `message` defined in the `Thought` class is inherited by `Advice`, but `Advice` overrides it with an alternative version. The new version of the method prints out an entirely different message and then invokes the parent's version of the `message` method using the `super` reference.

The object that is used to invoke a method determines which version of the method is actually executed. When `message` is invoked using the `parked` object in the `main` method, the `Thought` version of `message` is executed. When `message` is invoked using the `dates` object, the `Advice` version of `message` is executed.

A method can be defined with the `final` modifier. A child class cannot override a final method. This technique is used to ensure that a derived class uses a particular definition of a method.

Method overriding is a key element in object-oriented design. It allows two objects that are related by inheritance to use the same naming conventions for methods that accomplish the same general task in different ways. Overriding

Listing 8.7

```
//********************************************************************
//  Messages.java       Java Foundations
//
//  Demonstrates the use of an overridden method.
//********************************************************************

public class Messages
{
   //-----------------------------------------------------------------
   //  Creates two objects and invokes the message method in each.
   //-----------------------------------------------------------------
   public static void main (String[] args)
   {
      Thought parked = new Thought();
      Advice dates = new Advice();

      parked.message();

      dates.message();  // overridden
   }
}
```

Output

```
I feel like I'm diagonally parked in a parallel universe.

Warning: Dates in calendar are closer than they appear.

I feel like I'm diagonally parked in a parallel universe.
```

becomes even more important when it comes to polymorphism, which is discussed in Chapter 9.

Shadowing Variables

It is possible, although not recommended, for a child class to declare a variable with the same name as one that is inherited from the parent. Note the distinction between redeclaring a variable and simply giving an inherited variable a particular value. If a variable of the same name is declared in a child class, it is called a *shadow variable*. It is similar in concept to the process of overriding methods but

Listing **8.8**

```
//********************************************************************
//  Thought.java       Java Foundations
//
//  Represents a stray thought. Used as the parent of a derived
//  class to demonstrate the use of an overridden method.
//********************************************************************

public class Thought
{
   //-----------------------------------------------------------------
   //  Prints a message.
   //-----------------------------------------------------------------
   public void message()
   {
      System.out.println ("I feel like I'm diagonally parked in a " +
                          "parallel universe.");

      System.out.println();
   }
}
```

creates confusing subtleties.

Because an inherited variable is already available to the child class, there is usually no good reason to redeclare it. Someone reading code with a shadowed variable will find two different declarations that seem to apply to a variable used in the child class. This confusion causes problems and serves no useful purpose. A redeclaration of a particular variable name could change its type, but that is usually unnecessary. In general, shadowing variables should be avoided.

8.3 Class Hierarchies

A child class derived from one parent can be the parent of its own child class. Furthermore, multiple classes can be derived from a single parent. Therefore, inheritance relationships often develop into *class hierarchies*. The diagram in Figure 8.4 shows a class hierarchy that includes the inheritance relationship between the `Mammal` and `Horse` classes, discussed earlier.

Listing 8.9

```
//********************************************************************
//  Advice.java       Java Foundations
//
//  Represents some thoughtful advice. Used to demonstrate the use
//  of an overridden method.
//********************************************************************

public class Advice extends Thought
{
   //-----------------------------------------------------------------
   //  Prints a message. This method overrides the parent's version.
   //-----------------------------------------------------------------
   public void message()
   {
      System.out.println ("Warning: Dates in calendar are closer " +
                          "than they appear.");

      System.out.println();

      super.message();  // explicitly invokes the parent's version
   }
}
```

There is no limit to the number of children a class can have or to the number of levels to which a class hierarchy can extend. Two children of the same parent are called *siblings*. Although siblings share the characteristics passed on by their

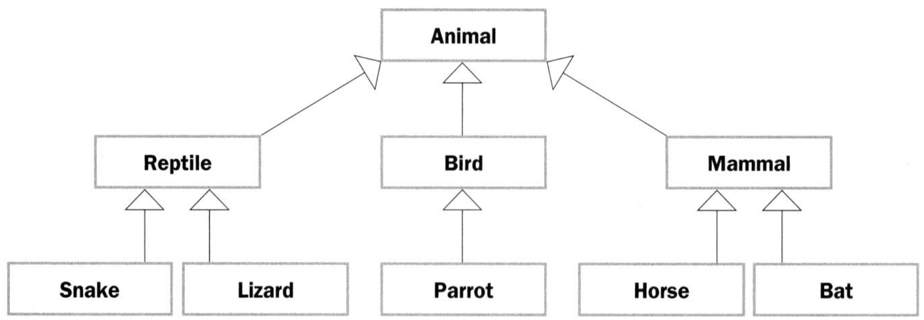

FIGURE 8.4 A class hierarchy

common parent, they are not related by inheritance because one is not used to derive the other.

In class hierarchies, common features should be kept as high in the hierarchy as reasonably possible. That way, the only characteristics explicitly established in a child class are those that make the class distinct from its parent and from its siblings. This approach maximizes the potential to reuse classes. It also facilitates maintenance activities because when changes are made to the parent, they are automatically reflected in the descendants. Always remember to maintain the is-a relationship when building class hierarchies.

The child of one class can be the parent of one or more other classes, creating a class hierarchy.

The inheritance mechanism is transitive. That is, a parent passes along a trait to a child class, and that child class passes it along to its children, and so on. An inherited feature might have originated in the immediate parent or possibly several levels higher in a more distant ancestor class.

Common features should be located as high in a class hierarchy as is reasonably possible.

There is no single best hierarchy organization for all situations. The decisions you make when you are designing a class hierarchy restrict and guide more detailed design decisions and implementation options, so you must make them carefully.

The class hierarchy shown in Figure 8.4 organizes animals by their major biological classifications, such as `Mammal`, `Bird`, and `Reptile`. In a different situation, however, it may be better to organize the same animals in a different way. For example, as shown in Figure 8.5, the class hierarchy might be organized around a function of the animals, such as their ability to fly. In this case, a `Parrot` class and a `Bat` class would be siblings derived from a general `FlyingAnimal` class. This class hierarchy is as valid and reasonable as the original one. The goals of the programs that use the classes are the determining factor, guiding the programmer to a hierarchy design that is best for the situation.

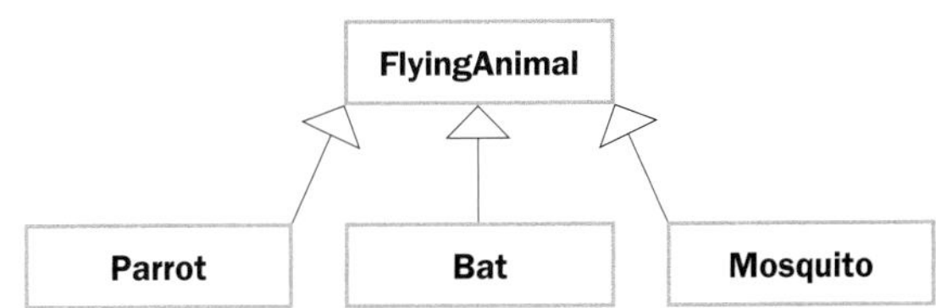

FIGURE 8.5 An alternative hierarchy for organizing animals

The Object Class

In Java, all classes are derived ultimately from the Object class. If a class definition doesn't use the extends clause to derive itself explicitly from another class, then that class is automatically derived from the Object class by default. Therefore, this class definition:

```
class Thing
{
   // whatever
}
```

is equivalent to this one:

```
class Thing extends Object
{
   // whatever
}
```

All Java classes are derived, directly or indirectly, from the Object class.

Because all classes are derived from Object, all public methods of Object are inherited by every Java class. They can be invoked through any object created in any Java program. The Object class is defined in the java.lang package of the Java standard class library. Figure 8.6 lists some of the methods of the Object class.

The toString and equals methods are inherited by every class in every Java program.

As it turns out, we've been using Object methods quite often in our examples. The toString method, for instance, is defined in the Object class, so the toString method can be called on any object. As we've seen several times, when a println method is called with an object parameter, toString is called to determine what to print.

```
boolean equals (Object obj)
```
Returns true if this object is an alias of the specified object.

```
String toString ()
```
Returns a string representation of this object.

```
Object clone ()
```
Creates and returns a copy of this object.

FIGURE 8.6 Some methods of the Object class

So when we define a `toString` method in a class, we are actually overriding an inherited definition. The definition for `toString` that is provided by the `Object` class returns a string containing the object's class name followed by a numeric value that is unique for that object. Usually, we override the `Object` version of `toString` to fit our own needs. The `String` class has overridden the `toString` method so that it returns its stored string value.

We are also overriding an inherited method when we define an `equals` method for a class. As we discussed in Chapter 4, the purpose of the `equals` method is to determine whether two objects are equal. The definition of the `equals` method provided by the `Object` class returns true if the two object references actually refer to the same object (that is, if they are aliases). Classes often override the inherited definition of the `equals` method in favor of a more appropriate definition. For instance, the `String` class overrides `equals` so that it returns true only if both strings contain the same characters in the same order.

Abstract Classes

An *abstract class* represents a generic concept in a class hierarchy. As the name implies, an abstract class represents an abstract entity that is usually insufficiently defined to be useful by itself. Instead, an abstract class may contain a partial description that is inherited by all of its descendants in the class hierarchy. An abstract class is just like any other class, except that it may have some methods that have not been defined yet. Its children, which are more specific, fill in the gaps.

An abstract class cannot be instantiated and usually contains one or more *abstract methods*, which have no definition. That is, there is no body of code defined for an abstract method, and therefore it cannot be invoked. An abstract class might also contain methods that are not abstract, meaning that the method definition is provided as usual. And an abstract class can contain data declarations as usual.

An abstract class cannot be instantiated. It represents a concept on which other classes can build their definitions.

A class is declared as abstract by including the `abstract` modifier in the class header. Any class that contains one or more abstract methods must be declared as abstract. In abstract classes, the `abstract` modifier must be applied to each abstract method. A class declared as abstract does not have to contain abstract methods, however.

Consider the class hierarchy shown in Figure 8.7. The `Vehicle` class at the top of the hierarchy may be too generic for a particular application. Therefore we

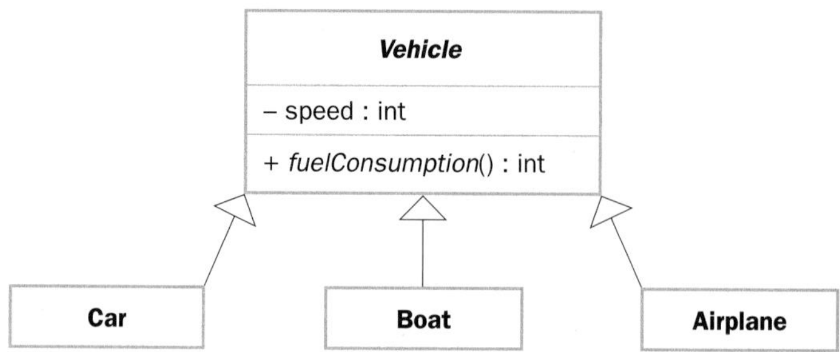

FIGURE 8.7 A vehicle class hierarchy

may choose to implement it as an abstract class. In UML diagrams, the names of abstract classes and abstract methods are shown in italics.

Concepts that apply to all vehicles can be represented in the `Vehicle` class and are inherited by its descendants. That way, each of its descendants doesn't have to define the same concept redundantly (and perhaps inconsistently). For example, in Figure 8.7 we declare a variable called `speed` in the `Vehicle` class, and all specific vehicles below it in the hierarchy automatically have that variable because of inheritance. Any change we make to the representation of the speed of a vehicle is automatically reflected in all descendant classes. Similarly, in `Vehicle` we declare an abstract method called `fuelConsumption`, whose purpose is to calculate how quickly fuel is being consumed by a particular vehicle. The `Vehicle` class establishes that all vehicles consume fuel and provides a consistent method interface for computing that value. But the implementation of the `fuelConsumption` method is left up to each subclass of `Vehicle` which can tailor its method accordingly.

Some concepts don't apply to all vehicles, so we wouldn't represent those concepts at the `Vehicle` level. For instance, we wouldn't include a variable called `numberOfWheels` in the `Vehicle` class, because not all vehicles have wheels. The child classes for which wheels are appropriate can add that concept at the appropriate level in the hierarchy.

A class derived from an abstract parent must override all of its parent's abstract methods, or the derived class will also be considered abstract.

There are no restrictions as to where in a class hierarchy an abstract class can be defined. Usually they are located at the upper levels of a class hierarchy. However, it is possible to derive an abstract class from a nonabstract parent.

Usually, a child of an abstract class will provide a specific definition for an abstract method inherited from its parent. Note that this is just a specific case of overriding a method, giving a different definition than the one the parent provides. If a child of an abstract class does not give a definition for every abstract method that it inherits from its parent, then the child class is also considered abstract.

It would be a contradiction for an abstract method to be modified as `final` or `static`. Because a final method cannot be overridden in subclasses, an abstract final method would have no way of being given a definition in subclasses. A static method can be invoked using the class name without declaring an object of the class. Because abstract methods have no implementation, an abstract static method would make no sense.

Choosing which classes and methods to make abstract is an important part of the design process. You should make such choices only after careful consideration. By using abstract classes wisely, you can create flexible, extensible software designs.

8.4 Visibility

As we mentioned earlier in this chapter, all variables and methods in a parent class, even those declared as private, are inherited by child classes. Private members exist for an object of a derived class, even though they can't be referenced directly. They can, however, be referenced indirectly.

Let's look at an example that demonstrates this situation. The program shown in Listing 8.10 contains a `main` method that instantiates a `Pizza` object and invokes a method to determine how many calories the pizza has per serving due to its fat content.

Private members are inherited by the child class, but cannot be referenced directly by name. They may be used indirectly, however.

The `FoodItem` class shown in Listing 8.11 represents a generic type of food. The constructor of `FoodItem` accepts the number of grams of fat and the number of servings of that food. The `calories` method returns the number of calories due to fat, which the `caloriesPerServing` method invokes to help compute the number of fat calories per serving.

The `Pizza` class, shown in Listing 8.12, is derived from the `FoodItem` class, but it adds no special functionality or data. Its constructor calls the constructor of `FoodItem` using the `super` reference, asserting that there are eight servings per pizza.

Listing **8.10**

```
//********************************************************************
//  FoodAnalyzer.java       Java Foundations
//
//  Demonstrates indirect access to inherited private members.
//********************************************************************

public class FoodAnalyzer
{
   //-----------------------------------------------------------------
   //  Instantiates a Pizza object and prints its calories per
   //  serving.
   //-----------------------------------------------------------------
   public static void main (String[] args)
   {
      Pizza special = new Pizza (275);

      System.out.println ("Calories per serving: " +
                          special.caloriesPerServing());
   }
}
```

Output

```
Calories per serving: 309
```

The `Pizza` object called `special` in the `main` method is used to invoke the method `caloriesPerServing`, which is defined as a public method of `FoodItem`. Note that `caloriesPerServing` calls `calories`, which is declared with private visibility. Furthermore, `calories` references the variable `fatGrams` and the constant `CALORIES_PER_GRAM`, which are also declared with private visibility.

Even though the `Pizza` class cannot explicitly reference `calories`, `fatGrams`, or `CALORIES_PER_GRAM`, they are available for use indirectly when the `Pizza` object needs them. A `Pizza` object cannot be used to invoke the `calories` method, but it can call a method that can. Note that a `FoodItem` object was never created or needed.

Listing **8.11**

```
//********************************************************************
//  FoodItem.java       Java Foundations
//
//  Represents an item of food. Used as the parent of a derived class
//  to demonstrate indirect referencing.
//********************************************************************

public class FoodItem
{
   final private int CALORIES_PER_GRAM = 9;
   private int fatGrams;
   protected int servings;

   //-----------------------------------------------------------------
   //  Sets up this food item with the specified number of fat grams
   //  and number of servings.
   //-----------------------------------------------------------------
   public FoodItem (int numFatGrams, int numServings)
   {
      fatGrams = numFatGrams;
      servings = numServings;
   }

   //-----------------------------------------------------------------
   //  Computes and returns the number of calories in this food item
   //  due to fat.
   //-----------------------------------------------------------------
   private int calories()
   {
      return fatGrams * CALORIES_PER_GRAM;
   }

   //-----------------------------------------------------------------
   //  Computes and returns the number of fat calories per serving.
   //-----------------------------------------------------------------
   public int caloriesPerServing()
   {
      return (calories() / servings);
   }
}
```

Listing **8.12**

```
//********************************************************************
//  Pizza.java       Java Foundations
//
//  Represents a pizza, which is a food item. Used to demonstrate
//  indirect referencing through inheritance.
//********************************************************************

public class Pizza extends FoodItem
{
   //-----------------------------------------------------------------
   //  Sets up a pizza with the specified amount of fat (assumes
   //  eight servings).
   //-----------------------------------------------------------------
   public Pizza (int fatGrams)
   {
      super (fatGrams, 8);
   }
}
```

8.5 Designing for Inheritance

Software design must carefully and specifically address inheritance.

As a major characteristic of object-oriented software, inheritance must be carefully and specifically addressed during software design. A little thought about inheritance relationships can lead to a far more elegant design, which pays huge dividends in the long term.

Throughout this chapter, several design issues have been addressed in the discussion of the nuts and bolts of inheritance in Java. The following list summarizes some of the inheritance issues that you should keep in mind during the program design stage:

- Every derivation should be an is-a relationship. The child should be a more specific version of the parent.
- Design a class hierarchy to capitalize on reuse, and potential reuse in the future.
- As classes and objects are identified in the problem domain, find their commonality. Push common features as high in the class hierarchy as appropriate for consistency and ease of maintenance.

- Override methods as appropriate to tailor or change the functionality of a child.
- Add new variables to the child class as needed, but don't shadow (redefine) any inherited variables.
- Allow each class to manage its own data. Therefore, use the `super` reference to invoke a parent's constructor and to call overridden versions of methods if appropriate.
- Design a class hierarchy to fit the needs of the application, with attention to how it may be useful in the future.
- Even if there are no current uses for them, override general methods such as `toString` and `equals` appropriately in child classes so that the inherited versions don't cause unintentional problems later.
- Use abstract classes to specify a common class interface for the concrete classes lower in the hierarchy.
- Use visibility modifiers carefully to provide the needed access in derived classes without violating encapsulation.

Restricting Inheritance

We've seen the `final` modifier used in declarations to create constants many times. The other uses of the `final` modifier involve inheritance and can have a significant influence on software design. Specifically, the `final` modifier can be used to curtail the abilities related to inheritance.

Earlier in this chapter we mentioned that a method can be declared as `final`, which means it cannot be overridden in any classes that extend the one it is in. A final method is often used to insist that particular functionality be used in all child classes.

The `final` modifier can also be applied to an entire class. A final class cannot be extended at all. Consider the following declaration:

The `final` modifier can be used to restrict inheritance.

```
public final class Standards
{
   // whatever
}
```

Given this declaration, the `Standards` class cannot be used in the `extends` clause of another class. The compiler will generate an error message in such a case. The `Standards` class can be used normally, but it cannot be the parent of another class.

Using the `final` modifier to restrict inheritance abilities is a key design decision. It should be done in situations in which a child class could possibly be used to change functionality that you, as the designer, specifically want to be handled a certain way. This issue comes up again in the discussion of polymorphism in Chapter 9.

Summary of Key Concepts

- Inheritance is the process of deriving a new class from an existing one.
- One purpose of inheritance is to reuse existing software.
- Inheritance creates an is-a relationship between the parent and child classes.
- Protected visibility provides the best possible encapsulation that permits inheritance.
- A parent's constructor can be invoked using the `super` reference.
- A child class can override (redefine) the parent's definition of an inherited method.
- The child of one class can be the parent of one or more other classes, creating a class hierarchy.
- Common features should be located as high in a class hierarchy as is reasonably possible.
- All Java classes are derived, directly or indirectly, from the `Object` class.
- The `toString` and `equals` methods are inherited by every class in every Java program.
- An abstract class cannot be instantiated. It represents a concept on which other classes can build their definitions.
- A class derived from an abstract parent must override all of its parent's abstract methods, or the derived class will also be considered abstract.
- Private members are inherited by the child class, but cannot be referenced directly by name. They may be used indirectly, however.
- Software design must carefully and specifically address inheritance.
- The `final` modifier can be used to restrict inheritance.

Self-Review Questions

SR 8.1 Describe the relationship between a parent class and a child class.

SR 8.2 How does inheritance support software reuse?

SR 8.3 What relationship should every class derivation represent?

SR 8.4 What does the `protected` modifier accomplish?

SR 8.5 Why is the `super` reference important to a child class?

SR 8.6 What is the difference between single inheritance and multiple inheritance?

SR 8.7 Why would a child class override one or more of the methods of its parent class?

SR 8.8 What is the significance of the `Object` class?

SR 8.9 What is the role of an abstract class?

SR 8.10 Are all members of a parent class inherited by the child? Explain.

SR 8.11 How can the `final` modifier be used to restrict inheritance?

Exercises

EX 8.1 Draw a UML class diagram showing an inheritance hierarchy containing classes that represent different types of clocks. Show the variables and method names for two of these classes.

EX 8.2 Show an alternative diagram for the hierarchy in exercise 8.1. Explain why it may be a better or worse approach than the original.

EX 8.3 Draw a UML class diagram showing an inheritance hierarchy containing classes that represent different types of cars, organized first by manufacturer. Show some appropriate variables and method names for at least two of these classes.

EX 8.4 Show an alternative diagram for the hierarchy in exercise 8.3 in which the cars are organized first by type (sports car, sedan, SUV, etc.). Show some appropriate variables and method names for at least two of these classes. Compare and contrast the two approaches.

EX 8.5 Draw a UML class diagram showing an inheritance hierarchy containing classes that represent different types of airplanes. Show some appropriate variables and method names for at least two of these classes.

EX 8.6 Draw a UML class diagram showing an inheritance hierarchy containing classes that represent different types of trees (oak, elm, etc.). Show some appropriate variables and method names for at least two of these classes.

EX 8.7 Draw a UML class diagram showing an inheritance hierarchy containing classes that represent different types of payment transactions at a store (cash, credit card, etc.). Show some appropriate variables and method names for at least two of these classes.

EX 8.8 Experiment with a simple derivation relationship between two classes. Put `println` statements in constructors of both the parent and child classes. Do not explicitly call the constructor of the parent in the child. What happens? Why? Change the child's constructor to explicitly call the constructor of the parent. Now what happens?

Programming Projects

PP 8.1 Design and implement a class called `MonetaryCoin` that is derived from the `Coin` class presented in Chapter 5. Store a value in the monetary coin that represents its value and add a method that returns its value. Create a driver class to instantiate and compute the sum of several `MonetaryCoin` objects. Demonstrate that a monetary coin inherits its parent's ability to be flipped.

PP 8.2 Design and implement a set of classes that define the employees of a hospital: doctor, nurse, administrator, surgeon, receptionist, janitor, and so on. Include methods in each class that are named according to the services provided by that person and that print an appropriate message. Create a driver class to instantiate and exercise several of the classes.

PP 8.3 Design and implement a set of classes that define various types of reading material: books, novels, magazines, technical journals, textbooks, and so on. Include data values that describe various attributes of the material, such as the number of pages and the names of the primary characters. Include methods that are named appropriately for each class and that print an appropriate message. Create a driver class to instantiate and exercise several of the classes.

myCodeMate

PP 8.4 Design and implement a set of classes that keep track of various sports statistics. Have each low-level class represent a specific sport. Tailor the services of the classes to the sport in question, and move common attributes to the higher-level classes as appropriate. Create a driver class to instantiate and exercise several of the classes.

PP 8.5 Design and implement a set of classes that keep track of demographic information about a set of people, such as age, nationality, occupation, income, and so on. Design each class to focus on a particular aspect of data collection. Create a driver class to instantiate and exercise several of the classes.

myCodeMate

PP 8.6 Design and implement a set of classes that define a series of three-dimensional geometric shapes. For each shape, store fundamental data about its size and provide methods to access and modify this data. In addition, provide appropriate methods to compute each shape's circumference, area, and volume. In your design, consider how shapes are related and thus where inheritance can be implemented. Create a driver class to instantiate several shapes of differing types and exercise the behavior you provided.

myCodeMate

PP 8.7 Design and implement a set of classes that define various types of electronics equipment (computers, cell phones, pagers, digital cameras, etc.). Include data values that describe various attributes of the electronics, such as the weight, cost, power usage, and name of the manufacturer. Include methods that are named appropriately for each class and that print an appropriate message. Create a driver class to instantiate and exercise several of the classes.

myCodeMate

PP 8.8 Design and implement a set of classes that define various courses in your curriculum. Include information about each course such as the title, number, description, and department which teaches the course. Consider the categories of classes that comprise your curriculum when designing your inheritance structure. Create a driver class to instantiate and exercise several of the classes.

Answers to Self-Review Questions

SR 8.1 A child class is derived from a parent class using inheritance. The methods and variables of the parent class automatically become a part of the child class, subject to the rules of the visibility modifiers used to declare them.

SR 8.2 Because a new class can be derived from an existing class, the characteristics of the parent class can be reused without the error-prone process of copying and modifying code.

SR 8.3 Each inheritance derivation should represent an is-a relationship: the child *is-a* more specific version of the parent. If this relationship does not hold, then inheritance is being used improperly.

SR 8.4 The `protected` modifier establishes a visibility level (like `public` and `private`) that takes inheritance into account. A variable or method declared with protected visibility can be referenced by name in the derived class, while retaining some level of encapsulation. Protected visibility allows access from any class in the same package.

SR 8.5 The `super` reference can be used to call the parent's constructor, which cannot be invoked directly by name. It can also be used to invoke the parent's version of an overridden method.

SR 8.6 With single inheritance, a class is derived from only one parent, whereas with multiple inheritance, a class can be derived from multiple parents, inheriting the properties of each. The problem with multiple inheritance is that collisions must be resolved in the cases when two or more parents contribute an attribute or method with the same name. Java only supports single inheritance.

SR 8.7 A child class may prefer its own definition of a method in favor of the definition provided for it by its parent. In this case, the child overrides (redefines) the parent's definition with its own.

SR 8.8 All classes in Java are derived, directly or indirectly, from the `Object` class. Therefore all public methods of the `Object` class, such as `equals` and `toString`, are available to every object.

SR 8.9 An abstract class is a representation of a general concept. Common characteristics and method signatures can be defined in an abstract class so that they are inherited by child classes derived from it.

SR 8.10 A class member is not inherited if it has private visibility, meaning that it cannot be referenced by name in the child class. However, such members do exist for the child and can be referenced indirectly.

SR 8.11 The `final` modifier can be applied to a particular method, which keeps that method from being overridden in a child class. It can also be applied to an entire class, which keeps that class from being extended at all.

Chapter Objectives

- Define polymorphism and explore its benefits.
- Discuss the concept of dynamic binding.
- Use inheritance to create polymorphic references.
- Explore the purpose and syntax of Java interfaces.
- Use interfaces to create polymorphic references.
- Discuss object-oriented design in the context of polymorphism.

Polymorphism

This chapter discusses polymorphism, another fundamental principle of object-oriented software. We first explore the concept of binding and discuss how it relates to polymorphism. Then we look at two distinct ways to implement a polymorphic reference in Java: inheritance and interfaces. Java interfaces are explored in general, establishing the similarities between them and abstract classes, and bringing the polymorphism discussion full circle. The chapter concludes with a discussion of the design issues related to polymorphism.

9.1 Late Binding

Often, the type of a reference variable exactly matches the class of the object to which it refers. For example, consider the following reference:

```
ChessPiece bishop;
```

The `bishop` variable may be used to point to an object that is created by instantiating the `ChessPiece` class. However, it doesn't have to. The variable type and the object it refers to must be compatible, but their types need not be exactly the same. The relationship between a reference variable and the object it refers to is more flexible than that.

A polymorphic reference can refer to different types of objects over time.

The term *polymorphism* can be defined as "having many forms." A *polymorphic reference* is a reference variable that can refer to different types of objects at different points in time. The specific method invoked through a polymorphic reference (the actual code executed) can change from one invocation to the next.

Consider the following line of code:

```
obj.doIt();
```

If the reference `obj` is polymorphic, it can refer to different types of objects at different times. So if that line of code is in a loop, or if it's in a method that is called more than once, that line of code could call a different version of the `doIt` method each time it is invoked.

At some point, the commitment is made to execute certain code to carry out a method invocation. This commitment is referred to as *binding* a method invocation to a method definition. In many situations, the binding of a method invocation to a method definition can occur at compile time. For polymorphic references, however, the decision cannot be made until run time. The method definition that is used is determined by the type of the object being referenced at the moment of invocation. This deferred commitment is called *late binding* or *dynamic binding*. It is slightly less efficient than binding at compile time because the decision is made during the execution of the program. This overhead is generally acceptable in light of the flexibility that a polymorphic reference provides.

The binding of a method invocation to its definition is performed at run time for a polymorphic reference.

We can create a polymorphic reference in Java in two ways: using inheritance and using interfaces. Let's look at each in turn.

9.2 Polymorphism via Inheritance

When we declare a reference variable using a particular class name, it can be used to refer to any object of that class. In addition, it can also refer to any object of any class that is related to its declared type by inheritance. For example, if the class `Mammal` is the parent of the class `Horse`, then a `Mammal` reference can be used to refer to an object of class `Horse`. This ability is shown in the following code segment:

```
Mammal pet;
Horse secretariat = new Horse();
pet = secretariat;  // a valid assignment
```

The ability to assign an object of one class to a reference of another class may seem like a deviation from the concept of strong typing discussed in Chapter 2, but it's not. Strong typing asserts that a variable can only be assigned a value consistent with its declared type. Well, that's what's happening here. Remember, inheritance establishes an is-a relationship. A horse *is-a* mammal. Therefore, assigning a `Horse` object to a `Mammal` reference is perfectly reasonable.

The reverse operation, assigning the `Mammal` object to a `Horse` reference, can also be done but it requires an explicit cast. Assigning a reference in this direction is generally less useful and more likely to cause problems because although a horse has all the functionality of a mammal, the reverse is not necessarily true.

A reference variable can refer to any object created from any class related to it by inheritance.

This relationship works throughout a class hierarchy. If the `Mammal` class were derived from a class called `Animal`, the following assignment would also be valid:

```
Animal creature = new Horse();
```

Carrying this idea to the limit, an `Object` reference can be used to refer to any object because ultimately all classes are descendants of the `Object` class.

The reference variable `creature` can be used polymorphically because at any point in time it can refer to an `Animal` object, a `Mammal` object, or a `Horse` object. Suppose that all three of these classes have a method called `move` that is implemented in different ways (because the child class overrode the definition it inherited). The following invocation calls the `move` method, but the particular version of the method it calls is determined at run time:

```
creature.move();
```

When this line is executed, if `creature` currently refers to an `Animal` object, the `move` method of the `Animal` class is invoked. Likewise, if `creature` currently refers to a Mammal object, the Mammal version of move is invoked. Similarly, if it currently refers to a Horse object, the Horse version of move is invoked.

The type of the object, not the type of the reference, determines which version of a method is invoked.

Of course, since Animal and Mammal represent general concepts, they may be defined as abstract classes. This situation does not eliminate the ability to have polymorphic references. Suppose the move method in the Mammal class is abstract, and is given unique definitions in the Horse, Dog, and Whale classes (all derived from Mammal). A Mammal reference variable can be used to refer to any objects created from any of the Horse, Dog, and Whale classes, and can be used to execute the move method on any of them, even though Mammal itself is abstract.

Let's look at another situation. Consider the class hierarchy shown in Figure 9.1. The classes in it represent various types of employees that might be employed at a particular company. Let's explore an example that uses this hierarchy to pay a set of employees of various types.

The Firm class shown in Listing 9.1 contains a main driver that creates a Staff of employees and invokes the payday method to pay them all. The program output includes information about each employee and how much each is paid (if anything).

The Staff class shown in Listing 9.2 maintains an array of objects that represent individual employees of various kinds. Note that the array is declared to hold StaffMember references, but it is actually filled with objects created from several other classes, such as Executive and Employee. These classes are all descendants of the StaffMember class, so the assignments are valid. The staffList array is filled with polymorphic references.

The payday method of the Staff class scans through the list of employees, printing their information and invoking their pay methods to determine how much each employee should be paid. The invocation of the pay method is polymorphic because each class has its own version of the pay method.

The StaffMember class shown in Listing 9.3 is abstract. It does not represent a particular type of employee and is not intended to be instantiated. Rather, it serves as the ancestor of all employee classes and contains information that applies to all employees. Each employee has a name, address, and phone number, so variables to store these values are declared in the StaffMember class and are inherited by all descendants.

The StaffMember class contains a toString method to return the information managed by the StaffMember class. It also contains an abstract method called pay, which takes no parameters and returns a value of type double. At the generic StaffMember level, it would be inappropriate to give a definition for this method. However, the descendants of StaffMember each provide their own specific definition for pay.

This example shows the essence of polymorphism. Each class knows best how it should handle a specific behavior, in this case paying an employee. Yet in one sense it's all the same behavior—the employee is getting paid. Polymorphism lets us treat similar objects in consistent but unique ways.

By defining `pay` abstractly in `StaffMember`, the `payday` method of `Staff` can pay each employee polymorphically. If the `pay` method had not been established in

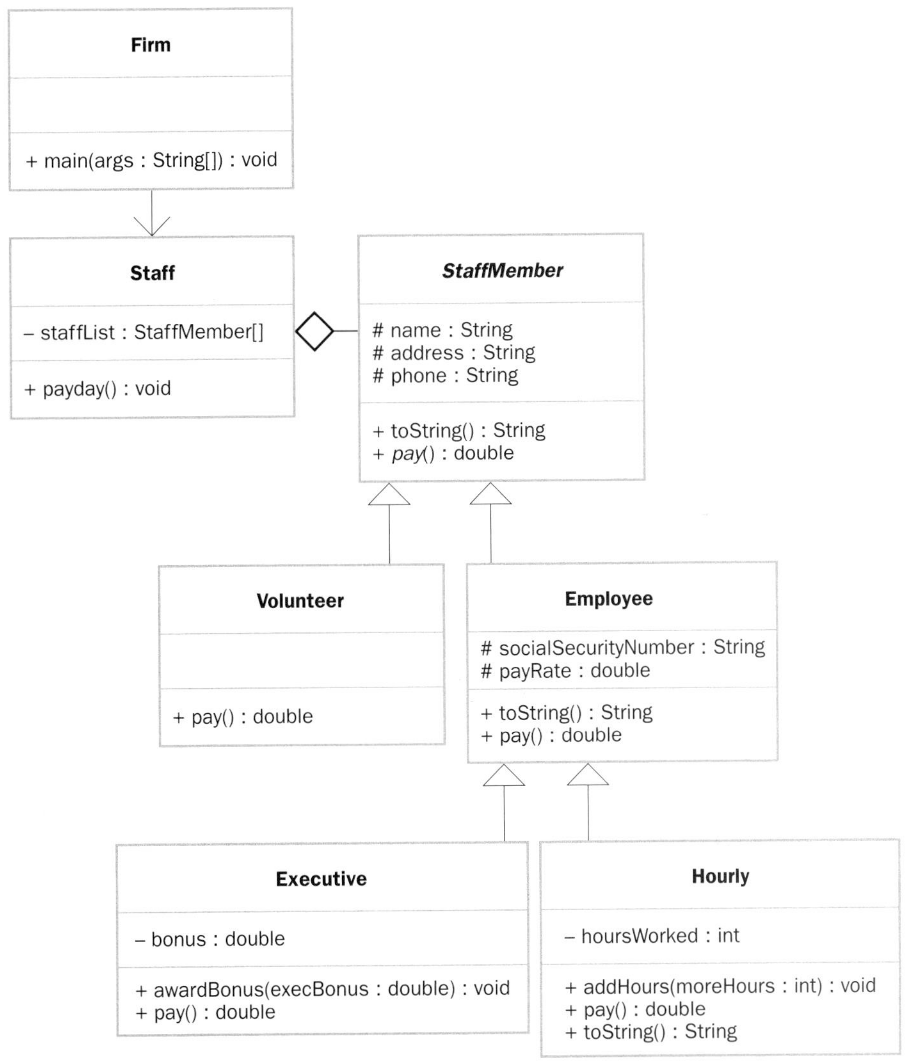

FIGURE 9.1 A class hierarchy of employees

Listing 9.1

```
//********************************************************************
//  Firm.java       Java Foundations
//
//  Demonstrates polymorphism via inheritance.
//********************************************************************

public class Firm
{
   //-----------------------------------------------------------------
   //  Creates a staff of employees for a firm and pays them.
   //-----------------------------------------------------------------
   public static void main (String[] args)
   {
      Staff personnel = new Staff();

      personnel.payday();
   }
}
```

Output

```
Name: Tony
Address: 123 Main Line
Phone: 555-0469
Social Security Number: 123-45-6789
Paid: 2923.07
-----------------------------------
Name: Paulie
Address: 456 Off Line
Phone: 555-0101
Social Security Number: 987-65-4321
Paid: 1246.15
-----------------------------------
Name: Vito
Address: 789 Off Rocker
Phone: 555-0000
Social Security Number: 010-20-3040
Paid: 1169.23
-----------------------------------
Name: Michael
Address: 678 Fifth Ave.
Phone: 555-0690
Social Security Number: 958-47-3625
```

Listing **9.1** continued

```
Current hours: 40
Paid: 422.0
-----------------------------------
Name: Adrianna
Address: 987 Babe Blvd.
Phone: 555-8374
Thanks!
-----------------------------------
Name: Benny
Address: 321 Dud Lane
Phone: 555-7282
Thanks!
-----------------------------------
```

Listing **9.2**

```
//********************************************************************
//  Staff.java       Java Foundations
//
//  Represents the personnel staff of a particular business.
//********************************************************************

public class Staff
{
   private StaffMember[] staffList;

   //-----------------------------------------------------------------
   //  Constructor: Sets up the list of staff members.
   //-----------------------------------------------------------------
   public Staff ()
   {
      staffList = new StaffMember[6];

      staffList[0] = new Executive ("Tony", "123 Main Line",
         "555-0469", "123-45-6789", 2423.07);
```

Listing **9.2** continued

```
      staffList[1] = new Employee ("Paulie", "456 Off Line",
         "555-0101", "987-65-4321", 1246.15);
      staffList[2] = new Employee ("Vito", "789 Off Rocker",
         "555-0000", "010-20-3040", 1169.23);

      staffList[3] = new Hourly ("Michael", "678 Fifth Ave.",
         "555-0690", "958-47-3625", 10.55);

      staffList[4] = new Volunteer ("Adrianna", "987 Babe Blvd.",
         "555-8374");
      staffList[5] = new Volunteer ("Benny", "321 Dud Lane",
         "555-7282");

      ((Executive)staffList[0]).awardBonus (500.00);

      ((Hourly)staffList[3]).addHours (40);
   }

   //-----------------------------------------------------------------
   //  Pays all staff members.
   //-----------------------------------------------------------------
   public void payday ()
   {
      double amount;

      for (int count=0; count < staffList.length; count++)
      {
         System.out.println (staffList[count]);

         amount = staffList[count].pay();  // polymorphic

         if (amount == 0.0)
            System.out.println ("Thanks!");
         else
            System.out.println ("Paid: " + amount);

         System.out.println ("-----------------------------------");
      }
   }
}
```

Listing 9.3

```
//********************************************************************
//  StaffMember.java       Java Foundations
//
//  Represents a generic staff member.
//********************************************************************

abstract public class StaffMember
{
   protected String name;
   protected String address;
   protected String phone;

   //-----------------------------------------------------------------
   //  Constructor: Sets up this staff member using the specified
   //  information.
   //-----------------------------------------------------------------
   public StaffMember (String eName, String eAddress, String ePhone)
   {
      name = eName;
      address = eAddress;
      phone = ePhone;
   }

   //-----------------------------------------------------------------
   //  Returns a string including the basic employee information.
   //-----------------------------------------------------------------
   public String toString()
   {
      String result = "Name: " + name + "\n";

      result += "Address: " + address + "\n";
      result += "Phone: " + phone;

      return result;
   }

   //-----------------------------------------------------------------
   //  Derived classes must define the pay method for each type of
   //  employee.
   //-----------------------------------------------------------------
   public abstract double pay();
}
```

StaffMember, the compiler would complain when pay was invoked through an element of the staffList array. The abstract method guarantees the compiler that any object referenced through the staffList array has a pay method defined for it.

The Volunteer class shown in Listing 9.4 represents a person that is not compensated monetarily for his or her work. We keep track only of a volunteer's basic information, which is passed into the constructor of Volunteer, which in turn passes it to the StaffMember constructor using the super reference. The pay method of Volunteer simply returns a zero pay value. If pay had not been overridden, the Volunteer class would have been considered abstract and could not have been instantiated.

Note that when a volunteer gets "paid" in the payday method of Staff, a simple expression of thanks is printed. In all other situations, where the pay value is greater than zero, the payment itself is printed.

Listing **9.4**

```
//********************************************************************
//  Volunteer.java       Java Foundations
//
//  Represents a staff member that works as a volunteer.
//********************************************************************

public class Volunteer extends StaffMember
{
   //-----------------------------------------------------------------
   //  Constructor: Sets up this volunteer using the specified
   //  information.
   //-----------------------------------------------------------------
   public Volunteer (String eName, String eAddress, String ePhone)
   {
      super (eName, eAddress, ePhone);
   }

   //-----------------------------------------------------------------
   //  Returns a zero pay value for this volunteer.
   //-----------------------------------------------------------------
   public double pay()
   {
      return 0.0;
   }
}
```

The `Employee` class shown in Listing 9.5 represents an employee that gets paid at a particular rate each pay period. The pay rate, as well as the employee's social security number, is passed along with the other basic information to the `Employee` constructor. The basic information is passed to the constructor of `StaffMember` using the `super` reference.

Listing 9.5

```
//********************************************************************
//  Employee.java       Java Foundations
//
//  Represents a general paid employee.
//********************************************************************

public class Employee extends StaffMember
{
   protected String socialSecurityNumber;
   protected double payRate;

   //-----------------------------------------------------------------
   //  Constructor: Sets up this employee with the specified
   //  information.
   //-----------------------------------------------------------------
   public Employee (String eName, String eAddress, String ePhone,
                    String socSecNumber, double rate)
   {
      super (eName, eAddress, ePhone);

      socialSecurityNumber = socSecNumber;
      payRate = rate;
   }

   //-----------------------------------------------------------------
   //  Returns information about an employee as a string.
   //-----------------------------------------------------------------
   public String toString()
   {
      String result = super.toString();

      result += "\nSocial Security Number: " + socialSecurityNumber;

      return result;
   }
```

Listing 9.5 continued

```
   //-----------------------------------------------------------------
   //  Returns the pay rate for this employee.
   //-----------------------------------------------------------------
   public double pay()
   {
      return payRate;
   }
}
```

The `toString` method of `Employee` is overridden to concatenate the additional information that `Employee` manages to the information returned by the parent's version of `toString`, which is called using the `super` reference. The `pay` method of an `Employee` simply returns the pay rate for that employee.

The `Executive` class shown in Listing 9.6 represents an employee that may earn a bonus in addition to his or her normal pay rate. The `Executive` class is derived from `Employee` and therefore inherits from both `StaffMember` and `Employee`. The constructor of `Executive` passes along its information to the `Employee` constructor and sets the executive bonus to zero.

A bonus is awarded to an executive using the `awardBonus` method. This method is called in the `payday` method in `Staff` for the only executive that is part of the `staffList` array. Note that the generic `StaffMember` reference must be cast into an `Executive` reference to invoke the `awardBonus` method (because it doesn't exist for a `StaffMember`).

The `Executive` class overrides the `pay` method so that it first determines the payment as it would for any employee, then adds the bonus. The `pay` method of the `Employee` class is invoked using `super` to obtain the normal payment amount. This technique is better than using just the `payRate` variable because if we choose to change how `Employee` objects get paid, the change will automatically be reflected in `Executive`. After the bonus is awarded, it is reset to zero.

The `Hourly` class shown in Listing 9.7 represents an employee whose pay rate is applied on an hourly basis. It keeps track of the number of hours worked in the current pay period, which can be modified by calls to the `addHours` method. This method is called from the `payday` method of `Staff`. The `pay` method of `Hourly` determines the payment based on the number of hours worked, and then resets the hours to zero.

Listing 9.6

```
//********************************************************************
//  Executive.java       Java Foundations
//
//  Represents an executive staff member, who can earn a bonus.
//********************************************************************

public class Executive extends Employee
{
   private double bonus;

   //-----------------------------------------------------------------
   //  Constructor: Sets up this executive with the specified
   //  information.
   //-----------------------------------------------------------------
   public Executive (String eName, String eAddress, String ePhone,
                     String socSecNumber, double rate)
   {
      super (eName, eAddress, ePhone, socSecNumber, rate);

      bonus = 0;  // bonus has yet to be awarded
   }

   //-----------------------------------------------------------------
   //  Awards the specified bonus to this executive.
   //-----------------------------------------------------------------
   public void awardBonus (double execBonus)
   {
      bonus = execBonus;
   }

   //-----------------------------------------------------------------
   //  Computes and returns the pay for an executive, which is the
   //  regular employee payment plus a one-time bonus.
   //-----------------------------------------------------------------
   public double pay()
   {
      double payment = super.pay() + bonus;

      bonus = 0;

      return payment;
   }
}
```

Listing 9.7

```
//********************************************************************
//  Hourly.java       Java Foundations
//
//  Represents an employee that gets paid by the hour.
//********************************************************************

public class Hourly extends Employee
{
   private int hoursWorked;

   //-----------------------------------------------------------------
   //  Constructor: Sets up this hourly employee using the specified
   //  information.
   //-----------------------------------------------------------------
   public Hourly (String eName, String eAddress, String ePhone,
                  String socSecNumber, double rate)
   {
      super (eName, eAddress, ePhone, socSecNumber, rate);

      hoursWorked = 0;
   }

   //-----------------------------------------------------------------
   //  Adds the specified number of hours to this employee's
   //  accumulated hours.
   //-----------------------------------------------------------------
   public void addHours (int moreHours)
   {
      hoursWorked += moreHours;
   }

   //-----------------------------------------------------------------
   //  Computes and returns the pay for this hourly employee.
   //-----------------------------------------------------------------
   public double pay()
   {
      double payment = payRate * hoursWorked;

      hoursWorked = 0;

      return payment;
   }
```

Listing **9.7** continued

```
   //-----------------------------------------------------------------
   //  Returns information about this hourly employee as a string.
   //-----------------------------------------------------------------
   public String toString()
   {
      String result = super.toString();

      result += "\nCurrent hours: " + hoursWorked;

      return result;
   }
}
```

9.3 Interfaces

In Chapter 5 we used the term interface to refer to the set of public methods through which we can interact with an object. That definition is consistent with our use of it in this section, but now we are going to formalize this concept using a Java language construct. Interfaces provide another way to create polymorphic references.

A Java *interface* is a collection of constants and abstract methods. As discussed in Chapter 8, an abstract method is a method that does not have an implementation. That is, there is no body of code defined for an abstract method. The header of the method, including its parameter list, is simply followed by a semicolon. An interface cannot be instantiated.

An interface is a collection of abstract methods and therefore cannot be instantiated.

Listing 9.8 shows an interface called `Encryptable`. It contains two abstract methods: `encrypt` and `decrypt`.

An abstract method can be preceded by the reserved word `abstract`, though in interfaces it usually is not. Methods in interfaces have public visibility by default.

A class *implements* an interface by providing method implementations for each of the abstract methods defined in the interface. The `Secret` class, shown in Listing 9.9, implements the `Encryptable` interface.

Listing 9.8

```
//********************************************************************
//  Encryptable.java       Java Foundations
//
//  Represents the interface for an object that can be encrypted
//  and decrypted.
//********************************************************************

public interface Encryptable
{
   public void encrypt();
   public String decrypt();
}
```

Listing 9.9

```
//********************************************************************
//  Secret.java       Java Foundations
//
//  Represents a secret message that can be encrypted and decrypted.
//********************************************************************

import java.util.Random;

public class Secret implements Encryptable
{
   private String message;
   private boolean encrypted;
   private int shift;
   private Random generator;

   //-----------------------------------------------------------------
   //  Constructor: Stores the original message and establishes
   //  a value for the encryption shift.
   //-----------------------------------------------------------------
   public Secret (String msg)
   {
      message = msg;
      encrypted = false;
```

Listing **9.9** continued

```
      generator = new Random();
      shift = generator.nextInt(10) + 5;
   }

   //-----------------------------------------------------------------
   //  Encrypts this secret using a Caesar cipher. Has no effect if
   //  this secret is already encrypted.
   //-----------------------------------------------------------------
   public void encrypt ()
   {
      if (!encrypted)
      {
         String masked = "";
         for (int index=0; index < message.length(); index++)
            masked = masked + (char)(message.charAt(index)+shift);
         message = masked;
         encrypted = true;
      }
   }

   //-----------------------------------------------------------------
   //  Decrypts and returns this secret. Has no effect if this
   //  secret is not currently encrypted.
   //-----------------------------------------------------------------
   public String decrypt()
   {
      if (encrypted)
      {
         String unmasked = "";
         for (int index=0; index < message.length(); index++)
            unmasked = unmasked + (char)(message.charAt(index)-shift);
         message = unmasked;
         encrypted = false;
      }

      return message;
   }

   //-----------------------------------------------------------------
   //  Returns true if this secret is currently encrypted.
   //-----------------------------------------------------------------
   public boolean isEncrypted()
   {
```

Listing 9.9 continued

```
      return encrypted;
   }

   //-----------------------------------------------------------------
   //  Returns this secret (may be encrypted).
   //-----------------------------------------------------------------
   public String toString()
   {
      return message;
   }
}
```

A class that implements an interface uses the reserved word `implements` followed by the interface name in the class header. If a class asserts that it implements a particular interface, it must provide a definition for all methods in the interface. The compiler will produce errors if any of the methods in the interface are not given a definition in the class.

In the class `Secret`, both the `encrypt` and `decrypt` methods are implemented, which satisfies the contract established by the interface. These methods must be declared with the same signatures as their abstract counterparts in the interface. In the `Secret` class, the encryption is implemented using a simple Caesar cipher, which shifts the characters of the message a certain number of places. Another class that implements the `Encryptable` interface may use a completely different technique for encryption.

Note that the `Secret` class also implements additional methods that are not part of the `Encryptable` interface. Specifically, it defines the methods `isEncrypted` and `toString`, which have nothing to do with the interface. The interface guarantees that the class implements certain methods, but it does not restrict it from having others. In fact, it is common for a class that implements an interface to have other methods.

Listing 9.10 shows a program called `SecretTest`, which creates some `Secret` objects.

An interface and its relationship to a class can be shown in a UML class diagram. An interface is represented similarly to a class node except that the designation `<<interface>>` is inserted above the interface name. A dotted arrow with

Listing **9.10**

```
//********************************************************************
//  SecretTest.java       Java Foundations
//
//  Demonstrates the use of a formal interface.
//********************************************************************

public class SecretTest
{
   //-----------------------------------------------------------------
   //  Creates a Secret object and exercises its encryption.
   //-----------------------------------------------------------------
   public static void main (String[] args)
   {
      Secret hush = new Secret ("Wil Wheaton is my hero!");
      System.out.println (hush);

      hush.encrypt();
      System.out.println (hush);

      hush.decrypt();
      System.out.println (hush);
   }
}
```

Output

```
Wil Wheaton is my hero!
asv*arok~yx*s}*w?*ro|y+
Wil Wheaton is my hero!
```

a triangular arrowhead is drawn from the class to the interface that it implements. Figure 9.2 shows a UML class diagram for the `SecretTest` program.

Multiple classes can implement the same interface, providing their own definitions for the methods. For example, we could implement a class called `Password` that also implements the `Encryptable` interface. And, as mentioned earlier, each class that implements an interface may do so in different ways. The interface specifies which methods are implemented, not how they are implemented.

A class can implement more than one interface. In these cases, the class must provide an implementation for all methods in all interfaces listed. To show that a

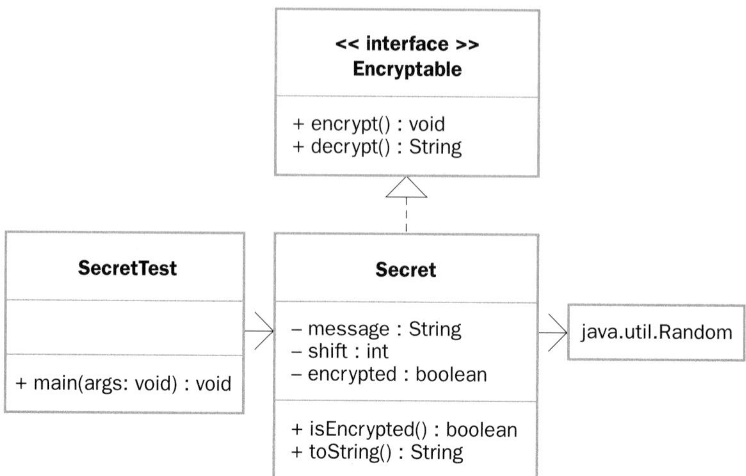

FIGURE 9.2 A UML class diagram for the `SecretTest` program

class implements multiple interfaces, they are listed in the `implements` clause, separated by commas. For example:

```
class ManyThings implements Interface1, Interface2, Interface3
{
   // implements all methods of all interfaces
}
```

In addition to, or instead of, abstract methods, an interface can contain constants, defined using the `final` modifier. When a class implements an interface, it gains access to all the constants defined in it.

Interface Hierarchies

Inheritance can be applied to interfaces so that one interface can be derived from another.

The concept of inheritance can be applied to interfaces as well as to classes. That is, one interface can be derived from another interface. These relationships can form an *interface hierarchy*, which is similar to a class hierarchy. Inheritance relationships between interfaces are shown in UML diagrams using the same connection (an arrow with an open arrowhead) as they are with classes.

When a parent interface is used to derive a child interface, the child inherits all abstract methods and constants of the parent. Any class that implements the child interface must implement all of the methods. There are no visibility issues when dealing with inheritance between interfaces (as there are with protected and private members of a class) because all members of an interface are public.

Class hierarchies and interface hierarchies do not overlap. That is, an interface cannot be used to derive a class, and a class cannot be used to derive an interface. A class and an interface interact only when a class is designed to implement a particular interface.

Before we see how interfaces support polymorphism, let's take a look at a couple of useful interfaces that are defined in the Java standard class library: `Comparable` and `Iterator`.

The `Comparable` Interface

The Java standard class library contains interfaces as well as classes. The `Comparable` interface, for example, is defined in the `java.lang` package. The `Comparable` interface contains only one method, `compareTo`, which takes an object as a parameter and returns an integer.

The purpose of this interface is to provide a common mechanism for comparing one object to another. One object calls the method and passes another as a parameter as follows:

```
if (obj1.compareTo(obj2) < 0)
   System.out.println ("obj1 is less than obj2");
```

As specified by the documentation for the interface, the integer that is returned from the `compareTo` method should be negative if `obj1` is less than `obj2`, 0 if they are equal, and positive if `obj1` is greater than `obj2`. It is up to the designer of each class to decide what it means for one object of that class to be less than, equal to, or greater than another.

In Chapter 4, we mentioned that the `String` class contains a `compareTo` method that operates in this manner. Now we can clarify that the `String` class has this method because it implements the `Comparable` interface. The `String` class implementation of this method bases the comparison of strings on the lexicographic ordering defined by the Unicode character set.

The `Iterator` Interface

The `Iterator` interface is another interface defined in the Java standard class library. It is used by a class that represents a collection of objects, providing a means to move through the collection one object at a time.

In Chapter 4, we defined the concept of an iterator, using a loop to process all elements in the collection. Most iterators, including objects of the `Scanner` class, are defined using the `Iterator` interface.

The two primary methods in the `Iterator` interface are `hasNext`, which returns a boolean result, and `next`, which returns an object. Neither of these methods takes any parameters. The `hasNext` method returns true if there are items left to process, and `next` returns the next object. It is up to the designer of the class that implements the `Iterator` interface to decide the order in which objects will be delivered by the `next` method.

We should note that, according to the spirit of the interface, the `next` method does not remove the object from the underlying collection; it simply returns a reference to it. The `Iterator` interface also has a method called `remove`, which takes no parameters and has a `void` return type. A call to the `remove` method removes the object that was most recently returned by the `next` method from the underlying collection.

We've seen how we can use iterators to process information from the `Scanner` class (in Chapter 4) and from arrays (in Chapter 7). Recall that the foreach version of the `for` loop simplifies this processing in many cases. We will continue to use iterators as appropriate. They are an important part of the development of collection classes, which we discuss in detail in the later chapters of this book (Chapters 14 and beyond).

9.4 Polymorphism via Interfaces

An interface name can be used to declare an object reference variable.

Now let's examine how we can create polymorphic references using interfaces. As we've seen many times, a class name can be used to declare the type of an object reference variable. Similarly, an interface name can be used as the type of a reference variable as well. An interface reference variable can be used to refer to any object of any class that implements that interface.

Suppose we declare an interface called `Speaker` as follows:

```
public interface Speaker
{
   public void speak();
   public void announce (String str);
}
```

The interface name, `Speaker`, can now be used to declare an object reference variable:

```
Speaker current;
```

The reference variable `current` can be used to refer to any object of any class that implements the `Speaker` interface. For example, if we define a class called `Philosopher` such that it implements the `Speaker` interface, we can then assign a `Philosopher` object to a `Speaker` reference as follows:

```
current = new Philosopher();
```

This assignment is valid because a `Philosopher` is a `Speaker`. In this sense the relationship between a class and its interface is the same as the relationship between a child class and its parent. It is an is-a relationship, similar to the relationship created via inheritance. And that relationship forms the basis of the polymorphism.

An interface reference can refer to any object of any class that implements that interface.

The flexibility of an interface reference allows us to create polymorphic references. As we saw earlier in this chapter, using inheritance, we can create a polymorphic reference that can refer to any one of a set of objects as long as they are related by inheritance. Using interfaces, we can create similar polymorphic references among objects that implement the same interface.

For example, if we create a class called `Dog` that also implements the `Speaker` interface, it can be assigned to a `Speaker` reference variable as well. The same reference variable, in fact, can at one point refer to a `Philosopher` object and then later refer to a `Dog` object. The following lines of code illustrate this:

```
Speaker guest;
guest = new Philosopher();
guest.speak();
guest = new Dog();
guest.speak();
```

In this code, the first time the `speak` method is called, it invokes the `speak` method defined in the `Philosopher` class. The second time it is called, it invokes the `speak` method of the `Dog` class. As with polymorphic references via inheritance, it is not the type of the reference that determines which method gets invoked; it is based on the type of the object that the reference points to at the moment of invocation.

Note that when we are using an interface reference variable, we can invoke only the methods defined in the interface, even if the object it refers to has other methods to which it can respond. For example, suppose the `Philosopher` class also defined a public method called `pontificate`. The second line of the following code segment would generate a compiler error, even though the object can in fact contain the `pontificate` method:

```
Speaker special = new Philosopher();
special.pontificate();  // generates a compiler error
```

The problem is that the compiler can determine only that the object is a `Speaker`, and therefore can guarantee only that the object can respond to the `speak` and `announce` methods. Because the reference variable `special` could refer to a `Dog` object (which cannot pontificate), it does not allow the invocation. If we know in a particular situation that such an invocation is valid, we can cast the object into the appropriate reference so that the compiler will accept it, as follows:

```
((Philosopher)special).pontificate();
```

A parameter to a method can be polymorphic, giving the method flexible control of its arguments.

As we can with polymorphic references based in inheritance, an interface name can be used as the type of a method parameter. In such situations, any object of any class that implements the interface can be passed into the method. For example, the following method takes a `Speaker` object as a parameter. Therefore both a `Dog` object and a `Philosopher` object can be passed into it in separate invocations:

```
public void sayIt (Speaker current)
{
   current.speak();
}
```

Using a polymorphic reference as the formal parameter to a method is a powerful technique. It allows the method to control the types of parameters passed into it, yet gives it the flexibility to accept arguments of various types.

Let's now examine a particular use of polymorphism via interfaces.

Event Processing

In Chapter 6 we examined the processing of events in a Java GUI. Recall that, in order to respond to an event, we must establish a relationship between an event listener object and a particular component that may fire the event. We establish the relationship between the listener and the component it listens to by making a method call that adds the listener to the component. This situation is actually an example of polymorphism.

Suppose a class called `MyButtonListener` represents an action listener. To set up a listener to respond to a `JButton` object, we might do the following:

```
JButton button = new JButton();
button.addActionListener (new MyButtonListener());
```

Once this relationship is established, the listener will respond whenever the button fires an action event (because the user pressed it). Now think about the `addActionListener` method carefully. It is a method of the `JButton` class, which was written by someone at Sun Microsystems years ago. On the other hand, we might have written the `MyButtonListener` class today. So how can a method written years ago take a parameter whose class was just written?

The answer is polymorphism. If you examine the source code for the `addActionListener` method, you'll discover that it accepts a parameter of type `ActionListener`, the interface. Therefore, instead of accepting a parameter of only one object type, the `addActionListener` method can accept any object of any class that implements the `ActionListener` interface. All other methods that add listeners work in similar ways.

Establishing the relationship between a listener and the component it listens to is accomplished using polymorphism.

The `JButton` object doesn't know anything particular about the object that is passed to the `addActionListener` method, except for the fact that it implements the `ActionListener` interface (otherwise the code wouldn't compile). The `JButton` object simply stores the listener object and invokes its `performAction` method when the event occurs.

In Chapter 6 we mentioned that we can also create a listener by extending an adaptor class. This is another example of polymorphism via interfaces, even though the listener class is created via inheritance. Each adaptor class is written to implement the appropriate listener interface, providing empty methods for all event handlers. So by extending an adaptor class, the new listener class automatically implements the corresponding listener interface. And that is what really makes it a listener such that it can be passed to an appropriate add listener method.

Thus, no matter how a listener object is created, we are using polymorphism via interfaces to set up the relationship between a listener and the component it listens to. GUI events are a wonderful example of the power and versatility provided by polymorphism.

Polymorphism, whether implemented via inheritance or interfaces, is a fundamental object-oriented technique that we will use as appropriate throughout the remainder of this book.

Summary of Key Concepts

- A polymorphic reference can refer to different types of objects over time.
- The binding of a method invocation to its definition is performed at run time for a polymorphic reference.
- A reference variable can refer to any object created from any class related to it by inheritance.
- The type of the object, not the type of the reference, determines which version of a method is invoked.
- An interface is a collection of abstract methods and therefore cannot be instantiated.
- Inheritance can be applied to interfaces so that one interface can be derived from another.
- An interface name can be used to declare an object reference variable.
- An interface reference can refer to any object of any class that implements that interface.
- A parameter to a method can be polymorphic, giving the method flexible control of its arguments.
- Establishing the relationship between a listener and the component it listens to is accomplished using polymorphism.

Self-Review Questions

SR 9.1 What is polymorphism?

SR 9.2 How does inheritance support polymorphism?

SR 9.3 How is overriding related to polymorphism?

SR 9.4 Why is the `StaffMember` class in the `Firm` example declared as abstract?

SR 9.5 Why is the `pay` method declared in the `StaffMember` class, given that it is abstract and has no body at that level?

SR 9.6 What is the difference between a class and an interface?

SR 9.7 How do class hierarchies and interface hierarchies intersect?

SR 9.8 Describe the `Comparable` interface.

SR 9.9 How can polymorphism be accomplished using interfaces?

Exercises

EX 9.1 Draw and annotate a class hierarchy that represents various types of faculty at a university. Show what characteristics would be represented in the various classes of the hierarchy. Explain how polymorphism could play a role in the process of assigning courses to each faculty member.

EX 9.2 Draw and annotate a class hierarchy that represents various types of animals in a zoo. Show what characteristics would be represented in the various classes of the hierarchy. Explain how polymorphism could play a role in guiding the feeding of the animals.

EX 9.3 Draw and annotate a class hierarchy that represents various types of sales transactions in a store (cash, credit, etc.). Show what characteristics would be represented in the various classes of the hierarchy. Explain how polymorphism could play a role in the payment process.

EX 9.4 What would happen if the `pay` method were not defined as an abstract method in the `StaffMember` class of the `Firm` program?

EX 9.5 Create an interface called `Visible` that includes two methods: `makeVisible` and `makeInvisible`. Both methods should take no parameters and should return a boolean result. Describe how a class might implement this interface.

EX 9.6 Draw a UML class diagram that shows the relationships among the elements of exercise 9.5.

EX 9.7 Create an interface called `VCR` that has methods that represent the standard operations on a video cassette recorder (play, stop, etc.). Define the method signatures any way you desire. Describe how a class might implement this interface.

EX 9.8 Draw a UML class diagram that shows the relationships among the elements of exercise 9.7.

EX 9.9 Explain how a call to the `addMouseListener` method in a GUI-based program represents a polymorphic situation.

Programming Projects

PP 9.1 Modify the `Firm` example from this chapter such that it accomplishes its polymorphism using an interface called `Payable`.

PP 9.2 Modify the `Firm` example from this chapter such that all employees can be given different vacation options depending on their classification. Modify the driver program to demonstrate this new functionality.

PP 9.3 Modify the `RationalNumber` class from Chapter 5 so that it implements the `Comparable` interface. To perform the comparison, compute an equivalent floating point value from the numerator and denominator for both `RationalNumber` objects, then compare them using a tolerance value of 0.0001. Write a `main` driver to test your modifications.

PP 9.4 Create a class called `Password` that implements the `Encryptable` interface from this chapter. Then create a `main` driver that instantiates a `Secret` object and a `Password` object, using the same reference variable, and exercises their methods. Use any type of encryption desired for `Password`, other than the Caesar cipher used by `Secret`.

PP 9.5 Implement the `Speaker` interface defined in this chapter. Create three classes that implement `Speaker` in various ways. Create a driver class whose `main` method instantiates some of these objects and tests their abilities.

PP 9.6 Design a Java interface called `Priority` that includes two methods: `setPriority` and `getPriority`. The interface should define a way to establish numeric priority among a set of objects. Design and implement a class called `Task` that represents a task (such as on a to-do list) that implements the `Priority` interface. Create a driver class to exercise some `Task` objects.

PP 9.7 Modify the `Task` class from programming projects 9.6 so that it also implements the `Comparable` interface from the Java standard class library. Implement the interface such that the tasks are ranked by priority. Create a driver class whose `main` method shows these new features of `Task` objects.

PP 9.8 Design a Java interface called `Lockable` that includes the following methods: `setKey`, `lock`, `unlock`, and `locked`. The `setKey`, `lock`, and `unlock` methods take an integer parameter that represents the key. The `setKey` method establishes the key. The `lock` and `unlock` methods lock and unlock the object, but only if the key passed in is correct. The `locked` method returns a boolean that indicates whether or not the object is locked. A `Lockable` object represents an object whose regular methods are protected: if the object is locked, the methods cannot be invoked; if it is unlocked, they can be invoked. Redesign and implement a version of the `Coin` class from Chapter 5 so that it is `Lockable`.

PP 9.9 Redesign and implement a version of the `Account` class from Chapter 5 so that it is `Lockable` as defined by programming project 9.8.

Answers to Self-Review Questions

SR 9.1 Polymorphism is the ability of a reference variable to refer to objects of various types at different times. A method invoked through such a reference is bound to different method definitions at different times, depending on the type of the object referenced.

SR 9.2 In Java, a reference variable declared using a parent class can be used to refer to an object of the child class. If both classes contain a method with the same signature, the parent reference can be polymorphic.

SR 9.3 When a child class overrides the definition of a parent's method, two versions of that method exist. If a polymorphic reference is used to invoke the method, the version of the method that is invoked is determined by the type of the object being referred to, not by the type of the reference variable.

SR 9.4 The `StaffMember` class is abstract because it is not intended to be instantiated. It serves as a placeholder in the inheritance hierarchy to help organize and manage the objects polymorphically.

SR 9.5 The `pay` method has no meaning at the `StaffMember` level, so it is declared as abstract. But by declaring it there we guarantee that every object of its children will have a `pay` method. This allows us to create an array of `StaffMember` objects, which is actually filled with various types of staff members, and pay each one. The details of being paid are determined by each class as appropriate.

SR 9.6 A class can be instantiated; an interface cannot. An interface can contain only abstract methods and constants. A class provides the implementation for an interface.

SR 9.7 Class hierarchies and interface hierarchies do not intersect. A class can be used to derive a new class, and an interface can be used to derive a new interface, but these two types of hierarchies do not overlap.

SR 9.8 The `Comparable` interface contains a single method called `compareTo`, which should return an integer that is less than zero, equal to zero, or greater than zero if the executing object is less than, equal to, or greater than the object to which it is being compared, respectively.

SR 9.9 An interface name can be used as the type of a reference. Such a reference variable can refer to any object of any class that implements that interface. Because all classes implement the same interface, they have methods with common signatures, which can be dynamically bound.

10

Exceptions

Chapter Objectives

- Discuss the purpose of exceptions.
- Examine exception messages and the call stack trace.
- Examine the `try-catch` statement for handling exceptions.
- Explore the concept of exception propagation.
- Describe the exception class hierarchy in the Java standard class library.
- Explore I/O exceptions and the ability to write text files.

Exception handling is an important part of an object-oriented software system. Exceptions represent problems or unusual situations that may occur in a program. Java provides various ways to handle exceptions when they occur. We explore the class hierarchy from the Java standard library used to define exceptions, as well as the ability to define our own exception objects. This chapter also discusses the use of exceptions when dealing with input and output, and presents an example that writes a text file.

10.1 Exception Handling

Errors and exceptions are objects that represent unusual or invalid processing.

As we've discussed briefly in other parts of the text, problems that arise in a Java program may generate exceptions or errors. An *exception* is an object that defines an unusual or erroneous situation. An exception is thrown by a program or the run-time environment and can be caught and handled appropriately if desired. An *error* is similar to an exception except that an error generally represents an unrecoverable situation and should not be caught.

Java has a predefined set of exceptions and errors that may occur during the execution of a program. If the predefined exceptions don't suffice, a programmer may choose to design a new class that represents an exception that is specific to a particular situation.

Problem situations represented by exceptions and errors can have various kinds of root causes. Here are some examples of situations that cause exceptions to be thrown:

- attempting to divide by zero
- an array index that is out of bounds
- a specified file that could not be found
- a requested I/O operation that could not be completed normally
- attempting to follow a null reference
- attempting to execute an operation that violates some kind of security measure

These are just a few examples. There are dozens of others that address very specific situations.

As many of these examples show, an exception can represent a truly erroneous situation. But, as the name implies, they may simply represent an exceptional situation. That is, an exception may represent a situation that won't occur under usual conditions. Exception handling is set up to be an efficient way to deal with such situations, especially given that they don't happen too often.

We have several options when it comes to dealing with exceptions. A program can be designed to process an exception in one of three ways. It can:

- not handle the exception at all,
- handle the exception where it occurs, or
- handle the exception at another point in the program.

We explore each of these approaches in the following sections.

10.2 Uncaught Exceptions

If a program does not handle the exception at all, it will terminate abnormally and produce a message that describes what exception occurred and where in the code it was produced. The information in an exception message is often helpful in tracking down the cause of a problem.

Let's look at the output of an exception. The program shown in Listing 10.1 throws an `ArithmeticException` when an invalid arithmetic operation is attempted. In this case, the program attempts to divide by zero.

Because there is no code in this program to handle the exception explicitly, it terminates when the exception occurs, printing specific information about the exception. Note that the last `println` statement in the program never executes because the exception occurs first.

The first line of the exception output indicates which exception was thrown and provides some information about why it was thrown. The remaining lines are the *call stack trace*; they indicate where the exception occurred. In this case, there is only one line in the call stack trace, but there may be several depending on where the exception originated. The first trace line indicates the method, file, and line number where the exception occurred. The other trace lines, if present, indicate the methods that were called to get to the method that produced the exception. In this program, there is only one method, and it produced the exception; therefore there is only one line in the trace.

The messages printed when an exception is thrown provide a method call stack trace.

The call stack trace information is also available by calling methods of the exception class that is being thrown. The method `getMessage` returns a string explaining the reason the exception was thrown. The method `printStackTrace` prints the call stack trace.

10.3 The `try-catch` Statement

Let's now examine how we catch and handle an exception when it is thrown. The *try-catch* statement identifies a block of statements that may throw an exception. A *catch clause*, which follows a `try` block, defines how a particular kind of exception is handled. A `try` block can have several `catch` clauses associated with it. Each `catch` clause is called an *exception handler*.

Listing **10.1**

```
//********************************************************************
//  Zero.java       Java Foundations
//
//  Demonstrates an uncaught exception.
//********************************************************************

public class Zero
{
   //-----------------------------------------------------------------
   //  Deliberately divides by zero to produce an exception.
   //-----------------------------------------------------------------
   public static void main (String[] args)
   {
      int numerator = 10;
      int denominator = 0;

      System.out.println ("Before the attempt to divide by zero.");

      System.out.println (numerator / denominator);

      System.out.println ("This text will not be printed.");
   }
}
```

Output

```
Before the attempt to divide by zero.
Exception in thread "main" java.lang.ArithmeticException: / by zero
        at Zero.main(Zero.java:19)
```

When a `try` statement is executed, the statements in the `try` block are executed. If no exception is thrown during the execution of the `try` block, processing continues with the statement following the `try` statement (after all of the `catch` clauses). This situation is the normal execution flow and should occur most of the time.

Each `catch` clause handles a particular kind of exception that may be thrown within the `try` block.

If an exception is thrown at any point during the execution of the `try` block, control is immediately transferred to the appropriate catch handler if it is present. That is, control transfers to the first `catch` clause whose exception class corresponds to the class

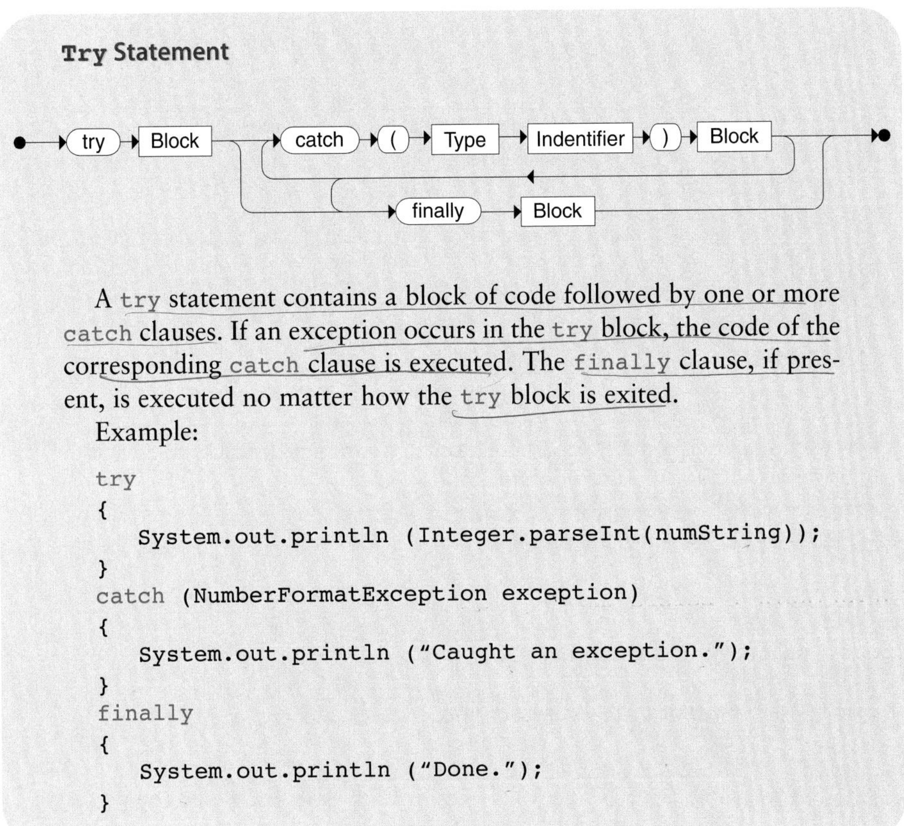

A try statement contains a block of code followed by one or more catch clauses. If an exception occurs in the try block, the code of the corresponding catch clause is executed. The finally clause, if present, is executed no matter how the try block is exited.

Example:

```
try
{
   System.out.println (Integer.parseInt(numString));
}
catch (NumberFormatException exception)
{
   System.out.println ("Caught an exception.");
}
finally
{
   System.out.println ("Done.");
}
```

of the exception that was thrown. After executing the statements in the catch clause, control transfers to the statement after the entire try-catch statement.

Let's look at an example. Suppose a hypothetical company uses codes to represent its various products. A product code includes, among other information, a character in the tenth position that represents the zone from which that product was made, and a four-digit integer in positions 4 through 7 that represents the district in which it will be sold. Due to some reorganization, products from zone R are banned from being sold in districts with a designation of 2000 or higher. The program shown in Listing 10.2 reads product codes from the user and counts the number of banned codes entered.

The programming statements in the try block attempt to pull out the zone and district information, and then determine whether it represents a banned product

Listing 10.2

```
//********************************************************************
//  ProductCodes.java       Java Foundations
//
//  Demonstrates the use of a try-catch block.
//********************************************************************

import java.util.Scanner;

public class ProductCodes
{
   //-----------------------------------------------------------------
   //  Counts the number of product codes that are entered with a
   //  zone of R and district greater than 2000.
   //-----------------------------------------------------------------
   public static void main (String[] args)
   {
      String code;
      char zone;
      int district, valid = 0, banned = 0;

      Scanner scan = new Scanner (System.in);

      System.out.print ("Enter product code (STOP to quit): ");
      code = scan.nextLine();

      while (!code.equals ("STOP"))
      {
         try
         {
            zone = code.charAt(9);
            district = Integer.parseInt(code.substring(3, 7));
            valid++;
            if (zone == 'R' && district > 2000)
               banned++;
         }
         catch (StringIndexOutOfBoundsException exception)
         {
            System.out.println ("Improper code length: " + code);
         }
         catch (NumberFormatException exception)
         {
            System.out.println ("District is not numeric: " + code);
         }
```

Listing **10.2** continued

```
            System.out.print ("Enter product code (STOP to quit): ");
            code = scan.nextLine();
         }

         System.out.println ("# of valid codes entered: " + valid);
         System.out.println ("# of banned codes entered: " + banned);
      }
   }
```

Output

```
Enter product code (STOP to quit): TRV2475A5R-14
Enter product code (STOP to quit): TRD1704A7R-12
Enter product code (STOP to quit): TRL2k74A5R-11
District is not numeric: TRL2k74A5R-11
Enter product code (STOP to quit): TRQ2949A6M-04
Enter product code (STOP to quit): TRV2105A2
Improper code length: TRV2105A2
Enter product code (STOP to quit): TRQ2778A7R-19
Enter product code (STOP to quit): STOP
# of valid codes entered: 4
# of banned codes entered: 2
```

code. If there is any problem extracting the zone and district information, the product code is considered to be invalid and is not processed further. For example, a `StringIndexOutOfBoundsException` could be thrown by either the `charAt` or `substring` method. Furthermore, a `NumberFormatException` will be thrown by the `parseInt` method if the `substring` method does not contain a valid integer. A particular message is printed depending on which exception is thrown. In either case, since the exception is caught and handled, processing continues normally.

Note that, for each code examined, the integer variable `valid` is incremented only if no exception is thrown. If an exception is thrown, control transfers immediately to the appropriate `catch` clause. Likewise, the zone and district are tested by the `if` statement only if no exception is thrown.

The `finally` Clause

The `finally` clause is executed whether the `try` block is exited normally or because of a thrown exception.

A `try-catch` statement can have an optional *finally clause*. The `finally` clause defines a section of code that is executed no matter how the `try` block is exited. Most often, a `finally` clause is used to manage resources or to guarantee that particular parts of an algorithm are executed.

If no exception is generated, the statements in the `finally` clause are executed after the `try` block is complete. If an exception is generated in the `try` block, control first transfers to the appropriate `catch` clause. After executing the exception-handling code, control transfers to the `finally` clause and its statements are executed. A `finally` clause, if present, must be listed after the `catch` clauses.

Note that a `try` block does not need to have a `catch` clause at all. If there are no `catch` clauses, a `finally` clause may be used by itself if that is appropriate for the situation.

10.4 Exception Propagation

We can design our software so that an exception is caught and handled at an outer level in the method calling hierarchy. If an exception is not caught and handled in the method where it occurs, control is immediately returned to the method that invoked the method that produced the exception. If it isn't caught there, control returns to the method that called it, and so on. This process is called *exception propagation.*

If an exception is not caught and handled where it occurs, it is propagated to the calling method.

An exception will be propagated until it is caught and handled or until it is passed out of the `main` method, which causes the program to terminate and produces an exception message. To catch an exception at any level, the method that produces the exception must be invoked inside a `try` block that has `catch` clauses to handle it.

The `Propagation` program shown in Listing 10.3 succinctly demonstrates the process of exception propagation. The `main` method invokes method `level1` in the `ExceptionScope` class (see Listing 10.4), which invokes `level2`, which invokes `level3`, which produces an exception. Method `level3` does not catch and handle the exception, so control is transferred back to `level2`. The `level2` method does not catch and handle the exception either, so control is transferred back to `level1`. Because the invocation of `level2` is made inside a `try` block (in method `level1`), the exception is caught and handled at that point.

Listing **10.3**

```
//********************************************************************
//  Propagation.java       Java Foundations
//
//  Demonstrates exception propagation.
//********************************************************************

public class Propagation
{
   //-----------------------------------------------------------------
   //  Invokes the level1 method to begin the exception demonstration.
   //-----------------------------------------------------------------
   static public void main (String[] args)
   {
      ExceptionScope demo = new ExceptionScope();

      System.out.println("Program beginning.");
      demo.level1();
      System.out.println("Program ending.");
   }
}
```

Output

```
Program beginning.
Level 1 beginning.
Level 2 beginning.
Level 3 beginning.

The exception message is: / by zero

The call stack trace:
java.lang.ArithmeticException: / by zero
        at ExceptionScope.level3(ExceptionScope.java:54)
        at ExceptionScope.level2(ExceptionScope.java:41)
        at ExceptionScope.level1(ExceptionScope.java:18)
        at Propagation.main(Propagation.java:17)

Level 1 ending.
Program ending.
```

Listing **10.4**

```
//********************************************************************
//  ExceptionScope.java       Java Foundations
//
//  Demonstrates exception propagation.
//********************************************************************

public class ExceptionScope
{
   //-----------------------------------------------------------------
   //  Catches and handles the exception that is thrown in level3.
   //-----------------------------------------------------------------
   public void level1()
   {
      System.out.println("Level 1 beginning.");

      try
      {
         level2();
      }
      catch (ArithmeticException problem)
      {
         System.out.println ();
         System.out.println ("The exception message is: " +
                             problem.getMessage());
         System.out.println ();
         System.out.println ("The call stack trace:");
         problem.printStackTrace();
         System.out.println ();
      }

      System.out.println("Level 1 ending.");
   }

   //-----------------------------------------------------------------
   //  Serves as an intermediate level.  The exception propagates
   //  through this method back to level1.
   //-----------------------------------------------------------------
   public void level2()
   {
      System.out.println("Level 2 beginning.");
      level3 ();
      System.out.println("Level 2 ending.");
   }
```

Listing 10.4 continued

```
   //-----------------------------------------------------------------
   //  Performs a calculation to produce an exception.  It is not
   //  caught and handled at this level.
   //-----------------------------------------------------------------
   public void level3 ()
   {
      int numerator = 10, denominator = 0;

      System.out.println("Level 3 beginning.");
      int result = numerator / denominator;
      System.out.println("Level 3 ending.");
   }
}
```

Note that the program output does not include the messages indicating that the methods `level3` and `level2` are ending. These `println` statements are never executed because an exception occurred and had not yet been caught. However, after method `level1` handles the exception, processing continues normally from that point, printing the messages indicating that method `level1` and the program are ending.

Note also that the `catch` clause that handles the exception uses the `getMessage` and `printStackTrace` methods to output that information. The stack trace shows the methods that were called when the exception occurred.

A programmer must carefully consider how and where exceptions should be handled, if at all.

A programmer must pick the most appropriate level at which to catch and handle an exception. There is no single best answer as to how to do this. It depends on the situation and the design of the system. Sometimes the right approach will be not to catch an exception at all and let the program terminate.

10.5 The Exception Class Hierarchy

The classes that define various exceptions are related by inheritance, creating a class hierarchy that is shown in part in Figure 10.1.

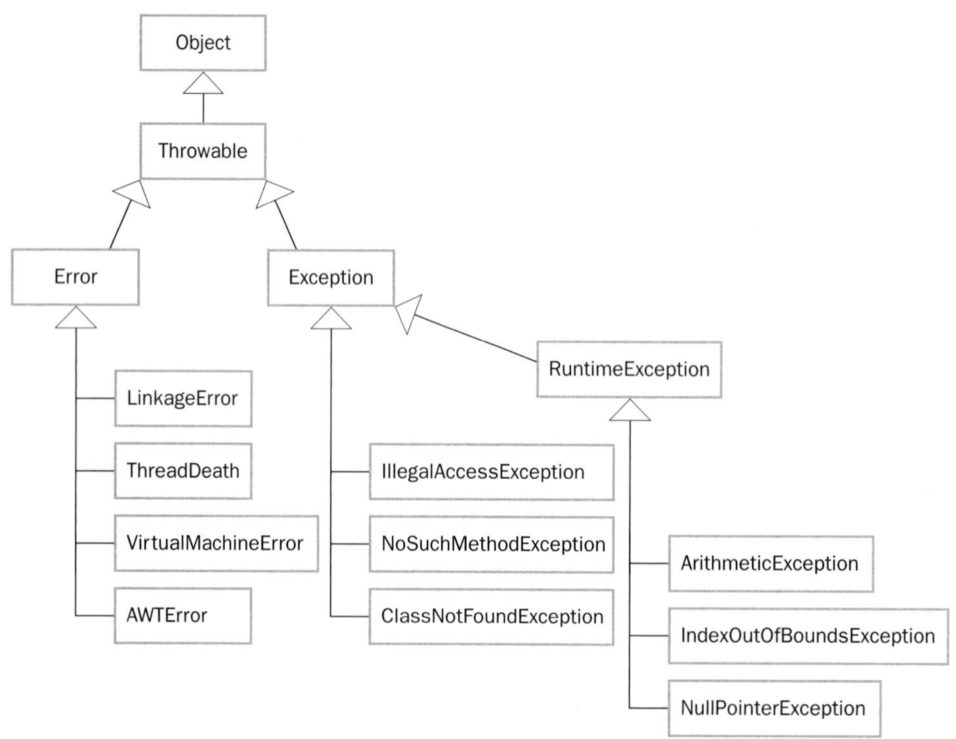

FIGURE 10.1 Part of the `Error` and `Exception` class hierarchy

The `Throwable` class is the parent of both the `Error` class and the `Exception` class. Many types of exceptions are derived from the `Exception` class, and these classes also have many children. Though these high-level classes are defined in the `java.lang` package, many child classes that define specific exceptions are part of other packages. Inheritance relationships can span package boundaries.

A new exception is defined by deriving a new class from the `Exception` class or one of its descendants.

We can define our own exceptions by deriving a new class from `Exception` or one of its descendants. The class we choose as the parent depends on what situation or condition the new exception represents.

The program in Listing 10.5 instantiates an exception object and throws it. The exception is created from the `OutOfRangeException` class, which is shown in Listing 10.6. This exception is not part of the Java standard class library. It was created to represent the situation in which a value is outside a particular valid range.

Listing 10.5

```
//********************************************************************
//  CreatingExceptions.java       Java Foundations
//
//  Demonstrates the ability to define an exception via inheritance.
//********************************************************************

import java.util.Scanner;

public class CreatingExceptions
{
   //-----------------------------------------------------------------
   //  Creates an exception object and possibly throws it.
   //-----------------------------------------------------------------
   public static void main (String[] args) throws OutOfRangeException
   {
      final int MIN = 25, MAX = 40;

      Scanner scan = new Scanner (System.in);

      OutOfRangeException problem =
         new OutOfRangeException ("Input value is out of range.");

      System.out.print ("Enter an integer value between " + MIN +
                        " and " + MAX + ", inclusive: ");
      int value = scan.nextInt();

      //  Determine if the exception should be thrown
      if (value < MIN || value > MAX)
         throw problem;

      System.out.println ("End of main method.");  // may never reach
   }
}
```

Output

```
Enter an integer value between 25 and 40, inclusive: 69
Exception in thread "main" OutOfRangeException:
        Input value is out of range.
        at CreatingExceptions.main(CreatingExceptions.java:20)
```

Listing **10.6**

```
//********************************************************************
//  OutOfRangeException.java       Java Foundations
//
//  Represents an exceptional condition in which a value is out of
//  some particular range.
//********************************************************************

public class OutOfRangeException extends Exception
{
   //-----------------------------------------------------------------
   //  Sets up the exception object with a particular message.
   //-----------------------------------------------------------------
   OutOfRangeException (String message)
   {
      super (message);
   }
}
```

After reading in an input value, the `main` method evaluates it to see whether it is in the valid range. If not, the *throw statement* is executed. A `throw` statement is used to begin exception propagation. Because the `main` method does not catch and handle the exception, the program will terminate if the exception is thrown, printing the message associated with the exception.

We created the `OutOfRangeException` class by extending the `Exception` class. Often, a new exception is nothing more than what you see in this example: an extension of some existing exception class that stores a particular message describing the situation it represents. The important point is that the class is ultimately a descendant of the `Exception` class and the `Throwable` class, which gives it the ability to be thrown using a `throw` statement.

The type of situation handled by this program, in which a value is out of range, does not need to be represented as an exception. We've previously handled such situations using conditionals or loops alone. Whether you handle a situation using an exception or take care of it in the normal flow of your program is an important design decision.

Checked and Unchecked Exceptions

Some exceptions are checked, whereas others are unchecked. A *checked exception* must either be caught by a method or be listed in the *throws clause* of any method that may throw or propagate it. A `throws` clause is appended to the header of a method definition to formally acknowledge that the method will throw or propagate a particular exception if it occurs. An *unchecked* exception requires no `throws` clause.

The `throws` clause on a method header must be included for checked exceptions that are not caught and handled in the method.

The only unchecked exceptions in Java are objects of type `RuntimeException` or any of its descendants. All other exceptions are considered checked exceptions. The `main` method of the `CreatingExceptions` program has a `throws` clause, indicating that it may throw an `OutOfRangeException`. This `throws` clause is required because the `OutOfRangeException` was derived from the `Exception` class, making it a checked exception.

10.6 I/O Exceptions

Processing input and output is a task that often produces tenuous situations, given that it relies on external resources such as user data and files. These resources can have various problems that lead to exceptions being thrown. Let's explore some I/O issues and the problems that may arise.

A *stream* is an ordered sequence of bytes. The term stream comes from the analogy that as we read and write information, the data flows from a source to a destination (or *sink*) as water flows down a stream. The source of the information is like a spring filling the stream, and the destination is like a cave into which the stream flows.

A stream is a sequential sequence of bytes; it can be used as a source of input or a destination for output.

In a program, we treat a stream as either an *input stream*, from which we read information, or as an *output stream*, to which we write information. A program can deal with multiple input and output streams at one time. A particular store of data, such as a file, can serve either as an input stream or as an output stream to a program, but it generally cannot be both at the same time.

There are three streams that are referred to as the standard I/O streams. They are listed in Figure 10.2. The `System` class contains three object reference variables (`in`, `out`, and `err`) that represent the three standard I/O streams. These references are declared as both `public` and `static`, which allows them to be accessed directly through the `System` class.

Three public reference variables in the `System` class represent the standard I/O streams.

Standard I/O Stream	Description
`System.in`	Standard input stream.
`System.out`	Standard output stream.
`System.err`	Standard error stream (output for error messages)

FIGURE10.2 Standard I/O streams

We've been using the standard output stream, with calls to `System.out.prinln` for instance, in examples throughout this book. We've also used the standard input stream to create a `Scanner` object when we want to process input read interactively from the user. The `Scanner` class manages the input read from the standard input stream in various ways that makes our programming tasks easier. It also processes various I/O exceptions internally, producing an `InputMismatchException` when needed.

The standard I/O streams, by default, represent particular I/O devices. `System.in` typically represents keyboard input, whereas `System.out` and `System.err` typically represent a particular window on the monitor screen. The `System.out` and `System.err` streams write output to the same window by default (usually the one in which the program was executed), though they could be set up to write to different places. The `System.err` stream is usually where error messages are sent.

In addition to the standard input streams, the `java.io` package of the Java standard class library provides many classes that let us define streams with particular characteristics. Some of the classes deal with files, others with memory, and others with strings. Some classes assume that the data they handle consists of characters, whereas others assume the data consists of raw bytes of binary information. Some classes provide the means to manipulate the data in the stream in some way, such as buffering the information or numbering it. By combining classes in appropriate ways, we can create objects that represent a stream of information that has the exact characteristics we want for a particular situation.

The Java class library contains many classes for defining I/O streams with various characteristics.

The broad topic of Java I/O, and the sheer number of classes in the `java.io` package, prohibits us from covering it in detail in this book. Our focus for the moment is on I/O exceptions.

Many operations performed by I/O classes can potentially throw an `IOException`. The `IOException` class is the parent of several exception classes that represent problems when trying to perform I/O.

An `IOException` is a checked exception. As described earlier in this chapter, that means that either the exception must be caught or all methods that propagate it must list it in a `throws` clause of the method header.

Because I/O often deals with external resources, many problems can arise in programs that attempt to perform I/O operations. For example, a file from which we want to read might not exist; when we attempt to open the file, an exception will be thrown because that file can't be found. In general, we should try to design programs to be as robust as possible when dealing with potential problems.

We've seen in previous examples how we can use the `Scanner` class to read and process input read from a text file. Now let's explore an example that writes data to a text output file. Writing output to a text file requires simply that we use the appropriate classes to create the output stream, then call the appropriate methods to write the data.

Suppose we want to test a program we are writing, but don't have the real data available. We could write a program that generates a test data file that contains random values. The program shown in Listing 10.7 generates a file that contains random integer values within a particular range. It also writes one line of standard output, confirming that the data file has been written.

Listing **10.7**

```
//********************************************************************
//  TestData.java       Java Foundations
//
//  Demonstrates I/O exceptions and the use of a character file
//  output stream.
//********************************************************************

import java.util.Random;
import java.io.*;

public class TestData
{
   //-----------------------------------------------------------------
   //  Creates a file of test data that consists of ten lines each
   //  containing ten integer values in the range 10 to 99.
   //-----------------------------------------------------------------
   public static void main (String[] args) throws IOException
   {
      final int MAX = 10;
```

Listing 10.7 continued

```
      int value;
      String file = "test.dat";

      Random rand = new Random();

      FileWriter fw = new FileWriter (file);
      BufferedWriter bw = new BufferedWriter (fw);
      PrintWriter outFile = new PrintWriter (bw);

      for (int line=1; line <= MAX; line++)
      {
         for (int num=1; num <= MAX; num++)
         {
            value = rand.nextInt (90) + 10;
            outFile.print (value + "   ");
         }
         outFile.println ();
      }

      outFile.close();
      System.out.println ("Output file has been created: " + file);
   }
}
```

Output

```
Output file has been created: test.dat
```

The `FileWriter` class represents a text output file, but has minimal method support for manipulating data. The `PrintWriter` class provides `print` and `println` methods similar to the standard I/O `PrintStream` class.

Although we do not need to do so for the program to work, we have added a layer in the file stream configuration to include a `BufferedWriter`. This addition simply gives the output stream buffering capabilities, which makes the processing more efficient. While buffering is not crucial in this situation, it is usually a good idea when writing text files.

Note that in the `TestData` program, we have eliminated explicit exception handling. That is, if something goes wrong, we simply allow the program to terminate instead of specifically catching and handling the problem. Because all `IOExceptions` are checked exceptions, we must include the `throws` clause on the method header to indicate that they may be thrown. For each program, we must carefully consider how best to handle the exceptions that may be thrown. This requirement is especially important when dealing with I/O, which is fraught with potential problems that cannot always be foreseen.

The `TestData` program uses nested `for` loops to compute random values and write them to the output file. After all values are printed, the file is closed. Output files must be closed explicitly to ensure that the data is retained. In general, it is good practice to close all file streams explicitly when they are no longer needed.

Output file streams should be explicitly closed or they may not correctly retain the data written to them

The data that is contained in the file `test.dat` after the `TestData` program is run might look like this:

```
85  90  93  15  82  79  52  71  70  98
74  57  41  66  22  16  67  65  24  84
86  61  91  79  18  81  64  41  68  81
98  47  28  40  69  10  85  82  64  41
23  61  27  10  59  89  88  26  24  76
33  89  73  36  54  91  42  73  95  58
19  41  18  14  63  80  96  30  17  28
24  37  40  64  94  23  98  10  78  50
89  28  64  54  59  23  61  15  80  88
51  28  44  48  73  21  41  52  35  38
```

Summary of Key Concepts

- Errors and exceptions are objects that represent unusual or invalid processing.
- The messages printed when an exception is thrown provide a method call stack trace.
- Each `catch` clause handles a particular kind of exception that may be thrown within the `try` block.
- The `finally` clause is executed whether the `try` block is exited normally or because of a thrown exception.
- If an exception is not caught and handled where it occurs, it is propagated to the calling method.
- A programmer must carefully consider how and where exceptions should be handled, if at all.
- A new exception is defined by deriving a new class from the `Exception` class or one of its descendants.
- The `throws` clause on a method header must be included for checked exceptions that are not caught and handled in the method.
- A stream is a sequential sequence of bytes; it can be used as a source of input or a destination for output.
- Three public reference variables in the `System` class represent the standard I/O streams.
- The Java class library contains many classes for defining I/O streams with various characteristics.
- Output file streams should be explicitly closed or they may not correctly retain the data written to them.

Self-Review Questions

SR 10.1 In what ways might a thrown exception be handled?

SR 10.2 What is a `catch` phrase?

SR 10.3 What happens if an exception is not caught?

SR 10.4 What is a `finally` clause?

SR 10.5 What is a checked exception?

SR 10.6 What is a stream?

SR 10.7 What are the standard I/O streams?

Exercises

EX 10.1 Create a UML class diagram for the `ProductCodes` program.

EX 10.2 Describe the output for the `ProductCodes` program if a `finally` clause were added to the `try` statement that printed the string `"Got here!"`.

EX 10.3 What would happen if the `try` statement were removed from the `level1` method of the `ExceptionScope` class in the `Propagation` program?

EX 10.4 What would happen if the `try` statement described in the previous exercise were moved to the `level2` method?

EX 10.5 What happens when the `Exception` class is used in a `catch` clause to catch an exception?

EX 10.6 Look up the following exception classes in the online Java API documentation and describe their purpose:

a. `ArithmeticException`

b. `NullPointerException`

c. `NumberFormatException`

d. `PatternSyntaxException`

EX 10.7 Describe the output file used in the `TestData` program in terms of the classes that were used to create it.

Programming Projects

PP 10.1 Design and implement a program that reads a series of 10 integers from the user and prints their average. Read each input value as a string, and then attempt to convert it to an integer using the `Integer.parseInt` method. If this process throws a `NumberFormatException` (meaning that the input is not a valid number), print an appropriate error message and prompt for the number again. Continue reading values until 10 valid integers have been entered.

PP 10.2 Design and implement a program that creates an exception class called `StringTooLongException`, designed to be thrown when a string is discovered that has too many characters in it. In the `main` driver of the program, read strings from the user until the user enters `"DONE"`. If a string is entered that has too many characters (say 20), throw the exception. Allow the thrown exception to terminate the program.

PP 10.3 Modify the solution to programming project 10.2 such that it catches and handles the exception if it is thrown. Handle the exception by printing an appropriate message, and then continue processing more strings.

PP 10.4 Design and implement a program that creates an exception class called `InvalidDocumentCodeException`, designed to be thrown when an improper designation for a document is encountered during processing. Suppose in a particular business all documents are given a two-character designation starting with U, C, or P, standing for unclassified, confidential, or proprietary. If a document designation is encountered that doesn't fit that description, the exception is thrown. Create a driver program to test the exception, allowing it to terminate the program.

PP 10.5 Modify the solution to programming project 10.4 such that it catches and handles the exception if it is thrown. Handle the exception by printing an appropriate message, and then continue processing.

PP 10.6 Write a program that reads strings from the user and writes them to an output file called `userStrings.dat`. Terminate processing when the user enters the string `"DONE"`. Do not write the sentinel string to the output file.

PP 10.7 Suppose a library is processing an input file containing the titles of books in order to remove duplicates. Write a program that reads all of the titles from an input file called `bookTitles.inp` and writes them to an output file called `noDuplicates.out`. When complete, the output file should contain all unique titles found in the input file.

Answers to Self-Review Questions

SR 10.1 A thrown exception can be handled in one of three ways: it can be ignored, which will cause a program to terminate, it can be handled where it occurs using a `try` statement, or it can be caught and handled higher in the method calling hierarchy.

SR 10.2 A `catch` phrase of a `try` statement defines the code that will handle a particular type of exception.

SR 10.3 If an exception is not caught immediately when thrown, it begins to propagate up through the methods that were called to get to the point where it was generated. The exception can be caught and handled at any point during that propagation. If it propagates out of the `main` method, the program terminates.

SR 10.4 The `finally` clause of a `try-catch` statement is executed no matter how the `try` block is exited. If no exception is thrown, the `finally` clause is executed after the `try` block is complete. If an exception is thrown, the appropriate `catch` clause is executed, then the `finally` clause is executed.

SR 10.5 A checked exception is an exception that must be either (1) caught and handled or (2) listed in the `throws` clause of any method that may throw or propagate it. This establishes a set of exceptions that must be formally acknowledged in the program one way or another. Unchecked exceptions can be ignored completely in the code if desired.

SR 10.6 A stream is a sequential series of bytes that serves as a source of input or a destination for output.

SR 10.7 The standard I/O streams in Java are `System.in`, the standard input stream; `System.out`, the standard output stream; and `System.err`, the standard error stream. Usually, standard input comes from the keyboard and standard output and errors go to a default window on the monitor screen.

Chapter Objectives

Introduce the JFMail application, a text-based mail-reading program.

Discuss the use and creation of packages in Java.

Investigate the use of the CLASSPATH environment variable.

Examine Java archive (jar) files.

Introduce build tools and create an ANT build file for our project.

Discuss various types of testing.

Introduce the JUnit testing framework.

Examine the process of debugging programs.

11 Building, Testing, and Debugging

As you become more proficient in software development, you will likely work on larger projects with more complex designs and a large amount of source code. Larger projects require better organization of code, better management of resources, and better approaches to testing and debugging. This chapter focuses on a number of concepts and activities that every programmer should master as they move into more advanced applications.

11.1 Building Larger Applications: JFMail

This chapter explores a variety of topics related to the process of developing large-scale software. First, we'll introduce an application that will provide a context for our discussions. The JFMail application is a text-based (non-GUI) program for reading email across the Internet. The program is still relatively small—four classes total—but it provides an excellent basis for us to discuss this chapter's topics.

The JFMail application is a basic *email client*, a program that communicates with an *email server* through which mail is sent and received. The server is a separate program running on a computer somewhere on the Internet. When an email message is sent to you, it is stored on the server computer, waiting for you to read it. You run an email client to retrieve your messages from the server and present them to you to read. When you send mail, you compose the message in your email client, which sends it out through the server. The relationship between the email client and server is depicted in Figure 11.1. In many cases, there are two different email servers, one to handle incoming mail and one to handle outgoing mail.

The JFMail application, as discussed in this chapter, is an email client for handling incoming mail. Extending the client to send outgoing mail to an email server is left as a programming project.

The JFMail application uses Sun's JavaMail API, a library of classes that will help us write a full-featured email client. The JavaMail API supports a number of communications protocols for reading email from a server, including IMAP and POP. These communications protocols establish the commands required to communicate with another machine for the purposes of reading mail (IMAP and POP) or sending mail (SMTP). The SMTP protocol is also included as part of the JavaMail API. The JFMail application will only have the capability to receive email—we leave the modifications for sending email up to you!

Figure 11.2 shows a UML class diagram for the JFMail application as it was developed.

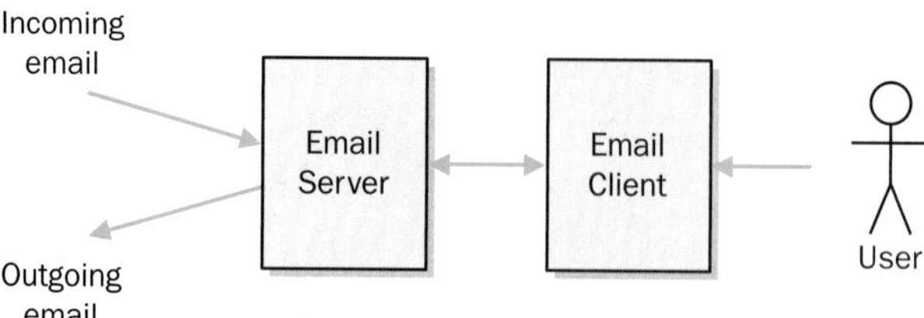

FIGURE 11.1 An email client and server

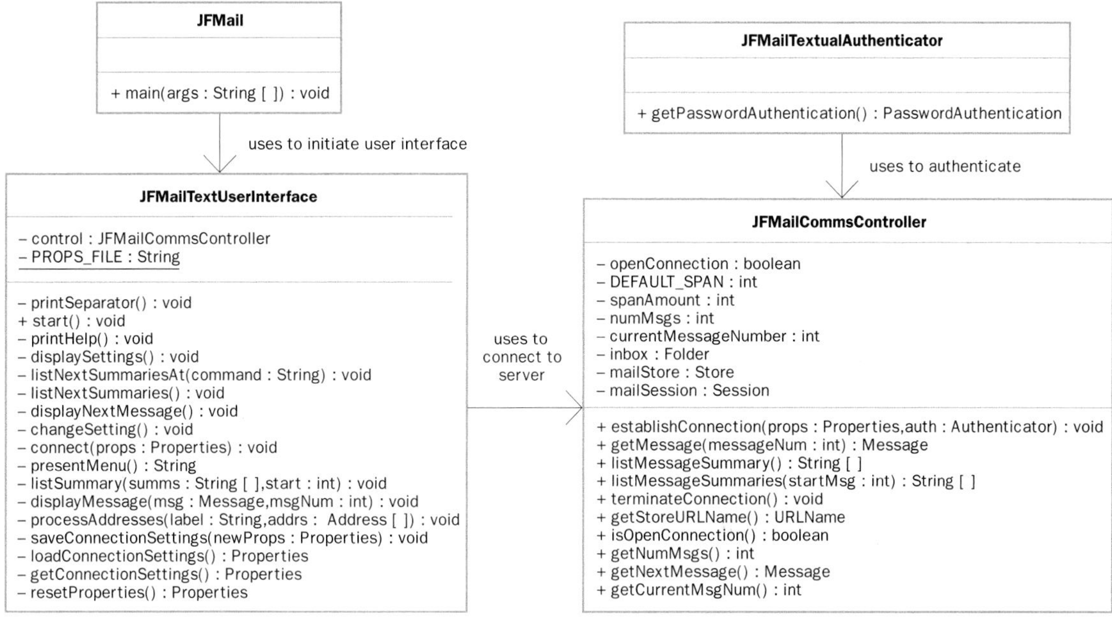

FIGURE 11.2 A UML class diagram for the JFMail program

Design Considerations

We'll examine the code in the JFMail program eventually, but let's first discuss some of the issues related to its design, as shown in Figure 11.2. The `JFMail` class instantiates a `JFMailCommsController` object and passes it to a `JFMailTextUserInterface` object. Since our user interface will be achieved entirely through plain printed text to the user's command shell, the `JFMailTextUserInterface` class is designed to do just that—handle all input from the user via the keyboard and produce all output to the screen through simple `println` statements to the `System.out` object.

Communications to the mail server are established and managed in the `JFMailCommsController` class. Its job is to provide a clean, consistent method for any type of user interface object to be able to obtain the information it needs. This includes establishing communications with the server, obtaining summaries of messages or messages themselves, and disconnecting from the server.

When we started the design of the JFMail application, we decided that our design should include the ability to swap out the text-based user interface with a GUI-based user interface. This activity is left as a programming project at the end of this chapter. However, to accomplish this swap capability, we carefully thought about the services the `JFMailCommsController` class provides to its clients (`JFMailUserInterface` or its replacement user interface). The `JFMailCommsController` class must therefore provide all communication capabilities on behalf of the application and be capable of providing requested data (`Message` objects, message summaries, status information, etc.) in a user interface-neutral approach.

The `JFMailTextualAuthenticator` class extends the `Authenticator` class located in the `javax.mail` package, to provide a text-based approach to query the user for their username and password during the connection to the mail server. `JFMailTextualAuthenticator`'s sole method, `getPasswordAuthentication`, is called by the JavaMail's `Session` object during the connection attempt at the point user authentication is required.

The JFMail application enables you to do the following capabilities once it is connected to a mail server:

- display a short summary of a specified message (including message number, who the message is from, and the subject of the message)
- display a summary of the next 10 messages
- display the contents of a specified message (including the message number, sender information, subject line, and plain text body of the message)
- display the contents of the next message
- display a short listing of each command option and its description
- display the current settings of the connection (hostname, username, and connection protocol)
- reset the current settings of the connection (including termination of the current connection and establishing a new connection—possibly to a different mail host)
- exit the application (including termination of the current connection)

The JFMail application will attempt to save the most recent set of successful configuration settings to a properties file named `jfMail.props` in the project's main directory. This file is written and read through the use of the `java.util.Properties` class. The `Properties` object creates a list of name and value pairs typically used to store application settings. In the JFMail application, we use this approach to quickly create a list of application settings that we wish to store, specifically the mail server hostname and the mail communications protocol used to communicate with the mail server. Once created, this list can easily be written to a plain text file and read back in again by the `Properties` class.

11.2 Packages

In Chapter 3, we briefly introduced the concept of a class library and the use of packages to organize the classes that the library contains. Software developers often organize the classes that make up a large program into packages of common functionality. Some packages may be general enough to be used in multiple programs. The source code you develop may not be destined for only one program, but rather a class library that you create and share (or sell) to other programmers. These programmers in turn use your packaging structure to quickly locate classes of use to them, organized by functionality.

Packages are used to organize source code based on functionality.

Code Organization Through Packaging

You've used classes from various packages as you have worked on projects in earlier chapters of this text. As we've seen, the `java.util` package contains a variety of classes for utility purposes, `java.lang` contains classes related to core aspects of the language, and `java.io` encompasses input and output functionality.

The JFMail application consists of three packages: `jfmail`, `jfmail.userInterface`, and `jfMail.communications`. The `JFMail` class is our driver class that contains the `main` method for the application. Its job is to instantiate the most fundamental objects required for program execution and to start the main body of processing. The `JFMail` class resides in the `jfmail` package, and therefore the fully qualified name of the class is `jfmail.JFMail`. In our `jfmail.userInterface` package, we find the two classes that comprise the functionality of the creation of our text-based interface, `JFMailTextUserInterface` and `JFMailTextualAuthenticator`, both discussed earlier. Note, however, that since both of these classes were related to the user interface, we gather them together into a single package. If we were to develop additional classes that support other types of user interfaces (for example, graphical user interfaces or perhaps a cell phone user interface), we would likely place those classes in this package as well.

Finally, we have the `jfmail.communications` package, which contains the `JFMailCommsController` and `JFCommsTesting` classes. We have placed this class in the `jfmail.communications` package because it is a class that supports the communications aspects of the mail application.

Creating Your Own Packages

The JFMail application's packaging is not overly complex—only three packages are involved. We create our own packages by creating subdirectories in our working area when authoring our applications, and by establishing which package a class belongs to in the source code.

Let's examine the directory structure for our JFMail application, shown in Figure 11.3. Our project is located in the `C:\Documents and Settings\Peter\Desktop\ch11` directory. The only file in this directory is named `build.xml` (an Ant build file, which we will discuss in section 11.3 of this chapter). Our `ch11` directory also contains a subdirectory named `jfmail`, which is the home of all the classes contained in the `jfmail` package. The `jfmail` package contains the `JFMail.java` source code file. Within the `jfmail` directory we also find the `communications` and `userInterface` directories, each containing their respective source code files.

If you recall the full name of the `userInterface` package, it is `jfmail.userInterface`. However, when we organize our source code, the package name is broken up into directories (sometimes nested within other package directories) based on the name of the package. Be careful here, because we don't use the full name of the package in the directory name if the package comprises more than one component. That is, our communications directory is not named `jfmail.communications`.

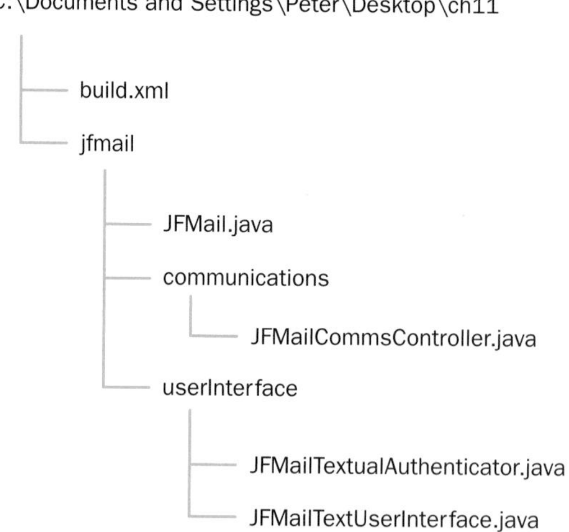

FIGURE 11.3 The directory structure for the JFMail application

Creating directories for our packaged source code is not enough, though. We also need to modify the source code file itself. Let's look at the source code for the `JFMail` class, more correctly known as the `jfmail.JFMail` class. Listing 11.1 shows the source code of the file. The first statement in the file (not the comments) is

```
package jfmail;
```

This statement indicates that the class contained in the file is part of the `jfmail` package. At compile time, the compiler will check the package declaration statement and the location of the source code file in the directory tree to ensure that the source code file is in the correct location.

Since the `JFMail` class uses both the `JFMailTextUserInterface` and `JFMailCommsController` classes in the body of the `main` method, the `JFMail` class needs to import these classes from their respective packages. So, we have

Listing 11.1

```
//*******************************************************************
//  JFMail.java        Java Foundations
//
//  Main driver for the JF Mail application.
//*******************************************************************
package jfmail;

import jfmail.communications.*;
import jfmail.userInterface.*;

public class JFMail
{
   //-----------------------------------------------------------------
   //  Instantiates and initiates the user interface for the mail
   //  application.
   //-----------------------------------------------------------------
   public static void main (String[] args)
   {
      JFMailCommsController comms = new JFMailCommsController();
      JFMailTextUserInterface ui = new JFMailTextUserInterface(comms);
      ui.start();
   }
}
```

also added the two `import` statements following the package declaration statement in the `JFMail` class.

We can also create packages elsewhere in the file system if we so choose. For example, if the JFMail application were to utilize additional classes that we had authored, such as the collections code we discuss in Chapter 14, we only need to tell the compiler (`javac`) and run-time environment (`java`) where in the file system to search for the additional packages.

Using CLASSPATH

An *environment variable* is a variable set up at the operating system level to establish a value needed by the overall computing system. The CLASSPATH environment variable is usually set in the command shell to indicate the list of paths (directories and other locations) where the compiler or run-time environment will look if it cannot find a class we reference in the source code. Recall that this happens automatically for classes in the Java API—such as `java.util.Scanner`, `java.lang.String`, and `java.net.URL`, for example.

The variable can be set through several mechanisms. The first is to modify it on the command line as an option to the compiler or run-time environment. For example, let's assume our JFMail application needed to import classes from our collections code in the `javafoundations` package. Additionally, let's assume the `javafoundations` package is located at `C:\javafoundations` on our system. At compile time, we will need to tell the compiler that there are two primary locations to search for any classes not provided by the API. To do this we add the `-cp` command-line option when invoking the compiler, as in:

```
javac -cp C:\javafoundations;. jfmail\JFMail.java
```

Following the `-cp` option, we specify the two locations we instruct the compiler to search in. The first is `C:\javafoundations`, where we have placed the collections code. The second location is specified as a period (`.`), the current working directory from which the `javac` command was issued. When searching for packages that contain the classes our program is using, the compiler looks first in the Java installation area (for API classes), then the `C:\javafoundations` directory, and then the current directory.

The CLASSPATH environment variable may also be modified for temporary use in the command shell (Windows command shell, or login shell in Unix/Linux) by first setting the variable name and value prior to executing other commands, such as compiling or executing the run-time environment. Under the Windows operating system, an environment variable can be temporarily set by issuing the set command. For example,

```
set CLASSPATH=.;C:\javafoundations
```

On Unix machines the process is somewhat more complex, depending on the type of shell you are using. Check with your instructor or system administrator to determine how to set an environment variable via the command line.

Shortly, we will temporarily set our environment variables to store the installation location of several additional software packages needed to successfully compile and execute the JFMail application. By setting these variables, we will be able to shorten our command line compilation and execution commands, as well as use them in other tools, such as the ANT build files we will introduce later in this chapter.

Finally, the CLASSPATH variable may be permanently set in the command shell by altering the variable in the Control Panel (Windows) or the shell's login configuration file (Unix/Linux). These modifications are easy to accomplish, but beyond the scope of this book, so we encourage you to look at our tutorial about this activity on the book's Web site. By setting an environment variable through the shell, we can access it in a variety of places, such as in programs, in scripts, and in the shell itself.

Regardless of how you achieve the modification to the CLASSPATH variable, you should note that in the examples above we set our CLASSPATH to be `C:\javafoundations;.` (including the dot that represents the current working directory). Items in the CLASSPATH variable are separated by a semicolon (`;`) in Windows and a colon (`:`) under Unix/Linux.

Often, the same classes that we need access to during compilation will be required at run time by the interpreter. So, in a similar fashion, we can modify the CLASSPATH via the command line for the interpreter. To get the JFMail application to execute, we would issue the following:

```
java -cp C:\javafoundations;. jfmail.JFMail
```

Had we set the CLASSPATH environment variable via the shell or the control panel, we could shorten our command to:

```
java jfmail.JFMail
```

Here, the value of the CLASSPATH is used by the Java run-time environment automatically, so we don't need to specify it via the `–cp` option.

Another item we need to point out is found here—the use of the package and directory names on the command line. When issuing the `javac` compiler command, we referred to the `JFMail.java` source code file by referencing it with its directory name (also its package name): `jfMail\JFMail.java`. When we issued the compiler command, the shell was working in the `ch11` directory and the source code we wished to compile was located in the `jfmail` directory. If we had used the full package name to specify the file to compile (as in `jfmail.JFMail`), the file would not have been found.

When we issued the command to start the execution of the JFMail application, we referred to the class by including the package name of the class (`jfmail.JFMail`). Here, we are not referring to a file name, but rather to a specific class in a specific package. Be careful when you issue each of these commands when working with your own programs. A common mistake is to always use the file name for both the `javac` and `java` programs, or to always use the fully qualified class name.

If you have attempted to download and execute the JFMail application, you may have run into an error when one or more classes were not found. This is due to the fact that the JFMail application relies on the JavaMail API, as we mentioned in section 11.1. So, you need to visit the JavaMail API Web site, agree to the license, and download and install the API to get the JFMail application to compile and execute. You can find the JavaMail API Web site at:

http://java.sun.com/products/javamail/downloads/index.html

Some of the functionality of the JavaMail API relies on another Java product known as the JavaBeans Activation Framework (JAF). So, you need to download and install this as well. You can find this product at the following Web site:

http://java.sun.com/products/javabeans/jaf/downloads/index.html

Both the JavaMail API and JAF are delivered as zip files, which you need to unzip and install into locations on your local machine's file system.

The JavaMail API and JAF provide a wealth of additional classes for our use. In addition to the classes, the zip files you downloaded contain documentation, demo programs, and other supporting files. We are mainly interested in the additional classes. Rather than delivering the classes as source code, only the class files are provided. Additionally, they are each packaged into a special file known as a jar file, and this is the subject of our next section.

Java Archive (Jar) Files

Programmers often wish to share their files with other individuals. For example, it is not uncommon to share the class files of our program with customers or other individuals so that they may run our Java program. Another scenario might include students who need to share their .java files with their instructors (for grading or debugging purposes). To accomplish this, we can collect the files we wish to share into an email as multiple attachments, but this is often sloppy for the recipient. Alternatively, we can package the files into a directory and burn them to a CD-ROM and give the physical media to our intended recipient.

A better solution is to package our files into a single file. This approach is commonly used by computer users the world over when we "zip" a group of files together into what is known as a "zip" file. Zip is an algorithm that is used to compress each file from a group and package them in a standard way as a single file. Java's implementation of this approach is known as a Java Archive or jar file.

The Java Standard Edition (SE) Development Kit (JDK) includes a program that is used to create, view, and explode jar files. Once packaged in this fashion, we can share our .class or .java files (and graphic images, sound files, etc.) with other users. Jar files are relatively easy to create and provide a number of other advanced functions that we will not delve into here. However, it is very useful for us to know how to build and use jar files.

Let's say, for example, that we wish to create a jar file for our JFMail application. Inside of this file we may wish to add all of our source code from the three different packages. To accomplish this, we'll use the `jar` program to build a new jar file:

```
C:\> jar -cf jfmail.jar jfmail\*.java
   jfmail\userInterface\*.java jfmail\communications\*.java
```

Note that we are passing two options to the `jar` tool program: `c` and `f`. The first (`c`), tells the program that we are creating a new jar file. The second (`f`) defines the name of the jar file (which follows the `f`) as `jfmail.jar`. Finally, the remainder of the command specifies which files we will add to the jar file—all .java files in the three different packaging directories.

If we wish to see the contents of a jar file, we can use the `jar` tool program with the `t`, `v`, and `f` options (to show the table of contents, verbosely display the information, and specify the jar file we wish to examine, respectively):

```
C:\> jar -tvf jfmail.jar
```

To extract all of the contents of a jar file, we can use the `jar` tool program with the `x`, `v`, and `f` options to specify extraction, specify verbose output (a report of the extraction process), and specify the jar file, respectively:

```
C:\> jar -xvf jfmail.jar
```

In addition to using the Java-provided `jar` tool, many popular IDEs come with the capability to help you build your jar files with the aid of a GUI wizard or window. Check with the documentation for your particular IDE to see if you can take advantage of this feature.

Using Another Developer's Packages

Often, jar files are used to share class files so that another individual can execute the application contained within the jar file, or so that another developer can write an application using the classes contained in the jar file.

Since our focus is on software development using Java, for now we'll turn our attention to using the jar file's contents in developing our own programs. The JFMail application requires the JavaMail API and JAF code, so we need to include the jar files for these two libraries in the CLASSPATH when we compile our project's code. In our case, we have installed the downloads in `C:\Program Files\Java\javamail-1.4` and `C:\Program Files\Java\jaf-1.1` on our local system. We also set two command shell environment variables named JAVAMAIL_HOME and JAF_HOME to be used a little later in this chapter. To achieve this we executed the following two commands in our shell:

```
set JAVAMAIL_HOME="C:\Program Files\Java\javamail-1.4"
set JAF_HOME="C:\Program Files\jaf-1.1"
```

Notice that we set each of the variables to the installation location of the downloaded libraries, and the use of the double quotes in the values. Since the path names to the installation locations contain spaces, we need to surround the locations with double quotes.

In reading through the JavaMail documentation, we find that we will require the `mail.jar` file from the JavaMail installation and the `activation.jar` file from the JAF installation. Actually, we only will need the `activation.jar` file when we execute our program, but we need the `mail.jar` file for both compilation and execution.

We'll leave the jar files in their respective installation directories for the time being, and modify how we compile our JFMail code. We can now compile our application with the following command, executed from the `C:\Documents and Settings\Peter\Desktop\ch11` directory on our system:

```
javac -cp %JAVAMAIL_HOME%\mail.jar;. jfmail\JFMail.java
```

Note the use of the percent signs (on our Windows-based system). These are used to replace the environment variable with its value.

Our execution command is even longer, since we have to include in the `activation.jar` file as well:

```
java -cp %JAF_HOME%\activation.jar;%JAVAMAIL_HOME\mail.jar;.jfmail.JFMail
```

We could make our lives a little easier and copy the two jar files to the project's directory (`C:\Documents and Settings\Peter\Desktop\ch11`). However, shortly we will make life much easier by using build files. So, we'll leave the jar files where they are.

If the purpose of a jar file is for an individual to execute the application in the jar file, we can achieve this in one of two ways. First, we can specify the name of the jar file and the class that contains the `main` method when you use the Java run-time environment (that is, when we execute a program using the Java interpreter). For example, if our jar file's name is `awesomeApp.jar` and the `main` method of the application resides in the `com.awesome.Driver` class, we can issue the following command:

```
java -jar awesomeApp.jar com.awesome.Driver
```

Our alternative approach relies on the jar file's developer. At the time the jar file is created, the developer can specify the location of the class that contains the `main` method of the application (also known as the "main class"). This information is encoded into the `MANIFEST.MF` file, which is placed in the `META-INF` (meta information) directory of the jar file. This too is beyond the scope of our discussion, so we'll leave the details of creating the manifest file correctly for you to find at another time. However, if the main class is declared in the manifest file (there's really no way to know without trying these steps), you can then either double-click on the jar file with your mouse (this works under Windows and some configurations of Unix/Linux) or issue the following command:

```
java -jar awesomeApp.jar
```

In this instance, we don't need to specify the location of the main class, as that information is encoded in the jar file.

11.3 Building Java Projects

As you can likely gather from the preceding discussion, it is very easy for large, complex applications to quickly have very ugly compilation and execution commands. Many software developers (and many students too) prefer to use integrated development environments (IDEs), such as NetBeans or Eclipse, that facilitate large-scale development. Both NetBeans and Eclipse are included on the book's accompanying CD. Typically, in addition to assistance with source code editing, IDEs will have a number of tools to assist with compilation, debugging, execution, packaging, and creation and use of jar files. If you are not interested in using an IDE (we know a number of programmers who prefer just a good editor and the command line), additional tools are available to assist with common Java software development tasks. Throughout the rest of this chapter, we will introduce you to just a few of them.

IDEs and the Classpath

Before we talk about the first tool that will make your software development activities easier, we should mention that IDEs do not insulate you from the issues related to the CLASSPATH environment variable that we have covered earlier in this chapter. Generally speaking, IDEs allow you to edit the CLASSPATH that the IDE uses during compilation and execution. This is most often performed through a properties or options window, and usually allows you to add directories and jar files to the path. As you evolve as a Java developer, you will undoubtedly be using jar files from other companies and developers. Assuming that you do select an IDE, be sure to investigate how it manages the CLASSPATH and what assistance it offers you in terms of the activities you will perform.

Build Tools and Ant

Build tools are used to simplify many common repeatable software development tasks.

It is not uncommon for software developers to want to simplify many of the tasks repeatedly performed when working on software development. Generally, developers turn to the use of tools to aid in the simplification process. One of the most popular classes of tools comprises what are known as *build tools*, which are used to define and execute a clear, consistent process for building software applications.

Often, developers wish to compile only those source code files that have been modified since the last successful compilation build. Rather than searching out those files by hand (or worse yet, based on the developer's memory), build tools can identify the modified files and invoke the compiler on the user's behalf. This is just one of the reasons we turn to build files to assist us as the size of our project grows.

Other motivating reasons include the need to standardize the compilation process or to add support for special compilation activities (such as moving the source code files, backing up copies of files, or automatically including information such as the date or time in the application during the build process). Another example of useful build behavior includes ensuring that when code dependencies exist (one portion of code depending on another), the dependency is recognized and compiled in an appropriate sequence. This last example is particularly relevant to C and C++ source code.

The most popular build tool for C and C++ is called *make*. Make uses *build files* known as *makefiles* to organize the structure of the build commands. Make's counterpart in Java is a tool known as Ant. Ant is an open source build tool for Java developed by the Apache Software Foundation (http://ant.apache.org). Like make, Ant uses build files, written in the Extensible Markup Language (XML) to describe the build activities you wish to define.

While we can't get into all of the ins and outs of Ant in this chapter, we will show you a simple, effective build file that provides two activities (known as *targets* in Ant) as well as a more complex build file that was used during the development of the JFMail application. Hopefully, you will agree that Ant is a powerful tool that you may wish to build your projects on and it will drive you to investigate Ant further.

A simple build file for Ant is shown in Listing 11.2. The build file contains two targets, named `compile` and `clean`. As you can likely guess from the listing, the `compile` target contains just one task—invoking the `javac` compiler application. In this task, we inform the compiler that all of our source code from the current directory (`.`) should be compiled, including code in subdirectories. Class files created from the compilation will be placed in the same directory as their associated source code files. Our second target, `clean`, deletes all files that have an extension of `.class` from the current directory and all subdirectories.

Ant permits us to modify the properties of the `javac` and `delete` tasks to change their behavior. For example, we might want to create a directory into which all of our .class files from a build are placed. A complete listing of each Ant task and its attributes can be found in the Ant documentation.

Listing 11.2

```
<project name="example" default="compile">
   <target name="compile">
      <javac srcdir="."/>
   </target>

   <target name="clean">
      <delete>
         <fileset dir="." includes="**/*.class"/>
      </delete>
   </target>
</project>
```

Listing 11.3 provides the Ant build file used to develop the JFMail application. In this build file, we use four targets to provide our core set of functionality to the user. Our `compile` target is enhanced from the version shown in Listing 11.2, as we have specified a modification to the CLASSPATH—the location of the JavaMail `mail.jar` file used to reference the classes provided by the JavaMail API.

Listing 11.3

```
<project name="JFMail" default="compile" basedir=".">
   <description>Build file for Java Foundations' Mail Application
   </description>

  <!-- set global properties for this build -->
  <property name="src" location="."/>
  <property name="dist"  location="dist"/>
  <property environment="env"/>

  <target name="compile" description="Compiles the source code of the project.">
    <!-- Compile the java code located in ${src} -->
    <javac srcdir="${src}">
      <classpath>
        <pathelement location="${env.JAVAMAIL_HOME}/mail.jar"/>
      </classpath>
    </javac>
```

Listing **11.3** continued

```
  </target>

  <target name="clean" description="Deletes all .class files and the distribution directory.">
    <!-- Delete the ${dist} directory -->
    <delete dir="${dist}"/>

    <delete>
      <fileset dir="${src}" includes="**/*.class"/>
    </delete>
  </target>

  <target name="dist" depends="compile" description="Generates the distribution (jar file).">
    <!-- Create the distribution directory -->
    <mkdir dir="${dist}"/>

    <!-- Set the format of the "today" property for use in naming the jar file -->
    <tstamp>
      <format property="today" pattern="yyMMdd" locale="en"/>
    </tstamp>

    <!-- Put everything in ${src} into the jfmail-${today}.jar file -->
    <jar jarfile="${dist}/jfmail-${today}.jar" basedir="${src}">
      <manifest>
        <attribute name="Built-By" value="Lewis, DePasquale, and Chase"/>
    </manifest>
    </jar>
  </target>

</project>
```

In the build file's compile target, we access the JAVAMAIL_HOME environment variable set in the shell (mentioned earlier) to locate the installation location of the JavaMail API. We then append the `/mail.jar` string to the installation location, defining the true location of the `mail.jar` file. By using the environment variable, rather than hard coding the path of the jar file in the build file, we can share our build file with other developers and not have to worry about their installation location of the JavaMail API. Our only requirement for the build file is then that anyone else using the build file will need to have installed the JavaMail API and set the JAVAMAIL_HOME environment variable (via the

Control Panel in Windows or a login configuration file in Unix). Using the environment variable in this fashion makes the build file flexible—easily used by others without unnecessary hard-coded paths in it.

There are some other interesting things worth noting about the build file. We can set property values (constant variables) by using the `property` task (shown near the start of the file, prior to any tasks). Property values are used throughout the build file to provide a singular location and value that might change as the build file evolves (just as we do for constant values in Java programs). Notice that we have established properties for the location of our source code (the `src` property), the location of our distribution directory (the `dist` property), and the inclusion of our environment variables present in the shell.

The `dist` target is used to create the `dist` subdirectory—a file system location in which our distributable jar files will be placed. Additionally, the `dist` target will create a property named `"today"`, which will be used in the subsequent task, creating a jar file whose name is based in part on the current date. The `dist` target has a dependency with the `compile` target. This dependency will force the execution of the `compile` target prior to the `dist` target executing. Dependencies can be used to create logical chains of targets to execute, simplifying the build process by decomposing it into a series of identifiable steps.

The `clean` target is used to remove the `dist` subdirectory from our workspace by using the `delete` task. We also delete all .class files found in the `src` area of our workspace. `${src}` is a reference to the `src` property value set near the top of the build file.

Once an Ant build file is created, we generally save it in the project's topmost directory with the file name `build.xml`. Other file names can be chosen, but that alters our execution command of Ant. To execute our build file, we issue the `ant` command on the command line. If our build file's name is `projectBuild.xml`, then we issue the `ant -f projectBuild.xml` command.

Ant processes our build file and executes the project's default target. A default target is named in the `project` task (see the first line of the build file), and should match one of the included targets in the build file. If no default target is named, or you wish to execute another target, you can issue the command `ant targetname`, where `targetname` is the name of the target you wish to execute. For example, to clean up our build and remove our .class files, we can issue the `ant clean` command.

11.4 Testing

The term *testing* can be applied in many ways to software development. Testing certainly includes its traditional definition: the act of running a completed program with various inputs to discover problems. But it also includes any evaluation that is performed by human or machine to assess the quality of the evolving system. These evaluations should occur long before a single line of code is written.

The goal of testing is to find errors. By finding errors and fixing them, we improve the quality of our program. It's likely that later on someone else will find any errors that remain hidden during development. The earlier the errors are found, the easier and cheaper they are to fix. Taking the time to uncover problems as early as possible is almost always worth the effort.

Testing a program can never guarantee the absence of errors.

Running a program with specific input and producing the correct results establishes only that the program works for that particular input. As more and more test cases execute without revealing errors, our confidence in the program rises, but we can never really be sure that all errors have been eliminated. There could always be another error still undiscovered. Because of that, it is important to thoroughly test a program in as many ways as possible and with well-designed test cases.

It is possible to prove that a program is correct, but that technique is enormously complex for large systems, and errors can be made in the proof itself. Therefore we generally rely on testing to determine the quality of a program.

After determining that an error exists, we determine the cause of the error and fix it. After a problem is fixed, we should run previous tests again to make sure that while fixing the problem we didn't create another. This technique is called *regression testing*.

Reviews

One technique used to evaluate design or code is called a *review*, which is a meeting in which several people carefully examine a design document or section of code. Presenting our design or code to others causes us to think more carefully about it and permits others to share their suggestions with us. The participants discuss its merits and problems, and create a list of issues that must be addressed. The goal of a review is to identify problems, not to solve them, which usually takes much more time.

A design review should determine whether the requirements are addressed. It should also assess the way the system is decomposed into classes and objects. A code review should determine how faithfully the design satisfies the requirements and how faithfully the implementation represents the design. It should identify any specific problems that would cause the design or the implementation to fail in its responsibilities.

Sometimes a review is called a *walkthrough* because its goal is to step carefully through a document and evaluate each section.

Defect Testing

Since the goal of testing is to find errors, it is often referred to as *defect testing*. With that goal in mind, a good test is one that uncovers any deficiencies in a program. This might seem strange, because we ultimately don't want to have problems in our system. But keep in mind that errors almost certainly exist. Our testing efforts should make every attempt to find them. We want to increase the reliability of our program by finding and fixing the errors that exist, rather than letting users discover them.

A good test is one that uncovers an error.

A *test case* is a set of inputs, user actions, or other initial conditions, and the expected output. A test case should be appropriately documented so that it can be repeated later as needed. Developers often create a complete *test suite*, which is a set of test cases that covers various aspects of the system.

Because programs operate on a large number of possible inputs, it is not feasible to create test cases for all possible input or user actions. Nor is it usually necessary to test every single situation. Two specific test cases may be so similar that they actually do not test unique aspects of the program. To do both would be a wasted effort. We'd rather execute a test case that stresses the program in some new way. Therefore we want to choose our test cases carefully. To that end, let's examine two approaches to defect testing: black-box testing and white-box testing.

It is not feasible to exhaustively test a program for all possible input and user actions.

As the name implies, *black-box testing* treats the thing being tested as a black box. In black-box testing, test cases are developed without regard to the internal workings. Black-box tests are based on inputs and outputs. An entire program can be tested using a black-box technique, in which case the inputs are the user-provided information and user actions such as button pushes. A test case is successful only if the input produces the expected output. A single class can also be tested using a black-box technique, which focuses on the system interface (its public methods) of the class. Certain parameters are passed in, producing certain results. Black-box test cases are often derived directly from the requirements of the system or from the stated purpose of a method.

The input data for a black-box test case is often selected by defining *equivalence categories*. An equivalence category is a collection of inputs that are expected to produce similar outputs. Generally, if a method will work for one value in the equivalence category, we have every reason to believe it will work for the others. For example, the input to a method that computes the square root of an integer can be divided into two equivalence categories: nonnegative integers and negative integers. If it works appropriately for one nonnegative value, it will likely work for all nonnegative values. Likewise, if it works appropriately for one negative value, it will likely work for all negative values.

Equivalence categories have defined boundaries. Because all values of an equivalence category essentially test the same features of a program, only one test case inside the equivalence boundary is needed. However, because programming often produces "off by one" errors, the values on and around the boundary should be tested exhaustively. For an integer boundary, a good test suite would include at least the exact value of the boundary, the boundary minus 1, and the boundary plus 1. Test cases that use these cases, plus at least one from within the general field of the category, should be defined.

Let's look at an example. Consider a method whose purpose is to validate that a particular integer value is in the range 0 to 99, inclusive. There are three equivalence categories in this case: values below 0, values in the range of 0 to 99, and values above 99. Black-box testing dictates that we use test values that surround and fall on the boundaries, as well as some general values from the equivalence categories. Therefore, a set of black-box test cases for this situation might be: –500, –1, 0, 1, 50, 98, 99, 100, and 500.

White-box testing, also known as *glass-box testing*, exercises the internal structure and implementation of a method. A white-box test case is based on the logic of the code. The goal is to ensure that every path through a program is executed at least once. A white-box test maps the possible paths through the code and ensures that the test cases cause every path to be executed. This type of testing is often called *statement coverage*.

Paths through code are controlled by various control flow statements that use conditional expressions, such as `if` statements. In order to have every path through the program executed at least once, the input data values for the test cases need to control the values for the conditional expressions. The input data of one or more test cases should cause the condition of an `if` statement to evaluate to `true` in at least one case and to `false` in at least one case. Covering both true and false values in an `if` statement guarantees that both the paths through the `if` statement will be executed. Similar situations can be created for loops and other constructs.

In both black-box and white-box testing, the expected output for each test should be established prior to running the test. It's too easy to be persuaded that the results of a test are appropriate if you haven't first carefully determined what the results should be.

Unit Testing

Another type of testing is known as *unit testing*. This approach creates a test case for each module of code (method) that has been authored. The goal of unit testing is to ensure correctness of the methods (units), one method at a time. Generally, we collect our unit tests together and execute each test and observe all of the results. We can also use these tests repeatedly as the source code changes, to observe the effect of our code changes on the results of the test (regression testing, discussed above).

Integration Testing

During *integration testing*, modules that were individually tested during unit testing are now tested as a collection. This form of testing looks at the larger picture and determines if there are bugs present when modules are brought together and integrated to work together. As with unit testing, we can use regression testing as the software changes to determine how our results may have changed as integration occurred and problems in the modules or integration approaches were modified. Typically, the goal of integration testing is to examine the correctness of large components of a system.

System Testing

System testing seeks to test the entire software system and how its implementation adheres to its requirements. You may be familiar with public alpha or beta testing of applications or operating systems. Alpha and beta tests are system tests occurring prior to the formal release and availability of a software product. Software development companies will partake in these types of public tests to increase the number of users testing a product, or to expand the hardware base that the product is tested on.

JUnit

JUnit (http://www.junit.org) is a testing framework for performing automated unit tests on Java applications. JUnit is one of the most widely used unit testing frameworks for Java developers, providing a series of classes that support the development and execution of one or more tests. The JUnit framework can execute your unit tests in either a text-based or GUI-based interface.

JUnit is a testing framework for performing automated unit tests.

In this section, we will explore the basics of creating a unit test in your application and demonstrate how to execute your tests in the GUI-based *runner* to observe the results of your test. For the purposes of this discussion we have downloaded and installed JUnit 3.8.2 from the JUnit Web site. We have also created another shell environment variable named JUNIT_HOME, which stores the installation location of JUnit on our machine (`C:\Program Files\junit3.8.2`).

Note that version 4.1 (or later) of JUnit has been released, but utilizes a number of language-specific issues that we won't be discussing in this textbook. Additionally, during the development of this textbook, Ant had not yet supported the 4.1 release of JUnit, making the discussion even more difficult. Thus, it was natural to stick with the version 3.8 release of JUnit.

We'll begin our unit testing by creating a new class in the `jfmail.communications` package named `JFCommsTesting`. This file is shown in Listing 11.4. Notice that we are importing a number of classes from the `JFMail` packages (`jfmail.userInterface`), `java.util`, `javax.mail`, and also `junit.framework`. The inclusion of classes from the `junit.framework` package will permit us to create our unit tests.

Listing 11.4

```
//********************************************************************
//  JFCommsTesting.java        Java Foundations
//
//  This class holds testing routines for the communications module.
//********************************************************************
package jfmail.communications;

import java.util.*;
import javax.mail.*;
import jfmail.userInterface.*;
import junit.framework.*;
```

Listing 11.4 continued

```
public class JFCommsTesting extends TestCase
{
   //-----------------------------------------------------------------
   //  Tests that a JFMailCommsController object is intialized
   //  correctly following instantiation.
   //-----------------------------------------------------------------
   public void testCommsInitialization ()
   {
      JFMailCommsController comms = new JFMailCommsController();
      Authenticator textAuth = new JFMailTextualAuthenticator();
      Properties props = new Properties();
      assertTrue(comms.getNumMsgs() == -1);
   }

   //-----------------------------------------------------------------
   //  Tests the establishment of a connection to a user-defined mail
   //  server.  This test will prompt for the entry of the hostname,
   //  protocol, username, and password prior to attempting to
   //  establish a connection.
   //-----------------------------------------------------------------
   public void testConnectionEstablished ()
   {
      JFMailCommsController comms = new JFMailCommsController();
      Authenticator textAuth = new JFMailTextualAuthenticator();
      Properties props = new Properties();

      try
      {
         Scanner scan = new Scanner(System.in);

         System.out.println("Enter the hostname of the mail server:");
         System.out.flush();
         scan.hasNextLine();
         props.setProperty("mail.host", scan.nextLine().trim());

         System.out.println("Enter the connection protocol type: ");
         System.out.flush();
         scan.hasNextLine();
         props.setProperty("mail.store.protocol", scan.nextLine());

         comms.establishConnection(props, textAuth);
         assertEquals(true, comms.isOpenConnection());
      }
```

Listing **11.4** continued

```
        catch(AuthenticationFailedException afe)
        {
           throw new AssertionFailedError ("Authentication failed "
              + " connecting to " + props.getProperty("mail.host"));
        }
        catch(MessagingException me)
        {
           throw new AssertionFailedError (me.toString());
        }
     }
  }
```

Our testing class extends the `TestCase` class from `junit.framework`. This will enable us to define one or more tests and execute them automatically. Our class currently implements two testing methods, `testCommsInitialization` and `testConnectionEstablished`. We have specifically named these methods to start with the word *test*. By doing so, our test runner (an application that will execute our tests and provide us feedback on the results of each test) will be able to find our tests based on the name using an advanced Java technology known as reflection. Reflection is a topic that is outside the scope of this textbook, so we won't delve into it here. However, all you really need to know is that when our test runner starts executing, it will locate all of our tests by searching for any methods whose name starts with *test*.

Let's take a closer look at the `testCommsInitialization` method. This test method simply creates a new instance of the `JFMailCommsController` class and obtains the value of the `numMsgs` instance variable. At the time of instantiation, the `numMsgs` variable should be set to `-1`, and once a connection is established to a mail server, this value will contain the number of messages in our inbox. Since our inbox may contain zero or more messages, we set this variable to be `-1` to indicate that we have yet to establish a connection.

Our test simply comprises the instantiation of the `JFMailCommsController` object and the testing of this instance variable. To actually perform the test, we *assert* that the value of this variable should be set to `-1`. We call the `assertTrue` method of the `Assert` class (the parent class of `TestCase`) to perform this assertion. If our assertion is indeed true, the method ends cleanly, and the test is

Assertions are used to verify that our expected test results match our actual test results.

considered *passed*. However, if the assertion is false, and the value of `numMsgs` is not `-1` during the assertion, then the `assertTrue` method will throw an `AssertionFailedError`. We don't need to catch this error within the testing method, as it will be propagated to the method that called the test, in this case, the framework.

Our second test is slightly more complex than our first. The `testConnectionEstablished` method creates both an instance of the `JFMailCommsController` class and an instance of the `JFMailTextualAuthenticator` class. Our goal is to prompt the user to enter a valid mail server hostname and password, establishing a connection to the server, which in turn will use the authenticator to prompt the user for the username and password. If the connection is correctly established, we should be able to execute another assertion on the result of the `isOpenConnection` method from the controller. Rather than use the `assertTrue` method, we'll demonstrate the use of another type of assertion, `assertEquals`. The `assertEquals` method will test that our expected result (the first parameter, `true`), is equal to the actual result (the value returned as the result of calling the `isOpenConnection` method contained in the `comms` object).

If, during the second test, an `AuthenticationException` is thrown by the `establishConnection` method in the `JFMailCommsController` object, we will catch the exception and force the test to fail by throwing an `AssertionFailedError`. Similarly, if we obtain a `MessagingException` during the connection process (for example, from a bad hostname), we will purposely fail the test.

Now that we have two unit tests, we'll execute them and ensure that it is possible for our tests to pass. Ideally, we are looking to establish that the instantiation of the `JFMailCommsController` object and `establishConnection` method go smoothly, and that our tests all pass.

To execute our tests, we'll need to add the `junit.jar` file to our CLASSPATH during compilation and execution. Ideally, our new compilation command will be

```
javac -cp %JAVAMAIL_HOME%\mail.jar;"C:\Program
   Files\junit3.8.2\junit.jar";.
   jfmail\communications\JFCommsTesting.java
```

Notice that we are starting our compilation with the `JFCommsTesting.java` file. By doing so, the compiler will compile `JFCommsTesting` and all classes that it refers to or requires. If you had performed this compilation with a "clean" project area (that contained no .class files), the `JFMail` and `JFMailTextUserInterface` classes would not have been compiled. Neither of those classes is required by `JFCommsTesting`, nor is either used by any class that `JFCommsTesting` uses.

Once again, our command-line compilation approach is getting cumbersome. That's certainly a lot of typing, and thus it's easy to introduce errors in getting the command correct. So, we'll modify our compile target of the build file to include the `junit.jar` file that we need. To do so, we can use the installation location of JUnit from our shell's environment variable, JUNIT_HOME:

```
<target name="compile" description="Compiles the source code of
the project.">
   <!-- Compile the java code located in ${src} -->
      <javac srcdir="${src}">
         <classpath>
            <pathelement path="${env.JAVAMAIL_HOME}/mail.jar"/>
            <pathelement path="${env.JUNIT_HOME}/junit.jar"/>
         </classpath>
   </javac>
</target>
```

Once compiled, we'll execute our tests in the GUI test runner by doing the following on the command line:

```
java -cp %JAVAMAIL_HOME%\mail.jar;"C:\Program
   Files\junit3.8.2\junit.jar";. junit.swingui.TestRunner
   jfmail.communications.JFCommsTesting
```

In the above command, we're actually calling the `main` method present in the `TestRunner` class provided as part of the JUnit API. In calling the `main` method, we're passing it the name of our class that contains the test methods (`jfmail.communications.JFCommsTesting`). When the test runner starts, we are presented with a GUI window that will provide status information on the state and results of our testing.

Our first test requires no user interaction, and should execute (and pass) quickly. The second test, `testConnectionEstablished`, will start, instantiate the required objects, and then prompt the user to enter the hostname and protocol of the mail server. At this point, the GUI of our test runner looks as though the program is hung or halted, with the second test being incomplete. Actually, the test runner is waiting for input from the user to proceed. The prompting for the required input can be found in the shell window from which we executed the command to start the test runner.

If you enter a valid hostname and protocol, the JFMail application will then prompt you to enter your username and password to complete the connection attempt. Assuming all of the user input is valid and correct, the second test should successfully complete, and the test runner will display the results. Figure 11.4 shows a screen shot of the JUnit tool after running our tests. In it, you can see that both of our tests passed (two successful tests out of a total of two). No errors or failures were present.

If we execute the test again, and purposely pass in a bad username, the test will fail, throwing an `AssertionFailedError`. This will result in the JUnit test runner completing two tests, failing the second, as shown in Figure 11.5.

Going Further with JUnit

Our discussion of testing touched upon only two different assertion types provided by JUnit-the `assertTrue` and `assertEquals` methods. However, there are many more that you can use while building your tests. The API includes support for `assertFalse`, `assertNotNull`, `assertNotSame`, `assertNull`, and `assertSame`.

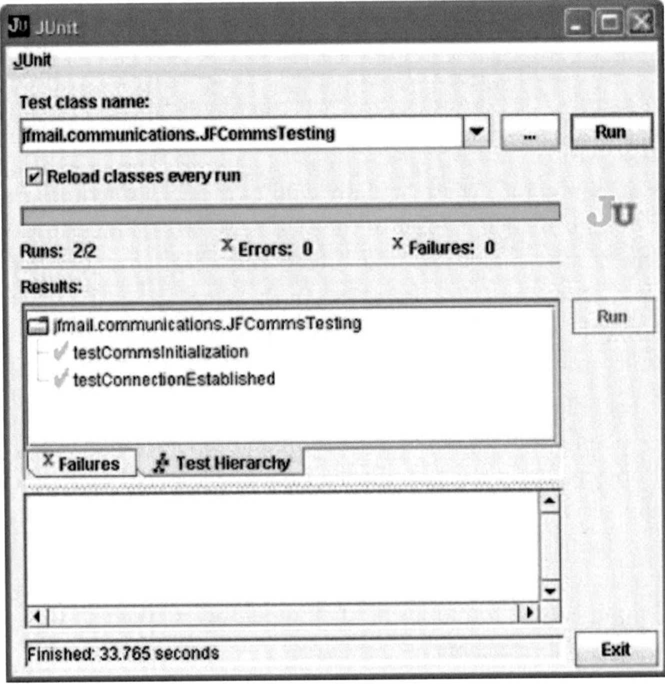

FIGURE 11.4 The JUnit tool

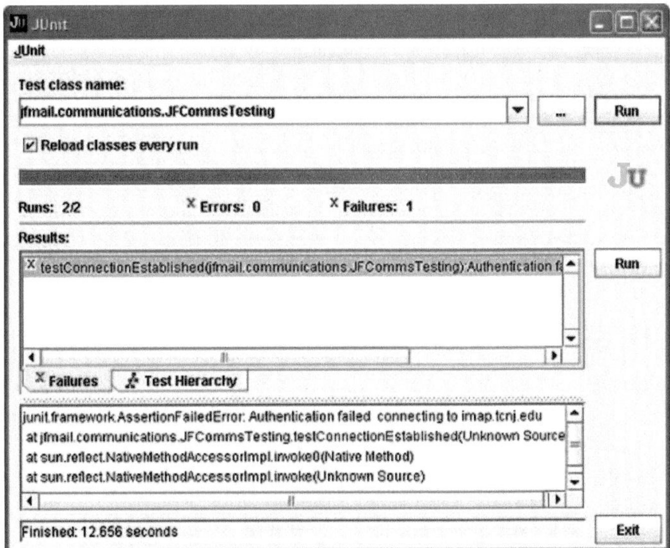

FIGURE 11.5 The JUnit tool showing a failed test

You'll likely want to read the API's documentation fully to determine which of these are appropriate for the types of testing you wish to accomplish.

The two tests that we have developed both rely on a `JFMailCommsController` object. Rather than instantiate the object within the body of each test method, we can include an instance variable for the object and perform the instantiation in another method prior to each test running. The method that creates the object(s) we will utilize and interact with during the execution of the test is known as the *test fixture*. We can establish the test fixture by adding a `setUp` method to our `JFCommsTesting` class and removing the declaration and instantiation of the `JFMailCommsController` object in both of our tests. In fact, we have done this and saved our changes in the `JFCommsTestingRevised.java` file shown in Listing 11.5. We can also add a `tearDown` method to remove or terminate any objects or settings prior to the end of the test. For example, we might want to open an output file in the `setUp` method, which is closed in the `tearDown` method.

You may have noticed that we have taken the development of our test fixture one step further and included the instantiation of a `JFMailTextualAuthenticator` object and a `Properties` object. These objects are used in the second test, but not the first. We did this primarily to remove the basic instantiation of objects from our test cases, so that the source code for the test cases would be kept to a minimum.

Listing **11.5**

```
//********************************************************************
//  JFCommsTestingRevised.java       Java Foundations
//
//  This class holds testing routines for the communications module.
//********************************************************************
package jfmail.communications;

import java.util.*;
import javax.mail.*;
import jfmail.userInterface.*;
import junit.framework.*;

public class JFCommsTestingRevised extends TestCase
{
   protected JFMailCommsController comms;
   protected Authenticator textAuth;
   protected Properties props;

   //-----------------------------------------------------------------
   //  Tests that a JFMailCommsController object is intialized
   //  correctly following instantiation.
   //-----------------------------------------------------------------
   public void testCommsInitialization ()
   {
      assertTrue(comms.getNumMsgs() == -1);
   }

   //-----------------------------------------------------------------
   //  Tests the establishment of a connection to a user-defined mail
   //  server.  This test will prompt for the entry of the hostname,
   //  protocol, username, and password prior to attempting to
   //  establish a connection.
   //-----------------------------------------------------------------
   public void testConnectionEstablished ()
   {
      try
      {
         Scanner scan = new Scanner(System.in);

         System.out.println("Enter the hostname of the mail server:");
         System.out.flush();
         scan.hasNextLine();
         props.setProperty("mail.host", scan.nextLine().trim());
```

Listing **11.5** continued

```
            System.out.println("Enter the connection protocol type: ");
            System.out.flush();
            scan.hasNextLine();
            props.setProperty("mail.store.protocol", scan.nextLine());

            comms.establishConnection(props, textAuth);
            assertEquals(true, comms.isOpenConnection());
        }
        catch(AuthenticationFailedException afe)
        {
            throw new AssertionFailedError ("Authentication failed "
                + " connecting to " + props.getProperty("mail.host"));
        }
        catch(MessagingException me)
        {
            throw new AssertionFailedError (me.toString());
        }
    }

    //-----------------------------------------------------------------
    //  Instantiates the objects required to execute the tests in this
    //  class.
    //-----------------------------------------------------------------
    protected void setUp ()
    {
        comms = new JFMailCommsController();
        textAuth = new JFMailTextualAuthenticator();
        props = new Properties();
    }
}
```

Test-Driven Development

Ideally, developers should be writing test cases at the same time as the development of the source code that our applications use. In fact, many developers have adopted a style in which they write their test cases first, and then implement only enough source code such that the test case will pass. This notion is known professionally as *test-driven development*.

In test-driven development, test cases are developed for code before the code is written.

The test-driven approach requires that the developer periodically (during development and implementation) test their code using the implemented test cases. If you were to look at the test-driven approach as a sequence of steps, you would generally find the following activities:

1. Create a test case that tests a specific method that has yet to be completed.
2. Execute all of the test cases present and verify that all test cases pass except for the most recently implemented test case.
3. Develop the method that the test case targets so that the test case will pass without errors.
4. Re-execute all of the test cases and verify that every test case passes, including the most recently implemented test case.
5. Clean up the code to eliminate any redundant portions introduced by the development of the most recent method. This step is known as *refactoring* the code.
6. Repeat the process starting with Step 1.

The test-driven approach is becoming increasingly popular in professional settings. Without a doubt, it requires an adjustment for many developers to stop and write test cases prior to writing methods that provide functionality to systems under development.

A Final Note About Testing and JFMail

Finding appropriate methods in your code to subject to testing can be difficult. One of the problems that we faced in adding testing code to our application is that many of the methods return values that are highly variable, subject to the status of the mailbox that we connect to at testing time. For instance, while we can establish if we have a connection to the mail server, the `getNextMessage` method in the `JFMailCommsController` class returned message objects if a next message was present. Since we don't always know the status of the mailbox, our test can check to see that the `getNextMessage` method returns either a null value (in the case in which there is no next message) or the message itself (in the case in which a next message exists). These types of tests didn't seem to provide much use to us in the development of the JFMail application.

Additionally, we know `JFMailTextUserInterface` class methods are difficult to test, since their primary function is to print text to the screen

(`System.out`). We found this a difficult place to insert tests as well because the text that is printed is variable, depending on the contents of the mailbox. Methods that have a return type of `void` are also problematic, since there is less to test. In cases like this, you generally want to determine if any instance variables were modified by the method under test. Again, our user interface didn't do much of that.

Testing should not usually be this challenging. However, this application brings to light that in some situations, finding appropriate locations to insert a unit test can be an exercise unto itself.

11.5 Debugging

Finally, we come to one of the most important concepts that you will likely come to master as a programmer—the art of *debugging* your programs. Debugging is the act of locating and correcting run-time and logic errors in your programs. We can locate errors in our programs through a number of different ways. You may notice a run-time error (the program terminating abnormally) when you execute your program and certain situations arise that you did not consider or design for. Also, you may notice a logic error in your program as it executes when your anticipated results do not match the actual results you obtain.

Debugging is the act of locating and correcting run-time and logic errors from your programs.

Ideally, through rigorous testing, we hope to discover all possible errors in our programs. However, typically a few errors slip through into the final program. Once you recognize that your program contains an error, you will want to locate the portion of code where the error is arising from. For example, if you determine that your program is terminating abnormally due to a divide-by-zero problem, you'll likely want to locate the exact line that it is happening at. You may also wish to observe the values of the variables involved in the division. The same may be true if you have a logic error (rather than a divide-by-zero problem) in that division operation.

Regardless of your motivation, often times it is very helpful to obtain detailed information about the values of variables, states of objects, and other inner workings of your program. This is where a debugger comes in. A *debugger* is a software application that allows us to observe these inner workings as the program executes. However, before we jump into discussing the debugger, we should first talk about simple debugging.

A debugger is a software program that permits developers to observe the execution of a program.

Simple Debugging with `print` Statements

One of the most simplistic approaches to debugging involves the use of printing. That is, scattered throughout our program can be `print` and `println` statements that output various information to either the screen or to an output file. Generally, this type of approach will serve to provide information on the value or state of a specific variable or object. Periodic printing of an object's string representation is considered to be a useful approach to observing the state of an object over time.

Other types of useful information can be printed as well. For example, sometimes we wish to know "how far our program got before it died." Programmers facing this challenge often print a series of "It got here." type of statements to output to monitor the exact path of execution of the program.

Consider the case of calling a method. It may be useful for us to print the value of each parameter after the method starts to observe how the method was called. This is particularly helpful when debugging recursive methods, discussed in the next chapter. We can also print the value of a variable prior to it being returned as the method ends.

Debugging Concepts

Debugging through printing can only take us so far. Most of the time this style of debugging can be effectively used to identify what is happening during execution or the value of a variable at a certain point in the program. However, a more powerful approach is to use a debugger in which our program will execute. The debugger can be used to control our program's execution and provide additional functionality to the developer that we simply can't get with simple debugging through `print` statements.

A debugger allows us to do the following:

- Set one or more *breakpoints* in our program. In the debugger, we can examine the source code and set special flags or triggers on one or more lines of code. When execution of the program comes across a statement that has been flagged, execution stops.
- Print the value of a variable or object. Once we have reached a breakpoint and execution has stopped, the debugger allows us to display the value of a variable or examine the state of an object. Generally these types of displays are to the screen and only within the confines of the debugger application.

- Step into or over a method. If we set a breakpoint at a statement that is a call to a method, when execution reaches this breakpoint and the program stops, the developer can choose to enter into the method and continue debugging or to step over the method, bypassing the display of the execution of the statements contained in the method. In stepping over the method, we should note that the method is still executed, but we have chosen not to delve into the method. Consider the call to the printing of a string of output to the screen. We likely don't need to step into the `println` method of the `System.out` object. It's likely already been fully debugged (and we can't change its behavior anyway).
- Execute the next single statement. After reaching a breakpoint, the developer can choose to execute the next single statement (also known as a *step*). By executing a single step, we can literally control the execution of our program one statement at a time. Developers often perform stepping to be sure they understand the flow of execution and to provide themselves the opportunity to display the value of a variable following each step, if desired.
- Continue execution. Once a program has stopped due to a breakpoint, or is waiting for the developer to decide if they will step into, step over, or single step, the developer can also continue execution. Continuing execution will result in the program running each statement without pausing until the program ends, it encounters another breakpoint, or a run-time error occurs.

Debuggers also offer a pile of additional features to assist in the debugging task. However, for the purposes of this discussion, we can limit ourselves to the set of activities listed above. Any debugger that is worth using has at a minimum these operations.

The Java Debugger (JDB)

As part of the JDK, Java comes with a debugger known as the `jdb` (Java debugger). The `jdb` application is a text-based program that provides all of the functionality listed above and more. We'll use both a small sample application and our JFMail application in our examples of how to use a debugger. In fact, the JFMail application presents a few additional interesting issues related to debugging.

Listing 11.6 is a small class that contains two static methods. The `main` method calls the `power` method, which returns a string showing the result of a value raised to an exponent.

Let's assume that we were authoring the `power` method and suspected that it was not returning the correct value. We will use the debugger to load and execute the program to locate our problem. First, we'll recompile the program and use the `-g` option to inform the compiler that we wish to include debugging information as part of the compilation. The added information will be included in the .class

Listing **11.6**

```
//********************************************************************
//  DebugTester.java       Java Foundations
//
//  This class is used to demonstrate the user of a debugger.
//********************************************************************
public class DebugTester
{
   //-----------------------------------------------------------------
   // The main method calls the static tester method and prints the
   // result returned from the power method.
   //-----------------------------------------------------------------
   public static void main (String[] args)
   {
      System.out.println(power(10, 4));
   }

   //-----------------------------------------------------------------
   //  The power method returns a string showing the result of a base
   //  value raised to an exponent.
   //-----------------------------------------------------------------
   public static String power (int base, int exponent)
   {
      int pow = 0;
      String result = base + " raised to the power of " + exponent;
      result += " is ";

      pow = base + exponent;

      return result + pow;
   }
}
```

files generated during the compilation. So, to compile the `DebugTest.java` file shown in Listing 11.6, we'll use the following command:

```
javac -g DebugTester.java
```

Of course, if your program requires the use of more than one class, you'll have a more complex compilation command to ensure that all of your source code files are compiled. Once the source code files have successfully compiled, we'll start the debugger by typing the following on the command line:

```
jdb DebugTester
```

When the debugger starts, you'll be presented with a startup message and a debugger prompt (>). We'll enter our first command to stop the debugger when our program enters the `main` method. To do this, enter `stop in DebugTester.main`. The debugger will inform us that the breakpoint will be set once the class is loaded. Next, we'll start execution of the `DebugTester` program by entering `run` at the debug prompt. The debugger will load the `DebugTester` class, set the breakpoint, execute the program, and halt execution at the start of the `main` method. The output produced should look something like

```
> run
run DebugTester
Set uncaught java.lang.Throwable
Set deferred uncaught java.lang.Throwable
>
VM Started: Set deferred breakpoint DebugTester.main

Breakpoint hit: "thread=main", DebugTester.main(), line=14
bci=0
14          System.out.println(power(10, 4));

main[1]
```

On the last line of the output, we have a debugger prompt indicating that we have paused execution. Executing the `list` command will show the source code around the first line of source code in the method:

```
main[1] list
10        // result returned from the power method.
11        //----------------------------------------
12        public static void main (String [] args)
13        {
14 =>        System.out.println(power(10, 4));
```

```
15        }
16
17        //-----------------------------------------------------
18        //  The power method returns a string showing the
result of a base
19        //  value raised to an exponent.
main[1]
```

If we execute the step command at this point, we will execute the next single instruction, calling the power method, and pause execution on the first line of the power method:

```
main[1] step
>
Step completed: "thread=main", DebugTester.power(), line=23
bci=0
23            int pow = 0;

main[1] list
19        //  value raised to an exponent.
20        //-----------------------------------------------------
21        public static String power (int base, int exponent)
22        {
23 =>         int pow = 0;
24            String result = base + " raised to the power of "
+ exponent;
25            result += " is ";
26
27            pow = base + exponent;
28
main[1]
```

The print command will allow us to display the value of a single variable, and the locals command will display the value of all of the local variables. If you enter the where command, the debugger will print a stack trace—a listing of each of the methods you have entered and not exited from. Each of these commands and their corresponding output are shown below:

```
main[1] print base
 base = 10
main[1] locals
Method arguments:
base = 10
exponent = 4
Local variables:
main[1] where
```

```
  [1] DebugTester.power (DebugTester.java:23)
  [2] DebugTester.main (DebugTester.java:14)
main[1]
```

Next, we'll set a breakpoint at the `return` statement of the `power` method. The `return` statement is on line 29 of the source code file, so we'll issue the command `stop at DebugTester:29`. By continuing execution (by using the `cont` command), the program should now execute the interim statements and pause execution again on line 29. At this point, we can examine the value of the `pow` variable by printing its value (`print pow`).

By performing these steps, we have learned that the value returned was miscalculated on line 27, just prior to the `return` statement. Our problem lies with the fact that the `pow` variable's value was incorrectly calculated by adding the two parameters together and not multiplying them.

Before we exit the debugger to correct our source code, we'll discuss two last commands. First, the `set` command allows us to change the value of a variable. By entering `set variableName = expression`, we can change the value of a variable to be the result of the expression. For example, we can perform a `set pow=10000` to set the correct result for this method. Changing the value of a variable can be handy if we continue to debug additional code from this program since we can affect the outcome of the program without correcting the error and recompiling.

Our last command is `help`. Entering `help` will display a summary of all the commands you can enter in the debugger. There are plenty of interesting options and commands that we can use while debugging. Be sure to explore the commands to get the most out of your debugging time.

Debugging the JFMail Application

To use the `jdb` debugger on the JFMail application, we'll need to adjust our approach slightly for a few wrinkles. Of course, we'll need to provide the large CLASSPATH to the debugger so that the execution environment can find all of the necessary classes at run time. This will once again require us to include the `mail.jar` and `activation.jar` files we downloaded earlier in the chapter.

The other primary issue we have to get around is the fact that the JFMail application requires the user to enter input from the keyboard once they have been prompted on the screen. In other words, it's a console application that requires our input. However, the `jdb` debugger is a console-based application that requires our input as well. Here lies the conflict. When the JFMail application is requesting input, our console won't know where the input should go.

For example, the output below shows a sequence of starting the JFMail application in the debugger, setting a breakpoint in the `establishCommunications` method of the `JFMailCommsController` class, and executing the application until it prompts for user input (the name of the host to connect to). When we enter the name of the host, the debugger intervenes and informs us that our hostname is not a debugger command (and to see help). This interaction will force us to take a slightly different approach.

```
C:\Documents and Settings\Peter\Desktop\Java
Foundations\ch11JFMail>jdb -classpath
%JAVAMAIL_HOME%\mail.jar;%JAF_HOME%\activation.jar;.
jfmail.JFMail
Initializing jdb. . .
> stop in
jfmail.communications.JFMailCommsController.establishConnection
Deferring breakpoint
jfmail.communications.JFMailCommsController.establishConnection.
It will be set after the class is loaded.
> run
run jfmail.JFMail
Set uncaught java.lang.Throwable
Set deferred uncaught java.lang.Throwable
>
VM Started: Set deferred breakpoint
jfmail.communications.JFMailCommsController.establishConnection

Welcome to the Java Foundations Mail Reader.

Enter the hostname of the mail server: mailserver.tcnj.edu
Unrecognized command: 'mailserver.tcnj.edu'. Try help...
>
```

How do we solve this? Fortunately, we can start the application in one shell window and start the debugger in another. The debugger will then be instructed to connect to the running application. Actually, we'll load the application but not really start execution until the debugger instructs the application to start. Once we have this configuration set, we can issue debugger commands in the debugger console window, and we can also provide input to the application through the application's console window.

Let's start the application in our first window. We'll issue the `java` command, providing a few additional options. The details of these options are beyond the scope of our discussion, so we'll avoid talking about them for now. However, notice that we started the run-time environment, passed it a CLASSPATH, and set a few transport properties in place when we started the `jfmail.JFMail` application. In particular note the `suspend=y` setting, which suspends (pauses) the application when the run-time environment loads the application. By doing this, the application won't start running while we move on to start the debugger.

```
java -classpath
   %JAVAMAIL_HOME%\mail.jar;%JAF_HOME%\activation.jar;.
   -agentlib:jdwp=transport=dt_shmem,server=y,suspend=y
   jfmail.JFMail
```

Once the run-time environment started and loaded up the JFMail application, we received the following message on the display:

```
Listening for transport dt_shmem at address: javadebug
```

Now let's start the debugger in another console window and connect it to our semi-running program:

```
jdb -attach javadebug
```

In the line above we have started the debugger and attached it to the semi-running application through a particular location in memory named `javadebug`.

Once connected, we can issue commands like `stop in`, `list`, `print`, `run`, etc. to the debugger, impacting how the JFMail application will execute. Don't forget to check the console window for the JFMail application. It might be waiting for you to enter the connection information!

The directions above demonstrate how to start an application and then attach a debugger to the executing application. We based these directions on the Windows platform. Similar capabilities exist under the Solaris and Linux operating systems with only minimal changes. Please refer to the `jdb` documentation to learn how to connect the debugger to a running Java application.

GUI-based Debuggers

Many IDE programs also include debuggers as part of the IDE application. Eclipse, NetBeans, DrJava, and other IDEs each come with the ability to debug the programs you develop with the IDE. From IDE to IDE, the commands to establish a debugging session vary widely, so you'll want to read the documentation of your IDE to determine if it includes a debugger and, if so, which commands you can use to debug your programs.

In Figure 11.6, we have started the DrJava IDE and created a project from the source code used to develop the JFMail application. We then set a breakpoint in

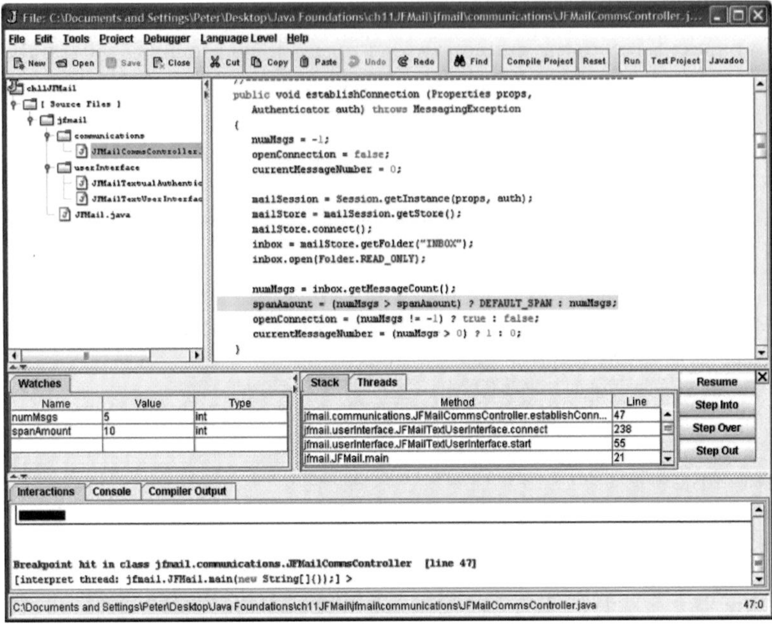

FIGURE 11.6 The debugger in DrJava

the `establishConnection` method, set the IDE into debug mode, and ran the `jfmail.JFMail.main` method to start the debugger. After reading the existing `jfMail.props` file to obtain the basic connection information, we were prompted to enter our username and password for the mail server. Once completed, the `establishConnection` method was called and the program paused at the line in the method where the `spanAmount` is calculated (highlighted in blue).

You may notice in the figure that we have two *watches* set to display the value of the `numMsgs` and `spanAmount` variables in the method. We achieved this by entering the variables' names in the Watches table. Each time the debugger pauses in the `establishConnection` method, the value of each variable in the Watches table is updated.

Generally speaking, most developers find graphical debuggers easier to use than text-based debuggers. However, all debuggers are different and there is likely to be a learning curve for any debugger you chose. We examined several debuggers during the writing of this chapter. Several we decided not to use due to the complexity of their interface, or the amount of time we would need to learn how to use it. Be sure to choose a debugger that you feel comfortable with. As you grow as a programmer, you will likely find that a good debugger is an indispensable tool for helping you author high-quality software.

Summary of Key Concepts

- Packages are used to organize source code based on functionality.
- Build tools are used to simplify many common repeatable software development tasks.
- Testing a program can never guarantee the absence of errors.
- A good test is one that uncovers an error.
- It is not feasible to exhaustively test a program for all possible input and user actions.
- JUnit is a testing framework for performing automated unit tests.
- Assertions are used to verify that our expected test results match our actual test results.
- In test-driven development, test cases are developed for code before the code is written.
- Debugging is the act of locating and correcting run-time and logic errors from your programs.
- A debugger is a software program that permits developers to observe the execution of a program.

Self-Review Questions

SR 11.1 What is the purpose of a package in Java?

SR 11.2 What is the CLASSPATH?

SR 11.3 What purpose does a jar file serve?

SR 11.4 Write the command-line option that will

a. specify that we wish to create a jar file.

b. specify that we wish to obtain the table of contents of a jar file.

c. specify that we wish to extract the contents of a jar file.

SR 11.5 What is a build tool?

SR 11.6 What is a defect test?

SR 11.7 What is white-box testing?

SR 11.8 What approach is used when performing unit testing?

SR 11.9 What sequence of steps is generally performed under test-driven development?

SR 11.10 What is a debugger?

Exercises

EX 11.1 Explore the following core Ant tasks: `echo`, `input`, `mail`, `move`, and `unjar`. What functionality does each of these tasks achieve? Describe how you could use each of them in a build file for your applications.

EX 11.2 Create at least three new targets in the JFMail build file that use the core Ant tasks shown in exercise 11.1.

EX 11.3 Modify the `JFCommsTestingRevised` class and add unit tests to support the testing of the following methods:

a. `JFMailCommsController.getMessage`

b. `JFMailCommsController.listMessageSummary`

EX 11.4 Create an additional testing class named `jfmail.userInterface.interfaceTesting` and add unit tests to support the testing of the following methods:

a. `JFMailTextUserInterface.presentMenu`

b. `JFMailTextUserInterface.loadConnectionSettings`

EX 11.5 Use a debugger to support the development of the unit tests in exercise 11.3.

Programming Projects

PP 11.1 Build the JFMail application from scratch on your own machine via the command line. Ensure that you can perform a successful build of the application without errors, and then execute the application and test the reading of your own email.

PP 11.2 Build the JFMail application using the Ant build file on your own machine. Ensure that you can perform a successful build of the application without errors and then execute the application and test the reading of your own email.

PP 11.3 Modify the JFMail application so that a crash does not occur when a bad hostname is entered by a user.

PP 11.4 Add the ability to send an email from the JFMail application. This will require in-depth reading about the JFMail API and investigation of your own campus email settings. Hint: You need to know the settings for the SMTP server.

PP 11.5 Modify the JFMail application to add a graphical user interface to replace the text user interface currently present.

PP 11.6 Modify the Ant build file so that the name of the jar file that is created is based upon the username of the user executing the build file.

PP 11.7 Modify the JFMail application so that the user can enter a new span amount (number of message summaries displayed when listing summaries) through the menu.

PP 11.8 Modify the JFMail application to support a command-line option that will ignore the use of a properties file, if present.

Answers to Self-Review Questions

SR 11.1 Java packages organize classes into packages of common functionality.

SR 11.2 The CLASSPATH indicates the list of paths (directories and other locations) where the compiler or run-time environment will look if it cannot find a class we reference in the source code.

SR 11.3 Jar files allow us to collect our source code, .class files, and other files into a single file for distribution.

SR 11.4 The command-line options are:

a. The `c` command-line option specifies to create a jar file.

b. The `t` command-line option specifies to obtain the table of contents of a jar file.

c. The `x` command-line option specifies to extract the contents of a jar file.

SR 11.5 Build tools are used to define and execute a clear, consistent process for building software applications.

SR 11.6 Defect testing is the act of testing to locate errors in a program.

SR 11.7 White-box testing exercises the internal structure and implementation of a method.

SR 11.8 When performing unit testing, we create a test case for each module of code (method) that has been authored.

SR 11.9 The test-driven development sequence is as follows:

1. Create a test case that tests a specific method that has yet to be completed.
2. Execute all of the test cases present, verifying that all test cases pass except for the most recently implemented test case.
3. Develop the method that the test case targets.
4. Re-execute all of the test cases, verifying that every test case passes.
5. Refactor the code.
6. Repeat the process starting with Step 1.

SR 11.10 A debugger is a software application that allows us to observe and manipulate the inner workings of a program as it executes.

Chapter Objectives

- Explain the underlying concepts of recursion.
- Explore examples that promote recursive thinking.
- Define infinite recursion and discuss ways to avoid it.
- Explain when recursion should and should not be used.
- Examine recursive methods and unravel their processing steps.
- Demonstrate the use of recursion to solve problems.

Recursion

Recursion is a powerful programming technique that provides elegant solutions to certain problems. This chapter provides an introduction to recursive processing. It contains an explanation of the basic concepts underlying recursion and then explores the use of recursion in programming.

12.1 Recursive Thinking

Recursion is a programming technique in which a method calls itself.

We know that one method can call another method to help it accomplish its goal. Similarly, a method can call itself as well. *Recursion* is a programming technique in which a method calls itself in order to fulfill its purpose.

Before we get into the details of how we use recursion in a program, we need to explore the general concept of recursion first. The ability to think recursively is essential to being able to use recursion as a programming technique.

A key to being able to program recursively is to learn to think recursively.

In general, recursion is the process of defining something in terms of itself. For example, consider the following definition of the word **decoration:**

decoration: n. any ornament or adornment used to decorate something

The word *decorate* is used to define the word *decoration.* You may recall your grade school teacher telling you to avoid such recursive definitions when explaining the meaning of a word. However, in many situations, recursion is an appropriate way to express an idea or definition. For example, suppose we wanted to formally define a list of one or more numbers, separated by commas. Such a list can be defined recursively as either a number or as a number followed by a comma followed by a list. This definition can be expressed as follows:

```
A LIST is a:  number
       or a:  number   comma   LIST
```

This recursive definition of a list defines each of the following lists of numbers:

```
24, 88, 40, 37
96, 43
14, 64, 21, 69, 32, 93, 47, 81, 28, 45, 81, 52, 69
70
```

No matter how long a list is, the recursive definition describes it. A list of one element, such as in the last example, is defined completely by the first (non-recursive) part of the definition. For any list longer than one element, the recursive part of the definition (the part which refers to itself) is used as many times as necessary until the last element is reached. The last element in the list is always defined by the non-recursive part of the definition. Figure 12.1 shows how one particular list of numbers corresponds to the recursive definition of LIST.

```
LIST: number   comma   LIST
        24        ,     88,  40,  37
                        number   comma   LIST
                          88       ,      40,  37
                                         number   comma   LIST
                                           40       ,      37
                                                          number
                                                            37
```

FIGURE 12.1 Tracing the recursive definition of a LIST

Infinite Recursion

Note that the definition of a list contains one option that is recursive and one option that is not. The part of the definition that is not recursive is called the *base case*. If all options had a recursive component, the recursion would never end. For example, if the definition of LIST was simply "a number followed by a comma followed by a LIST," then no list could ever end. This problem is called *infinite recursion*. It is similar to an infinite loop except that the "loop" occurs in the definition itself.

As in the infinite loop problem, a programmer must be careful to design algorithms so that they avoid infinite recursion. Any recursive definition must have a base case that does not result in a further recursion. The base case of the LIST definition is a single number that is not followed by anything. In other words, when the last number in the list is reached, the base case option terminates the recursion.

Any recursive definition must have a non-recursive part, called the base case, which permits the recursion to eventually end.

Recursion in Math

Let's look at an example of recursion in mathematics. The value referred to as N! (pronounced *N factorial*) is defined for any positive integer N as the product of all integers between 1 and N inclusive. Therefore, 3! is defined as:

```
3!  =  3*2*1  =  6
```

and 5! is defined as:

```
5!  =  5*4*3*2*1  =  120.
```

Mathematical formulas are often expressed recursively. The definition of N! can be expressed recursively as:

```
1! = 1
N! = N * (N-1)! for N > 1
```

Mathematical problems and formulas are often expressed recursively.

The base case of this definition is 1!, which is defined as 1. All other values of N! (for $N > 1$) are defined recursively as N times the value (N–1)!. The recursion is that the factorial function is defined in terms of the factorial function.

Using this definition, 50! is equal to 50 * 49!. And 49! is equal to 49 * 48!. And 48! is equal to 48 * 47!. This process continues until we get to the base case of 1. Because N! is defined only for positive integers, this definition is complete and will always conclude with the base case.

The next section describes how recursion is accomplished in programs.

12.2 Recursive Programming

Let's use a simple mathematical operation to demonstrate the concept of recursive programming. Consider the process of summing the values between 1 and N inclusive, where N is any positive integer. The sum of the values from 1 to N can be expressed as N plus the sum of the values from 1 to N–1. That sum can be expressed similarly, as shown in Figure 12.2.

For example, the sum of the values between 1 and 20 is equal to 20 plus the sum of the values between 1 and 19. Continuing this approach, the sum of the values between 1 and 19 is equal to 19 plus the sum of the values between 1 and 18. This may sound like a strange way to think about this problem, but it is a straightforward example that can be used to demonstrate how recursion is programmed.

$$
\begin{aligned}
\sum_{i=1}^{N} i &= N + \sum_{i=1}^{N-1} i = N + N-1 + \sum_{i=1}^{N-2} i \\
&= N + N-1 + N-2 + \sum_{i=1}^{N-3} i \\
&\;\;\vdots \\
&= N + N-1 + N-2 + \cdots + 2 + 1
\end{aligned}
$$

FIGURE 12.2 The sum of the numbers 1 through N, defined recursively

In Java, as in many other programming languages, a method can call itself. Each call to the method creates a new environment in which to work. That is, all local variables and parameters are newly defined with their own unique data space every time the method is called. Each parameter is given an initial value based on the new call. Each time a method terminates, processing returns to the method that called it (which may be an earlier invocation of the same method). These rules are no different from those governing any "regular" method invocation.

Each recursive call to a method creates new local variables and parameters.

A recursive solution to the summation problem is defined by the following recursive method called sum:

```
// This method returns the sum of 1 to num
public int sum (int num)
{
   int result;
   if (num == 1)
      result = 1;
   else
      result = num + sum (num-1);
   return result;
}
```

This method embodies our recursive definition that the sum of the numbers between 1 and N is equal to N plus the sum of the numbers between 1 and N–1. The `sum` method is recursive because `sum` calls itself. The parameter passed to `sum` is decremented each time `sum` is called until it reaches the base case of 1. Recursive methods usually contain an `if-else` statement, with one of the branches representing the base case.

Suppose the `main` method calls `sum`, passing it an initial value of 1, which is stored in the parameter `num`. Since `num` is equal to 1, the result of 1 is returned to `main` and no recursion occurs.

Now let's trace the execution of the `sum` method when it is passed an initial value of 2. Since `num` does not equal 1, `sum` is called again with an argument of `num-1`, or 1. This is a new call to the method `sum`, with a new parameter `num` and a new local variable `result`. Since this `num` is equal to 1 in this invocation, the result of 1 is returned without further recursive calls. Control returns to the first version of `sum` that was invoked. The return value of 1 is added to the initial value of `num` in that call to `sum`, which is 2. Therefore, `result` is assigned the value 3, which is returned to the `main` method. The method called from `main` correctly calculates the sum of the integers from 1 to 2 and returns the result of 3.

The base case in the summation example is when N equals 1, at which point no further recursive calls are made. The recursion begins to fold back into the earlier versions of the sum method, returning the appropriate value each time. Each return value contributes to the computation of the sum at the higher level. Without the base case, infinite recursion would result. Each call to a method requires additional memory space; therefore infinite recursion often results in a run-time error indicating that memory has been exhausted.

Trace the sum function with different initial values of num until this processing becomes familiar. Figure 12.3 illustrates the recursive calls when main invokes sum to determine the sum of the integers from 1 to 4. Each box represents a copy of the method as it is invoked, indicating the allocation of space to store the formal parameters and any local variables. Invocations are shown as solid lines, and returns as dotted lines. The return value result is shown at each step. The recursive path is followed completely until the base case is reached; the calls then begin to return their result up through the chain.

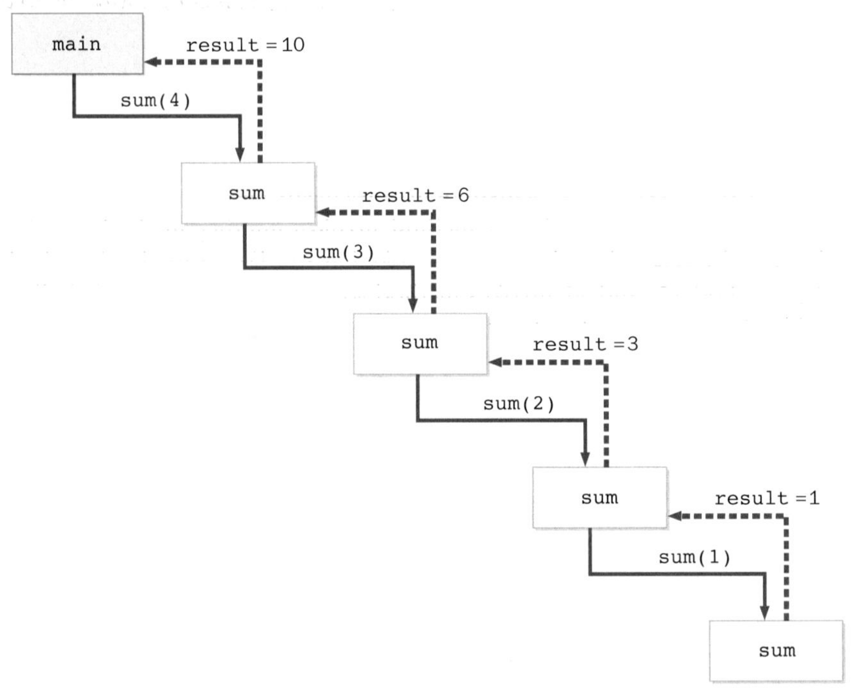

FIGURE 12.3 Recursive calls to the sum method

Recursion vs. Iteration

Of course, there is a non-recursive solution to the summation problem we just explored. One way to compute the sum of the numbers between 1 and `num` inclusive in an iterative manner is as follows:

```
sum = 0;
for (int number = 1; number <= num; number++)
   sum += number;
```

This solution is certainly more straightforward than the recursive version. We used the summation problem to demonstrate recursion because it is simple, not because you would use recursion to solve it under normal conditions. Recursion has the overhead of multiple method invocations and, in this case, presents a more complicated solution than its iterative counterpart.

Recursion is the most elegant and appropriate way to solve some problems, but for others it is less intuitive than an iterative solution.

A programmer must learn when to use recursion and when not to use it. Determining which approach is best depends on the problem being solved. All problems can be solved in an iterative manner, but in some cases the iterative version is much more complicated. Recursion, for some problems, allows us to create relatively short, elegant programs.

Direct vs. Indirect Recursion

Direct recursion occurs when a method invokes itself, such as when `sum` calls `sum`. *Indirect recursion* occurs when a method invokes another method, eventually resulting in the original method being invoked again. For example, if method `m1` invokes method `m2`, and `m2` invokes method `m1`, we can say that `m1` is indirectly recursive. The amount of indirection could be several levels deep, as when `m1` invokes `m2`, which invokes `m3`, which invokes `m4`, which invokes `m1`. Figure 12.4 depicts a situation with indirect recursion. Method invocations are shown with solid lines, and returns are shown with dotted lines. The entire invocation path is followed, and then the recursion unravels following the return path.

Indirect recursion requires all of the same attention to base cases that direct recursion requires. Furthermore, indirect recursion can be more difficult to trace because of the intervening method calls. Therefore extra care is warranted when designing or evaluating indirectly recursive methods. Ensure that the indirection is truly necessary and clearly explained in the program's documentation.

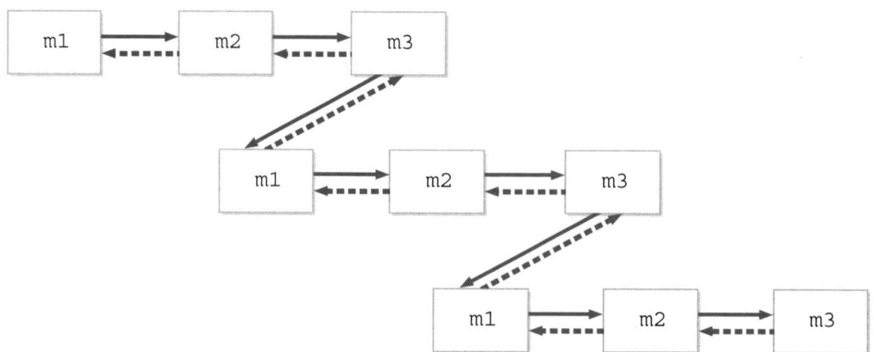

FIGURE 12.4 Indirect recursion

12.3 Using Recursion

The following sections describe problems that we then solve using recursion. For each one, we examine exactly how recursion plays a role in the solution and how a base case is used to terminate the recursion. As you examine these examples, consider how complicated a non-recursive solution for each problem would be.

Traversing a Maze

Solving a maze involves a great deal of trial and error: following a path, backtracking when you cannot go farther, and then trying other previously untried options. Such activities often are handled nicely using recursion. The program shown in Listing 12.1 creates a `Maze` object and attempts to traverse it.

Listing 12.1

```
//********************************************************************
//  MazeSearch.java       Java Foundations
//
//  Demonstrates recursion by solving a maze traversal.
//********************************************************************

public class MazeSearch
{
```

Listing **12.1** continued

```
   //-----------------------------------------------------------------
   //  Creates a new maze, prints its original form, attempts to
   //  solve it, and prints out its final form.
   //-----------------------------------------------------------------
   public static void main (String[] args)
   {
      Maze labyrinth = new Maze();

      System.out.println (labyrinth);

      if (labyrinth.traverse (0, 0))
         System.out.println ("The maze was successfully traversed!");
      else
         System.out.println ("There is no possible path.");

      System.out.println (labyrinth);
   }
}
```

Output

```
1110110001111
1011101111001
0000101010100
1110111010111
1010000111001
1011111101111
1000000000000
1111111111111

The maze was successfully traversed!

7770110001111
3077707771001
0000707070300
7770777070333
7070000773003
7077777703333
7000000000000
7777777777777
```

The `Maze` class shown in Listing 12.2 uses a two-dimensional array of integers to represent the maze. The goal is to move from the top-left corner (the entry point) to the bottom-right corner (the exit point). Initially, a 1 indicates a clear path and a 0 indicates a blocked path. As the maze is solved, these array elements are changed to other values to indicate attempted paths and ultimately a successful path through the maze if one exists.

Listing 12.2

```
//********************************************************************
//  Maze.java        Java Foundations
//
//  Represents a maze of characters. The goal is to get from the
//  top left corner to the bottom right, following a path of 1's.
//********************************************************************

public class Maze
{
   private final int TRIED = 3;
   private final int PATH = 7;

   private int[][] grid = { {1,1,1,0,1,1,0,0,0,1,1,1,1},
                            {1,0,1,1,1,0,1,1,1,1,0,0,1},
                            {0,0,0,0,1,0,1,0,1,0,1,0,0},
                            {1,1,1,0,1,1,1,0,1,0,1,1,1},
                            {1,0,1,0,0,0,0,1,1,1,0,0,1},
                            {1,0,1,1,1,1,1,1,0,1,1,1,1},
                            {1,0,0,0,0,0,0,0,0,0,0,0,0},
                            {1,1,1,1,1,1,1,1,1,1,1,1,1} };

   //-----------------------------------------------------------------
   //  Attempts to recursively traverse the maze. Inserts special
   //  characters indicating locations that have been tried and that
   //  eventually become part of the solution.
   //-----------------------------------------------------------------
   public boolean traverse (int row, int column)
   {
      boolean done = false;

      if (valid (row, column))
      {
         grid[row][column] = TRIED;  // this cell has been tried

         if (row == grid.length-1 && column == grid[0].length-1)
            done = true;  // the maze is solved
```

Listing **12.2** continued

```
         else
         {
            done = traverse (row+1, column);      // down
            if (!done)
               done = traverse (row, column+1);   // right
            if (!done)
               done = traverse (row-1, column);   // up
            if (!done)
               done = traverse (row, column-1);   // left
         }

         if (done)  // this location is part of the final path
            grid[row][column] = PATH;
      }

      return done;
   }

   //-----------------------------------------------------------------
   //  Determines if a specific location is valid.
   //-----------------------------------------------------------------
   private boolean valid (int row, int column)
   {
      boolean result = false;

      // check if cell is in the bounds of the matrix
      if (row >= 0 && row < grid.length && column >= 0 &&
         column < grid[row].length)

         //  check if cell is not blocked and not previously tried
         if (grid[row][column] == 1)
            result = true;

      return result;
   }

   //-----------------------------------------------------------------
   //  Returns a string representation of the maze.
   //-----------------------------------------------------------------
   public String toString ()
   {
      String result = "\n";
```

Listing 12.2 continued

```
      for (int row = 0; row < grid.length; row++)
      {
         for (int column=0; column < grid[row].length; column++)
            result += grid[row][column] + "";
         result += "\n";
      }

      return result;
   }
}
```

The only valid moves through the maze are in the four primary directions: down, right, up, and left. No diagonal moves are allowed. In this example, the maze is 8 rows by 13 columns, although the code is designed to handle a maze of any size.

Let's think this through recursively. The maze can be traversed successfully if it can be traversed successfully from position (0, 0). Therefore, the maze can be traversed successfully if it can be traversed successfully from any positions adjacent to (0, 0), namely position (1, 0), position (0, 1), position (–1, 0), or position (0, –1). Picking a potential next step, say (1, 0), we find ourselves in the same type of situation we were in before. To successfully traverse the maze from the new current position, we must successfully traverse it from an adjacent position. At any point, some of the adjacent positions may be invalid, may be blocked, or may represent a possible successful path. We can continue this process recursively from each new position. If the base case, position (7, 12), is reached, the maze has been traversed successfully.

The recursive method in the `Maze` class is called `traverse`. It returns a boolean value that indicates whether a solution was found. First the method determines whether a move to the specified row and column is valid. A move is considered valid if it stays within the grid boundaries and if the grid contains a 1 in that location, indicating that a move in that direction is not blocked. The initial call to `traverse` passes in the upper-left location (0, 0).

If the move is valid, the grid entry is changed from a 1 to a 3, marking this location as visited so that later we don't retrace our steps. The `traverse` method then determines whether the maze has been completed by having reached the bottom-right location. Therefore, there are actually three possibilities of the base case for this problem that will terminate any particular recursive path:

- an invalid move because the move is out of bounds
- an invalid move because the move has been tried before
- a move that arrives at the final location

If the current location is not the bottom-right corner, we search for a solution in each of the primary directions, if necessary. First, we look down by recursively calling the `traverse` method and passing in the new location. The logic of the `traverse` method starts all over again using this new position. It's as if each call to `traverse` is attempting to solve a new, slightly smaller, maze.

A solution is either ultimately found by first attempting to move down from the current location, or it's not found. If a solution is not found by moving down, we try moving right. If that fails, we try up. Finally, we try left. If no direction from the current location yields a correct solution, then there is no path from this location, and `traverse` returns false. If the very first invocation of the `traverse` method returns false, then there is no possible path through the maze.

If a solution is found from the current location, the grid entry is changed to a 7. The first 7 is placed in the bottom-right corner. The next 7 is placed in the location that led to the bottom-right corner, and so on until the final 7 is placed in the upper-left corner. Therefore, when the final maze is printed, the zeros still indicate a blocked path, a 1 indicates an open path that was never tried, a 3 indicates a path that was tried but failed to yield a correct solution, and a 7 indicates a part of the final solution of the maze.

Note that there are several opportunities for recursion in each call to the `traverse` method. Any or all of them might be followed, depending on the maze configuration. Although there may be many paths through the maze, the recursion terminates when a path is found. Carefully trace the execution of this code while examining the maze array to see how the recursion solves the problem. Then consider the difficulty of producing a non-recursive solution.

The Towers of Hanoi

The *Towers of Hanoi* puzzle was invented in the 1880s by Edouard Lucas, a French mathematician. It has become a favorite among computer scientists because its solution is an excellent demonstration of recursive elegance.

The puzzle consists of three upright pegs and a set of disks with holes in the middle so that they slide onto the pegs. Each disk has a different diameter.

Initially, all of the disks are stacked on one peg in order of size such that the largest disk is on the bottom, as shown in Figure 12.5.

The goal of the puzzle is to move all of the disks from their original (first) peg to the destination (third) peg. We can use the "extra" peg as a temporary place to put disks, but we must obey the following three rules:

- We can move only one disk at a time.
- We cannot place a larger disk on top of a smaller disk.
- All disks must be on some peg except for the disk in transit between pegs.

These rules imply that we must move smaller disks "out of the way" in order to move a larger disk from one peg to another. Figure 12.6 shows the step-by-step solution for the Towers of Hanoi puzzle using three disks. In order to ultimately move all three disks from the first peg to the third peg, we first have to get to the point where the smaller two disks are out of the way on the second peg so that the largest disk can be moved from the first peg to the third peg.

The first three moves shown in Figure 12.6 can be thought of as moving the smaller disks out of the way. The fourth move puts the largest disk in its final place. The last three moves then put the smaller disks in their final place on top of the largest one.

Let's use this idea to form a general strategy. To move a stack of N disks from the original peg to the destination peg:

- Move the topmost N–1 disks from the original peg to the extra peg.
- Move the largest disk from the original peg to the destination peg.
- Move the N–1 disks from the extra peg to the destination peg.

This strategy lends itself nicely to a recursive solution. The step to move the N–1 disks out of the way is the same problem all over again: moving a stack of disks. For this subtask, though, there is one less disk, and our destination peg is

FIGURE 12.5 The Towers of Hanoi puzzle

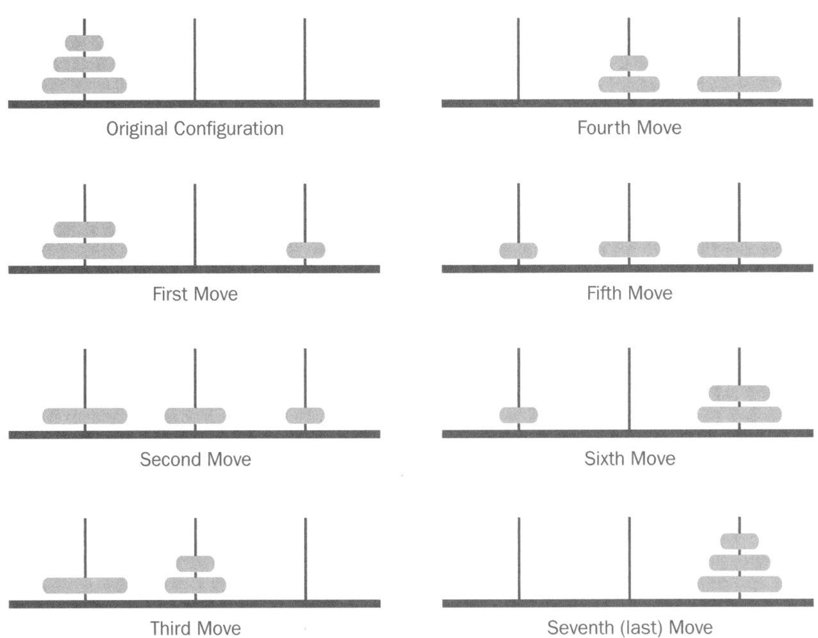

FIGURE 12.6 A solution to the three-disk Towers of Hanoi puzzle

what we were originally calling the extra peg. A similar situation occurs after we've moved the largest disk and we have to move the original N–1 disks again.

The base case for this problem occurs when we want to move a "stack" that consists of only one disk. That step can be accomplished directly and without recursion.

The program in Listing 12.3 creates a `TowersOfHanoi` object and invokes its `solve` method. The output is a step-by-step list of instructions that describes how the disks should be moved to solve the puzzle. This example uses four disks, which is specified by a parameter to the `TowersOfHanoi` constructor.

The `TowersOfHanoi` class shown in Listing 12.4 uses the `solve` method to make an initial call to `moveTower`, the recursive method. The initial call indicates that all of the disks should be moved from peg 1 to peg 3, using peg 2 as the extra position.

The `moveTower` method first considers the base case (a "stack" of one disk). When that occurs, it calls the `moveOneDisk` method that prints a single line describing that particular move. If the stack contains more than one disk, we call `moveTower` again to get the N–1 disks out of the way, then move the largest disk, then move the N–1 disks to their final destination with yet another call to `moveTower`.

Listing **12.3**

```
//********************************************************************
//  SolveTowers.java       Java Foundations
//
//  Demonstrates recursion by solving the classic Towers of Hanoi
//  puzzle.
//********************************************************************

public class SolveTowers
{
   //-----------------------------------------------------------------
   //  Creates a TowersOfHanoi puzzle and solves it.
   //-----------------------------------------------------------------
   public static void main (String[] args)
   {
      TowersOfHanoi towers = new TowersOfHanoi (4);
      towers.solve();
   }
}
```

Output

```
Move one disk from 1 to 2
Move one disk from 1 to 3
Move one disk from 2 to 3
Move one disk from 1 to 2
Move one disk from 3 to 1
Move one disk from 3 to 2
Move one disk from 1 to 2
Move one disk from 1 to 3
Move one disk from 2 to 3
Move one disk from 2 to 1
Move one disk from 3 to 1
Move one disk from 2 to 3
Move one disk from 1 to 2
Move one disk from 1 to 3
Move one disk from 2 to 3
```

Listing 12.4

```
//********************************************************************
//  TowersOfHanoi.java       Java Foundations
//
//  Represents the classic Towers of Hanoi puzzle.
//********************************************************************

public class TowersOfHanoi
{
   private int totalDisks;

   //-----------------------------------------------------------------
   //  Sets up the puzzle with the specified number of disks.
   //-----------------------------------------------------------------
   public TowersOfHanoi (int disks)
   {
      totalDisks = disks;
   }

   //-----------------------------------------------------------------
   //  Performs the initial call to moveTower to solve the puzzle.
   //  Moves the disks from tower 1 to tower 3 using tower 2.
   //-----------------------------------------------------------------
   public void solve ()
   {
      moveTower (totalDisks, 1, 3, 2);
   }

   //-----------------------------------------------------------------
   //  Moves the specified number of disks from one tower to another
   //  by moving a subtower of n-1 disks out of the way, moving one
   //  disk, then moving the subtower back. Base case of 1 disk.
   //-----------------------------------------------------------------
   private void moveTower (int numDisks, int start, int end, int temp)
   {
      if (numDisks == 1)
         moveOneDisk (start, end);
      else
```

Listing 12.4 continued

```
      {
         moveTower (numDisks-1, start, temp, end);
         moveOneDisk (start, end);
         moveTower (numDisks-1, temp, end, start);
      }
   }

   //-----------------------------------------------------------------
   //  Prints instructions to move one disk from the specified start
   //  tower to the specified end tower.
   //-----------------------------------------------------------------
   private void moveOneDisk (int start, int end)
   {
      System.out.println ("Move one disk from " + start + " to " +
         end);
   }
}
```

Note that the parameters to `moveTower` describing the pegs are switched around as needed to move the partial stacks. This code follows our general strategy and uses the `moveTower` method to move all partial stacks. Trace the code carefully for a stack of three disks to understand the processing. Compare the processing steps to Figure 12.6.

The Towers of Hanoi solution has exponential complexity, which is very inefficient. Yet the implementation of the solution is incredibly short and elegant.

Contrary to its short and elegant implementation, the solution to the Towers of Hanoi puzzle is terribly inefficient. To solve the puzzle with a stack of N disks, we have to make $2^N–1$ individual disk moves. This situation is an example of *exponential complexity*. As the number of disks increases, the number of required moves increases exponentially. Techniques for analyzing the efficiency of algorithms are discussed further in Chapter 14.

Legend has it that priests of Brahma are working on this puzzle in a temple at the center of the world. They are using 64 gold disks, moving them between pegs of pure diamond. The downside is that when the priests finish the puzzle, the world will end. The upside is that even if they move one disk every second of every day, it will take them over 584 billion years to complete it. That's with a puzzle of only 64 disks! It is certainly an indication of just how intractable exponential algorithmic complexity is.

Summary of Key Concepts

- Recursion is a programming technique in which a method calls itself.
- A key to being able to program recursively is to be able to think recursively.
- Any recursive definition must have a non-recursive part, called the base case, which permits the recursion to eventually end.
- Mathematical problems and formulas are often expressed recursively.
- Each recursive call to a method creates new local variables and parameters.
- Recursion is the most elegant and appropriate way to solve some problems, but for others it is less intuitive than an iterative solution.
- The Towers of Hanoi solution has exponential complexity, which is very inefficient. Yet the implementation of the solution is incredibly short and elegant.

Self-Review Questions

SR 12.1 What is recursion?

SR 12.2 What is infinite recursion?

SR 12.3 When is a base case needed for recursive processing?

SR 12.4 Is recursion necessary?

SR 12.5 When should recursion be avoided?

SR 12.6 What is indirect recursion?

SR 12.7 Under what conditions does the recursion stop in the `MazeSearch` program?

SR 12.8 Explain the general approach to solving the Towers of Hanoi puzzle. How does it relate to recursion?

Exercises

EX 12.1 Write a recursive definition of a valid Java identifier (see Chapter 1).

EX 12.2 Write a recursive definition of x^y (x raised to the power y), where x and y are integers and $y > 0$.

EX 12.3 Write a recursive definition of $i \times j$ (integer multiplication), where $i > 0$. Define the multiplication process in terms of integer addition. For example, 4×7 is equal to 7 added to itself 4 times.

EX 12.4 Write a recursive definition of the Fibonacci numbers. The Fibonacci numbers are a sequence of integers, each of which is the sum of the previous two numbers. The first two numbers in the sequence are 0 and 1. Explain why you would not normally use recursion to solve this problem.

EX 12.5 Modify the method that calculates the sum of the integers between 1 and N shown in this chapter. Have the new version match the following recursive definition: The sum of 1 to N is the sum of 1 to (N/2) plus the sum of (N/2 + 1) to N. Trace your solution using an N of 7.

EX 12.6 Write a recursive method that returns the value of N! (N factorial) based on the definition given in this chapter. Explain why you would not normally use recursion to solve this problem.

EX 12.7 Write a recursive method to reverse a string. Explain why you would not normally use recursion to solve this problem.

EX 12.8 Design or generate a new maze for the `MazeSearch` program in this chapter and rerun the program. Explain the processing in terms of your new maze, giving examples of a path that was tried but failed, a path that was never tried, and the ultimate solution.

EX 12.9 Annotate the lines of output of the `SolveTowers` program in this chapter to show the recursive steps.

EX 12.10 Produce a chart showing the number of moves required to solve the Towers of Hanoi puzzle using the following number of disks: 2, 3, 4, 5, 6, 7, 8, 9, 10, 15, 20, and 25.

Programming Projects

PP 12.1 Design and implement a recursive version of the `PalindromeTester` program from Chapter 4.

PP 12.2 Design and implement a program that implements Euclid's algorithm for finding the greatest common divisor of two positive integers. The greatest common divisor is the largest integer that divides both values without producing a remainder. An iterative version of this method was part of the `RationalNumber` class presented in Chapter 5. In a class called `DivisorCalc`, define a static method called `gcd` that accepts two integers, `num1` and `num2`. Create a driver to test your implementation. The recursive algorithm is defined as follows:

- `gcd(num1, num2)` is `num2` if `num2 <= num1` and `num2` divides `num1`
- `gcd(num1, num2)` is `gcd(num2, num1)` if `num1 < num2`
- `gcd(num1, num2)` is `gcd(num2, num1%num2)` otherwise

PP 12.3 Modify the `Maze` class so that it prints out the path of the final solution as it is discovered without storing it.

PP 12.4 Design and implement a program that traverses a 3D maze.

PP 12.5 Design and implement a recursive program that solves the Non-Attacking Queens problem. That is, write a program to determine how eight queens can be positioned on an eight-by-eight chessboard so that none of them is in the same row, column, or diagonal as any other queen. There are no other chess pieces on the board.

PP 12.6 In the language of an alien race, all words take the form of Blurbs. A Blurb is a Whoozit followed by one or more Whatzits. A Whoozit is the character 'x' followed by zero or more 'y's. A Whatzit is a 'q' followed by either a 'z' or a 'd', followed by a Whoozit. Design and implement a recursive program that generates random Blurbs in this alien language.

PP 12.7 Design and implement a recursive program to determine whether a string is a valid Blurb as defined in programming project 12.6.

PP 12.8 Design and implement a recursive program to determine and print the Nth line of Pascal's Triangle, as shown on page 22. Each interior value is the sum of the two values above it. *Hint:* Use an array to store the values on each line.

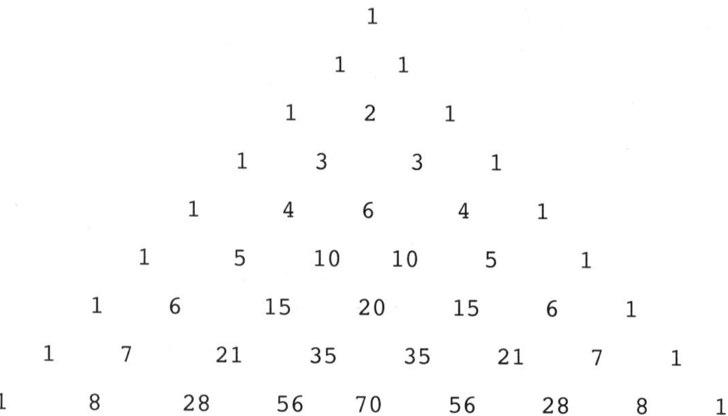

PP 12.9 Design and implement a graphic version of the Towers of Hanoi puzzle. Allow the user to set the number of disks used in the puzzle. The user should be able to interact with the puzzle in two main ways. The user can move the disks from one peg to another using the mouse, in which case the program should ensure that each move is legal. The user can also watch a solution take place as an animation, with pause/resume buttons. Permit the user to control the speed of the animation.

PP 12.10 Write a program that prompts the user for a list of cities, where each city has a name and *x* and *y* coordinates. After all cities have been entered, the program should use a recursive algorithm to print the length of all possible routes that start at the first city entered, end at the last city entered, and visit every city in the list. For each route, the program should print the name of each city visited, followed by the length of the route.

Answers to Self-Review Questions

SR 12.1 Recursion is a programming technique in which a method calls itself, solving a smaller version of the problem each time, until the terminating condition is reached.

SR 12.2 Infinite recursion occurs when there is no base case that serves as a terminating condition or when the base case is improperly specified. The recursive path is followed forever. In a recursive program, infinite recursion will often result in an error that indicates that available memory has been exhausted.

SR 12.3 A base case is always required to terminate recursion and begin the process of returning through the calling hierarchy. Without the base case, infinite recursion results.

SR 12.4 Recursion is not necessary. Every recursive algorithm can be written in an iterative manner. However, some problem solutions are much more elegant and straightforward when written recursively.

SR 12.5 Avoid recursion when the iterative solution is simpler and more easily understood and programmed. Recursion has the overhead of multiple method calls, is not always intuitive, and can be very inefficient.

SR 12.6 Indirect recursion occurs when a method calls another method, which calls another method, and so on until one of the called methods invokes the original. Indirect recursion is usually more difficult to trace than direct recursion, in which a method calls itself.

SR 12.7 The `MazeSearch` program recursively processes each of the four positions adjacent to the "current" one unless either (1) the current position is outside of the playing grid or (2) the final destination position is reached.

SR 12.8 The Towers of Hanoi puzzle of N disks is solved by moving N–1 disks out of the way onto an extra peg, moving the largest disk to its destination, then moving the N–1 disks from the extra peg to the destination. This solution is inherently recursive because, to move the substack of N–1 disks, we can use the same process.

Chapter Objectives

- Examine the linear and binary search algorithms.
- Examine the selection, insertion, bubble, quick, and merge sort algorithms.
- Discuss the techniques for analyzing the complexity of algorithms.
- Explore the complexity of the search and sort algorithms.

13 Searching and Sorting

Two common tasks in the world of software development are searching for a particular element within a group and sorting a group of elements into a particular order. There are a variety of algorithms that can be used to accomplish these tasks, and the differences between them are worth exploring carefully. This chapter also introduces the formal concept of algorithm analysis, and uses these concepts to explore the efficiency of the searching and sorting algorithms.

13.1 Searching

Searching is the process of finding a designated target within a group of items or determining that it doesn't exist.

Searching is the process of finding a designated *target element* within a group of items, or determining that the target does not exist within the group. The group of items to be searched is sometimes called the *search pool.*

This section examines two common approaches to searching: a linear search and a binary search. In this chapter we restrict ourselves to searching an array of items. In later chapters of the book we explore other search techniques that organize data in different ways.

An efficient search minimizes the number of comparisons made.

Our goal is to perform the search as efficiently as possible. In terms of algorithm analysis, we want to minimize the number of comparisons we have to make to find the target. In general, the more items there are in the search pool, the more comparisons it will take to find the target. Thus, the size of the problem is defined by the number of items in the search pool.

To be able to search for an object, we must be able to compare one object to another. Our implementations of these algorithms search an array of `Comparable` objects. Therefore, the elements involved must implement the `Comparable` interface and be comparable to each other.

Recall that the `Comparable` interface contains one method, `compareTo`, which is designed to return an integer that is less than zero, equal to zero, or greater than zero (respectively) if the object is less than, equal to, or greater than (respectively) the object to which it is being compared. Therefore, any class that implements the `Comparable` interface defines the relative order of any two objects of that class.

For our examples, we'll search an array of `Contact` objects. The `Contact` class is shown in Listing 13.1. Each `Contact` object represents a person with a last name, a first name, and a phone number.

The `Contact` class implements the `Comparable` interface and therefore provides a definition of the `compareTo` method. In this case, the contacts are sorted by last name; if two contacts have the same last name, their first names are used to determine the order.

There is a version of the `Comparable` interface that uses *generics*, a technique we explore in the next chapter. For now, we are using the basic interface. This may cause some warnings to be issued by the compiler when this class is used, but they do not prevent an executable version of the program from being created. Don't worry about them at this point.

Listing **13.1**

```
//********************************************************************
//  Contact.java       Java Foundations
//
//  Represents a phone contact that implements Comparable.
//********************************************************************

public class Contact implements Comparable
{
   private String firstName, lastName, phone;

   //-----------------------------------------------------------------
   //  Sets up this contact with the specified information.
   //-----------------------------------------------------------------
   public Contact (String first, String last, String telephone)
   {
      firstName = first;
      lastName = last;
      phone = telephone;
   }

   //-----------------------------------------------------------------
   //  Returns a string representation of this contact.
   //-----------------------------------------------------------------
   public String toString ()
   {
      return lastName + ", " + firstName + ":  " + phone;
   }

   //-----------------------------------------------------------------
   //  Uses both last and first names to determine lexical ordering.
   //-----------------------------------------------------------------
   public int compareTo (Object other)
   {
      int result;

      if (lastName.equals(((Contact)other).lastName))
         result = firstName.compareTo(((Contact)other).firstName);
      else
         result = lastName.compareTo(((Contact)other).lastName);

      return result;
   }
}
```

The program in Listing 13.2 creates an array of `Contact` objects representing tennis players, and then searches for a particular player. It creates a `target` object to use in the search that contains only the values that contribute to the comparison of `Contact` objects, in this case the first and last name of the person. When the search algorithm finds that person in the list, it returns a reference to the original `Contact` object in the list. If the reference that is returned is `null`, then the target was not found in the list.

It may seem like overkill to create a target object that is so close to the one being sought, but imagine a much more complex `Contact` object that contains many more attributes and methods. In that case creating a placeholder target object with only a first and last name is a simple way to indicate which object is being sought.

The `SearchPlayerList` program searches for a particular `Contact` object by calling the static `linearSearch` method of the `Searching` class. Let's explore the idea of a linear search in more detail.

Linear Search

If the search pool is organized into a list of some kind, as it is with an array, one straightforward way to perform the search is to start at the beginning of the list and compare each value in turn to the target element. Eventually, we will either find the target or come to the end of the list and conclude that the target doesn't exist in the group. This approach is called a *linear search* because it begins at one end and scans the search pool in a linear manner. This process is depicted in Figure 13.1.

The `Searching` class is shown in Listing 13.3. It contains two static methods, one that searches for an item using a linear search algorithm, and one that searches for an item using a binary search algorithm. We explore the binary search algorithm in the next section.

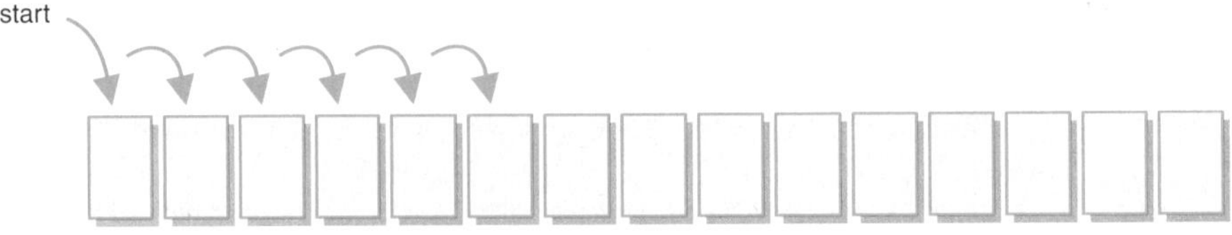

FIGURE 13.1 A linear search

Listing **13.2**

```
//********************************************************************
//  SearchPlayerList.java       Java Foundations
//
//  Demonstrates a linear search of Comparable objects.
//********************************************************************

public class SearchPlayerList
{
   //-----------------------------------------------------------------
   //  Creates an array of Contact objects, then searches for a
   //  particular player.
   //-----------------------------------------------------------------
   public static void main (String[] args)
   {
      Contact[] players = new Contact[7];

      players[0] = new Contact ("Rodger", "Federer", "610-555-7384");
      players[1] = new Contact ("Andy", "Roddick", "215-555-3827");
      players[2] = new Contact ("Maria", "Sharapova", "733-555-2969");
      players[3] = new Contact ("Venus", "Williams", "663-555-3984");
      players[4] = new Contact ("Lleyton", "Hewitt", "464-555-3489");
      players[5] = new Contact ("Eleni", "Daniilidou", "322-555-2284");
      players[6] = new Contact ("Serena", "Williams", "243-555-2837");

      Contact target = new Contact ("Eleni", "Daniilidou", "");

      Contact found = (Contact)Searching.linearSearch(players, target);

      if (found == null)
         System.out.println ("Player was not found.");
      else
         System.out.println ("Found: " + found);
   }
}
```

Output

```
Found: Daniilidou, Eleni:  322-555-2284
```

Listing **13.3**

```
//********************************************************************
//  Searching.java       Java Foundations
//
//  Contains various search algorithms that operate on an array of
//  Comparable objects.
//********************************************************************

public class Searching
{
   //-----------------------------------------------------------------
   //  Searches the specified array of objects using a linear search
   //  algorithm. Returns null if the target is not found.
   //-----------------------------------------------------------------
   public static Comparable linearSearch (Comparable[] data,
                                          Comparable target)
   {
      Comparable result = null;
      int index = 0;

      while (result == null && index < data.length)
      {
         if (data[index].compareTo(target) == 0)
            result = data[index];
         index++;
      }

      return result;
   }

   //-----------------------------------------------------------------
   //  Searches the specified array of objects using a binary search
   //  algorithm. Returns null if the target is not found.
   //-----------------------------------------------------------------
   public static Comparable binarySearch (Comparable[] data,
                                          Comparable target)
   {
      Comparable result = null;
      int first = 0, last = data.length-1, mid;

      while (result == null && first <= last)
      {
         mid = (first + last) / 2;  // determine midpoint
         if (data[mid].compareTo(target) == 0)
            result = data[mid];
```

Listing **13.3** continued

```
            else
               if (data[mid].compareTo(target) > 0)
                  last = mid - 1;
               else
                  first = mid + 1;
         }

         return result;
      }
}
```

The `linearSearch` method accepts the array of elements to be searched and the target item sought. The method returns a reference to the item that was found, which will be `null` if the item was not found in the list.

Note that the parameters and return type of `linearSearch` refer to `Comparable` objects, not `Contact` objects. That is, the `linearSearch` method is implemented in terms of `Comparable` objects, not in terms of any particular class. Recall from Chapter 9 that this situation is an example of *polymorphism*. The references to `Comparable` objects can take on any class of any object that implements the `Comparable` interface. Thus, the `linearSearch` method can be used to search any array of `Comparable` objects, and is another example that shows the versatility and beauty of polymorphism.

The `Comparable` interface allows an algorithm to be implemented polymorphically, without regard to a particular class.

The `while` loop in the `linearSearch` method steps through the elements of the array, terminating when either the element is found or the end of the array is reached. If the target is found, the value of `result` is set to the element in the array, the loop terminates, and the reference is returned. If the entire array is searched without finding the element, the value of `result` stays `null` and is returned, indicating that the target element was not in the list.

The linear search algorithm is fairly easy to understand, though it is not particularly efficient. Note that a linear search does not require the elements in the search pool to be in any particular order within the array. The only criterion is that we must be able to examine them, based on their implementation of `Comparable`, one at a time in turn.

The binary search algorithm, described next, improves on the efficiency of the search process, but only works if the search pool is ordered.

Binary Search

A binary search capitalizes on the fact that the search pool is sorted.

If the group of items in the search pool is sorted, then our approach to searching can be much more efficient than that of a linear search. A *binary search* algorithm eliminates large parts of the search pool with each comparison by capitalizing on the fact that the search pool is in sorted order.

Instead of starting the search at one end of the list, a binary search begins in the middle. If the target element is not found at that middle element, then the search continues. And because the list is sorted, we know that if the target is in the list, it will be on one side of the array or the other, depending on whether the target is less than or greater than the middle element. Thus, because the list is sorted, we eliminate half of the search pool with one carefully chosen comparison. The remaining half of the list represents the *viable candidates* in which the target element may yet be found.

The search continues in this same manner, examining the middle element of the viable candidates, eliminating half of them. Each comparison reduces the viable candidates by half until eventually the target element is found or there are no more viable candidates, which means the target element is not in the search pool. The process of a binary search is depicted in Figure 13.2.

Let's explore the idea of a binary search using a simple sorted list of integers:

```
10 12 18 22 31 34 40 46 59 67 69 72 80 84 98
```

Suppose we were trying to determine if the number 67 is in the list. Initially, the target could be anywhere in the list. That is, initially all items in the search pool are viable candidates.

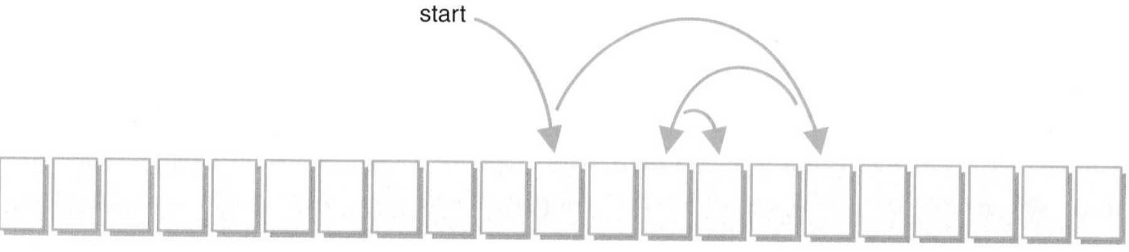

FIGURE 13.2 A binary search

The binary search approach begins by examining the middle element, in this case 46. That element is not our target, so we must continue searching. But since we know that the list is sorted, we know that if 67 is in the list, it must be in the second half of the data, because all data items to the left of the middle have values of 46 or less. This leaves the following viable candidates to search (shown in blue):

```
10 12 18 22 31 34 40 46 59 67 69 72 80 84 98
```

Continuing the same approach, we examine the middle value of the viable candidates (72). Again, this is not our target value, so we must continue the search. This time we can eliminate all values higher than 72, leaving:

```
10 12 18 22 31 34 40 46 59 67 69 72 80 84 98
```

Note that, in only two comparisons, we have reduced the viable candidates from 15 items down to 3 items. Employing the same approach again, we select the middle element, 67, and find the element we are seeking. If it had not been our target, we would have continued with this process until we either found the value or eliminated all possible data.

With each comparison, a binary search eliminates approximately half of the remaining data to be searched (it also eliminates the middle element as well). Therefore, a binary search eliminates half of the data with the first comparison, another quarter of the data with the second comparison, another eighth of the data with the third comparison, and so on.

A binary search eliminates half of the viable candidates with each comparison.

The static `binarySearch` method of the `Searching` class in Listing 13.3 implements a binary search. Like the `linearSearch` method, it accepts an array of `Comparable` objects to be searched and the target value being sought.

The values of the integer variables `first` and `last` represent the range of indexes that make up the viable candidates at any given point during the algorithm. Initially they are set to encompass the entire array.

Similar to the linear search, the `while` loop in the `binarySearch` method continues until the target element is found or the viable data is exhausted. If the target is found, the value of `result` is set and the loop terminates. On the other hand, if the value of `first` ever exceeds the value of `last`, then all viable candidates have been eliminated, the loop terminates, and a `null` value is returned.

In each iteration of the loop, the midpoint of the viable candidates is calculated by taking the average of the `first` and `last` indexes (using integer division). If the target value is found, the return value `result` is set to the original element from the array. Otherwise, the value of `first` or `last` is adjusted to either side of the midpoint, depending on which half of the candidates remains viable, and the search continues.

This version of the binary search algorithm is implemented iteratively. It can also be implemented recursively, which is left as a programming project.

In general, a binary search is more efficient than a linear search because it eliminates many candidates with each comparison. But a binary search requires that the list be in sorted order, whereas a linear search does not. A formal comparison of the efficiency of these search algorithms is presented in the last section of this chapter.

13.2 Sorting

Sorting is the process of arranging a list of items into a defined order based on some criteria.

Sorting is the process of arranging a group of items into a defined order, either ascending or descending, based on some criteria. For example, you may want to alphabetize a list of names or put a list of survey results into descending numeric order. Many sort algorithms have been developed and critiqued over the years. In fact, sorting is considered to be a classic area of study in computer science.

In this section we examine five different sorting algorithms: selection sort, insertion sort, bubble sort, quick sort, and merge sort. The first three are roughly equal in terms of efficiency, but approach the problem from different perspectives. The last two are much more efficient, though a bit more complicated. The last section of this chapter explores ways to examine the efficiency of algorithms, and formally compares these sorting algorithms.

As we did with our search algorithms, we currently restrict ourselves to sorting an array of objects. Other sorting techniques are examined later in the book based on alternative ways to structure our data.

The program in Listing 13.4 creates an array of `Contact` objects just like the array used in our example of search algorithms in Listing 13.2. This time, however, after populating the array, we invoke a method that sorts the elements and then prints them out in order. This example uses the same `Contact` class shown back in Listing 13.1 and relies on its implementation of the `Comparable` interface to determine the relative order of the objects. Note that when two `Contact` objects contain the same last name, the first name is used to determine the order.

Listing 13.4

```
//********************************************************************
//  SortPlayerList.java       Java Foundations
//
//  Demonstrates a selection sort of Comparable objects.
//********************************************************************

public class SortPlayerList
{
   //-----------------------------------------------------------------
   //  Creates an array of Contact objects, sorts them, then prints
   //  them.
   //-----------------------------------------------------------------
   public static void main (String[] args)
   {
      Contact[] players = new Contact[7];

      players[0] = new Contact ("Rodger", "Federer", "610-555-7384");
      players[1] = new Contact ("Andy", "Roddick", "215-555-3827");
      players[2] = new Contact ("Maria", "Sharapova", "733-555-2969");
      players[3] = new Contact ("Venus", "Williams", "663-555-3984");
      players[4] = new Contact ("Lleyton", "Hewitt", "464-555-3489");
      players[5] = new Contact ("Eleni", "Daniilidou", "322-555-2284");
      players[6] = new Contact ("Serena", "Williams", "243-555-2837");

      Sorting.selectionSort(players);

      for (Comparable player : players)
         System.out.println (player);
   }
}
```

Output

```
Daniilidou, Eleni:  322-555-2284
Federer, Rodger:  610-555-7384
Hewitt, Lleyton:  464-555-3489
Roddick, Andy:  215-555-3827
Sharapova, Maria:  733-555-2969
Williams, Serena:  243-555-2837
Williams, Venus:  663-555-3984
```

The `SortPlayerList` program invokes the static `selectionSort` method of the `Sorting` class, shown in Listing 13.5. However, any of the sorting methods in that class could be used to sort the list of `Contact` objects by changing the name of the method invoked.

Let's explore each of these algorithms in turn.

Listing 13.5

```
//********************************************************************
//  Sorting.java       Java Foundations
//
//  Contains various sort algorithms that operate on an array of
//  Comparable objects.
//********************************************************************

public class Sorting
{
   //-----------------------------------------------------------------
   //  Sorts the specified array of integers using the selection
   //  sort algorithm.
   //-----------------------------------------------------------------
   public static void selectionSort (Comparable[] data)
   {
      int min;

      for (int index = 0; index < data.length-1; index++)
      {
         min = index;
         for (int scan = index+1; scan < data.length; scan++)
            if (data[scan].compareTo(data[min]) < 0)
               min = scan;

         swap (data, min, index);
      }
   }

   //-----------------------------------------------------------------
   //  Swaps two elements in the specified array.
   //-----------------------------------------------------------------
   private static void swap (Comparable[] data, int index1, int index2)
   {
      Comparable temp = data[index1];
      data[index1] = data[index2];
      data[index2] = temp;
   }
```

Listing 13.5 continued

```
   //-----------------------------------------------------------------
   //  Sorts the specified array of objects using an insertion
   //  sort algorithm.
   //-----------------------------------------------------------------
   public static void insertionSort (Comparable[] data)
   {
      for (int index = 1; index < data.length; index++)
      {
         Comparable key = data[index];
         int position = index;

         // Shift larger values to the right
         while (position > 0 && data[position-1].compareTo(key) > 0)
         {
            data[position] = data[position-1];
            position--;
         }

         data[position] = key;
      }
   }

   //-----------------------------------------------------------------
   //  Sorts the specified array of objects using a bubble sort
   //  algorithm.
   //-----------------------------------------------------------------
   public static void bubbleSort (Comparable[] data)
   {
      int position, scan;

      for (position = data.length - 1; position >= 0; position--)
      {
         for (scan = 0; scan <= position - 1; scan++)
            if (data[scan].compareTo(data[scan+1]) > 0)
               swap (data, scan, scan+1);
      }
   }

   //-----------------------------------------------------------------
   //  Sorts the specified array of objects using the quick sort
   //  algorithm.
   //-----------------------------------------------------------------
```

Listing 13.5 continued

```
   public static void quickSort (Comparable[] data, int min, int max)
   {
      int pivot;

      if (min < max)
      {
         pivot = partition (data, min, max);  // make partitions
         quickSort(data, min, pivot-1);  // sort left partition
         quickSort(data, pivot+1, max);  // sort right partition
      }
   }

   //-----------------------------------------------------------------
   //  Creates the partitions needed for quick sort.
   //-----------------------------------------------------------------
   private static int partition (Comparable[] data, int min, int max)
   {
      // Use first element as the partition value
      Comparable partitionValue = data[min];

      int left = min;
      int right = max;

      while (left < right)
      {
         // Search for an element that is > the partition element
         while (data[left].compareTo(partitionValue) <= 0 && left < right)
            left++;

         // Search for an element that is < the partitionelement
         while (data[right].compareTo(partitionValue) > 0)
            right--;

         if (left < right)
            swap(data, left, right);
      }

      // Move the partition element to its final position
      swap (data, min, right);

      return right;
   }
```

Listing **13.5** continued

```
//-----------------------------------------------------------------
//  Sorts the specified array of objects using the merge sort
//  algorithm.
//-----------------------------------------------------------------
public static void mergeSort (Comparable[] data, int min, int max)
{
   if (min < max)
   {
      int mid = (min + max) / 2;
      mergeSort (data, min, mid);
      mergeSort (data, mid+1, max);
      merge (data, min, mid, max);
   }
}

//-----------------------------------------------------------------
//  Sorts the specified array of objects using the merge sort
//  algorithm.
//-----------------------------------------------------------------
public static void merge (Comparable[] data, int first, int mid,
   int last)
{
   Comparable[] temp = new Comparable[data.length];

   int first1 = first, last1 = mid;  // endpoints of first subarray
   int first2 = mid+1, last2 = last;  // endpoints of second subarray
   int index = first1;  // next index open in temp array

   //  Copy smaller item from each subarray into temp until one
   //  of the subarrays is exhausted
   while (first1 <= last1 && first2 <= last2)
   {
     if (data[first1].compareTo(data[first2]) < 0)
     {
        temp[index] = data[first1];
        first1++;
     }
     else
     {
        temp[index] = data[first2];
        first2++;
     }
     index++;
   }
```

Listing 13.5 continued

```
        //  Copy remaining elements from first subarray, if any
        while (first1 <= last1)
        {
           temp[index] = data[first1];
           first1++;
           index++;
        }

        //  Copy remaining elements from second subarray, if any
        while (first2 <= last2)
        {
           temp[index] = data[first2];
           first2++;
           index++;
        }

        //  Copy merged data into original array
        for (index = first; index <= last; index++)
           data[index] = temp[index];
     }
  }
```

Selection Sort

Best, n^2
Avg, n^2
worst n^2

The selection sort algorithm sorts a list of values by repeatedly putting a particular value into its final, sorted position.

The *selection sort* algorithm sorts a list of values by repetitively putting a particular value into its final, sorted position. In other words, for each position in the list, the algorithm selects the value that should go in that position and then puts it there.

The general strategy of the selection sort algorithm is as follows: Scan the entire list to find the smallest value. Exchange that value with the value in the first position of the list. Scan the rest of the list (all but the first value) to find the smallest value, and then exchange it with the value in the second position of the list. Scan the rest of the list (all but the first two values) to find the smallest value, and then exchange it with the value in the third position of the list. Continue this process for each position in the list. When complete, the list is sorted. The selection sort process is illustrated in Figure 13.3.

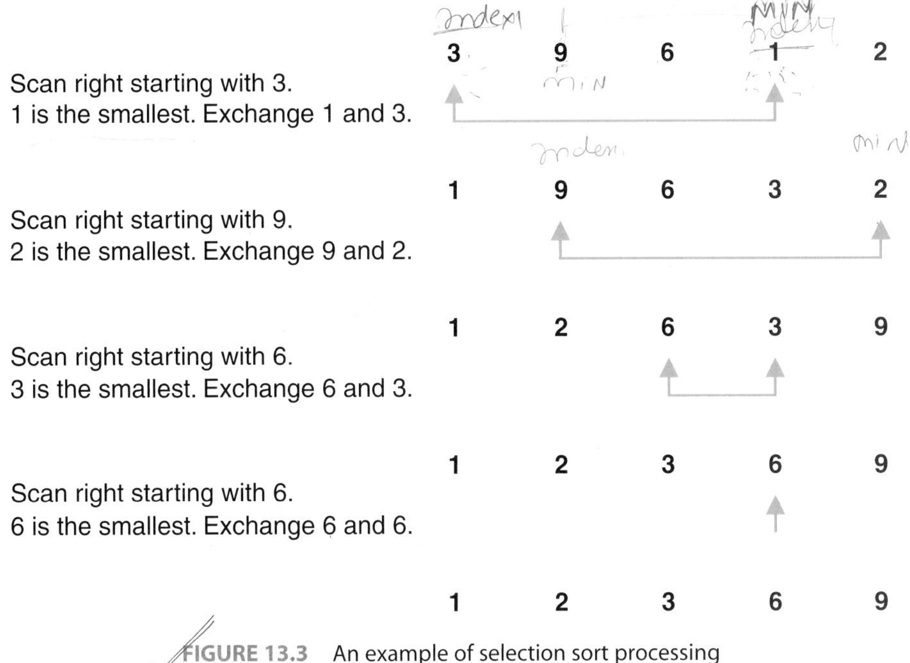
3 9 6 1 2
Scan right starting with 3.
1 is the smallest. Exchange 1 and 3.
1 9 6 3 2
Scan right starting with 9.
2 is the smallest. Exchange 9 and 2.
1 2 6 3 9
Scan right starting with 6.
3 is the smallest. Exchange 6 and 3.
1 2 3 6 9
Scan right starting with 6.
6 is the smallest. Exchange 6 and 6.
1 2 3 6 9

FIGURE 13.3 An example of selection sort processing

The `selectionSort` method accepts an array of `Comparable` objects as a parameter. When control returns to the calling method, the elements within the array are sorted. The method uses two loops to sort an array. The outer loop controls the position in the array where the next smallest value will be stored. The inner loop finds the smallest value in the rest of the list by scanning all positions greater than or equal to the index specified by the outer loop. When the smallest value is determined, it is exchanged with the value stored at `index`.

The exchange of two elements in the array, called *swapping*, is accomplished with a call to a support method called `swap`. Many of the sort algorithms we examine in this chapter swap elements and make use of this method. The `swap` method uses three assignment statements to make the exchange.

Note that because this algorithm finds the smallest value during each iteration, the result is an array sorted in ascending order (i.e., smallest to largest). The algorithm can easily be changed to put values in descending order by finding the largest value each time through the loop.

Insertion Sort

The *insertion sort* algorithm sorts a list of values by repetitively inserting a particular value into a subset of the list that has already been sorted. One at a time, each unsorted element is inserted at the appropriate position in that sorted subset until the entire list is in order.

The insertion sort algorithm sorts a list of values by repetitively inserting a particular value into a subset of the list that has already been sorted.

The general strategy of the insertion sort algorithm is as follows: Sort the first two values in the list relative to each other by exchanging them if necessary. Insert the list's third value into the appropriate position relative to the first two (sorted) values. Then insert the fourth value into its proper position relative to the first three values in the list. Each time an insertion is made, the number of values in the sorted subset increases by one. Continue this process until all values in the list are completely sorted. The insertion process requires that the other values in the array shift to make room for the inserted element. Figure 13.4 illustrates the insertion sort process.

Similar to the selection sort implementation, the `insertionSort` method uses two loops to sort an array of objects. In the insertion sort, however, the outer loop controls the index in the array of the next value to be inserted. The inner loop compares the current insert value with values stored at lower indexes (which make up a sorted subset of the entire list). If the current insert value is less than the value at `position`, then that value is shifted to the right. Shifting continues until the proper position is "opened" to accept the insert value. Each iteration of the outer loop adds one more value to the sorted subset of the list, until the entire list is sorted.

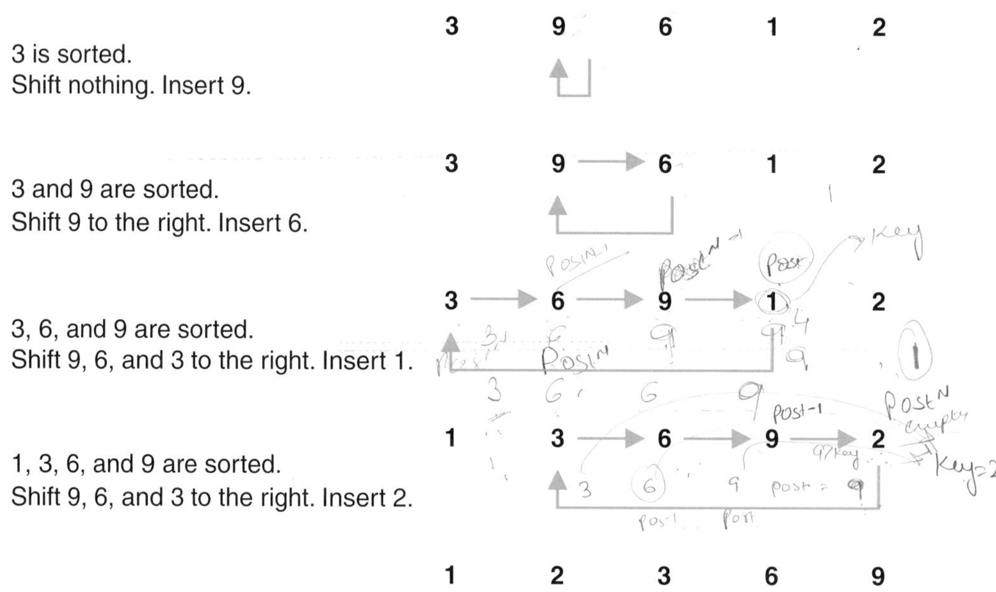

3 9 6 1 2
3 is sorted.
Shift nothing. Insert 9.
3 9 6 1 2
3 and 9 are sorted.
Shift 9 to the right. Insert 6.
3 6 9 1 2
3, 6, and 9 are sorted.
Shift 9, 6, and 3 to the right. Insert 1.
1 3 6 9 2
1, 3, 6, and 9 are sorted.
Shift 9, 6, and 3 to the right. Insert 2.
1 2 3 6 9

FIGURE 13.4 An example of insertion sort processing

Bubble Sort

A *bubble sort* sorts values by repeatedly comparing neighboring elements in the list and swapping their position if they are not in order relative to each other.

The bubble sort algorithm sorts a list by repeatedly comparing neighboring elements and swapping them if necessary.

The general strategy of the bubble sort algorithm is as follows: Scan through the list comparing adjacent elements and swap them if they are not in relative order. This has the effect of "bubbling" the largest value to the last position in the list, which is its appropriate position in the final, sorted list. Then scan through the list again, bubbling up the second-to-last value. This process continues until all elements have been bubbled into their correct positions.

Each pass through the bubble sort algorithm moves one value to its final position. A pass may also reposition other elements as well. Let's follow this process for a small list of integers. Suppose we started with this list:

```
9  6  8  12  3  1  7
```

We would first compare 9 and 6 and, finding them not in the correct order, swap them, yielding:

```
6  9  8  12  3  1  7
```

Then we would compare 9 to 8 and, again, finding them not in the correct order, swap them, yielding:

```
6  8  9  12  3  1  7
```

Then we would compare 9 to 12. Since they are in the correct order, we don't swap them. Instead, we move on to the next pair of values. That is, we then compare 12 and 3. Since they are not in order, we swap them, yielding:

```
6  8  9  3  12  1  7
```

We then compare 12 to 1 and swap them, yielding:

```
6  8  9  3  1  12  7
```

We then compare 12 to 7 and swap them, yielding:

```
6  8  9  3  1  7  12
```

This completes one pass through the data to be sorted. After this first pass, the largest value in the list (12) is in its correct position. The next pass will bubble the value 9 up to its final position. Each subsequent pass through the data guarantees that one more element is put into the correct position. Thus we make n–1 passes through the data, because if n–1 elements are in the correct, sorted positions, the nth item must also be in the correct location.

The `bubbleSort` method in the `Sorting` class implements this approach. The outer `for` loop represents the n–1 passes through the data. The inner `for` loop scans through the data, performing the pair-wise comparisons of the neighboring data and swapping them if necessary. The support method `swap` is used to perform the exchange of two elements, just as we used it in the `selectionSort` method.

Note that the outer loop also has the effect of decreasing the position that represents the maximum index to examine in the inner loop. That is, after the first pass, which puts the last value in its correct position, there is no need to consider that value in future passes through the data. After the second pass, we can forget about the last two, and so on. Thus the inner loop examines one less value on each pass.

Quick Sort

The sort algorithms we have discussed thus far in this chapter (selection sort, insertion sort, and bubble sort) are relatively simple, but they are generally inefficient. They each use a pair of nested loops and require roughly n^2 comparisons to sort a list of n elements. Let's now turn our attention to more efficient sorts.

The *quick sort* algorithm sorts a list by partitioning the list based on an arbitrarily chosen *partition element* and then recursively sorting the sublists on either side of the partition element.

The quick sort algorithm sorts a list by partitioning the list and then recursively sorting the two partitions.

The general strategy of the quick sort algorithm is as follows: First, choose one element of the list to act as a partition element. Next, partition the list so that all elements less than the partition element are to the left of that element and all elements greater than the partition element are to the right. Finally, apply this quick sort strategy (recursively) to both partitions.

If the items to be sorted are in random order initially, the choice of the partition element is arbitrary, and we will use the first element in the list. For efficiency reasons, it would be nice if the partition element divided the list roughly in half, but the algorithm will work no matter what element is chosen as the partition.

Let's look at an example of creating a partition. Suppose we start with the following list:

```
90 65 7 305 120 110 8
```

We choose 90 as our partition element, and then rearrange the list, putting the elements that are less than 90 to the left side and those that are greater than 90 to the right side, yielding two partitions (in blue):

```
8 65 7 90 120 110 305
```

The relative order of the elements in each partition doesn't matter at this point, as long as every value in the left partition is less than 90 and every value in the right partition is greater than 90. Note that, after creating the two partitions, the partition element (90) is in its final position in the array, and we no longer have to consider or move it again.

We then apply the quick sort algorithm separately to both partitions. This process continues until a partition contains only one element, which is inherently sorted. Thus, after the algorithm is applied recursively to either side, the entire list is sorted.

The `quickSort` method in the `Sorting` class implements the quick sort algorithm. It accepts an array of objects to sort and the minimum and maximum index values used for a particular call to the method. For the initial call to the method, the values of `min` and `max` would encompass the entire set of elements to be sorted.

The `quickSort` method calls a support method called `partition`, which partitions the elements on either side of the partition element and returns the final index of the partition element (the pivot point). The `quickSort` method then calls itself twice more recursively to sort the two partitions. The `if` statement terminates the recursion when the size of the partition is one or less.

The `partition` method works by scanning in from each end of the current partition toward the middle until it finds two elements that are on the wrong side, and then swaps them. When this scanning process meets at the partition point, the partitions have been created.

The integer variables `left` and `right` are used to track the positions in the array as we scan in from either end of the current partition. The two inner loops are used to find elements that are in the wrong partitions. The first inner loop scans from left to right looking for an element that is greater than the partition element. The second inner loop scans from right to left looking for an element that is less than the partition element. When these two elements are found, they are swapped. This process continues until the right and left indexes meet in the "middle" of the list, and the outer loop terminates. The location where they meet also indicates where the partition element should reside. At the end of the method, the partition element is moved from its initial location to its final position in the sorted array.

Merge Sort

The merge sort algorithm sorts a list by recursively dividing the list in half until each sublist has one element and then merging these sublists into the sorted order.

The *merge sort* algorithm sorts a list by recursively dividing the list in half until each sublist has one element and then recombining these sublists in order.

The general strategy of the merge sort algorithm is as follows: Begin by dividing the list in two roughly equal parts and then recursively calling itself with each of those lists. Continue the recursive decomposition of the list until the base case of the recursion is reached, where the list is divided into lists of length one, which are inherently sorted. Then, as control passes back up the recursive calling structure, the algorithm merges the two sorted sublists resulting from the two recursive calls into one sorted list.

Suppose we started with the following initial list (the same example we used in the previous section):

```
90 65 7 305 120 110 8
```

The merge sort algorithm divides the list in half, and then divides each of those lists in half, and so on until a list of length one is reached, as shown in Figure 13.5.

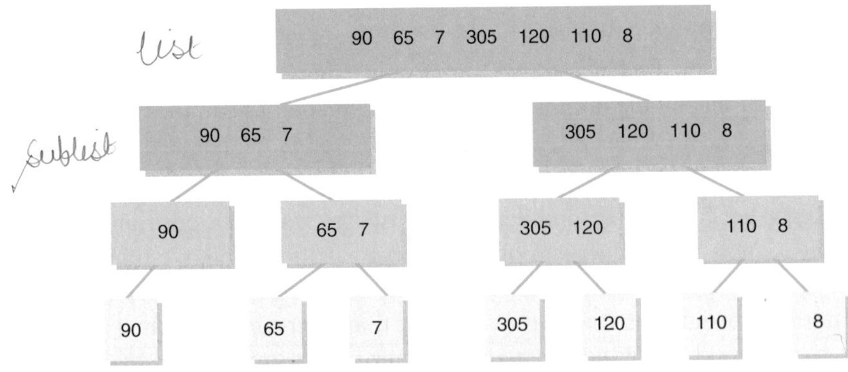

FIGURE 13.5 The decomposition of merge sort

The merge portion of the algorithm then recombines the lists as shown in Figure 13.6. When each sublist is merged together, their elements are kept in sorted order.

The `mergeSort` method in the `Sorting` class in Listing 13.5 implements this strategy. The midpoint of the list to be sorted is determined, and then `mergeSort` is called twice again recursively to sort those two halves. The recursion is terminated by the `if` statement when a sublist has a length of one or less. As the recursion unfolds, the two sorted sublists are merged by the `merge` support method.

The `merge` method accepts three integers that define the two sublists within the array that have already been sorted. The values in the array from index `first` to index `mid` are in sorted order, and the values in the array from index `mid+1` to index `last` are in sorted order. The job of the `merge` method is to merge these two sublists into one larger, sorted list.

As the merge occurs, values are moved from one sublist or the other into a temporary array. Then when the merge is complete, the values are copied from the temporary array back into the original.

The first `while` loop in the `merge` method scans through the two sublists, copying the smaller values found from either list into the `temp` array. This process continues until all values from one sublist or the other have been copied into the `temp` array. Then the remaining values are moved from the other sublist into the `temp` array. Since we don't know which sublist has been exhausted, both are checked (but only one or the other will be needed for any given execution of the sort).

The `for` loop at the end of the `merge` method copies all data put into the `temp` array, which is now sorted, back into the original array.

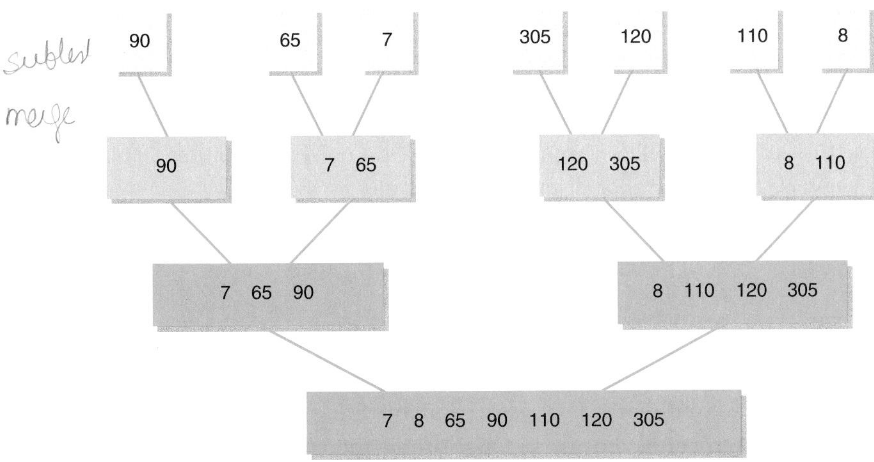

FIGURE 13.6 The merge portion of the merge sort algorithm

13.3 Analysis of Algorithms

One of the most important resources is CPU time. The efficiency of an algorithm we use to accomplish a particular task is a major factor that determines how fast a program executes. Although we can analyze an algorithm relative to the amount of memory it uses, CPU time is usually the more interesting issue.

This section introduces the concept of formal algorithm analysis to assess efficiency. Let's start with an everyday example: washing dishes by hand. If washing a dish takes 30 seconds and drying a dish takes an additional 30 seconds, then we can see that it would take n minutes to wash and dry n dishes. This computation could be expressed as follows:

$$\begin{aligned} \textit{Time (n dishes)} &= n * (30 \text{ seconds wash time} + 30 \text{ seconds dry time}) \\ &= 60n \text{ seconds} \end{aligned}$$

Now let's extend this example to a ridiculous extreme. Suppose we were careless while washing the dishes and splashed too much water around, so much so that each time we washed a dish, we had to dry not only that dish but also all of the dishes we had washed and dried before that one. It would still take 30 seconds to wash each dish, but now it would take 30 seconds to dry the last dish (once), 2 * 30 or 60 seconds to dry the second-to-last dish (twice), 3 * 30 or 90 seconds to dry the third-to-last dish (three times), and so on. This computation could be expressed as follows:

$$\begin{aligned} &= n * (30 \text{ seconds wash time}) + \sum_{i=1}^{n} (i * 30) \\ \textit{Time (n dishes)} &= 30n + \frac{30n(n+1)}{2} \\ &= 15n^2 + 45n \text{ seconds} \end{aligned}$$

If there were 30 dishes to wash, the first approach would take 30 minutes, whereas the second (careless) approach would take 247.5 minutes. The more dishes we wash the worse that discrepancy becomes.

Growth Functions and Big O() Notation

For every algorithm we want to analyze, we need to define the size of the problem. For our dishwashing example, the size of the problem is the number of dishes to be washed and dried. For a search algorithm, the size of the problem is the size of the search pool. For a sort algorithm, the size of the problem is the number of elements to be sorted.

We also need to think in terms of the key processing steps that define our use of CPU time. That is, we want to find a processing step that we can minimize. For dishwashing, we want to minimize the number of times a dish has to be washed and dried. For search and sort algorithms, we can express the processing in terms of the number of comparisons between elements that have to be made in order to find the target or sort the list.

The overall amount of time spent at the task is directly related to how many times we have to perform the key processing step. Thus an algorithm's efficiency can be defined in terms of the problem size and the key processing step.

The efficiency of an algorithm is a function of the problem size and a key processing step.

A *growth function* shows the relationship between the size of the problem (n) and the value we hope to optimize. This function represents the *time complexity* or *space complexity* of the algorithm. As we mentioned earlier, time complexity is generally more important, so we will continue to focus on that aspect.

A growth function shows time or space utilization relative to the problem size.

The growth function for our second dishwashing algorithm is

$$t(n) = 15n^2 + 45n$$

However, it is not typically necessary to know the exact growth function for an algorithm. Instead, we are mainly interested in the *asymptotic complexity* of an algorithm. That is, we want to focus on the general nature of the function as n increases. This characteristic is based on the *dominant term* of the expression—the term that increases most quickly as n increases. As n gets very large, the value of the dishwashing growth function approaches n^2 because the n^2 term grows much faster than the n term. The constants and the secondary term quickly become irrelevant as n increases.

The asymptotic complexity is called the *order* of the algorithm. Thus, our dishwashing algorithm is said to have order n^2 time complexity, which is written $O(n^2)$. This is referred to as Big O() or Big-Oh notation. Figure 13.7 lists several growth functions and their asymptotic complexity.

Growth Function	Order	Complexity
$t(n) = 17$	$O(1)$	constant
$t(n) = 20n - 4$	$O(n)$	linear
$t(n) = 12n \log n + 100n$	$O(n \log n)$	logarithmic
$t(n) = 3n^2 + 5n - 2$	$O(n^2)$	polynomial (quadratic)
$t(n) = 2^n + 18n^2 + 3n$	$O(2^n)$	exponential

FIGURE 13.7 Some growth functions and their asymptotic complexity

A growth function that executes in a set amount of time regardless of the size of the problem is said to have O(1), or *constant complexity*. Algorithms that solve problems in direct proportion to their problem size are said to operate in *linear time*. Many computing algorithms execute with *logarithmic complexity*, a function of $\log_2 n$. Other algorithms execute with *polynomial complexity*, in which n is raised to a particular value, such as $O(n^2)$ or $O(n^3)$. Worse yet are those algorithms that run with *exponential complexity*, in which the value of n is in the exponent, such as $O(2^n)$.

Because the order of the function is the main factor, the other terms and constants are often not even mentioned. All algorithms within a given order are considered to be generally equivalent in terms of efficiency. For example, all sorting algorithms of $O(n^2)$ are considered to be equally efficient in general.

Comparing Growth Functions

One might assume that, with the advances in the speed of processors and the availability of large amounts of inexpensive memory, algorithm analysis would no longer be necessary. However, nothing could be farther from the truth. Processor speed and memory cannot make up for the differences in efficiency of algorithms.

A faster processor cannot compensate for an inefficient algorithm as the size of the problem increases.

The table in Figure 13.8 compares four algorithms with various time complexities and the effects of speeding up the processor by a factor of 10. Algorithm A_1, with a time complexity of n, is indeed improved by a factor of 10. However, algorithm A_2, with a time complexity of n^2, is only improved by a factor of 3.16. Similarly, algorithm A_3 is only improved by a factor of 2.15. The rate of improvement due to processing speed is no match for the degradation caused by inefficient algorithms. In the grand scheme of things, if an algorithm is inefficient, speeding up the processor will not help.

Figure 13.9 shows various growth functions graphically. Note that when n is small, there is little difference between the algorithms. That is, if you can guarantee a very small problem size (5 or less), it doesn't really matter which algorithm

Algorithm	Time Complexity	Max Problem Size Before Speedup	Max Problem Size After Speedup
A_1	n	s_1	$10s_1$
A_2	n^2	s_2	$3.16s_2$
A_3	n^3	s_3	$2.15s_3$
A_4	n^4	s_4	$s_4 + 3.3$

FIGURE 13.8 Increase in problem size with a tenfold increase in processor speed

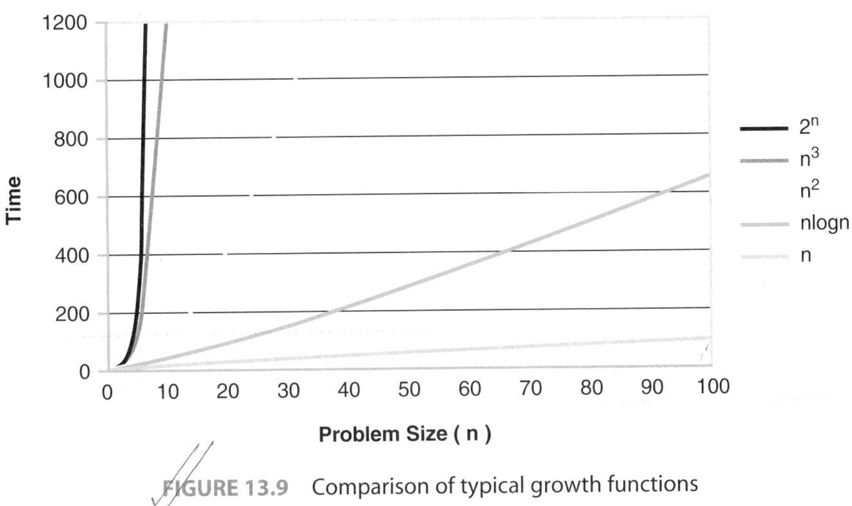

FIGURE 13.9 Comparison of typical growth functions

is used. However, as n gets larger, the differences between the growth functions become significant quickly.

Analyzing Loop Execution

Analyzing algorithm complexity often requires analyzing the execution of loops.

To determine the order of an algorithm, we often have to determine how often a particular statement or set of statements gets executed. Therefore, we often have to determine how many times the body of a loop is executed. To analyze loop execution, first determine the order of the body of the loop, and then multiply that by the number of times the loop will execute relative to n. Keep in mind that n represents the problem size.

Assuming that the body of a loop is O(1), then a loop such as this:

```
for (int count = 0; count < n; count++)
{
   // some sequence of O(1) steps
}
```

would have O(n) time complexity. This is due to the fact that the body of the loop has O(1) complexity but is executed n times by the loop structure. In general, if a loop structure steps through n items in a linear fashion and the body of the loop is O(1), then the loop is O(n). Even in a case where the loop is designed to skip some number of elements, as long as the progression of elements to skip is linear, the loop is still O(n). For example, if the preceding loop skipped every other number, the growth function of the loop would be n/2, but since constants don't affect the asymptotic complexity, the order is still O(n).

Let's look at another example. If the progression of the loop is logarithmic such as the following:

```
count = 1
while (count < n)
{
    count *= 2;
    // some sequence of O(1) steps
}
```

then the loop is said to be O(log n). Note that when we use a logarithm to express an algorithm's complexity, we almost always mean log base 2. This can be explicitly written as $O(\log_2 n)$. Since each time through the loop the value of `count` is multiplied by 2, the number of times the loop is executed is $\log_2 n$.

When loops are nested, we must multiply the complexity of the outer loop by the complexity of the inner loop to find the resulting complexity. For example, consider the following nested loops:

```
for (int count = 0; count < n; count++)
    for (int count2 = 0; count2 < n; count2++)
    {
        // some sequence of O(1) steps
    }
```

The analysis of nested loops must take into account both the inner and outer loops.

This code has complexity $O(n^2)$. Both the inner and outer loops have complexity O(n), which, when multiplied together, results in $O(n^2)$. When you think that through, it makes sense: each time the outer loop is executed (which happens n times), the inner loop is executed n times.

What is the complexity of the following nested loop?

```
for (int count = 0; count < n; count++)
    for (int count2 = count; count2 < n; count2++)
    {
        // some sequence of O(1) steps
    }
```

In this case, the inner loop index is initialized to the current value of the index for the outer loop. The outer loop executes n times. The inner loop executes n times the first time, n–1 times the second time, etc. However, remember that we are only interested in the dominant term, not in constants or any lesser terms. If the progression is linear, regardless of whether some elements are skipped, the order is still O(n). Thus the resulting complexity for this code is $O(n^2)$.

Analyzing Recursive Algorithms

Determining the order of a recursive algorithm is a matter of determining the order of the recursion (the number of times the recursive definition is followed) and multiplying that by the order of the body of the recursive method.

Consider the following recursive method that computes the sum of the integers from 1 to some positive value (we saw this example in Chapter 12):

```
public int sum (int num)
{
   int result;
   if (num == 1)
      result = 1;
   else
      result = num + sum (num-1);
   return result;
}
```

We realize that this is not a good example of the use of recursion, but it's a good first example to consider as we analyze the algorithm's complexity. The size of this problem is naturally expressed as the number of values to be summed. Because we are summing the integers from 1 to `num`, the number of values to be summed is `num`. In this case the operation of interest is the act of adding two values together. The body of the recursive method performs one addition operation, and therefore is O(1). Each time the recursive method is invoked, the value of `num` is decreased by 1. Therefore, the recursive method is called `num` times, so the order of the recursion is O(n). Thus, since the body is O(1) and the recursion is O(n), the order of the entire algorithm is O(n). So it is no more inefficient than the iterative version to sum the values, though it certainly is less intuitive.

Now let's revisit the Towers of Hanoi puzzle discussed in Chapter 12 (review it if necessary). The size of the puzzle is naturally the number of disks, and the processing operation of interest is the step of moving one disk from one peg to another. Each recursive call to `moveTower` results in one disk being moved. Unfortunately, except for the base case, each recursive call also results in calling itself twice more, with each call operating on a stack of disks that is only one less than before. Thus, calling `moveTower` with 1 disk results in 1 disk being moved, calling `moveTower` with 2 disks results in 3 disks being moved, calling `moveTower` with 3 disks results in 7 disks being moved, calling `moveTower` with 4 disks results in 15 disks being moved, etc. Looking at it another way, if f(n) is the growth function for this problem, then:

```
f(n)     =    1 when n is equal to 1
```

and, for n > 1:

```
f(n)      =    2 *(f(n-1) + 1)
          =    2^n - 1
```

Thus, the Towers of Hanoi puzzle has exponential complexity, $O(2^n)$.

13.4 Analyzing Searching and Sorting Algorithms

Now that we've introduced the ideas behind algorithm analysis, let's apply those concepts to the searching and sorting algorithms presented earlier in this chapter. Keep in mind that what we're most interested in is the asymptotic complexity of an algorithm as the size of the problem grows. That is, although we could painstakingly quantify the effort represented by each line of code (assignment statements, increments, comparisons), they individually contribute some constant to the growth function, and those constants become irrelevant in the big picture. The thing that matters is the way the algorithm behaves in terms of the problem size (n).

Another issue to consider is the *best-case* and *worst-case* situations for each algorithm. For some problems, such as our dishwashing scenario or the Towers of Hanoi puzzle, there essentially is no best or worst case. Solving these problems will always require the same amount of effort for a given problem size. But in the case of searching, the effort depends on the particular value being sought. You could be "lucky" and find it quickly, or "unlucky" and not find it until late in the processing. Similarly, some sorting algorithms may be more efficient in a particular situation depending on the original configuration of the data to be sorted.

Thinking through the best-case and worst-case scenarios often helps us appreciate the *expected-case* (or *average-case*) situation for a given algorithm, which is generally the focus of algorithm analysis.

Comparing Search Algorithms

For a linear search, the best case occurs when the target element happens to be the first item we examine in the group. The worst case occurs when the target is not in the group, and we have to examine every element before we determine that it isn't present. The expected case is that we would have to search half of the list before we find the element. That is, if there are n elements in the search pool, on average we would have to examine n/2 elements before finding the one for which we were searching.

Therefore, the linear search algorithm has a linear time complexity of O(n). Because the elements are searched one at a time in turn, the complexity is linear—in direct proportion to the number of elements to be searched.

A binary search, on the other hand, is generally much faster. Because we can eliminate half of the remaining data with each comparison, we can find the element much more quickly. The best case is that we find the target in one comparison—that is, the target element happens to be at the midpoint of the array. The worst case occurs if the element is not present in the list, in which case we have to make approximately $\log_2 n$ comparisons before we eliminate all of the data. Thus, the expected case for finding an element that is in the search pool is approximately $(\log_2 n)/2$ comparisons.

Therefore, a binary search is a logarithmic algorithm and has a time complexity of O(log n). Compared to a linear search, a binary search is much faster for large values of n.

A binary search has logarithmic complexity, making it very efficient for a large search pool.

The question might be asked, if a logarithmic search is more efficient than a linear search, why would we ever use a linear search? First, a linear search is generally simpler than a binary search, and thus easier to program and debug. Second, a linear search does not require the additional overhead of sorting the search list. There is a trade-off between the effort to keep the search pool sorted and the efficiency of the search.

For small problems, there is little practical difference between the two types of algorithms. However, as n gets larger, the binary search becomes increasingly attractive. Suppose a given set of data contains one million elements. In a linear search, we'd have to examine each of the one million elements to determine that a particular target element is not in the group. In a binary search, we could make that conclusion after approximately 20 comparisons.

Comparing Sort Algorithms

Although selection sort, insertion sort, and bubble sort each solve the problem with a different technique, they all do so with approximately the same efficiency. All three of those algorithms use two loops, one nested within the other, to arrange the elements in order, and the details all lead to an $O(n^2)$ running time.

Selection sort, for instance, has an outer loop that iterates n–1 times. For each iteration of the outer loop, the inner loop iterates over a portion of the array (how much depends on which iteration of the outer loop we're doing, but it's always less than n). And there is some constant effort in each inner iteration. So the growth function of this algorithm can be expressed:

```
f(n)    =    (n-1) * (some constant * n + another constant)
        =    an² + bn + c
```

for irrelevant constants a, b, and c. For Big-Oh analysis, only the n^2 term matters, leaving sequential sort with a complexity of $O(n^2)$.

The average running time complexity for selection sort, insertion sort, and bubble sort is $O(n^2)$.

Similar arguments can be made for the insertion sort and bubble sort algorithms. The details would vary, but the analysis would conclude that they also have quadratic complexity.

Now consider the best- and worst-case scenarios for each of these algorithms. For selection and bubble sorts, the processing is fundamentally independent of the original configuration of the elements to be sorted. There will be slight differences in the number of swaps that occur depending on the data, but the best, worst, and average cases for both selection and bubble sorts are all $O(n^2)$.

Insertion sort, on the other hand, is based on the original configuration. The worst case for insertion sort, when the original array is in reverse sorted order, will process the inner loop fully, so it is basically the same as the average case, $O(n^2)$. However, if the array is already sorted in the correct order, the inner loop of the insertion sort will make only one comparison, and thus the best case for insertion sort is $O(n)$. While starting with a fully sorted array initially is not likely, starting with a partially sorted array may be likely depending on the situation, and the insertion sort is quicker in those cases as well.

Now let's consider the quick sort algorithm. Ideally, the partition element chosen each time will divide the elements in half, so that each recursive call to `quickSort` will operate on about half of the current data, as depicted in Figure 13.10. In this case, there will be $\log_2 n$ levels in the recursion. The act of partitioning the elements at each level requires one pass through the data, so the effort to partition an entire level of Figure 13.10 is $O(n)$. Thus, the effort to sort the entire array is $O(n \log n)$.

Figure 13.10 depicts the best case for quick sort. And if we pick a good partition element, that is the expected case as well. The worst-case scenario for quick sort is if it consistently picks a partition element that does not partition the data at all, which means each level of the recursion only handles one element. In that case the running time degrades to $O(n^2)$.

The key to quick sort is picking a good partition element.

Thus the key to quick sort is picking a good partition element. In our implementation, we simply chose the first element in the partition. If the original configuration of the array is truly random,

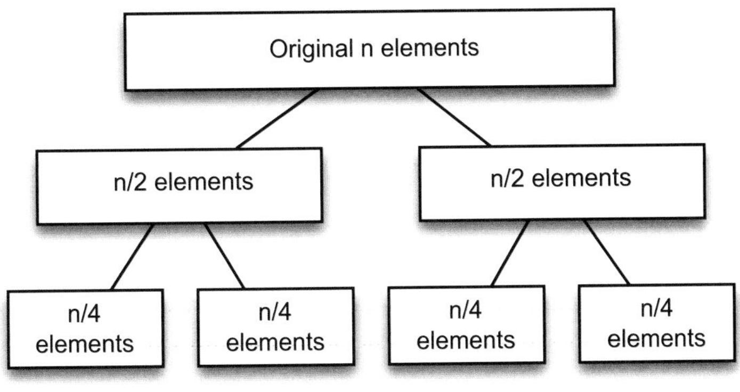

FIGURE 13.10 The ideal decomposition of quick sort

this value would be as good as any other. One way to improve the likelihood of picking a good partition element is to pick three values at random and use the median of those three.

Merge sort has a maximum running time complexity of O(n log n).

The analysis of merge sort is similar to that of quick sort, except that we are guaranteed that the recursive decomposition for merge sort will always divide the data in half. Therefore in a scenario similar to the one in Figure 13.10, the number of levels is $\log_2 n$. For the merge portion of the algorithm, one pass is needed through the data to merge two sublists. So the effort to merge an entire level is O(n). Therefore, the effort of merge sort is O(n log n) in the best, worst, and average cases.

The primary downside to the merge sort algorithm is the need for temporary data space to perform the merge operation. In general, the guaranteed savings in running time usually makes up for this expense.

Summary of Key Concepts

- Searching is the process of finding a designated target within a group of items or determining that it doesn't exist.
- An efficient search minimizes the number of comparisons made.
- The `Comparable` interface allows an algorithm to be implemented polymorphically, without regard to a particular class.
- A binary search capitalizes on the fact that the search pool is sorted.
- A binary search eliminates half of the viable candidates with each comparison.
- Sorting is the process of arranging a list of items into a defined order based on some criteria.
- The selection sort algorithm sorts a list of values by repeatedly putting a particular value into its final, sorted position.
- The insertion sort algorithm sorts a list of values by repetitively inserting a particular value into a subset of the list that has already been sorted.
- The bubble sort algorithm sorts a list by repeatedly comparing neighboring elements and swapping them if necessary.
- The quick sort algorithm sorts a list by partitioning the list and then recursively sorting the two partitions.
- The merge sort algorithm sorts a list by recursively dividing the list in half until each sublist has one element and then merging these sublists into the sorted order.
- The efficiency of an algorithm is a function of the problem size and a key processing step.
- A growth function shows time or space utilization relative to the problem size.
- A faster processor cannot compensate for an inefficient algorithm as the size of the problem increases.
- Analyzing algorithm complexity often requires analyzing the execution of loops.
- The analysis of nested loops must take into account both the inner and outer loops.
- A binary search has logarithmic complexity, making it very efficient for a large search pool.

- The average running time complexity for selection sort, insertion sort, and bubble sort is $O(n^2)$.
- The key to quick sort is picking a good partition element.
- Merge sort has a maximum running time complexity of $O(n \log n)$.

Self-Review Questions

SR 13.1 How does the `Comparable` interface facilitate the implementation of search and sort algorithms?

SR 13.2 Which search algorithm requires that the list be sorted? Why?

SR 13.3 What are the viable candidates in a binary search?

SR 13.4 What is swapping?

SR 13.5 How does selection sort work in general?

SR 13.6 How does quick sort work in general?

SR 13.7 What is a growth function?

SR 13.8 Can a faster computer eliminate the need to analyze an algorithm's efficiency? Explain.

SR 13.9 Which is more efficient, linear or binary search?

SR 13.10 Which is more efficient, selection sort, insertion sort, or bubble sort?

SR 13.11 Which is more efficient, quick sort or merge sort?

Exercises

EX 13.1 Which value does the `binarySearch` method use as the midpoint if the number of viable candidates is even? Explain.

EX 13.2 Trace a binary search for Eleni Daniilidou conducted on the data from the `SearchPlayerList` program. How many comparisons does it perform?

EX 13.3 Compare and contrast the linear search and binary search algorithms by searching for the numbers 45 and 54 in the following list:

```
3  8  12  34  54  84  91  110
```

EX 13.4 The `swap` method uses three assignment statements to swap two values. Can it be done with fewer assignment statements? Explain.

EX 13.5 Using the list from Exercise 13.3, construct a table showing the number of comparisons required to sort that list for each of the sort algorithms (selection sort, insertion sort, bubble sort, quick sort, and merge sort).

EX 13.6 Using the list from Exercise 13.3 as an example, discuss what happens to the number of comparisons for each of the sort algorithms if the list is already sorted?

EX 13.7 Given the following list:

```
90   8   7   56   123   235   9   1   653
```

trace the execution for:

a. selection sort

b. insertion sort

c. bubble sort

d. quick sort

e. merge sort

EX 13.8 Given the resulting sorted list from Exercise 13.7, trace the execution for a binary search, searching for the number 235.

EX 13.9 Describe the modifications needed to make the `selectionSort` method sort in descending order.

EX 13.10 Draw a UML class diagram for the `SortPlayerList` program.

EX 13.11 What is the complexity of the following code?

```
for (int num = 1; num <= n; num++)
{
   val1 = num * 3;
   val2 = (num – 14) / (num + 69);
   System.out.println (val1 + " and  " + val2);
}
```

EX 13.12 What is the complexity of the following code?

```
for (int num = 1; num <= n; num++)
   for (int num2 = 1; num2 <= n; num2+=2)
      System.out.println (num + num2);
```

Programming Projects

PP 13.1 Modify the `SearchPlayerList` driver program to first call the `selectionSort` method of the `Sorting` class, and then call the `binarySearch` method looking for Maria Sharapova.

PP 13.2 Create a version of the `Contact` class that determines the relative ordering of contacts based on their telephone numbers instead of their names. Modify the driver program accordingly, and test both the linear and binary search algorithms.

PP 13.3 Add a recursive implementation of the binary search algorithm to the `Searching` class. Create a driver to demonstrate this implementation.

PP 13.4 The bubble sort algorithm shown in this chapter is less efficient than it could be. If a pass is made through the list without exchanging any elements, this means that the list is sorted and there is no reason to continue. Modify this algorithm so that it will stop as soon as it recognizes that the list is sorted. *Do not* use a `break` statement.

PP 13.5 There is a variation of the bubble sort algorithm called *gap sort* that, rather than comparing neighboring elements each time through the list, compares elements that are some number (i) positions apart, where i is an integer less than n. For example, the first element would be compared to the (i+1) element, the second element would be compared to the (i+2) element, the nth element would be compared to the (n–i) element, etc. A single iteration is completed when all of the elements that can be compared, have been compared. On the next iteration, i is reduced by some number greater than 1 and the process continues until i is less than 1. Implement a gap sort and create a driver program to exercise it.

PP 13.6 Modify the sorts listed in the chapter (selection sort, insertion sort, bubble sort, quick sort, and merge sort) by adding code to each to tally the total number of comparisons and total execution time of each algorithm. Execute the sort algorithms against the same list, recording information for the total number of comparisons and total execution time for each algorithm. Try several different lists, including at least one that is already in sorted order.

PP 13.7 Design and implement a class called `TVShow` that represents a particular television program. Have `TVShow` implement `Comparable`, so that it determines the relative order of the shows alphabetically by title. Create a driver program that populates an array of `TVShow` objects and exercises various searching and sorting algorithms.

PP 13.8 Modify the `TVShow` class from programming project 13.7 so that it takes the day the show is presented into account when comparing them. That is, have all shows on Sunday come before all shows on Monday, etc. Within a day, sort by title alphabetically. Create a driver program that demonstrates this new ability.

PP 13.9 The search and sort algorithms were implemented in this chapter as static methods of the classes `Searching` and `Sorting`, respectively. Sometimes such methods are incorporated into the classes of the objects upon which they operate. Create a class called `ContactList` that manages an array of `Contact` objects. In the `ContactList` class, implement a `selectionSort` method that operates without the need to pass the array as a parameter.

PP 13.10 Modify the `ContactList` class from programming project 13.9 so that it implements a merge sort.

Answers to Self-Review Questions

SR 13.1 The `Comparable` interface provides a specific and separate way to define the relative ordering of any particular class of objects. It is up to the class to implement the `compareTo` method appropriately. The search and sort methods don't particularly "care" what type of objects they operate on, as long as they're `Comparable` objects. This is a classic application of the object-oriented concept of polymorphism.

SR 13.2 Binary search requires the elements to be sorted because it starts in the middle of the list and eliminates half of the data with one comparison.

SR 13.3 In a binary search, the viable candidates are the elements in the search pool in which the target may still be found. For a binary search, each comparison divides the size of the viable candidates in half.

SR 13.4 Swapping is the process of exchanging the position of two elements in an array. The need to swap two elements occurs in several sorting algorithms.

SR 13.5 Selection sort repeatedly puts a particular value into its final, sorted position. On each pass, it selects one value, such as the smallest value, and puts it in the correct place.

SR 13.6 Quick sort partitions a list of elements into two groups, those smaller than a particular partition element, and those larger than the partition element. Then it recursively sorts the two partitions.

SR 13.7 A growth function of an algorithm expresses the time or space usage of the algorithm relative to the size of the problem it is solving.

SR 13.8 A faster processor cannot compensate for an inefficient algorithm. For small data sets, the algorithm used may not matter, but as the size of the problem increases, the differences in algorithm efficiency become significant quickly. The speed increase due to a faster processor pales in comparison to impact of inefficient algorithms.

SR 13.9 The binary search, at O(log n), is more efficient than a linear search, which is O(n). However, the binary search requires that the search pool be sorted.

SR 13.10 Selection sort, insertion sort, and bubble sort all have an average run time of $O(n^2)$ and are generally considered to be of equal efficiency. Insertion sort, however, does have a better run time if the original data is in partially sorted order.

SR 13.11 Quick sort and merge sort are both O(n log n) algorithms, with basically equal efficiency. They are much better than the quadratic sorts (selection, insertion, and bubble). Merge sort has the added benefit of guaranteeing O(n log n) even in the worst case, whereas quick sort can degrade to $O(n^2)$ if bad choices are made for the partition element.

Collections and Linked Lists

Chapter Objectives

- Explore the concept of a collection.
- Stress the importance of separating the interface from the implementation.
- Explore generic types and their use in collection classes.
- Examine the difference between fixed and dynamic implementations.
- Define and use dynamically linked lists.
- Discuss the Java Collections API.

This chapter explores collections, objects that are designed to organize and manage other objects in specific ways. We'll examine how collections can be implemented in various ways, and introduce the concept of a linked list. This chapter lays the foundation for collections in general, and the remaining chapters in this book explore specific collections and their implementations.

14.1 Introduction to Collections

In our everyday lives, we're used to having collections of things: collections of books, CDs, stamps, key chains, etc. Hopefully we organize and store the items in a collection in a way that makes it easy to access and use the items when needed. We're now going to apply that concept to the design of our programs. We want to organize objects in our programs in ways that help us solve problems.

A *collection* is an object that serves as a repository for other objects. It provides services to add, remove, and otherwise manage the elements it contains. In many previous examples, we've used arrays to organize groups of objects, but a collection takes it a step further, providing a specific interface to the collection that permits only valid manipulations of the elements it contains. The underlying *data structure* used to implement the collection is independent of the operations the collection provides. We will, in fact, use arrays as one technique for implementing a collection. And later in this chapter we'll explore a way to implement collections using object references as dynamic links.

Collections can be separated into two broad categories: *linear* and *nonlinear*. As the name implies, a linear collection is one in which the elements of the collection are organized in a straight line. A nonlinear collection is one in which the elements are organized in something other than a straight line, such as a hierarchy or a graph.

The organization of the elements in a collection, relative to each other, is usually determined by one of two things:

- The order in which they were added to the collection
- Some inherent relationship among the elements themselves

For example, a particular linear collection may always add new elements to one end of the list, so the order of the elements is determined by the order in which they are added. Another linear collection may keep elements in sorted order based on some characteristic of the elements. For example, a list of people may be kept in alphabetical order by name. The specific organization of the elements in a nonlinear collection can be determined in either of these two ways as well.

Separating Interface from Implementation

An *abstract data type* (ADT) is a set of data and the particular operations that are allowed on that data. An ADT has a name, a domain of values, and a set of operations that can be performed on those values. An ADT is considered abstract because the operations you can perform on it are separated from the underlying implementation. That is, the details of how an ADT stores its data and accomplishes its methods are separate from the concept that it embodies.

A collection is an abstract data type. Like any well-designed object, a collection is an abstraction. A collection defines the interface operations through which the user can manage the objects in the collection, such as adding and removing elements. The user interacts with the collection through this interface. However, the details of how a collection is implemented to fulfill that definition should be an independent issue. A class that implements the collection's interface must fulfill the conceptual definition of the collection, but can do so in many ways. Figure 14.1 depicts this crucial separation.

Keeping a collection's interface independent of its underlying implementation is a crucial design criteria.

This figure is not unlike one we saw back in Chapter 5 when discussing objects in general. Objects are perfectly suited for implementing collections. An object, by definition, has a well-defined interface whose implementation is hidden in the class. The way the data is represented and the operations that manage the data are encapsulated inside the object. This type of object is reusable and reliable, because its interaction with the rest of the system is controlled.

An object, with its well-defined interface, is a perfect mechanism for implementing a collection.

For every collection that we examine, we should consider the following:

- How does the collection operate, conceptually?
- What operations are included in the interface to the collection?
- What kinds of problems does the collection help us solve?
- How might the collection be implemented?
- How do the implementations compare from an efficiency point of view?

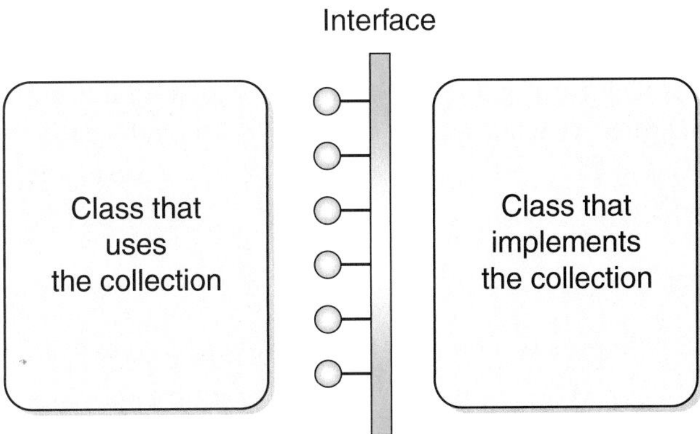

FIGURE 14.1 A well-defined interface masks the implementation of a collection.

The Java Collections API

The Java standard class library includes several classes that define collections. They are referred to as the Java Collections API. The classes in the Java Collections API define a few specific collections, implemented in various ways.

You might wonder why we spend time studying the design and implementation of collections if a set of collections has already been provided for us. There are several reasons. First, the Java Collections API provides only a subset of the collections you may want to use. Second, the classes they provide may not implement the collections you want in ways you desire. Third, and perhaps most important, the study of software development requires a deep understanding of the issues involved in the design of collections and the data structures used to implement them.

As we explore various types of collections, we will also examine the appropriate classes of the Java Collections API.

Generic Types

Before we explore collections further, let's discuss a programming technique that will facilitate their development. Java enables us to define a class based on a *generic type*. That is, we can define a class so that it stores, operates on, and manages objects whose type is not specified until the class is instantiated. Generic types are sometimes called *parameterized types*.

Suppose we wanted to define a class called `Group` that stores and manages a group of objects. Using polymorphism, we could simply define `Group` so that internally it stores references to the `Object` class. Then, any type of object could be stored in the group. In fact, multiple types of unrelated objects could be stored in the group. The extreme flexibility that comes from using `Object` references brings with it a loss of control.

A better approach is to define the `Group` class to store a generic type `T`. (We can use any identifier we want for the generic type, though using `T` has become a convention.) The header of the class contains a reference to the type in angle brackets. For example:

```
class Group<T>
{
   // declarations and code that manage objects of type T
}
```

Then, when a `Group` is needed, it is instantiated with a specific class used in place of `T`. For example, if we wanted a group of `Product` objects, we could use the following declaration:

```
Group<Product> group1 = new Group<Product>;
```

The type of the `group1` variable is `Group<Product>`. In essence, for the `group1` object, the `Group` class replaces `T` with `Product`. Now suppose we wanted a `Group` in which to store `Friend` objects. We could make the following declaration:

```
Group<Friend> group2 = new Group<Friend>;
```

For `group2`, the `Group` class essentially replaces `T` with `Friend`. So, although the `group1` and `group2` objects are both `Group` objects, they have different types because the generic type is taken into account. One is a group of products, the other is a group of friends.

Generic classes ensure type compatibility among the objects stored by the collection.

Using generics provides a safer implementation, because with these declarations we cannot use `group1` to store `Friend` objects, nor could we use `group2` to store `Product` objects. This approach ensures type compatibility among the objects in a particular collection.

A generic type such as `T` cannot be instantiated. It is merely a placeholder to allow us to define the class that will manage a specific type of object that is established when the class is instantiated.

In some collections, it's desirable to store items that are `Comparable`, so that they can be kept in order relative to each other. That is, we may want to combine the concept of storing a generic type `T` with the restriction that `T` be a type that implements the `Comparable` interface. To do this for the `Group` class, we declare it as follows:

```
class Group<T extends Comparable<T>>
{
   // declarations and code that manage objects of type T
}
```

Note that the `Comparable` interface itself is defined using a generic type. In Chapter 13, when we used `Comparable` during our exploration of sorting and searching algorithms, we used it without specifying the type. Now that we've explored generics, we can take full advantage of them when we use `Comparable`.

The classes of the Java Collections API are implemented as generic types.

The collection classes in the Java Collections API are all implemented using generic types. Throughout the rest of the book, we use generics to define collections as well.

14.2 A Bag Collection

Let's look at an example of a collection. A *bag* is a collection that facilitates the selection of random elements from the group. Conceptually, a bag is nonlinear, in that the elements contained in a bag have no particular positional relationship to each other. A bag is appropriately named in that it is similar to a physical bag into which the elements are placed. Once in the bag, there is no guarantee about where that element is in relation to any other element in the bag. Figure 14.2 depicts a bag collection.

Of course, the underlying implementation will store the elements of a bag in some particular way, perhaps in an array or using some other technique. For now, though, let's focus on the conceptual nature of a bag, the operations it permits, and how it might be used. We'll discuss the implementation of a bag collection in the next section.

Java interfaces, as discussed in Chapter 9, provide a nice mechanism for defining the set of operations that can be performed on a collection. Recall that an interface defines the set of methods that a particular class must implement. Listing 14.1 shows an interface for a bag collection. Any class that implements the `Bag` interface must implement all of the listed methods.

Using generics, the `Bag` interface is defined to operate on a generic type `T`. The `add` method, for instance, accepts a parameter of type `T` specifying the element to

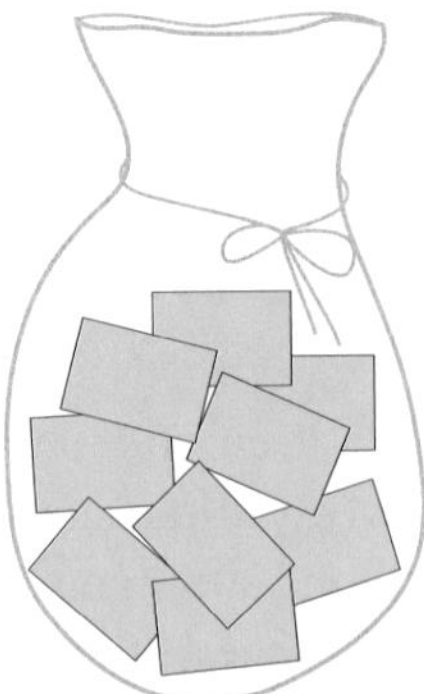

FIGURE 14.2 The conceptual view of a bag collection

Listing **14.1**

```
//********************************************************************
//  Bag.java       Java Foundations
//
//  Defines the interface to a bag collection.
//********************************************************************

package javafoundations;

public interface Bag<T> extends Iterable<T>
{
   //  Adds the specified element to the bag.
   public void add (T element);

   //  Removes and returns a random element from the bag.
   public T remove();

   //  Returns true if the bag contains no elements and false
   //  otherwise.
   public boolean isEmpty();

   //  Returns the number of elements in the bag.
   public int size();

   //  Returns a string representation of the bag.
   public String toString();
}
```

be added to the bag. The `remove` method returns a reference of type `T`. Keep in mind that when an object that satisfies this interface is instantiated, it specifies what `T` is. So we might have a bag of `Coin` objects, or a bag of `Book` objects, etc.

For a bag collection, there is no inherent relationship among the elements stored in the collection. So there is no need in this case to make the type `T` be `Comparable`. In other collections that may be an important characteristic to establish.

The `Bag` interface contains an `isEmpty` method, which returns a `boolean` that indicates if the bag is currently empty. The `size` method returns an integer that indicates how many elements are currently in the bag. The `toString` method, as normal, returns a string representation of the bag collection, and provides a convenient way to get a snapshot of the current status of the bag. These methods are common operations found in many collections.

Note that the `Bag` interface extends the `Iterable` interface. The `Iterable` interface is part of the Java standard class library in the `java.lang` package. It contains only one method, `iterator`, which returns an `Iterator` object. Recall from Chapter 4 that an `Iterator` object provides `hasNext` and `next` methods that allow the user to scan through a collection of objects. By implementing `Iterable`, the collection can be processed using the for-each version of the `for` loop. We'll discuss this further when we examine the implementation.

The operations defined for a bag collection are not rigidly defined. We might have added others, but this definition will help us explore the issues related to using and implementing collections.

Let's look at an example that uses a bag. In the game of Bingo, players have a card containing a grid of numbers, such as the one depicted in Figure 14.3. Each player has a different card, and each card contains a different set and configuration of numbers. The numbers in the range of 1 to 15 are associated with the letter B, 16 to 30 with the letter I, 31 to 45 with the letter N, 46 to 60 with the letter G, and 61 to 75 with the letter O.

The person running the game (the "caller") manages a set of balls that are each marked with a letter/number combination. The caller selects a ball randomly and

B	I	N	G	O
9	25	34	48	69
15	19	31	59	74
2	28	FREE	52	62
7	16	41	58	70
12	20	38	47	64

FIGURE 14.3 A Bingo card

announces it to the players. Players mark the square on their cards corresponding to the called number. The goal is to mark five squares in a row (vertically, horizontally, or diagonally), at which point the player calls out BINGO! and wins the game.

A bag collection is perfectly suited to assist the caller in running a Bingo game. The program in Listing 14.2 instantiates a bag of `BingoBall` objects, fills it, and then extracts some at random. The bag is actually an object of the `ArrayBag` class, which we'll examine in the next section. The `ArrayBag` class implements the `Bag` interface.

Note that the `ArrayBag` object is instantiated using `BingoBall` as its parameterized type. When an element of the bag is removed, it doesn't have to be cast as a `BingoBall` object, because that's the only type of object that could have been put into this particular bag. The `BingoBall` class is shown in Listing 14.3.

Listing **14.2**

```
//********************************************************************
//  Bingo.java       Java Foundations
//
//  Demonstrates the use of a bag collection.
//********************************************************************

import javafoundations.ArrayBag;

public class Bingo
{
   //-----------------------------------------------------------------
   //  Creates all 75 Bingo balls and stores them in a bag. Then
   //  pulls several balls from the bag at random and prints them.
   //-----------------------------------------------------------------
   public static void main (String[] args)
   {
      final int NUM_BALLS = 75, NUM_PULLS = 20;

      ArrayBag<BingoBall> bingoBag = new ArrayBag<BingoBall>();
      BingoBall ball;

      for (int num = 1; num <= NUM_BALLS; num++)
         bingoBag.add (new BingoBall(num));

      System.out.println ("Size: " + bingoBag.size() + "\n");
```

Listing **14.2** continued

```
      for (int num = 1; num <= NUM_PULLS; num++)
      {
         ball = bingoBag.remove();
         System.out.println (ball);
      }
   }
}
```

Output

```
Size: 75

N 35
I 19
B 1
N 40
G 52
I 21
O 62
B 13
B 14
O 71
B 5
B 2
I 27
B 9
B 4
O 67
O 74
O 64
B 15
N 37
```

Listing **14.3**

```
//********************************************************************
//  BingoBall.java       Java Foundations
//
//  Represents a ball used in a Bingo game.
//********************************************************************

public class BingoBall
{
   private char letter;
   private int number;

   //-----------------------------------------------------------------
   //  Sets up this Bingo ball with the specified number and the
   //  appropriate letter.
   //-----------------------------------------------------------------
   public BingoBall (int num)
   {
      number = num;

      if (num <= 15)
         letter = 'B';
      else
         if (num <= 30)
           letter = 'I';
         else
            if (num <= 45)
               letter = 'N';
            else
               if (num <= 60)
                  letter = 'G';
               else
                  letter = 'O';
   }

   //-----------------------------------------------------------------
   //  Returns a string representation of this Bingo ball.
   //-----------------------------------------------------------------
   public String toString ()
   {
      return (letter + " " + number);
   }
}
```

14.3 An Array Implementation of a Bag

Now that we've seen what a bag collection is and how it can be used, let's consider how it might be implemented. An array, as we've seen many times before, could be used to store the elements of the collection.

An important issue to consider is that an array has a fixed size once it is created, and we don't want to limit the number of elements that can be put into a bag. Collections can be, and sometimes are, implemented to have a fixed capacity. If so, the collection can become "full" at some point, and this situation must be taken into account when the user tries to add an element to a full collection. But there is no good reason to limit the capacity in this case.

The `ArrayBag` class is shown in Listing 14.4. The names of the classes in the Java Collections API indicate both the collection and the underlying data structure used to implement it. We follow this naming convention as well. Thus, the `ArrayBag` class represents an array-based implementation of a bag collection.

Listing 14.4

```
//********************************************************************
//  ArrayBag.java        Java Foundations
//
//  Represents an array implementation of bag collection.
//********************************************************************

package javafoundations;

import java.util.*;
import javafoundations.exceptions.EmptyCollectionException;

public class ArrayBag<T> implements Bag<T>
{
   private final int DEFAULT_CAPACITY = 10;
   private int count;
   private T[] contents;
   private static Random rand = new Random();

   //-----------------------------------------------------------------
   //  Creates an empty bag using the default capacity.
   //-----------------------------------------------------------------
   public ArrayBag()
   {
```

Listing **14.4** continued

```
      count = 0;
      contents = (T[]) (new Object[DEFAULT_CAPACITY]);
   }

   //-----------------------------------------------------------------
   //  Adds the specified element to this bag by storing the element
   //  at the end of the list, expanding the array capacity if needed.
   //-----------------------------------------------------------------
   public void add (T element)
   {
      if (count == contents.length)
         expandCapacity();

      contents[count] = element;
      count++;
   }

   //-----------------------------------------------------------------
   //  Removes a random element from this bag, shifting the last
   //  element into its place to keep the list contiguous. Throws
   //  EmptyCollectionException if this bag is empty.
   //-----------------------------------------------------------------
   public T remove() throws EmptyCollectionException
   {
      if (count == 0)
         throw new EmptyCollectionException ("Remove operation " +
            "failed. The bag is empty.");

      int index = rand.nextInt(count);
      T result = contents[index];

      count--;
      contents[index] = contents[count];
      contents[count] = null;

      return result;
   }

   //-----------------------------------------------------------------
   //  Returns true if this bag contains no elements, and false
   //  otherwise.
   //-----------------------------------------------------------------
   public boolean isEmpty()
```

Listing **14.4** continued

```
   {
      return (count == 0);
   }

   //-----------------------------------------------------------------
   //  Returns the number of elements in this bag.
   //-----------------------------------------------------------------
   public int size()
   {
      return count;
   }

   //-----------------------------------------------------------------
   //  Returns an iterator for this bag.
   //-----------------------------------------------------------------
   public Iterator<T> iterator()
   {
      ArrayIterator<T> iter = new ArrayIterator<T>();
      for (int index = 0; index < count; index++)
         iter.add(contents[index]);

      return iter;
   }

   //-----------------------------------------------------------------
   //  Returns a string representation of this bag.
   //-----------------------------------------------------------------
   public String toString()
   {
      String result = "Bag Contents:\n";

      for (int index=0; index < count; index++)
         result += contents[index] + "\n";

      return result;
   }

   //-----------------------------------------------------------------
   //  Creates a new array to store the contents of this bag with
   //  twice the capacity of the old one.
   //-----------------------------------------------------------------
   private void expandCapacity()
   {
```

Listing **14.4** continued

```
        T[] larger = (T []) (new Object[contents.length*2]);

        int location = 0;
        for (T element : contents)
           larger[location++] = element;

        contents = larger;
    }
}
```

The ArrayBag class is declared to be part of the javafoundations package. We've set up this package to hold all of the classes from this book that are used to define collections. As discussed in Chapter 11, it's often good practice to organize related classes into appropriate packages.

The ArrayBag class, which implements the Bag<T> interface, manages generic T objects. The elements in the bag are stored in an array called contents, and an integer variable called count is used to keep track of the number of elements currently in the bag. Note that the Random object (used to pick random elements from the bag) is declared as a static variable, and is instantiated in its declaration (rather than in the constructor). Because it is static, it is shared among all instances of the ArrayBag class, which avoids the problem of creating two bags that have random-number generators using the same seed value.

The ArrayBag constructor instantiates the contents array using a default capacity. We cannot instantiate an array of a generic type, or an array of generic types. So instead, we instantiate an array of Object references and cast it into the type T[]. When we compile this class, the compiler warns us that this is an unchecked cast, meaning that it is not sure that the array of objects is really an array of T objects. At this point, the array is newly created and empty, so there is no problem. And the rest of the class is designed such that only elements of type T are stored in the array. It is safe to ignore these warnings in these situations.

The add method accepts an element of type T and stores it in the array. It must first check to make sure the capacity of the array is not exceeded. If the current array used to store the bag elements is full, the private support method expandCapacity is called. It creates a new array twice as large as the old one and copies the existing elements into it. At this point it will be safe to store the new element. Note that the current size of the array and the need to increase it is not something the user of the collection has to know or manage. It's handled automatically as needed.

The value of the variable `count` actually represents two related pieces of information. In addition to indicating how many elements are currently in the collection, it also represents the next available slot in the array into which we can store the new element (because arrays start at index 0).

Note that it is possible to store a null reference as an element in a bag. This may be helpful, depending on what problem the user is using the collection to solve. Another implementation may choose to make it impossible to store null elements. This is an important design decision.

The `remove` method returns a random element from the bag. First, it checks to see that there is at least one element in the bag. If not, the `remove` method throws an `EmptyCollectionException` and returns immediately to the calling method. The `EmptyCollectionException` is defined as part of the `javafoundations.exceptions` package.

If there is at least one element to pick from, a random index is computed and the corresponding element is stored to be returned. The `remove` method actually takes the element out of the collection, though, so it must be removed from the array. The `count` of elements is decremented, and the last element in the array is put into the now vacated location that was randomly selected. This overwrites the removed element and keeps the elements in the bag contiguous in the array. Since there is no inherent relationship among the elements stored in a bag, it doesn't matter where in the array the elements are kept.

The `isEmpty`, `size`, and `toString` methods are fairly straightforward. There is no particularly interesting way to present the contents of a bag, so the `toString` method creates its return string in the order in which the elements are stored in the array.

Collection Iterators

It's common to *traverse* the elements of a collection, "visiting" each one in turn. The user decides what processing is done when each element is visited. For example, a collection may be traversed to print out its current contents.

We introduced the concept of an iterator object in Chapter 4, which allows the user to step through a set of objects one at a time. We'll use iterators in our collections to perform various kinds of traversals as appropriate.

The `iterator` method in the `ArrayBag` class satisfies the `Iterable` interface (from which the `Bag` interface is derived). The return type of the `iterator` method is `Iterator`, which is another interface. So the `iterator` method has to return an object created from some class that implements the `Iterator` interface. The `ArrayIterator` class, shown in Listing 14.5, was created for exactly this purpose.

Listing **14.5**

```
//********************************************************************
//  ArrayIterator.java       Java Foundations
//
//  Represents an iterator over the elements of a collection.
//********************************************************************

package javafoundations;

import java.util.*;

public class ArrayIterator<T> implements Iterator<T>
{
   private int DEFAULT_CAPACITY = 10;
   private int count;    // the number of elements in the iterator
   private int current;  // the current position in the iteration
   private T[] items;    // the iterator's storage for elements

   //-----------------------------------------------------------------
   //  Sets up this iterator.
   //-----------------------------------------------------------------
   public ArrayIterator()
   {
      items = (T[]) (new Object[DEFAULT_CAPACITY]);
      count = 0;
      current = 0;
   }

   //-----------------------------------------------------------------
   //  Adds the specified item to this iterator.
   //-----------------------------------------------------------------
   public void add (T item)
   {
      if (count == items.length)
```

Listing 14.5 continued

```
         expandCapacity();

      items[count] = item;
      count++;
   }

   //-----------------------------------------------------------------
   //  Returns true if this iterator has at least one more element to
   //  deliver in the iteration.
   //-----------------------------------------------------------------
   public boolean hasNext()
   {
      return (current < count);
   }

   //-----------------------------------------------------------------
   //  Returns the next element in the iteration. If there are no more
   //  elements in this iteration, a NoSuchElementException is thrown.
   //-----------------------------------------------------------------
   public T next()
   {
      if (! hasNext())
         throw new NoSuchElementException();

      current++;

      return items[current - 1];
   }

   //-----------------------------------------------------------------
   //  The remove operation is not supported in this collection.
   //-----------------------------------------------------------------
   public void remove() throws UnsupportedOperationException
   {
     throw new UnsupportedOperationException();
   }

   //-----------------------------------------------------------------
   //  Expands the capacity of the storage array
   //-----------------------------------------------------------------
   private void expandCapacity()
   {
      T[] larger = (T []) (new Object[items.length*2]);
```

Listing 14.5 continued

```
        int location = 0;
        for (T element : items)
            larger[location++] = element;

        items = larger;
    }
}
```

Any class that implements the `Iterator` interface must include the `hasNext`, `next`, and `remove` methods. The `ArrayIterator` class is so named because it uses an array as the underlying structure to hold the elements in the iterator. As such, it is very similar to the `ArrayBag` collection class.

The value of `current` starts at zero (the first index in the array) and gets incremented each time an element is obtained using the `next` method. Once the elements in the iterator are exhausted, the `next` method throws a `NoSuchElementException`.

It's generally not a good idea to remove an element from a collection using an iterator, so we have implemented the `remove` method of `ArrayIterator` to throw an `UnsupportedOperationException` in all cases.

Collections that provide iterators make it easy to traverse and process each element in the collection. Another advantage of making a collection `Iterable` is that then it can be processed using the for-each version of the `for` loop.

As we'll see in later chapters, some collections conceptually do not allow access to its elements except through the collection's operations. In these cases we will not make the collection `Iterable`.

14.4 Linked Lists

An array is only one way in which a linear collection can be represented. As we've seen, arrays are limited in one sense because they have a fixed size throughout their existence, so allowances have to be made to manage the capacity carefully. This does not necessarily yield an efficient implementation.

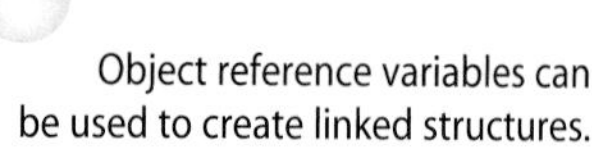

Object reference variables can be used to create linked structures.

A *linked structure* is a data structure that uses object reference variables to create links between objects. A linked structure is the primary alternative to an array-based implementation of a collection. After discussing various issues involved in linked structures, we will examine a new implementation of a bag collection that uses an underlying linked data structure.

Recall that an object reference variable holds the address of an object, indicating where the object is stored in memory. The following declaration creates a variable called `obj` that is only large enough to hold the numeric address of an object:

```
Object obj;
```

Usually the specific address that an object reference variable holds is irrelevant. That is, while it is important to be able to use the reference variable to access an object, the specific location in memory where it is stored is unimportant. Therefore, instead of showing addresses, we usually depict a reference variable as a name that "points to" an object, as shown in Figure 14.4. A reference variable, used in this context, is sometimes called a *pointer*.

Consider the situation in which a class defines as instance data a reference to another object of the same class. For example, suppose we have a class named `Person` that contains a person's name, address, and other relevant information. Now suppose that in addition to this data, the `Person` class also contains a reference variable to another `Person` object:

```
public class Person
{
   private String name;
   private String address;
   private Person next; // a link to another Person object
   // whatever else
}
```

Using only this one class, a linked structure can be created. One `Person` object contains a link to a second `Person` object. This second object contains a reference to another `Person`, which contains another, and so on. This type of object is sometimes called *self-referential*.

FIGURE 14.4 An object reference variable pointing to an object

This kind of relationship forms the basis of a *linked list*, which is a linked structure in which one object refers to the next, creating a linear ordering of the objects in the list. Figure 14.5 shows a linked list. Often the objects stored in a linked list are referred to generically as the *nodes* of the list.

A linked list is composed of objects that each point to the next object in the list.

Note that a separate reference variable is needed to indicate the first node in the list. The list is terminated in a node whose `next` reference is null.

A simple linked list is only one kind of linked structure. In a *doubly linked list*, as illustrated in Figure 14.6, each node in the list stores both a reference to the next element and a reference to the previous one. This is convenient when the processing involves moving back and forth between elements in the list. Usually, in addition to a separate reference to the front of the list, a doubly linked list maintains a reference to the last node in the list as well.

If a class is set up to have multiple references to objects, a more complex, nonlinear structure can be created, such as the one depicted in Figure 14.7. The way in which the links are managed dictates the specific organization of the structure. We'll see examples of nonlinear structures in later chapters.

Unlike an array, which has a fixed size, a linked list has no upper bound on its capacity other than the limitations of memory in the computer. A linked list is considered to be a *dynamic structure* because its size grows and shrinks as needed to accommodate the number of elements stored.

A linked list dynamically grows as needed and essentially has no capacity limitations.

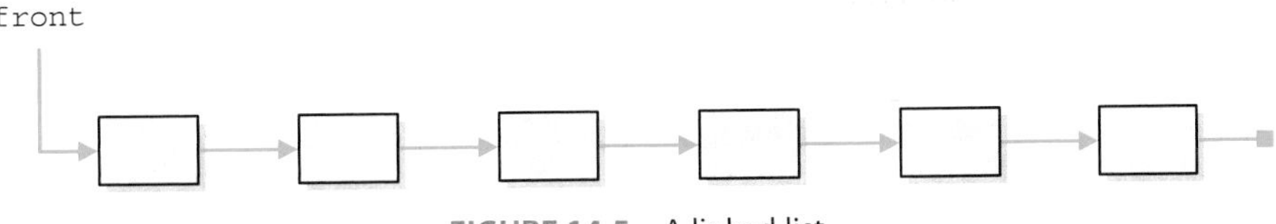

FIGURE 14.5 A linked list

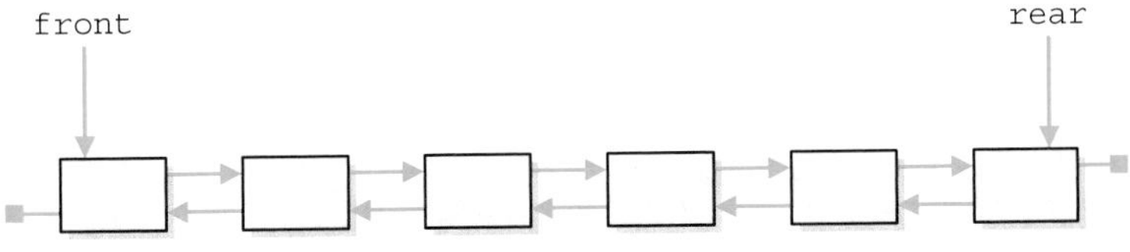

FIGURE 14.6 A doubly linked list

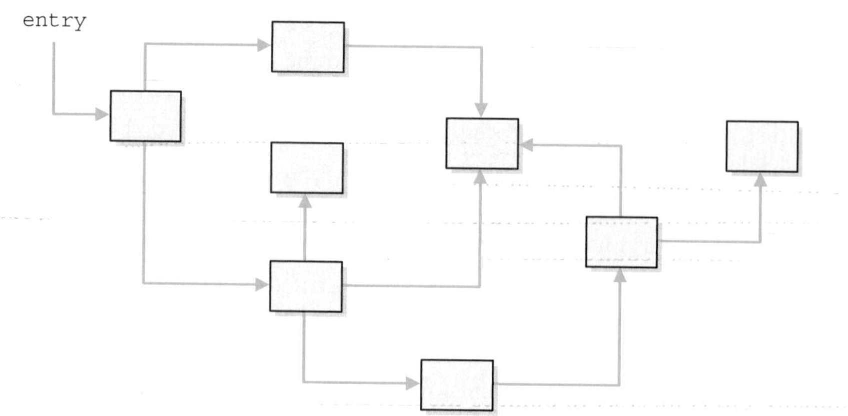

FIGURE 14.7 A nonlinear linked structure

Managing Linked Lists

No matter what a linked list is used to store, there are a few basic techniques involved in managing the nodes on the list. Specifically, nodes are added to a list and they are removed from the list. Special care must be taken when dealing with the first node in the list so that the reference to the entire list is maintained appropriately.

A node may be inserted into a linked list at any location: at the front of the list, among the interior nodes in the middle of the list, or at the end of the list. Adding a node to the front of the list requires resetting the reference to the entire list, as shown in Figure 14.8. First, the `next` reference of the added node is set to point to the current first node in the list. Second, the reference to the front of the list is reset to point to the newly added node.

The order in which references are changed is crucial to maintaining a linked list.

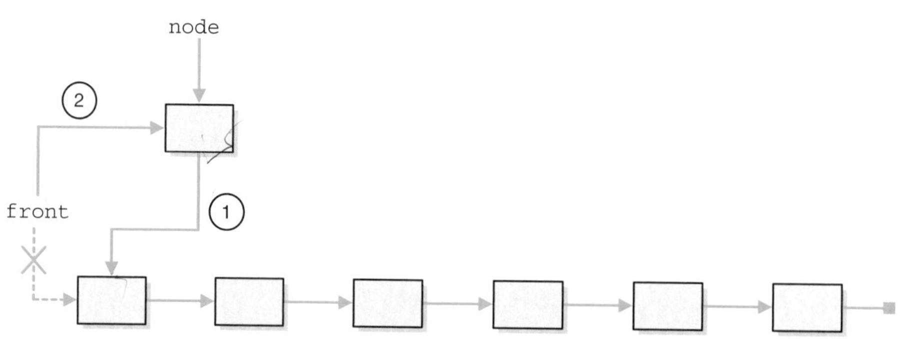

FIGURE 14.8 Inserting a node at the front of a linked list

Note that difficulties would arise if these steps were reversed. If we were to reset the `front` reference first, we would lose the only reference to the existing list and it could not be retrieved.

Inserting a node into the middle of a list requires some additional processing. First we have to find the node in the list that will immediately precede the new node being inserted. Unlike an array, in which we can access elements using subscripts, a linked list requires that we use a separate reference to move through the nodes of the list until we find the one we want. This type of reference is often called `current`, because it indicates the current node in the list that is being examined.

Initially, `current` is set to point to the first node in the list. Then a loop is used to move the `current` reference along the list of nodes until the desired node is found. Once it is found, the new node can be inserted, as shown in Figure 14.9.

First, the `next` reference of the new node is set to point to the node *following* the one to which `current` refers. Then, the `next` reference of the current node is reset to point to the new node. Once again, the order of these steps is important.

This process will work wherever the node is to be inserted along the list, including making it the new second node in the list or making it the last node in the list. If the new node is inserted immediately after the first node in the list, then `current` and `front` will refer to the same (first) node. If the new node is inserted at the end of the list, the `next` reference of the new node is set to `null`. The only special case occurs when the new node is inserted as the first node in the list.

Any node in the list can be deleted. We must maintain the integrity of the list no matter which node is deleted. As with the process of inserting a node, dealing with the first node in the list represents a special case.

Dealing with the first node in a linked list often requires special handling.

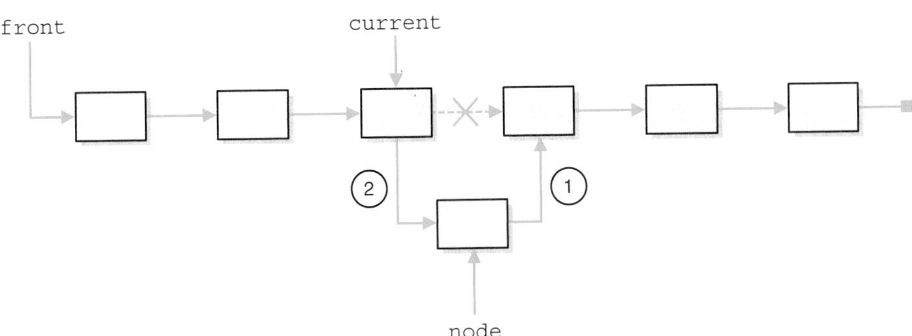

FIGURE 14.9 Inserting a node in the middle of a linked list

To delete the first node in a linked list, the reference to the front of the list is reset so that it points to the current second node in the list. This process is shown in Figure 14.10. If the deleted node is needed elsewhere, a separate reference to it must be set up before resetting the front reference.

To delete a node from the interior of the list, we must first find the node in front of the node that is to be deleted. This processing often requires the use of two references: one to find the node to be deleted and another to keep track of the node immediately preceding that one. Thus, they are often called `current` and `previous`, as shown in Figure 14.11.

Once these nodes have been found, the `next` reference of the previous node is reset to point to the node pointed to by the `next` reference of the current node. The deleted node can then be used as needed.

Elements Without Links

Now that we've explored some of the techniques needed to manage the nodes of a linked list, we can turn our attention to using a linked list as an alternative implementation approach for a collection. However, to do so we need to carefully examine one other key aspect of linked lists. We must separate the details of the linked list structure from the elements that the list stores.

Objects that are stored in a collection should not contain any implementation details of the underlying data structure.

Earlier in this chapter we discussed the idea of a `Person` class that contains, among its other data, a link to another `Person` object. The flaw in this approach is that the self-referential `Person` class must be designed so that it "knows" it may become a node in a linked list of `Person` objects. This assumption is impractical,

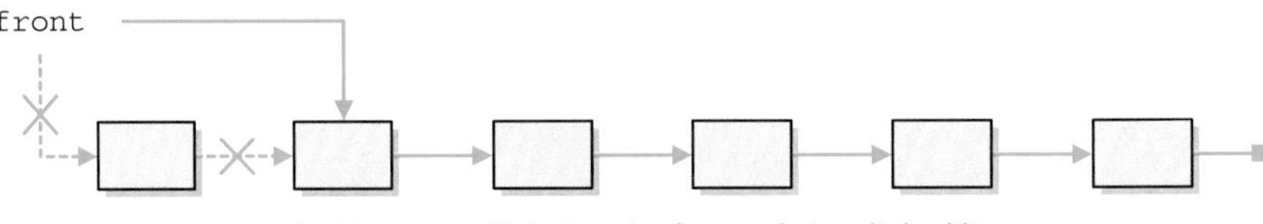

FIGURE 14.10 Deleting the first node in a linked list

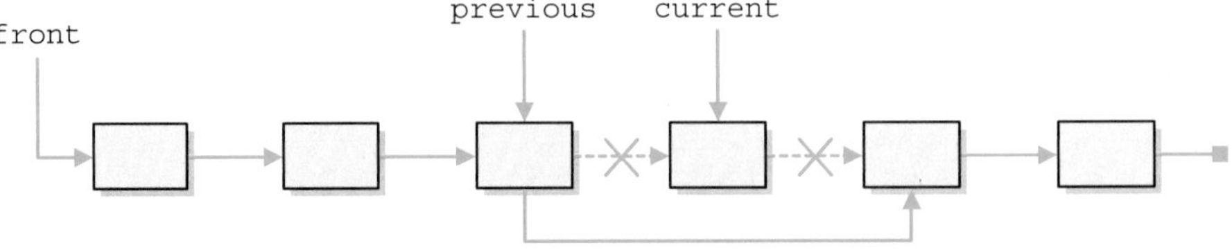

FIGURE 14.11 Deleting an interior node from a linked list

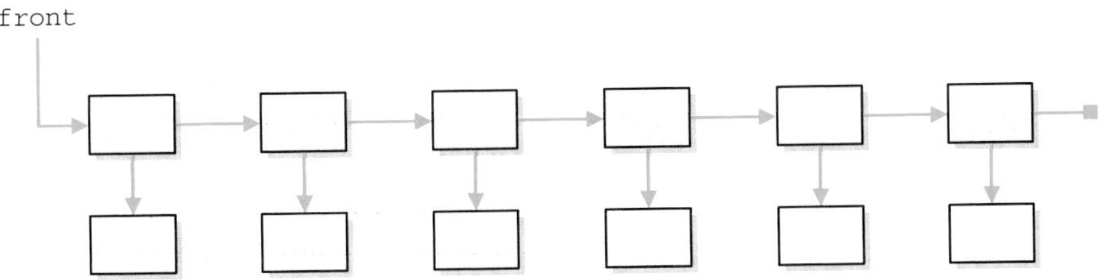

FIGURE 14.12 Using separate node objects to store and link elements

and it violates our goal of separating the implementation details from the parts of the system that use the collection.

The solution to this problem is to define a separate node class that serves to link the elements together. A node class is fairly simple, containing only two important references: one to the next node in the linked list and another to the element that is being stored in the list. This approach is depicted in Figure 14.12.

The linked list of nodes can still be managed using the techniques discussed in the previous section. The only additional aspect is that the actual elements stored in the list are accessed using a separate reference in the node objects.

14.5 A Linked Implementation of a Bag

Let's explore a linked implementation of a bag collection. First, since we don't expect the elements in our bag to be self-referential, we'll create a separate class to represent the nodes in the linked list. The `LinearNode` class, shown in Listing 14.6, holds a reference to an element and a reference to the next node in the list.

Listing 14.6

```
//********************************************************************
//  LinearNode.java        Java Foundations
//
//  Represents a node in a linked list.
//********************************************************************

package javafoundations;
```

Listing 14.6 continued

```
public class LinearNode<T>
{
   private LinearNode<T> next;
   private T element;

   //-----------------------------------------------------------------
   //  Creates an empty node.
   //-----------------------------------------------------------------
   public LinearNode()
   {
      next = null;
      element = null;
   }

   //-----------------------------------------------------------------
   //  Creates a node storing the specified element.
   //-----------------------------------------------------------------
   public LinearNode (T elem)
   {
      next = null;
      element = elem;
   }

   //-----------------------------------------------------------------
   //  Returns the node that follows this one.
   //-----------------------------------------------------------------
   public LinearNode<T> getNext()
   {
      return next;
   }

   //-----------------------------------------------------------------
   //  Sets the node that follows this one.
   //-----------------------------------------------------------------
   public void setNext (LinearNode<T> node)
   {
      next = node;
   }

   //-----------------------------------------------------------------
   //  Returns the element stored in this node.
   //-----------------------------------------------------------------
   public T getElement()
```

Listing **14.6** continued

```
   {
      return element;
   }

   //-----------------------------------------------------------------
   //  Sets the element stored in this node.
   //-----------------------------------------------------------------
   public void setElement (T elem)
   {
      element = elem;
   }
}
```

The `LinkedBag` class is shown in Listing 14.7, with some operations left as programming projects. As with our array-based implementation, the `LinkedBag` class uses an integer variable to keep track of the number of elements in the collection. The reference variable `contents` is a pointer to the head of the linked list of nodes storing the elements in the bag collection.

Listing **14.7**

```
//********************************************************************
//  LinkedBag.java        Java Foundations
//
//  Represents a linked implementation of a bag collection.
//********************************************************************

package javafoundations;

import java.util.*;
import javafoundations.exceptions.EmptyCollectionException;

public class LinkedBag<T> implements Bag<T>
{
   private int count = 0;
   private LinearNode<T> contents;
   private static Random rand = new Random();
```

Listing 14.7 continued

```
   //-----------------------------------------------------------------
   //  Creates an empty list.
   //-----------------------------------------------------------------
   public LinkedBag()
   {
      count = 0;
      contents = null;
   }

   //-----------------------------------------------------------------
   //  Adds the specified element to this bag by putting it on the
   //  front of the list.
   //-----------------------------------------------------------------
   public void add (T element)
   {
      LinearNode<T> node = new LinearNode<T>(element);
      node.setNext(contents);
      contents = node;
      count++;
   }

   //-----------------------------------------------------------------
   //  Removes a random element from this bag. Throws an
   //  EmptyCollectionException if this bag is empty.
   //-----------------------------------------------------------------
   public T remove() throws EmptyCollectionException
   {
      T result = null;

      if (count == 0)
         throw new EmptyCollectionException ("Remove operation "
            + "failed. The bag is empty.");

      int choice = rand.nextInt(count) + 1;
      if (choice == 1)
      {
         result = contents.getElement();
         contents = contents.getNext();
      }
      else
      {
         LinearNode<T> current = contents;
```

Listing **9.7** continued

```
            for (int i=1; i < choice-1; i++)
                current = current.getNext();
            result = current.getNext().getElement();
            current.setNext(current.getNext().getNext());
        }

        return result;
    }

    //-----------------------------------------------------------------
    //  Returns an iterator for this bag.
    //-----------------------------------------------------------------
    public Iterator<T> iterator()
    {
        ArrayIterator<T> iter = new ArrayIterator<T>();
        LinearNode<T> current = contents;

        while (current != null)
        {
            iter.add(current.getElement());
            current = current.getNext();
        }

        return iter;
    }

    //-----------------------------------------------------------------
    //  The following methods are left as programming projects.
    //-----------------------------------------------------------------
    // public boolean isEmpty() { }
    // public int size() { }
    // public String toString() { }
}
```

The `add` method creates a new `LinearNode`, storing the element in it, and inserts it at the front of the list. This approach creates an ordering opposite to that of the `ArrayBag` implementation, but given that a bag maintains no specific order among the elements, the simplest solution is best.

As we did with the ArrayBag implementation, the remove method throws an EmptyCollectionException if an attempt is made to remove an element from an empty bag. Otherwise, an element is chosen by picking a random number from 1 to the number of elements in the bag. If the first element is picked, the reference to the front of the list is updated. If not, a loop is used to update the value of the current reference until it points the node before the node being removed. After storing the element to be returned, the node is deleted from the linked list by updating the next pointer of the previous node. Trace this processing carefully to see how it works in various scenarios.

The processing of the remove method is similar to that shown in Figure 14.11, except that we did not use a previous reference. In this case, we knew the number of the node being deleted, and so could stop one node before the one being removed. In other cases, when the nodes themselves must be examined to find the one to delete, a previous reference would be helpful.

The iterator method creates an ArrayIterator object and populates it with the elements from the collection, just as we did in the ArrayBag class. In this case, it accesses the elements by scanning through the linked list using a current reference. Note that this linked implementation uses an array-based iterator. As a programming project you are asked to create a iterator with an underlying linked implementation. That linked iterator then could be used in either the ArrayBag or LinkedBag class.

Compare the two implementations that we've explored for a bag collection. One uses an array, and so can access its elements directly using an index, but must deal with a finite array capacity. In the LinkedBag implementation, there is no maximum capacity to worry about, but the remove method had to use a loop to access the element to delete. There are often such tradeoffs when comparing alternative implementation strategies. Sometimes, those differences are crucial.

Once again, let's point out that we have a clean separation between the collection interface (the methods defined in the Bag interface) and its underlying implementation. The Bingo program, for example, could make use of the LinkedBag class instead of the ArrayBag class by simply changing the name of the class used. Since they both behave as a bag collection should, the way they get the job done is irrelevant to the program that uses the collection.

The isEmpty, size, and toString methods of the LinkedBag class are left as programming projects.

Summary of Key Concepts

- Keeping a collection's interface independent of its underlying implementation is a crucial design criteria.
- An object, with its well-defined interface, is a perfect mechanism for implementing a collection.
- Generic classes ensure type compatibility among the objects stored by the collection.
- The classes of the Java Collections API are implemented as generic types.
- Object reference variables can be used to create linked structures.
- A linked list is composed of objects that each point to the next object in the list.
- A linked list dynamically grows as needed and essentially has no capacity limitations.
- The order in which references are changed is crucial to maintaining a linked list.
- Dealing with the first node in a linked list often requires special handling.
- Objects that are stored in a collection should not contain any implementation details of the underlying data structure.

Self-Review Questions

SR 14.1 What is a collection?

SR 14.2 Why are objects particularly well suited for implementing collections?

SR 14.3 What is the Java Collections API?

SR 14.4 What is a generic type and how does it relate to collections?

SR 14.5 What is a bag collection?

SR 14.6 What is the `javafoundations` package?

SR 14.7 What is the `Iterable` interface?

SR 14.8 What is a linked list?

SR 14.9 Why should a separate node class be used when implementing a collection using a linked list?

SR 14.10 What advantages does an array-based implementation have over a linked-based implementation?

SR 14.11 What advantages does a linked-based implementation have over an array-based implementation?

Exercises

EX 14.1 Use the online Java API documentation to find and describe three classes that are part of the Java Collections API.

EX 14.2 Write a declaration that instantiates a group of `Book` objects, using the `Group` class described in this chapter.

EX 14.3 Why isn't the bag collection described in this chapter designed to hold `Comparable` objects?

EX 14.4 Why is a separate array created in the `expandCapacity` method of the `ArrayBag` class?

EX 14.5 Explain the relationship between an iterator and a traversal.

EX 14.6 Does an array-based implementation of a collection need to use an array-based iterator? Explain.

EX 14.7 Explain the steps for inserting a node in the middle of a linked list.

EX 14.8 Explain the steps for deleting a node from the middle of a linked list.

EX 14.9 What two special cases are considered in the `remove` method of the `LinkedBag` class?

EX 14.10 Given identical operations on a bag collection, would the `iterator` method in `ArrayBag` produce the same iteration as the `iterator` method in `LinkedBag`? Explain.

Programming Projects

PP 14.1 Design and implement a program that uses a bag collection to store a set of `ContestEntry` objects, then chooses five winners at random.

PP 14.2 Complete the implementation of the LinkedBag class presented in this chapter. Specifically, complete the implementations of the isEmpty, size, and toString operations.

PP 14.3 Modify the Bingo program so that it uses a LinkedBag implementation instead of an ArrayBag implementation.

PP 14.4 Design and implement a class called LinkedIterator that satisfies the Iterator interface and uses a linked list as its underlying structure.

PP 14.5 Modify the ArrayBag class so that it uses the LinkedIterator class created in programming project 14.4 instead of an ArrayIterator.

PP 14.6 The elements in an *indexed list* collection can be accessed using a numeric index. Create an IndexedList interface that contains the operations described in the table below, then create a class called ArrayIndexedList that implements it using an array-based strategy.

Operation	Description
insert	Inserts an element at a particular index, shifting existing elements as necessary. Throws an exception if the index specified is greater than the current highest index + 1.
set	Stores an element at a particular index, overwriting the element currently stored there. Throws an exception if the index specified is greater than the current highest index.
get	Returns the element at a particular index without removing it from the list. Throws an exception if the index is greater than the current highest index.
remove	Removes and returns the element at a particular index. Throws an exception if the index is greater than the current highest index.
contains	Returns true if the list contains a particular element, and false otherwise.
isEmpty	Returns true if the list is empty, and false otherwise.
size	Returns the current number of elements in the list.

PP 14.7 Create a class called LinkedIndexedList that implements the IndexedList interface defined in programming project 14.6 using an underlying linked strategy.

PP 14.8 An *ordered list* collection keeps its `Comparable` elements in the order specified by their `compareTo` method, independent of the order in which they are added to the collection. Create an `OrderedList` interface that contains the operations described in the table below, then create a class called `ArrayOrderedList` that implements it using an array-based strategy.

Operation	Description
`add`	Adds an element to the list, keeping the elements in order.
`remove`	Removes and returns the specified target element. Throws an exception if the target is not found in the list.
`first`	Returns the first element in the list without removing it. Throws an exception if the list is empty.
`last`	Returns the last element in the list without removing it. Throws an exception if the list is empty.
`contains`	Returns `true` if the list contains a particular element, and `false` otherwise.
`isEmpty`	Returns `true` if the list is empty, and `false` otherwise.
`size`	Returns the current number of elements in the list.

PP 14.9 Create a class called `LinkedOrderedList` that implements the `OrderedList` interface defined in programming project 14.8 using an underlying linked strategy.

Answers to Self-Review Questions

SR 14.1 A collection is an object whose purpose is to store and organize other objects. Some collections represent classic data structures that are helpful in particular problem solving situations.

SR 14.2 As an abstract data type (ADT), a collection must separate its interface from its underlying implementation. This permits the implementation to be changed without affecting the programs that use the collection. That criteria is identical to that of any well-designed object, which makes an object-oriented approach ideal for creating collections.

SR 14.3 The Java Collections API is a set of classes in the Java standard class library that represents collections of various types.

SR 14.4 A generic type is a placeholder that allows a class to be defined to operate on a particular type, but defer naming that type until the object is instantiated. That makes the use of generics ideally suited for implementing collections. Generics provide some compile-time control over the types of objects that are added to the collection, and eliminates the need to cast the objects when they are removed from the collection.

SR 14.5 A bag is a non-linear collection that facilitates the selection of random elements from the group. There is no particular ordering among the elements stored in a bag.

SR 14.6 The `javafoundations` package was created to organize the various collection classes discussed in the last few chapters of this book. It was created by the authors of this book and is not part of the Java standard class library.

SR 14.7 The `Iterable` interface contains a single method, `iterator`, that returns an object that satisfies the `Iterator` interface. By implementing a collection to satisfy the `Iterable` interface, we provide at least one technique for traversing the collection, and make it available for use with the for-each loop. However, providing an iterator is not appropriate for all collections.

SR 14.8 A linked list is a set of objects that use references to create a linear ordering. Each object refers to the next object in the list.

SR 14.9 If the elements stored in a collection contain the references necessary to make a linked list, we've blurred the distinction between the collection and the elements it stores. The elements should not have to be designed with collection implementation details in mind. By using a separate node to create the linked list, any element can be stored in the collection.

SR 14.10 An array-based implementation can use its indexes to directly access the elements stored in the array, whereas a linked-based implementation must traverse the list to find a desired element.

SR 14.11 A linked-based implementation does not have to worry about the underlying data structure becoming full, whereas an array-based implementation has a fixed capacity that must be checked and expanded as needed.

Chapter Objectives

- Discuss how stacks and queues work conceptually.
- Define stack and queue abstract data types.
- Demonstrate how stacks and queues can be used to solve problems.
- Examine various stack and queue implementations.
- Analyze and compare stack and queue implementations.

Stacks and Queues

This chapter examines two classic and useful collections: stacks and queues. Common examples of stacks include a stack of plates or a stack of trays in a cafeteria. In a stack, items are added and removed from the top of the stack. A queue is another collection with which we are inherently familiar. A queue is a waiting line, such as the line of customers waiting in a bank for their opportunity to talk to a teller. Other examples of queues include the check-out line at the grocery store or cars waiting at a stoplight. In a queue, an item enters on one end and leaves from the other.

15.1 Stacks

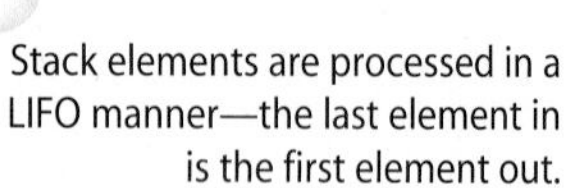

Stack elements are processed in a LIFO manner—the last element in is the first element out.

A *stack* is a linear collection whose elements are added and removed from the same end. We say that a stack is processed in a *last in, first out* (LIFO) manner. That is, the last element to be put on a stack will be the first one that gets removed. Said another way, the elements of a stack are removed in the reverse order of their placement on it.

The processing of a stack is shown in Figure 15.1. Usually a stack is depicted vertically, and we refer to the *top* of the stack as the end to which elements are added and from which they are removed.

The operations for a stack are listed in Figure 15.2. In stack terminology, we *push* an element onto a stack and we *pop* an element off a stack. We can also *peek* at the top element of a stack, examining it or using it as needed, without actually removing it from the collection. Similar to the operations defined for the indexed list in Chapter 14, there are also general operations to determine if the stack is empty and to obtain the number of elements the stack currently contains.

There are many programming situations in which a stack is helpful. For example, the undo operation in a word processor is usually implemented using a stack. As we make changes to a document (add data, delete data, make format changes, etc.), the word processor keeps track of each operation by pushing some representation of it onto a stack. If we choose to undo an operation, the word processing software pops the most recently performed operation off the stack and

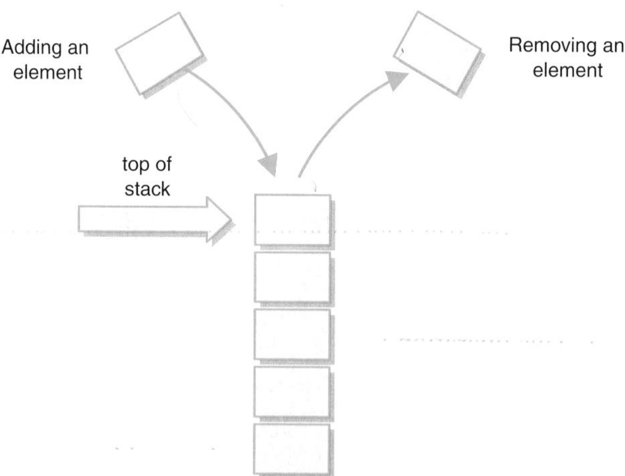

FIGURE 15.1 A conceptual view of a stack

Operation	Description
`push`	Adds an element to the top of the stack.
`pop`	Removes an element from the top of the stack.
`peek`	Examines the element at the top of the stack.
`isEmpty`	Determines if the stack is empty.
`size`	Determines the number of elements on the stack.

FIGURE 15.2 The operations on a stack

reverses it. If we choose to undo again (undoing the second-to-last operation we performed), another element is popped from the stack and reversed.

Keep in mind that the definition of a collection is not universal. Sometimes there are variations on the naming conventions for the operations on a collection. For a stack, for instance, the use of the terms `push` and `pop` is relatively standard, but the `peek` operation is sometimes referred to as `top`. Sometimes additional operations are defined in one version of a collection that you won't find in another version. We've been very careful in this book to define the operations on each collection so that they are consistent with its purpose.

For example, note that none of the stack operations in Figure 15.2 allow us to reach down into the stack to remove or reorganize the elements in the stack. That addresses the very nature of a stack—all activity occurs at one end. If we discover that to solve a particular problem, we need to access the elements in the middle or at the bottom of the collection, then a stack is not the appropriate collection to use.

A programmer should choose the collection that is appropriate for the type of data management needed.

Listing 15.1 shows the operations of a stack defined using a Java interface. Any class that implements the `Stack` interface must provide a definition for the methods listed in the interface. The methods of this interface refer to a generic type `T`, which allows us to instantiate a stack to store any type of object.

As we did with the bag collection in Chapter 14, we also provide a `toString` operation in the `Stack` interface. This is not a classic operation defined for a stack, but it provides a convenient means to view the stack's contents without modifying it. This operation is often helpful during testing and debugging.

Later in this chapter we examine two classes that implement these operations in different ways. Before we dive into those details, however, let's look at an example that uses a stack to solve a particular problem.

Listing **15.1**

```
//********************************************************************
//  Stack.java       Java Foundations
//
//  Defines the interface to a stack collection.
//********************************************************************

package javafoundations;

public interface Stack<T>
{
   //  Adds the specified element to the top of the stack.
   public void push (T element);

   //  Removes and returns the top element from the stack.
   public T pop();

   //  Returns a reference to the top element of this stack
   //  without removing it.
   public T peek();

   //  Returns true if the stack contains no elements and false
   //  otherwise.
   public boolean isEmpty();

   //  Returns the number of elements in the stack.
   public int size();

   //  Returns a string representation of the stack.
   public String toString();
}
```

15.2 Evaluating Postfix Expressions

Traditionally, arithmetic expressions are written in *infix* notation, meaning that the operator is placed between its operands in the form

<operand> <operator> <operand>

such as in the expression

```
4 + 5
```

When evaluating an infix expression, we rely on precedence rules to determine the order of operator evaluation. For example, the expression

```
4 + 5 * 2
```

evaluates to 14 rather than 18 because of the precedence rule that says in the absence of parentheses, multiplication evaluates before addition.

In a *postfix* expression, the operator comes after its two operands. Therefore, a postfix expression takes the form

<operand> <operand> <operator>

For example, the postfix expression

```
6 9 -
```

is equivalent to the infix expression

```
6 – 9
```

A postfix expression is generally easier to evaluate than an infix expression because precedence rules and parentheses do not have to be taken into account. The order of the values and operators in the expression are sufficient to determine the result. Programming language compilers and run-time environments often use postfix expressions in their internal calculations for this reason.

The process of evaluating a postfix expression can be stated in one simple rule: Scanning from left to right, apply each operation to the two operands immediately preceding it and replace the operator with the result. At the end we are left with the final value of the expression.

Consider the infix expression we looked at earlier:

```
4 + 5 * 2
```

In postfix notation, this expression would be written

```
4 5 2 * +
```

Let's use our evaluation rule to determine the final value of this expression. We scan from the left until we encounter the multiplication (`*`) operator. We apply this operator to the two operands immediately preceding it (`5` and `2`) and replace it with the result (`10`), leaving us with

```
4 10 +
```

Continuing our scan from left to right, we immediately encounter the plus (`+`) operator. Applying this operator to the two operands immediately preceding it (`4` and `10`) yields `14`, which is the final value of the expression.

Let's look at a slightly more complicated example. Consider the following infix expression:

```
(3 * 4 – (2 + 5)) * 4 / 2
```

The equivalent postfix expression is

```
3 4 * 2 5 + - 4 * 2 /
```

Applying our evaluation rule results in:

```
12 2 5 + - 4 * 2 /
```

then `12 7 – 4 * 2 /`
then `5 4 * 2 /`
then `20 2 /`
then `10`

Now let's think about the design of a program that will evaluate a postfix expression. The evaluation rule relies on being able to retrieve the previous two operands whenever we encounter an operator. Furthermore, a large postfix expression will have many operators and operands to manage. It turns out that a stack is the perfect collection to use in this case. The operations provided by a stack coincide nicely with the process of evaluating a postfix expression.

A stack is the ideal collection to use when evaluating a postfix expression.

The algorithm for evaluating a postfix expression using a stack can be expressed as follows: Scan the expression from left to right, identifying each token (operator or operand) in turn. If it is an operand, push it onto the stack. If it is an operator, pop the top two elements off of the stack, apply the operation to them, and push the result onto the stack.

When we reach the end of the expression, the element remaining on the stack is the result of the expression. If at any point we attempt to pop two elements off of the stack but there are not two elements on the stack, then our postfix expression was not properly formed. Similarly, if we reach the end of the expression and more than one element remains on the stack, then our expression was not well formed. Figure 15.3 depicts the use of a stack to evaluate a postfix expression.

The program in Listing 15.2 evaluates multiple postfix expressions entered by the user. It uses the `PostfixEvaluator` class shown in Listing 15.3.

To keep things simple, this program assumes that the operands to the expression are integers and are literal values (not variables). When executed, the program repeatedly accepts and evaluates postfix expressions until the user chooses to terminate the program.

The `evaluate` method performs the evaluation algorithm described earlier, supported by the private `isOperator` and `evalSingleOp` methods. Note that in the `evaluate` method, only operands are pushed onto the stack. Operators are used as they are encountered and are never put on the stack.

In this example, the operands are `int` primitive values, but they are being pushed onto a stack that is designed to handle objects of generic type `T`. This is an example of autoboxing, which we discussed in Chapter 3. In Java, when an object is needed but a primitive type is provided, the value is automatically converted into an object of the appropriate wrapper class. In this case, the `int` value is converted into an object of type `Integer`, and that object is then stored in the stack. When the object is popped from the stack, the reverse operation (unboxing) occurs, resulting in the original `int` value.

When an operator is encountered, the most recent two operands are popped off of the stack. Note that the first operand popped is actually the second operand in the expression, and the second operand popped is the first operand in the expression. This order doesn't matter in the cases of addition and multiplication, but it certainly matters for subtraction and division.

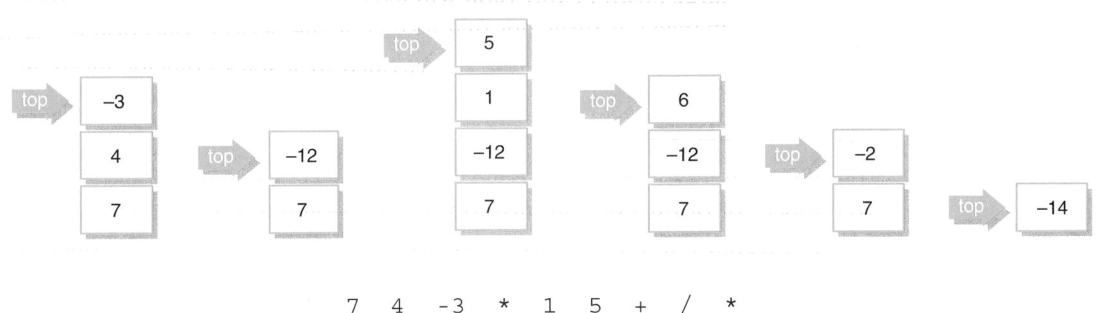

FIGURE 15.3 Using a stack to evaluate a postfix expression

Listing 15.2

```
//********************************************************************
//  Postfix.java       Java Foundations
//
//  Demonstrates the use of a stack to evaluate postfix expressions.
//********************************************************************
import java.util.Scanner;

public class Postfix
{
   //-----------------------------------------------------------------
   //  Reads and evaluates multiple postfix expressions.
   //-----------------------------------------------------------------
   public static void main (String[] args)
   {
      String expression, again;
      int result;

      try
      {
         Scanner in = new Scanner(System.in);

         do
         {
            PostfixEvaluator evaluator = new PostfixEvaluator();
            System.out.println ("Enter a valid postfix expression: ");
            expression = in.nextLine();

            result = evaluator.evaluate (expression);
            System.out.println();
            System.out.println ("That expression equals " + result);

            System.out.print ("Evaluate another expression [Y/N]? ");
            again = in.nextLine();
            System.out.println();
         }
         while (again.equalsIgnoreCase("y"));
      }
      catch (Exception IOException)
      {
         System.out.println("Input exception reported");
      }
   }
}
```

Listing 15.2 continued

Output

```
Enter a valid postfix expression:
7 4 -3 * 1 5 + / *

That expression equals -14
Evaluate another expression [Y/N]? Y

Enter a valid postfix expression:
12 4 - 3 7 * 19 - /

That expression equals 4
Evaluate another expression [Y/N]? N
```

Listing 15.3

```
//********************************************************************
//  PostfixEvaluator.java       Java Foundations
//
//  Represents an integer evaluator of postfix expressions. Assumes
//  the operands are constants.
//********************************************************************

import javafoundations.LinkedStack;
import java.util.Scanner;

public class PostfixEvaluator
{
   private final char ADD = '+', SUBTRACT = '-';
   private final char MULTIPLY = '*', DIVIDE = '/';
   private LinkedStack<Integer> stack;

   //-----------------------------------------------------------------
   //  Sets up this evaluator by creating a new stack.
   //-----------------------------------------------------------------
   public PostfixEvaluator()
   {
      stack = new LinkedStack<Integer>();
   }
```

Listing 15.3 continued

```
   //-----------------------------------------------------------------
   //  Evaluates the specified postfix expression. If an operand is
   //  encountered, it is pushed onto the stack. If an operator is
   //  encountered, two operands are popped, the operation is
   //  evaluated, and the result is pushed onto the stack.
   //-----------------------------------------------------------------
   public int evaluate (String expr)
   {
      int op1, op2, result = 0;
      String token;
      Scanner tokenizer = new Scanner (expr);

      while (tokenizer.hasNext())
      {
         token = tokenizer.next();

         if (isOperator(token))
         {
            op2 = (stack.pop()).intValue();
            op1 = (stack.pop()).intValue();
            result = evalSingleOp (token.charAt(0), op1, op2);
            stack.push (result);
         }
         else
            stack.push (Integer.parseInt(token));
      }

      return result;
   }

   //-----------------------------------------------------------------
   //  Determines if the specified token is an operator.
   //-----------------------------------------------------------------
   private boolean isOperator (String token)
   {
      return (token.equals("+") || token.equals("-") ||
         token.equals("*") || token.equals("/"));
   }

   //-----------------------------------------------------------------
   // Performs integer evaluation on a single expression consisting of
   // the specified operator and operands.
   //-----------------------------------------------------------------
```

Listing **15.3** continued

```
    private int evalSingleOp (char operation, int op1, int op2)
    {
        int result = 0;

        switch (operation)
        {
            case ADD:
                result = op1 + op2;
                break;
            case SUBTRACT:
                result = op1 - op2;
                break;
            case MULTIPLY:
                result = op1 * op2;
                break;
            case DIVIDE:
                result = op1 / op2;
        }

        return result;
    }
}
```

Note also that this program assumes that the postfix expression entered is valid, meaning that it contains a properly organized set of operators and operands. A postfix expression is invalid if either (1) two operands are not available on the stack when an operator is encountered or (2) there is more than one value on the stack when the tokens in the expression are exhausted. Either situation indicates that there was something wrong with the format of the expression, and both can be caught by examining the state of the stack at the appropriate point in the program. Checking for these problems is left as a programming project.

The stack used to solve the postfix evaluation problem was instantiated in this example by the class `ArrayStack`. We discuss the details of this class in the next section. Figure 15.4 shows a UML class diagram for the postfix expression evaluation program.

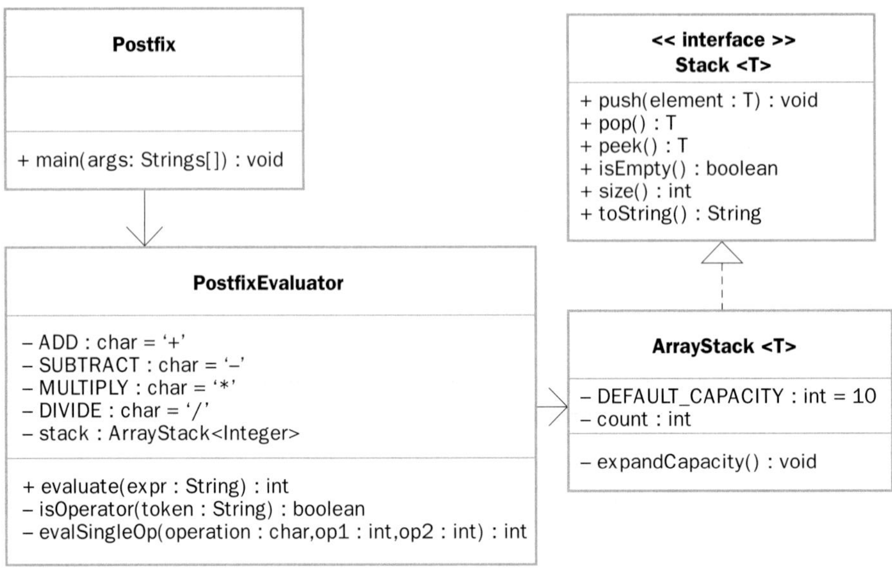

FIGURE 15.4 A UML class diagram for the `Postfix` program

Keep in mind that this program could have used any class that implemented a stack as long as it performed the stack operations appropriately. From the point of view of evaluating postfix expressions, the manner in which the stack is implemented is largely irrelevant.

15.3 Implementing Stacks with Arrays

For efficiency, an array-based stack implementation keeps the bottom of the stack at index 0.

It turns out that implementing a stack using an array is an efficient and fairly straightforward solution if certain decisions are made carefully. In particular, given that all activity on a stack occurs at one end, fixing the bottom of the stack at array index 0 makes the implementation of the various operations relatively easy.

Figure 15.5 illustrates this configuration for an array-based stack that currently contains the elements A, B, C, and D, assuming that they have been pushed on in that order. To simplify the figure, the elements are shown in the array itself rather than as objects referenced from the array. The integer variable `count` is used to indicate the number of elements that are currently on the stack, and it also represents the index in the array where the next item pushed onto the stack will be stored.

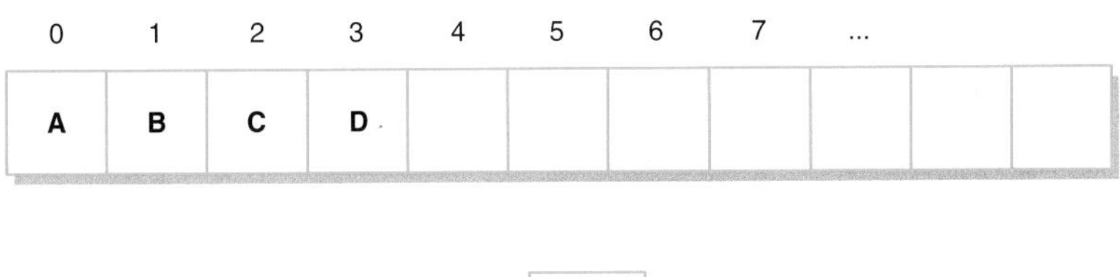

FIGURE 15.5 An array implementation of a stack

Consistent with the naming convention we established in Chapter 14, we define our array-based version of a stack in a class called `ArrayStack`. This class is shown in part in Listing 15.4; some methods are left to be implemented as part of the programming projects at the end of the chapter. The array that holds the stack elements stores object references of generic type `T`, whose specific type is established when the `ArrayStack` object is instantiated.

Listing 15.4

```
//********************************************************************
//  ArrayStack.java        Java Foundations
//
//  Represents an array implementation of a stack. The bottom of
//  the stack is kept at array index 0.
//********************************************************************

package javafoundations;

import javafoundations.exceptions.*;

public class ArrayStack<T> implements Stack<T>
{
   private final int DEFAULT_CAPACITY = 10;
   private int count;
   private T[] stack;

   //-----------------------------------------------------------------
   //  Creates an empty stack using the default capacity.
   //-----------------------------------------------------------------
   public ArrayStack()
   {
      count = 0;
```

Listing **15.4** continued

```
      stack = (T[]) (new Object[DEFAULT_CAPACITY]);
   }

   //-----------------------------------------------------------------
   //  Adds the specified element to the top of this stack, expanding
   //  the capacity of the stack array if necessary.
   //-----------------------------------------------------------------
   public void push (T element)
   {
      if (count == stack.length)
         expandCapacity();

      stack[count] = element;
      count++;
   }

   //-----------------------------------------------------------------
   //  Returns a string representation of this stack.
   //-----------------------------------------------------------------
   public String toString()
   {
      String result = "<top of stack>\n";

      for (int index=count-1; index >= 0; index--)
         result += stack[index] + "\n";

      return result + "<bottom of stack>";
   }

   //-----------------------------------------------------------------
   //  Creates a new array to store the contents of this stack with
   //  twice the capacity of the old one.
   //-----------------------------------------------------------------
   private void expandCapacity()
   {
      T[] larger = (T[])(new Object[stack.length*2]);

      for (int index=0; index < stack.length; index++)
         larger[index] = stack[index];

      stack = larger;
   }
```

Listing **15.4** continued

```
   //-----------------------------------------------------------------
   //  The following methods are left as programming projects.
   //-----------------------------------------------------------------
   //  public T pop () throws EmptyCollectionException { }
   //  public T peek () throws EmptyCollectionException { }
   //  public boolean isEmpty() { }
   //  public int size() { }
}
```

The push method inserts the new element in the next available position in the array, which is specified by the current value of count. Before doing so, however, we must determine if the array has been filled to its capacity and, if so, expand it. After storing the value, the value of count is updated so that it continues to represent the number of elements in the stack.

Note that the push method is virtually identical to the add method from the ArrayBag class in Chapter 14. One adds to the top of a stack and the other adds to the end of a list. They are conceptually two different ideas, but in this case are implemented in the same way. Think about the similarities and differences of these two classes and how they implement their respective collections.

Similarly, the expandCapacity method is implemented in the same way as it is in the ArrayBag class. This will not always be the case, depending on the details of the implementation strategy used for a given collection. The expandCapacity method serves only to support the push method and therefore is implemented with private visibility.

Figure 15.6 illustrates the result of pushing an element E onto the stack that was depicted in Figure 15.5.

The pop operation removes and returns the element at the top of the stack. For an array implementation, that means returning the element at index count–1. Before attempting to return an element, however, the pop method must ensure that there is at least one element in the stack to return, and throw an EmptyCollectionException if there is not. Popping an element from the stack shown in Figure 15.6 would return the stack to the configuration shown in Figure 15.5.

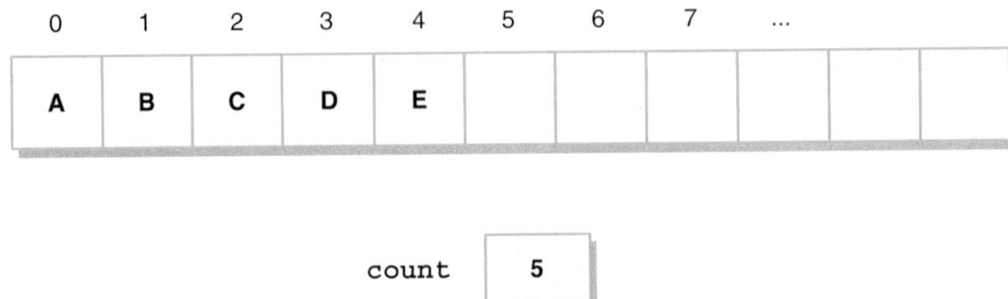

FIGURE 15.6 The stack after pushing element E.

The `peek` operation is similar to `pop`, but does not actually remove the element from the stack. It too must ensure that there is at least one element on the stack.

The `pop`, `peek`, `isEmpty`, and `size` operations are left as programming projects.

Note that the implementation of `toString` in the `ArrayStack` class presents the elements from the top down, which better reflects the conceptual notion of a stack. Thus the loop moves through the array from the higher indexes down to 0.

In this implementation, the bottom of the stack is always held at index 0 of the array, and the stack grows and shrinks at the higher indexes. This is considerably more efficient than if the stack were reversed within the array. Consider the processing that would be necessary for each operation if the top of the stack were kept at index 0.

15.4 Implementing Stacks with Links

A linked implementation of a stack adds and removes elements from one end of the linked list.

Let's now explore a linked implementation of a stack. Because a stack is a linear structure, the elements of a stack can be maintained using a linked list. A reference can be kept to the top element of the stack, where all push and pop activity will take place. Each node points to the next element (below it) in the stack.

As with the linked bag solution, we'll use a separate node to manage the links in the list. In fact, our solution can reuse the `LinearNode` class from Chapter 14. Figure 15.7 illustrates this configuration for a stack containing four elements, A, B, C, and D, that have been pushed onto the stack in that order. An integer variable called `count` is used to keep track of the number of elements currently in the stack.

The `LinkedStack` class is shown in Listing 15.5, with some operations left as programming projects.

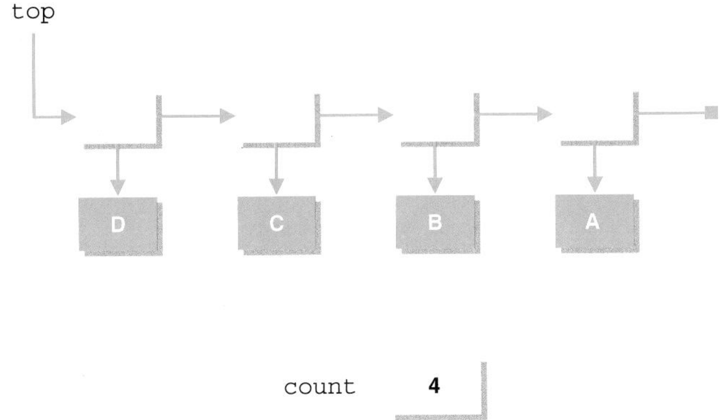

FIGURE 15.7 A linked implementation of a stack

Listing 15.5

```
//********************************************************************
//  LinkedStack.java         Java Foundations
//
//  Represents a linked implementation of a stack.
//********************************************************************

package javafoundations;

import javafoundations.exceptions.*;

public class LinkedStack<T> implements Stack<T>
{
   private int count;
   private LinearNode<T> top;

   //-----------------------------------------------------------------
   //  Creates an empty stack using the default capacity.
   //-----------------------------------------------------------------
   public LinkedStack()
   {
      count = 0;
      top = null;
   }

   //-----------------------------------------------------------------
   //  Removes the element at the top of this stack and returns a
```

Listing **15.5** continued

```
   //  reference to it. Throws an EmptyCollectionException if the
   //  stack contains no elements.
   //-----------------------------------------------------------------
   public T pop() throws EmptyCollectionException
   {
      if (count == 0)
         throw new EmptyCollectionException ("Pop operation failed. "
            + "The stack is empty.");

      T result = top.getElement();
      top = top.getNext();
      count--;

      return result;
   }

   //-----------------------------------------------------------------
   //  Returns a string representation of this stack.
   //-----------------------------------------------------------------
   public String toString()
   {
      String result = "<top of stack>\n";
      LinearNode current = top;

      while (current != null)
      {
         result += current.getElement() + "\n";
         current = current.getNext();
      }

      return result + "<bottom of stack>";
   }

   //-----------------------------------------------------------------
   //  The following methods are left as programming projects.
   //-----------------------------------------------------------------
   //  public void push () { }
   //  public T peek () throws EmptyCollectionException { }
   //  public boolean isEmpty() { }
   //  public int size() { }
}
```

Every time a new element is pushed onto the stack, a new `LinearNode` object is created to store it in the linked list. To position the newly created node at the top of the stack, its `next` reference is set to the current top of the stack, and the `top` reference is reset to point to the new node. The value of `count` is incremented to reflect the new element. Figure 15.8 shows the result of pushing the element E onto the stack depicted in Figure 15.7.

The `pop` operation requires that the stack contain at least one element. If the stack is empty, an `EmptyCollectionException` is thrown. Otherwise, it stores a reference to the element currently stored at the top of the stack and resets the `top` reference to the next element in the list (which is now the new top of the stack). The value of `count` is decremented to reflect the deleted element. Popping an element from the stack shown in Figure 15.8 would return the stack to the configuration shown in Figure 15.7.

In a linked implementation, the `peek` operation is implemented by returning a reference to the element pointed to by the node pointed to by the top pointer. The `push`, `peek`, `isEmpty`, and `size` operations are left as programming projects.

As we discussed in the previous section, there is an advantage to keeping the bottom of the stack at index 0 in the array implementation of a stack. There is a similar advantage in the linked organization described in this section. Consider the ramifications of replacing the `top` reference with one that keeps track of the bottom of the stack instead.

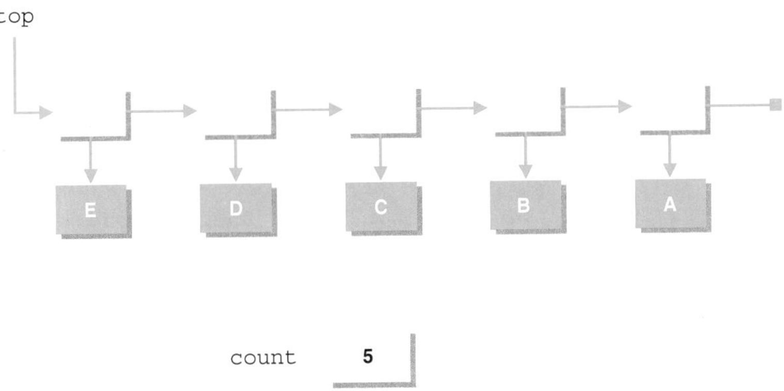

FIGURE 15.8 The stack after pushing element E

15.5 The `java.util.Stack` Class

In Chapter 14 we introduced the Java Collections API, a set of classes in the Java standard class library that provide implementations of various collections. The Java Collections API includes the `java.util.Stack` class, an implementation of a stack with similar operations to the ones that we have been discussing:

- The `push` operation accepts a parameter item that is a reference to an object to be placed on the stack.
- The `pop` operation removes the object on top of the stack and returns a reference to it.
- The `peek` operation returns a reference to the object on top of the stack.
- The `empty` operation returns true if the stack is empty, just like the `isEmpty` operation that we have been discussing.
- The `size` operation returns the number of elements in the stack.

The `java.util.Stack` class provides an additional operation called `search`. Given an object to search for, the `search` operation returns the distance from the top of the stack to the first occurrence of that object on the stack. If the object is found at the top of the stack, the `search` method returns the value 1. If the object is not found on the stack, `search` returns the value –1.

The `java.util.Stack` class is derived from the `java.util.Vector` class, which in turn is derived from a series of other classes in the Java standard class library. It also implements several interfaces. Figure 15.9 depicts these relationships.

Capitalizing on its inherited characteristics, the `java.util.Stack` class stores the stack elements using the `Vector` internal structure. This implementation keeps track of the top of the stack using an index similar to an array implementation.

The `java.util.Stack` class is derived from `Vector`, which gives a stack inappropriate operations.

Unfortunately, since the `java.util.Stack` implementation is derived from the `Vector` class, it inherits the full set of operations defined for `Vector`. In some cases, these additional capabilities violate the basic assumptions of a stack. That is, an object instantiated from the `java.util.Stack` class provides services that are completely contrary to the conceptual notion of a stack. For example, a `java.util.Stack` object provides methods that allow the user to reach down into the stack and retrieve or modify elements other than the one at the top.

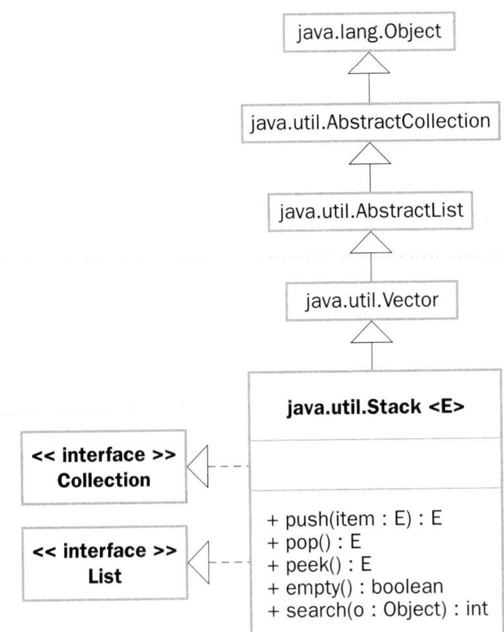

FIGURE 15.9 The derivation of the `java.util.Stack` class

The developers did this for convenience, and most software engineers consider this a bad use of inheritance. Since a stack is not everything a vector is, it is not a proper is-a relationship. And it violates the basic premise of a well-designed collection class. Well-disciplined developers can, of course, limit themselves to only those operations appropriate to a stack. Luckily, most of the other classes in the Java Collections API have a better design.

15.6 Queues

Let's explore another fundamental collection. A *queue* is a linear collection whose elements are added on one end and removed from the other. Therefore, we say that queue elements are processed in a *first in, first out* (FIFO) manner. Elements are removed from a queue in the same order in which they are placed on the queue.

Queue elements are processed in a FIFO manner—the first element in is the first element out.

This is consistent with the general concept of a waiting line. When a customer arrives at a bank, he or she begins waiting at the end of the line. When a teller becomes available, the customer at the beginning of the line leaves the line to receive service. Eventually every customer that started out at the end of the line moves to the front of the line and exits. For any given set of customers, the first person to get in line is the first person to leave it.

The processing of a queue is pictured in Figure 15.10. Usually a queue is depicted horizontally. One end is established as the *front* of the queue and the other as the *rear* of the queue. Elements go onto the rear of the queue and come off of the front. Sometimes the front of the queue is called the *head* and the rear of the queue the *tail*.

Compare and contrast the processing of a queue to the LIFO (last in, first out) processing of a stack, which was discussed in section 15.1. In a stack, the processing occurs at only one end of the collection. In a queue, processing occurs at both ends.

The operations defined for a queue are listed in Figure 15.11. The term *enqueue* is used to refer to the process of adding a new element to the end of a queue. Likewise, *dequeue* refers to removing the element at the front of a queue. The *first* operation allows the user to examine the element at the front of the queue without removing it from the collection.

Remember that naming conventions are not universal for collection operations. Sometimes `enqueue` is simply called `add` or `insert`. The `dequeue` operation is sometimes called `remove` or `serve`. The `first` operation is sometimes called `front`.

There is a general similarity between the operations of a queue and those of a stack. The `enqueue`, `dequeue`, and `first` operations correspond to the stack operations `push`, `pop`, and `peek`. Similar to a (well-designed) stack, there are no operations that allow the user to "reach into" the middle of a queue and reorganize or remove elements. If that type of processing is required, perhaps the appropriate collection to use is a list of some kind.

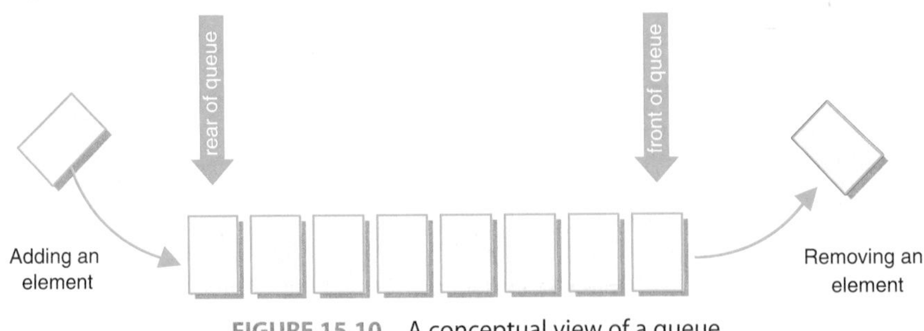

FIGURE 15.10 A conceptual view of a queue

Operation	Description
`enqueue`	Adds an element to the rear of the queue.
`dequeue`	Removes an element from the front of the queue.
`first`	Examines the element at the front of the queue.
`isEmpty`	Determines if the queue is empty.
`size`	Determines the number of elements on the queue.

FIGURE 15.11 The operations on a queue

Listing 15.6 shows a Java interface defining the queue operations. We included a `toString` method, as we did with previous collections. It is included for convenience and is not generally considered a classic operation on a queue.

Listing **15.6**

```
//********************************************************************
//  Queue.java       Java Foundations
//
//  Defines the interface to a queue collection.
//********************************************************************

package javafoundations;

public interface Queue<T>
{
   //  Adds the specified element to the rear of the queue.
   public void enqueue (T element);

   //  Removes and returns the element at the front of the queue.
   public T dequeue();

   //  Returns a reference to the element at the front of the queue
   //  without removing it.
   public T first();

   //  Returns true if the queue contains no elements and false
   //  otherwise.
   public boolean isEmpty();
```

Listing 15.6 continued

```
    //  Returns the number of elements in the queue.
    public int size();

    //  Returns a string representation of the queue.
    public String toString();
}
```

Queues have a wide variety of applications within computing. Before exploring various ways to implement a queue, let's look at an example in which a queue is used for its particular characteristics.

15.7 Radix Sort

A radix sort is inherently based on queue processing.

Queues are particularly helpful when implementing a *radix sort.* We examined a variety of sorting algorithms in Chapter 13, but radix sort was not covered there because it is not a comparison sort and thus has very little in common with those techniques.

A sort is based on some particular value, called the *sort key*. For example, a set of people might be sorted by their last name. A radix sort, rather than comparing items by sort key, is based on the structure of the sort key. Separate queues are created for each possible value of each digit or character of the sort key. The number of queues, or the number of possible values, is called the *radix*. For example, if we were sorting strings made up of lowercase alphabetic characters, the radix would be 26. We would use 26 separate queues, one for each possible character. If we were sorting decimal numbers, then the radix would be 10, one for each digit 0 through 9.

Let's walk through an example that uses a radix sort to put 10 three-digit numbers in order. To keep things manageable, we'll restrict the digits of these numbers to 0 through 5, which means we'll need only six queues.

Each three-digit number has a 1s position (right digit), a 10s position (middle digit), and a 100s position (left digit). The radix sort makes three passes through the values, one for each digit position. On the first pass, each number is put on the queue corresponding to its 1s digit. On the second pass, each number is put on the queue corresponding to its 10s digit. And finally, on the third pass, each number is put on the queue corresponding to its 100s digit.

Originally, the numbers are loaded into the queues from the original list. On the second pass, the numbers are taken from the queues in a particular order. They are retrieved from the digit 0 queue first, and then the digit 1 queue, etc. For each queue, the numbers are processed in the order in which they come off the queue. This processing order is crucial to the operation of a radix sort. Likewise, on the third pass, the numbers are again taken from the queues in the same way. When the numbers are pulled off of the queues after the third pass, they will be completely sorted.

Figure 15.12 shows the processing of a radix sort of 10 three-digit numbers. First, the number 442 is taken from the original list and put onto the queue corresponding to digit 2. Then 503 is put onto the queue corresponding to digit 3. Then 312 is put onto the queue corresponding to digit 2 (following 442). This process continues for all values, resulting in the set of queues for the 1s position.

Assume, as we begin the second pass, that we have a fresh set of six empty digit queues. In actuality, the queues can be used over again if processed carefully. To begin the second pass, the numbers are taken from the 0 digit queue

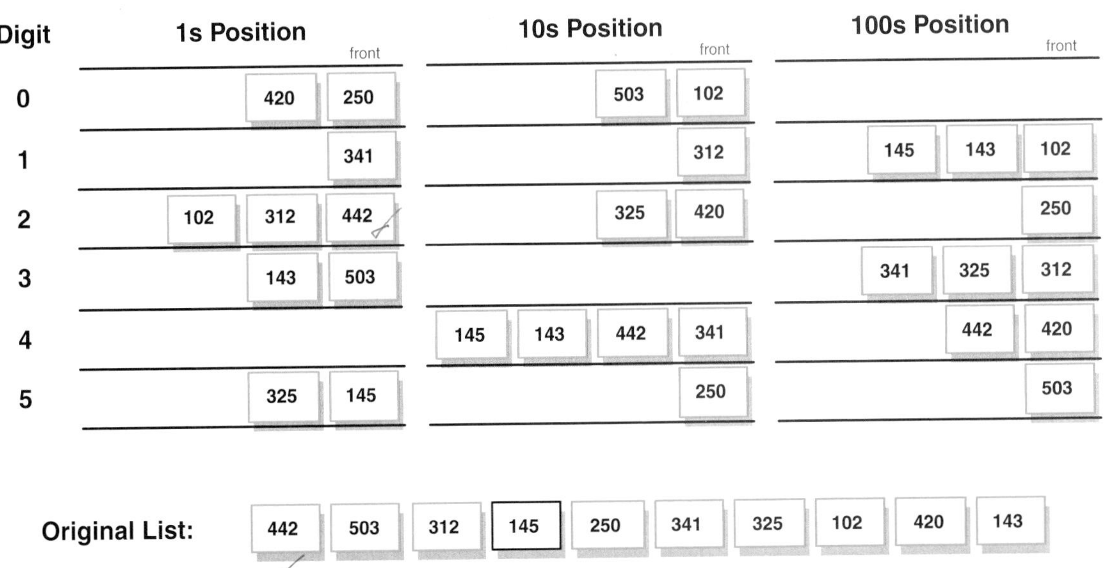

FIGURE 15.12 A radix sort of 10 three-digit numbers

first. The number 250 is put onto the queue for digit 5, and then 420 is put onto the queue for digit 2. Then we can move to the next queue, taking 341 and putting it onto the queue for digit 4. This process continues until all numbers have been taken off of the 1s position queues and put on the appropriate queue for the 10s position.

For the third pass, the process is repeated. First, 102 is put onto the queue for digit 1, then 503 is put onto the queue for digit 5, then 312 is put onto the queue for digit 3. This process continues until we have the final set of digit queues for the 100s position. The numbers are now in sorted order if taken off of each queue in turn.

Let's now look at a program that implements the radix sort. The program in Listing 15.7 sorts a set of four-digit numbers. In this example we don't restrict the digits used in those numbers. Using an array of 10 queue objects (one for each digit 0 through 9), the processing steps of a radix sort are carried out, resulting in a final sorted list.

In the `RadixSort` program, we cannot create an array of queues to hold integers because of the restriction that prevents the instantiation of arrays of generic types. Instead, we create an array of `ArrayQueue` and then cast that as an array of `ArrayQueue<Integer>`.

The numbers are originally stored in an array called `list`. After each pass, the numbers are pulled off of the queues and stored back into the `list` array in the proper order. This allows the program to reuse the original array of 10 queues for each pass of the sort.

The concept of a radix sort can be applied to any type of data as long as the sort key can be dissected into well-defined positions. Note that unlike the sorts we discussed in Chapter 13, it's not reasonable to create a generic radix sort for any object, because dissecting the key values is an integral part of the process.

Figure 15.13 shows a UML class diagram of the `RadixSort` program. This particular program used an array-based implementation of a queue, but of course alternate implementations can be substituted without having to change anything else about the program. This is yet another example that shows the value of separating the interface of a collection from its underlying implementation.

The following three sections look at various ways a queue might be implemented.

Listing **15.7**

```
//********************************************************************
//  RadixSort.java       Java Foundations
//
//  Demonstrates the use of queues in the execution of a radix sort.
//********************************************************************

import javafoundations.ArrayQueue;

public class RadixSort
{
   //-----------------------------------------------------------------
   //  Perform a radix sort on a set of numeric values.
   //-----------------------------------------------------------------
   public static void main (String[] args)
   {
      int[] list = {7843, 4568, 8765, 6543, 7865, 4532, 9987, 3241,
                    6589, 6622, 1211};
      String temp;
      int digit, num;

      ArrayQueue<Integer>[] digitQueues =
         (ArrayQueue<Integer>[])(new ArrayQueue[10]);

      for (int digitVal = 0; digitVal <= 9; digitVal++)
         digitQueues[digitVal] = new ArrayQueue<Integer>();

      // sort the list
      for (int position=0; position <= 3; position++)
      {
         for (int scan = 0; scan < list.length; scan++)
         {
            temp = String.valueOf (list[scan]);
            digit = Character.digit (temp.charAt(3-position), 10);
            digitQueues[digit].enqueue (list[scan]);
         }

         // gather numbers back into list
         num = 0;
         for (int digitVal = 0; digitVal <= 9; digitVal++)
         {
            while (!(digitQueues[digitVal].isEmpty()))
            {
               list[num] = digitQueues[digitVal].dequeue().intValue();
```

Listing **15.7** continued

```
                  num++;
               }
            }
         }

         // output the sorted list
         for (int scan = 0; scan < list.length; scan++)
            System.out.println (list[scan]);
      }
   }
```

Output

```
1211
3241
4532
4568
6543
6589
6622
7843
7865
8765
9987
```

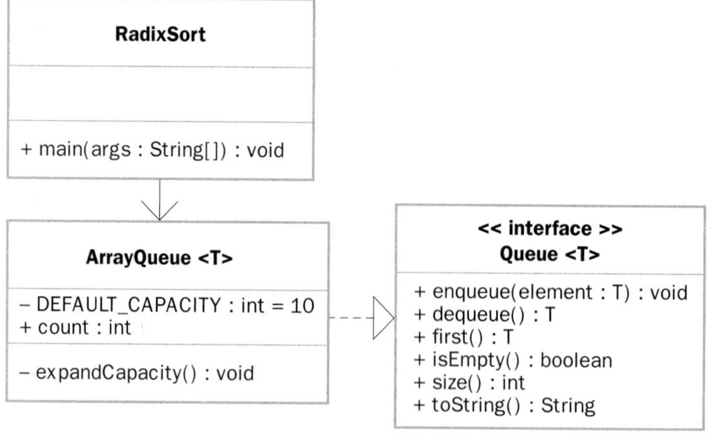

FIGURE 15.13 A UML class diagram of the `RadixSort` program

15.8 Implementing Queues with Arrays

One array-based strategy for implementing a queue is to fix one end of the queue (say, the front) at index 0 of the array. Figure 15.14 depicts a queue organized in this manner, assuming elements A, B, C, and D have been added to the queue in that order. The integer variable `count` represents the number of elements currently in the queue. Its value also indicates the next open cell in the array.

The `ArrayQueue` class is shown in Listing 15.8, with some operations left as programming projects.

The `enqueue` operation adds a new element to the rear of the queue, which in this implementation strategy is stored at the high end of the array. If there is room in the array for an additional element, it can be stored in the location indicated by the integer `count`. This implementation can use the same technique for expanding the capacity of the queue array as the one used for other collections.

Figure 15.15 shows the queue implementation of Figure 15.14 after element E is enqueued.

Because queue operations modify both ends of the collection, fixing one end at index 0 requires that the elements be shifted.

Unlike a stack, which operates at one end of the collection, a queue operates at both ends. In this implementation strategy, the first element in the queue is always stored at index 0 of the array. Therefore, when an element is removed from the queue, we must shift the elements in the array to put the new front element in position 0. (In the next section of this chapter, we examine a different array-based implementation that eliminates element shifting.)

The `dequeue` method first checks to see if the queue has at least one element to dequeue. If not, it throws an `EmptyCollectionException`, consistent with how we've been dealing with such situations in other collections. If there is at least one element, it is stored so that it can be returned, and the value of `count`

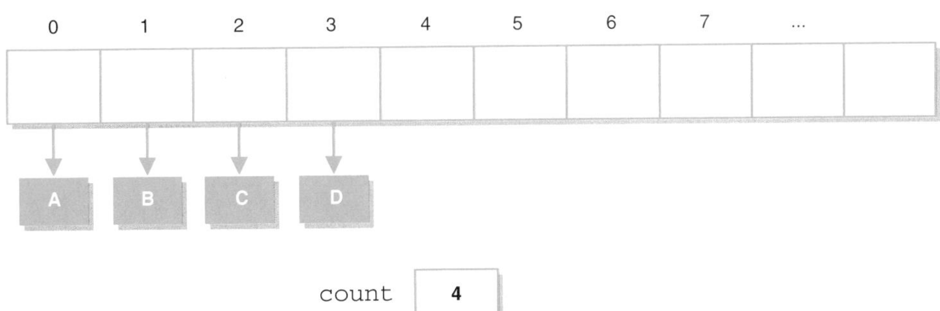

FIGURE 15.14 An array implementation of a queue

Listing 15.8

```
//********************************************************************
//  ArrayQueue.java       Java Foundations
//
//  Represents an array implementation of a queue. The front of
//  the queue is kept at array index 0.
//********************************************************************

package javafoundations;

import javafoundations.exceptions.*;

public class ArrayQueue<T> implements Queue<T>
{
   private final int DEFAULT_CAPACITY = 10;
   private int count;
   private T[] queue;

   //-----------------------------------------------------------------
   //  Creates an empty queue using the default capacity.
   //-----------------------------------------------------------------
   public ArrayQueue()
   {
      count = 0;
      queue = (T[]) (new Object[DEFAULT_CAPACITY]);
   }

   //-----------------------------------------------------------------
   //  Removes the element at the front of this queue and returns a
   //  reference to it. Throws an EmptyCollectionException if the
   //  queue is empty.
   //-----------------------------------------------------------------
   public T dequeue() throws EmptyCollectionException
   {
      if (count == 0)
         throw new EmptyCollectionException ("Dequeue operation failed. "
            + "The queue is empty.");

      T result = queue[0];

      count--;

      // shift the elements to keep the front element at index 0
      for (int index=0; index < count; index++)
```

Listing **15.8** continued

```
            queue[index] = queue[index+1];

        queue[count] = null;

        return result;
    }

    //-----------------------------------------------------------------
    //  The following methods are left as programming projects.
    //-----------------------------------------------------------------
    //  public void enqueue (T element) { }
    //  public T first () throws EmptyCollectionException { }
    //  public boolean isEmpty() { }
    //  public int size() { }
    //  public String toString() { }
}
```

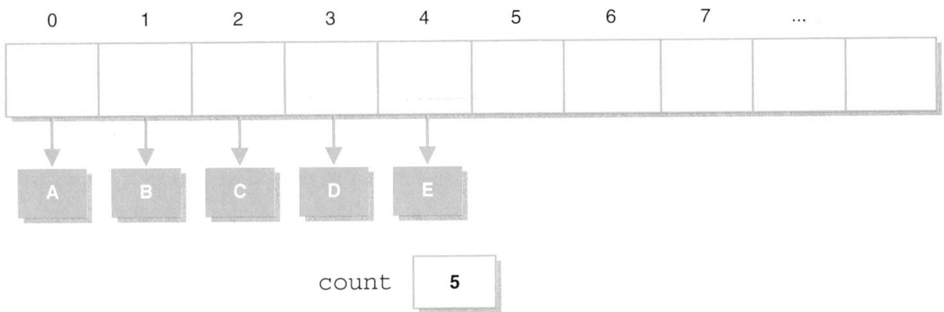

FIGURE 15.15 The queue after adding element E

is decremented to reflect that we now have one less element in the queue. Then the elements are shifted one position, moving the second element up to the first position, and so on. For completeness, the copy of the reference to the last element in the queue is overwritten with `null`.

Figure 15.16 illustrates the results of the `dequeue` operation on the queue from Figure 15.15. Note that, unlike the `pop` and `push` operations on a stack, the `dequeue` operation is not the inverse of `enqueue`. That is, Figure 15.16 is not identical to our original configuration shown in Figure 15.14, because the `enqueue` and `dequeue` operations are working on opposite ends of the collection.

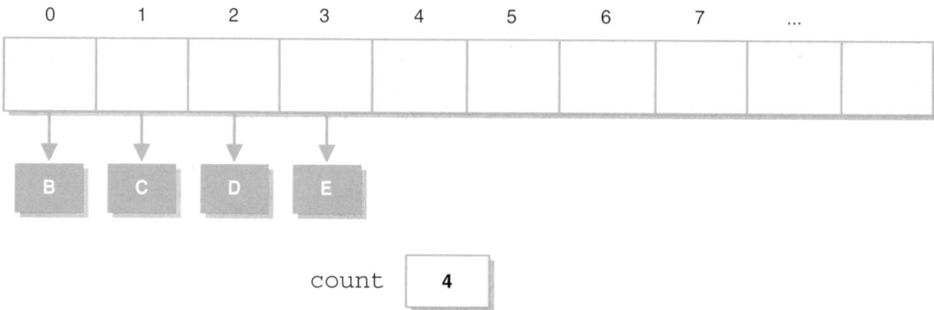

FIGURE 15.16 The queue after removing the first element

The implementation of the `enqueue`, `first`, `isEmpty`, `size`, and `toString` operations using this strategy are left as programming projects. Remember that the `enqueue` operation will need support to expand the capacity of the array if necessary.

15.9 Implementing Queues with Circular Arrays

The main problem with the array-based strategy discussed in the previous section is that the front end of the queue is fixed at index 0. Therefore, every time a `dequeue` operation is performed, all elements stored in the queue array have to be shifted down one position. If the queue is large, or if many `dequeue` operations are performed, this creates a lot of shifting operations that we'd like to avoid. This section describes another array-based approach that eliminates the shifting of elements.

Turning around the queue so that the rear of the queue is at index 0 does not solve the problem. That approach would simply cause the element shifting to occur in the `enqueue` method (before the element is added) rather than in the `dequeue` method (after the element is removed).

The key is to not fix either end at a certain position. As elements are `dequeued`, the front of the queue will move further into the array. As elements are `enqueued`, the rear of the queue will also move further into the array. With this strategy, extra variables are needed to keep track of the location of the front and rear of the queue, but no shifting is needed.

The challenge comes when the rear of the queue reaches the end of the array. Enlarging the array at this point is not a practical solution, and does not make use of the now empty space in the lower indexes of the array.

To make this solution work, we will use a *circular array* to implement the queue. A circular array is not a new construct—it is just a way to think about the array that is used to store the collection. Conceptually, the array is used as a circle, whose last index is followed by the first index. A circular array storing a queue is shown in Figure 15.17.

Treating arrays as circular eliminates the need to shift elements in an array queue implementation.

Like the previous array strategy, we use an integer variable called `count` to represent the number of elements currently in the queue. However, `count` no longer represents the location for adding new elements. Two additional integer values are used to represent the front and rear of the queue, which change as elements are added and removed. Note that the value of `front` represents the location where the first element in the queue is stored, and the value of `rear` represents the next available slot in the array (not where the last element is stored). Using `rear` in this manner is consistent with our other array implementation.

When the rear of the queue reaches the end of the list, it "wraps around" to the front of the array. The elements of the queue can therefore straddle the end of the array, as shown in Figure 15.18, which assumes the array can store 100 elements.

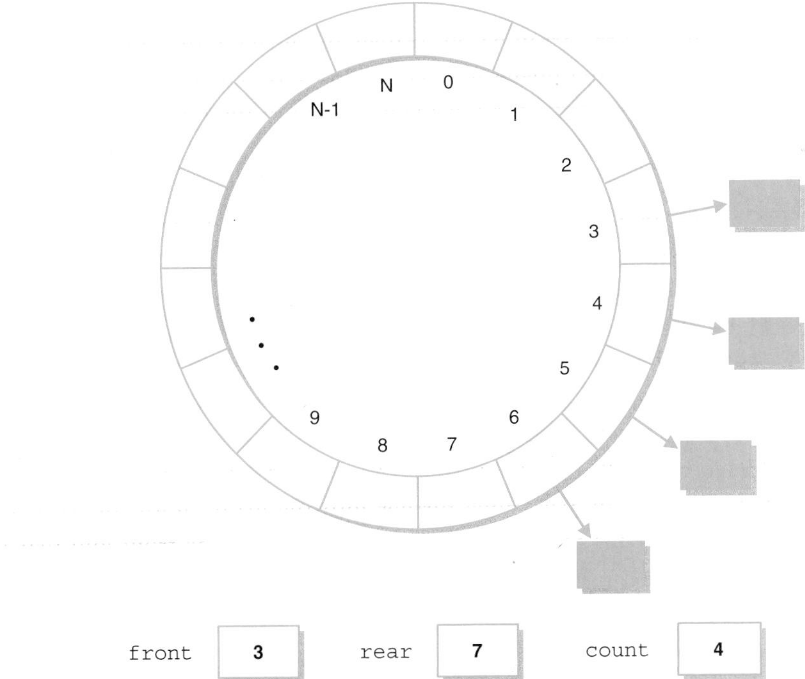

FIGURE 15.17 A circular array implementation of a queue

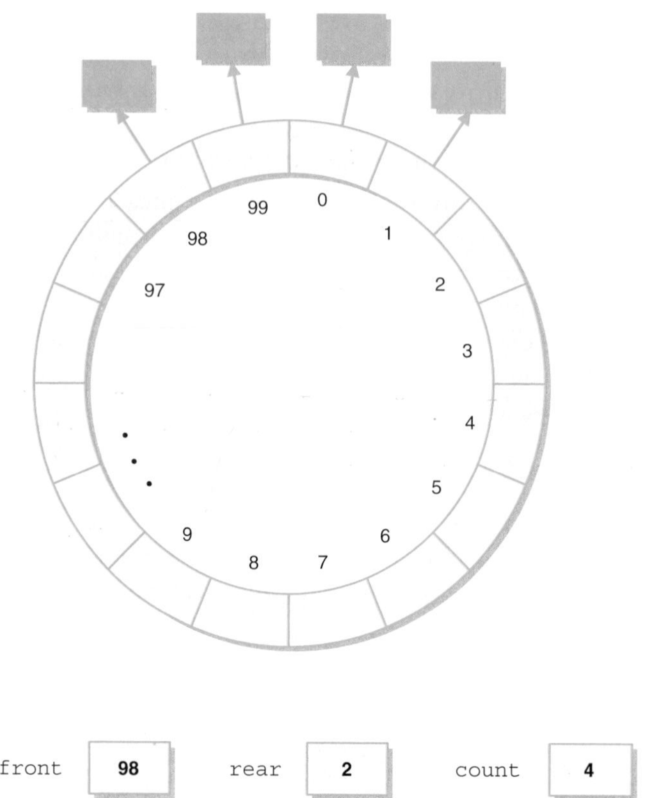

FIGURE 15.18 A queue straddling the end of a circular array

Using this strategy, once an element has been added to the queue, it stays in one location in the array until it is removed with a `dequeue` operation. No elements need to be shifted as elements are added or removed. However, this approach requires that we carefully manage the values of `front` and `rear`.

Let's look at another example. Figure 15.19 shows a circular array (drawn linearly) with a capacity of 10 elements. Initially it is shown after elements A through H have been enqueued. It is then shown after the first four elements (A through D) have been dequeued. Finally, it is shown after elements I, J, K, and L have been enqueued, which causes the queue to wrap around the end of the array.

Listing 15.9 shows a class called `CircularArrayQueue`, which contains a partial implementation of a queue using a circular array. Some operations are left as programming projects. Note that the structure of the array holding the

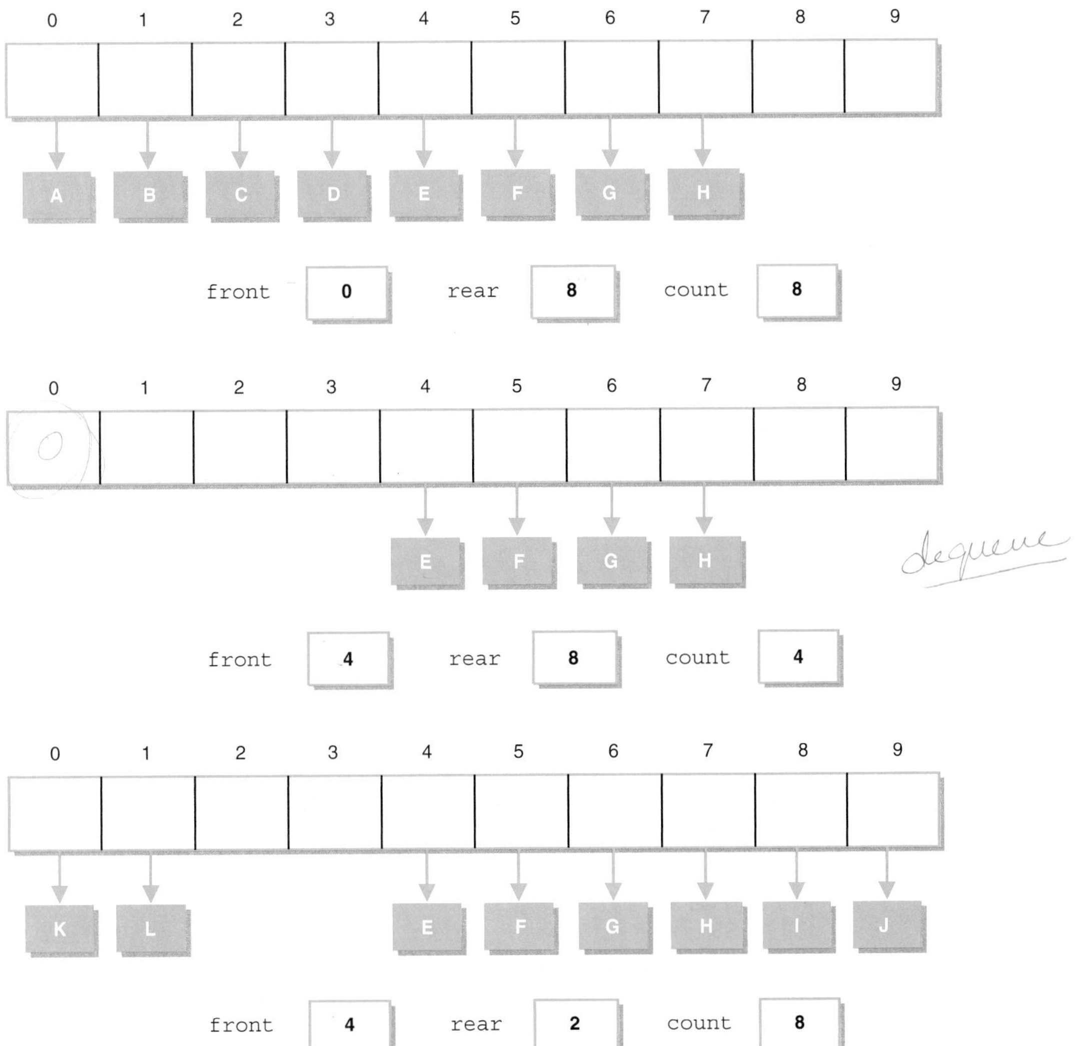

FIGURE 15.19 The changing state of a queue implemented using a circular array

queue elements is no different than the one used in the `ArrayQueue` class from the previous section. The underlying structure is not different, but the way we manage it is.

Listing **15.9**

```
//********************************************************************
//  CircularArrayQueue.java       Java Foundations
//
//  Represents an array implementation of a queue in which neither
//  end of the queue is fixed in the array. The variables storing the
//  indexes of the front and rear of the queue continually increment
//  as elements are removed and added, cycling back to 0 when they
//  reach the end of the array.
//********************************************************************

package javafoundations;

import javafoundations.exceptions.*;

public class CircularArrayQueue<T> implements Queue<T>
{
   private final int DEFAULT_CAPACITY = 10;
   private int front, rear, count;
   private T[] queue;

   //-----------------------------------------------------------------
   //  Creates an empty queue using the default capacity.
   //-----------------------------------------------------------------
   public CircularArrayQueue()
   {
      front = rear = count = 0;
      queue = (T[]) (new Object[DEFAULT_CAPACITY]);
   }

   //-----------------------------------------------------------------
   //  Adds the specified element to the rear of this queue, expanding
   //  the capacity of the queue array if necessary.
   //-----------------------------------------------------------------
   public void enqueue (T element)
   {
      if (count == queue.length)
         expandCapacity();

      queue[rear] = element;
      rear = (rear+1) % queue.length;
      count++;
   }
```

Listing **15.9** continued

```
    //-----------------------------------------------------------------
    //  Creates a new array to store the contents of this queue with
    //  twice the capacity of the old one.
    //-----------------------------------------------------------------
    public void expandCapacity()
    {
       T[] larger = (T[])(new Object[queue.length*2]);

       for (int index=0; index < count; index++)
          larger[index] = queue[(front+index) % queue.length];

       front = 0;
       rear = count;
       queue = larger;
    }

    //-----------------------------------------------------------------
    //  The following methods are left as programming projects.
    //-----------------------------------------------------------------
    //  public T dequeue () throws EmptyCollectionException { }
    //  public T first () throws EmptyCollectionException { }
    //  public boolean isEmpty() { }
    //  public int size() { }
    //  public String toString() { }
}
```

The enqueue method checks to see if the array capacity needs to be expanded, then adds the element to the rear of the queue and updates the values of `rear` and `count`. Note the interesting calculation used to compute the new value of `rear`. In general, after an element is enqueued, the value of `rear` is incremented. But when an `enqueue` operation fills the last cell of the array (at the largest index), the value of `rear` must be set to 0, indicating that the next element should be stored at index 0.

The appropriate update to the value of `rear` is accomplished in a calculation using the remainder operator (`%`). Recall that the remainder operator returns the remainder after dividing the first operand by the second. Let's try this calculation, assuming we have an array of size 10. If `rear` is currently 5, it will be set to

6%10, or 6. If `rear` is currently 9, it will be set to 10%10 or 0. Try this calculation using various situations to see that it works no matter how big the array is.

As with any array-based implementation, all cells in the array may become filled. This implies that the rear of the queue has "caught up" to the front of the queue. To add another element, the array would have to be enlarged. Keep in mind, however, that the elements of the existing array must be copied into the new array in their proper order in the queue, not necessarily the order in which they appear in the current array. The easiest way to do that is to copy them into the array starting at index 0 and updating the values of `front` and `rear` accordingly, as shown in the `expandCapacity` method.

As usual, the `dequeue` operation must ensure that the collection is not empty. Then it must store the element at the front of the queue to be returned, remove the element from the array, and update the values of `front` and `count` appropriately. After an element is dequeued, the value of `front` is incremented. But after enough `dequeue` operations, the value of `front` will reach the last index of the array. After removing the element at the largest index, the value of `front` must be set to 0 instead of being incremented. So the update of the `front` variable is similar to the calculation done for `rear` in `enqueue`.

The `toString` operation becomes a bit more complicated than usual using this approach because the elements are not stored starting at index 0 and may wrap around the end of the array. The operations `dequeue`, `first`, `isEmpty`, `size`, and `toString` are left as programming projects.

15.10 Implementing Queues with Links

Because a queue is a linear collection, we can implement a queue as a linked list of `LinearNode` objects, as we did with stacks. The primary difference is that we will have to operate on both ends of the list. Therefore, in addition to a reference (called `front`) pointing to the first element in the list, we will also keep track of a second reference (called `rear`) that points to the last element in the list. We will also use an integer variable called `count` to keep track of the number of elements in the queue.

A linked implementation of a queue is facilitated by references to the first and last elements of the linked list.

Figure 15.20 depicts this strategy for implementing a queue. It shows a queue that has had the elements A, B, C, and D added to the queue, in that order. Remember that Figure 15.20 depicts the general case. We always have to be careful to accurately maintain our references in special cases. For an empty queue, the `front` and `rear` references are both null and the count is zero. If there is exactly

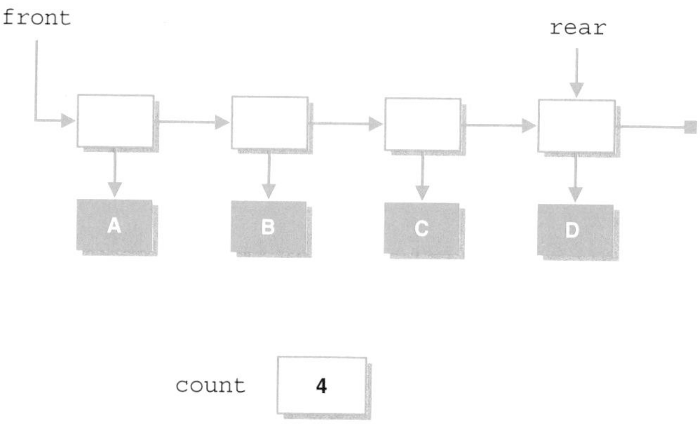

FIGURE 15.20 A linked implementation of a queue

one element in the queue, both the `front` and `rear` references point to the same object.

Listing 15.10 shows the `LinkedQueue` class, with some operations left as programming projects.

The `enqueue` operation requires that we put the new element on the rear of the list. In the general case, that means setting the `next` reference of the current last element to the new one, and resetting the `rear` reference to the new last element. However, if the queue is currently empty, the `front` reference must also be set to the new (and only) element.

Note that if the queue is empty, the `next` reference of the new node need not be set, because it has already been set to null in the `LinearNode` class. The `rear` reference is set to the new node in either case, and the `count` is incremented.

Figure 15.21 shows the linked list implementation of the queue from Figure 15.20 after element E has been added.

The `dequeue` operation must ensure that there is at least one element to return. Then it must consider the situation in which there is only one element in the queue. If, after removing the front element, the queue is now empty, the `rear` reference must be set to null. Note that in this case, the `front` reference will be null because it was set equal to the `next` reference of the last element in the list.

Figure 15.22 shows the result of a `dequeue` operation on the queue from Figure 15.21. The element A at the front of the list is removed and returned to the user. As with our array-based implementation, the `dequeue` operation does not bring us back to the original configuration shown in Figure 15.20 because `enqueue` and `dequeue` modify opposite ends of the queue.

Listing 15.10

```
//********************************************************************
//  LinkedQueue.java        Java Foundations
//
//  Represents a linked implementation of a queue.
//********************************************************************

package javafoundations;

import javafoundations.exceptions.*;

public class LinkedQueue<T> implements Queue<T>
{
   private int count;
   private LinearNode<T> front, rear;

   //-----------------------------------------------------------------
   //  Creates an empty queue.
   //-----------------------------------------------------------------
   public LinkedQueue()
   {
      count = 0;
      front = rear = null;
   }

   //-----------------------------------------------------------------
   //  Adds the specified element to the rear of this queue.
   //-----------------------------------------------------------------
   public void enqueue (T element)
   {
      LinearNode<T> node = new LinearNode<T>(element);

      if (count == 0)
         front = node;
      else
         rear.setNext(node);

      rear = node;
      count++;
   }

   //-----------------------------------------------------------------
   //  The following methods are left as programming projects.
   //-----------------------------------------------------------------
```

Listing **15.10** continued

```
//  public T dequeue () throws EmptyCollectionException { }
//  public T first () throws EmptyCollectionException { }
//  public boolean isEmpty() { }
//  public int size() { }
//  public String toString() { }
}
```

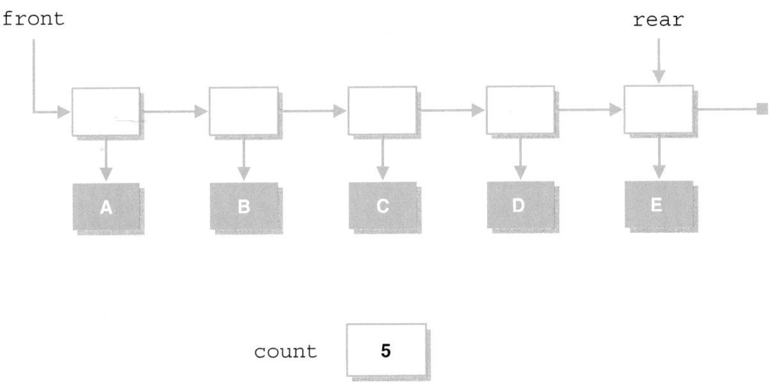

FIGURE 15.21 The queue after adding element E

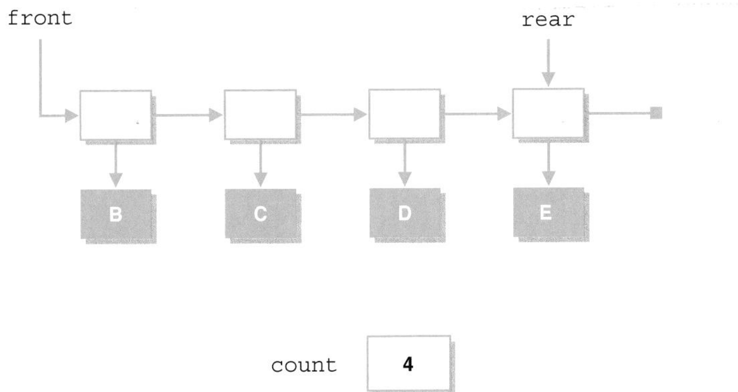

FIGURE 15.22 The queue after a dequeue operation

The remaining operations in the linked queue implementation are fairly straightforward and are similar to the stack collection. The operations `dequeue`, `first`, `isEmpty`, `size`, and `toString` are left as programming projects.

15.11 Analysis of Stack and Queue Implementations

As discussed in Chapter 14, we can evaluate algorithms based on the memory space they use and the CPU time they consume, where time is usually the more important criteria. The space issues for stacks and queues are similar to those we saw with the bag collection in Chapter 14. Let's now examine the CPU time requirements for stack and queue operations.

It turns out that stacks and queues can be implemented very efficiently. In almost all cases, the implemented operations on these collections are not affected by the number of elements in the collection. There is usually a small number of set steps to take to accomplish an operation, and traversing the set of elements in the collection is rarely necessary.

All operations for a stack (`push`, `pop`, etc.) are O(1). Review the implementations of both the `ArrayStack` and `LinkedStack` classes to confirm this. One reason for the efficiency in the array-based version of a stack is our choice to keep the bottom of the stack at index 0. Since all processing on a stack occurs at one end, that decision is significant from an efficiency point of view.

The shifting of elements in a noncircular array implementation creates an O(n) complexity.

Similarly, almost all operations for a queue (`enqueue`, `dequeue`, etc.) are O(1). The only interesting exception is the `dequeue` operation for the `ArrayQueue` class. In this version, when an element is dequeued, the remaining elements are shifted one position to keep the front element at index 0. Because of this traversal, the `dequeue` operation for an array-based queue is O(n).

That inefficiency is why we discussed the circular array version of a queue. By treating the array as circular in our implementation, we were able to eliminate the need to shift the elements. Thus, the order of the `dequeue` operation is O(1) for the `CircularArrayQueue` class.

Summary of Key Concepts

- Stack elements are processed in a LIFO manner—the last element in is the first element out.
- A programmer should choose the structure that is appropriate for the type of data management needed.
- A stack is the ideal collection to use when evaluating a postfix expression.
- For efficiency, an array-based stack implementation keeps the bottom of the stack at index 0.
- A linked implementation of a stack adds and removes elements from one end of the linked list.
- The `java.util.Stack` class is derived from `Vector`, which gives a stack inappropriate operations.
- Queue elements are processed in a FIFO manner—the first element in is the first element out.
- A radix sort is inherently based on queue processing.
- Because queue operations modify both ends of the collection, fixing one end at index 0 requires that the elements be shifted.
- Treating arrays as circular eliminates the need to shift elements in an array queue implementation.
- A linked implementation of a queue is facilitated by references to the first and last elements of the linked list.
- The shifting of elements in a noncircular array implementation creates an O(n) complexity.

Self-Review Questions

SR 15.1 What is the characteristic behavior of a stack?

SR 15.2 What are the five basic operations on a stack?

SR 15.3 What are the advantages of the `java.util.Stack` implementation of a stack?

SR 15.4 What is the potential problem with the `java.util.Stack` implementation?

SR 15.5 What is the difference between a queue and a stack?

SR 15.6 What are the five basic operations on a queue?

SR 15.7 How many queues would it take to use a radix sort to sort names stored as all lowercase?

SR 15.8 Is it possible for the `front` and `rear` references in a non-circular array implementation of a queue to be equal?

SR 15.9 Is it possible for the `front` and `rear` references in a circular array implementation of a queue to be equal?

SR 15.10 Is it possible for the `front` and `rear` references in a linked implementation of a queue to be equal?

SR 15.11 Which implementation of stacks and queues has the worst time complexity?

Exercises

EX 15.1 Hand trace the stack `myStack` through the following operations, assuming it is initially empty:

```
myStack.push(new Integer(4));
myStack.push(new Integer(3));
Integer num = myStack.pop();
myStack.push(new Integer(7));
myStack.push(new Integer(2));
myStack.push(new Integer(5));
myStack.push(new Integer(9));
Integer num = myStack.pop();
myStack.push(new Integer(3));
myStack.push(new Integer(9));
```

EX 15.2 Given the resulting stack `myStack` from the previous exercise, what would be the result of each of the following?

a. `num = myStack.peek();`

b. `num = myStack.pop();`

   `num2 = myStack.peek();`

c. `num = myStack.pop();`

   `num2 = myStack.peek();`

EX 15.3 What would be the time complexity of the `size` operation for the linked implementation of a stack if there were no `count` variable? Explain.

EX 15.4 Show how the undo operation in a word processor can be supported by the use of a stack. Give specific examples and draw the contents of the stack after various actions are taken.

EX 15.5 In the postfix expression evaluation example, the two most recent operands are popped when an operator is encountered so that the subexpression can be evaluated. The first operand popped is treated as the second operand in the subexpression, and the second operand popped is the first. Give and explain an example that demonstrates the importance of this aspect of the solution.

EX 15.6 Draw an example using the five integers (12, 23, 1, 45, 9) of how a stack could be used to reverse the order of these elements.

EX 15.7 Explain what would happen to the algorithms and the time complexity of an array implementation of the stack if the top of the stack were at position 0.

EX 15.8 Name five everyday examples of a queue other than those discussed in this chapter.

EX 15.9 Hand trace a queue `myQueue` through the following operations:

```
myQueue.enqueue(new Integer(4));
myQueue.enqueue(new Integer(1));
Integer num = myQueue.dequeue();
myQueue.enqueue(new Integer(8));
myQueue.enqueue(new Integer(2));
myQueue.enqueue(new Integer(5));
myQueue.enqueue(new Integer(3));
Integer num = myQueue.dequeue();
myQueue.enqueue(new Integer(4));
myQueue.enqueue(new Integer(9));
```

EX 15.10 Given the resulting queue `myQueue` from exercise 15.9, what would be the result of each of the following?

a. `myQueue.front();`

b. `num = myQueue.dequeue();`

   `myQueue.front();`

c. `num = myQueue.dequeue();`

   `myQueue.front();`

EX 15.11 What would be the time complexity of the `size` operation for each of the three implementations if there were not a `count` variable?

EX 15.12 Hand trace a radix sort for the following list of five-digit student ID numbers, assuming that each digit must be between 1 and 5: 13224 32131 54355 12123 22331 21212 33333 54312.

EX 15.13 What is the time complexity of a radix sort?

EX 15.14 Compare and contrast the `enqueue` method of the `LinkedQueue` class to the `push` method of the `LinkedStack` class.

EX 15.15 Describe two different ways the `isEmpty` method of the `LinkedQueue` class could be implemented.

EX 15.16 Explain why the array implementation of a stack does not require elements to be shifted but the noncircular array implementation of a queue does.

EX 15.17 Suppose the `count` variable was not used in the `CircularArrayQueue` class. Explain how you could use the values of `front` and `rear` to compute the number of elements in the list.

Programming Projects

PP 15.1 Complete the implementation of the `ArrayStack` class presented in this chapter. Specifically, complete the implementations of the `pop`, `peek`, `isEmpty`, and `size` operations.

PP 15.2 Complete the implementation of the `LinkedStack` class presented in this chapter. Specifically, complete the implementations of the `push`, `peek`, `isEmpty`, and `size` operations.

PP 15.3 Design and implement an application that reads a sentence from the user and prints the sentence with the characters of each word backwards. Use a stack to reverse the characters of each word.

PP 15.4 Modify the solution to the postfix expression evaluation problem so that it checks for the validity of the expression that is entered by the user. Issue an appropriate error message when an erroneous situation is encountered.

PP 15.5 Create a version of the `MazeSearch` program from Chapter 12 that uses a stack to track the exploration of the maze instead of using recursion.

PP 15.6 Create a version of the `ArrayStack` class that, instead of using a variable called `count` to track the number of elements, uses a variable called `top` that holds the index of the top element of the stack.

PP 15.7 The linked implementation of a stack uses a variable called `count` to keep track of the number of elements in the stack. Rewrite the linked implementation without using such a variable.

PP 15.8 A collection called a *drop-out stack* behaves like a stack in every respect except that it can hold a maximum number of elements (n), and when the n+1 element is pushed, the element at the bottom of the stack is lost. Implement a drop-out stack using a circular array implementation, and create a driver program to demonstrate its processing.

PP 15.9 Implement a drop-out stack as described in programming project 15.8 using a linked implementation.

PP 15.10 Implement an integer adder using three stacks. Create a driver program to demonstrate its processing.

PP 15.11 Implement an infix-to-postfix expression translator using stacks. Create a driver program to demonstrate its processing.

PP 15.12 Complete the implementation of the `ArrayQueue` class presented in this chapter. Specifically, complete the implementations of the `enqueue`, `first`, `isEmpty`, `size`, and `toString` operations.

PP 15.13 Complete the implementation of the `CircularArrayQueue` class presented in this chapter. Specifically, complete the implementations of the `dequeue`, `first`, `isEmpty`, `size`, and `toString` operations.

PP 15.14 Complete the implementation of the `LinkedQueue` class presented in this chapter. Specifically, complete the implementations of the `dequeue`, `first`, `isEmpty`, `size`, and `toString` operations.

PP 15.15 Implement a version of the `ArrayQueue` class that keeps the rear of the queue fixed at index 0. Create a driver program to demonstrate its processing.

PP 15.16 Implement a version of the `CircularArrayQueue` class that grows the list in the opposite direction from which the version described in this chapter grows the list. Create a driver program to demonstrate its processing.

PP 15.17 Implement a version of the `CircularArrayQueue` class without a `count` variable. Create a driver program to demonstrate its processing.

PP 15.18 A *deque* (pronounced "deck") is a collection that is closely related to a queue. The name deque stands for double-ended queue. The difference between the two is that with a deque, you can insert or remove from either end of the queue. Create an array-based implementation of a deque and demonstrate its processing.

PP 15.19 Implement a deque as described in programming project 15.18 using links. (Hint: Each node will need a `next` and a `previous` reference.)

PP 15.20 Design a program to simulate vehicles at an intersection. Assume that there is one lane going in each of four directions, with stoplights facing each direction. Vary the arrival time of vehicles randomly in each direction and set up a regular frequency of the light changes. Run your simulation for a set period of time to view the "behavior" of the intersection.

PP 15.21 Design a program that uses a stack and a queue to test whether a given string is a palindrome. See the `PalindromeTester` program from Chapter 4 for the basic premise.

Answers to Self-Review Questions

SR 15.1 A stack is a last in, first out (LIFO) structure.

SR 15.2 The operations are:

`push`—adds an element to the end of the stack

`pop`—removes an element from the front of the stack

`peek`—returns a reference to the element at the front of the stack

`isEmpty`—returns `true` if the stack is empty, returns `false` otherwise

`size`—returns the number of elements in the stack

SR 15.3 Since the `java.util.Stack` implementation is an extension of the `Vector` class, it can keep track of the positions of elements in the stack using an index and thus does not require each node to store an additional pointer. This implementation also allocates space only as it is needed, like the linked implementation.

SR 15.4 The `java.util.Stack` implementation is an extension of the `Vector` class and thus inherits a large number of operations that violate the basic assumptions of a stack.

SR 15.5 A queue is a first in, first out (FIFO) collection, whereas a stack is a last in, first out (LIFO) collection.

SR 15.6 The basic queue operations are:

`enqueue`—adds an element to the end of the queue

`dequeue`—removes an element from the front of the queue

`first`—returns a reference to the element at the front of the queue

`isEmpty`—returns `true` if the queue is empty, returns `false` otherwise

`size`—returns the number of elements in the queue

SR 15.7 A radix sort based on the alphabet would require 27 queues, one for each of the 26 letters in the alphabet and 1 to store the whole list before, during, and after sorting.

SR 15.8 There is no `front` reference in the noncircular queue implementation. The first element in the queue is always in position 0 of the array. However, when the queue is empty, the `rear` also points to position 0.

SR 15.9 Yes, the `front` and `rear` references are the same in the circular array version of a queue under two circumstances: when the queue is empty, and when the queue is full.

SR 15.10 Yes, in the linked version of a queue, the `front` and `rear` references are the same when the queue is empty (both `front` and `rear` are null) and when there is only one element on the queue.

SR 15.11 The noncircular array implementation with an O(n) dequeue operation has the worst time complexity.

Trees

Chapter Objectives

- Define the terms associated with trees.
- Discuss possible strategies for implementing trees.
- Discuss the various ways trees can be traversed.
- Explore an implementation of a binary tree.
- Use binary trees to represent decision trees.

This chapter begins our exploration of nonlinear collections, and trees in particular. Trees are used in many situations in computing. In this chapter we discuss the use and implementation of trees, define the terms associated with trees, analyze possible tree implementations, and look at examples of implementing and using trees. Based on this core material, Chapter 17 continues the exploration of trees.

16.1 Tree Terminology

A tree is a nonlinear structure whose elements are organized into a hierarchy.

The collections we examined in Chapter 15 (stacks, queues, and lists) are linear data structures, meaning their elements are arranged in order one after another. A *tree* is a nonlinear structure in which elements are organized into a hierarchy. This section describes trees in general and establishes some important terminology.

A tree is composed of a set of *nodes* in which elements are stored, and *edges* that connect one node to another. Each node is at a particular *level* in the tree hierarchy. The root of the tree is the only node at the top level of the tree. There is only one root node in a tree. Figure 16.1 illustrates some tree terminology.

The nodes at lower levels of the tree are the *children* of nodes at the previous level. In Figure 16.1, the nodes labeled B, C, D, and E are the children of A. Nodes F and G are the children of B. A node can have only one parent, but a node may have multiple children. Nodes that have the same parent are called *siblings*. Thus, nodes H, I, and J are siblings because they are all children of D.

The root node is the only node in a tree that does not have a parent. A node that does not have any children is called a *leaf*. A node that is not the root and has at least one child is called an *internal node*. Note that the tree analogy is upside-down. Our trees "grow" from the root at the top of the tree to the leaves toward the bottom of the tree.

A *subtree* is a tree structure that makes up part of another tree. The tree in Figure 16.1 is made up of subtrees with roots B, C, D, and E. In turn, the subtree with root B has subtrees of its own with roots F and G.

We can follow a *path* through a tree from parent to child, starting at the root. For example, the path from node A to N in Figure 16.1 is A, D, I, N. A node is the *ancestor* of another node if it is above it on the path from the root. Thus the

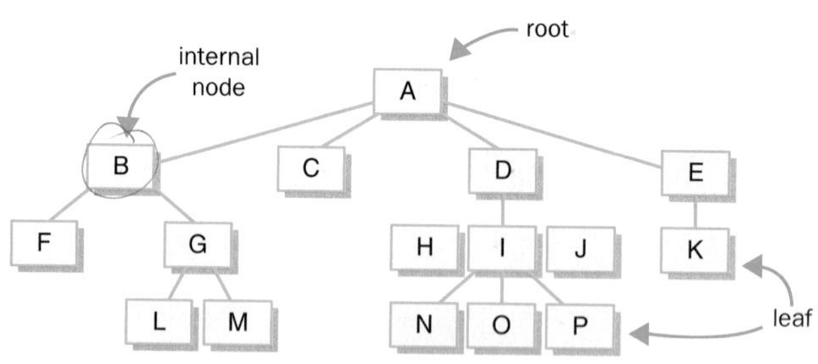

FIGURE 16.1 Some tree terminology

root is the ultimate ancestor of all nodes in a tree. Nodes that can be reached by following a path from a particular node are the *descendants* of that node.

The level of a node is also the length of the path from the root to the node. This *path length* is determined by counting the number of edges that must be followed to get from the root to the node. The root is considered to be level 0, the children of the root are at level 1, the grandchildren of the root are at level 2, and so on. Path length and level are depicted in Figure 16.2.

The *height* (or *depth*) of a tree is the length of the longest path from the root to a leaf. Thus the height of the tree in Figure 16.2 is 3, because the path length from the root to leaf F (or G) is 3. The height of a particular node is defined by the level it is on. Thus the height of node B is 1.

Tree Classifications

Trees can be classified in many ways. One important criterion is the maximum number of children any node in the tree may have. This value is sometimes referred to as the *order of the tree*. A tree that has no limit to the number of children a node may have is called a *general tree*. A tree that limits each node to no more than n children is referred to as an *n-ary tree*.

The order of a tree specifies the maximum number of children any node in the tree may have.

A tree in which nodes may have at most two children is called a *binary tree*. This type of tree is particularly helpful in many situations. Much of our exploration of trees will focus on binary trees.

Another way to classify a tree is whether it is balanced or not. A tree is considered to be *balanced* if all of the leaves of the tree are on the same level or at least within one level of each other. Thus, the tree shown on the left in Figure 16.3 is balanced, while the one on the right is not. A balanced n-ary tree with m elements will have a height of $\log_n m$. Thus, a balanced binary tree with n nodes has

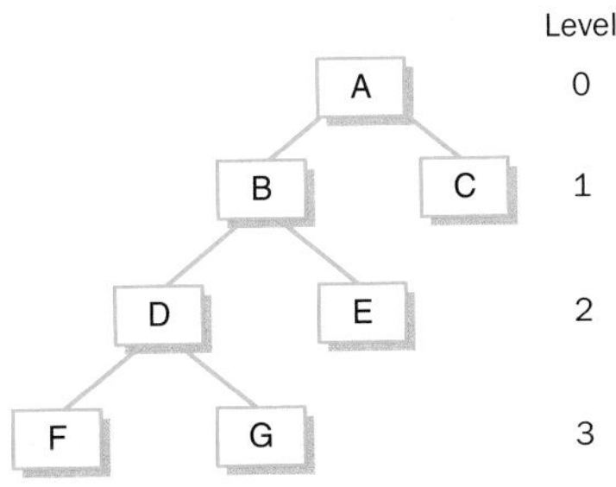

FIGURE 16.2 Path length and level

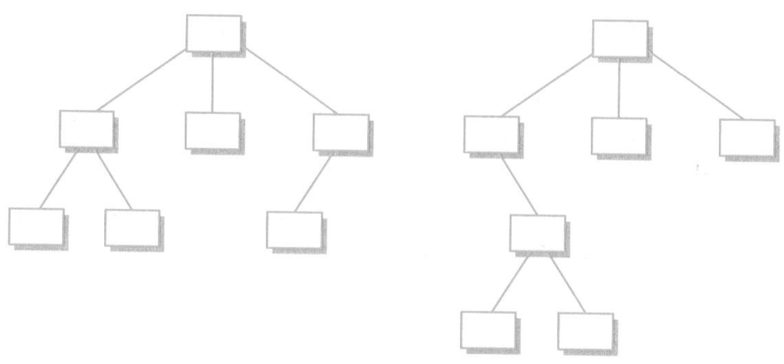

FIGURE 16.3 Balanced and unbalanced trees

A balanced n-ary tree with m elements will have height $\log_n m$.

a height of $\log_2 n$, a fact we used to our advantage in the analysis of certain sorting algorithms in Chapter 13.

An n-ary tree is *full* if all leaves of the tree are at the same level and every nonleaf node has exactly n children. A tree is *complete* if it is full, or full to the next-to-last level with all leaves at the bottom level on the left side of the tree. In Figure 16.4, the first two trees (a and b) are complete, but not full. The third tree (c) is both complete and full. As we'll see, full and complete trees can be implemented efficiently using certain techniques.

16.2 Tree Traversals

Because a tree is a nonlinear structure, the concept of traversing a tree is generally more interesting than the concept of traversing a linear structure. There are four basic ways to traverse a tree, all starting at the root node:

- *Preorder traversal* — visit the root, then traverse the subtrees from left to right
- *Inorder traversal* — traverse the left subtree, then visit the root, then traverse the remaining subtrees from left to right
- *Postorder traversal* — traverse the subtrees from left to right, then visit the root
- *Level-order traversal* — visit each node at each level of the tree from top (root) to bottom and left to right

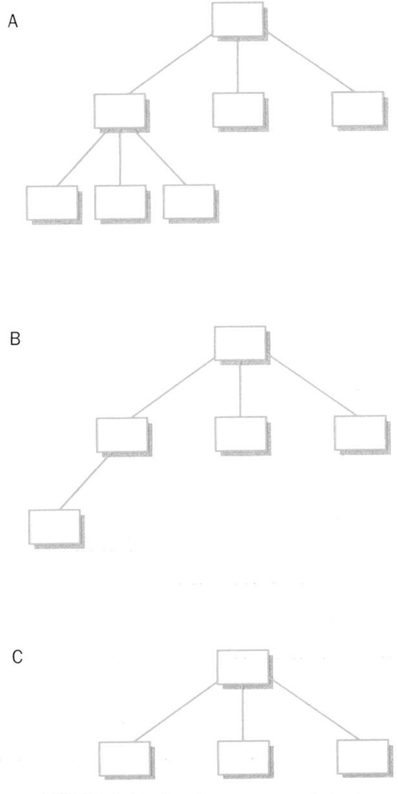

FIGURE 16.4 Some complete trees

There are four basic techniques for traversing a tree.

Recall from our earlier discussions of collections that the concept of "visiting" a node during a traversal is deliberately vague. What a program does when visiting a node is up to the developer. A particular type of traversal simply dictates the order in which the elements of a collection are accessed.

The first three traversal definitions in this list are inherently recursive. For instance, when a subtree is traversed in a preorder traversal, it is traversed in a preorder fashion. The traversal techniques do not intersect. A level-order traversal is not recursive in nature because it's processing is based on the tree's levels, not on subtrees.

These definitions apply to trees of any order. For example, if a particular node had four children, an inorder traversal would traverse the node's leftmost subtree, then visit the node, then traverse the second subtree completely, then the third subtree, and then the fourth. However, to simplify the following example, we focus on how each of these definitions applies to a binary tree.

Figure 16.5 shows a binary tree and its four traversals. Let's walk through the processing of each type of traversal.

Preorder Traversal

In a preorder traversal, the nodes are visited before any subtrees are visited. So for the binary tree in Figure 16.5, the root A is visited, then the entire subtree with root B is traversed, and then the entire subtree with root C is traversed. Note that all nodes in the left subtree are listed in the traversal before the nodes in the right subtree. This can be summarized in the following pseudocode:

```
Visit node
Traverse(left-subtree)
Traverse(right-subtree)
```

And remember, every subtree is traversed using a preorder approach. To traverse the subtree with root B, the root B is visited, then the entire subtree with root D is traversed, then the entire subtree with root E is traversed.

Let's walk through the preorder traversal from the beginning. First A is visited, followed by B, D, and H as the left subtree of each node is traversed. At this point, there is no left subtree of H, so we're ready to traverse the right subtree of H. But there is no child there either. So, having completely traversed the left subtree of D, we turn to the right subtree of D. After visiting I and finding that it has no children, the subtree with root D is finished. Next we traverse the right subtree

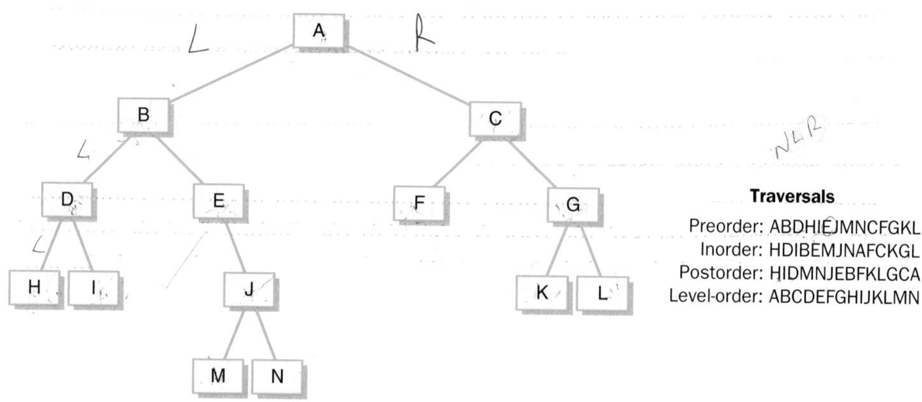

FIGURE 16.5 Four traversals of a tree

of B, first visiting node E. Then, because there is no left subtree of E, we process its right subtree, yielding J, M, and N.

At this point, the entire left subtree with root B has been traversed, and the right subtree with root C is processed next. This yields C, F, G, K, and L.

Take a few minutes to study the tree in Figure 16.5 and its preorder traversal, tracing the route the traversal takes through the tree.

Inorder Traversal

For a binary tree, an inorder traversal visits the root in between the traversals of the left and right subtrees. This is shown in the following pseudocode:

```
Traverse(left-subtree)
Visit node
Traverse(right-subtree)
```

Compare this pseudocode to that of the preorder traversal. The recursive logic is the same, but the first two steps are reversed.

To perform an inorder traversal of the tree in Figure 16.5, we first traverse the left subtree of A completely, then visit the root A, then traverse the entire right subtree of A. Applying that logic recursively, we first follow the leftmost path down the tree to H, where there is no left subtree to process. Then the node H is visited, followed by its right subtree (which doesn't exist). Having processed the entire left subtree of D, we visit D, then process its right subtree, yielding I. Now, with the entire subtree with root D finished, we visit B, then process its right subtree. There is no left subtree of E, so we visit E, then traverse its right subtree. This yields M, J, and N.

At this point, the entire left subtree of A is finished, so we visit A, then traverse its right subtree. That yields F, C, K, G, and L.

Note that in the results of a preorder traversal, the root of the tree comes first. But in an inorder traversal, the root is visited in the "middle" of the traversal (depending on how balanced the tree is). This observation can be made for any subtree as well.

Postorder Traversal

After embracing the preorder and inorder traversals, the postorder traversal is nothing new. The only difference, once again, is the order in which the root is visited relative to the subtrees. In a postorder traversal, the root is visited last, as shown in the following pseudocode:

```
Traverse(left-subtree)
Traverse(right-subtree)
Visit node
```

To perform a postorder traversal of the tree in Figure 16.5, we first traverse the entire left subtree of A, then traverse the entire right subtree of A, then finally visit the root. Applying this approach recursively, we follow the leftmost path down to H, find no children on either side, then visit node H. Next comes the traversal of the right subtree of D, yielding I, then visiting D. With the left subtree of B finished, we traverse its right subtree, yielding M, N, J, and E. Then B is visited, finishing the left subtree of A. We then traverse the right subtree of A, yielding F, K, L, G, and C. Finally, the last node visited is the root of the entire tree, A.

Compare the results of the preorder and postorder traversals. In a preorder traversal, the root always comes first. In a postorder traversal, the root comes last. And again, this effect can be seen for all subtrees.

Level-Order Traversal

A level-order traversal is quite different from the other three because it traverses the tree across levels instead of down subtrees. Each node on each level is visited from left to right. For the tree in Figure 16.5, the level-order traversal is easy to see. We first visit the root A. Then we visit B and C on the next level. Then we visit D, E, F, and G on the next level, and so on.

But producing a level-order traversal by looking at a tree and producing it algorithmically are two different things. Recursive processing of subtrees won't work because a level-order traversal does not follow the parent/child relationships that exist inherently between the nodes of a tree. Instead, it cuts across subtrees horizontally, requiring a bit of processing to access the nodes in the proper order.

Our solution relies on the use of a queue to help manage the nodes as we encounter them. The algorithm for producing a level-order traversal can be expressed as follows:

```
Enqueue the root node of the tree
While the queue is not empty
{
   Dequeue node
```

```
        Visit node
        Enqueue left child of node
        Enqueue right child of node
    }
```

Follow the logic of this algorithm as applied to the tree in Figure 16.5. The root, A, is enqueued, and the loop begins. Node A is dequeued and visited, then B and C are enqueued in that order. Processing the loop body again, node B is dequeued and visited, and D and E are enqueued (behind C). Then C is dequeued and visited, and its children, F and G, are enqueued. This process continues for each level of the tree.

A queue can be used to store the elements of a tree during a level-order traversal.

16.3 Strategies for Implementing Trees

Before getting into the details, let's discuss some general strategies for implementing trees. Because a tree is a nonlinear structure, it may not seem reasonable to attempt to implement it using an underlying linear structure such as an array. However, sometimes array-based implementations are useful, though almost certainly a less obvious choice. We'll briefly discuss two array-based approaches. Perhaps the most obvious implementation of a tree is a linked structure, with object references pointing from each tree node to its children.

Computed Links in an Array

For certain types of trees, specifically full or complete binary trees, a computational strategy can be used for representing a tree using an array. One possible strategy is as follows: For any element stored in position n of the array, the element's left child is stored in position (2n + 1) and the element's right child is stored in position (2 * (n + 1)). The capacity of the array can be managed in much the same way that we managed capacity for the array implementations of queues and stacks. This strategy is illustrated in Figure 16.6.

One strategy for implementing binary trees using an array places the left child of element n at position (2n +1) and the right child at position (2*(n+1)).

Despite the conceptual elegance of this solution, it is not without drawbacks. If the represented tree is not complete or relatively complete, this implementation strategy can waste large amounts of memory allocated in the array for positions of the tree that do not contain data.

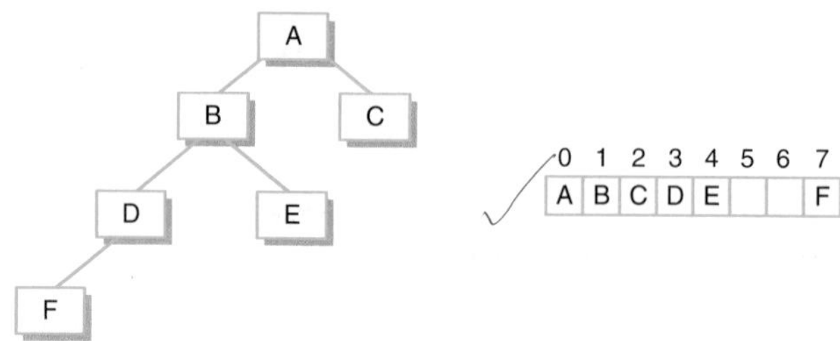

FIGURE 16.6 An array implementation of a binary tree using computed links

Stored Links in an Array

Another possible array implementation of trees is modeled after the way operating systems manage memory. Instead of assigning elements of the tree to array positions based on their location in the tree, array positions are allocated contiguously on a first-come, first-served basis. Each element of the array is an object that stores a reference to the tree element and the array index of each child. This approach, illustrated in Figure 16.7, allows elements to be stored contiguously in the array so that space is not wasted. The order of the elements in the array is determined simply by their entry order into the tree. In this case, the entry order is assumed to have been A, C, B, E, D, F.

A stored link strategy for an array-based tree implementation allows array positions to be allocated contiguously regardless of the completeness of the tree.

This approach increases the overhead for deleting elements in the tree, because it requires either that remaining elements be shifted to remain contiguous or that a list of unused locations be maintained.

This same strategy can also be used when tree structures need to be stored directly on disk. In this case, rather than using an array index as a pointer, each node stores the relative position in the file of its children so that an offset can be calculated given the base address of the file.

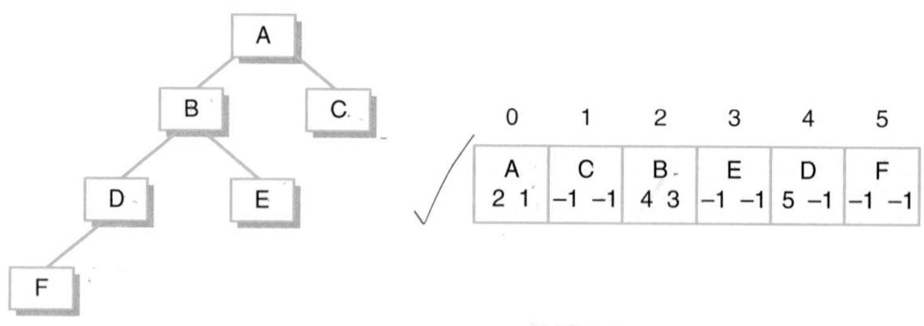

FIGURE 16.7 An array implementation of a binary tree using stored links

Linked Nodes

In a classic linked implementation, each tree node can be defined using a separate class, similar to what we did with the `LinearNode` class for linked lists. Each node would contain a reference to the element to be stored in that node and, instead of simply a `next` reference to the next node in the list, references for each of the possible children of the node.

If the tree being represented is a binary tree, the node can simply keep track of references to the left and right child nodes. However, if the implementation is for an n-ary or general tree, with many possible children per node, more child references will be needed. And at that point it would almost certainly be best to store an array or linked list of references to the child nodes instead of using individual references.

Trees organized in this way lend themselves to recursive processing for many operations. Each node can be thought of as the root of a subtree. This concept is depicted in Figure 16.8. We explore this implementation approach for a binary tree in the following section.

16.4 A Binary Tree Implementation

One possible set of operations for a binary tree is shown in the `BinaryTree` interface in Listing 16.1. Keep in mind that the definition of a collection is not universal. You will find variations in the operations defined for specific collections from one book to another.

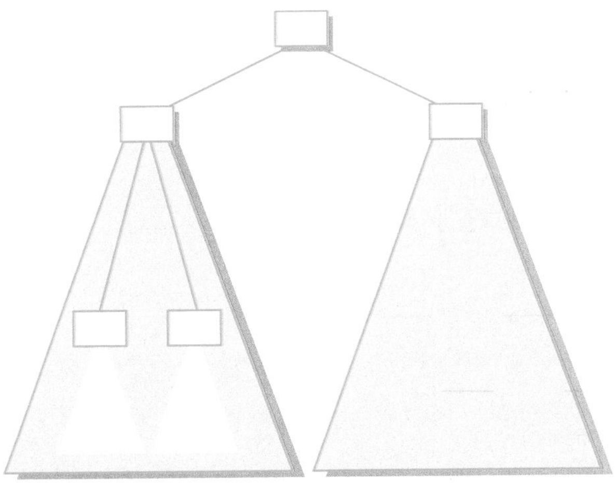

FIGURE 16.8 A tree and its subtrees

Listing 16.1

```
//********************************************************************
//  BinaryTree.java       Java Foundations
//
//  Defines the interface to a binary tree collection.
//********************************************************************

package javafoundations;

import java.util.Iterator;

public interface BinaryTree<T> extends Iterable<T>
{
   //  Returns the element stored in the root of the tree.
   public T getRootElement();

   //  Returns the left subtree of the root.
   public BinaryTree<T> getLeft();

   //  Returns the right subtree of the root.
   public BinaryTree<T> getRight();

   //  Returns true if the binary tree contains an element that
   //  matches the specified element and false otherwise.
   public boolean contains (T target);

   //  Returns a reference to the element in the tree matching
   //  the specified target.
   public T find (T target);

   //  Returns true if the binary tree contains no elements, and
   //  false otherwise.
   public boolean isEmpty();

   //  Returns the number of elements in this binary tree.
   public int size();

   //  Returns the string representation of the binary tree.
   public String toString();

   //  Returns a preorder traversal on the binary tree.
   public Iterator<T> preorder();
```

Listing **16.1** continued

```
    //  Returns an inorder traversal on the binary tree.
    public Iterator<T> inorder();

    //  Returns a postorder traversal on the binary tree.
    public Iterator<T> postorder();

    //  Performs a level-order traversal on the binary tree.
    public Iterator<T> levelorder();
}
```

Note that the `BinaryTree` interface has no methods to add a particular element to the tree, or to remove a particular element from the tree. In more refined versions of a binary tree, such as those described in the next chapter, the characteristics of those trees will dictate the semantics of adding and removing particular elements. For the general binary tree described here, the emphasis is on more basic operations. Even so, as we'll see, this type of tree is useful in certain situations.

How elements are added to and removed from a general binary tree depends on the tree's purpose.

Let's examine some of the issues related to implementing the `BinaryTree` interface. We'll focus on a linked implementation, using a recursive definition of a tree as discussed in the previous section.

The `LinkedBinaryTree` class, shown in Listing 16.2, provides an implementation of a binary tree with some operations left as programming projects. The tree stores elements of a generic type `T`, as we've done with previous collections. Like all well-designed collections, the user of the binary tree does not have to know anything about details of the underlying implementation.

The instance data of the `LinkedBinaryTree` class is a single link to the root node of the tree, represented by the `BTNode` class. The `BTNode` class, shown in Listing 16.3, is similar to the `LinearNode` class used in linked lists, but stores links to the left and right children of each node. This organization is depicted in Figure 16.9. The `LinkedBinaryTree` class provides the formal implementation of the `BinaryTree` interface, but its underlying structure relies heavily on the recursive `BTNode` structure.

There are three overloaded constructors for the `LinkedBinaryTree` class: one that creates an empty binary tree, one that creates a binary tree with a single root

Listing **16.2**

```
//********************************************************************
//  LinkedBinaryTree.java       Java Foundations
//
//  Implements a binary tree using a linked representation.
//********************************************************************

package javafoundations;

import java.util.Iterator;
import javafoundations.*;
import javafoundations.exceptions.*;

public class LinkedBinaryTree<T> implements BinaryTree<T>
{
   protected BTNode<T> root;

   //-----------------------------------------------------------------
   //  Creates an empty binary tree.
   //-----------------------------------------------------------------
   public LinkedBinaryTree()
   {
      root = null;
   }

   //-----------------------------------------------------------------
   //  Creates a binary tree with the specified element as its root.
   //-----------------------------------------------------------------
   public LinkedBinaryTree (T element)
   {
      root = new BTNode<T>(element);
   }

   //-----------------------------------------------------------------
   //  Creates a binary tree with the two specified subtrees.
   //-----------------------------------------------------------------
   public LinkedBinaryTree (T element, LinkedBinaryTree<T> left,
      LinkedBinaryTree<T> right)
   {
      root = new BTNode<T>(element);
      root.setLeft(left.root);
      root.setRight(right.root);
   }
```

Listing **16.2** continued

```
//-----------------------------------------------------------------
//  Returns the element stored in the root of the tree. Throws an
//  EmptyCollectionException if the tree is empty.
//-----------------------------------------------------------------
public T getRootElement()
{
   if (root == null)
      throw new EmptyCollectionException ("Get root operation "
         + "failed. The tree is empty.");

   return root.getElement();
}

//-----------------------------------------------------------------
//  Returns the left subtree of the root of this tree.
//-----------------------------------------------------------------
public LinkedBinaryTree<T> getLeft()
{
   if (root == null)
      throw new EmptyCollectionException ("Get left operation "
         + "failed. The tree is empty.");

   LinkedBinaryTree<T> result = new LinkedBinaryTree<T>();
   result.root = root.getLeft();

   return result;
}

//-----------------------------------------------------------------
//  Returns the element in this binary tree that matches the
//  specified target. Throws a ElementNotFoundException if the
//  target is not found.
//-----------------------------------------------------------------
public T find (T target)
{
   BTNode<T> node = null;

   if (root != null)
      node = root.find(target);

   if (node == null)
      throw new ElementNotFoundException("Find operation failed. "
         + "No such element in tree.");
```

Listing 16.2 continued

```
      return node.getElement();
   }

   //-----------------------------------------------------------------
   //  Returns the number of elements in this binary tree.
   //-----------------------------------------------------------------
   public int size()
   {
      int result = 0;

      if (root != null)
         result = root.count();

      return result;
   }

   //-----------------------------------------------------------------
   //  Populates and returns an iterator containing the elements in
   //  this binary tree using an inorder traversal.
   //-----------------------------------------------------------------
   public Iterator<T> inorder()
   {
      ArrayIterator<T> iter = new ArrayIterator<T>();

      if (root != null)
         root.inorder (iter);

      return iter;
   }

   //-----------------------------------------------------------------
   //  Populates and returns an iterator containing the elements in
   //  this binary tree using a levelorder traversal.
   //-----------------------------------------------------------------
   public Iterator<T> levelorder()
   {
      LinkedQueue<BTNode<T>> queue = new LinkedQueue<BTNode<T>>();
      ArrayIterator<T> iter = new ArrayIterator<T>();
```

Listing **16.2** continued

```
      if (root != null)
      {
         queue.enqueue(root);
         while (!queue.isEmpty())
         {
            BTNode<T> current = queue.dequeue();

            iter.add (current.getElement());

            if (current.getLeft() != null)
               queue.enqueue(current.getLeft());
            if (current.getRight() != null)
               queue.enqueue(current.getRight());
         }
      }

      return iter;
   }

   //-----------------------------------------------------------------
   //  Satisfies the Iterable interface using an inorder traversal.
   //-----------------------------------------------------------------
   public Iterator<T> iterator()
   {
      return inorder();
   }

   //-----------------------------------------------------------------
   //  The following methods are left as programming projects.
   //-----------------------------------------------------------------
   // public LinkedBinaryTree<T> getRight() { }
   // public boolean contains (T target) { }
   // public boolean isEmpty() { }
   // public String toString() { }
   // public Iterator<T> preorder() { }
   // public Iterator<T> postorder() { }
}
```

Listing 16.3

```
//********************************************************************
//  BTNode.java       Java Foundations
//
//  Represents a node in a binary tree with a left and right child.
//  Therefore this class also represents the root of a subtree.
//********************************************************************

package javafoundations;

public class BTNode<T>
{
   protected T element;
   protected BTNode<T> left, right;

   //-----------------------------------------------------------------
   //  Creates a new tree node with the specified data.
   //-----------------------------------------------------------------
   public BTNode (T element)
   {
      this.element = element;
      left = right = null;
   }

   //-----------------------------------------------------------------
   //  Returns the element stored in this node.
   //-----------------------------------------------------------------
   public T getElement()
   {
      return element;
   }

   //-----------------------------------------------------------------
   //  Sets the element stored in this node.
   //-----------------------------------------------------------------
   public void setElement (T element)
   {
      this.element = element;
   }

   //-----------------------------------------------------------------
   //  Returns the left subtree of this node.
   //-----------------------------------------------------------------
   public BTNode<T> getLeft()
```

Listing **16.3** continued

```
   {
      return left;
   }

   //-----------------------------------------------------------------
   //  Sets the left child of this node.
   //-----------------------------------------------------------------
   public void setLeft (BTNode<T> left)
   {
      this.left = left;
   }

   //-----------------------------------------------------------------
   //  Returns the right subtree of this node.
   //-----------------------------------------------------------------
   public BTNode<T> getRight()
   {
      return right;
   }

   //-----------------------------------------------------------------
   //  Sets the right child of this node.
   //-----------------------------------------------------------------
   public void setRight (BTNode<T> right)
   {
      this.right = right;
   }

   //-----------------------------------------------------------------
   //  Returns the element in this subtree that matches the
   //  specified target. Returns null if the target is not found.
   //-----------------------------------------------------------------
   public BTNode<T> find (T target)
   {
      BTNode<T> result = null;

      if (element.equals(target))
         result = this;
      else
      {
         if (left != null)
            result = left.find(target);
         if (result == null && right != null)
```

Listing **16.3** continued

```
            result = right.find(target);
        }

        return result;
    }

    //-----------------------------------------------------------------
    //  Returns the number of nodes in this subtree.
    //-----------------------------------------------------------------
    public int count()
    {
        int result = 1;

        if (left != null)
            result += left.count();

        if (right != null)
            result += right.count();

        return result;
    }

    //-----------------------------------------------------------------
    //  Performs an inorder traversal on this subtree, updating the
    //  specified iterator.
    //-----------------------------------------------------------------
    public void inorder (ArrayIterator<T> iter)
    {
        if (left != null)
            left.inorder (iter);

        iter.add (element);

        if (right != null)
            right.inorder (iter);
    }

    //-----------------------------------------------------------------
    //  The following methods are left as programming projects.
    //-----------------------------------------------------------------
    // public void preorder(ArrayIterator<T> iter) { }
    // public void postorder(ArrayIterator<T> iter) { }
}
```

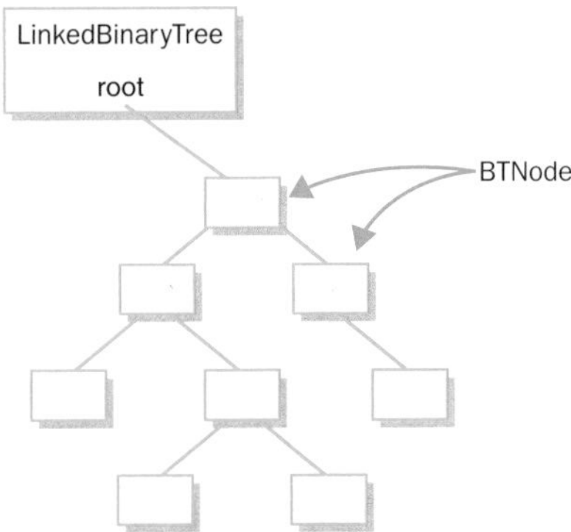

FIGURE 16.9 The implementation strategy for a linked binary tree

node but no children, and one that creates a binary tree with a root node and two subtrees. In the last case, either parameter representing the subtrees could be null.

Without any methods to add elements to the tree, the tree must be created from the bottom up using the `LinkedBinaryTree` constructors. That is, the lowest subtrees are constructed first, and used to create larger subtrees. The last step is to create the tree that holds the root element of the entire tree.

The `getRootElement` method provides access to the element stored in the node. The `getLeft` method returns the entire left subtree as a newly constructed `LinkedBinaryTree` object. The `getRight` method would operate similarly. Note that the `BTNode` class has its own version of `getLeft` and `getRight`, which return `BTNode` objects.

The `find` method in `LinkedBinaryTree` throws an exception if the target element is not found or the tree is empty. The actual search is performed in the find method of the `BTNode` class. It checks to see if the target element is stored in the current node, then calls `find` on the subtrees as needed. It uses the `equals` method of the stored element to determine equality. Like we've seen in other collections, this approach puts the definition of equality under the control of the class being stored in the tree. The `find` method in `BSTNode` returns `null` if the target element is not found. The `contains` method in `LinkedBinaryTree`, which is left as a programming project, could use the `find` method to determine if the target element exists in the tree.

The number of elements in the tree is equal to the number of nodes in the left subtree plus the number of nodes in the right subtree plus 1 (for the root). The `size` method in `LinkedBinaryTree` calls the `count` method in `BTNode`, which computes this value recursively. It's possible to use an integer variable to keep track of the number of elements in the collection, as we did in previous collections, but we chose to show this approach here.

The `inorder` method returns an iterator that allows the user to step through the elements of the tree in an inorder traversal. It uses an `ArrayIterator` object, as we've used in previous collections, to store the elements in the proper order. The initial call to the `inorder` method sets up an empty `ArrayIterator` object, then populates it with a call to the version of `inorder` in `BTNode` that recursively processes the subtrees. When the node is "visited," it is added to the iterator. The `preorder` and `postorder` methods will follow similar logic, visiting the nodes in the proper order for each traversal.

The `levelorder` method produces a similar iterator, with the elements in the proper order for a level-order traversal. This method follows the algorithm described earlier in this chapter, using a queue to store the nodes during processing. Unlike the other traversals, the `levelorder` method does not rely on a corresponding method in the `BTNode` class.

Finally, the `iterator` method is included to satisfy the `Iterable` interface. It simply returns the iterator produced by the `inorder` method. There is no particular reason for choosing an inorder traversal—any of the other three traversals could have been used.

The `getRight`, `contains`, `isEmpty`, `toString`, `preorder`, and `postorder` methods in `LinkedBinaryTree` are left as programming projects, which require some methods in `BTNode` as well.

16.5 Decision Trees

Let's use the binary tree implementation to solve a particular problem. A *decision tree* is a tree whose nodes represent decision points, and whose children represent the options available at that point. The leaves of a decision tree represent the possible conclusions that might be drawn based on the answers.

A simple decision tree, with yes/no questions, can be modeled by a binary tree. Figure 16.10 shows a decision tree that helps to diagnose the cause of back pain. For each question, the left child represents the answer No and the right child represents the answer Yes. To perform a diagnosis, begin with the question at the root, following the appropriate path based on the answers until a leaf is reached.

Decision trees are sometimes used as a basis for an *expert system*, which is software that attempts to represent the knowledge of an expert in a particular field. For instance, a particular expert system might be used to model the expertise of a

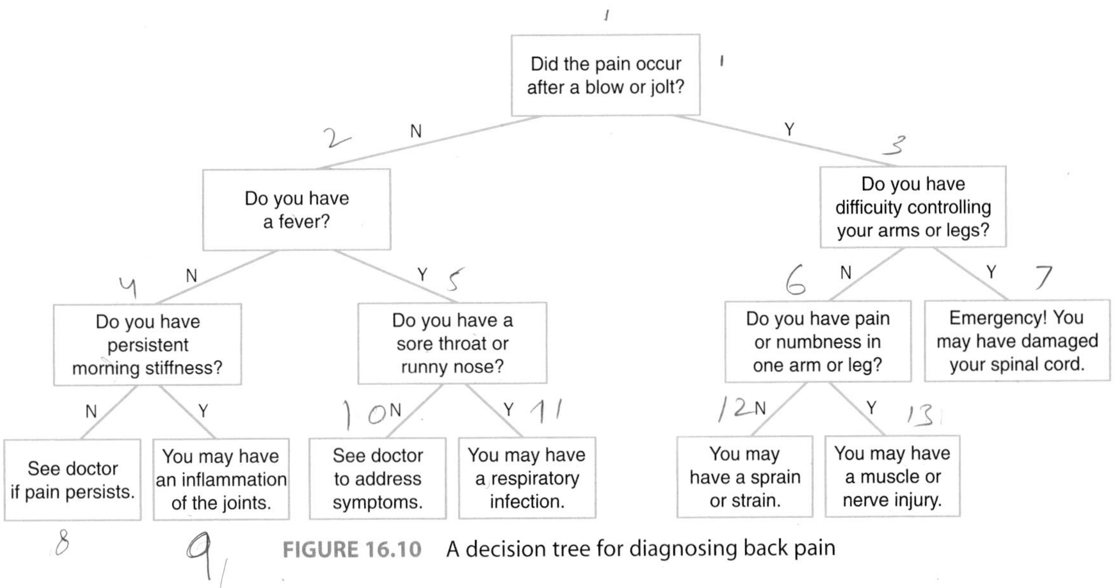

FIGURE 16.10 A decision tree for diagnosing back pain

doctor, car mechanic, or accountant. Obviously, the greatly simplified decision tree in Figure 16.10 is not fleshed out enough to do a good job diagnosing the real cause of back pain, but it should give you a feel for how such systems might work.

A decision tree can be used as the basis for an expert system.

Let's look at an example that uses the `LinkedBinaryTree` implementation discussed in the previous section to represent a decision tree. The program in Listing 16.4 uses the tree pictured in Figure 16.9 to hold a dialog with the user and draw a conclusion.

The tree is constructed and used in the `BackPainExpert` class, shown in Listing 16.5. The only instance data is the variable `tree` that represents the entire decision tree, which is defined to store `String` objects as elements.

The constructor of `BackPainExpert` first defines the various string elements to be stored in the tree nodes. Then the nodes themselves are created, with no children for the leaves and with previously defined nodes (or subtrees) as children for internal nodes. The tree is basically created from the bottom up.

The `diagnose` method uses the variable `current` to indicate the current node in the tree being processed, beginning at the root. The `while` loop continues until a leaf is found. The current question is printed, and the answer is read from the user. If the answer is No, `current` is updated to point to the left child. Otherwise, it is updated to point to the right child. After falling out of the loop, the element stored in the leaf (the conclusion) is printed.

Listing **16.4**

```
//********************************************************************
//  BackPainAnalyzer.java       Java Foundations
//
//  Demonstrates the use of a binary tree.
//********************************************************************

public class BackPainAnalyzer
{
   //-----------------------------------------------------------------
   //  Asks questions of the user to diagnose a medical problem.
   //-----------------------------------------------------------------
   public static void main (String[] args)
   {
      BackPainExpert expert = new BackPainExpert();
      expert.diagnose();
   }
}
```

Output

```
=====================================================
So, you're having back pain.
Did the pain occur after a blow or jolt?
Y
Do you have difficulty controlling your arms or legs?
N
Do you have pain or numbness in one arm or leg?
Y
You may have a muscle or nerve injury.
=====================================================
```

Listing 16.5

```
//********************************************************************
//  BackPainExpert.java       Java Foundations
//
//  Represents a simple expert system for back pain diagnosis.
//********************************************************************

import javafoundations.*;
import java.util.Scanner;

public class BackPainExpert
{
   private LinkedBinaryTree<String> tree;

   //-----------------------------------------------------------------
   //  Sets up the diagnosis question tree.
   //-----------------------------------------------------------------
   public BackPainExpert()
   {
      String e1 = "Did the pain occur after a blow or jolt?";
      String e2 = "Do you have a fever?";
      String e3 = "Do you have difficulty controlling your arms or legs?";
      String e4 = "Do you have persistent morning stiffness?";
      String e5 = "Do you have a sore throat or runny nose?";
      String e6 = "Do you have pain or numbness in one arm or leg?";
      String e7 = "Emergency! You may have damaged your spinal cord.";
      String e8 = "See doctor if pain persists.";
      String e9 = "You may have an inflammation of the joints.";
      String e10 = "See doctor to address symptoms.";
      String e11 = "You may have a respiratory infection.";
      String e12 = "You may have a sprain or strain.";
      String e13 = "You may have a muscle or nerve injury.";

      LinkedBinaryTree<String> n2, n3, n4, n5, n6, n7, n8, n9,
         n10, n11, n12, n13;

      n8 = new LinkedBinaryTree<String>(e8);
      n9 = new LinkedBinaryTree<String>(e9);
      n4 = new LinkedBinaryTree<String>(e4, n8, n9);

      n10 = new LinkedBinaryTree<String>(e10);
      n11 = new LinkedBinaryTree<String>(e11);
      n5 = new LinkedBinaryTree<String>(e5, n10, n11);
```

Listing **16.5** continued

```
        n12 = new LinkedBinaryTree<String>(e12);
        n13 = new LinkedBinaryTree<String>(e13);
        n6 = new LinkedBinaryTree<String>(e6, n12, n13);

        n7 = new LinkedBinaryTree<String>(e7);

        n2 = new LinkedBinaryTree<String>(e2, n4, n5);
        n3 = new LinkedBinaryTree<String>(e3, n6, n7);

        tree = new LinkedBinaryTree<String>(e1, n2, n3);
    }

    //-----------------------------------------------------------------
    //  Follows the diagnosis tree based on user responses.
    //-----------------------------------------------------------------
    public void diagnose()
    {
        Scanner scan = new Scanner(System.in);
        LinkedBinaryTree<String> current = tree;

        System.out.println ("So, you're having back pain.");
        while (current.size() > 1)
        {
            System.out.println (current.getRootElement());
            if (scan.nextLine().equalsIgnoreCase("N"))
                current = current.getLeft();
            else
                current = current.getRight();
        }

        System.out.println (current.getRootElement());
    }
}
```

Summary of Key Concepts

- A tree is a nonlinear structure whose elements are organized into a hierarchy.
- The order of a tree specifies the maximum number of children any node in the tree may have.
- A balanced n-ary tree with m elements will have height $\log_n m$.
- There are four basic techniques for traversing a tree.
- A queue can be used to store the elements of a tree during a level-order traversal.
- One strategy for implementing binary trees using arrays places the left child of element n at position (2n +1) and the right child at position (2*(n+1)).
- A stored link strategy for an array-based tree implementation allows array positions to be allocated contiguously regardless of the completeness of the tree.
- How elements are added to and removed from a general binary tree depends on the tree's purpose.
- A decision tree can be used as the basis for an expert system.

Self-Review Questions

SR 16.1 What is a tree?

SR 16.2 What is a node?

SR 16.3 What is the root of a tree?

SR 16.4 What is a leaf?

SR 16.5 What is an internal node?

SR 16.6 Define the height of a tree.

SR 16.7 Define the level of a node.

SR 16.8 What is a binary tree?

SR 16.9 Describe a balanced tree.

SR 16.10 Describe a complete tree.

SR 16.11 Describe a full tree.

SR 16.12 Compare and contrast preorder and postorder tree traversals.

SR 16.13 What are the advantages and disadvantages of implementing binary trees using computed links?

SR 16.14 What is a decision tree?

Exercises

Use the following tree to answer Exercises 16.1–16.16.

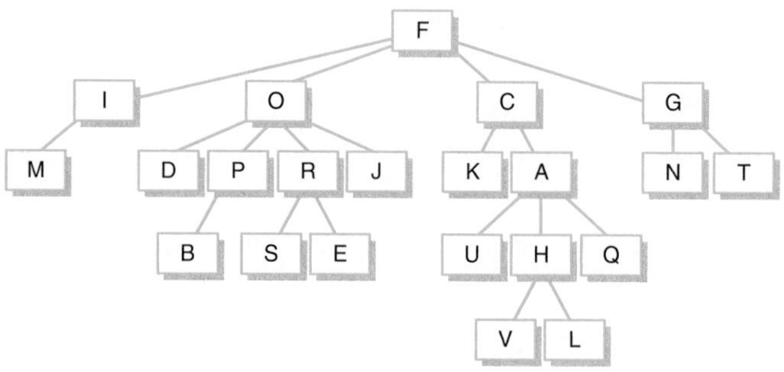

EX 16.1 Which node is the root? Explain.

EX 16.2 Which nodes are leaves?

EX 16.3 What are the siblings of node R?

EX 16.4 What are the siblings of node B?

EX 16.5 Is G an internal node? Explain.

EX 16.6 Draw the subtrees of node C.

EX 16.7 What are the descendents of node A?

EX 16.8 What are the ancestors of node S?

EX 16.9 What is the path from the root to node L?

EX 16.10 What nodes are at level 1 of the tree?

EX 16.11 What is the height of this tree?

EX 16.12 Is this tree a binary tree? Explain.

EX 16.13 What is the minimum order of this tree, based on the picture?

EX 16.14 Is this tree balanced? Explain.

EX 16.15 Is this tree complete? Explain.

EX 16.16 Is this tree full? Explain.

Use the following binary tree to answer Exercises 16.17–16.21.

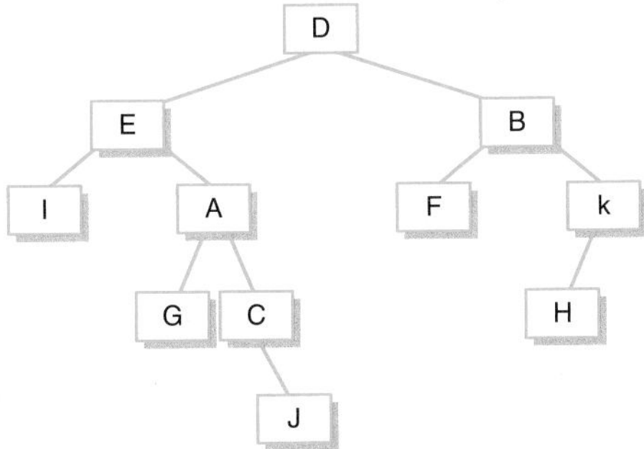

EX 16.17 Produce a preorder traversal of this tree.

EX 16.18 Produce an inorder traversal of this tree.

EX 16.19 Produce a postorder traversal of this tree.

EX 16.20 Produce a level-order traversal of this tree.

EX 16.21 Draw an array similar to the one shown in Figure 16.6 to represent this tree using the computed links implementation strategy.

EX 16.22 Is a full tree necessarily a complete tree? Explain.

EX 16.23 What do we mean when we say a traversal "visits" a tree node?

EX 16.24 Are trees of the type discussed in this chapter appropriate for modeling a family tree? Explain.

EX 16.25 What is the time complexity of the `find` operation in the `LinkedBinaryTree` class?

EX 16.26 What is the time complexity of the `inorder` operation in the `LinkedBinaryTree` class?

Programming Projects

PP 16.1 Complete the implementation of the `LinkedBinaryTree` class presented in this chapter. Specifically, complete the implementations of the `getRight`, `contains`, `isEmpty`, `toString`, `preorder`, and `postorder` operations. Some of these operations will require corresponding methods in the `BTNode` class.

PP 16.2 Implement a class called `CLArrayBinaryTree` that satisfies the `BinaryTree` interface. The class should represent the tree using the computed link implementation strategy described in this chapter.

PP 16.3 Implement a class called `SLArrayBinaryTree` that satisfies the `BinaryTree` interface. The class should represent the tree using the stored link implementation strategy described in this chapter.

PP 16.4 Modify the `BackPainAnalyzer` program so that the tree used has three additional questions (don't worry about the accuracy of the medical expertise).

PP 16.5 Design and implement a program that uses a decision tree to represent the process a car mechanic might use to determine the cause of an automotive problem.

PP 16.6 In the game called 20 Questions, one person thinks of an object, and another person tries to determine what the object is by asking yes-or-no questions. The goal is to determine the object in as few questions as possible. Design and implement a program that uses a decision tree to play a version of the 20 Questions game, based on a predetermined set of possible objects.

PP 16.7 An *ancestor tree* illustrates a person's biological heritage. Design and implement a program that uses a binary tree to represent an ancestor tree. Each node represents a person, and a node's two children represent that person's parents.

PP 16.8 Recall from Chapter 2 that an *expression tree* can be used to represent an arithmetic expression. Design and implement a program that uses a binary tree to represent an expression tree. Provide a method that evaluates the tree to determine the result of the expression.

Answers to Self-Review Questions

SR 16.1 A tree is a nonlinear collection defined by the concept that each node in the tree, other than the first node or root node, has exactly one parent.

SR 16.2 A node in a tree refers to a location in the tree where an element is stored.

SR 16.3 The root of a tree is the node at the top of the tree that does not have a parent. The root node is considered to be the "entry point" into the tree.

SR 16.4 A leaf is a tree node that does not have any children.

SR 16.5 An internal node is any non-root node that has at least one child.

SR 16.6 The height of the tree is the length of the longest path from the root to a leaf.

SR 16.7 The level of a node is measured by the number of links that must be followed to reach that node from the root.

SR 16.8 A binary tree is a tree whose nodes can have no more than two children. Binary trees are quite useful in many problem-solving situations.

SR 16.9 A balanced tree is a tree whose leaf nodes are all on one level or at most two adjacent levels.

SR 16.10 A complete tree is a balanced tree in which all leaf nodes are as far left in the tree as possible.

SR 16.11 A full tree is an n-ary tree in which all leaf nodes are at the same level and every node is either a leaf or has exactly n children.

SR 16.12 Tree traversals visit each element in the tree. The type of traversal dictates when a node is visited. A preorder traversal visits the root before visiting either subtree, and a postorder traversal visits the root after visiting both subtrees.

SR 16.13 The computed link strategy does not have to store the links between a parent to child node since that relationship is determined by its position in the array. However, this strategy may lead to substantial wasted space for trees that are not balanced and/or not complete.

SR 16.14 A decision tree is a tree used to represent the questions and responses that can be used to determine an appropriate conclusion. A decision tree can be used as the basis of an expert system, such as a medical diagnosis system.

Search Trees and Heaps

Chapter Objectives

- Discuss the nature of a binary search tree.
- Explore a linked implementation of a binary search tree.
- Discuss binary search tree rotations.
- Discuss how search trees are implemented in the Java Collections API.
- Define a heap and discuss its implementation.
- Discuss a heap sort.

Search trees, especially binary search trees, and heaps are among the most useful software structures. In this chapter, we first explore the concept of a binary search tree and its implementation. We examine algorithms for adding and removing elements from binary search trees and for maintaining balanced trees. We then explore heaps, another extension of binary trees, and their implementation.

17.1 Binary Search Trees

A *search tree* is a tree whose elements are organized to facilitate finding a particular element when needed. That is, the elements in a search tree are stored in a particular way relative to each other so that finding an element doesn't require searching the entire tree.

A *binary search tree* is a binary tree that, for each node n, the left subtree of n contains elements less than the element stored in n, and the right subtree of n contains elements that are greater than or equal to the element stored in n.

A binary search tree is a binary tree in which, for each node, the elements in the left subtree are less than the parent, and the elements in the right subtree are greater than or equal to the parent.

Figure 17.1 shows a binary search tree containing integer values. Examine it carefully, noting the relationships among the nodes. Every element in the left subtree of the root is less than 45, and every element in the right subtree of the root is greater than 45. This relationship is true for every node in the tree.

Equal values are stored in the right subtree, as in the case of 42 in Figure 17.1. This decision, however, is arbitrary. Equal values could be stored to the left as long as all operations managing the tree were consistent with that decision.

To determine if a particular target element exists in the tree, we follow the appropriate path starting at the root, moving left or right from the current node, depending on whether the target is less than or greater than the element in that node. We will eventually either find the element we're looking for or encounter the end of the path, which means the target is not in the tree.

This process should remind you of the binary search algorithm we discussed in Chapter 13. It is, in fact, the same logic. In Chapter 13, we searched a sorted

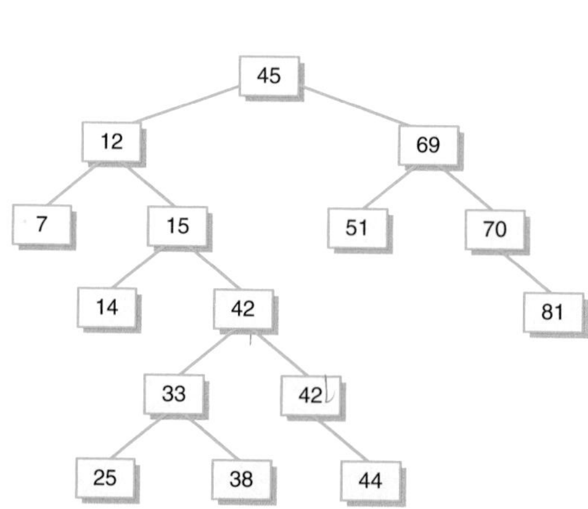

FIGURE 17.1 A binary search tree of integers

array and jumped to an appropriate index. With a binary search tree, the structure of the tree itself provides the search path.

The binary search tree in Figure 17.1 is only one of many that could be constructed using the same elements. The particular shape a binary search tree has depends on the order in which elements were added to the tree (as we explore in the next section) and on any additional processing used to reshape it. The most efficient binary search trees are balanced, so that approximately half of the viable candidates are eliminated with each comparison.

The most efficient binary search trees are balanced, so that half of the viable candidates are eliminated with each comparison.

Of course, binary search trees can hold any kind of data or object, as long as we have a way to determine their relative ordering. Objects that implement the `Comparable` interface, for instance, can be put into a binary search tree because we can determine, using the `compareTo` method, which object comes before another. For simplicity, we will use integers in the examples in this chapter.

Note that if you perform an inorder traversal (as described in Chapter 16) on a binary search tree, the elements will be visited in sorted order, ascending.

Adding an Element to a Binary Search Tree

The process of adding a new element to a binary search tree is similar to the process of searching the tree. A new element is added as a leaf node on the tree. Starting at the root, follow the path dictated by the elements in each node until there is no child node in the appropriate direction. At that point, add the new element as a leaf.

For example, let's add the following elements, in order, to a new binary search tree:

77 24 58 82 17 40 97

The first value, 77, becomes the root of our new tree. Next, because 24 is less than 77, it is added as the left child of the root. The next value, 58, is less than 77, so it goes in the left subtree of the root, but it is greater than 24, so it is added as the right child of 24. The value 82 is greater than the root value of 77, and thus is added as its right child. The value 17 is less than 77 and less than 24, so it is added as the left child of 24. This process is shown in Figure 17.2, and continues for the remaining items in our example.

Without any additional processing to change the shape of the tree, the order in which the values are added dictates its shape. If that order is particularly skewed one way or another, the resulting tree is not particularly useful. For example, adding the following values in order creates the tree depicted in Figure 17.3:

20 24 37 28 44 47 69

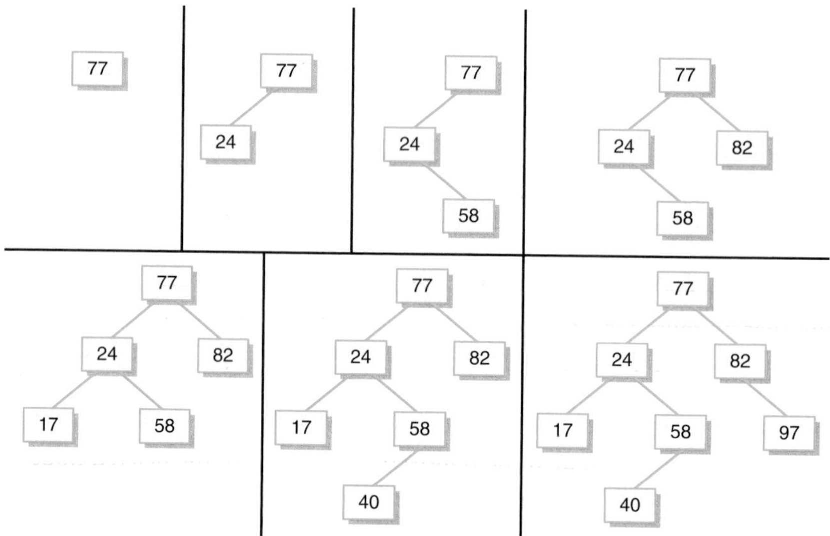

FIGURE 17.2 Adding elements to a binary search tree

Without any additional processing, the shape of a binary search tree is dictated by the order in which elements are added to it.

The tree in Figure 17.3 is called a *degenerate tree* because it is highly unbalanced. If the input is completely sorted, the binary search tree essentially degenerates into a sorted linked list. The value of a binary search tree comes from being able to exclude large amounts of the data with each comparison, and a degenerate tree eliminates that value.

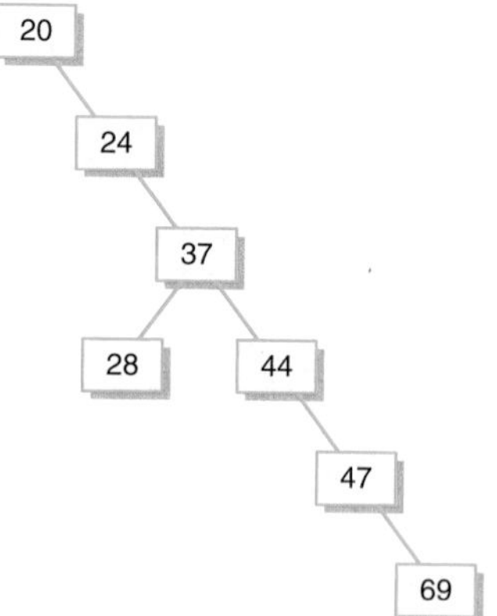

FIGURE 17.3 A degenerate binary search tree

Removing an Element from a Binary Search Tree

In linear data structures, removing a target element generally involved finding the element, then resetting a reference so that the node before the target pointed to the node after the target. For binary search trees, the process is not as simple, because there are potentially two children for each node. Keep in mind that after removing the element, the resulting tree must still be a valid binary search tree, with appropriate relationships among all the elements.

Consider the binary search tree shown in Figure 17.4. It points out the three situations that we must consider when removing an element from a binary search tree:

- Situation 1: If the node to be removed is a leaf (has no children), it can simply be deleted.
- Situation 2: If the node to be removed has one child, the deleted node is replaced by its child.
- Situation 3: If the node to be removed has two children, an appropriate node is found from lower in the tree and used to replace the node. The children of the removed node become the children of the replacement node.

There are three situations to consider when removing an element from a binary search tree, two of which are straightforward.

The first situation is trivial. If we want to remove a leaf node, such as 88 or 67, it can simply be deleted. The resulting tree remains a valid binary search tree.

The second situation is pretty straightforward too. If we want to remove a node with only one child, such as 51 or 62, the child can replace the deleted parent. That is, 57 could replace 51, and

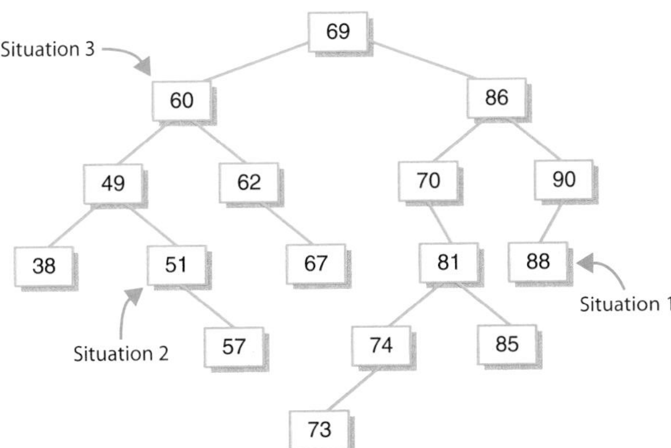

FIGURE 17.4 The three situations to consider when removing an element from a binary search tree

67 could replace 62. The child's relationship to the rest of the tree will remain intact. This solution works even if the child has subtrees of its own. The node containing 70, for instance, could be replaced by 81, even though 81 has its own children. The entire subtree has the appropriate relationship to the new parent (86).

The third situation is the most interesting. Suppose we want to remove a node that has two children, such as 60. Neither child can be used as a replacement without a significant reconstruction of the tree. A good choice to replace the node is its *inorder successor*, which is the element that would follow the deleted element in an inorder traversal (the next highest value). For example, in the tree in Figure 17.4, the inorder successor of 60 is 62, the inorder successor of 70 is 73, and the inorder successor of 69 is 70.

When removing a node with two children from a binary search tree, the inorder successor is a good choice to replace it.

So to remove a node that has two children, we first remove its inorder successor from the tree, and then use it to replace the node that's actually being removed. The existing children of the node being removed become the children of the replacement node.

But what about the existing children of the inorder successor? Well, it's guaranteed that the inorder successor of a node will not have a left child. If it did, that child would be the inorder successor. Therefore, the inorder successor will either be a leaf or have one (right) child. So removing the inorder successor falls under one of the first two situations for removing a node.

For example, to remove element 86 from the tree in Figure 17.4, we find its inorder successor (88), remove it from the tree (which is trivial because it's a leaf), and replace 86 with it. The node containing 70 becomes the left child of 88, and the node containing 90 becomes the right child of 88.

Let's walk through another example of removing a node with two children. Starting over with the tree in Figure 17.4, let's delete the root (69). First we find its inorder successor (70) and remove it from the tree, moving the subtree with root 81 up to replace it. Then the element 69 is replaced with the element 70. The resulting tree is shown in Figure 17.5.

17.2 Binary Search Tree Implementation

Having explored the conceptual nature of a binary search tree and discussed the techniques for some key operations, let's now discuss its implementation. Because the essence of a binary search tree is a binary tree, we can base our implementation on the `BinaryTree` interface and `LinkedBinaryTree` class that we discussed in Chapter 16.

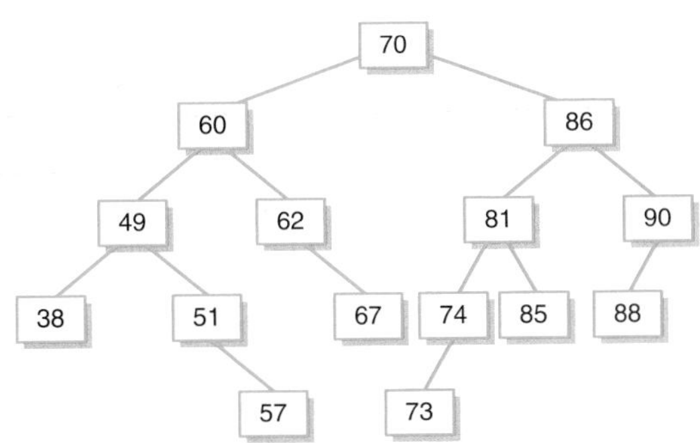

FIGURE 17.5 The resulting tree after the root is removed

Listing 17.1 shows the `BinarySearchTree` interface, which is derived from the `BinaryTree` interface. This relationship is shown in the UML diagram in Figure 17.6. The search tree interface includes methods to add an element to the tree, to find a target element in the tree, and to remove an element from the tree. As a convenience, we also choose to include methods that find the minimum and maximum values in the tree.

Listing 17.1

```
//********************************************************************
//  BinarySearchTree.java       Java Foundations
//
//  Defines the interface to a binary search tree.
//********************************************************************

package javafoundations;

public interface BinarySearchTree<T extends Comparable<T>> extends BinaryTree<T>
{
   //  Adds the specified element to the tree.
   public void add (T element);

   //  Finds and returns the element in the tree matching the
   //  specified target. Overrides the find method of BinaryTree.
   public T find (T target);

   //  Returns the minimum value in the binary search tree.
```

Listing 17.1 continued

```
    public T findMin();

    //  Returns the maximum value in the binary search tree.
    public T findMax();

    //  Removes and returns the specified element from the tree.
    public T remove (T target);
}
```

The `BinarySearchTree` interface is defined to operate on a generic type `T`, which extends `Comparable`. All elements added to a binary search tree must be `Comparable` in order to determine their relative position within the tree. Generic types were introduced in Chapter 14.

The `LinkedBinarySearchTree` class is shown in Listing 17.2, with some methods left as programming projects. It extends the `LinkedBinaryTree` class (from Chapter 16), inheriting the classic methods such as `size` and `isEmpty`, as well as the various iterator methods that provide various traversals of the tree. It also inherits the instance data, including the `left` and `right` references to the child nodes.

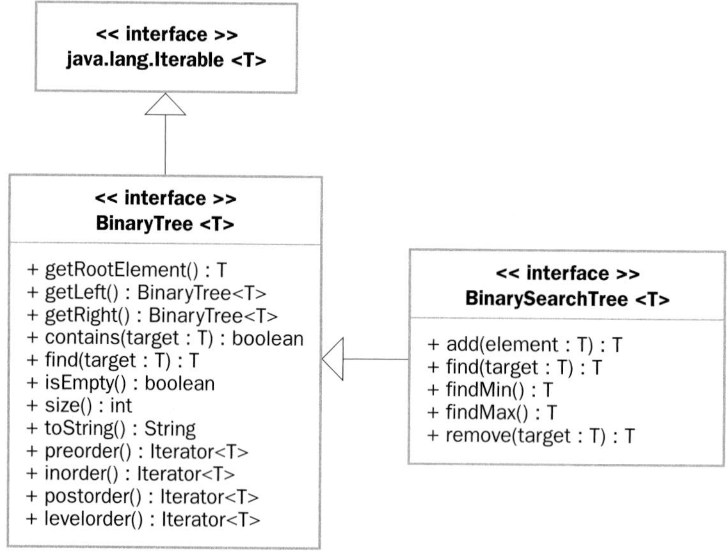

FIGURE 17.6 A UML diagram of the `BinarySearchTree` interface

Listing 17.2

```
//*******************************************************************
//  LinkedBinarySearchTree.java       Java Foundations
//
//  Implements the binary tree using a linked representation.
//*******************************************************************

package javafoundations;

import javafoundations.*;
import javafoundations.exceptions.*;

public class LinkedBinarySearchTree<T extends Comparable<T>>
   extends LinkedBinaryTree<T> implements BinarySearchTree<T>
{
   //-----------------------------------------------------------------
   //  Creates an empty binary search tree.
   //-----------------------------------------------------------------
   public LinkedBinarySearchTree()
   {
      super();
   }

   //-----------------------------------------------------------------
   //  Creates a binary search tree with the specified element at its
   //  root.
   //-----------------------------------------------------------------
   public LinkedBinarySearchTree (T element)
   {
      root = new BSTNode<T>(element);
   }

   //-----------------------------------------------------------------
   //  Adds the specified element to this binary search tree.
   //-----------------------------------------------------------------
   public void add (T item)
   {
      if (root == null)
         root = new BSTNode<T>(item);
      else
         ((BSTNode)root).add(item);
   }
```

Listing 17.2 continued

```
   //-----------------------------------------------------------------
   //  Removes and returns the element matching the specified target
   //  from this binary search tree. Throws an ElementNotFoundException
   //  if the target is not found.
   //-----------------------------------------------------------------
   public T remove (T target)
   {
      BSTNode<T> node = null;

      if (root != null)
         node = ((BSTNode)root).find(target);

      if (node == null)
         throw new ElementNotFoundException ("Remove operation failed. "
            + "No such element in tree.");

      root = ((BSTNode)root).remove(target);

      return node.getElement();
   }

   //-----------------------------------------------------------------
   //  The following methods are left as programming projects.
   //-----------------------------------------------------------------
   // public T findMin() { }
   // public T findMax() { }
}
```

Similar to our approach to the implementation of a general binary tree, the `LinkedBinarySearchTree` interacts with a separate set of objects that represent the nodes of the tree. The `BSTNode` class, shown in Listing 17.3, is derived from the `BTNode` class from Chapter 16. Like `LinkedBinarySearchTree`, the `BSTNode` class manages `Comparable` elements.

The `LinkedBinarySearchTree` class inherits the reference to the root node from `LinkedBinaryTree`. Similarly, the `BSTNode` class inherits the `left` and `right` references to child nodes from the `BTNode` class. Because of their original declarations, these references will need to be cast into their true class to be able to carry out certain operations.

Listing 17.3

```
//*******************************************************************
//  BSTNode.java        Java Foundations
//
//  Represents a node in a binary search tree, storing Comparable
//  elements.
//*******************************************************************

package javafoundations;

public class BSTNode<T extends Comparable<T>> extends BTNode<T>
{
   //-----------------------------------------------------------------
   //  Creates a new tree node with the specified data.
   //-----------------------------------------------------------------
   public BSTNode (T element)
   {
      super(element);
   }

   //-----------------------------------------------------------------
   //  Adds a new node containing the specified element at the
   //  appropriate place in this tree.
   //-----------------------------------------------------------------
   public void add (T item)
   {
      if (item.compareTo(element) < 0)
         if (left == null)
            left = new BSTNode (item);
         else
            ((BSTNode)left).add (item);
      else
         if (right == null)
            right = new BSTNode (item);
         else
            ((BSTNode)right).add (item);
   }

   //-----------------------------------------------------------------
   //  Returns the node in this subtree whose element matches the
   //  specified target. Returns null if the target is not found.
   //  Overrides the find method of BTNode to capitalize on the
   //  binary search tree characteristics.
   //-----------------------------------------------------------------
```

Listing **17.3** continued

```
public BSTNode<T> find (T target)
{
   BSTNode<T> result = null;

   if (target.compareTo(element) == 0)
      result = this;
   else
   {
      if (target.compareTo(element) < 0)
      {
         if (left != null)
            result = ((BSTNode)left).find (target);
      }
      else
         if (right != null)
            result = ((BSTNode)right).find (target);
   }

   return result;
}

//-----------------------------------------------------------------
//  Removes the specified target from this subtree. Returns a
//  reference to the revised tree. The tree will be unchanged if
//  the target is not found.
//-----------------------------------------------------------------
public BSTNode<T> remove(T target)
{
   BSTNode<T> result = this;

   if (target.compareTo(element) == 0)
   {
      if (left == null && right == null)
         result = null;
      else if (left != null && right == null)
         result = (BSTNode)left;
      else if (left == null && right != null)
         result = (BSTNode)right;
      else
      {
         result = getSuccessor();
         result.left = left;
         result.right = right;
```

Listing 17.3 continued

```
         }
      }
      else
         if (target.compareTo(element) < 0)
            if (left != null)
               left = ((BSTNode)left).remove(target);
         else
            if (right != null)
               right = ((BSTNode)right).remove(target);

      return result;
   }

   //-----------------------------------------------------------------
   //  Finds and returns the node containing the inorder successor of
   //  this node, and then removes the successor from its original
   //  location in the tree.
   //-----------------------------------------------------------------
   protected BSTNode<T> getSuccessor()
   {
      BSTNode<T> successor = (BSTNode)right;

      while (successor.getLeft() != null)
         successor = (BSTNode) successor.getLeft();

      ((BSTNode)right).remove (successor.getElement());

      return successor;
   }
}
```

The first constructor of the `LinkedBinarySearchTree` class simply invokes the parent's constructor using the `super` reference. The parent constructor sets the element and child references to null. The second constructor creates a new `BSTNode` object, storing the element.

The `add` method of `LinkedBinarySearchTree` creates a new root node if the tree is currently empty. Otherwise, it invokes the `add` method of `BSTNode`, which searches for the location to add the new element as a leaf. It does so by first checking to see if the new element is less than the current root element. If so, it checks if a left child exists. If there is no left child, it creates a new node containing the new element, and adds it as the new left child. If the left subtree exists, the `add` method is invoked again to add the child to the left subtree. Similar logic is used to add the new element to the right subtree if appropriate. Note that this code ensures that if the new element and root element are equal, the new node is added to the right subtree.

The `LinkedBinarySearchTree` class relies on the `find` method inherited from the `LinkedBinaryTree` class to satisfy that operation in the interface. However, it invokes the `find` method in `BSTNode`, which overrides the version inherited from its parent. This version of the `find` method first checks if the current element is a match, and if so returns that node. If not, it determines if the target would lie in the left or right subtree, and calls `find` again on the subtree. If the appropriate child does not exist, then the element does not exist in the tree, and a `null` value is returned.

It's important to understand why the `find` method in `BSTNode` overrides the version of the `find` method provided by the `BTNode` class. Because the elements in a general binary tree are not ordered, the `find` method of the `BTNode` class examines every element in the tree if necessary. The `find` method of `BSTNode` is much more efficient, narrowing down the search considerably with each comparison. This distinction is the essence of a binary search tree.

The `remove` method in `LinkedBinarySearchTree` obtains the target element using the `find` method so that it can return the removed value. If the tree is empty, or the target element is not found, an exception is thrown. If the element is found, the `remove` method of `BSTNode` is called to delete the specified element and return a reference to the revised tree. This return value is key to the processing of this method. As the recursive calls to the `remove` method unfold, the tree is essentially "rebuilt" with potentially revised subtrees. Keep in mind that it may be the root node that is removed. The returned tree will be unchanged if the target element is not found in the tree.

The outer `if` statement in the `remove` method in `BSTNode` determines if the element to be removed matches the root element. If not, the `else` portion determines if the target will be found in the left or right subtree, and calls the `remove` method again appropriately. This logic is similar to the processing in the `find` method.

If the target matches the root element, the `remove` method deletes the node. To do so, it determines which of the three situations described in the previous section applies. If neither child exists, the return value is set to `null`. When the method returns, the appropriate parent's child reference is set to `null`, effectively deleting the node. If either the left or right subtree exists (but not both), the return value is set to that subtree. Thus, when the method returns, the subtree is "moved up" to replace the deleted node.

If none of those situations applies, then both child nodes must exist, which is the interesting third situation. When that happens, the `getSuccessor` support method is called, which returns a reference to the node containing the inorder successor of the element to be removed. The `left` and `right` child references of the replacement node are set to the corresponding subtrees of the node being deleted. The successor node, with its new subtrees, is returned from the `remove` method to replace the parent node's reference to the now deleted child.

In casual terms, the inorder successor of a node can be found by "going right" once, then "going left" as far as possible. Therefore, the `getSuccessor` method first sets the reference `successor` to the right child of the node. (This node is guaranteed to exist or we wouldn't be processing this situation.) Then the `getSuccessor` method uses a `while` loop to traverse a straight path down the left child nodes until there is no left child. Note that this step is not recursive. Before returning a reference to this node, the successor node is removed from the tree using another call to the `remove` method. As discussed in the previous section, deleting this node is guaranteed to be one of the two straightforward situations (zero or one child).

Spend some time looking at situations that occur in Figure 17.4 and trace the logic of the `remove` method carefully.

The `findMin` and `findMax` methods are left as programming projects.

17.3 Balanced Binary Search Trees

We've mentioned that a balanced binary search tree is more efficient than searching a degenerate tree. The search and add operations on a balanced tree of n nodes have an efficiency of $O(\log_2 n)$ comparisons (the length of the longest path). The more degenerate the tree becomes, the search and add operations approach $O(n)$, which eliminates the benefits of using a search tree.

The implementation of a binary search tree that we explored in the previous section does not guarantee a balanced tree. The shape of the tree is determined solely on the order in which the elements are added to the tree.

There are more sophisticated implementations of binary search trees that ensure the trees stay balanced. AVL trees and red/black trees are two such approaches, though we do not explore them in this book. Instead, we will simply explore the general concept of performing *rotations* on a binary search tree, which are operations

Rotations can be performed on a binary search tree to help rebalance them.

that assist in the process of keeping a tree balanced. These rotations do not solve all problems created by unbalanced trees, but they show the basic algorithmic processes that are used to manipulate trees in this way.

Right Rotation

Figure 17.7 shows a binary search tree that is not balanced and the processing steps necessary to rebalance it. To get this tree into balance, we need to

- Make the left child element of the root the new root element.
- Make the former root element the right child element of the new root.
- Make the right child of what was the left child of the former root the new left child of the former root.

This process is referred to as a *right rotation*. This kind of rotation can be done at any level of a tree, around the root of any subtree. This rotation corrects an imbalance caused by a long path in the left subtree of the left child of the root.

Left Rotation

Figure 17.8 shows another binary search tree that is not balanced, and the steps to correct it. However, this time the long path is in the right subtree of the right child of the root. To get this tree into balance, we need to

- Make the right child element of the root the new root element.
- Make the former root element the left child element of the new root.
- Make the left child of what was the right child of the former root the new right child of the former root.

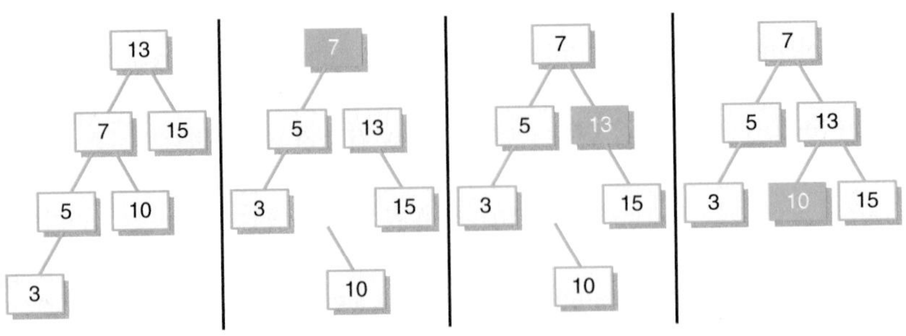

FIGURE 17.7 A right rotation on a binary search tree

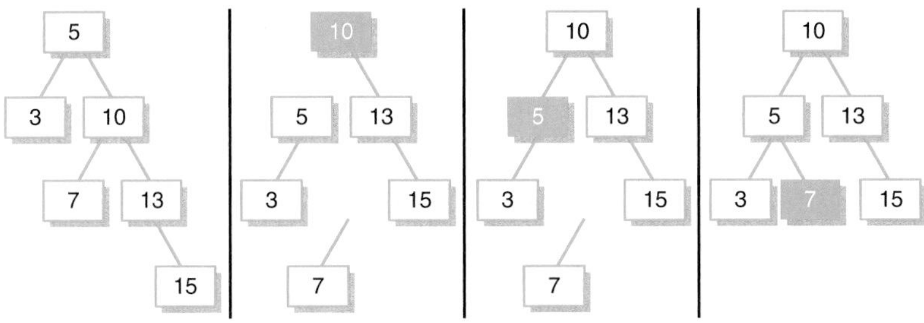

FIGURE 17.8 A left rotation on a binary search tree

This is referred to as a *left rotation*. It is essentially the mirror of a right rotation. As with a right rotation, a left rotation can be done at any level of the tree.

Right-Left Rotation

Unfortunately, not all imbalances can be solved by a single rotation. If the imbalance is caused by a long path in the left subtree of the right child of the root, we must first perform a right rotation around the offending subtree, and then perform a left rotation around the root. This is called a *right-left rotation*. Figure 17.9 illustrates this process.

First, a right rotation is performed around the subtree with root 13, yielding the second tree in the figure. Then a left rotation is performed around the root of the tree (5), yielding the final tree.

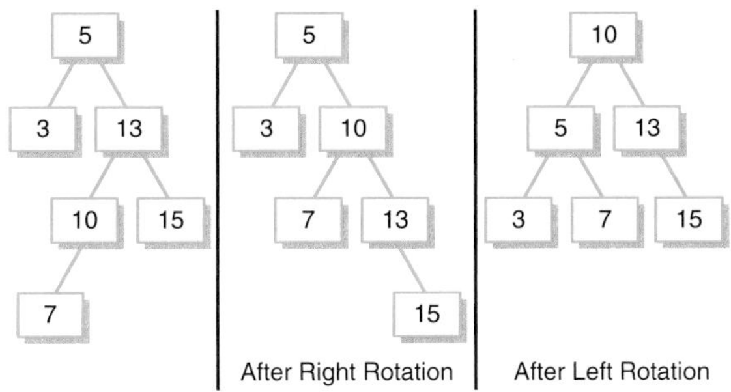

FIGURE 17.9 A right-left rotation on a binary search tree

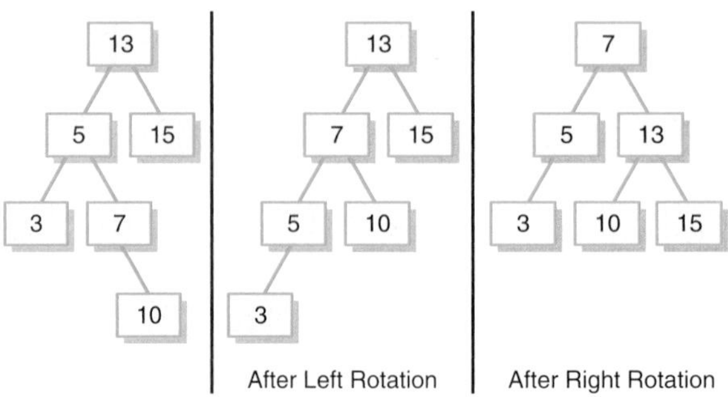

FIGURE 17.10 A left-right rotation on a binary search tree

Left-Right Rotation

Similarly, if the imbalance is caused by a long path in the right subtree of the left child of the root, we can perform a *left-right rotation*. First perform a left rotation of the offending subtree, and then perform a right rotation around the root. Figure 17.10 illustrates this process.

17.4 Heaps

A heap is a complete binary tree in which each element is greater than or equal to both of its children.

So far in this chapter we've focused on binary search trees, which are based on the concept of a general binary tree, discussed in the previous chapter. Let's now turn our attention to another structure that is also fundamentally an extension of a binary tree. A *heap* is a complete binary tree in which each element is greater than or equal to both of its children.

Note that there are two interesting extensions to a general binary tree in the heap definition. The first is that it is a complete tree (recall that a complete tree is balanced with all leaves as far left in the tree as possible). The second is the constraint on the relationship among elements. The element at the root of the tree is always the largest element in the tree, and every path from the root encounters successively decreasing values. Figure 17.11 shows a heap, using integer elements for simplicity.

As with binary search trees, there are many possible heap configurations for a given set of elements. The elements in the heap in Figure 17.11 could be organized into a different heap, as long as the properties of a heap are maintained.

To be more precise, our definition describes a *maxheap*. A heap can also be a *minheap*, in which each element is greater than or equal to its children. We will

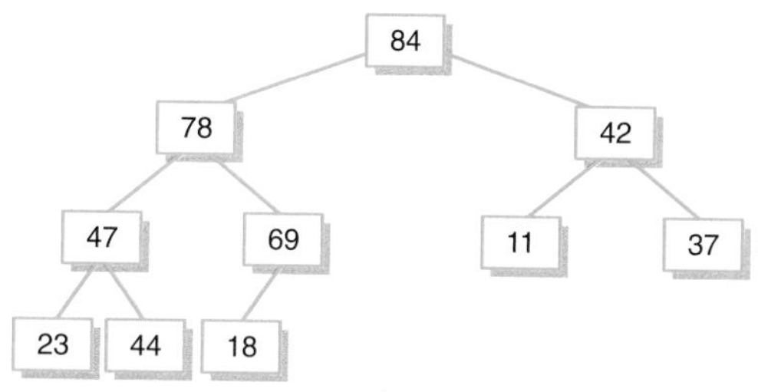

FIGURE 17.11 A heap

focus our discussion in this chapter on maxheaps. All of the same operations work for minheaps by reversing the comparisons.

A heap keeps the largest value of a set of elements readily available, and is useful in any situation in which that value is the dominant criteria. A heap has three primary operations: add a new element to the heap, find the maximum value, and remove the maximum value. The find operation is trivial, since the maximum value is always held in the root of the tree. Let's discuss the add and remove operations.

Adding an Element to a Heap

The strategy for adding a new element to a heap is to add the element as a new leaf, keeping the tree complete, and then moving the element up toward the root, exchanging positions with its parent, until the relationship among the elements is appropriate. This approach guarantees that the resulting tree will conform to the heap criteria.

Adding an element to a heap can be accomplished by adding the element as a leaf, then moving it upward as appropriate.

An example of this process is shown in Figure 17.12. The original heap is complete with appropriate relationships among the elements. The new element, 39, is added to the tree as a new leaf, as far left as possible. The tree is no longer a heap at this point—it is complete, but the relationship among the elements is not right. Because 39 is greater than its parent, 28, we switch them. Then, because 39 is greater than 33, those elements are switched. This results in the tree becoming a valid heap once again, with the new element incorporated.

The relationship among the elements determines how much movement is needed after the new element is added as a leaf. It may not move at all if its parent is already greater than it. It may move part way up the tree, or perhaps all the way up to become the new root of the tree, as it did in Figure 17.12.

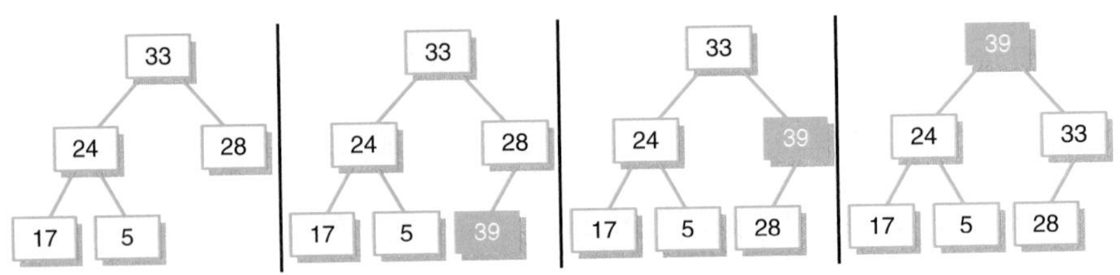

FIGURE 17.12 Adding an element to a heap

Removing the Largest Element from a Heap

Because of the characteristics of a heap, we know that the largest element is in the root of the tree. So removing that element requires deleting the root node, then reconstructing a heap from the two disjoint subtrees that remain.

Removing the maximum element from the heap can be accomplished by replacing the root with the last leaf, then moving it downward as appropriate.

The strategy for reconstructing the heap is to move the "last leaf" of the tree (the rightmost leaf on the last level) to the root position, then move it down through the tree as needed until the relationships among the elements are appropriate. This is somewhat the reverse of the process used to add a new element to the tree.

To determine if the new root element should move down, we compare it to its children. If the root element is smaller than the larger of its children, they are exchanged. This process continues until both children are less than or equal to the element being moved.

Figure 17.13 shows an example of removing the largest element from a heap. The current root element, 43, is guaranteed to be the largest value in the tree. It is deleted, leaving two disjoint subtrees. (Note that these subtrees are heaps themselves.) The last leaf of the tree, 25, is then moved up to become the new root of the tree. At this point the tree is no longer a heap. The new root element is

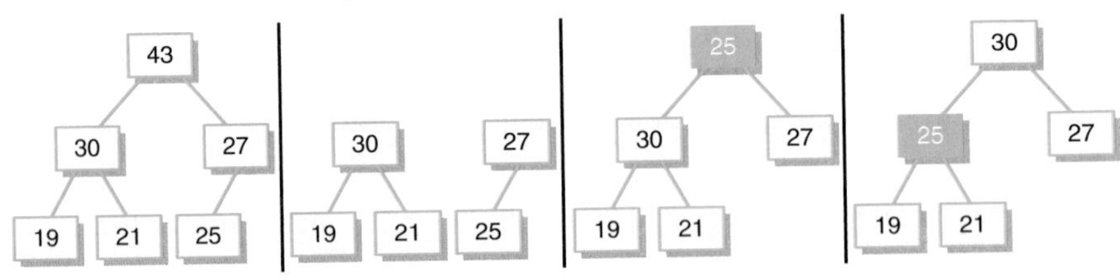

FIGURE 17.13 Removing the largest element from a heap

switched with the larger of its children, in this case 30. At this point, because 25 is greater than both of its children (19 and 21), the tree is now a heap once again.

As with the add operation, how many times the new root value moves down through the tree depends on the relationship among the elements. In our example, the new root value only moved one level down, but it will often take more steps.

17.5 Heap Implementation

Listing 17.4 shows the `MaxHeap` interface. For heaps, we commit at the interface level whether the heap is a maxheap or a minheap. The interface contains methods for adding a new element to the heap, getting the highest value, and removing the highest value.

Because a heap is a binary tree, its implementation can be based on the `LinkedBinaryTree` class defined in Chapter 16 (as we did with the implementa-

Listing 17.4

```
//********************************************************************
//  MaxHeap.java        Java Foundations
//
//  Defines the interface to a max heap.
//********************************************************************

package javafoundations;

public interface MaxHeap<T extends Comparable<T>> extends BinaryTree<T>
{
   //  Adds the specified object to the heap.
   public void add (T obj);

   //  Returns a reference to the element with the highest value in
   //  the heap.
   public T getMax ();

   //  Removes and returns the element with the highest value in the
   //  heap.
   public T removeMax ();
}
```

tion of a binary search tree). That's the version we'll explore now. However, because a heap is a complete tree, it also lends itself to an array-based implementation.

The `LinkedMaxHeap` class is shown in Listing 17.5, with one operation left as a programming project. Like our binary search tree implementation,

Listing 17.5

```
//********************************************************************
//  LinkedMaxHeap.java        Java Foundations
//
//  Implements a max heap using a linked representation.
//********************************************************************

package javafoundations;

import javafoundations.exceptions.*;

public class LinkedMaxHeap<T extends Comparable<T>>
   extends LinkedBinaryTree<T> implements MaxHeap<T>
{
   private HeapNode<T> last;

   //-----------------------------------------------------------------
   //  Creates a max heap with the specified element as its root.
   //-----------------------------------------------------------------
   public LinkedMaxHeap ()
   {
      super();
      last = null;
   }

   //-----------------------------------------------------------------
   //  Creates a max heap with the specified element as its root.
   //-----------------------------------------------------------------
   public LinkedMaxHeap (T element)
   {
      root = new HeapNode<T>(element);
      last = (HeapNode<T>)root;
   }
```

Listing **17.5** continued

```
//-----------------------------------------------------------------
//  Adds the specified element to this heap by adding it as a leaf
//  then reestablishing the heap relationships.
//-----------------------------------------------------------------
public void add (T element)
{
   HeapNode<T> node = new HeapNode<T>(element);
   HeapNode<T> newParent = null;

   if (root == null)
      root = node;
   else
   {
      newParent = ((HeapNode<T>)root).getParentAdd(last);

      if (newParent.left == null)
         newParent.setLeft(node);
      else
         newParent.setRight(node);
   }

   node.setParent(newParent);
   last = node;

   ((HeapNode<T>)root).heapifyAdd(last);
}

//-----------------------------------------------------------------
//  Remove the element with the largest value in this heap and
//  returns a reference to it.
//-----------------------------------------------------------------
public T removeMax()
{
   if (root == null)
      throw new EmptyCollectionException ("Remove max operation " +
         "failed. Tree is empty.");

   T maxElement = root.getElement();

   if (root.count() == 1)
      root = last = null;
```

Listing 17.5 continued

```
        else
        {
           HeapNode<T> newLast = ((HeapNode<T>)root).getNewLastNode(last);
           if (last.parent.left == last)
              last.parent.left = null;
           else
              last.parent.right = null;

           root.setElement(last.getElement());
           last = newLast;
           ((HeapNode<T>)root).heapifyRemove((HeapNode<T>)root);
        }

        return maxElement;
     }

     //-----------------------------------------------------------------
     //  The following method is left as a programming project.
     //-----------------------------------------------------------------
     // public T getMax() { }
}
```

`LinkedMaxHeap` extends `LinkedBinaryTree` and operates on a generic type `T`, which extends the `Comparable` interface.

The `LinkedMaxHeap` class inherits the `root` reference from `LinkedBinaryTree`. It also keeps track of the "last node" in the heap—that is, the last leaf in the complete tree. Since there is only one last node in the tree, this reference is maintained in the `LinkedMaxHeap` class and is not duplicated for every node.

The `LinkedMaxHeap` class relies on the `HeapNode` class, shown in Listing 17.6. In addition to the inherited references `left` and `right`, a `HeapNode` also keeps a reference to its parent node, which allows us to move up the tree paths. The constructors in `LinkedMaxHeap` set up empty or one-node heaps, as appropriate.

Consider the process of adding a new element as the "last leaf" in the complete tree. For any given tree, there is only one possible position to add that leaf. But keep in mind that that position might be on the level of current leaves, or it could

Listing 17.6

```
//********************************************************************
//  HeapNode.java        Java Foundations
//
//  Represents a node, and the root of a subtree, in a heap.
//********************************************************************

package javafoundations;

public class HeapNode<T extends Comparable<T>> extends BTNode<T>
{
   HeapNode<T> parent;

   //-----------------------------------------------------------------
   //  Creates a new heap node with the specified data.
   //-----------------------------------------------------------------
   public HeapNode (T element)
   {
      super(element);
      parent = null;
   }

   //-----------------------------------------------------------------
   //  Returns the parent node of this node.
   //-----------------------------------------------------------------
   public HeapNode<T> getParent()
   {
      return parent;
   }

   //-----------------------------------------------------------------
   //  Returns the parent node of this node.
   //-----------------------------------------------------------------
   public void setParent(HeapNode<T> parent)
   {
      this.parent = parent;
   }

   //-----------------------------------------------------------------
   //  Returns the node that will be the parent of the new node.
   //-----------------------------------------------------------------
```

Listing 17.6 continued

```
   public HeapNode<T> getParentAdd (HeapNode<T> last)
   {
      HeapNode<T> result = last;

      while ((result.parent != null) && (result.parent.left != result))
         result = result.parent;

      if (result.parent != null)
         if (result.parent.right == null)
            result = result.parent;
         else
         {
            result = (HeapNode<T>) result.parent.right;
            while (result.left != null)
               result = (HeapNode<T>) result.left;
         }
      else
         while (result.left != null)
            result = (HeapNode<T>) result.left;

      return result;
   }

   //-----------------------------------------------------------------
   //  Moves a newly added leaf up the tree as far as appropriate to
   //  reestablish the heap.
   //-----------------------------------------------------------------
   public void heapifyAdd (HeapNode<T> last)
   {
      T temp;
      HeapNode<T> current = last;

      while ((current.parent != null) &&
         ((current.element).compareTo(current.parent.element) > 0))
      {
         temp = current.element;
         current.element = current.parent.element;
         current.parent.element = temp;
         current = current.parent;
      }
   }
```

Listing **17.6** continued

```
//-----------------------------------------------------------------
//  Returns the node that will be the new last node after a remove.
//-----------------------------------------------------------------
public HeapNode<T> getNewLastNode(HeapNode<T> last)
{
   HeapNode<T> result = last;

   while ((result.parent != null) && (result.parent.left == result))
      result = result.parent;

   if (result.parent != null)
      result = (HeapNode<T>) result.parent.left;

   while (result.right != null)
      result = (HeapNode<T>) result.right;

   return result;
}

//-----------------------------------------------------------------
//  Reorders this heap after removing the root element.
//-----------------------------------------------------------------
public void heapifyRemove(HeapNode<T> root)
{
   T temp;
   HeapNode<T> current = root;
   HeapNode<T> next = largerChild (current);

   while (next != null && next.element.compareTo(current.element) > 0)
   {
      temp = current.element;
      current.element = next.element;
      next.element = temp;

      current = next;
      next = largerChild (current);
   }
}

//-----------------------------------------------------------------
//  Returns the larger of the two children of the specified node.
//-----------------------------------------------------------------
```

Listing 17.6 continued

```
   public HeapNode<T> largerChild (HeapNode<T> node)
   {
      HeapNode<T> larger = null;

      if (node.left == null && node.right == null)
         larger = null;
      else if (node.left == null)
         larger = (HeapNode<T>)node.right;
      else if (node.right == null)
         larger = (HeapNode<T>)node.left;
      else if (((HeapNode<T>)node.left).element.compareTo(((HeapNode<T>)
      node.right).element) > 0)
         larger = (HeapNode<T>)node.left;
      else
         larger = (HeapNode<T>)node.right;

      return larger;
   }
}
```

be the first position of the next level if the tree is currently full. Figure 17.14 shows two heaps and the next insertion point for a new leaf.

The `add` method of `LinkedMaxHeap` relies on two support methods in `HeapNode`. One (`getParentAdd`) gets the parent of the new node to be added, and the other (`heapifyAdd`) reestablishes the heap after the leaf is added. This processing is consistent with our discussion of adding a new element to a heap presented in the previous section of this chapter.

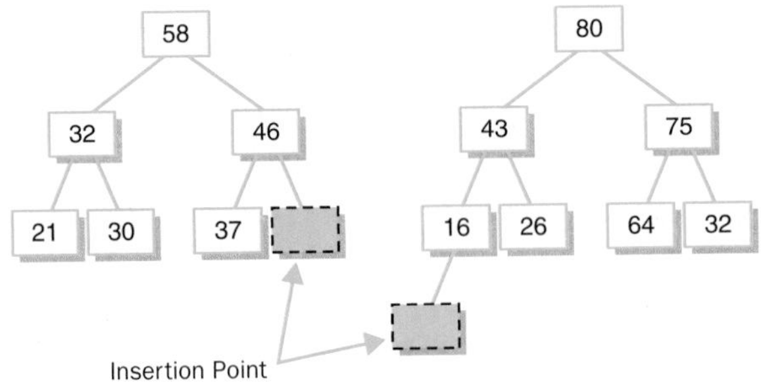

FIGURE 17.14 Insertion points in a heap

Starting at the last node in the tree, the `getParentAdd` method considers all possibilities, looking for the node that will serve as the parent of the new node being added. First it looks up the tree until it discovers it is a left child of some node, or until it hits the root. If it reaches the root, then the new parent is the leftmost descendent of the root (and the new leaf begins a new level). If it does not reach the root, it looks for the leftmost descendent of the right child.

Once the new leaf has been added to the tree, the `heapifyAdd` method uses the `parent` references to move up the tree, swapping elements as needed. Note that it doesn't move the nodes themselves around—it just exchanges the elements stored in them.

The `removeMax` method in `LinkedMaxHeap` removes the root of the heap, which is guaranteed to hold the largest value, and returns the element. If there is only one node in the heap, this step is straightforward. Otherwise, the `removeMax` method replaces the root with the last node in the tree, then reestablishes the heap characteristics of the tree (as described in the previous section). It relies on two support methods from `HeapNode` to accomplish this task. The `getNewLastNode` method returns the node that will be the new "last node" after the element has been removed. The `heapifyRemove` method starts at the root, swapping the element with the larger of its children, until the heap characteristic is once again established.

The `getMax` operation is left as a programming project.

17.6 Heap Sort

In Chapter 13 we introduced a variety of sorting techniques, some of which were sequential sorts (bubble sort, selection sort, and insertion sort) and some of which were logarithmic sorts (merge sort and quick sort). Given the ordering property of a heap, it is natural to think of using a heap to sort a list of numbers.

A *heap sort* sorts a set of elements by adding each one to a heap, then removing them one at a time. Because the largest element comes off of a heap first (in a maxheap), the sequence of elements coming off the heap will be in sorted order, descending. Similarly, a minheap can be used to sort the values in ascending order.

A heap sort makes use of the primary characteristic of a heap to sort a set of elements.

Implementing a heap sort is left as a programming project.

Summary of Key Concepts

- A binary search tree is a binary tree in which, for each node, the elements in the left subtree are less than the parent, and the elements in the right subtree are greater than or equal to the parent.
- The most efficient binary search trees are balanced, so that half of the viable candidates are eliminated with each comparison.
- Without any additional processing, the shape of a binary search tree is dictated by the order in which elements are added to it.
- There are three situations to consider when removing an element from a binary search tree, two of which are straightforward.
- When removing a node with two children from a binary search tree, the inorder successor is a good choice to replace it.
- Rotations can be performed on a binary search tree to help rebalance them.
- A heap is a complete binary tree in which each element is greater than or equal to both of its children.
- Adding an element to a heap can be accomplished by adding the element as a leaf, then moving it upward as appropriate.
- Removing the maximum element from the heap can be accomplished by replacing the root with the last leaf, then moving it downward as appropriate.
- A heap sort makes use of the primary characteristic of a heap to sort a set of elements.

Self-Review Questions

SR 17.1 What is the difference between a binary tree and a binary search tree?

SR 17.2 Compare a binary search tree to the binary search algorithm discussed in Chapter 13.

SR 17.3 Which method of traversing a binary search tree would result in a sorted list?

SR 17.4 What is the process of adding an element to a binary search tree?

SR 17.5 What is a degenerate tree?

SR 17.6 Why is it important for a binary search tree to be balanced (or close to balanced)?

SR 17.7 What is the most interesting situation when removing an element from a binary search tree? Explain.

SR 17.8 What is a binary search tree rotation?

SR 17.9 What is the difference between a heap and a binary search tree?

SR 17.10 What is the difference between a minheap and a maxheap?

SR 17.11 How is an element added to a heap?

SR 17.12 How is the largest element removed from a heap?

SR 17.13 What is a heap sort?

Exercises

EX 17.1 Draw a binary search tree containing the same elements as those stored in Figure 17.1, but with a different structure.

EX 17.2 Will two equal elements in a binary search tree always be in a direct parent/child relationship to each other (as the two 42 values are in Figure 17.1)? Explain.

EX 17.3 Show the binary search tree that results when the following values are added, in order, to the tree shown in Figure 17.1.

57 90 42 11 31 66

EX 17.4 Show the binary search tree that results when the following values are added, in order, to a new tree.

24 61 28 17 72 4 23 49 24 80 10 36 16

EX 17.5 Show the binary search tree that results after deleting the following elements, in order, from the tree that is produced in Exercise 17.4.

23 4 61

EX 17.6 Show the binary search tree that results when the following values are added, in order, to a new tree.

14 45 28 49 69 12 84 76 31 69 88 79

EX 17.7 Show the binary search tree that results after deleting the following elements, in order, from the tree that is produced in Exercise 17.6.

49 14 31 84

EX 17.8 When deleting a node with two children from a binary search tree, we chose to replace it with its inorder successor. What other value would be an equally reasonable choice? Explain.

EX 17.9 Given that a `find` method is defined in the `BinaryTree` interface, did the `find` method need to be declared in the `BinarySearchTree` interface? Explain.

EX 17.10 Show the binary search tree that results after balancing the following tree using the rotation technique(s) described in this chapter.

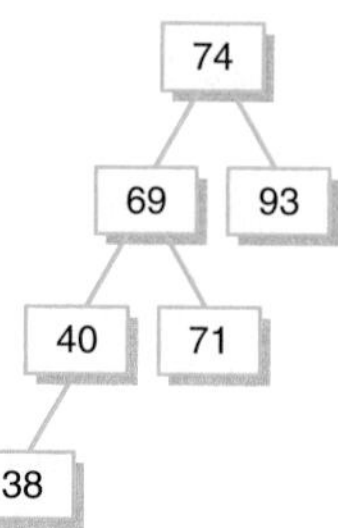

EX 17.11 Show the binary search tree that results after balancing the following tree using the rotation technique(s) described in this chapter.

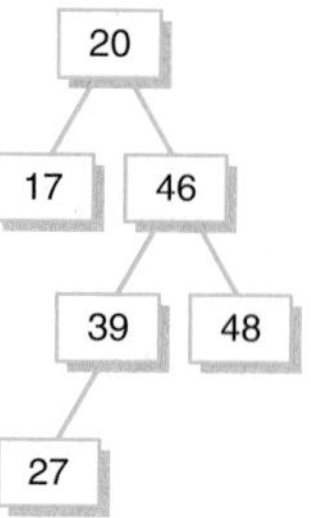

EX 17.12 Show the binary search tree that results after balancing the following tree using the rotation technique(s) described in this chapter.

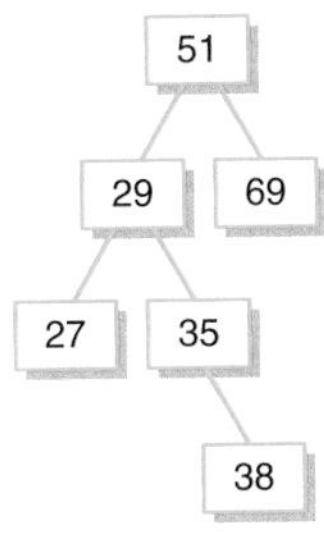

EX 17.13 Does a heap ever need rebalancing, as we discussed doing for binary search trees? Explain.

EX 17.14 Draw a heap containing the same elements as those stored in Figure 17.11, but with a different structure.

EX 17.15 In a heap, does it matter which subtree (left or right) holds equal values? Explain.

EX 17.16 Show the maxheap that results when the following values are added, in order, to the heap shown in Figure 17.11.

81 25 22 86

EX 17.17 Show the maxheap that results when the following values are added, in order, to a new heap.

28 19 41 35 50 37 10 39 55

EX 17.18 Show the maxheap that results after deleting the three highest elements, in order, from the heap that is produced in Exercise 17.17.

EX 17.19 Show the maxheap that results when the following values are added, in order, to a new heap.

12 31 7 38 34 81 36 29 67 77 79

EX 17.20 Show the maxheap that results after deleting the three highest elements, in order, from the heap that is produced in Exercise 17.19.

Programming Projects

PP 17.1 Complete the implementation of the `LinkedBinarySearchTree` class presented in this chapter. Specifically, complete the implementations of the `findMin` and `findMax` operations.

PP 17.2 Implement a class called `CLArrayBinarySearchTree` that satisfies the `BinarySearchTree` interface. The class should represent the tree using the computed link implementation strategy and be derived from the `CLArrayBinaryTree` class from programming project 16.2 in Chapter 16.

PP 17.3 Implement a class called `SLArrayBinarySearchTree` that satisfies the `BinarySearchTree` interface. The class should represent the tree using the stored link implementation strategy and be derived from the `SLArrayBinaryTree` class from programming project 16.3 in Chapter 16.

PP 17.4 Design a `ClubMember` class that represents a member of a social club. Use a binary search tree to store a set of club members based on their membership ID number.

PP 17.5 Modify the `ClubMember` class created in programming project 17.4 so that ClubMembers are ordered by their last name. Demonstrate that the same binary search tree collection can manage them without modification.

PP 17.6 Complete the implementation of the `LinkedMaxHeap` class presented in this chapter. Specifically, complete the implementation of the `getMax` operation.

PP 17.7 Design and implement a minheap collection, with an appropriate interface, implementing class, and node class. Use a linked implementation strategy.

PP 17.8 Implement a class called `CLArrayMaxHeap` that satisfies the `MaxHeap` interface. The class should represent the tree using the computed link implementation strategy and be derived from the `CLArrayBinaryTree` class from programming project 16.2 in Chapter 16.

PP 17.9 Implement a class called `SLArrayMaxHeap` that satisfies the `MaxHeap` interface. The class should represent the tree using the stored link implementation strategy and be derived from the `SLArrayBinaryTree` class from programming project 16.3 in Chapter 16.

PP 17.10 A *priority queue* is a collection that allows integer priority value to be associated with any object stored in the queue, then produces the items with the highest priority first. Design and implement a priority queue collection, using a maxheap as its underlying implementation.

PP 17.11 Implement a heap sort and demonstrate its functionality.

Answers to Self-Review Questions

SR 17.1 A binary search tree is a binary tree, with the added ordering property that each node is less than its left child and greater than or equal to its right child. A general binary tree has no constraints on the relationships among its elements.

SR 17.2 A binary search tree and the binary search algorithm from Chapter 13 have the same intent: to organize and process data so that approximately half of the data is removed from consideration with each comparison. The binary search algorithm works on a sorted array, while the binary search tree uses its structure to organize the data.

SR 17.3 An inorder traversal of a binary search tree produces the elements in sorted, ascending order.

SR 17.4 Adding an element to a binary search tree involves navigating the tree based on the relationship between the new element and the node elements until a location is found to add the new element as a leaf.

SR 17.5 A degenerate tree is a binary search tree that is significantly skewed one way or another, defeating the value of the tree structure.

SR 17.6 If a binary search tree is balanced, approximately half of the elements are eliminated from consideration with each comparison. The more unbalanced the tree, the closer it gets to a linear structure, which is much less efficient.

SR 17.7 The most interesting situation when removing an element from a binary search tree occurs when the element has two children, because there is no simple option to replace the element (as there are if it has one child or no children).

SR 17.8 A binary search tree rotation is an operation that helps put a binary search tree back into a balanced state.

SR 17.9 A binary search tree and a heap are both binary trees that have constraints on the relationships among their elements. The nodes in a binary search tree are less than their left child and greater than or equal to their right child, whereas the nodes in a heap (maxheap) are greater than or equal to both children.

SR 17.10 A minheap keeps the smallest value in the tree at the root, whereas a maxheap keeps the largest value at the root. Otherwise, their strategies and implementations are similar.

SR 17.11 An element is added to a heap by inserting it as a new leaf, then moving that element up the tree as appropriate to reassert the proper relationships among the elements.

SR 17.12 The maximum element is removed from a heap (maxheap) by replacing the root with the last leaf of the tree, then moving that element down the tree as appropriate to reassert the proper relationships among the elements.

SR 17.13 A heap sort is a sorting algorithm that sorts values by adding them to a heap, then removing them in sorted order.

Chapter Objectives

- Discuss directed and undirected graphs.
- Define weighted graphs and explore their use.
- Define breadth-first and depth-first traversals of a graph.
- Define a minimum spanning tree.
- Discuss strategies for implementing graphs.

18 Graphs

We've seen that trees, as discussed in Chapters 16 and 17, are nonlinear structures with a single root node. This chapter introduces graphs, nonlinear structures in which nodes may be connected to many other nodes, with no particular parent/child relationships. The exploration of graphs and graph theory is an entire subdiscipline of both mathematics and computer science. In this chapter we introduce the basic concepts of graphs and their implementation.

18.1 Undirected Graphs

As we discussed in previous chapters, a tree is a nonlinear structure defined by the concept that each node in the tree, other than the root node, has exactly one parent. If we were to violate that premise and allow each node in the tree to be connected to a variety of other nodes with no notion of parent or child, the result would be a graph.

An undirected graph is a graph where the pairings representing the edges are unordered.

Like trees, a graph is made up of nodes and the connections between those nodes. In graph terminology, we refer to the nodes as *vertices* and refer to the connections among them as *edges*. Vertices are typically referenced by a name or a label. For example, we might label vertices A, B, C, and D. Edges are referenced by a pairing of the vertices that they connect. For example, we might have an edge (A, B), which means there is an edge from vertex A to vertex B.

An *undirected graph* is a graph where the pairings representing the edges are unordered. Thus, listing an edge as (A, B) means that there is a connection between A and B that can be traversed in either direction. Thus, in an undirected graph, listing an edge as (A, B) means exactly the same thing as listing the edge as (B, A). Figure 18.1 illustrates an undirected graph.

Two vertices in a graph are adjacent if there is an edge connecting them.

Two vertices in a graph are *adjacent* if there is an edge connecting them. For example, in the graph of Figure 18.1, vertices A and B are adjacent while vertices A and D are not. Adjacent vertices are sometimes referred to as *neighbors*. An edge of a graph that connects a vertex to itself is called a *self-loop* or a *sling*.

An undirected graph is considered complete if it has the maximum number of edges connecting vertices.

An undirected graph is considered *complete* if it has the maximum number of edges connecting vertices. For the first vertex, it requires (n–1) edges to connect it to the other vertices. For the second vertex, it requires only (n–2) edges since it is already connected to the first vertex. For the third vertex, it requires (n–3) edges. This sequence continues until the final vertex requires no

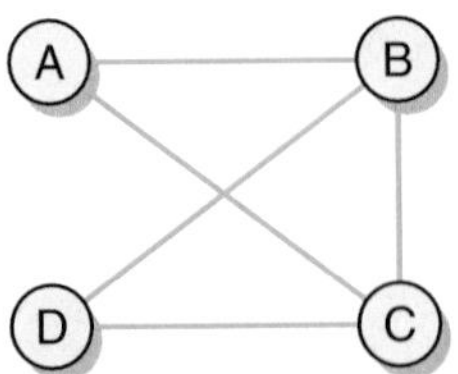

FIGURE 18.1 An undirected graph

additional edges because all the other vertices have already been connected to it. Mathematically, this is the summation:

$$\sum_{i=1}^{n-1} = \frac{n(n-1)}{2}$$

A *path* is a sequence of edges that connects two vertices in a graph. For example, in our graph from Figure 18.1, A, B, D is a path from A to D. Notice that each sequential pair, (A, B) and then (B, D), is an edge. A path in an undirected graph is bi-directional. For example, A, B, D is the path from A to D but since the edges are undirected, the inverse, D, B, A is also the path from D to A. The *length* of a path is the number of edges in the path (or the number of vertices – 1). So for our previous example, the path length is 2. Notice that this definition of path length is identical to the definition that we used in discussing trees. In fact, trees are graphs.

A path is a sequence of edges that connects two vertices in a graph.

An undirected graph is considered *connected* if for any two vertices in the graph there is a path between them. Our graph from Figure 18.1 is connected. The same graph with a minor modification is not connected, as illustrated in Figure 18.2.

A cycle is a path in which the first and last vertices are the same and none of the edges are repeated.

A *cycle* is a path in which the first and last vertices are the same and none of the edges are repeated. In Figure 18.2, we would say that the path A, B, C, A is a cycle. A graph that has no cycles is called *acyclic*. Earlier we mentioned the relationship between graphs and trees. Now that we have introduced these definitions, we can formalize that relationship. An undirected tree is a connected, acyclic, undirected graph with one element designated as the root.

18.2 Directed Graphs

A *directed graph*, sometimes referred to as a *digraph*, is a graph where the edges are ordered pairs of vertices. This means that the edges (A, B) and (B, A) are separate, directional edges in a

In a directed graph, the edges are ordered pairs of vertices.

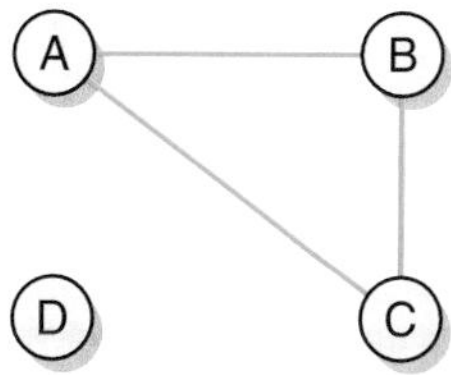

FIGURE 18.2 An example undirected graph that is not connected

directed graph. In our previous example we had the following description for an undirected graph:

Vertices: A, B, C, D

Edges: (A, B), (A, C), (B, C), (B, D), (C, D)

A path in a directed graph is a sequence of directed edges that connects two vertices in a graph.

Figure 18.3 shows what happens if we interpret this earlier description as a directed graph. We represent each of the edges now with the direction of traversal specified by the ordering of the vertices. For example, the edge (A, B) allows traversal from A to B but not the other direction.

Our previous definitions change slightly for directed graphs. For example, a path in a directed graph is a sequence of directed edges that connects two vertices in a graph. In our undirected graph we listed the path A, B, D, as the path from A to D, and that is still true in our directed interpretation of the graph description. However, paths in a directed graph are not bi-directional, so the inverse is no longer true: D, B, A is not a valid path from D to A.

Our definition of a connected directed graph sounds the same as it did for undirected graphs. A directed graph is connected if for any two vertices in the graph there is a path between them. However, keep in mind that our definition of path is different. Look at the two graphs shown in Figure 18.4. The first one is connected. The second one, however, is not connected because there is no path from any other vertex to vertex 1.

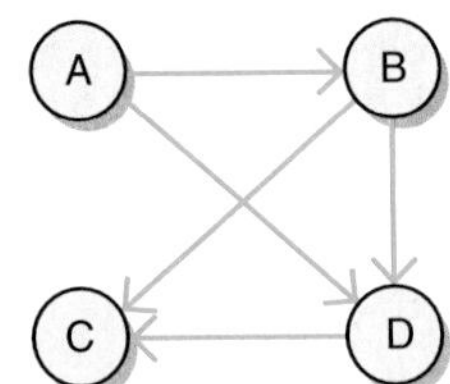

FIGURE 18.3 A directed graph

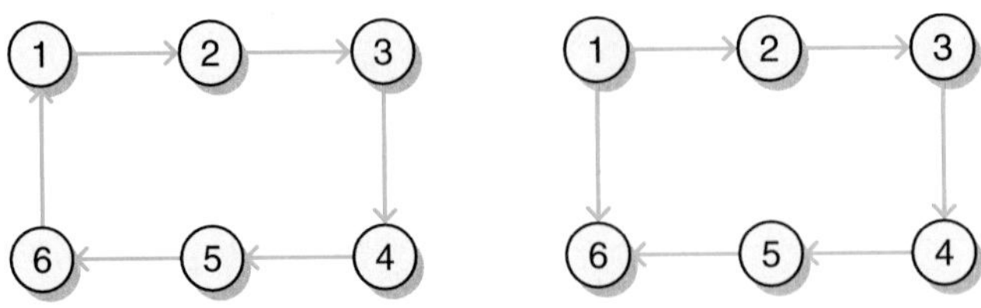

FIGURE 18.4 Directed edges determining connectivity

If a directed graph has no cycles, it is possible to arrange the vertices such that vertex A precedes vertex B if an edge exists from A to B. The order of vertices resulting from this arrangement is called *topological order* and is very useful for examples such as course prerequisites.

As we discussed earlier, trees are graphs. In fact, most of our previous work with trees actually focused on directed trees. A directed tree is a directed graph that has an element designated as the root and has the following properties:

- There are no connections from other vertices to the root.
- Every non-root element has exactly one connection to it.
- There is a path from the root to every other vertex.

18.3 Weighted Graphs

A weighted graph is a graph with costs associated with each edge.

A *weighted graph*, sometimes called a *network*, is a graph with weights or costs associated with each edge. Figure 18.5 shows an undirected weighted graph of the connections and the airfares between cities. This graph could then be used to determine the cheapest path from one city to another. The weight of a path in a weighted graph is the sum of the weights of the edges in the path.

Weighted graphs may be either undirected or directed depending upon the need. Take our airfare example from Figure 18.5. What if the airfare to fly from New York to Boston is one price but the airfare to fly from Boston to New York is a different price? This would be an excellent application of a directed weighted graph, as illustrated in Figure 18.6.

For weighted graphs, we represent each edge with a triple including the starting vertex, ending vertex, and the weight. Keep in mind, for undirected weighted graphs, the starting and ending vertices could be swapped with no impact.

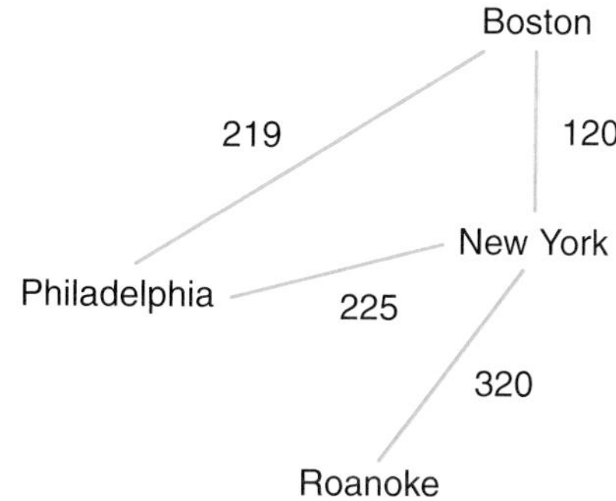

FIGURE 18.5 An undirected weighted graph

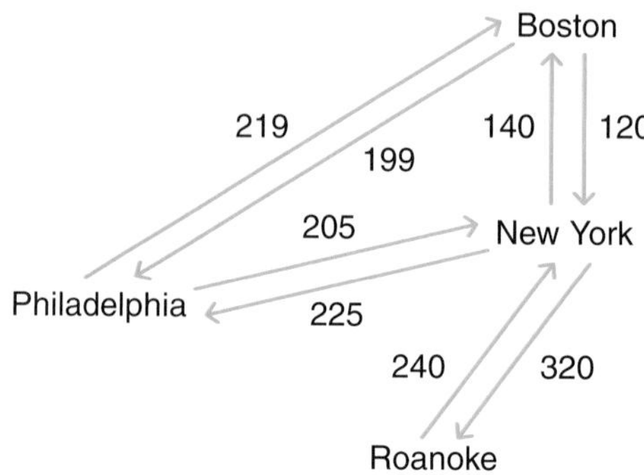

FIGURE 18.6 A directed weighted graph

However, for directed graphs, a triple must be included for every directional connection. For example, the weighted graph of Figure 18.6 would be represented as follows:

Vertices: Boston, New York, Philadelphia, Roanoke

Edges: (Boston, New York, 120), (Boston, Philadelphia, 199), (New York, Boston, 140), (New York, Philadelphia, 225), (New York, Roanoke, 320), (Philadelphia, Boston, 219), (Philadelphia, New York, 205), (Roanoke, New York, 240)

18.4 Common Graph Algorithms

There are a number of common graph algorithms that may apply to undirected graphs, directed graphs, and/or weighted graphs. These include various traversal algorithms similar to those we explored with trees, as well as algorithms for finding the shortest path, algorithms for finding the least costly path in a network, and algorithms to answer simple questions about the graph such as whether or not the graph is connected or what the shortest path is between two vertices.

Traversals

In our discussion of trees in Chapter 16, we defined four types of traversals (preorder, inorder, postorder, and level-order). There are generally two types of graph traversals: a *breadth-first traversal*, which behaves very much like the level-order traversal of a tree, and a *depth-first traversal*, which behaves very much like the preorder traversal of a tree. One difference is that there is no root node present in a graph. Thus, our traversals may start at any vertex in the graph.

We can construct a breadth-first traversal for a graph using a queue and an iterator. We will use the queue (`traversalQueue`) to manage the traversal and use the iterator (`iter`) to build our result. The first step is to enqueue the starting vertex into the queue and mark the starting vertex as visited. We then begin a loop that will continue until the queue is empty. Within this loop we will take the first vertex off of the queue and add that vertex to the iterator. Next, we will enqueue each of the vertices that are adjacent to the current one, and have not already been marked as visited, into the queue, mark each of them as visited, and then repeat the loop. We simply repeat this process for each of the visited vertices until the queue is empty, meaning we can no longer reach any new vertices. The iterator now contains the vertices in breadth-first order from the given starting point. Very similar logic can be used to construct a depth-first iterator.

The following method shows an iterative algorithm for a breadth-first traversal using an array implementation of a graph. The determination of vertices that are adjacent to the current one depends upon the implementation we choose to represent edges in a graph. We will discuss this further in section 18.4.

```
//-----------------------------------------------------------------
//  Returns an iterator that performs a breadth-first search
//  traversal starting at the given index.
//-----------------------------------------------------------------
public Iterator<T> iteratorBFS(int startIndex)
{
   int currentVertex;
   LinkedQueue<Integer> traversalQueue = new
      LinkedQueue<Integer>();
   ArrayIterator<T> iter = new ArrayIterator<T>();

   if (!indexIsValid(startIndex))
      return iter;

   boolean[] visited = new boolean[numVertices];
   for (int vertexIndex = 0; vertexIndex < numVertices;
      vertexIndex++)
      visited[vertexIndex] = false;

   traversalQueue.enqueue(startIndex);
   visited[startIndex] = true;

   while (!traversalQueue.isEmpty())
   {
      currentVertex = traversalQueue.dequeue();
      iter.add(vertices[currentVertex]);
```

```
      for (int vertexIndex = 0; vertexIndex < numVertices;
         vertexIndex++)
         if (adjMatrix[currentVertex][vertexIndex] &&
            !visited[vertexIndex])
         {
            traversalQueue.enqueue(vertexIndex);
            visited[vertexIndex] = true;
         }
   }
   return iter;
}
```

A depth-first traversal for a graph can be constructed using virtually the same logic by simply replacing the queue with a stack. One other difference in the algorithm, however, is that we do not want to mark a vertex as visited until it has been added to the iterator. The `iteratorDFS` method below illustrates this algorithm for an array implementation of a graph.

```
//-----------------------------------------------------------------
//  Returns an iterator that performs a depth-first search
//  traversal starting at the given index.
//-----------------------------------------------------------------
public Iterator<T> iteratorDFS(int startIndex)
{
   int currentVertex;
   LinkedStack<Integer> traversalStack =
      new LinkedStack<Integer>();
   ArrayIterator<T> iter = new ArrayIterator<T>();
   boolean[] visited = new boolean[numVertices];
   boolean found;

   if (!indexIsValid(startIndex))
      return iter;

   for (int vertexIdx = 0; vertexIdx < numVertices;
      vertexIdx++)
      visited[vertexIdx] = false;

   traversalStack.push(startIndex);
   iter.add (vertices[startIndex]);
   visited[startIndex] = true;

   while (!traversalStack.isEmpty())
   {
      currentVertex = traversalStack.peek();
      found = false;
```

```
      for (int vertexIdx = 0; vertexIdx < numVertices && !found;
         vertexIdx++)
         if (adjMatrix[currentVertex][vertexIdx] && !visited[vertexIdx])
         {
            traversalStack.push(vertexIdx);
            iter.add(vertices[vertexIdx]);
            visited[vertexIdx] = true;
            found = true;
         }

      if (!found && !traversalStack.isEmpty())
         traversalStack.pop();
   }
   return iter;
}
```

The main difference between a depth-first traversal of a graph and a breadth-first traversal is the use of a stack instead of a queue to manage the traversal.

Let's look at an example. Figure 18.7 shows a sample undirected graph where each vertex is labeled with an integer. For a breadth-first traversal starting from vertex 9, we do the following:

1. Add 9 to the queue and mark it as visited.
2. Dequeue 9 from the queue.
3. Add 9 on the iterator.
4. Add 6, 7, and 8 to the queue, marking each of them as visited.
5. Dequeue 6 from the queue.
6. Add 6 on the iterator.

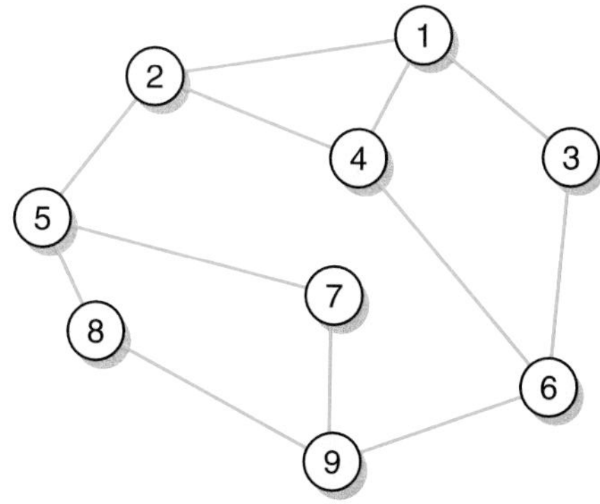

FIGURE 18.7 A traversal example

7. Add 3 and 4 to the queue, marking them both as visited.
8. Dequeue 7 from the queue and add it to the iterator.
9. Add 5 to the queue, marking it as visited.
10. Dequeue 8 from the queue and add it to the iterator. (We do not add any new vertices to the queue since there are no neighbors of 8 that have not already been visited.)
11. Dequeue 3 from the queue and add it to the iterator.
12. Add 1 to the queue, marking it as visited.
13. Dequeue 4 from the queue and add it to the iterator.
14. Add 2 to the queue, marking it as visited.
15. Dequeue 5 from the queue and add it to the iterator. (Since there are no unvisited neighbors, we continue without adding anything to the queue.)
16. Dequeue 1 from the queue and add it to the iterator. (Since there are no unvisited neighbors, we continue without adding anything to the queue.)
17. Dequeue 2 from the queue and add it to the iterator.

Thus, the iterator now contains the breadth-first order starting at vertex 9: 9, 6, 7, 8, 3, 4, 5, 1, and 2. Trace a depth-first search on the same graph from Figure 18.7.

Of course, both of these algorithms could also be expressed recursively. For example, the following algorithm recursively defines a depth-first search:

```
depthFirstSearch(node x)
{
   visit(x)
   for each node y adjacent to x
      if y not visited
         depthFirstSearch(y)
}
```

Testing for Connectivity

In our earlier discussion, we defined a graph as *connected* if for any two vertices in the graph, there is a path between them. This definition holds true for both undirected and directed graphs. Let's now put that in terms of the breadth-first traversal we just discussed: A graph is connected if and only if for each vertex v in a graph containing n vertices, the size of the result of a breadth-first traversal starting at v is n.

A graph is connected if and only if the number of vertices in the breadth-first traversal is the same as the number of vertices in the graph regardless of the starting vertex.

Let's look at the example undirected graphs in Figure 18.8. We stated earlier that the graph on the left is connected and that the graph on the right is not. Let's confirm that by following our algorithm. Figure 18.9 shows the breadth-first traversals for the graph on the left using each of the vertices as a starting point. As you can see, each of the traversals yield n = 4 vertices, thus the graph is connected. Figure 18.10 shows the breadth-first traversals for the graph on the right using each of the vertices as a starting point. Notice that not only do none of the traversals contain n = 4 vertices, but the one starting at vertex D has only the one vertex. Thus the graph is not connected.

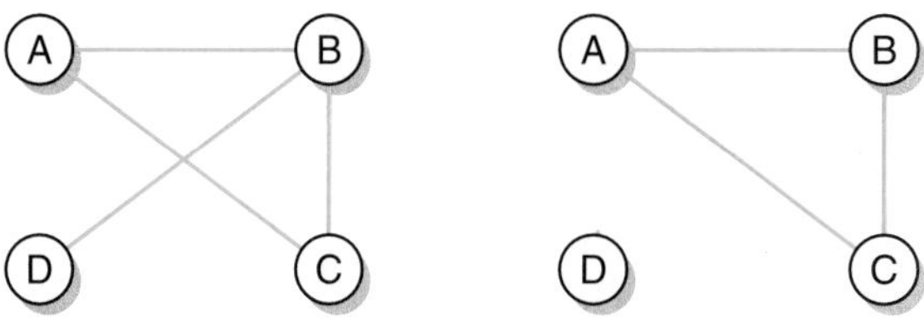

FIGURE 18.8 Connectivity in an undirected graph

Starting Vertex	Breadth-First Traversal
A	A, B, C, D
B	B, A, D, C
C	C, B, A, D
D	D, B, A, C

FIGURE 18.9 Breadth-first traversals for a connected undirected graph

Starting Vertex	Breadth-First Traversal
A	A, B, C
B	B, A, C
C	C, B, A
D	D

FIGURE 18.10 Breadth-first traversals for an unconnected undirected graph

Minimum Spanning Trees

A spanning tree is a tree that includes all of the vertices of a graph and some, but possibly not all, of the edges.

A *spanning tree* is a tree that includes all of the vertices of a graph and some, but possibly not all, of the edges. Since trees are also graphs, for some graphs, the graph itself will be a spanning tree, and thus the only spanning tree for that graph will include all of the edges. Figure 18.11 shows a spanning tree for our graph from Figure 18.7.

A minimum spanning tree is a spanning tree where the sum of the weights of the edges is less than or equal to the sum of the weights for any other spanning tree for the same graph.

One interesting application of spanning trees is to find a *minimum spanning tree* for a weighted graph. A minimum spanning tree is a spanning tree where the sum of the weights of the edges is less than or equal to the sum of the weights for any other spanning tree for the same graph.

The algorithm for developing a minimum spanning tree was developed by Prim (1957) and is quite elegant. As we discussed earlier, each edge is represented by a triple including the starting

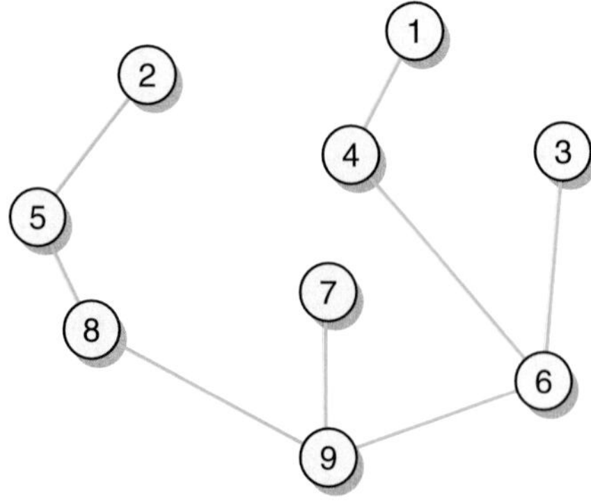

FIGURE 18.11 A spanning tree

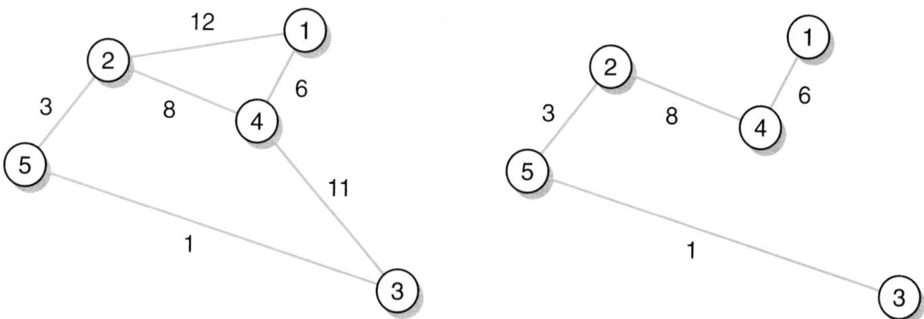

FIGURE 18.12 A weighted graph and its associated minimum spanning tree

vertex, ending vertex, and the weight. We then pick an arbitrary starting vertex (it does not matter which one) and add it to our minimum spanning tree (MST). Next we add all of the edges that include our starting vertex to a minheap ordered by weight. Keep in mind that if we are dealing with a directed graph, we will only add edges that start at the given vertex.

Next we remove the minimum edge from the minheap and add the edge and the new vertex to our MST. Next we add to our minheap all of the edges that include this new vertex and whose other vertex is not already in our MST. We continue this process until either our MST includes all of the vertices in our original graph or the minheap is empty. Figure 18.12 shows a weighted network and its associated minimum spanning tree. Shown below is the `getMST` method, which illustrates this algorithm.

```
//-----------------------------------------------------------------
//  Returns a minimum spanning tree of the graph.
//-----------------------------------------------------------------
public Graph getMST()
{
   int x, y;
   int[] edge = new int[2];
   LinkedStack<int[]> vertexStack = new LinkedStack<int[]>();
   Graph<T> resultGraph = new Graph<T>();

   if (isEmpty() || !isConnected())
      return resultGraph;

   resultGraph.adjMatrix = new
      boolean[numVertices][numVertices];

   for (int i = 0; i < numVertices; i++)
      for (int j = 0; j < numVertices; j++)
         resultGraph.adjMatrix[i][j] = false;
```

```
resultGraph.vertices = (T[])(new Object[numVertices]);
boolean[] visited = new boolean[numVertices];

for (int i = 0; i < numVertices; i++)
   visited[i] = false;

edge[0] = 0;
resultGraph.vertices[0] = this.vertices[0];
resultGraph.numVertices++;
visited[0] = true;

//  Add all edges that are adjacent to vertex 0 to the stack.
for (int i = 0; i < numVertices; i++)
{
   if (!visited[i] && this.adjMatrix[0][i])
   {
      edge[1] = i;
      vertexStack.push(edge.clone());
      visited[i] = true;
   }
}

while ((resultGraph.size() < this.size()) &&
!vertexStack.isEmpty())
{
   //  Pop an edge off the stack and add it to the resultGraph.
   edge = vertexStack.pop();
   x = edge[0];
   y = edge[1];
   resultGraph.vertices[y] = this.vertices[y];
   resultGraph.numVertices++;
   resultGraph.adjMatrix[x][y] = true;
   resultGraph.adjMatrix[y][x] = true;
   visited[y] = true;

   for (int i = 0; i < numVertices; i++)
   {
      if (!visited[i] && this.adjMatrix[i][y])
      {
         edge[0] = y;
         edge[1] = i;
         vertexStack.push(edge.clone());
         visited[i] = true;
      }
   }
```

```
    }

    return resultGraph;
}
```

Determining the Shortest Path

There are two possibilities for determining the "shortest" path in a graph. The first, and perhaps simplest, possibility is to determine the literal shortest path between a starting vertex and a target vertex, meaning the least number of edges between the two vertices. This turns out to be a simple variation of our earlier breadth-first traversal algorithm.

To convert this algorithm to find the shortest path, we simply store two additional pieces of information for each vertex during our traversal: the path length from the starting vertex to this vertex, and the vertex that is the predecessor of this vertex in that path. Then we modify our loop to terminate when we reach our target vertex. The path length for the shortest path is simply the path length to the predecessor of the target + 1, and if we wish to output the vertices along the shortest path, we can simply backtrack along the chain of predecessors.

The second possibility for determining the shortest path is to look for the cheapest path in a weighted graph. Dijkstra (1959) developed an algorithm for this possibility that is similar to our previous algorithm. However, instead of using a queue of vertices that causes us to progress through the graph in the order we encounter vertices, we use a minheap or a priority queue storing vertex, weight pairs based upon total weight (the sum of the weights from the starting vertex to this vertex) so that we always traverse through the graph following the cheapest path first. For each vertex, we must store the label of the vertex, the weight of the cheapest path (thus far) to that vertex from our starting point, and the predecessor of that vertex along that path. On the minheap, we will store vertex, weight pairs for each possible path that we have encountered but not yet traversed. As we remove a vertex, weight pair from the minheap, if we encounter a vertex with a weight less than the one already stored with the vertex, we update the cost.

18.5 Strategies for Implementing Graphs

As we have done in the previous two chapters, we will present algorithms and strategies for the implementation of graphs but leave the implementations as programming projects. Let us begin our discussion of implementation strategies by examining what operations would need to be available for a graph. Of course, we would need to be able to add and remove vertices, and add and remove edges from the graph. There will need to be traversals (perhaps breadth first and depth first) beginning with a particular vertex, and these might be implemented as iterators, as we did for binary trees. Other operations like `size`, `isEmpty`, `toString`, and `find` will be useful as well. In addition to these, operations to determine the shortest path from a particular vertex to a particular target vertex, to determine the adjacency of two vertices, to construct a minimum spanning tree, and to test for connectivity would all likely need to be implemented.

Whatever storage mechanism we use for vertices must allow us to mark vertices as visited during traversals and other algorithms. This can be accomplished by simply adding a boolean variable to the class representing the vertices.

Adjacency Lists

Since trees are graphs, perhaps the best introduction to how we might implement graphs is to consider the discussions and examples that we have already seen concerning the implementation of trees. One might immediately think of using a set of nodes where each node contains an element and perhaps a linked list of up to n–1 links to other nodes. When we used this strategy with trees, the number of connections from any given node was limited by the order of the tree (e.g., a maximum of two directed edges starting at any particular node in a binary tree). Because of this limitation, we were able to specify, for example, that a binary-node had a left and a right child pointer. Even if the binary-node was a leaf, the pointer still existed. It was simply set to null.

In the case of a *graph-node*, since each node could have up to n–1 edges connecting it to other nodes, it would be better to use a dynamic structure such as a linked list to store the edges within each node. This list is called an *adjacency list*. In the case of a weighted graph, each edge would be stored as a triple including the weight. In the case of an undirected graph, an edge (A, B) would appear in the adjacency list of both vertex A and vertex B.

Adjacency Matrices

Keep in mind that we must somehow efficiently (both in terms of space and access time) store both vertices and edges. Since vertices are just elements, we can use any of our collections to store the vertices. In fact, we often talk about a "set of vertices," the term set implying an implementation strategy. However, another solution for storing edges is motivated by our use of array implementations of trees, but instead of using a one-dimensional array, we will use a two-dimensional array that we call an *adjacency matrix*. In an adjacency matrix, each position of the two-dimensional array represents an intersection between two vertices in the graph. Each of these intersections is represented by a boolean value indicating whether or not the two vertices are connected. Figure 18.13 shows an undirected graph and its adjacency matrix.

For any position (row, column) in the matrix, that position is true if and only if the edge (v_{row}, v_{column}) is in the graph. Since edges in an undirected graph are bi-directional, if (A, B) is an edge in the graph, then (B, A) is also in the graph.

Notice that this matrix is symmetrical—that is, each side of the diagonal is a mirror image of the other. The reason for this is that we are representing an undirected graph. For undirected graphs, it may not be necessary to represent the entire matrix but simply one side or the other of the diagonal.

However, for directed graphs, since all of the edges are directional, the result can be quite different. Figure 18.14 shows a directed graph and its adjacency matrix.

Adjacency matrices may also be used with weighted graphs by simply storing an object at each position of the matrix to represent the weight of the edge. Positions in the matrix where edges do not exist would simply be set to null.

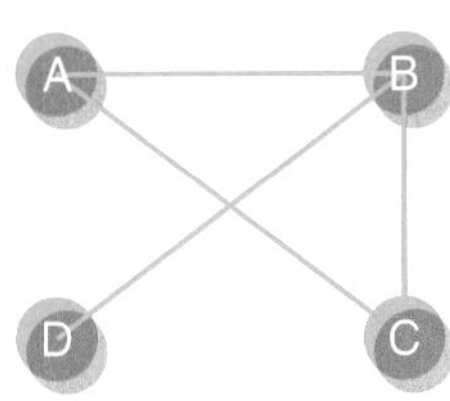

	A	B	C	D
A	F	T	T	F
B	T	F	T	T
C	T	T	F	F
D	F	T	F	F

FIGURE 18.13 An undirected graph and its adjacency matrix

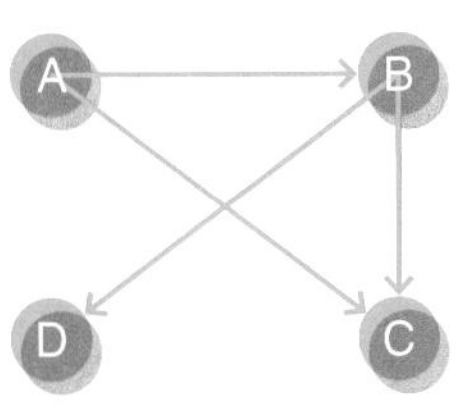

	A	B	C	D
A	F	T	T	F
B	F	F	T	T
C	F	F	F	F
D	F	F	F	F

FIGURE 18.14 A directed graph and its adjacency matrix

Summary of Key Concepts

- An undirected graph is a graph where the pairings representing the edges are unordered.
- Two vertices in a graph are adjacent if there is an edge connecting them.
- An undirected graph is considered complete if it has the maximum number of edges connecting vertices.
- A path is a sequence of edges that connects two vertices in a graph.
- A cycle is a path in which the first and last vertices are the same and none of the edges are repeated.
- In a directed graph, the edges are ordered pairs of vertices.
- A path in a directed graph is a sequence of directed edges that connects two vertices in a graph.
- A weighted graph is a graph with costs associated with each edge.
- The main difference between a depth-first traversal of a graph and a breadth-first traversal is the use of a stack instead of a queue to manage the traversal.
- A graph is connected if and only if the number of vertices in the breadth-first traversal is the same as the number of vertices in the graph regardless of the starting vertex.
- A spanning tree is a tree that includes all of the vertices of a graph and some, but possibly not all, of the edges.
- A minimum spanning tree is a spanning tree where the sum of the weights of the edges is less than or equal to the sum of the weights for any other spanning tree for the same graph.

Self-Review Questions

SR 18.1 What is the difference between a graph and a tree?

SR 18.2 What is an undirected graph?

SR 18.3 What is a directed graph?

SR 18.4 What does it mean to say that a graph is complete?

SR 18.5 What is the maximum number of edges for an undirected graph? A directed graph?

SR 18.6 What is the definition of a path? A cycle?

SR 18.7 What is the difference between a weighted graph and a graph?

SR 18.8 What is a spanning tree? A minimum spanning tree?

Exercises

EX 18.1 Draw the undirected graph that is represented by the following:

vertices: 1, 2, 3, 4, 5, 6, 7

edges: (1, 2), (1, 4), (2, 3), (2, 4), (3, 7), (4, 7), (4, 6), (5, 6), (5, 7), (6, 7)

EX 18.2 Is the graph from Exercise 18.1 connected? Complete?

EX 18.3 List all of the cycles in the graph from Exercise 18.1.

EX 18.4 Draw a spanning tree for the graph of Exercise 18.1.

EX 18.5 Using the same data from Exercise 18.1, draw the resulting directed graph.

EX 18.6 Is the directed graph of Exercise 18.5 connected? Complete?

EX 18.7 List all of the cycles in the graph of Exercise 18.5.

EX 18.8 Draw a spanning tree for the graph of Exercise 18.5.

EX 18.9 Consider the weighted graph shown in Figure 18.10. List all of the possible paths from vertex 2 to vertex 3 along with the total weight of each path.

Programming Projects

PP 18.1 Implement an undirected graph using whatever underlying data structure you prefer. Keep in mind that you must store both vertices and edges. Your implementation should include methods for adding and removing vertices, adding and removing edges, `size` (which should return the number of vertices), `isEmpty`, a breadth-first iterator, and a depth-first iterator.

PP 18.2 Repeat programming project 18.1 for a directed graph.

PP 18.3 Implement a shortest path method to go along with your implementation for programming project 18.1 that will either return the length of the shortest path or return –1 if no path is found.

PP 18.4 Repeat programming project 18.3 for the directed graph implementation of programming project 18.2.

PP 18.5 Extend your implementation from programming project 18.1 to create a weighted, undirected graph and add a method to return a minimum spanning tree.

PP 18.6 Extend your implementation from programming project 18.2 to create a weighted, directed graph and add a method to return a minimum spanning tree.

PP 18.7 Create a limited airline scheduling system that will allow a user to enter city to city connections and their prices. Your system should then allow a user to enter two cities and should return the shortest path and the cheapest path between the two cities. Your system should report if there is no connection between two cities. Use an undirected weighted graph.

PP 18.8 Repeat programming project 18.7 assuming a directed weighted graph.

PP 18.9 Create a computer network routing system that, given the point-to-point connections in the network and the costs of utilizing each, will produce cheapest-path connections from each point to each point in the network, pointing out any disconnected locations.

Answers to Self-Review Questions

SR 18.1 A graph is the more general concept without the restriction that each node has one and only one parent except for the root, which does not have a parent. In the case of a graph, there is no root, and each vertex can be connected to up to n–1 other vertices.

SR 18.2 An undirected graph is a graph where the pairings representing the edges are unordered.

SR 18.3 A directed graph, sometimes referred as a digraph, is a graph where the edges are ordered pairs of vertices.

SR 18.4 A graph is considered complete if it has the maximum number of edges connecting vertices.

SR 18.5 The maximum number of edges for an undirected graph is n(n–1)/2. For a directed graph, it is n(n–1).

SR 18.6 A path is a sequence of edges that connects two vertices in a graph. A cycle is a path in which the first and last vertices are the same and none of the edges are repeated.

SR 18.7 A weighted graph is a graph, either directed or undirected, with weights or costs associated with each edge.

SR 18.8 A spanning tree is a tree that includes all of the vertices of a graph and some, but possibly not all, of the edges. A minimum spanning tree is a spanning tree where the sum of the weights of the edges is less than or equal to the sum of the weights for any other spanning tree for the same graph.

Glossary

abstract—A Java reserved word that serves as a modifier for classes, interfaces, and methods. An `abstract` class cannot be instantiated and is used to specify bodiless abstract methods that are given definitions by derived classes. Interfaces are inherently abstract.

abstract class—*See* abstract.

abstract data type (ADT)—A collection of data and the operations that are defined on that data. An abstract data type might be implemented in a variety of ways, but the interface operations are consistent.

abstract method—*See* abstract.

Abstract Windowing Toolkit (AWT)—The package in the Java API (`java.awt`) that contains classes related to graphics and GUIs. *See also* Swing.

abstraction—The concept of hiding details. If the right details are hidden at the right times, abstraction can significantly help control complexity and focus attention on appropriate issues.

access—The ability to reference a variable or invoke a method from outside the class in which it is declared. Controlled by the visibility modifier used to declare the variable or method. Also called the level of encapsulation. *See also* visibility modifier.

access modifier—*See* visibility modifier.

actual parameter—The value passed to a method as a parameter. *See also* formal parameter.

adaptor class—*See* listener adaptor class.

address—(1) A numeric value that uniquely identifies a particular memory location in a computer's main memory. (2) A designation that uniquely identifies a computer among all others on a network.

adjacency list—A list of all of the edges in a graph grouped by the vertices that each edge touches. *See also* edge, graph, vertex.

adjacency matrix—A matrix (two-dimensional array) that stores the list of edges in a graph. Each position in the array represents an intersection between two vertices in the graph. *See also* array, edge, graph, vertex.

ADT—*See* abstract data type.

aggregate object—An object that contains variables that are references to other objects. *See also* has-a relationship.

aggregation—Something that is composed, at least in part, of other things. *See also* aggregate object.

algorithm—A step-by-step process for solving a problem. A program is based on one or more algorithms.

alias—A reference to an object that is currently also referred to by another reference. Each reference is an alias of the other.

analog—A representation that is in direct proportion to the source of the information. *See also* digital.

animation—A series of images or drawings that gives the appearance of movement when displayed in order at a particular speed.

ANT—A build tool generally used with Java program development. *See also* build tool.

API—*See* application programming interface (API).

applet—A Java program that is linked into an HTML document, then retrieved and executed using a Web browser, as opposed to a stand-alone Java application.

appletviewer—A software tool that interprets and displays Java applets through links in HTML documents. Part of the Java Development Kit.

application—(1) A generic term for any program. (2) A Java program that can be run without the use of a Web browser, as opposed to a Java applet.

application programming interface (API)—A set of classes that defines services for a programmer. Not part of the language itself, but often relied on to perform even basic tasks. *See also* class library.

arc angle—When defining an arc, the radial distance that defines the arc's length. *See also* start angle.

architectural design—A high-level design that identifies the large portions of a software system and key data structures. *See also* detailed design.

architecture—*See* computer architecture.

architecture neutral—Not specific to any particular hardware platform. Java code is considered architecture neutral because it is compiled into bytecode and then interpreted on any machine with a Java interpreter. *See also* bytecode.

arithmetic operator—An operator that performs a basic arithmetic computation, such as addition or multiplication.

arithmetic promotion—The act of promoting the type of a numeric operand to be consistent with the other operand.

array—A programming language construct used to store an ordered list of primitive values or objects. Each element in the array is referenced using a numerical index from 0 to $N-1$, where N is the size of the array.

array element—A value or object that is stored in an array.

array element type—The type of the values or objects that are stored in an array.

ASCII—A popular character set used by many programming languages. ASCII stands for American Standard Code for Information Interchange. It is a subset of the Unicode character set, which is used by Java.

assembly language—A low-level language that uses mnemonics to represent program commands.

assert—A Java reserved word that is used to make an assertion that a condition is fulfilled. *See also* assertion.

assertion—A programming language construct that is used to declare a programmatic assumption (that is usually true). Assertions are used by JUnit for the purposes of unit testing. *See also* JUnit, unit testing.

assignment conversion—Some data types can be converted to another data type in an assignment statement. *See* widening conversion.

assignment operator—An operator that results in an assignment to a variable. The = operator performs basic assignment. Many other assignment operators perform additional operations prior to the assignment, such as the *= operator.

association—A relationship between two classes in which one uses the other or relates to it in some way. *See also* operator association, use relationship.

asymptotic complexity—The order, or dominant term, of a growth function. *See also* dominant term, growth function.

AWT—*See* Abstract Windowing Toolkit.

background color—(1) The color of the background of a GUI component. (2) The color of the background of an HTML page. *See also* foreground color.

bag—A collection that facilitates the selection of random elements from a group. *See also* collection.

balanced tree—A tree whose leaves are all on the same level or within one level of each other. *See also* leaf, tree.

base—The numerical value on which a particular number system is based. It determines the number of digits available in that number system and the place value of each digit in a number. *See also* binary, decimal, hexadecimal, octal, place value.

base 2—*See* binary.

base 8—*See* octal.

base 10—*See* decimal.

base 16—*See* hexadecimal.

base case—The situation that terminates recursive processing, allowing the active recursive methods to begin returning to their point of invocation.

base class—*See* superclass.

behavior—The functional characteristics of an object, defined by its methods. *See also* identity, state.

binary—The base-2 number system. Modern computer systems store information as strings of binary digits (bits).

binary operator—An operator that uses two operands.

binary search—A searching algorithm that requires that the list be sorted. It repetitively compares the "middle" element of the list to the target value, narrowing the scope of the search each time. *See also* linear search.

binary search tree—A binary tree with the added property that, for each node, the left child is less than the parent, and the right child is greater than or equal to the parent. *See also* node, tree.

binary string—A series of binary digits (bits).

binary tree—A tree data structure in which each node can have no more than two child nodes.

binding—The process of associating an identifier with the construct that it represents. For example, the process of binding a method name to the specific definition that it invokes.

bit—A binary digit, either 0 or 1.

bit shifting—The act of shifting the bits of a data value to the left or right, losing bits on one end and inserting bits on the other.

bits per second (bps)—A measurement rate for data transfer devices.

bitwise operator—An operator that manipulates individual bits of a value, either by calculation or by shifting.

black-box testing—Producing and evaluating test cases based on the input and expected output of a software component. The test cases focus on covering the equivalence categories and boundary values of the input. *See also* white-box testing.

block—A group of programming statements and declarations delimited by braces (`{}`).

boolean—A Java reserved word representing a logical primitive data type that can only take the values `true` or `false`.

boolean expression—An expression that evaluates to a true or false result, primarily used as conditions in selection and repetition statements.

boolean operator—Any of the bitwise operators AND (`&`), OR (`|`), or XOR (`^`) when applied to `boolean` operands. The results are equivalent to their logical counterparts, except that boolean operators are not short-circuited.

border—A graphical edge around a GUI component to enhance its appearance or to group components visually. An empty border creates a buffer of space around a component.

boundary values—The input values corresponding to the edges of equivalence categories. Used in black-box testing.

bounding rectangle—A rectangle that delineates a region in which an oval or arc is defined.

bounds checking—The process of determining whether an array index is in bounds, given the size of the array. Java performs automatic bounds checking.

bps—*See* bits per second.

breadth-first traversal—A graph traversal that starts at a given vertex, then visits all neighboring vertices one edge from the starting vertex, then visits all vertices two edges from the starting vertex, and so on. *See also* depth-first traversal, graph, vertex.

break—A Java reserved word used to interrupt the flow of control by breaking out of the current loop or `switch` statement.

breakpoints—A special flag or tag in a debugger that pauses execution of the program being debugged when the execution reaches the breakpoint.

browser—Software that retrieves HTML documents across network connections and formats them for viewing. A browser is the primary vehicle for accessing the World Wide Web. *See also* Netscape Navigator.

bubble sort—A sorting algorithm in which values are repeatedly compared to neighboring elements in the list and their positions are swapped if they are not in order relative to each other. *See also* heap sort, insertion sort, merge sort, quick sort, radix sort, selection sort.

bug—A slang term for a defect or error in a computer program.

build-and-fix approach—An approach to software development in which a program is created without any significant planning or design, then modified until it reaches some level of acceptance. It is a prevalent, but unwise, approach.

build tool—A software application used to automate, define, and execute a consistent process for building software applications.

bus—A group of wires in the computer that carries data between components such as the CPU and main memory.

button—A GUI component that allows the user to initiate an action, set a condition, or choose an option with a mouse click. There are several kinds of GUI buttons. *See also* check box, push button, radio button.

byte—(1) A unit of binary storage equal to 8 bits. (2) A Java reserved word that represents a primitive integer type, stored using 8 bits in two's complement format.

byte stream—An I/O stream that manages 8-bit bytes of raw binary data. *See also* character stream.

bytecode—The low-level format into which the Java compiler translates Java source code. The bytecode is interpreted and executed by the Java interpreter, perhaps after transportation over the Internet.

capacity—*See* storage capacity.

case—(1) A Java reserved word that is used to identify each unique option in a `switch` statement. (2) The orientation of an alphabetic character (uppercase or lowercase).

case sensitive—Differentiating between the uppercase and lowercase versions of an alphabetic letter. Java is case sensitive; therefore the identifier `total` and the identifier `Total` are considered to be different identifiers.

cast—A Java operation expressed using a type or class name in parentheses to explicitly convert and return a value of one data type into another.

catch—A Java reserved word that is used to specify an exception handler, defined after a `try` block.

CD-Recordable (CD-R)—A compact disc on which information can be stored once using a home computer with an appropriate drive. *See also* CD-Rewritable, CD-ROM.

CD-Rewritable (CD-RW)—A compact disc on which information can be stored and rewritten multiple times using a home computer with an appropriate drive. *See also* CD-Recordable, CD-ROM.

CD-ROM—An optical secondary memory medium that stores binary information in a manner similar to a musical compact disc.

central processing unit (CPU)—The hardware component that controls the main activity of a computer, including the flow of information and the execution of commands.

char—A Java reserved word that represents the primitive character type. All Java characters are members of the Unicode character set and are stored using 16 bits.

character font—A specification that defines the distinct look of a character when it is printed or drawn.

character set—An ordered list of characters, such as the ASCII or Unicode character sets. Each character corresponds to a specific, unique numeric value within a given character set. A programming language adopts a particular character set to use for character representation and management.

character stream—An I/O stream that manages 16-bit Unicode characters. *See also* byte stream.

character string—A series of ordered characters. Represented in Java using the `String` class and string literals such as `"hello"`.

check box—A GUI component that allows the user to set a boolean condition with a mouse click. A check box can be used alone or independently among other check boxes. *See also* radio button.

checked exception—A Java exception that must be either caught or explicitly thrown to the calling method. *See also* unchecked exception.

child class—*See* subclass.

circular array—Conceptually, an array whose last index is followed by the first index.

class—(1) A Java reserved word used to define a class. (2) The blueprint of an object—the model that defines the variables and methods an object will contain when instantiated.

class diagram—A diagram that shows the relationships between classes, including inheritance and use relationships. *See also* Unified Modeling Language.

class hierarchy—A tree-like structure created when classes are derived from other classes through inheritance. *See also* interface hierarchy.

class library—A set of classes that defines useful services for a programmer. *See also* application programming interface (API).

class method—A method that can be invoked using only the class name. An instantiated object is not required as it is with instance methods. Defined in a Java program by using the `static` reserved word.

class variable—A variable that is shared among all objects of a class. It can also be referenced through the class name, without instantiating any object of that class. Defined in a Java program by using the `static` reserved word.

CLASSPATH—An operating system setting that determines where the Java interpreter searches for class files.

client-server model—A manner in which to construct a software design based on objects (clients) making use of the services provided by other objects (servers).

coding guidelines—A series of conventions that describe how programs should be constructed. They make programs easier to read, exchange, and integrate. Sometimes referred to as coding standards, especially when they are enforced.

coding standard—*See* coding guidelines.

cohesion—The strength of the relationship among the parts within a software component. *See also* coupling.

collection—An object that serves as a repository for other objects.

collision—The process of two hash values producing the same hash code. *See also* hash code, hashing.

color chooser—A GUI component, often displayed as a dialog box, that allows the user to select or specify a color.

combo box—A GUI component that allows the user to select one of several options. A combo box displays the most recent selection. *See also* list.

command-line arguments—The values that follow the program name on the command line. Accessed within a Java program through the `String` array parameter to the `main` method.

command shell—A text-based user interface for issuing commands to a computer operating system.

comment—A programming language construct that allows a programmer to embed human-readable annotations into the source code. *See also* documentation.

compile-time error—Any error that occurs during the compilation process, often indicating that a program does not conform to the language syntax or that an operation was attempted on an inappropriate data type. *See also* logical error, run-time error, syntax error.

compiler—A program that translates code from one language to equivalent code in another language. The Java compiler translates Java source code into Java bytecode. *See also* interpreter.

complete tree—A tree that is balanced and all of whose leaves at the bottom level are on the left side of the tree. *See also* balanced tree, leaf.

component—Any portion of a software system that performs a specific task, transforming input to output. *See also* GUI component.

computer architecture—The structure and interaction of the hardware components of a computer.

concatenation—*See* string concatenation.

condition—A boolean expression used to determine whether the body of a selection or repetition statement should be executed.

conditional coverage—A strategy used in white-box testing in which all conditions in a program are executed, producing both `true` and `false` results. *See also* statement coverage.

conditional operator—A Java ternary operator that evaluates one of two expressions based on a condition.

conditional statement—*See* selection statement.

connected graph—A graph in which a path exists between any two vertices. *See also* graph, path, vertex.

const—A Java reserved word that is not currently used.

constant—An identifier that contains a value that cannot be modified. Used to make code more readable and to facilitate changes. Defined in Java using the `final` modifier.

constant complexity—A growth function of an algorithm that executes in a set amount of time regardless of the size of the problem. *See also* growth function.

constructor—A special method in a class that is invoked when an object is instantiated from the class. Used to initialize the object.

container—A Java GUI component that can hold other components. *See also* containment hierarchy.

containment hierarchy—The relationships among graphical components of a user interface. *See also* container.

content pane—The part of a top-level container to which components are added.

control characters—*See* nonprintable characters.

controllers—Hardware devices that control the interaction between a computer system and a particular kind of peripheral.

coupling—The strength of the relationship between two software components. *See also* cohesion.

CPU—*See* central processing unit.

cycle—A path in a graph in which the first and last vertices are the same and none of the edges are repeated. *See also* graph.

data stream—An I/O stream that represents a particular source or destination for data, such as a file. *See also* processing stream.

data structure—Any programming construct, either defined in the language or by a programmer, used to organize data into a format to facilitate access and processing. Arrays, linked lists, and stacks can all be considered data structures.

data transfer device—A hardware component that allows information to be sent between computers, such as a modem.

data type—A designation that specifies a set of values (which may be infinite). For example, each variable has a data type that specifies the kinds of values that can be stored in it.

debugger—A software tool that allows a programmer to step through an executing program and examine the value of variables at any point. *See also* jdb.

debugging—The act of locating and correcting run-time and logic errors in your programs.

decimal—The base-10 number system, which humans use in everyday life. *See also* binary.

default—A Java reserved word that is used to indicate the default case of a `switch` statement, used if no other cases match.

default visibility—The level of access designated when no explicit visibility modifier is used to declare a class, interface, method, or variable. Sometimes referred to as package visibility. Classes and interfaces declared with default visibility can be used within their package. A method or variable declared with default visibility is inherited and accessible by all subclasses in the same package.

defect testing—Testing designed to uncover errors in a program.

defined—Existing for use in a derived class, even if it can only be accessed indirectly. *See also* inheritance.

degenerate tree—A tree whose nodes are located primarily on one side. *See also* tree.

delimiter—Any symbol or word used to set the boundaries of a programming language construct, such as the braces (`{}`) used to define a Java block.

deprecated—Something, such as a particular method, that is considered old-fashioned and should not be used.

depth-first traversal—A graph traversal that starts at a given vertex, and traverses as far as possible along a sequence of edges before backtracking and traversing alternative, skipped edges. *See also* breadth-first traversal, graph, vertex.

derived class—*See* subclass.

design—(1) The plan for implementing a program, which includes a specification of the classes and objects used and an expression of the important program algorithms. (2) The process of creating a program design.

desk check—A type of review in which a developer carefully examines a design or program to find errors.

detailed design—(1) The low-level algorithmic steps of a method. (2) The development stage at which low-level algorithmic steps are determined.

development stage—The software life-cycle stage in which a software system is first created, preceding use, maintenance, and eventual retirement.

dialog box—A graphical window that pops up to allow brief, specific user interaction.

digital—A representation that breaks information down into pieces, which are in turn represented as numbers. All modern computer systems are digital.

digitize—The act of converting an analog representation into a digital one by breaking it down into pieces.

digraph—*See* directed graph.

dimension—The number of index levels of a particular array.

direct recursion—The process of a method invoking itself. *See also* indirect recursion.

directed graph—A graph data structure in which each edge has a specific direction. *See also* edge.

disable—Make a GUI component inactive so that it cannot be used. A disabled component is grayed to indicate its disabled status. *See also* enable.

DNS—*See* Domain Name System.

do—A Java reserved word that represents a repetition construct. A `do` statement is executed one or more times. *See also* for, while.

documentation—Supplemental information about a program, including comments in a program's source code and printed reports such as a user's guide.

domain name—The portion of an Internet address that specifies the organization to which the computer belongs.

Domain Name System (DNS)—Software that translates an Internet address into an IP address using a domain server.

domain server—A file server that maintains a list of Internet addresses and their corresponding IP addresses.

dominant term—The term in a growth function that increases the most as the problem size (n) increases. The dominant term is the basis of determining the order of an algorithm. *See also* growth function, order.

double—A Java reserved word that represents a primitive floating point numeric type, stored using 64 bits in IEEE 754 format.

doubly linked list—A linked list with two references in each node: one that refers to the next node in the list and one that refers to the previous node in the list.

dynamic binding—The process of associating an identifier with its definition during run time. *See also* binding.

dynamic structure—A set of objects that are linked using references, which can be modified as needed during program execution.

edge—A connector (in a linked structure, a reference) between two nodes in a tree or graph. *See also* graph, node, tree.

editor—A software tool that allows the user to enter and store a file of characters on a computer. Often used by programmers to enter the source code of a program.

efficiency—The characteristic of an algorithm that specifies the required number of a particular operation in order to complete its task. For example, the efficiency of a sort can be measured by the number of comparisons required to sort a list. *See also* order.

element—A value or object stored in another object such as an array.

element type—*See* array element type.

else—A Java reserved word that designates the portion of code in an `if` statement that will be executed if the condition is false.

enable—Make a GUI component active so that it can be used. *See also* disable.

encapsulation—The characteristic of an object that limits access to the variables and methods contained in it. All interaction with an object occurs through a well-defined interface that supports a modular design.

environment variable—A variable located in the system's settings or command shell that can store a value (typically the path to a file or directory). Environment variables can be used within a command shell or program for configuration purposes. *See also* command shell.

equality operator—One of two Java operators that returns a boolean result based on whether two values are equal (`==`) or not equal (`!=`).

equivalence category—A range of functionally equivalent input values as specified by the requirements of the software component. Used when developing black-box test cases.

error—(1) Any defect in a design or program. (2) An object that can be thrown and processed by special `catch` blocks, though usually errors should not be caught. *See also* compile-time error, exception, logical error, run-time error, syntax error.

escape sequence—In Java, a sequence of characters beginning with the backslash character (\), used to indicate a special situation when printing values. For example, the escape sequence `\t` specifies that a horizontal tab should be printed.

exception—(1) A situation that arises during program execution that is erroneous or out of the ordinary. (2) An object that can be thrown and processed by special `catch` blocks. *See also* error.

exception handler—The code in a `catch` clause of a `try` statement, executed when a particular type of exception is thrown.

exception propagation—The process that occurs when an exception is thrown: control returns to each calling method in the stack trace until the exception is caught and handled or until the exception is thrown from the `main` method, terminating the program.

exponent—The portion of a floating point value's internal representation that specifies how far the decimal point is shifted. *See also* mantissa.

exponential complexity—An equation that specifies the efficiency of an algorithm whose dominant term contains the problem size as an exponent (e.g., 2^n). *See also* growth function.

expression—A combination of operators and operands that produces a result.

extends—A Java reserved word used to specify the parent class in the definition of a child class.

event—(1) A user action, such as a mouse click or key press. (2) An object that represents a user action, to which the program can respond. *See also* event-driven programming.

event-driven programming—An approach to software development in which the program is designed to acknowledge that an event has occurred and to act accordingly. *See also* event.

factorial—The product of all integers between 1 and any positive integer N (written N!).

false—A Java reserved word that serves as one of the two boolean literals (`true` and `false`).

fetch-decode-execute—The cycle through which the CPU continually obtains instructions from main memory and executes them.

FIFO—*See* first-in, first-out.

file—A named collection of data stored on a secondary storage device such as a disk. *See also* text file.

file chooser—A GUI component, usually displayed as a dialog box, that allows the user to select a file from a storage device.

file server—A computer in a network, usually with a large secondary storage capacity, that is dedicated to storing software needed by many network users.

filtering stream—*See* processing stream.

final—A Java reserved word that serves as a modifier for classes, methods, and variables. A final class cannot be used to derive a new class. A final method cannot be overridden. A final variable is a constant.

finalize—A Java method defined in the `Object` class that can be overridden in any other class. It is called after the object becomes a candidate for garbage collection and before it is destroyed. It can be used to perform "clean-up" activity that is not performed automatically by the garbage collector.

finalizer method—A Java method, called `finalize`, that is called before an object is destroyed. *See also* finalize.

finally—A Java reserved word that designates a block of code to be executed when an exception is thrown, after any appropriate catch handler is processed.

first-in, first-out (FIFO)—A data management technique in which the first value that is stored in a data structure is the first value that comes out. *See also* last-in, first-out; queue.

float—A Java reserved word that represents a primitive floating point numeric type, stored using 32 bits in IEEE 754 format.

flushing—The process of forcing the contents of the output buffer to be displayed on the output device.

font—*See* character font.

for—A Java reserved word that represents a repetition construct. A `for` statement is executed zero or more times and is usually used when a precise number of iterations is known.

foreground color—The color in which any current drawing will be rendered. *See also* background color.

formal parameter—An identifier that serves as a parameter name in a method. It receives its initial value from the actual parameter passed to it. *See also* actual parameter.

fourth-generation language—A high-level language that provides built-in functionality such as automatic report generation or database management, beyond that of traditional high-level languages.

full tree—An n-ary tree whose leaves are all on the same level and in which every node is a leaf or has exactly *n* children. *See also* leaf, level, node, tree.

function—A named group of declarations and programming statements that can be invoked (executed) when needed. A function that is part of a class is called a method. Java has no functions because all code is part of a class.

garbage—(1) An unspecified or uninitialized value in a memory location. (2) An object that cannot be accessed anymore because all references to it have been lost.

garbage collection—The process of reclaiming unneeded, dynamically allocated memory. Java performs automatic garbage collection of objects that no longer have any valid references to them.

general tree—A tree with no limit to the number of children a node may contain or reference. *See also* node, tree.

generic type—A class designed so that it stores, operates on, and manages objects whose type is not specified until the class is instantiated.

gigabyte (GB)—A unit of binary storage, equal to 2^{30} (approximately 1 billion) bytes.

glass-box testing—*See* white-box testing.

goto—(1) A Java reserved word that is not currently used. (2) An unconditional branch.

grammar—A representation of language syntax that specifies how reserved words, symbols, and identifiers can be combined into valid programs.

graph—A nonlinear data structure made up of vertices and edges that connect the vertices. *See also* directed graph, undirected graph, vertex, edge.

graphical user interface (GUI)—Software that provides the means to interact with a program or operating system by making use of graphical images and point-and-click mechanisms such as buttons and text fields.

graphics context—The drawing surface and related coordinate system on which a drawing is rendered or GUI components are placed.

growth function—A function that shows the complexity of an algorithm relative to the size of the problem (n). A growth function can represent the time complexity or space complexity of the algorithm. *See also* order.

GUI component—A visual element, such as a button or text field, that is used to make up a GUI.

hardware—The tangible components of a computer system, such as the keyboard, monitor, and circuit boards.

has-a relationship—The relationship between two objects in which one is composed, at least in part, of one or more of the other. *See also* aggregate object, is-a relationship.

hash code—An integer value calculated from any given data value or object, used to determine where a value should be stored in a hash table. Also called a hash value. *See also* hashing.

hash method—A method that calculates a hash code from a data value or object. The same data value or object will always produce the same hash code. Also called a hash function. *See also* hashing.

hash table—A data structure in which values are stored for efficient retrieval. *See also* hashing.

hashing—A technique for storing items so that they can be found efficiently. Items are stored in a hash table at a position specified by a calculated hash code. *See also* hash method.

heap—A complete binary tree in which each element is greater than or equal to both of its children. *See also* binary tree, minheap.

heap sort—A sorting algorithm in which a set of elements is sorted by adding each one to a heap, then removing them one at a time. *See also* bubble sort, merge sort, quick sort, radix sort, selection sort.

hexadecimal—The base-16 number system, often used as an abbreviated representation of binary strings.

hierarchy—An organizational technique in which items are layered or grouped to reduce complexity.

high-level language—A programming language in which each statement represents many machine-level instructions.

HTML—*See* HyperText Markup Language.

hybrid object-oriented language—A programming language that can be used to implement a program in a procedural manner or an object-oriented manner, at the programmer's discretion. *See also* pure object-oriented language.

hypermedia—The concept of hypertext extended to include other media types such as graphics, audio, video, and programs.

hypertext—A document representation that allows a user to easily navigate through it in other than a linear fashion. Links to other parts of the document are embedded at the appropriate places to allow the user to jump from one part of the document to another. *See also* hypermedia.

HyperText Markup Language (HTML)—The notation used to define Web pages. *See also* browser, World Wide Web.

icon—A small, fixed-sized picture, often used to decorate a GUI. *See also* image.

IDE—*See* integrated development environment.

identifier—Any name that a programmer makes up to use in a program, such as a class name or variable name.

identity—The designation of an object, which, in Java, is an object's reference name. See also *state, behavior.*

IEEE 754—A standard for representing floating point values. Used by Java to represent `float` and `double` data types.

if—A Java reserved word that specifies a simple conditional construct. *See also* else.

image—A picture, often specified using a GIF or JPEG format. *See also* icon.

IMAP—*See* Internet Message Access Protocol.

immutable—The characteristic of something that does not change. For example, the contents of a Java character string are immutable once the string has been defined.

implementation—(1) The process of translating a design into source code. (2) The source code that defines a method, class, abstract data type, or other programming entity.

implements—A Java reserved word that is used in a class declaration to specify that the class implements the methods specified in a particular interface.

import—A Java reserved word that is used to specify the packages and classes that are used in a particular Java source code file.

index—The integer value used to specify a particular element in an array.

index operator—The brackets (`[]`) in which an array index is specified.

indirect recursion—The process of a method invoking another method, which eventually results in the original method being invoked again. *See also* direct recursion.

infinite loop—A loop that does not terminate because the condition controlling the loop never becomes false.

infinite recursion—A recursive series of invocations that does not terminate because the base case is never reached. *See also* base case.

infix expression—An expression in which the operators are positioned between the operands on which they work. *See also* postfix expression.

inheritance—The ability to derive a new class from an existing one. Inherited variables and methods of the original (parent) class are available in the new (child) class as if they were declared locally.

initialize—To give an initial value to a variable.

initializer list—A comma-separated list of values, delimited by braces (`{}`), used to initialize and specify the size of an array.

inline documentation—Comments that are included in the source code of a program.

inner class—A nonstatic, nested class.

inorder traversal—A tree traversal that is accomplished by visiting the left child of the node, then the node, then any remaining nodes. *See also* level-order traversal, postorder traversal, preorder traversal.

input/output buffer—A storage location for data on its way from the user to the computer (input buffer) or from the computer to the user (output buffer).

input/output devices—Hardware components that allow the human user to interact with the computer, such as a keyboard, mouse, and monitor.

input/output stream—A sequence of bytes that represents a source of data (input stream) or a destination for data (output stream).

insertion sort—A sorting algorithm in which each value, one at a time, is inserted into a sorted subset of the entire list. *See also* bubble sort, heap sort, merge sort, quick sort, radix sort, selection sort.

inspection—*See* walkthrough.

instance—An object created from a class. Multiple objects can be instantiated from a single class.

instance method—A method that must be invoked through a particular instance of a class, as opposed to a class method.

instance variable—A variable that must be referenced through a particular instance of a class, as opposed to a class variable.

instanceof—A Java reserved word that is also an operator, used to determine the class or type of a variable.

instantiation—The act of creating an object from a class.

int—A Java reserved word that represents a primitive integer type, stored using 32 bits in two's complement format.

integrated development environment (IDE)—A software application used by software developers to create and debug programs.

integration test—The process of testing software components that are made up of other interacting components. Stresses the communication between components rather than the functionality of individual components.

interface—(1) A Java reserved word that is used to define a set of abstract methods that will be implemented by particular classes. (2) The set of messages to which an object responds, defined by the methods that can be invoked from outside of the object. (3) The techniques through which a human user interacts with a program, often graphically. *See also* graphical user interface.

interface hierarchy—A tree-like structure created when interfaces are derived from other interfaces through inheritance. *See also* class hierarchy.

internal node—A tree node that is not the root node and that has at least one child. *See also* node, root, tree.

Internet—The most pervasive wide-area network in the world; it has become the primary vehicle for computer-to-computer communication. *See also* wide-area network.

Internet address—A designation that uniquely identifies a particular computer or device on the Internet.

Internet Message Access Protocol (IMAP)—Protocol that defines the communications commands required to communicate with another machine for the purposes of reading email.

Internet Naming Authority—The governing body that approves all Internet addresses.

interpreter—A program that translates and executes code on a particular machine. The Java interpreter translates and executes Java bytecode. *See also* compiler.

invisible component—A GUI component that can be added to a container to provide buffering space between other components.

invocation—*See* method invocation.

I/O devices—*See* input/output devices.

IP address—A series of several integer values, separated by periods (`.`), that uniquely identifies a particular computer or device on the Internet. Each Internet address has a corresponding IP address.

is-a relationship—The relationship created through properly derived classes via inheritance. The subclass *is-a* more specific version of the superclass. *See also* has-a relationship.

ISO-Latin-1—A 128-character extension to the ASCII character set defined by the International Organization for Standardization (ISO). The characters correspond to the numeric values 128 through 255 in both ASCII and Unicode.

iteration—(1) One execution of the body of a repetition statement. (2) One pass through a cyclic process, such as an iterative development process.

iteration statement—*See* repetition statement.

iterative development process—A step-by-step approach for creating software, which contains a series of stages that are performed repetitively.

jar—A file format used by Java to package and compress a group of files and directories, suitable for exchanging with another computer. The jar file format is based on the zip file format. *See also* zip.

java—The Java command-line interpreter, which translates and executes Java bytecode. Part of the Java Development Kit (JDK).

Java—The programming language used throughout this text to demonstrate software development concepts. Described by its developers as object oriented, robust, secure, architecture neutral, portable, high-performance, interpreted, threaded, and dynamic.

Java API—*See* application programming interface (API).

Java Development Kit (JDK)—A collection of software tools available free from Sun Microsystems, the creators of the Java programming language. *See also* Software Development Kit.

Java Virtual Machine (JVM)—The conceptual device, implemented in software, on which Java bytecode is executed. Bytecode, which is architecture neutral, does not run on a particular hardware platform; instead, it runs on the JVM.

javac—The Java command-line compiler, which translates Java source code into Java bytecode. Part of the Java Development Kit.

javadoc—A software tool that creates external documentation in HTML format about the contents and structure of a Java software system. Part of the Java Development Kit.

javah—A software tool that generates C header and source files, used for implementing `native` methods. Part of the Java Development Kit.

javap—A software tool that disassembles a Java class file, containing unreadable bytecode, into a human-readable version. Part of the Java Development Kit.

jdb—The Java command-line debugger. Part of the Java Development Kit.

JDK—*See* Java Development Kit.

JUnit—A unit testing framework for Java applications. *See also* unit testing.

JVM—*See* Java Virtual Machine.

kilobit (Kb)—A unit of binary storage, equal to 2^{10}, or 1024, bits.

kilobyte (K or KB)—A unit of binary storage, equal to 2^{10}, or 1024, bytes.

label—(1) A GUI component that displays text, an image, or both. (2) An identifier in Java used to specify a particular line of code. The `break` and `continue` statements can jump to a specific, labeled line in the program.

LAN—*See* local-area network.

last-in, first-out (LIFO)—A data management technique in which the last value that is stored in a data structure is the first value that comes out. *See also* first-in, first-out; stack.

layout manager—An object that specifies the presentation of GUI components. Each container is governed by a particular layout manager.

leaf—A tree node that has no children. *See also* node, tree.

level—A conceptual horizontal line in a tree on which all elements of the same distance from the root node are located.

level-order traversal—A tree traversal that is accomplished by visiting all of the nodes at each level, one level at a time. *See also* inorder traversal, level, postorder traversal, preorder traversal.

lexicographic ordering—The ordering of characters and strings based on a particular character set such as Unicode.

life cycle—The stages through which a software product is developed and used.

LIFO—*See* last-in, first-out.

linear search—A search algorithm in which each item in the list is compared to the target value until the target is found or the list is exhausted. *See also* binary search.

link—(1) A designation in a hypertext document that "jumps" to a new document (or to a new part of the same document) when clicked. (2) An object reference used to connect two items in a dynamically linked structure.

linked list—A structure in which one object refers to the next, creating a linear ordering of the objects in the list. *See also* linked structure.

linked structure—A dynamic data structure in which objects are connected using references.

Linux—A computer operating system, similar to Unix, developed by hobbyists and generally available for free. *See also* operating system, Unix.

list—(1) A GUI component that presents a list of items from which the user can choose. The current selection is highlighted in the list. *See also* combo box. (2) A collection of objects arranged in a linear manner. *See also* linked list.

listener—An object that is set up to respond to an event when it occurs.

listener adaptor class—A class defined with empty methods corresponding to the methods invoked when particular events occur. A listener object can be derived from an adaptor class. *See also* listener interface.

listener interface—A Java interface that defines the methods invoked when particular events occur. A listener object can be created by implementing a listener interface. *See also* listener adaptor class.

literal—A primitive value used explicitly in a program, such as the numeric literal `147` or the string literal "`hello`".

local-area network (LAN)—A computer network designed to span short distances and connect a relatively small number of computers. *See also* wide-area network.

local variable—A variable, defined within a method, that does not exist except during the execution of the method.

logarithmic complexity—An equation that specifies the efficiency of an algorithm whose dominant term contains the problem size as the base of a logarithm (e.g. $\log_2 n$). *See also* growth function.

logical error—A problem stemming from inappropriate processing in the code. It does not cause an abnormal termination of the program, but it produces incorrect results. *See also* compile-time error, run-time error, syntax error.

logical line of code—A logical programming statement in a source code program, which may extend over multiple physical lines. *See also* physical line of code.

logical operator—One of the operators that perform a logical NOT (`!`), AND (`&&`), or OR (`||`), returning a boolean result. The logical operators are short-circuited, meaning that if their left operand is sufficient to determine the result, the right operand is not evaluated.

long—A Java reserved word that represents a primitive integer type, stored using 64 bits in two's complement format.

loop—*See* repetition statement.

loop control variable—A variable whose value specifically determines how many times a loop body is executed.

low-level language—Either machine language or assembly language, considered "low" because they are conceptually close to the basic processing of a computer when compared to high-level languages.

machine language—The native language of a particular CPU. Any software that runs on a particular CPU must be translated into its machine language.

main memory—The volatile hardware storage device where programs and data are held when they are actively needed by the CPU. *See also* secondary memory.

maintenance—(1) The process of fixing errors in or making enhancements to a released software product. (2) The software life-cycle phase in which the software is in use and changes are made to it as needed.

make—A build tool generally used with C and C++ program development. *See also* build tool.

mantissa—The portion of a floating point value's internal representation that specifies the magnitude of the number. *See also* exponent.

max heap—A complete binary tree in which each element is greater than or equal to both of its children. *See also* binary tree, min heap.

megabyte (MB)—A unit of binary storage, equal to 2^{20} (approximately 1 million) bytes.

member—A variable or method in an object or class.

memory—Hardware devices that store programs and data. *See also* main memory, secondary memory.

memory location—An individual, addressable cell inside main memory into which data can be stored.

memory management—The process of controlling dynamically allocated portions of main memory, especially the act of returning allocated memory when it is no longer required. *See also* garbage collection.

merge sort—A sorting algorithm in which a list is recursively divided in half until each sublist has one element. Then, the sublists are recombined in order. *See also* bubble sort, heap sort, insertion sort, quick sort, radix sort, selection sort.

method—A named group of declarations and programming statements that can be invoked (executed) when needed. A method is part of a class.

method call conversion—The automatic widening conversion that can occur when a value of one type is passed to a formal parameter of another type.

method definition—The specification of the code that gets executed when the method is invoked. The definition includes declarations of local variables and formal parameters.

method invocation—A line of code that causes a method to be executed. It specifies any values that are passed to the method as parameters.

method overloading—*See* overloading.

min heap—A complete binary tree in which each element is less than or equal to both of its children. *See also* binary tree, max heap.

minimum spanning tree—A spanning tree where the sum of the weights of the edges is less than or equal to the sum of the weights for any other spanning tree for the same graph. *See also* edge, spanning tree.

mnemonic—(1) A word or identifier that specifies a command or data value in an assembly language. (2) A keyboard character used as a alternative means to activate a GUI component such as a button.

modal—Having multiple modes (such as a dialog box).

modem—A data transfer device that allows information to be sent along a telephone line.

modifier—A designation used in a Java declaration that specifies particular characteristics to the construct being declared.

monitor—The screen in the computer system that serves as an output device.

multidimensional array—An array that uses more than one index to specify a value stored in it.

multiple inheritance—Deriving a class from more than one parent, inheriting methods and variables from each. Multiple inheritance is not supported in Java.

multiplicity—The numeric relationship between two objects, often shown in class diagrams.

n-ary tree—A tree that limits to the value of *n* the number of children a node can contain or reference.

NaN—An abbreviation that stands for "not a number," which is the designation for an inappropriate or undefined numeric value.

narrowing conversion—A conversion between two values of different but compatible data types. Narrowing conversions could lose information because the converted type usually has an internal representation smaller than the original storage space. *See also* widening conversion.

native—A Java reserved word that serves as a modifier for methods. A native method is implemented in another programming language.

natural language—A language that humans use to communicate, such as English or French.

negative infinity—A special floating point value that represents the "lowest possible" value. *See also* positive infinity.

nested class—A class declared within another class in order to facilitate implementation and restrict access.

nested if statement—An `if` statement that has as its body another `if` statement.

Netscape Navigator—A World Wide Web browser.

network—(1) Two or more computers connected together so that they can exchange data and share resources. (2) *See* weighted graph.

network address—*See* address.

new—A Java reserved word that is also an operator, used to instantiate an object from a class.

newline character—A nonprintable character that indicates the end of a line.

nodes—Objects in a collection that generally manage the structure of the collection. Nodes can be found in linked implementations of graphs, linked structures, and trees. *See also* graph, linked structure, trees.

nonprintable characters—Any character, such as an escape or newline character, that does not have a symbolic representation that can be displayed on a monitor or printed by a printer. *See also* printable characters.

nonvolatile—The characteristic of a memory device that retains its stored information even after the power supply is turned off. Secondary memory devices are nonvolatile. *See also* volatile.

null—A Java reserved word that is a reference literal, used to indicate that a reference does not currently refer to any object.

number system—A set of values and operations defined by a particular base value that determines the number of digits available and the place value of each digit.

object—(1) The primary software construct in the object-oriented paradigm. (2) An encapsulated collection of data variables and methods. (3) An instance of a class.

object diagram—A visual representation of the objects in a program at a given point in time, often showing the status of instance data.

object-oriented programming—An approach to software design and implementation that is centered around objects and classes. *See also* procedural programming.

octal—The base-8 number system, sometimes used to abbreviate binary strings. *See also* binary, hexadecimal.

off-by-one error—An error caused by a calculation or condition being off by one, such as when a loop is set up to access one too many array elements.

operand—A value on which an operator performs its function. For example, in the expression 5 + 2, the values 5 and 2 are operands.

operating system—The collection of programs that provides the primary user interface to a computer and manages its resources, such as memory and the CPU.

operator—A symbol that represents a particular operation in a programming language, such as the addition operator (+).

operator association—The order in which operators within the same precedence level are evaluated, either right to left or left to right. *See also* operator precedence.

operator overloading—Assigning additional meaning to an operator. Operator overloading is not supported in Java, though method overloading is.

operator precedence—The order in which operators are evaluated in an expression as specified by a well-defined hierarchy.

order—The dominant term in an equation that specifies the efficiency of an algorithm. For example, selection sort is of order n^2.

order of tree—The maximum number of children a tree node may contain or reference. *See also* node, tree.

overflow—A problem that occurs when a data value grows too large for its storage size, which can result in inaccurate arithmetic processing. *See also* underflow.

overloading—Assigning additional meaning to a programming language construct, such as a method or operator. Method overloading is supported by Java but operator overloading is not.

overriding—The process of modifying the definition of an inherited method to suit the purposes of the subclass. *See also* shadowing variables.

package—A Java reserved word that is used to specify a group of related classes.

package visibility—*See* default visibility.

panel—A GUI container that holds and organizes other GUI components.

parameter—(1) A value passed from a method invocation to its definition. (2) The identifier in a method definition that accepts the value passed to it when the method is invoked. *See also* actual parameter, formal parameter.

parameter list—The list of actual or formal parameters to a method.

parameterized type—*See* generic type.

parent class—*See* superclass.

partition element—An arbitrarily chosen element in a list of values that is used by the quick sort algorithm to partition the list for recursive processing. *See also* quick sort.

pass by reference—The process of passing a reference to a value into a method as the parameter. In Java, all objects are managed using references, so an object's formal parameter is an alias to the original. *See also* pass by value.

pass by value—The process of making a copy of a value and passing the copy into a method. Therefore any change made to the value inside the method is not reflected in the original value. All Java primitive types are passed by value.

path—A sequence of edges in a tree or graph that connects two nodes. *See* also edge, graph, node, tree.

PDL—*See* Program Design Language.

peripheral—Any hardware device other than the CPU or main memory.

persistence—The ability of an object to stay in existence after the executing program that creates it terminates. *See also* serialize.

physical line of code—A line in a source code file, terminated by a newline or similar character. *See also* logical line of code.

pixel—A picture element. A digitized picture is made up of many pixels.

place value—The value of each digit position in a number, which determines the overall contribution of that digit to the value. *See also* number system.

point-to-point connection—The link between two networked devices that are connected directly by a wire.

pointer—A variable that can hold a memory address. Instead of pointers, Java uses references, which provide essentially the same functionality as pointers but without the complications.

polyline—A shape made up of a series of connected line segments. A polyline is similar to a polygon, but the shape is not closed.

polymorphism—An object-oriented technique by which a reference that is used to invoke a method can result in different methods being invoked at different times. All Java method invocations are potentially polymorphic in that they invoke the method of the object type, not the reference type.

polynomial complexity—An equation that specifies the efficiency of an algorithm whose dominant term contains the problem size raised to a power (e.g., n^2). *See also* growth function.

POP—*See* Post Office Protocol.

portability—The ability of a program to be moved from one hardware platform to another without having to change it. Because Java bytecode is not related to any particular hardware environment, Java programs are considered portable. *See also* architecture neutral.

positive infinity—A special floating point value that represents the "highest possible" value. *See also* negative infinity.

Post Office Protocol—Protocol that defines the communications commands required to communicate with another machine for the purposes of reading email.

postfix expression—An expression in which an operator is positioned after the operands on which it works. *See also* infix expression.

postfix operator—In Java, an operator that is positioned behind its single operand, whose evaluation yields the value prior to the operation being performed. Both the increment (++) and decrement (—) operators can be applied postfix. *See also* prefix operator.

postorder traversal—A tree traversal that is accomplished by visiting the children, then the node. *See also* inorder traversal, level-order traversal, preorder traversal.

precedence—*See* operator precedence.

prefix operator—In Java, an operator that is positioned in front of its single operand, whose evaluation yields the value after the operation has been performed. Both the increment (++) and decrement (—) operators can be applied prefix. *See also* postfix operator.

preorder traversal—A tree traversal which is accomplished by visiting each node, followed by its children. *See also* inorder traversal, level-order traversal, postorder traversal.

primitive data type—A data type that is predefined in a programming language.

printable characters—Any character that has a symbolic representation that can be displayed on a monitor or printed by a printer. *See also* nonprintable characters.

private—A Java reserved word that serves as a visibility modifier for methods and variables. Private methods and variables are not inherited by subclasses, and can only be accessed in the class in which they are declared.

procedural programming—An approach to software design and implementation that is centered around procedures (or functions) and their interaction. *See also* object-oriented programming.

processing stream—An I/O stream that performs some type of manipulation on the data in the stream. Sometimes called a filtering stream. *See also* data stream.

program—A series of instructions executed by hardware, one after another.

Program Design Language (PDL)—A language in which a program's design and algorithms are expressed. *See also* pseudocode.

programming language—A specification of the syntax and semantics of the statements used to create a program.

programming language statement—An individual instruction in a given programming language.

prompt—A message or symbol used to request information from the user.

propagation—*See* exception propagation.

protected—A Java reserved word that serves as a visibility modifier for methods and variables. Protected methods and variables are inherited by all subclasses and are accessible from all classes in the same package.

prototype—A program used to explore an idea or prove the feasibility of a particular approach.

pseudocode—Structured and abbreviated natural language used to express the algorithmic steps of a program. *See also* Program Design Language.

pseudo-random number—A value generated by software that performs extensive calculations based on an initial seed value. The result is not truly random because it is based on a calculation, but it is usually random enough for most purposes.

public—A Java reserved word that serves as a visibility modifier for classes, interfaces, methods, and variables. A public class or interface can be used anywhere. A public method or variable is inherited by all subclasses and is accessible anywhere.

pure object-oriented language—A programming language that enforces, to some degree, software development using an object-oriented approach. *See also* hybrid object-oriented language.

push button—A GUI component that allows the user to initiate an action with a mouse click. *See also* check box, radio button.

queue—An abstract data type that manages information in a first-in, first-out manner.

quick sort—A sorting algorithm in which the list to sort is partitioned based on an arbitrarily chosen element. Then, the sublists on either side of the partition element are recursively sorted. *See also* bubble sort, heap sort, insertion sort, merge sort, radix sort, selection sort.

radio button—A GUI component that allows the user to choose one of a set of options with a mouse click. A radio button is useful only as part of a group of other radio buttons. *See also* check box.

radix—The base, or number of possible unique digits, of a number system.

radix sort—A sorting algorithm that utilizes a series of queues. *See also* bubble sort, heap sort, insertion sort, merge sort, selection sort, quick sort.

RAM—*See* random access memory.

random access device—A memory device whose information can be directly accessed. *See also* random access memory, sequential access device.

random access memory (RAM)—A term basically interchangeable with main memory. Should probably be called read-write memory, to distinguish it from read-only memory.

random-number generator—Software that produces a pseudo-random number, generated by calculations based on a seed value.

read-only memory (ROM)—Any memory device whose stored information is stored permanently when the device is created. It can be read from, but not written to.

recursion—The process of a method invoking itself, either directly or indirectly. Recursive algorithms sometimes provide elegant, though perhaps inefficient, solutions to a problem.

refactoring—The process of modifying existing source code to clean up redundant portions introduced during the development of additional source code.

reference—A variable that holds the address of an object. In Java, a reference can be used to interact with an object, but its address cannot be accessed, set, or operated on directly.

refinement—One iteration of an evolutionary development cycle in which a particular aspect of the system, such as the user interface or a particular algorithm, is addressed.

refinement scope—The specific issues that are addressed in a particular refinement during evolutionary software development.

register—A small area of storage in the CPU of the computer.

regression testing—The process of re-executing test cases following the addition of a new feature or the correcting of an existing bug to ensure that code modifications did not introduce any new problems.

relational operator—One of several operators that determine the ordering relationship between two values: less than (<), less than or equal to (<=), greater than (>), and greater than or equal to (>=). *See also* equality operator.

release—A version of a software product that is made available to the customer.

repetition statement—A programming construct that allows a set of statements to be executed repetitively as long as a particular condition is true. The body of the repetition statement should eventually make the condition false. Also called an iteration statement or loop. *See also* do, for, while.

requirements—(1) The specification of what a program must and must not do. (2) An early phase of the software development process in which the program requirements are established.

reserved word—A word that has special meaning in a programming language and cannot be used for any other purpose.

retirement—The phase of a program's life cycle in which the program is taken out of active use.

return—A Java reserved word that causes the flow of program execution to return from a method to the point of invocation.

return type—The type of value returned from a method, specified before the method name in the method declaration. Could be `void`, which indicates that no value is returned.

reuse—Using existing software components to create new ones.

review—The process of critically examining a design or program to discover errors. There are many types of reviews. *See also* desk check, walkthrough.

RGB value—A collection of three values that defines a color. Each value represents the contribution of the primary colors red, green, and blue.

ROM—*See* read-only memory.

rotation—An operation on a tree that seeks to relocate nodes in an attempt to assist in the balance of the tree. *See also* balanced tree, node.

run-time error—A problem that occurs during program execution that causes the program to terminate abnormally. *See also* compile-time error, logical error, syntax error.

scope—The areas within a program in which an identifier, such as a variable, can be referenced. *See also* access.

scroll pane—A GUI container that offers a limited view of a component and provides horizontal and/or vertical scroll bars to change that view.

SDK—*See* Software Development Kit.

search pool—A group of items over which a search is performed.

search tree—A tree whose elements are structured to facilitate finding a particular element when needed. *See also* tree.

searching—The process of determining the existence or location of a target value within a list of values. *See also* binary search, linear search.

secondary memory—Hardware storage devices, such as magnetic disks or tapes, that store information in a relatively permanent manner. *See also* main memory.

seed value—A value used by a random-number generator as a base for the calculations that produce a pseudo-random number.

selection sort—A sorting algorithm in which each value, one at a time, is placed in its final, sorted position. *See also* bubble sort, heap sort, insertion sort, merge sort, quick sort, radix sort.

selection statement—A programming construct that allows a set of statements to be executed if a particular condition is true. *See also* if, switch.

self-loop—An edge of a graph that connects a vertex to itself.

self-referential object—An object that contains a reference to a second object of the same type.

semantics—The interpretation of a program or programming construct.

sentinel value—A specific value used to indicate a special condition, such as the end of input.

serialize—The process of converting an object into a linear series of bytes so it can be saved to a file or sent across a network. *See also* persistence.

service methods—Methods in an object that are declared with public visibility and define a service that the object's client can invoke.

shadowing variables—The process of defining a variable in a subclass that supersedes an inherited version.

shell—*See* command shell.

short—A Java reserved word that represents a primitive integer type, stored using 16 bits in two's complement format.

siblings—Two items in a tree or hierarchy, such as a class inheritance hierarchy, that have the same parent.

sign bit—A bit in a numeric value that represents the sign (positive or negative) of that value.

signed numeric value—A value that stores a sign (positive or negative). All Java numeric values are signed. A Java character is stored as an unsigned value.

signature—The number, types, and order of the parameters of a method. Overloaded methods must each have a unique signature.

Simple Mail Transfer Protocol—Protocol that defines the communications commands required to send email.

slider—A GUI component that allows the user to specify a numeric value within a bounded range by moving a knob to the appropriate place in the range.

sling—*See* self-loop.

SMTP—See *Simple Mail Transfer Protocol.*

software—(1) Programs and data. (2) The intangible components of a computer system.

software component—*See* component.

Software Development Kit (SDK)—A collection of software tools that assists in the development of software. The Java Software Development Kit is another name for the Java Development Kit.

software engineering—The discipline within computer science that addresses the process of developing high-quality software within practical constraints.

sort key—A particular value present in each member of a collection of objects upon which a sort is based.

sorting—The process of putting a list of values into a well-defined order. *See also* bubble sort, heap sort, insertion sort, merge sort, radix sort, selection sort, quick sort.

spanning tree—A tree that includes all of the vertices of a graph and some, but possibly not all, of the edges. *See also* edge, vertex.

split pane—A GUI container that displays two components, either side by side or one on top of the other, separated by a moveable divider bar.

stack—An abstract data type that manages data in a last-in, first-out manner.

stack trace—The series of methods called to reach a certain point in a program. When an exception is thrown, the stack trace can be analyzed to assist the programmer in tracking down the problem.

standard I/O stream—One of three common I/O streams representing standard input (usually the keyboard), standard output (usually the monitor screen), and standard error (also usually the monitor). *See also* stream.

start angle—When defining an arc, the angle at which the arc begins. *See also* arc angle.

state—The state of being of an object, defined by the values of its data. *See also* behavior, identity.

statement—*See* programming language statement.

statement coverage—A strategy used in white-box testing in which all statements in a program are executed. *See also* condition coverage.

static—A Java reserved word that serves as a modifier for methods and variables. A static method is also called a class method and can be referenced without an instance of the class. A static variable is also called a class variable and is common to all instances of the class.

static data structure—A data structure that has a fixed size and cannot grow and shrink as needed. *See also* dynamic data structure.

step—The execution of a single program statement in a debugger. *See also* debugger.

storage capacity—The total number of bytes that can be stored in a particular memory device.

stream—A source of input or a destination for output.

strictfp—A Java reserved word that is used to control certain aspects of floating point arithmetic.

string—*See* character string.

string concatenation—The process of attaching the beginning of one character string to the end of another, resulting in one longer string.

strongly typed language—A programming language in which each variable is associated with a particular data type for the duration of its existence. Variables are not allowed to take on values or be used in operations that are inconsistent with their type.

structured programming—An approach to program development in which each software component has one entry and exit point and in which the flow of control does not cross unnecessarily.

stub—A method that simulates the functionality of a particular software component. Often used during unit testing. *See also* unit testing.

subclass—A class derived from another class via inheritance. Also called a derived class or child class. *See also* superclass.

subscript—*See* index.

super—A Java reserved word that is a reference to the parent class of the object making the reference. Often used to invoke a parent's constructor.

super reference—*See* super.

superclass—The class from which another class is derived via inheritance. Also called a base class or parent class. *See also* subclass.

support methods—Methods in an object that are not intended for use outside the class. They provide support functionality for service methods. As such, they are usually not declared with public visibility.

swapping—The process of exchanging the values of two variables.

Swing—The package in the Java API (`javax.swing`) that contains classes related to GUIs. Swing provides alternative components from those in the Abstract Windowing Toolkit package, but does not replace it.

switch—A Java reserved word that specifies a compound conditional construct.

synchronization—The process of ensuring that data shared among multiple threads cannot be accessed by more than one thread at a time. *See also* synchronized.

synchronized—A Java reserved word that serves as a modifier for methods. Separate threads of a process can execute concurrently in a method, unless the method is synchronized, making it a mutually exclusive resource. Methods that access shared data should be synchronized.

syntax error—An error produced by the compiler because a program did not conform to the syntax of the programming language. Syntax errors are a subset of compile-time errors. *See also* compile-time error, logical error, run-time error, syntax rules.

syntax rules—The set of specifications that govern how the elements of a programming language can be put together to form valid statements.

system test—The process of testing an entire software system. Alpha and beta tests (also known as alpha and beta releases of software applications) are system tests.

tabbed pane—A GUI container that presents a set of cards from which the user can choose. Each card contains its own GUI components.

target element—*See* target value.

target value—The value that is sought when performing a search on a collection of data.

targets—User-defined groups of actions present in an ANT build file.

TCP/IP—Software that controls the movement of messages across the Internet. The acronym stands for Transmission Control Protocol/Internet Protocol.

terabyte (TB)—A unit of binary storage, equal to 2^{40} (approximately 1 trillion) bytes.

termination—The point at which a program stops executing.

ternary operator—An operator that uses three operands.

test case—A set of input values and user actions, along with a specification of the expected output, used to find errors in a system.

test-driven development—A software development style that encourages the developer to write test cases first, and then develop just enough source code to see the test cases pass.

test fixture—A method used to instantiate objects used during a test.

test suite—A set of tests that covers various aspects of the system.

testing—(1) The process of running a program with various test cases in order to discover problems. (2) The process of critically evaluating a design or program.

text area—A GUI component that displays, or allows the user to enter, multiple lines of data.

text field—A GUI component that displays, or allows the user to enter, a single line of data.

text file—A file that contains data formatted as ASCII or Unicode characters.

this—A Java reserved word that is a reference to the object executing the code making the reference.

thread—An independent process executing within a program. A Java program can have multiple threads running in a program at one time.

throw—A Java reserved word that is used to start an exception propagation.

throws—A Java reserved word that specifies that a method may throw a particular type of exception.

timer—An object that generates an event at regular intervals.

token—A portion of a string defined by a set of delimiters.

tool tip—A short line of text that appears when the mouse pointer is allowed to rest on top of a particular component. Usually, tool tips are used to inform the user of the component's purpose.

top-level domain—The last part of a network domain name, such as edu or com.

transient—A Java reserved word that serves as a modifier for variables. A transient variable does not contribute to the object's persistent state, and therefore does not need to be saved. *See also* serialize.

tree—A nonlinear data structure that forms a hierarchy stemming from a single root node.

true—A Java reserved word that serves as one of the two boolean literals (`true` and `false`).

truth table—A complete enumeration of all permutations of values involved in a boolean expression, as well as the computed result.

try—A Java reserved word that is used to define the context in which certain exceptions will be handled if they are thrown.

two-dimensional array—An array that uses two indices to specify the location of an element. The two dimensions are often thought of as the rows and columns of a table. *See also* multidimensional array.

two's complement—A technique for representing numeric binary data. Used by all Java integer primitive types (`byte`, `short`, `int`, `long`).

type—*See* data type.

UML—*See* Unified Modeling Language.

unary operator—An operator that uses only one operand.

unchecked exception—A Java exception that does not need to be caught or dealt with if the programmer so chooses.

underflow—A problem that occurs when a floating point value becomes too small for its storage size, which can result in inaccurate arithmetic processing. *See also* overflow.

undirected graph—A graph data structure in which each edge can be traversed in either direction. *See also* edge.

Unicode—The international character set used to define valid Java characters. Each character is represented using a 16-bit unsigned numeric value.

Unified Modeling Language (UML)—A graphical notation for visualizing relationships among classes and objects. There are many types of UML diagrams. *See also* class diagrams.

uniform resource locator (URL)—A designation for a resource that can be located through a Web browser.

unit testing—The process of testing an individual software component. May require the creation of stub modules to simulate other system components.

Unix—A computer operating system developed by AT&T Bell Labs. *See also* Linux, operating system.

unsigned numeric value—A value that does not store a sign (positive or negative). The bit usually reserved to represent the sign is included in the value, doubling the magnitude of the number that can be stored. Java characters are stored as unsigned numeric values, but there are no primitive numeric types that are unsigned.

URL—*See* uniform resource locator.

use relationship—A relationship between two classes, often shown in a class diagram, that establishes that one class uses another in some way, such as relying on its services. *See also* association.

user interface—The manner in which the user interacts with a software system, which is often graphical. *See also* graphical user interface.

variable—An identifier in a program that represents a memory location in which a data value is stored.

vertex—A node in a graph. *See also* graph.

visibility modifier—A Java modifier that defines the scope in which a construct can be accessed. The Java visibility modifiers are `public`, `protected`, `private`, and default (no modifier used).

void—A Java reserved word that can be used as a return value for a method, indicating that no value is returned.

volatile—(1) A Java reserved word that serves as a modifier for variables. A volatile variable might be changed asynchronously and therefore indicates that the compiler should not attempt optimizations on it. (2) The characteristic of a memory device that loses stored information when the power supply is interrupted. Main memory is a volatile storage device. *See also* nonvolatile.

von Neumann architecture—The computer architecture named after John von Neumann in which programs and data are stored together in the same memory devices.

walkthrough—A form of review in which a group of developers, managers, and quality assurance personnel examines a design or program in order to find errors. Sometimes referred to as an inspection. *See also* desk check.

WAN—*See* wide-area network.

waterfall model—One of the earliest software development process models. It defines a basically linear interaction between the requirements, design, implementation, and testing stages.

Web—*See* World Wide Web.

weighted graph—A graph with weights or costs associated with each edge. Weighted graphs are also sometimes known as networks.

while—A Java reserved word that represents a repetition construct. A `while` statement is executed zero or more times. *See also* do, for.

white-box testing—Producing and evaluating test cases based on the interior logic of a software component. The test cases focus on stressing decision points and ensuring coverage. *See also* black-box testing, condition coverage, statement coverage.

white space—Spaces, tabs, and blank lines that are used to set off sections of source code to make programs more readable.

wide-area network (WAN)—A computer network that connects two or more local-area networks, usually across long geographic distances. *See also* local-area network.

widening conversion—A conversion between two values of different but compatible data types. Widening conversions usually leave the data value intact because the converted type has an internal representation equal to or larger than the original storage space. *See also* narrowing conversion.

word—A unit of binary storage. The size of a word varies by computer, and is usually 2, 4, or 8 bytes. The word size indicates the amount of information that can be moved through the machine at one time.

World Wide Web (WWW or Web)—Software that makes the exchange of information across a network easier by providing a common GUI for multiple types of information. Web browsers are used to retrieve and format HTML documents.

wrapper class—A class designed to store a primitive type in an object. Usually used when an object reference is needed and a primitive type would not suffice.

WWW—*See* World Wide Web.

zip—A file format used to compress and store one or more files and directories into a single file suitable for exchanging to another computer.

Number Systems

This appendix contains a detailed introduction to number systems and their underlying characteristics. The particular focus is on the binary number system, its use with computers, and its similarities to other number systems. This introduction also covers conversions between bases.

In our everyday lives, we use the *decimal number system* to represent values, to count, and to perform arithmetic. The decimal system is also referred to as the *base-10 number system*. We use 10 digits (0 through 9) to represent values in the decimal system.

Computers use the *binary number system* to store and manage information. The binary system, also called the *base-2 number system*, has only two digits (0 and 1). Each 0 and 1 is called a *bit*, short for binary digit. A series of bits is called a *binary string*.

There is nothing particularly special about either the binary or decimal systems. Long ago, humans adopted the decimal number system probably because we have 10 fingers on our hands. If humans had 12 fingers, we would probably be using a base-12 number system regularly and find it as easy to deal with as we do the decimal system now. It all depends on what you get used to. As you explore the binary system, it will become more familiar and natural.

Binary is used for computer processing because the devices used to manage and store information are less expensive and more reliable if they have to represent only two possible values. Computers have been made that use the decimal system, but they are not as convenient.

There are an infinite number of number systems, and they all follow the same basic rules. You already know how the binary number system works, but you just might not be aware that you do. It all goes back to the basic rules of arithmetic.

Place Value

In decimal, we represent the values of 0 through 9 using only one digit. To represent any value higher than 9, we must use more than one digit. The position of each digit has a *place value* that indicates the amount it contributes to the overall value. In decimal, we refer to the one's column, the ten's column, the hundred's column, and so on forever.

Each place value is determined by the *base* of the number system, raised to increasing powers as we move from right to left. In the decimal number system, the place value of the digit furthest to the right is 10^0, or 1. The place value of the next digit is 10^1, or 10. The place value of the third digit from the right is 10^2, or 100, and so on. Figure B.1 shows how each digit in a decimal number contributes to the value.

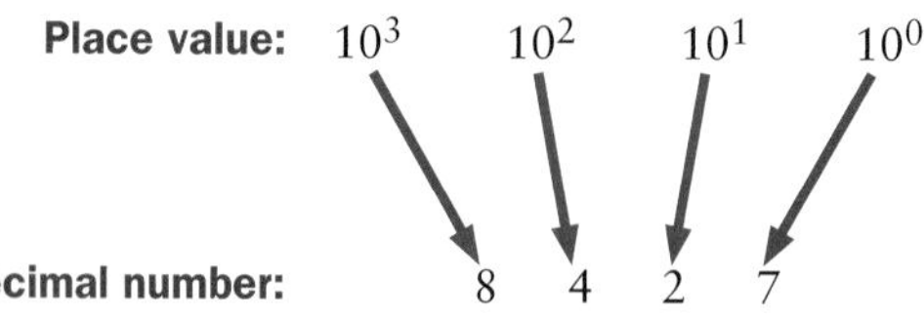

Decimal number: $8 * 10^3 + 4 * 10^2 + 2 * 10^1 + 7 * 10^0 =$

$8 * 1000 + 4 * 100 + 2 * 10 + 7 * 1 = 8427$

FIGURE B.1 Place values in the decimal number system

The binary number system works the same way except that we exhaust the available digits much sooner. We can represent 0 and 1 with a single bit, but to represent any value higher than 1, we must use multiple bits.

The place values in binary are determined by increasing powers of the base as we move right to left, just as they are in the decimal system. However, in binary, the base value is 2. Therefore the place value of the bit furthest to the right is 2^0, or 1. The place value of the next bit is 2^1, or 2. The place value of the third bit from the right is 2^2, or 4, and so on. Figure B.2 shows a binary number and its place values.

The number 1101 is a valid binary number, but it is also a valid decimal number as well. Sometimes to make it clear which number system is being used, the base value is appended as a subscript to the end of a number. Therefore you can distinguish between 1101_2, which is equivalent to 13 in decimal, and 1101_{10} (one thousand one hundred and one), which in binary is represented as 10001001101_2.

A number system with base N has N digits (0 through N–1). As we have seen, the decimal system has 10 digits (0 through 9), and the binary system has two digits (0 and 1). They all work the same way. For instance, the base-5 number system has five digits (0 through 4).

Note that, in any number system, the place value of the digit furthest to the right is 1, since any base raised to the zero power is 1. Also notice that the value 10, which we refer to as "ten" in the decimal system, always represents the base value in any number system. In base 10, 10 is one 10 and zero 1's. In base 2, 10 is one 2 and zero 1's. In base 5, 10 is one 5 and zero 1's.

You may have seen the following geeky joke on a t-shirt: There are 10 types of people in the world, those who understand binary, and those who don't.

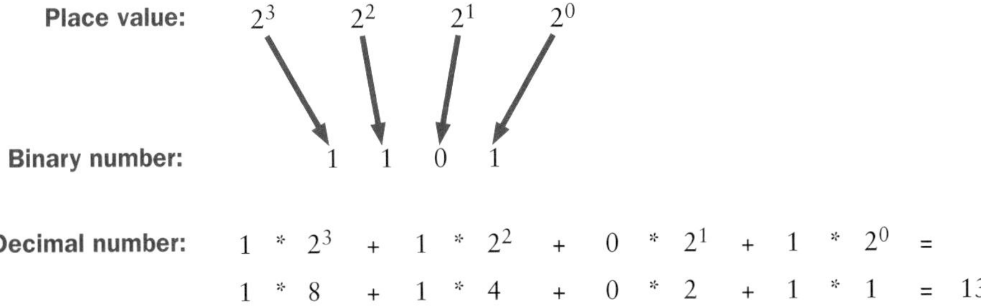

FIGURE B.2 Place values in the binary number system

Bases Higher Than 10

Since all number systems with base N have N digits, then base 16 has 16 digits. But what are they? We are used to the digits 0 through 9, but in bases higher than 10, we need a single digit, a single symbol, that represents the decimal value 10. In fact, in *base 16,* which is also called *hexadecimal,* we need digits that represent the decimal values 10 through 15.

For number systems higher than 10, we use alphabetic characters as single digits for values greater than 9. The hexadecimal digits are 0 through F, where 0 through 9 represent the first 10 digits, and A represents the decimal value 10, B represents 11, C represents 12, D represents 13, E represents 14, and F represents 15.

Therefore the number 2A8E is a valid hexadecimal number. The place values are determined as they are for decimal and binary, using increasing powers of the base. So in hexadecimal, the place values are powers of 16. Figure B.3 shows how the place values of the hexadecimal number 2A8E contribute to the overall value.

All number systems with bases greater than 10 use letters as digits. For example, base 12 has the digits 0 through B and base 19 has the digits 0 through I. However, beyond having a different set of digits and a different base, the rules governing each number system are the same.

Keep in mind that when we change number systems, we are simply changing the way we represent values, not the values themselves. If you have 18_{10} pencils, it may be written as 10010 in binary or as 12 in hexadecimal, but it is still the same number of pencils.

Figure B.4 shows the representations of the decimal values 0 through 20 in several bases, including *base 8,* which is also called *octal.* Note that the larger the base, the higher the value that can be represented in a single digit.

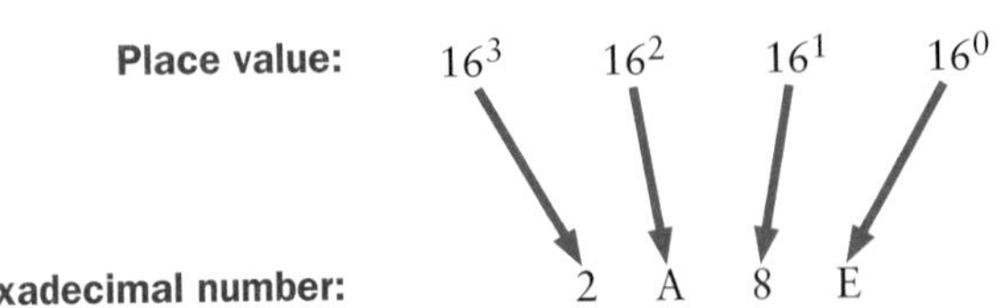

Decimal number: $2 * 16^3 + 10 * 16^2 + 8 * 16^1 + 14 * 16^0 =$

$2 * 4096 + 10 * 256 + 8 * 16 + 14 * 1 = 10893$

FIGURE B.3 Place values in the hexadecimal number system

Binary (base 2)	Octal (base 8)	Decimal (base 10)	Hexadecimal (base 16)
0	0	0	0
1	1	1	1
10	2	2	2
11	3	3	3
100	4	4	4
101	5	5	5
110	6	6	6
111	7	7	7
1000	10	8	8
1001	11	9	9
1010	12	10	A
1011	13	11	B
1100	14	12	C
1101	15	13	D
1110	16	14	E
1111	17	15	F
10000	20	16	10
10001	21	17	11
10010	22	18	12
10011	23	19	13
10100	24	20	14

FIGURE B.4 Counting in various number systems

Conversions

We've already seen how a number in another base is converted to decimal by determining the place value of each digit and computing the result. This process can be used to convert any number in any base to its equivalent value in base 10.

Now let's reverse the process, converting a base-10 value to another base. First, find the highest place value in the new number system that is less than or equal to the original value. Then divide the original number by that place value to determine the digit that belongs in that position. The remainder is the value that must be represented in the remaining digit positions. Continue this process, position by position, until the entire value is represented.

For example, Figure B.5 shows the process of converting the decimal value 180 into binary. The highest place value in binary that is less than or equal to 180 is 128 (or 2^7), which is the eighth bit position from the right. Dividing 180 by 128 yields 1 with 52 remaining. Therefore the first bit is 1, and the decimal value 52 must be represented in the remaining seven bits. Dividing 52 by 64, which is the next place value (2^6), yields 0 with 52 remaining. So the second bit is 0. Dividing 52 by 32 yields 1 with 20 remaining. So the third bit is 1 and the remaining five bits must represent the value 20. Dividing 20 by 16 yields 1 with 4 remaining. Dividing 4 by 8 yields 0 with 4 remaining. Dividing 4 by 4 yields 0 with 0 remaining.

Since the number has been completely represented, the rest of the bits are zero. Therefore 180_{10} is equivalent to 10110100 in binary. This can be confirmed by converting the new binary number back to decimal to make sure we get the original value.

This process works to convert any decimal value to any target base. For each target base, the place values and possible digits change. If you start with the correct place value, each division operation will yield a valid digit in the new base.

In the example in Figure B.5, the only digits that could have resulted from each division operation were 1 or 0, since we were converting to binary. However, when we are converting to other bases, any valid digit in the new base could result. For example, Figure B.6 shows the process of converting the decimal value 1967 into hexadecimal.

Place value	Number	Digit
128	180	1
64	52	0
32	52	1
16	20	1
8	4	0
4	4	1
2	0	0
1	0	0

$180_{10} = 10110100_2$

FIGURE B.5 Converting a decimal value into binary

Place value	Number	Digit
256	1967	7
16	175	A
1	15	F

$1967_{10} = 7AF_{16}$

FIGURE B.6 Converting a decimal value into hexadecimal

The place value 256, which is 16^2, is the highest place value less than or equal to the original number, since the next highest place value is 16^3 or 4096. Dividing 1967 by 256 yields 7 with 175 remaining. Dividing 175 by 16 yields 10 with 15 remaining. Remember that 10 in decimal can be represented as the single digit A in hexadecimal. The 15 remaining can be represented as the digit F. Therefore 1967_{10} is equivalent to 7AF in hexadecimal.

Shortcut Conversions

We have established techniques for converting any value in any base to its equivalent representation in base 10, and from base 10 to any other base. Therefore you can now convert a number in any base to any other base by going through base 10. However, an interesting relationship exists between the bases that are powers of 2, such as binary, octal, and hexadecimal, which allows very quick conversions between them.

To convert from binary to hexadecimal, for instance, you can simply group the bits of the original value into groups of four, starting from the right, then convert each group of four into a single hexadecimal digit. The example in Figure B.7 demonstrates this process.

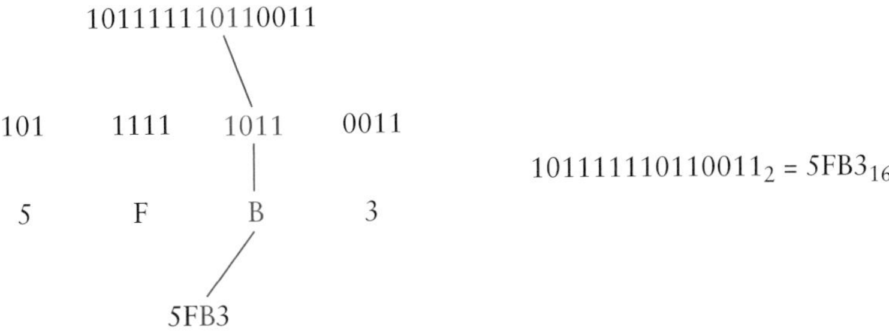

FIGURE B.7 A shortcut conversion from binary to hexadecimal

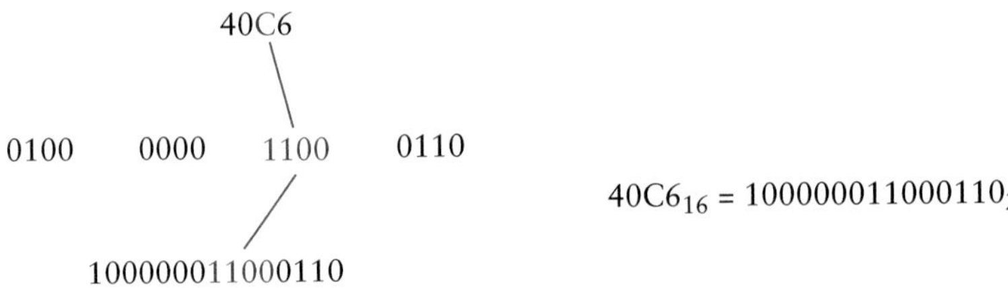

FIGURE B.8 A shortcut conversion from hexadecimal to binary

To go from hexadecimal to binary, we reverse this process, expanding each hexadecimal digit into four binary digits. Note that you may have to add leading zeros to the binary version of each expanded hexadecimal digit if necessary to make four binary digits. Figure B.8 shows the conversion of the hexadecimal value 40C6 to binary.

Why do we use groups of four bits when converting between binary and hexadecimal? The answer comes from the relationship between the bases 2 and 16. We use groups of four bits because $2^4 = 16$. The shortcut conversions work between binary and any base that is a power of 2. We section the bits into groups of that power.

Therefore, converting from binary to octal is the same process except that the bits are sectioned into groups of three, since $2^3 = 8$. Likewise, when converting from octal to binary, we expand each octal digit into three bits.

To convert between, say, hexadecimal and octal is now a process of doing two shortcut conversions. First convert from hexadecimal to binary, then take that result and perform a shortcut conversion from binary to octal.

By the way, these types of shortcut conversions can be performed between any base B and any base that is a power of B. For example, conversions between base 3 and base 9 can be accomplished using the shortcut grouping technique, sectioning or expanding digits into groups of two, since $3^2 = 9$.

Exercises

EX B.1 What is the difference between the binary and decimal number systems?

EX B.2 Why do modern computers use a binary number system to represent information?

EX B.3 How many digits are used in the base-6 number system? What are they?

EX B.4 How many digits are used in the base-12 number system? What are they?

EX B.5 Convert the following binary numbers to decimal.

a. 10

b. 10110

c. 11100

d. 10101010

e. 11001011

f. 10000000001

EX B.6 Convert the following octal numbers to decimal.

a. 10

b. 125

c. 5401

d. 7777

e. 46034

f. 65520

EX B.7 Convert the following hexadecimal numbers to decimal.

a. 10

b. 904

c. 6C3

d. ABC

e. 5D0BF

f. FFF

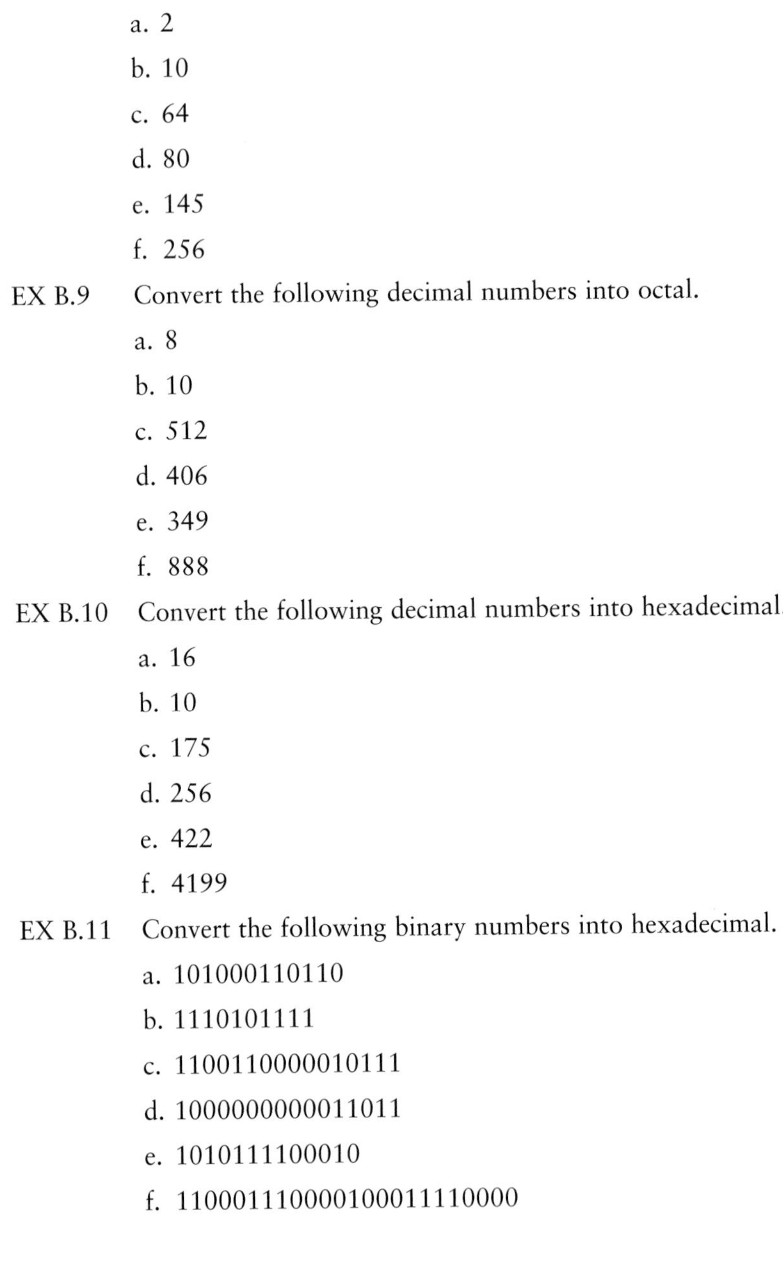

EX B.8 Convert the following decimal numbers into binary.

a. 2
b. 10
c. 64
d. 80
e. 145
f. 256

EX B.9 Convert the following decimal numbers into octal.

a. 8
b. 10
c. 512
d. 406
e. 349
f. 888

EX B.10 Convert the following decimal numbers into hexadecimal.

a. 16
b. 10
c. 175
d. 256
e. 422
f. 4199

EX B.11 Convert the following binary numbers into hexadecimal.

a. 101000110110
b. 1110101111
c. 1100110000010111
d. 1000000000011011
e. 1010111100010
f. 110001110000100011110000

EX B.12 Convert the following binary numbers into octal.

a. 101011111011

b. 1001101011

c. 111111000101110

d. 110100001101111110001

e. 1111101011000011010001

f. 1100010001110101111011100111

EX B.13 Convert the following hexadecimal numbers into binary.

a. 555

b. B74

c. 47A9

d. FDCB

e. 10101010

f. 5B60F9D

EX B.14 Convert the following octal numbers into binary.

a. 555

b. 760

c. 152

d. 3032

e. 76543

f. 6351732

Appendix C

The Unicode Character Set

The Java programming language uses the Unicode character set for managing text. A *character set* is simply an ordered list of characters, each corresponding to a particular numeric value. Unicode is an international character set that contains letters, symbols, and ideograms for languages all over the world. Each character is represented as a 16-bit unsigned numeric value. Unicode, therefore, can support over 65,000 unique characters. Only about half of those values have characters assigned to them at this point. The Unicode character set continues to be refined as characters from various languages are included.

Many programming languages still use the ASCII character set. ASCII stands for the American Standard Code for Information Interchange. The 8-bit extended ASCII set is quite small, so the developers of Java opted to use Unicode in order to support international users. However, ASCII is essentially a subset of Unicode, including the corresponding numeric values, so programmers used to ASCII should have no problems with Unicode.

Figure C.1 shows a list of commonly used characters and their Unicode numeric values. These characters also happen to be ASCII characters. All of the characters in Figure C.1 are called *printable characters* because they have a symbolic representation that can be displayed on a monitor or printed by a printer. Other characters are called *nonprintable characters* because they have no such symbolic representation. Note that the space character (numeric value 32) is considered a printable character, even though no symbol is printed when it is displayed. Nonprintable characters are sometimes called *control characters* because many of them can be generated by holding down the control key on a keyboard and pressing another key.

The Unicode characters with numeric values 0 through 31 are nonprintable characters. Also, the delete character, with numeric value 127, is a nonprintable character. All of these characters are ASCII characters as well. Many of them have

Value	Char	Value	Char	Value	Char	Value	Char	Value	Char
32	*space*	51	3	70	F	89	Y	108	l
33	!	52	4	71	G	90	Z	109	m
34	"	53	5	72	H	91	[	110	n
35	#	54	6	73	I	92	\	111	o
36	$	55	7	74	J	93	]	112	p
37	%	56	8	75	K	94	^	113	q
38	&	57	9	76	L	95	_	114	r
39	'	58	:	77	M	96	`	115	s
40	(	59	;	78	N	97	a	116	t
41	)	60	<	79	O	98	b	117	u
42	*	61	=	80	P	99	c	118	v
43	+	62	>	81	Q	100	d	119	w
44	,	63	?	82	R	101	e	120	x
45	-	64	@	83	S	102	f	121	y
46	.	65	A	84	T	103	g	122	z
47	/	66	B	85	U	104	h	123	{
48	0	67	C	86	V	105	i	124	|
49	1	68	D	87	W	106	j	125	}
50	2	69	E	88	X	107	k	126	~

FIGURE C.1 The printable ASCII subset of the Unicode character set

fairly common and well-defined uses, while others are more general. The table in Figure C.2 lists a small sample of the nonprintable characters.

Nonprintable characters are used in many situations to represent special conditions. For example, certain nonprintable characters can be stored in a text document to indicate, among other things, the beginning of a new line. An editor will process these characters by starting the text that follows it on a new line, instead of printing a symbol to the screen. Various types of computer systems use different nonprintable characters to represent particular conditions.

Except for having no visible representation, nonprintable characters are essentially equivalent to printable characters. They can be stored in a Java character variable and be part of a character string. They are stored using 16 bits, can be converted to their numeric value, and can be compared using relational operators.

The first 128 characters of the Unicode character set correspond to the common ASCII character set. The first 256 characters correspond to the ISO-Latin-1 extended ASCII character set. Many operating systems and Web browsers will handle these characters, but they may not be able to print the other Unicode characters.

The Unicode character set contains most alphabets in use today, including Greek, Hebrew, Cyrillic, and various Asian ideographs. It also includes Braille, and several sets of symbols used in mathematics and music. Figure C.3 shows a few characters from non-Western alphabets.

Value	Character
0	*null*
7	*bell*
8	*backspace*
9	*tab*
10	*line feed*
12	*form feed*
13	*carriage return*
27	*escape*
127	*delete*

FIGURE C.2 Some nonprintable characters in the Unicode character set

Value	Character	Source
1071	Я	Russian (Cyrillic)
3593	ฉ	Thai
5098	Ꮺ	Cherokee
8478	℞	Letterlike Symbols
8652	⇌	Arrows
10287	⠯	Braille
13407	㑟	Chinese/Japanese/Korean (Common)

FIGURE C.3 Some non-Western characters in the Unicode character set

Appendix D

Java Operators

Java operators are evaluated according to the precedence hierarchy shown in Figure D.1. Operators at low precedence levels are evaluated before operators at higher levels. Operators within the same precedence level are evaluated according to the specified association, either right to left (R to L) or left to right (L to R). Operators in the same precedence level are not listed in any particular order.

The order of operator evaluation can always be forced by the use of parentheses. It is sometimes a good idea to use parentheses even when they are not required, to make it explicitly clear to a human reader how an expression is evaluated.

Precedence Level	Operator	Operation	Associates
1	[ ] . (*parameters*) ++ --	array indexing object member reference parameter evaluation and method invocation postfix increment postfix decrement	L to R
2	++ -- + - ~ !	prefix increment prefix decrement unary plus unary minus bitwise NOT logical NOT	R to L
3	new (*type*)	object instantiation cast	R to L
4	* / %	multiplication division remainder	L to R
5	+ + -	addition string concatenation subtraction	L to R
6	<< >> >>>	left shift right shift with sign right shift with zero	L to R
7	< <= > >= instanceof	less than less than or equal greater than greater than or equal type comparison	L to R
8	== !=	equal not equal	L to R

FIGURE D.1 Java operator precedence

For some operators, the operand types determine which operation is carried out. For instance, if the + operator is used on two strings, string concatenation is performed, but if it is applied to two numeric types, they are added in the arithmetic sense. If only one of the operands is a string, the other is converted to a string, and string concatenation is performed. Similarly, the operators &, ^, and | perform bitwise operations on numeric operands but boolean operations on boolean operands.

<table>
<tr><th>Precedence Level</th><th>Operator</th><th>Operation</th><th>Associates</th></tr>
<tr><td>9</td><td>&
&</td><td>bitwise AND
boolean AND</td><td>L to R</td></tr>
<tr><td>10</td><td>^
^</td><td>bitwise XOR
boolean XOR</td><td>L to R</td></tr>
<tr><td>11</td><td>|
|</td><td>bitwise OR
boolean OR</td><td>L to R</td></tr>
<tr><td>12</td><td>&&</td><td>logical AND</td><td>L to R</td></tr>
<tr><td>13</td><td>||</td><td>logical OR</td><td>L to R</td></tr>
<tr><td>14</td><td>?:</td><td>conditional operator</td><td>R to L</td></tr>
<tr><td>15</td><td>=
+=
+=
-=
*=
/=
%=
<<=
>>=
>>>=
&=
&=
^=
^=
|=
|=</td><td>assignment
addition, then assignment
string concatenation, then assignment
subtraction, then assignment
multiplication, then assignment
division, then assignment
remainder, then assignment
left shift, then assignment
right shift (sign), then assignment
right shift (zero), then assignment
bitwise AND, then assignment
boolean AND, then assignment
bitwise XOR, then assignment
boolean XOR, then assignment
bitwise OR, then assignment
boolean OR, then assignment</td><td>R to L</td></tr>
</table>

FIGURE D.1 Java operator precedence, continued

The boolean operators & and | differ from the logical operators && and || in a subtle way. The logical operators are "short-circuited" in that if the result of an expression can be determined by evaluating only the left operand, the right operand is not evaluated. The boolean versions always evaluate both sides of the expression. There is no logical operator that performs an exclusive OR (XOR) operation.

Java Bitwise Operators

The Java *bitwise operators* operate on individual bits within a primitive value. Because they are not discussed in the chapters of this book, we explore them here further. The bitwise operators are defined only for integers and characters. They

Operator	Description
~	bitwise NOT
&	bitwise AND
|	bitwise OR
^	bitwise XOR
<<	left shift
>>	right shift with sign
>>>	right shift with zero fill

FIGURE D.2 The Java bitwise operators

are unique among all Java operators because they let us work at the lowest level of binary storage. Figure D.2 lists the Java bitwise operators.

Three of the bitwise operators are similar to the logical operators `!`, `&&`, and `||`. The bitwise NOT, AND, and OR operations work basically the same way as their logical counterparts, except they work on individual bits of a value. The rules are essentially the same. Figure D.3 shows the results of bitwise operators on all combinations of two bits. Compare this chart to the truth tables for the logical operators in Chapter 4 to see the similarities.

The bitwise operators include the XOR operator, which stands for *exclusive OR*. The logical || operator is an *inclusive OR* operation, which means it returns true if both operands are true. The | bitwise operator is also inclusive and yields a 1 if both corresponding bits are 1. However, the exclusive OR operator (^) yields a 0 if both operands are 1. There is no logical exclusive OR operator in Java.

When the bitwise operators are applied to integer values, the operation is performed individually on each bit in the value. For example, suppose the integer variable `number` is declared to be of type `byte` and currently holds the value 45. Stored as an 8-bit byte, it is represented in binary as `00101101`. When the bitwise

a	b	~ a	a & b	a | b	a ^ b
0	0	1	0	0	0
0	1	1	0	1	1
1	0	0	0	1	1
1	1	0	1	1	0

FIGURE D.3 Bitwise operations on individual bits

complement operator (~) is applied to `number`, each bit in the value is inverted, yielding `11010010`. Since integers are stored using two's complement representation, the value represented is now negative, specifically –46.

Similarly, for all bitwise operators, the operations are applied bit by bit, which is where the term "bitwise" comes from. For binary operators (with two operands), the operations are applied to corresponding bits in each operand. For example, assume `num1` and `num2` are `byte` integers, `num1` holds the value 45, and `num2` holds the value 14. Figure D.4 shows the results of several bitwise operations.

The operators `&`, `|`, and `^` can also be applied to boolean values, and they have basically the same meaning as their logical counterparts. When used with boolean values, they are called *boolean operators*. However, unlike the operators `&&` and `||`, which are "short-circuited," the boolean operators are not short-circuited. Both sides of the expression are evaluated every time.

Like the other bitwise operators, the three bitwise shift operators manipulate the individual bits of an integer value. They all take two operands. The left operand is the value whose bits are shifted; the right operand specifies how many positions they should move. Prior to performing a shift, `byte` and `short` values are promoted to `int` for all shift operators. Furthermore, if either of the operands is `long`, the other operand is promoted to `long`. For readability, we use only 16 bits in the examples in this section, but the concepts are the same when carried out to 32- or 64-bit strings.

When bits are shifted, some bits are lost off one end, and others need to be filled in on the other. The *left-shift* operator (`<<`) shifts bits to the left, filling the right bits with zeros. For example, if the integer variable `number` currently has the value 13, then the statement

```
number = number << 2;
```

stores the value 52 into `number`. Initially, `number` contains the bit string `0000000000001101`. When shifted to the left, the value becomes

num1 & num2	num1 | num2	num1 ^ num2
00101101	00101101	00101101
& 00001110	| 00001110	^ 00001110
= 00001100	= 00101111	= 00100011

FIGURE D.4 Bitwise operations on bytes

`0000000000110100`, or 52. Notice that for each position shifted to the left, the original value is multiplied by 2.

The sign bit of a number is shifted along with all of the others. Therefore the sign of the value could change if enough bits are shifted to change the sign bit. For example, the value –8 is stored in binary two's complement form as `1111111111111000`. When shifted left two positions, it becomes `1111111111100000`, which is –32. However, if enough positions are shifted, a negative number can become positive and vice versa.

There are two forms of the right-shift operator: one that preserves the sign of the original value (>>) and one that fills the leftmost bits with zeros (>>>).

Let's examine two examples of the *right-shift-with-sign-fill* operator. If the `int` variable `number` currently has the value 39, the expression `(number >> 2)` results in the value 9. The original bit string stored in `number` is `0000000000100111`, and the result of a right shift two positions is `0000000000001001`. The leftmost sign bit, which in this case is a zero, is used to fill from the left.

If `number` has an original value of –16, or `1111111111110000`, the right-shift (with sign fill) expression `(number >>> 3)` results in the binary string `1111111111111110`, or –2. The leftmost sign bit is a 1 in this case and is used to fill in the new left bits, maintaining the sign.

If maintaining the sign is not desirable, the *right-shift-with-zero-fill* operator (>>>) can be used. It operates similarly to the >> operator but fills with zero no matter what the sign of the original value is.

Java Modifiers

This appendix summarizes the modifiers that give particular characteristics to Java classes, interfaces, methods, and variables. For discussion purposes, the set of all Java modifiers is divided into two groups: visibility modifiers and all others.

Java Visibility Modifiers

The table in Figure E.1 describes the effect of Java visibility modifiers on various constructs. Some relationships are not applicable (N/A). For instance, a class cannot be declared with protected visibility. Note that each visibility modifier operates in the same way on classes and interfaces and in the same way on methods and variables.

Default visibility means that no visibility modifier was explicitly used. Default visibility is sometimes called *package visibility*, but you cannot use the reserved word `package` as a modifier. Classes and interfaces can have default or public visibility; this visibility determines whether a class or interface can be referenced outside of its package. Only an inner class can have private visibility, in which case only the enclosing class may access it.

A Visibility Example

Consider the situation depicted in Figure E.2. Class `P` is the parent class that is used to derive child classes `C1` and `C2`. Class `C1` is in the same package as `P`, but `C2` is not. Class `P` contains four methods, each with different visibility modifiers. One object has been instantiated from each of these classes.

The `public method a()` has been inherited by `C1` and `C2`, and any code with access to object `x` can invoke `x.a()`. The `private method d()` is not visible to `C1` or `C2`, so objects `y` and `z` have no such method available to them. Furthermore, `d()` is fully encapsulated and can only be invoked from within object `x`.

The `protected method b()` is visible in both `C1` and `C2`. A method in `y` could invoke `x.b()`, but a method in `z` could not. Furthermore, an object of any class

Modifier	Classes and interfaces	Methods and variables
default (no modifier)	Visible in its package.	Visible to any class in the same package as its class.
`public`	Visible anywhere.	Visible anywhere.
`protected`	N/A	Visible by any class in the same package as its class.
`private`	Visible to the enclosing class only	Not visible by any other class.

FIGURE E.1 Java visibility modifiers

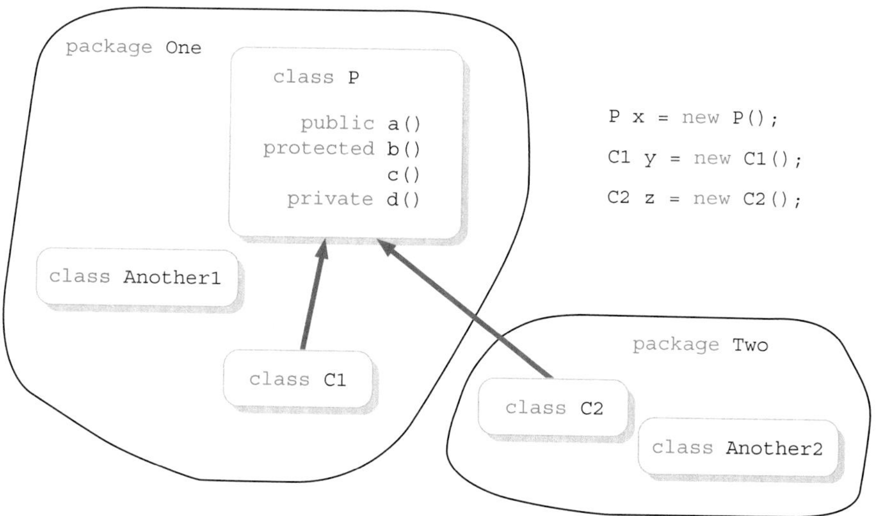

FIGURE E.2 A situation demonstrating Java visibility modifiers

in package `One` could invoke `x.b()`, even those that are not related to class `P` by inheritance, such as an object created from class `Another1`.

Method `c()` has `default` visibility, since no visibility modifier was used to declare it. Therefore object `y` can refer to the method `c()` as if it were declared locally, but object `z` cannot. Object `y` can invoke `x.c()`, as can an object instantiated from any class in package `One`, such as `Another1`. Object `z` cannot invoke `x.c()`.

These rules generalize in the same way for variables. The visibility rules may appear complicated initially, but they can be mastered with a little effort.

Other Java Modifiers

Figure E.3 summarizes the rest of the Java modifiers, which address a variety of issues. These modifiers have different effects on classes, interfaces, methods, and variables. Some modifiers cannot be used with certain constructs and therefore are listed as not applicable (N/A).

The `transient` modifier is used to indicate data that need not be stored in a persistent (serialized) object. That is, when an object is written to a serialized stream, the object representation will include all data that is not specified as transient.

Modifier	Class	Interface	Method	Variable
`abstract`	The class may contain abstract methods. It cannot be instantiated.	All interfaces are inherently abstract. The modifier is optional.	No method body is defined. The method requires implementation when inherited.	N/A
`final`	The class cannot be used to drive new classes.	N/A	The method cannot be overridden.	The variable is a constant, whose value cannot be changed once initially set.
`native`	N/A	N/A	No method body is necessary since implementation is in another language.	N/A
`static`	N/A	N/A	Defines a class method. It does not require an instantiated object to be invoked. It cannot reference non-static methods or variables. It is implicitly final.	Defines a class variable. It does not require an instantiated object to be referenced. It is shared (common memory space) among all instances of the class.
`synchronized`	N/A	N/A	The execution of the method is mutually exclusive among all threads.	N/A
`transient`	N/A	N/A	N/A	The variable will not be serialized.
`volatile`	N/A	N/A	N/A	The variable is changed asynchronously. The compiler should not perform optimizations on it.

FIGURE E.3 The rest of the Java modifiers

Java Graphics

Chapter 6 covers the issues related to developing a graphical user interface (GUI) for a Java program but does not discuss the mechanisms for drawing shapes and managing color. This appendix is provided to introduce the concepts and techniques used to manage Java graphics.

A picture is represented on a computer by breaking it down into *pixels*, a term that is short for picture elements. A complete picture is stored by storing the color of each individual pixel. The more pixels used to represent a picture, the more realistic it looks when it is reproduced. The number of pixels used to represent a picture is called the *picture resolution*. The number of pixels that can be displayed by a monitor is called the *monitor resolution*.

Coordinate Systems

When drawn, each pixel is mapped to a pixel on the monitor screen. Each computer system and programming language defines a coordinate system so that we can refer to particular pixels.

A traditional two-dimensional Cartesian coordinate system has two axes that meet at the origin. Values on either axis can be negative or positive. The Java programming language has a relatively simple coordinate system in which all of the visible coordinates are positive. Figure F.1 compares a traditional coordinate system to the Java coordinate system.

Each point in the Java coordinate system is represented using an (x, y) pair of values. Each graphical component in a Java program, such as a panel, has its own coordinate system, with the origin in the top-left corner at coordinates (0, 0). The *x*-axis coordinates get larger as you move to the right, and the *y*-axis coordinates get larger as you move down.

Representing Color

There are various ways to represent the color of a pixel. In the Java programming language, every color is represented as a mix of three *primary colors*: red, green, and blue. A color is specified using three numbers that are collectively referred to as an *RGB value*. RGB stands for Red-Green-Blue. Each number represents the relative contribution of a primary color.

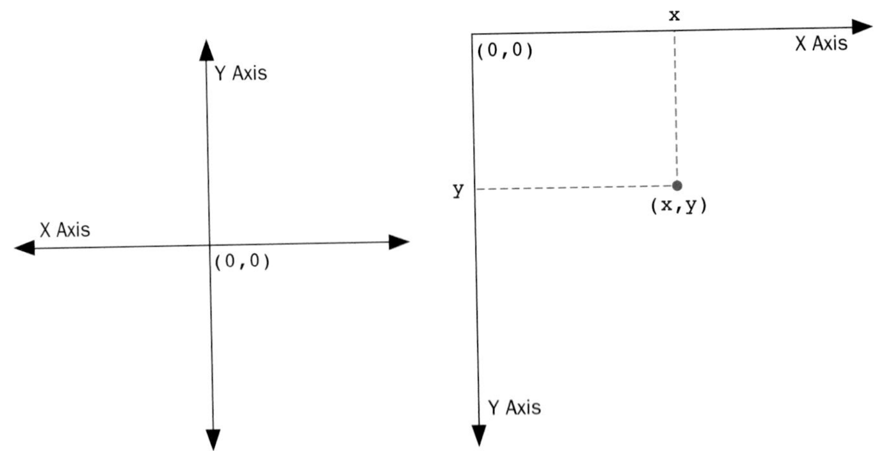

FIGURE F.1 A traditional coordinate system and the Java coordinate system

Color	Object	RGB Value
black	`Color.black`	0, 0, 0
blue	`Color.blue`	0, 0, 255
cyan	`Color.cyan`	0, 255, 255
gray	`Color.gray`	128, 128, 128
dark gray	`Color.darkGray`	64, 64, 64
light gray	`Color.lightGray`	192, 192, 192
green	`Color.green`	0, 255, 0
magenta	`Color.magenta`	255, 0, 255
orange	`Color.orange`	255, 200, 0
pink	`Color.pink`	255, 175, 175
red	`Color.red`	255, 0, 0
white	`Color.white`	255, 255, 255
yellow	`Color.yellow`	255, 255, 0

FIGURE F.2 Predefined colors in the `Color` class

Using 1 byte (8 bits) to store each of the three components of an RGB value, the numbers can range from 0 to 255. The level of each primary color determines the overall color. For example, high values of red and green combined with a low level of blue results in a shade of yellow.

In Java, a programmer uses the `Color` class, which is part of the `java.awt` package, to define and manage colors. Each object of the `Color` class represents a single color. The class contains several instances of itself to provide a basic set of predefined colors. Figure F.2 lists the predefined colors of the `Color` class. It also contains methods to define and manage many other colors.

Drawing Shapes

The Java standard class library provides many classes that let us present and manipulate graphical information. The `Graphics` class, which is defined in the `java.awt` package, is fundamental to all such processing.

The `Graphics` class contains various methods that allow us to draw shapes, including lines, rectangles, and ovals. Figure F.3 lists some of the fundamental drawing methods of the `Graphics` class. These methods also let us draw circles and squares, which are just specific types of ovals and rectangles, respectively.

```
void drawLine (int x1, int y1, int x2, int y2)
```
Paints a line from point (x1, y1) to point (x2, y2).

```
void drawRect (int x, int y, int width, int height)
```
Paints a rectangle with upper left corner (x, y) and dimensions width and height.

```
void drawOval (int x, int y, int width, int height)
```
Paints an oval bounded by the rectangle with an upper left corner of (x, y) and dimensions width and height.

```
void drawString (String str, int x, int y)
```
Paints the character string str at point (x, y), extending to the right.

```
void drawArc (int x, int y, int width, int height, int
startAngle, int arcAngle)
```
Paints an arc along the oval bounded by the rectangle defined by x, y, width, and height. The arc starts at startAngle and extends for a distance defined by arcAngle.

```
void fillRect (int x, int  y, int width, int height)
```
Same as their draw counterparts, but filled with the current foreground color.

```
void fillOval (int x, int y, int width, int height)

void fillArc (int x, int y, int width, int height,
int startAngle, int arcAngle)

Color getColor ()
```
Returns this graphics context's foreground color.

```
void setColor (Color color)
```
Sets this graphics context's foreground color to the specified color.

FIGURE F.3 Some methods of the `Graphics` class

The methods of the `Graphics` class allow us to specify whether we want a shape filled or unfilled. An unfilled shape shows only the outline of the shape and is otherwise transparent (you can see any underlying graphics). A filled shape is solid between its boundaries and covers any underlying graphics.

Many of these methods accept parameters that specify the coordinates at which the shape should be drawn. Shapes drawn at coordinates that are outside the visible area will not be seen.

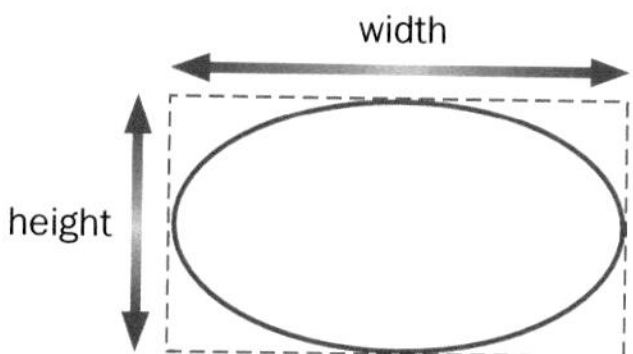

FIGURE F.4 An oval and its bounding rectangle

Many of the `Graphics` drawing methods are self-explanatory, but some require a little more discussion. Note, for instance, that an oval drawn by the `drawOval` method is defined by the coordinate of the upper-left corner and dimensions that specify the width and height of a *bounding rectangle*. Shapes with curves, such as ovals, are often defined by a rectangle that encompasses their perimeters. Figure F.4 depicts a bounding rectangle for an oval.

An arc can be thought of as a segment of an oval. To draw an arc, we specify the oval of which the arc is a part and the portion of the oval in which we're interested. The starting point of the arc is defined by the *start angle* and the ending point of the arc is defined by the *arc angle*. The arc angle does not indicate where the arc ends, but rather its range. The start angle and the arc angle are measured in degrees. The origin for the start angle is an imaginary horizontal line passing through the center of the oval and can be referred to as 0°, as shown in Figure F.5.

Every graphics context has a current *foreground color* that is used whenever shapes or strings are drawn. Every surface that can be drawn on has a *background*

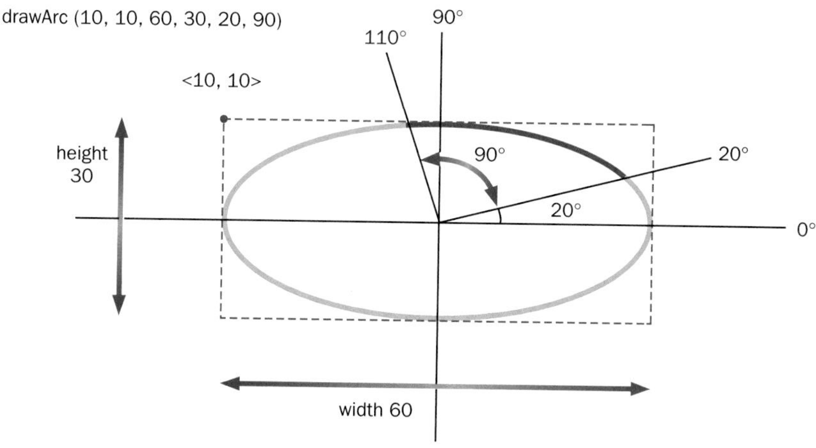

FIGURE F.5 An arc defined by an oval, a start angle, and an arc angle

color. The foreground color is set using the `setColor` method of the `Graphics` class, and the background color is set using the `setBackground` method of the component on which we are drawing, such as the panel.

Listing F.1 shows a program that uses various drawing and color methods to draw a winter scene featuring a snowman. The drawing is done on a `JPanel`, defined by the `SnowmanPanel` class, which is shown in Listing F.2.

The `paintComponent` method of a graphical component is called automatically when the component is rendered on the screen. Note that the `paintComponent` method accepts a `Graphics` object as a parameter. A `Graphics` object defines a particular *graphics context* with which we can interact. The graphics context passed into a panel's `paintComponent` method represents the graphics context in which the panel is drawn.

Listing **F.1**

```
//********************************************************************
//  Snowman.java        Java Foundations
//
//  Demonstrates the use of basic drawing methods.
//********************************************************************

import javax.swing.JFrame;

public class Snowman
{
   //-----------------------------------------------------------------
   //  Displays a winter scene featuring a snowman.
   //-----------------------------------------------------------------
   public static void main (String[] args)
   {
      JFrame frame = new JFrame ("Snowman");
      frame.setDefaultCloseOperation (JFrame.EXIT_ON_CLOSE);

      frame.getContentPane().add(new SnowmanPanel());

      frame.pack();
      frame.setVisible(true);
   }
}
```

Listing **F.1** continued

Display

Listing **F.2**

```
//********************************************************************
//  SnowmanPanel.java       Java Foundations
//
//  Represents the primary drawing panel for the Snowman application.
//********************************************************************

import java.awt.*;
import javax.swing.*;

public class SnowmanPanel extends JPanel
{
    private final int MID = 150;
    private final int TOP = 50;
```

Listing F.2 continued

```
   //-----------------------------------------------------------------
   //  Sets up the snowman panel.
   //-----------------------------------------------------------------
   public SnowmanPanel ()
   {
      setPreferredSize (new Dimension(300, 225));
      setBackground (Color.cyan);
   }

   //-----------------------------------------------------------------
   //  Draws a snowman.
   //-----------------------------------------------------------------
   public void paintComponent (Graphics page)
   {
      super.paintComponent (page);
      page.setColor (Color.blue);
      page.fillRect (0, 175, 300, 50);  // ground

      page.setColor (Color.yellow);
      page.fillOval (-40, -40, 80, 80);  // sun

      page.setColor (Color.white);
      page.fillOval (MID-20, TOP, 40, 40);      // head
      page.fillOval (MID-35, TOP+35, 70, 50);   // upper torso
      page.fillOval (MID-50, TOP+80, 100, 60);  // lower torso

      page.setColor (Color.black);
      page.fillOval (MID-10, TOP+10, 5, 5);   // left eye
      page.fillOval (MID+5, TOP+10, 5, 5);    // right eye

      page.drawArc (MID-10, TOP+20, 20, 10, 190, 160);   // smile

      page.drawLine (MID-25, TOP+60, MID-50, TOP+40);  // left arm
      page.drawLine (MID+25, TOP+60, MID+55, TOP+60);  // right arm

      page.drawLine (MID-20, TOP+5, MID+20, TOP+5);  // brim of hat
      page.fillRect (MID-15, TOP-20, 30, 25);        // top of hat
   }
}
```

The drawing of the snowman figure is based on two constant values called `MID` and `TOP`, which define the midpoint of the snowman (left to right) and the top of the snowman's head. The entire snowman figure is drawn relative to these values. Using constants like these makes it easier to create the snowman and to make modifications later. For example, to shift the snowman to the right or left in our picture, only one constant declaration would have to change.

The call to the `super.paintComponent` method as the first line in the `paintComponent` method ensures that the background color will be painted. The version of `paintComponent` defined in the `JPanel` class handles the display of the panel's background. The examples in Chapter 6, which add graphical components such as buttons to a panel, do not need this call. If a panel contains graphical components, the parent's `paintComponent` method is automatically called.

Listing **F.3**

```
//********************************************************************
//  Splat.java       Java Foundations
//
//  Demonstrates the use of graphical objects.
//********************************************************************

import javax.swing.JFrame;

public class Splat
{
   //-----------------------------------------------------------------
   //  Presents a set of circles.
   //-----------------------------------------------------------------
   public static void main (String[] args)
   {
      JFrame frame = new JFrame ("Splat");
      frame.setDefaultCloseOperation (JFrame.EXIT_ON_CLOSE);

      frame.getContentPane().add(new SplatPanel());

      frame.pack();
      frame.setVisible(true);
   }
}
```

Listing **F.3** continued

Display

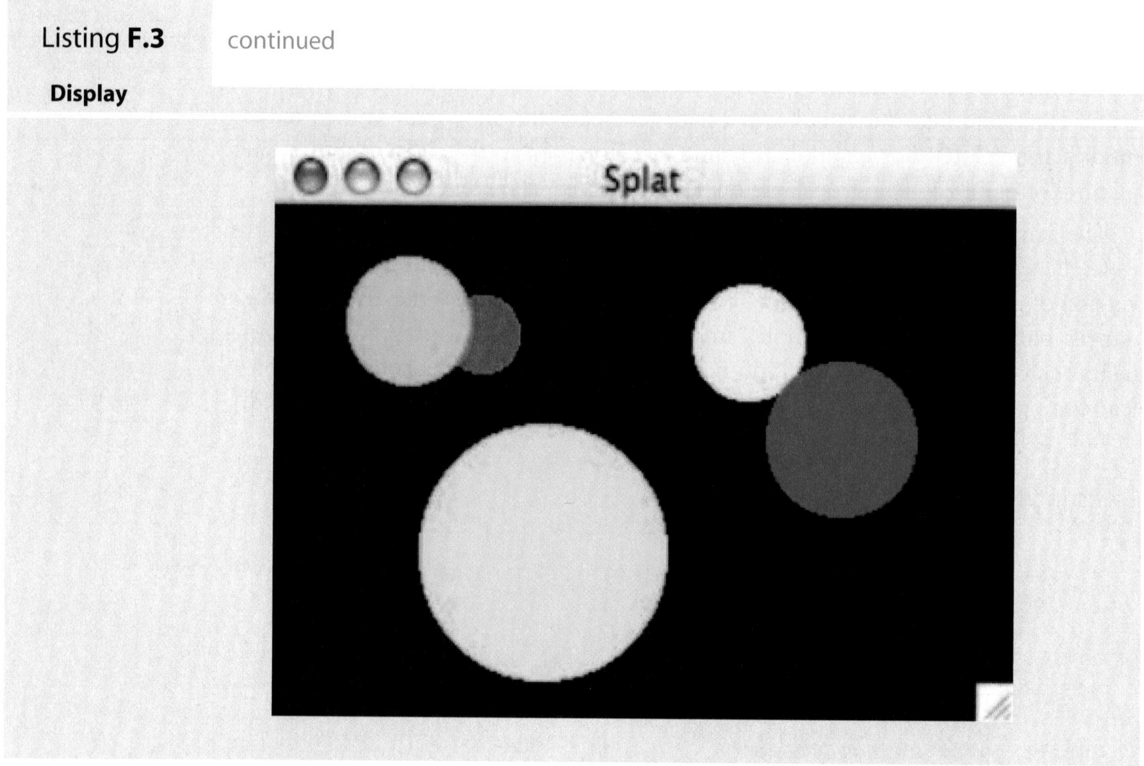

This is a key distinction between drawing on a component and adding a component to a container.

Let's look at another example. The `Splat` class shown in Listing F.3 simply draws a few filled circles. The interesting thing about this program is not what it does, but how it does it—each circle drawn in this program is represented by its own object.

The `main` method instantiates a `SplatPanel` object and adds it to the frame. The `SplatPanel` class is shown in Listing F.4. It is derived from `JPanel`, and holds as instance data five `Circle` objects, which are instantiated in the panel's constructor. The `paintComponent` method in the `SplatPanel` class draws the panel by calling the `draw` method of each circle.

The `Circle` class is shown in Listing F.5. It defines instance data to store the size of the circle, its (x, y) location, and its color. The `draw` method of the `Circle` class simply draws the circle based on the values of its instance data.

Listing F.4

```
//********************************************************************
//  SplatPanel.java       Java Foundations
//
//  Demonstrates the use of graphical objects.
//********************************************************************

import javax.swing.*;
import java.awt.*;

public class SplatPanel extends JPanel
{
   private Circle circle1, circle2, circle3, circle4, circle5;

   //-----------------------------------------------------------------
   //  Creates five Circle objects.
   //-----------------------------------------------------------------
   public SplatPanel()
   {
      circle1 = new Circle (30, Color.red, 70, 35);
      circle2 = new Circle (50, Color.green, 30, 20);
      circle3 = new Circle (100, Color.cyan, 60, 85);
      circle4 = new Circle (45, Color.yellow, 170, 30);
      circle5 = new Circle (60, Color.blue, 200, 60);

      setPreferredSize (new Dimension(300, 200));
      setBackground (Color.black);
   }

   //-----------------------------------------------------------------
   //  Draws this panel by requesting that each circle draw itself.
   //-----------------------------------------------------------------
   public void paintComponent (Graphics page)
   {
      super.paintComponent(page);

      circle1.draw(page);
      circle2.draw(page);
      circle3.draw(page);
      circle4.draw(page);
      circle5.draw(page);
   }
}
```

Listing F.5

```
//********************************************************************
//  Circle.java       Java Foundations
//
//  Represents a circle with a particular position, size, and color.
//********************************************************************

import java.awt.*;

public class Circle
{
   private int diameter, x, y;
   private Color color;

   //-----------------------------------------------------------------
   //  Sets up this circle with the specified values.
   //-----------------------------------------------------------------
   public Circle (int size, Color shade, int upperX, int upperY)
   {
      diameter = size;
      color = shade;
      x = upperX;
      y = upperY;
   }

   //-----------------------------------------------------------------
   //  Draws this circle in the specified graphics context.
   //-----------------------------------------------------------------
   public void draw (Graphics page)
   {
      page.setColor (color);
      page.fillOval (x, y, diameter, diameter);
   }
}
```

The design of the `Splat` program embodies fundamental object-oriented thinking. Each circle manages itself and will draw itself in whatever graphics context you pass it. The `Circle` class is defined in a way that can be used in other situations and programs. There is a clean separation between the object being drawn and the component on which it is drawn.

Polygons and Polylines

A polygon is a multisided shape that is defined in Java using a series of (x, y) points that indicate the vertices of the polygon. Arrays are often used to store the list of coordinates.

Polygons are drawn using methods of the `Graphics` class, similar to how we draw rectangles and ovals. Like these other shapes, a polygon can be drawn filled or unfilled. The methods used to draw a polygon are called `drawPolygon` and `fillPolygon`. Both of these methods are overloaded. One version uses arrays of integers to define the polygon, and the other uses an object of the `Polygon` class to define the polygon. We discuss the `Polygon` class later in this appendix.

In the version that uses arrays, the `drawPolygon` and `fillPolygon` methods take three parameters. The first is an array of integers representing the x coordinates of the points in the polygon, the second is an array of integers representing the corresponding y coordinates of those points, and the third is an integer that indicates how many points are used from each of the two arrays. Taken together, the first two parameters represent the (x, y) coordinates of the vertices of the polygons.

A polygon is always closed. A line segment is always drawn from the last point in the list to the first point in the list.

Similar to a polygon, a *polyline* contains a series of points connected by line segments. Polylines differ from polygons in that the first and last coordinates are not automatically connected when they are drawn. Since a polyline is not closed, it cannot be filled. Therefore there is only one method, called `drawPolyline`, used to draw a polyline. The parameters of the `drawPolyline` method are similar to those of the `drawPolygon` method.

The program shown in Listing F.6 uses polygons to draw a rocket. In the `RocketPanel` class, shown in Listing F.7, the arrays called `xRocket` and `yRocket` define the points of the polygon that make up the main body of the rocket. The first point in the arrays is the upper tip of the rocket, and the points progress clockwise from there. The `xWindow` and `yWindow` arrays specify the points for the polygon that form the window in the rocket. Both the rocket and the window are drawn as filled polygons.

The `xFlame` and `yFlame` arrays define the points of a polyline that are used to create the image of flame shooting out of the tail of the rocket. Because it is drawn as a polyline, and not a polygon, the flame is not closed or filled.

Listing F.6

```
//********************************************************************
//  Rocket.java       Java Foundations
//
//  Demonstrates the use of polygons and polylines.
//********************************************************************

import javax.swing.JFrame;

public class Rocket
{
   //-----------------------------------------------------------------
   //  Displays a rocket in flight.
   //-----------------------------------------------------------------
   public static void main (String[] args)
   {
      JFrame frame = new JFrame ("Rocket");
      frame.setDefaultCloseOperation (JFrame.EXIT_ON_CLOSE);

      frame.getContentPane().add(new RocketPanel());

      frame.pack();
      frame.setVisible(true);
   }
}
```

Display

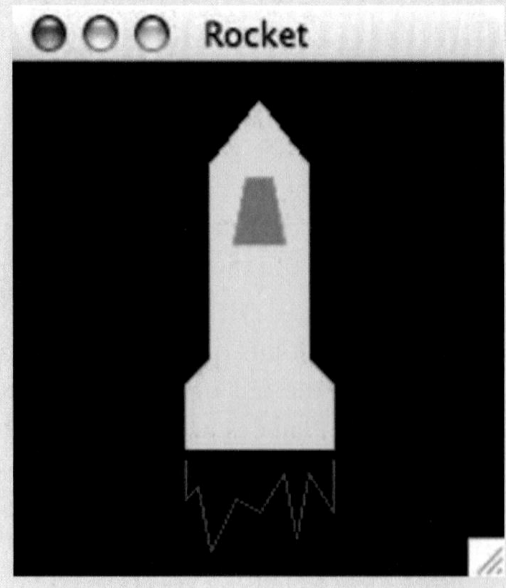

Listing **F.7**

```
//********************************************************************
//  RocketPanel.java        Java Foundations
//
//  Demonstrates the use of polygons and polylines.
//********************************************************************

import javax.swing.JPanel;
import java.awt.*;

public class RocketPanel extends JPanel
{
   private int[] xRocket = {100, 120, 120, 130, 130, 70, 70, 80, 80};
   private int[] yRocket = {15, 40, 115, 125, 150, 150, 125, 115, 40};

   private int[] xWindow = {95, 105, 110, 90};
   private int[] yWindow = {45, 45, 70, 70};

   private int[] xFlame = {70, 70, 75, 80, 90, 100, 110, 115, 120,
                           130, 130};
   private int[] yFlame = {155, 170, 165, 190, 170, 175, 160, 185,
                           160, 175, 155};

   //-----------------------------------------------------------------
   //  Sets up the basic characteristics of this panel.
   //-----------------------------------------------------------------
   public RocketPanel()
   {
      setBackground (Color.black);
      setPreferredSize (new Dimension(200, 200));
   }

   //-----------------------------------------------------------------
   //  Draws a rocket using polygons and polylines.
   //-----------------------------------------------------------------
   public void paintComponent (Graphics page)
   {
      super.paintComponent (page);

      page.setColor (Color.cyan);
      page.fillPolygon (xRocket, yRocket, xRocket.length);

      page.setColor (Color.gray);
      page.fillPolygon (xWindow, yWindow, xWindow.length);
```

Listing **F.7** continued

```
        page.setColor (Color.red);
        page.drawPolyline (xFlame, yFlame, xFlame.length);
    }
}
```

The `Polygon` Class

A polygon can also be defined explicitly using an object of the `Polygon` class, which is defined in the `java.awt` package of the Java standard class library. Two versions of the overloaded `drawPolygon` and `fillPolygon` methods take a single `Polygon` object as a parameter.

A `Polygon` object encapsulates the coordinates of the polygon sides. The constructors of the `Polygon` class allow the creation of an initially empty polygon, or one defined by arrays of integers representing the point coordinates. The `Polygon` class contains methods to add points to the polygon and to determine whether a given point is contained within the polygon shape. It also contains methods to get a representation of a bounding rectangle for the polygon, as well as a method to translate all of the points in the polygon to another position. Figure F.6 lists these methods.

`Polygon ()`
Constructor: Creates an empty polygon.

`Polygon (int[] xpoints, int[] ypoints, int npoints)`
Constructor: Creates a polygon using the (*x*, *y*) coordinate pairs in corresponding entries of `xpoints` and `ypoints`.

`void addPoint (int x, int y)`
Appends the specified point to this polygon.

`boolean contains (int x, int y)`
Returns true if the specified point is contained in this polygon.

`boolean contains (Point p)`
Returns true if the specified point is contained in this polygon.

`Rectangle getBounds ()`
Gets the bounding rectangle for this polygon.

`void translate (int deltaX, int deltaY)`
Translates the vertices of this polygon by `deltaX` along the *x* axis and `deltaY` along the *y* axis.

FIGURE F.6 Some methods of the `Polygon` class

Exercises

EX F.1 Compare and contrast a traditional coordinate system and the coordinate system used by Java graphical components.

EX F.2 How many bits are needed to store a color picture that is 400 pixels wide and 250 pixels high? Assume color is represented using the RGB technique described in this appendix and that no special compression is done.

EX F.3 Assuming you have a `Graphics` object called `page`, write a statement that will draw a line from point (20, 30) to point (50, 60).

EX F.4 Assuming you have a `Graphics` object called `page`, write a statement that will draw a rectangle with height 70 and width 35, such that its upper-left corner is at point (10, 15).

EX F.5 Assuming you have a `Graphics` object called `page`, write a statement that will draw a circle centered on point (50, 50) with a radius of 20 pixels.

EX F.6 The following lines of code draw the eyes of the snowman in the `Snowman` program. The eyes seem centered on the face when drawn, but the first parameters of each call are not equally offset from the midpoint. Explain.

```
page.fillOval (MID-10, TOP+10, 5, 5);

page.fillOval (MID+5, TOP+10, 5, 5);
```

EX F.7 Write a method called `randomColor` that creates and returns a `Color` object that represents a random color.

EX F.8 Write a method called `drawCircle` that draws a circle based on the method's parameters: a `Graphics` object through which to draw the circle, two integer values representing the (x, y) coordinates of the center of the circle, another integer that represents the circle's radius, and a `Color` object that defines the circle's color. The method does not return anything.

Programming Projects

PP F.1 Create a revised version of the `Snowman` program with the following modifications:

- Add two red buttons to the upper torso.

- Make the snowman frown instead of smile.
- Move the sun to the upper-right corner of the picture.
- Display your name in the upper-left corner of the picture.
- Shift the entire snowman 20 pixels to the right.

PP F.2 Write a program that writes your name using the `drawString` method.

PP F.3 Write a program that draws the Big Dipper. Add some extra stars in the night sky.

PP F.4 Write a program that draws some balloons tied to strings. Make the balloons various colors.

PP F.5 Write a program that draws the Olympic logo. The circles in the logo should be colored, from left to right, blue, yellow, black, green, and red.

PP F.6 Write a program that displays a business card of your own design. Include both graphics and text.

PP F.7 Write a program that shows a pie chart with eight equal slices, all colored differently.

PP F.8 Write a program that draws a house with a door (and doorknob), windows, and a chimney. Add some smoke coming out of the chimney and some clouds in the sky.

PP F.9 Modify the program from programming project F.8 to include a simple fence with vertical, equally spaced slats backed by two horizontal support boards. Make sure the house is visible between the slats in the fence.

PP F.10 Write a program that draws 20 horizontal, evenly spaced parallel lines of random length.

PP F.11 Write a program that draws the side view of stair steps from the lower left to the upper right.

PP F.12 Write a program that draws 100 circles of random color and random diameter in random locations. Ensure that in each case the entire circle appears in the visible area of the applet.

PP F.13 Write a program that draws 10 concentric circles of random radius.

PP F.14 Write a program that draws a brick wall pattern in which each row of bricks is offset from the row above and below it.

PP F.15 Design and implement a program that draws a rainbow. Use tightly spaced concentric arcs to draw each part of the rainbow in a particular color.

PP F.16 Design and implement a program that draws 20,000 points in random locations within the visible area. Make the points on the left half of the panel appear in red and the points on the right half of the panel appear in green. Draw each point by drawing a line with a length of only one pixel.

PP F.17 Design and implement a program that draws 10 circles of random radius in random locations. Fill in the largest circle in red.

PP F.18 Write a program that draws a quilt in which a simple pattern is repeated in a grid of squares.

PP F.19 Modify the program from programming project F.18 such that it draws a quilt using a separate class called `Pattern` that represents a particular pattern. Allow the constructor of the `Pattern` class to vary some characteristics of the pattern, such as its color scheme. Instantiate two separate `Pattern` objects and incorporate them in a checkerboard layout in the quilt.

PP F.20 Design and implement a class called `Building` that represents a graphical depiction of a building. Allow the parameters to the constructor to specify the building's width and height. Each building should be colored black, and contain a few random windows of yellow. Create a program that draws a random skyline of buildings.

PP F.21 Write a program that displays a graphical seating chart for a dinner party. Create a class called `Diner` (as in one who dines) that stores the person's name, gender, and location at the dinner table. A diner is graphically represented as a circle, color-coded by gender, with the person's name printed in the circle.

PP F.22 Create a class called `Crayon` that represents one crayon of a particular color and length (height). Design and implement a program that draws a box of crayons.

PP F.23 Create a class called `Star` that represents a graphical depiction of a star. Let the constructor of the star accept the number of points in the star (4, 5, or 6), the radius of the star, and the center point location. Write a program that draws a sky containing various types of stars.

PP F.24 Design and implement an application that displays an animation of a horizontal line segment moving across the screen, eventually passing across a vertical line. As the vertical line is passed, the horizontal line should change color. The change of color should occur while the horizontal line crosses the vertical one; therefore, while crossing, the horizontal line will be two different colors.

PP F.25 Create a class that represents a spaceship, which can be drawn (side view) in any particular location. Use it to create a program that displays the spaceship so that it follows the movement of the mouse. When the mouse button in pressed down, have a laser beam shoot out of the front of the spaceship (one continuous beam, not a moving projectile) until the mouse button is released.

Appendix G

Java Applets

There are two kinds of Java programs: Java applications and Java applets. A Java *application* is a stand-alone program that can be executed using a Java interpreter. The programs presented in the main chapters of this book are Java applications. A Java *applet* is a Java program that is intended to be embedded into an HTML document, transported across a network, and executed using a Web browser. This appendix explores Java applets.

The Web enables users to send and receive various types of media, such as text, graphics, and sound, using a point-and-click interface that is extremely convenient and easy to use. Java applets are considered just another type of media that can be exchanged across the Web.

When we surf the Web, we tend to think in terms of visiting a site. Of course, the reality is that we are downloading a page to our local computer to view it. Therefore, security is an issue with applets. As you browse Web pages, you may download a page containing an applet and suddenly an unknown program is executing on your machine. Because of the dangers inherent in that process,

applets are restricted in the kinds of operations they can perform. For instance, an applet cannot write data to a local drive.

Though Java applets are generally intended to be transported across a network, they don't have to be. They can be viewed locally using a Web browser. For that matter, they don't even have to be executed through a Web browser at all. A tool in Sun's Java Software Development Kit called *appletviewer* can be used to interpret and execute an applet. We use appletviewer to display applets in this appendix. However, usually the point of making a Java applet is to provide a link to it on a Web page and allow it to be retrieved and executed by Web users anywhere in the world.

Java bytecode (not Java source code) is linked to an HTML document and sent across the Web. A version of the Java interpreter embedded in a Web browser is used to execute the applet once it reaches its destination. A Java applet must be compiled into bytecode format before it can be used with the Web.

There are some important differences between the structure of a Java applet and the structure of a Java application. Because the Web browser that executes an applet is already running, applets can be thought of as a part of a larger program. As such they do not have a `main` method where execution starts. The `paint` method in an applet is automatically invoked when the applet program executes. Consider the program in Listing G.1, in which the `paint` method is used to draw a few shapes and write a quotation by Albert Einstein to the screen.

Listing G.1

```
//********************************************************************
//  Einstein.java       Java Foundations
//
//  Demonstrates a basic applet.
//********************************************************************

import javax.swing.JApplet;
import java.awt.*;

public class Einstein extends JApplet
{
   //-----------------------------------------------------------------
   //  Draws a quotation by Albert Einstein among some shapes.
   //-----------------------------------------------------------------
   public void paint (Graphics page)
```

Listing **G.1** continued

```
    {
        page.drawRect (50, 50, 40, 40);     // square
        page.drawRect (60, 80, 225, 30);    // rectangle
        page.drawOval (75, 65, 20, 20);     // circle
        page.drawLine (35, 60, 100, 120);   // line

        page.drawString ("Out of clutter, find simplicity.", 110, 70);
        page.drawString ("-- Albert Einstein", 130, 100);
    }
}
```

Display

Applet Viewer: Einstein.class

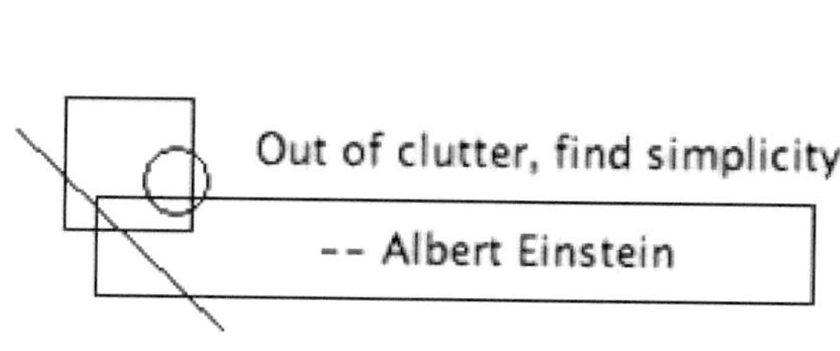

Applet started.

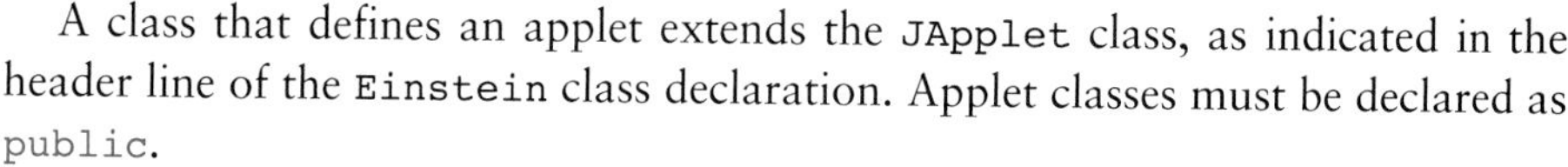

A class that defines an applet extends the `JApplet` class, as indicated in the header line of the `Einstein` class declaration. Applet classes must be declared as `public`.

The `paint` method is one of several applet methods that have particular significance. It is invoked automatically whenever the graphic elements of the applet need to be painted to the screen, such as when the applet is first run or when another window that was covering it is moved.

Note that the `paint` method accepts a `Graphics` object as a parameter. As discussed in Appendix F, a `Graphics` object defines the *graphics context* of a component and provides a variety of methods for drawing shapes on a component.

The graphics context passed into an applet's `paint` method represents the applet window.

Embedding Applets in HTML

In order for the applet to be executed, either by the appletviewer or by being transmitted over the Web and executed by a browser, it must be referenced in a HyperText Markup Language (HTML) document. An HTML document contains *tags* that specify formatting instructions and identify the special types of media that are to be included in a document.

An HTML tag is enclosed in angle brackets. The following is an example of an applet tag:

```
<applet code="Einstein.class" width="350" height="175">
</applet>
```

This tag dictates that the bytecode stored in the file `Einstein.class` should be transported over the network and executed on the machine that wants to view this particular HTML document. The applet tag also indicates the width and height of the applet.

There are other tags that can be used to reference an applet in an HTML file, including the `<object>` tag and the `<embed>` tag. The `<object>` tag is actually the tag that should be used, according to the World Wide Web Consortium (W3C). However, browser support for the `<object>` tag is not consistent. For now, the most reliable solution is to use the `<applet>` tag.

Note that the applet tag refers to the bytecode file of the `Einstein` applet, not to the source code file. Before an applet can be transported using the Web, it must be compiled into its bytecode format. Then, as shown in Figure G.1, the document can be loaded using a Web browser, which will automatically interpret and execute the applet.

More Applet Methods

An applet has several other methods that perform specific duties. Because an applet is designed to work with Web pages, some applet methods are specifically designed with that concept in mind. Figure G.2 lists several applet methods.

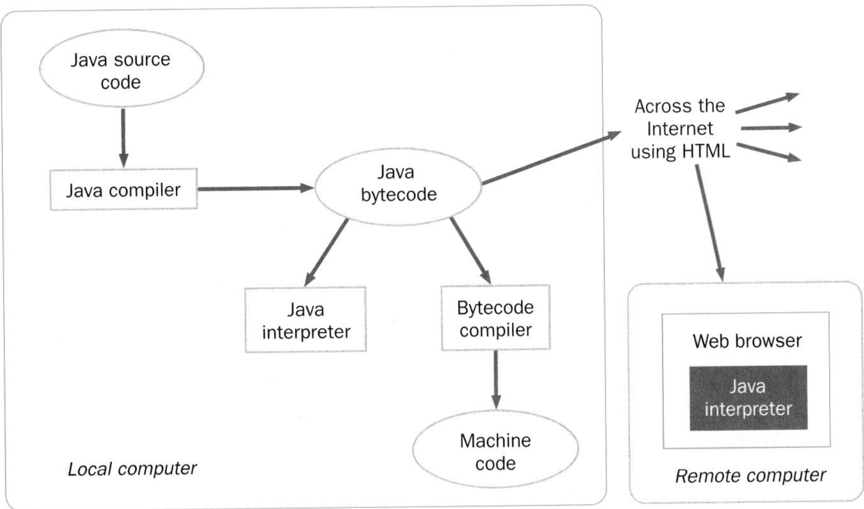

FIGURE G.1 The Java translation and execution process, including applets

```
public void init ()
```
Initializes the applet. Called just after the applet is loaded.

```
public void start ()
```
Starts the applet. Called just after the applet is made active.

```
public void stop ()
```
Stops the applet. Called just after the applet is made inactive.

```
public void destroy ()
```
Destroys the applet. Called when the browser is exited.

```
public URL getCodeBase ()
```
Returns the URL at which this applet's bytecode is located.

```
public URL getDocumentBase ()
```
Returns the URL at which the HTML document containing this applet is located.

```
public AudioClip getAudioClip (URL url, String name)
```
Retrieves an audio clip from the specified URL.

```
public Image getImage (URL url, String name)
```
Retrieves an image from the specified URL.

FIGURE G.2 Some methods of the `JApplet` class

The `init` method is executed once when the applet is first loaded, such as when the browser or appletviewer initially views the applet. Therefore the `init` method is the place to initialize the applet's environment and permanent data.

The `start` and `stop` methods of an applet are called when the applet becomes active or inactive, respectively. For example, after we use a browser to initially load an applet, the applet's `start` method is called. We may then leave that page to visit another one, at which point the applet becomes inactive and the `stop` method is called. If we return to the applet's page, the applet becomes active again and the `start` method is called again.

Note that the `init` method is called once when the applet is loaded, but `start` may be called several times as the page is revisited. It is good practice to implement `start` and `stop` for an applet if it actively uses CPU time, such as when it is showing an animation, so that CPU time is not wasted on an applet that is not visible.

Note that reloading the Web page in the browser does not necessarily reload the applet. To force the applet to reload, most browsers provide some key combination for that purpose. For example, in Netscape Navigator, holding down the Shift key while pressing the Reload button with the mouse not only reloads the Web page, it also reloads (and reinitializes) all applets linked to that page.

The `getCodeBase` and `getDocumentBase` methods are useful to determine where the applet's bytecode or HTML document resides. An applet could use the appropriate URL to retrieve additional resources, such as an image or audio clip, using the methods `getImage` or `getAudioClip`.

Let's look at another example of an applet. Carefully examine the display for the `TiledPictures` applet shown in Listing G.2. There are actually three unique images among the menagerie. The entire area is divided into four equal quadrants. A picture of the world (with a circle indicating the Himalayan mountain region) is shown in the bottom-right quadrant. The bottom-left quadrant contains a picture of Mt. Everest. In the top-right quadrant is a picture of a mountain goat.

The interesting part of the picture is the top-left quadrant. It contains a copy of the entire collage, including itself. In this smaller version you can see the three simple pictures in their three quadrants. And again, in the top-left corner, the picture is repeated (including itself). This repetition continues for several levels. It is similar to the effect you can create when looking at a mirror in the reflection of another mirror.

This visual effect is created using recursion. The applet's `init` method initially loads the three images. The `paint` method then invokes the `drawPictures`

Listing G.2

```
//********************************************************************
//  TiledPictures.java       Java Foundations
//
//  Demonstrates an applet.
//********************************************************************

import java.awt.*;
import javax.swing.JApplet;

public class TiledPictures extends JApplet
{
   private final int APPLET_WIDTH = 320;
   private final int APPLET_HEIGHT = 320;
   private final int MIN = 20;  // smallest picture size

   private Image world, everest, goat;

   //-----------------------------------------------------------------
   //  Loads the images.
   //-----------------------------------------------------------------
   public void init()
   {
      world = getImage (getDocumentBase(), "world.gif");
      everest = getImage (getDocumentBase(), "everest.gif");
      goat = getImage (getDocumentBase(), "goat.gif");

      setSize (APPLET_WIDTH, APPLET_HEIGHT);
   }

   //-----------------------------------------------------------------
   //  Draws the three images, then calls itself recursively.
   //-----------------------------------------------------------------
   public void drawPictures (int size, Graphics page)
   {
      page.drawImage (everest, 0, size/2, size/2, size/2, this);
      page.drawImage (goat, size/2, 0, size/2, size/2, this);
      page.drawImage (world, size/2, size/2, size/2, size/2, this);

      if (size > MIN)
         drawPictures (size/2, page);
   }
```

Listing **G.2** continued

```
   //-----------------------------------------------------------------
   //  Performs the initial call to the drawPictures method.
   //-----------------------------------------------------------------
   public void paint (Graphics page)
   {
      drawPictures (APPLET_WIDTH, page);
   }
}
```

Display

method, which accepts a parameter that defines the size of the area in which pictures are displayed. It draws the three images using the `drawImage` method, with parameters that scale the picture to the correct size and location. The `drawPictures` method is then called recursively to draw the upper-left quadrant.

On each invocation, if the drawing area is large enough, the `drawPictures` method is invoked again, using a smaller drawing area. Eventually, the drawing area becomes so small that the recursive call is not performed. Note that `drawPictures` assumes the origin (0, 0) coordinate as the relative location of the new images, no matter what their size is.

The base case of the recursion in this problem specifies a minimum size for the drawing area. Because the size is decreased each time, the base case eventually is reached and the recursion stops. This is why the upper-left corner is empty in the smallest version of the collage.

GUIs in Applets

In Chapter 6, we explored issues related to the development of programs that use graphical user interfaces (GUIs). The examples in those sections are presented as Java applications, using `JFrame` components as the primary heavyweight container. An applet can also be used to present GUI-based programs. Like a `JFrame`, a `JApplet` is a heavyweight container.

Let's look at an applet that contains interactive components. Our example will contain buttons that determine the level of a displayed fractal. A *fractal* is a geometric shape that can be made up of the same pattern repeated at different scales and orientations. The nature of a fractal lends itself to a recursive definition. Interest in fractals has grown immensely in recent years, largely due to Benoit Mandelbrot, a Polish mathematician born in 1924. He demonstrated that fractals occur in many places in mathematics and nature. Computers have made fractals much easier to generate and investigate. Over the past quarter century, the bright, interesting images that can be created with fractals have come to be considered as much an art form as a mathematical interest.

One particular example of a fractal is called the Koch snowflake, named after Helge von Koch, a Swedish mathematician. It begins with an equilateral triangle, which is considered to be the Koch fractal of order 1. Koch fractals of higher orders are constructed by repeatedly modifying all of the line segments in the shape.

To create the next higher order Koch fractal, each line segment in the shape is modified by replacing its middle third with a sharp protrusion made of two line

FIGURE G.3 Several orders of the Koch snowflake

segments, each having the same length as the replaced part. Relative to the entire shape, the protrusion on any line segment always points outward. Figure G.3 shows several orders of Koch fractals. As the order increases, the shape begins to look like a snowflake.

The applet shown in Listing G.3 draws a Koch snowflake of several different orders. The buttons at the top of the applet allow the user to increase and decrease the order of the fractal. Each time a button is pressed, the fractal image is redrawn. The applet serves as the listener for the buttons.

Listing G.3

```
//********************************************************************
//  KochSnowflake.java       Java Foundations
//
//  Demonstrates the use of recursion in graphics.
//********************************************************************

import java.awt.*;
import java.awt.event.*;
import javax.swing.*;

public class KochSnowflake extends JApplet implements ActionListener
{
   private final int APPLET_WIDTH = 400;
   private final int APPLET_HEIGHT = 440;

   private final int MIN = 1, MAX = 9;

   private JButton increase, decrease;
   private JLabel titleLabel, orderLabel;
   private KochPanel drawing;
   private JPanel appletPanel, tools;
```

Listing **G.3** continued

```
   //-----------------------------------------------------------------
   //  Sets up the components for the applet.
   //-----------------------------------------------------------------
   public void init()
   {
      tools = new JPanel ();
      tools.setLayout (new BoxLayout(tools, BoxLayout.X_AXIS));
      tools.setPreferredSize (new Dimension (APPLET_WIDTH, 40));
      tools.setBackground (Color.yellow);
      tools.setOpaque (true);

      titleLabel = new JLabel ("The Koch Snowflake");
      titleLabel.setForeground (Color.black);

      increase = new JButton (new ImageIcon ("increase.gif"));
      increase.setPressedIcon (new ImageIcon ("increasePressed.gif"));
      increase.setMargin (new Insets (0, 0, 0, 0));
      increase.addActionListener (this);

      decrease = new JButton (new ImageIcon ("decrease.gif"));
      decrease.setPressedIcon (new ImageIcon ("decreasePressed.gif"));
      decrease.setMargin (new Insets (0, 0, 0, 0));
      decrease.addActionListener (this);

      orderLabel = new JLabel ("Order: 1");
      orderLabel.setForeground (Color.black);

      tools.add (titleLabel);
      tools.add (Box.createHorizontalStrut (40));
      tools.add (decrease);
      tools.add (increase);
      tools.add (Box.createHorizontalStrut (20));
      tools.add (orderLabel);

      drawing = new KochPanel (1);

      appletPanel = new JPanel();
      appletPanel.add (tools);
      appletPanel.add (drawing);

      getContentPane().add (appletPanel);

      setSize (APPLET_WIDTH, APPLET_HEIGHT);
   }
```

Listing G.3 continued

```
   //-----------------------------------------------------------------
   //  Determines which button was pushed, and sets the new order
   //  if it is in range.
   //-----------------------------------------------------------------
   public void actionPerformed (ActionEvent event)
   {
      int order = drawing.getOrder();

      if (event.getSource() == increase)
         order++;
      else
         order--;

      if (order >= MIN && order <= MAX)
      {
         orderLabel.setText ("Order: " + order);
         drawing.setOrder (order);
         repaint();
      }
   }
}
```

Display

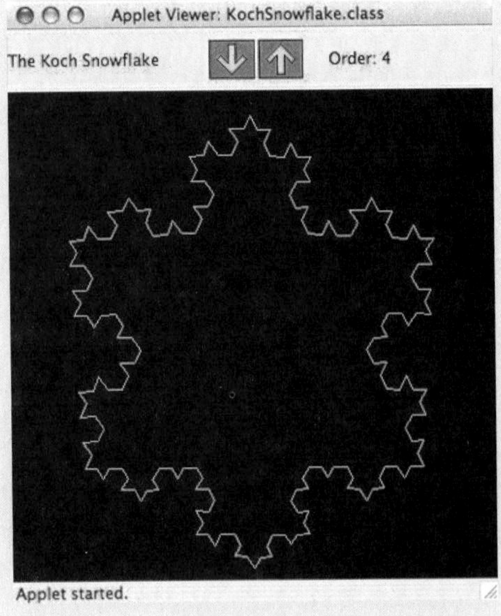

The fractal image is drawn on a panel defined by the `KochPanel` class shown in Listing G.4. The `paint` method makes the initial calls to the recursive method `drawFractal`. The three calls to `drawFractal` in the paint method represent the original three sides of the equilateral triangle that make up a Koch fractal of order 1.

Listing G.4

```
//********************************************************************
//  KochPanel.java       Java Foundations
//
//  Represents a drawing surface on which to paint a Koch Snowflake.
//********************************************************************

import java.awt.*;
import javax.swing.JPanel;

public class KochPanel extends JPanel
{
   private final int PANEL_WIDTH = 400;
   private final int PANEL_HEIGHT = 400;

   private final double SQ = Math.sqrt(3.0) / 6;

   private final int TOPX = 200, TOPY = 20;
   private final int LEFTX = 60, LEFTY = 300;
   private final int RIGHTX = 340, RIGHTY = 300;

   private int current;  // current order

   //-----------------------------------------------------------------
   //  Sets the initial fractal order to the value specified.
   //-----------------------------------------------------------------
   public KochPanel (int currentOrder)
   {
      current = currentOrder;
      setBackground (Color.black);
      setPreferredSize (new Dimension(PANEL_WIDTH, PANEL_HEIGHT));
   }

   //-----------------------------------------------------------------
   //  Draws the fractal recursively. The base case is order 1 for
   //  which a simple straight line is drawn. Otherwise three
   //  intermediate points are computed, and each line segment is
   //  drawn as a fractal.
   //-----------------------------------------------------------------
```

Listing **G.4** continued

```
   public void drawFractal (int order, int x1, int y1, int x5, int y5,
                            Graphics page)
   {
      int deltaX, deltaY, x2, y2, x3, y3, x4, y4;

      if (order == 1)
         page.drawLine (x1, y1, x5, y5);
      else
      {
         deltaX = x5 - x1;  // distance between end points
         deltaY = y5 - y1;

         x2 = x1 + deltaX / 3;  // one third
         y2 = y1 + deltaY / 3;

         x3 = (int) ((x1+x5)/2 + SQ * (y1-y5));  // tip of projection
         y3 = (int) ((y1+y5)/2 + SQ * (x5-x1));

         x4 = x1 + deltaX * 2/3;  // two thirds
         y4 = y1 + deltaY * 2/3;

         drawFractal (order-1, x1, y1, x2, y2, page);
         drawFractal (order-1, x2, y2, x3, y3, page);
         drawFractal (order-1, x3, y3, x4, y4, page);
         drawFractal (order-1, x4, y4, x5, y5, page);
      }
   }

   //-----------------------------------------------------------------
   //  Performs the initial calls to the drawFractal method.
   //-----------------------------------------------------------------
   public void paintComponent (Graphics page)
   {
      super.paintComponent (page);

      page.setColor (Color.green);

      drawFractal (current, TOPX, TOPY, LEFTX, LEFTY, page);
      drawFractal (current, LEFTX, LEFTY, RIGHTX, RIGHTY, page);
      drawFractal (current, RIGHTX, RIGHTY, TOPX, TOPY, page);
   }
```

Listing **G.4** continued

```
   //-----------------------------------------------------------------
   //  Sets the fractal order to the value specified.
   //-----------------------------------------------------------------
   public void setOrder (int order)
   {
      current = order;
   }

   //-----------------------------------------------------------------
   //  Returns the current order.
   //-----------------------------------------------------------------
   public int getOrder ()
   {
      return current;
   }
}
```

The variable `current` represents the order of the fractal to be drawn. Each recursive call to `drawFractal` decrements the order by 1. The base case of the recursion occurs when the order of the fractal is 1, which results in a simple line segment between the coordinates specified by the parameters.

If the order of the fractal is higher than 1, three additional points are computed. In conjunction with the parameters, these points form the four line segments of the modified fractal. Figure G.4 shows the transformation.

Based on the position of the two end points of the original line segment, a point one-third of the way and a point two-thirds of the way between them are computed. The calculation of <x3, y3>, the point at the tip of the protrusion, is more convoluted and uses a simplifying constant that incorporates multiple geometric relationships. The calculations to determine the three new points actually have nothing to do with the recursive technique used to draw the fractal, and so we won't discuss the details of these computations here.

An interesting mathematical feature of a Koch snowflake is that it has an infinite perimeter but a finite area. As the order of the fractal increases, the perimeter grows exponentially larger, with a mathematical limit of infinity. However, a rectangle large enough to surround the second-order fractal for the Koch snowflake is large enough to contain all higher-order fractals. The shape is restricted forever in area, but its perimeter gets infinitely longer.

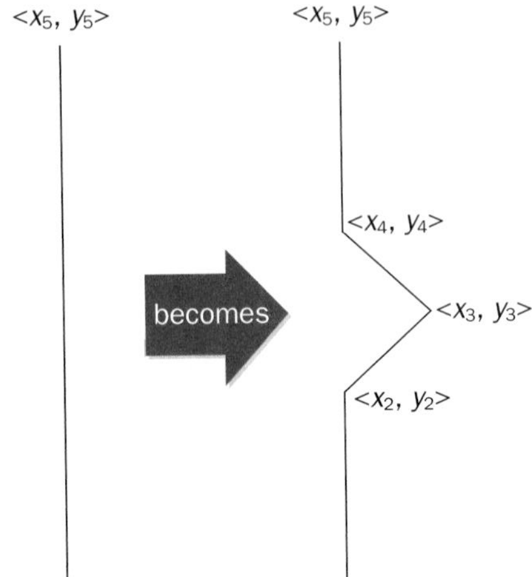

FIGURE G.4 The transformation of each line segment of a Koch snowflake

Programming Projects

PP G.1 Convert any of the applications described by the programming projects in Appendix F (Graphics) into applets.

PP G.2 Convert any of the applications described by the programming projects in Chapter 7 (GUIs) into applets, excluding those that require data written to a file.

Appendix

H

Regular Expressions

Throughout the book we've used the `Scanner` class to read interactive input from the user and parse strings into individual tokens such as words. In Chapter 4 we also used it to read input from a data file. Usually we used the default whitespace delimiters for tokens in the scanner input.

The `Scanner` class can also be used to parse its input according to a *regular expression*, which is a character string that represents a pattern. A regular expression can be used to set the delimiters used when extracting tokens, or it can be used in methods like `findInLine` to match a particular string.

Some of the general rules for constructing regular expressions include:

- The dot (`.`) character matches any single character.
- The asterisk (`*`) character, which is called the Kleene star, matches zero or more characters.

- A string of characters in brackets (`[ ]`) matches any single character in the string.
- The \ character followed by a special character (such as the ones in this list) matches the character itself.
- The \ character followed by a character matches the pattern specified by that character (see Figure H.1).

For example, the regular expression `B.b*` matches `Bob`, `Bubba`, and `Baby`. The regular expression `T[aei]*ing` matches `Taking`, `Tickling`, and `Telling`.

Figure H.1 shows some of the patterns that can be matched in a Java regular expression. This list is not complete—see the online documentation for the `Pattern` class for a complete list.

Regular Expression	Matches
x	The character x
.	Any character
[abc]	a, b, or c
[^abc]	Any character except a, b, or c (negation)
[a-z][A-Z]	a through z or A through Z, inclusive (range)
[a-o[m-p]]	a through d or m through p (union)
[a-z&&[def]]	d, e, or f (intersection)
[a-z&&[^bc]]	a through z, except for b and c (subtraction)
[a-z&&[^m-p]]	a through z but not m through p (subtraction)
\d	A digit: [0–9]
\D	A non-digit: [^0–9]
\s	A whitespace character
\S	A non-whitespace character
^	The beginning of a line
$	The end of a line

FIGURE H.1 Some patterns that can be specified in a Java regular expression

Javadoc Documentation Generator

Javadoc is a tool for creating documentation about Java source code in HTML format by examining the source code itself. The utility extracts specially marked information from the comments in the source code, and then produces Web pages that summarize the software.

Documentation comments, also referred to as doc comments, specify the format for comments processed by the javadoc tool. Special labels called *tags* are also parsed by the javadoc tool. Together, doc comments and tags can be used to construct a complete Java application programming interface (API) specification, which describes how to work with a set of classes.

Javadoc can be run on packages or individual files (or both). It produces a well-structured, integrated set of HTML documents each time it is run. However, javadoc does not support incremental additions.

Javadoc comes as a standard part of the Java Software Development Kit (SDK). The tool executable, javadoc.exe, resides in the bin folder of the installation directory along with the javac compiler and java run-time tool. Therefore, if you are able to compile and execute your code using the command line, javadoc should also work.

Using javadoc is simple in its plain form; it is very much like compiling a Java source file. The javadoc command can be issued from the command line. For example:

```
> javadoc myfile.java
```

The source file name must contain the .java extension (similar to the javac compiler command). Various options can be used with the javadoc command as well.

Doc Comments

The document comments are made up of descriptions and tags. Descriptions should be written to provide an overview of the functionality of the code. Tags address the specifics of the functionality, such as code version (for classes or interfaces) or return types (for methods).

Javadoc comments begin with `/**` and end with `*/`. Any comments written in this form will be examined and processed by the javadoc tool. Like regular comments that begin with `/*` and end with `*/`, javadoc comments may span multiple lines. However, each intermediate line begins with a * character, which is, along with any white space before it, discarded by the tool. These comments are allowed to contain HTML tags. For example:

```
/**
*     This is an <strong>example</strong> document comment.
*/
```

Javadoc comments should be constructed carefully. The javadoc tool automatically copies the first sentence from each comment to a summary at the top of the HTML document. The sentence begins after any white space following the * character and ends at the first period. Document comments are recognized only if they are placed immediately before a class, constructor, method, interface, or field declaration.

The use of HTML inside the description should be limited to proper comment separation and display rather than styling. Javadoc automatically structures the document based on certain HTML elements, such as heading tags. Appropriate use of paragraph or list elements should result in proper formatting.

Tags

Tags may be included in a javadoc comment. Each tag must start on a separate line, hence it must be preceded by the `*` character. Tags are case sensitive and begin with the `@` symbol.

Certain tags are required in some situations. The `@param` tag must be supplied for every parameter to a method and is used to describe the purpose of the parameter. The `@return` tag must be supplied for every method that returns a value other than `void`, to describe what the method returns. The `@author` and the `@version` tags are required for classes and interfaces only.

Figure I.1 lists the various tags used in javadoc comments.

Note the two different types of tags listed in Figure I.1. The *block tags*, which begin with the `@` symbol (such as `@author`), must be placed in the tag section following the main description. The *inline tags*, enclosed in `{` and `}` delimiters, can be placed anywhere in the description section or in the comments for block tags. For example:

```
/**
* This is an <strong>example</strong> document comment.
* The {@link Glossary} provides definitions of types used.
*
* @author Sebastian Niezgoda
*/
```

Files Generated

The javadoc tool analyzes a Java source file or package and produces a three-part HTML document for each class. The HTML file is often referred to as a documentation file. It contains cleanly organized information about the class file derived from the javadoc comments included in the code.

Tag Name	Description
@author	Inserts an "Author" entry with the specified text.
{ @code}	Same as <code>{@literal}</code>.
@deprecated	Inserts a bold "Deprecated" entry with the specified text.
{ @docRoot}	Relative link to the root of the document.
@exception	See @throws.
{ @inheritDoc}	Copies documentation from the closest inherited class or implemented interface where used allowing for more general comments of hierarchically higher classes to be reused.
{ @link}	Inserts a hyperlink to an HTML document. Use: {@link name url}.
{ @linkPlain}	Same as { @link} but is displayed as plain text. Use: {@linkPlain link label}.
{ @literal}	Text enclosed in the tag is denoted literally, as containing any HTML. For example, {@literal <td> TouchDown} would be displayed as <td> TouchDown (<td> not interpreted as a table cell).
@param	Inserts a "Parameters" section, which lists and describes parameters for a particular constructor/method.
@return	Inserts a "Returns" section, which lists and describes any return values for a particular constructor/method. Use: @return description. An error will be thrown if included in a comment of a method with the void return type.
@see	Included a "See Also" comment with a link pointing to a document with more information. Use: @see link.
@serial	Used for a serializable field. Use: @serial text.
@serialData	Used to document used to describe data written by the writeObject, readObject, writeExternal, and readExternal methods. Use: @serialdata text.
@serialField	Used to comment on the ObjectStreamField. Use: @serialField name type description.
@since	Inserts a new "Since" heading that is used to denote when particular features were first introduced. Use: @since text.
@throws	Includes a "Throws" heading. Use: @throws name description.
{ @value}	Returns the value of a code element it refers to. Use: @value code-member label.
@version	Add a "Version" heading when the -version command–line option is used. Use: @version text.

FIGURE I.1 Various tags used in javadoc comments

The first part of the document contains an overall description of the class. The class name appears first followed by a graphical representation of the inheritance relationships. A general description is displayed next, which is extracted from the first sentence of each doc comment entity (as discussed previously).

Next, a list of constructors and methods is provided. The signatures of all the constructors and methods included in the source file are listed along with one-sentence descriptions. The name of the constructor/method is a hyperlink to a more detailed description in the third part of the document.

Third, a complete description of each method is provided. Again, the signature is provided first followed by an explanation of the method (this time without the one-sentence limit), which is obtained from the javadoc comments. If applicable, a list of parameters and return values, along with their descriptions, is provided in the respective sections.

The HTML document makes extensive use of hyperlinks to provide necessary additional information, using the `@see` tag for example, and for navigational purposes. The header and the footer of the page are navigation bars, with the following links:

- *Package* provides a list of classes included in the package along with a short purpose and description of each class.
- *Tree* presents a visual hierarchy of the classes within the package. Each class name is a link to the appropriate documentation HTML file.
- *Deprecated* lists functionality that is considered deprecated that is used in any of the class files contained in the package.
- *Index* provides an alphabetical listing of classes, constructors, and methods in the package. The class name is also associated with a short purpose and description of the class. Each appearance of the class name is a link to the appropriate HTML documentation. The signature of every constructor and method is a link to the appropriate detailed description. A one-sentence description presented next to the signature associates the constructor/method with the appropriate class.
- *Help* loads a help page with how-to instructions for using and navigating the HTML documentation.

All pages could be viewed with or without the use of HTML frames. Each class summary has links that can be used to quickly access any of the parts of the document.

The output content can be modified by command-line options used when executing the javadoc tool. By default, if no options are specified, the output returned is equivalent to using the `protected` option. The options include:

- `private` shows all classes, methods, and variables.
- `public` shows only public classes, methods, and variables.
- `protected` shows only protected and public classes, methods, and variables.
- `help` presents the online help.
- `keywords` includes HTML meta tags to the output file generated to assist with searching.

Java Syntax

This appendix contains syntax diagrams that collectively describe the way in which Java language elements can be constructed. Rectangles indicate something that is further defined in another syntax diagram, and ovals indicate a literal word or character. Though largely complete, not all Java constructs are represented in this collection of syntax diagrams.

Compilation Unit

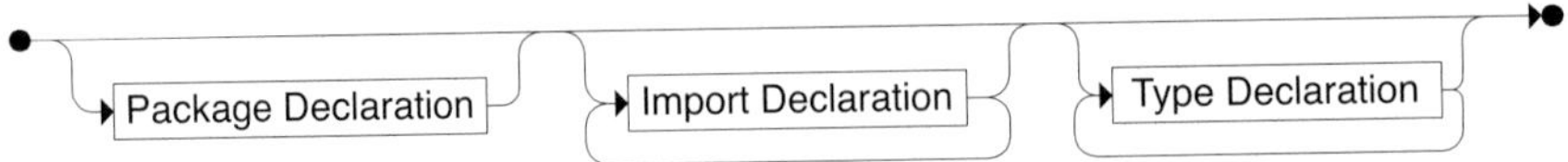

Package Declaration

Import Declaration

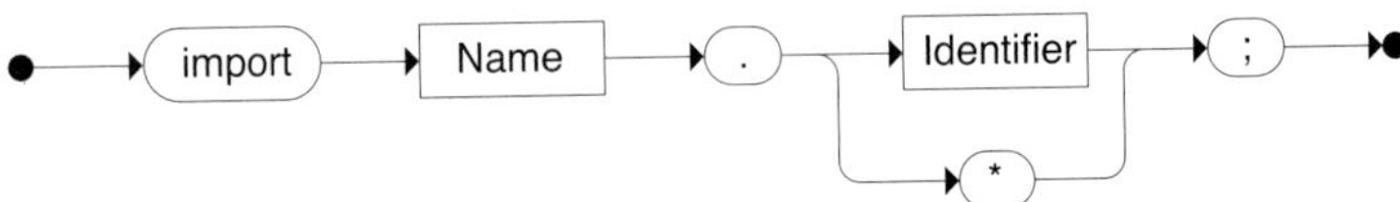

Type Declaration

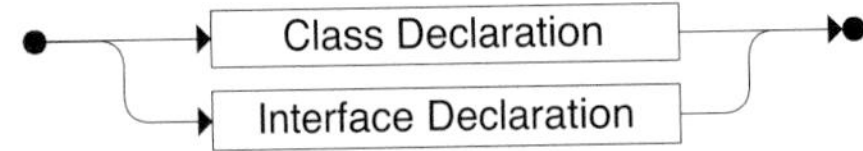

Class Declaration

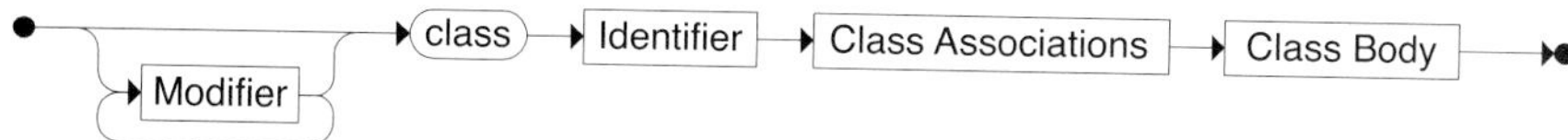

Class Associations

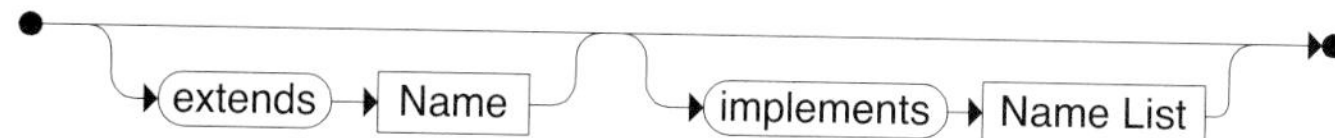

Class Body

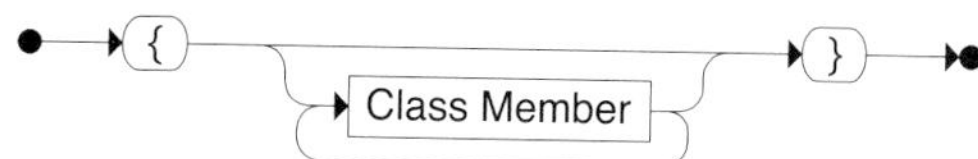

Class Member

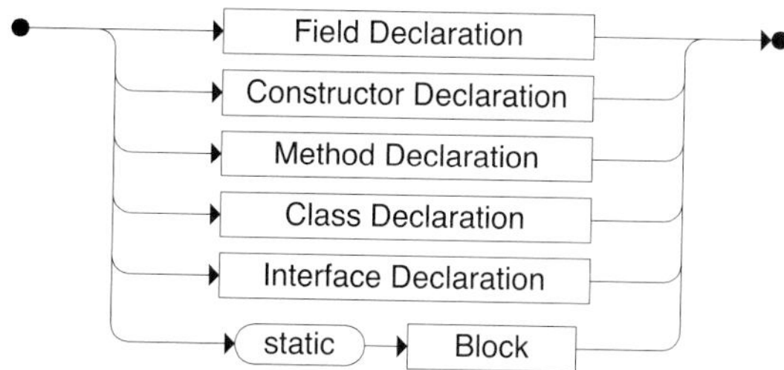

Interface Declaration

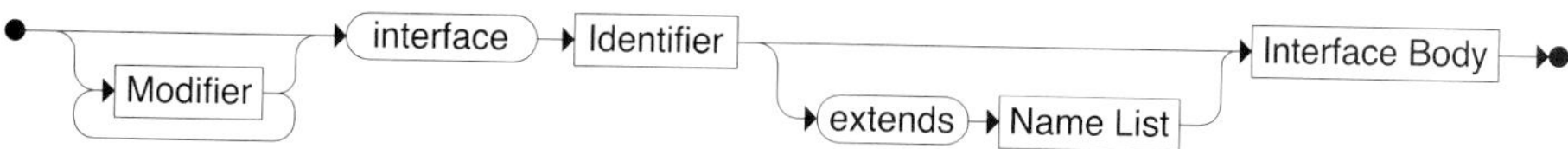

Interface Body

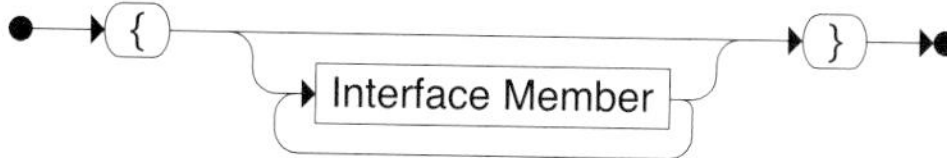

Interface Member

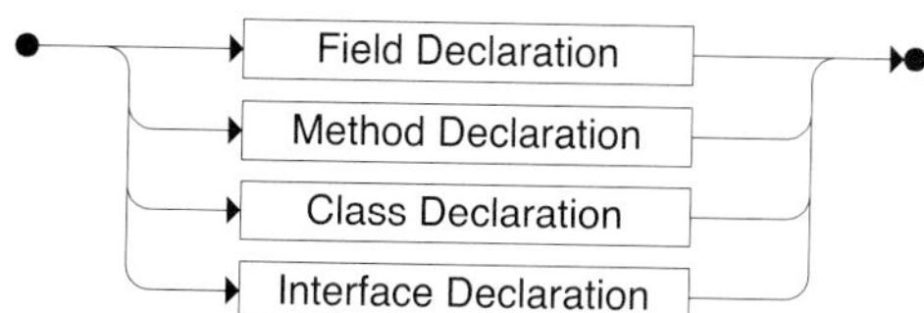

Field Declaration

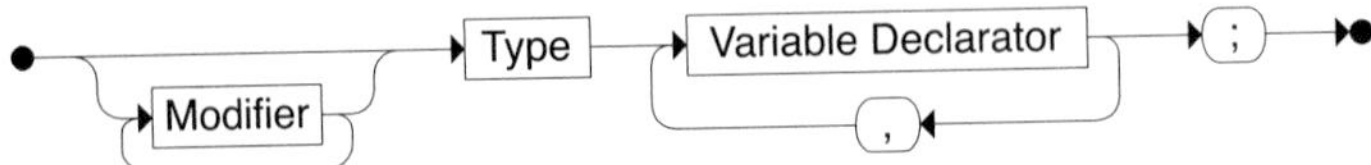

Variable Declarator

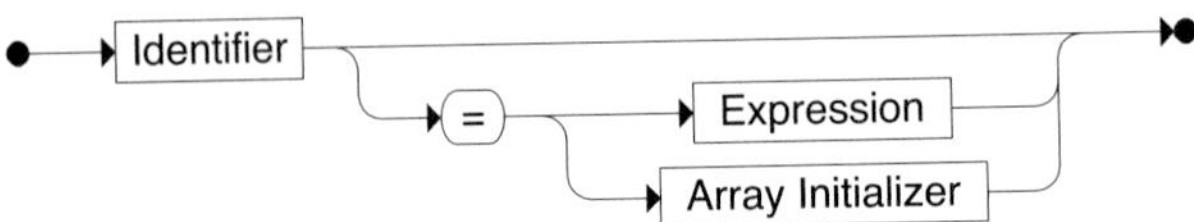

Type

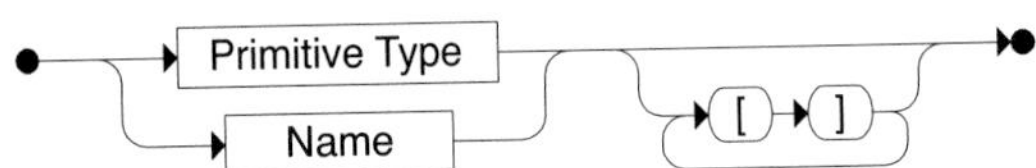

Modifier

Primitive Type

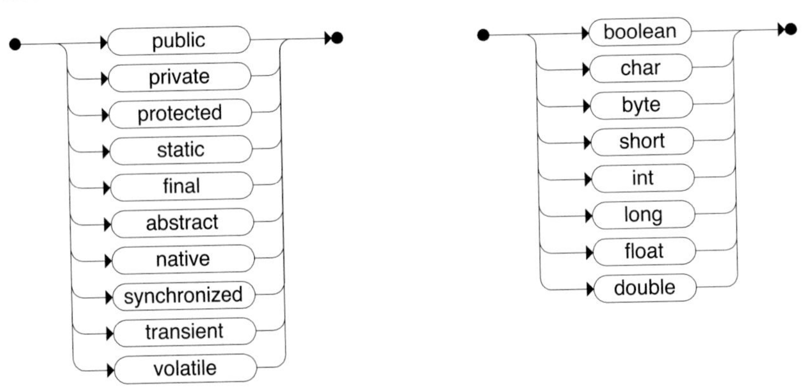

Array Initializer

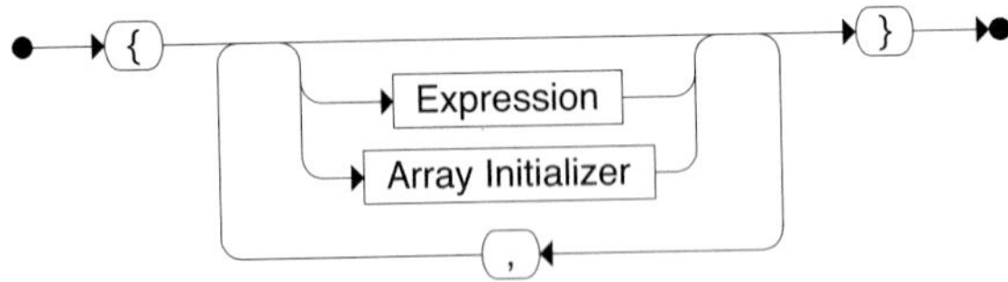

Name

Name List

Method Declaration

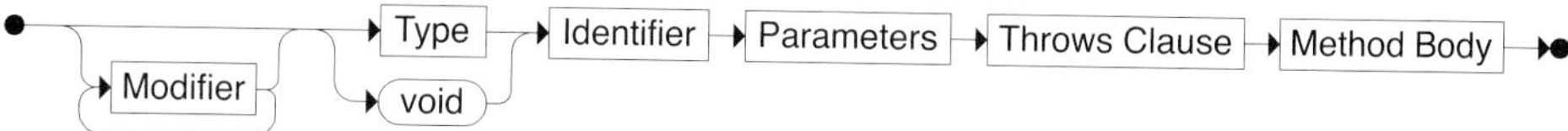

Parameters

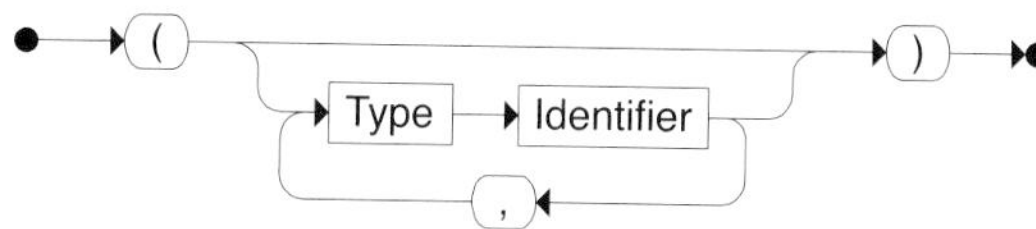

Throws Clause

Method Body

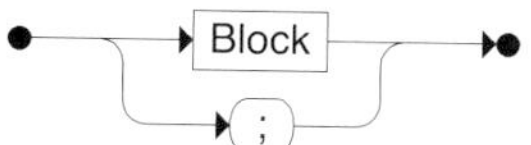

Constructor Declaration

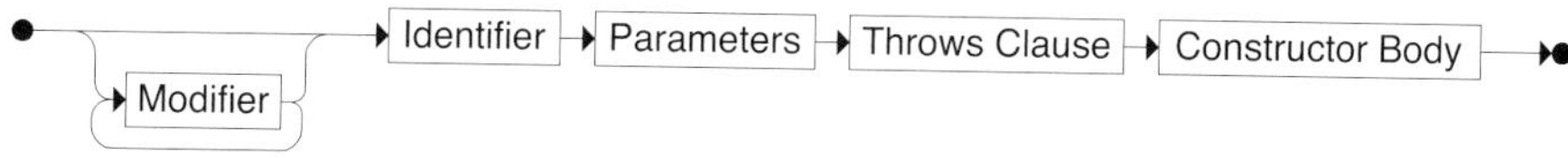

Constructor Body

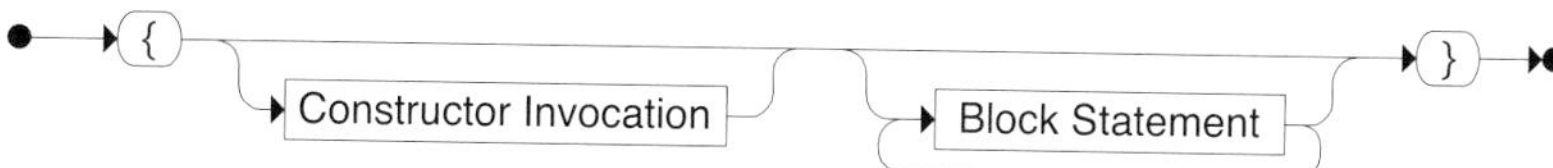

Constructor Invocation

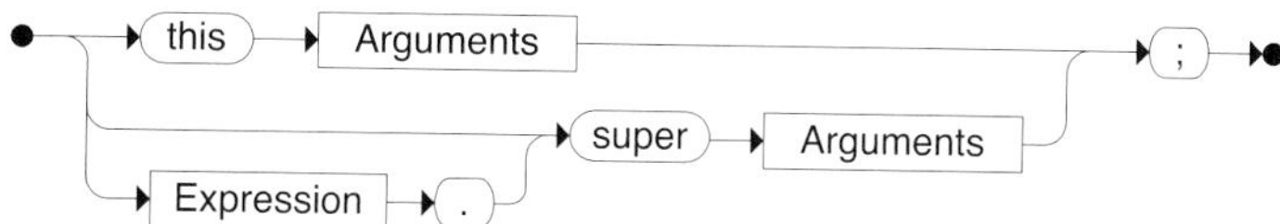

Block

Block Statement

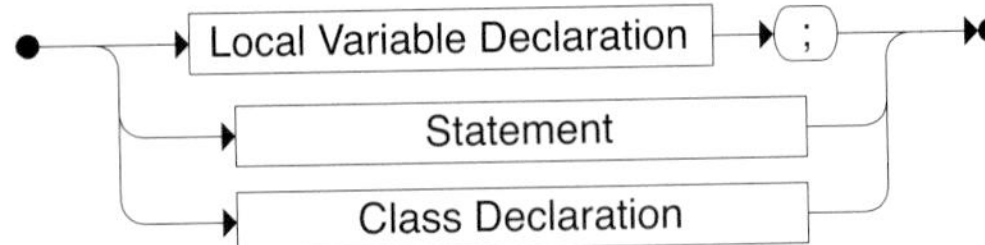

Local Variable Declaration

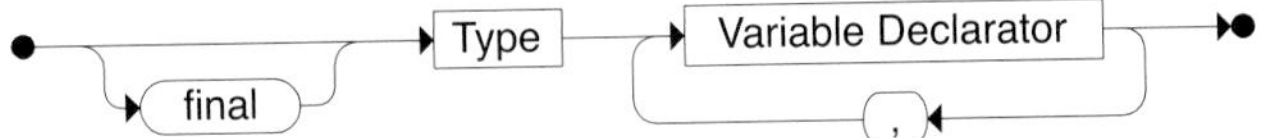

Statement

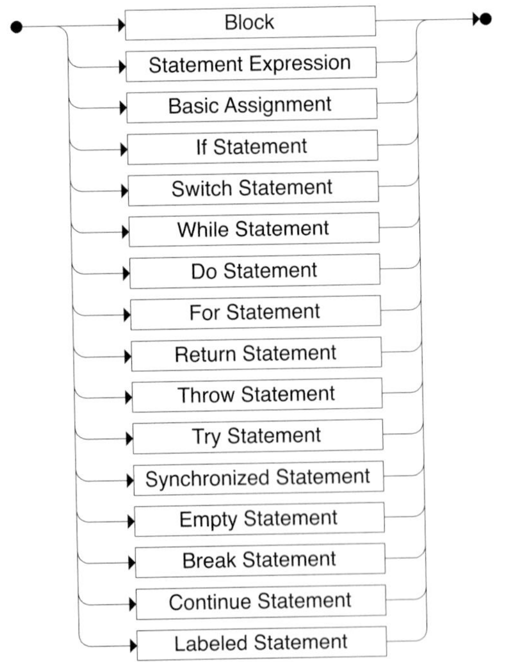

If Statement

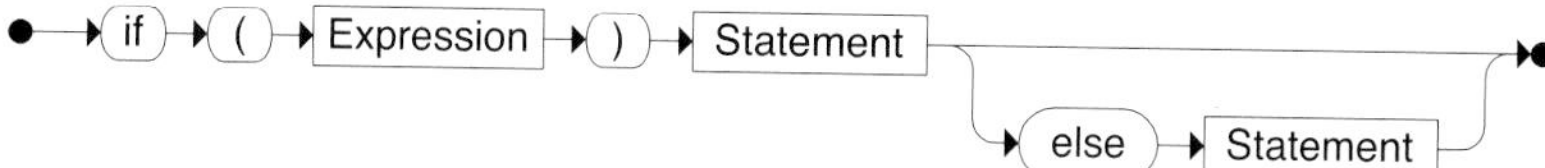

Switch Statement

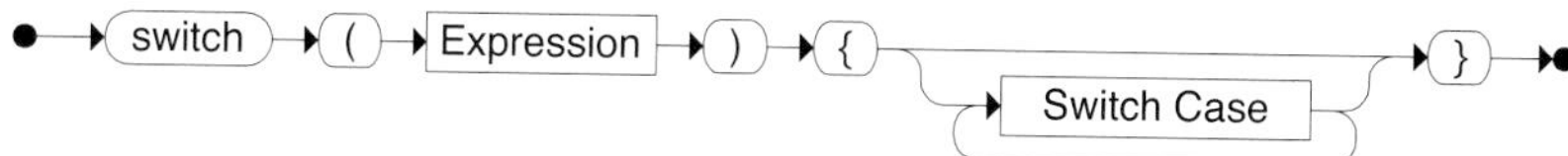

Switch Case

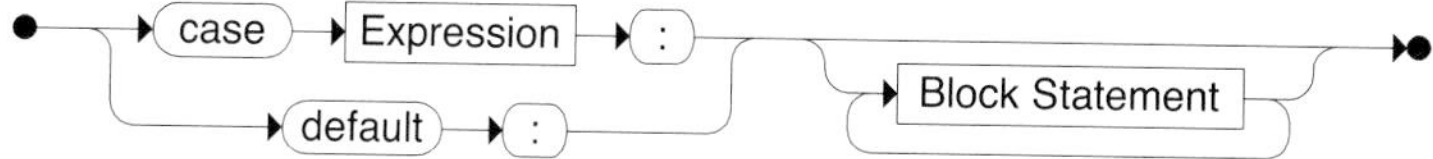

While Statement

Do Statement

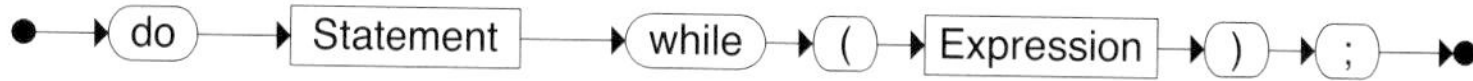

For Statement

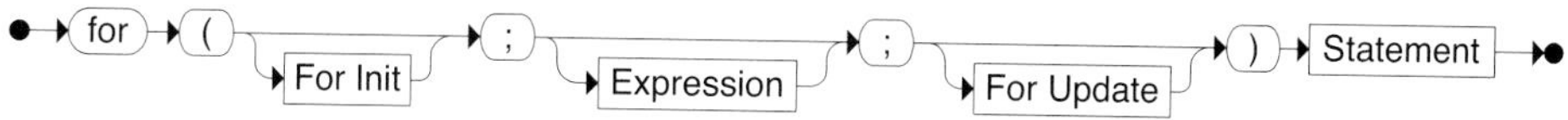

For Init

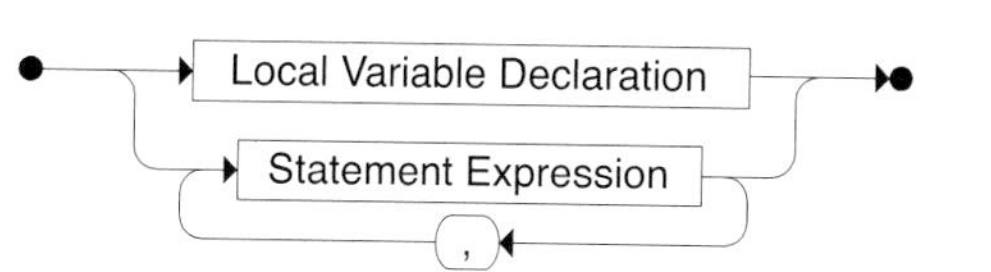

For Update

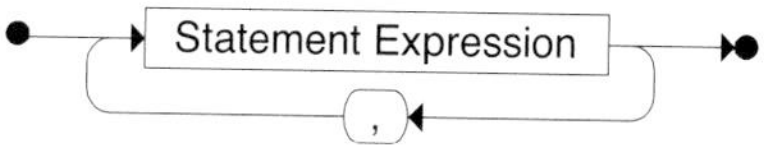

Statement Expression

,

Basic Assignment

Return Statement

Throw Statement

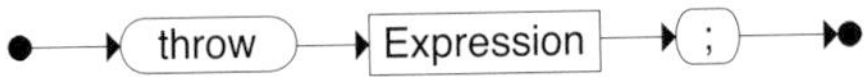

Try Statement

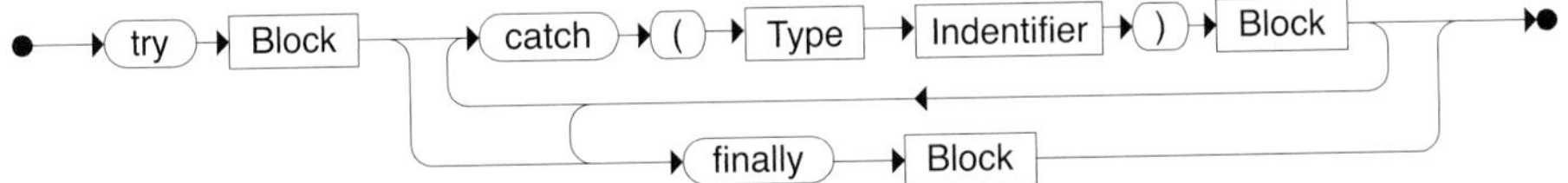

Synchronized Statement

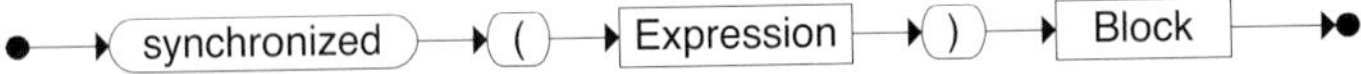

Empty Statement

Break Statement

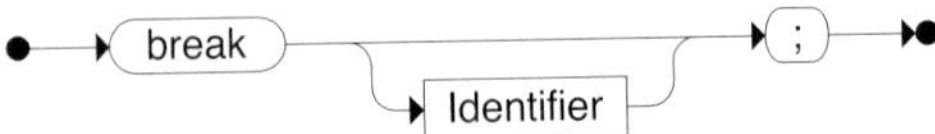

Continue Statement

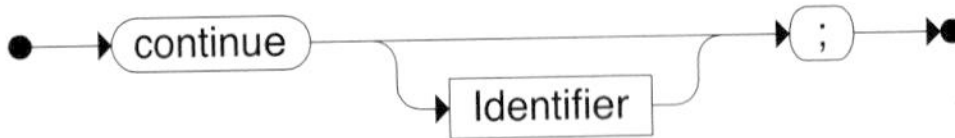

Labeled Statement

Expression

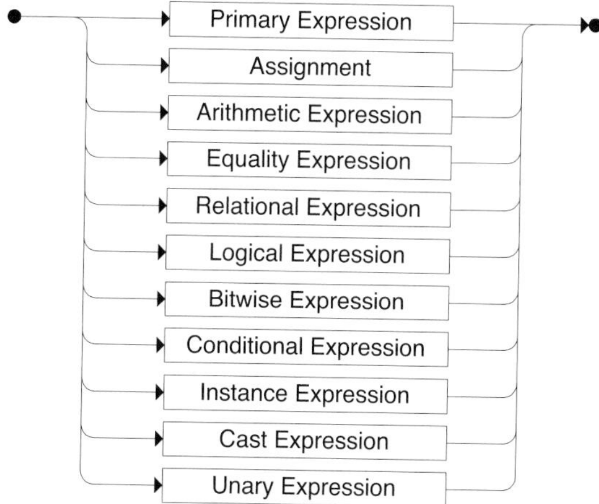

Primary Expression

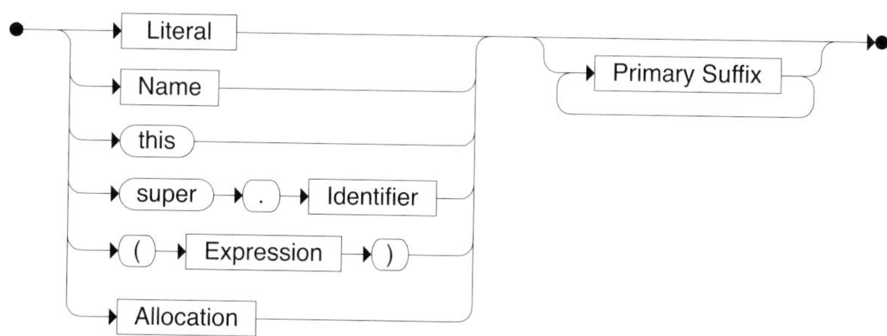

Primary Suffix

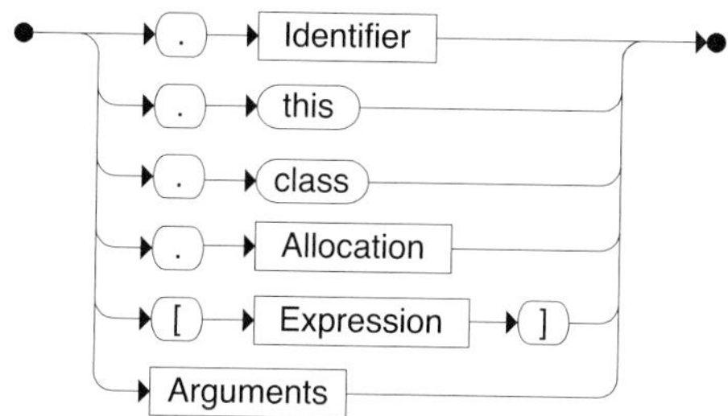

Arguments

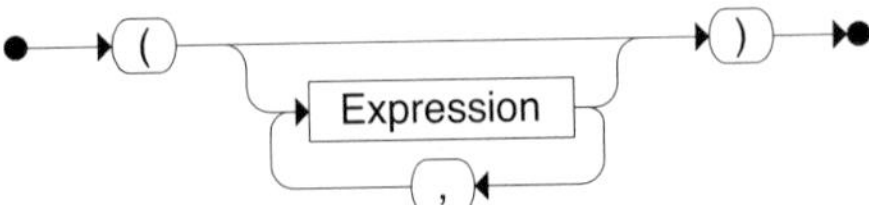

Allocation

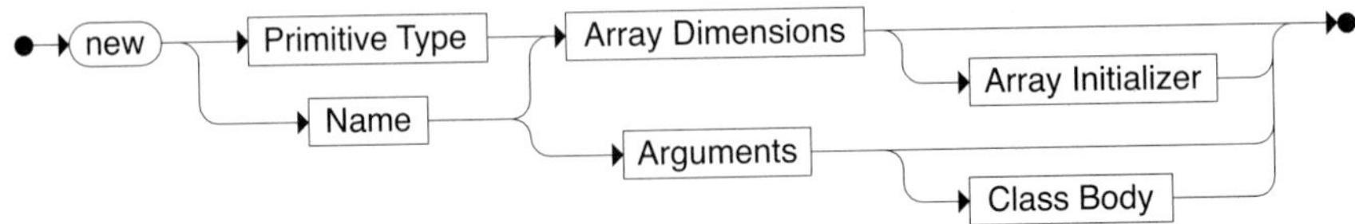

Array Dimensions

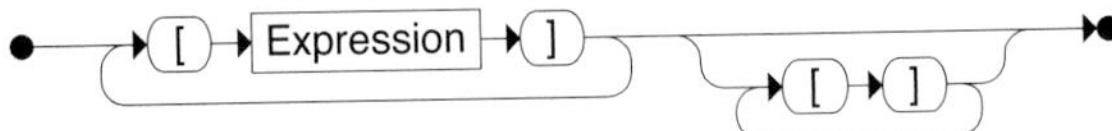

Statement Expression

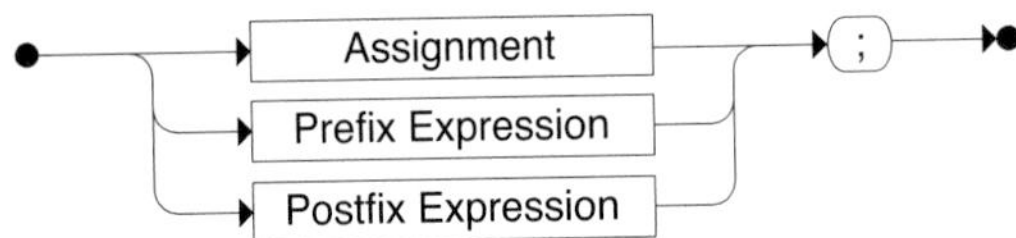

Assignment

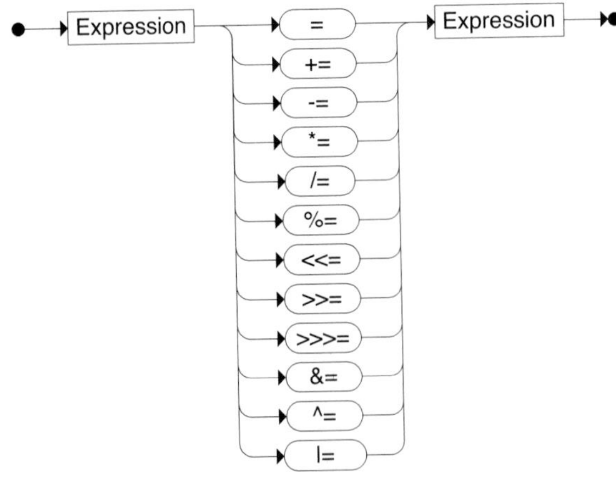

Arithmetic Expression

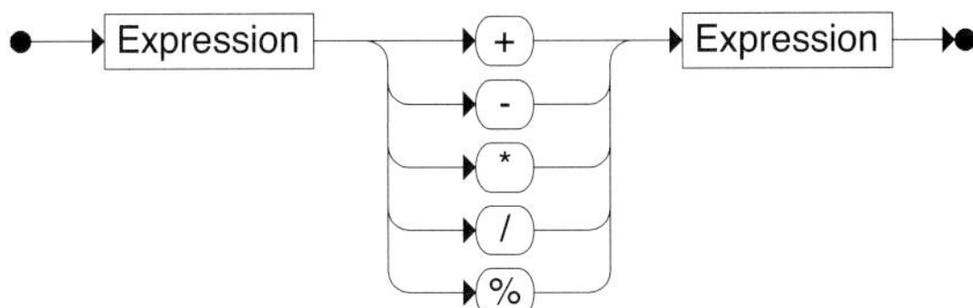

Equality Expression

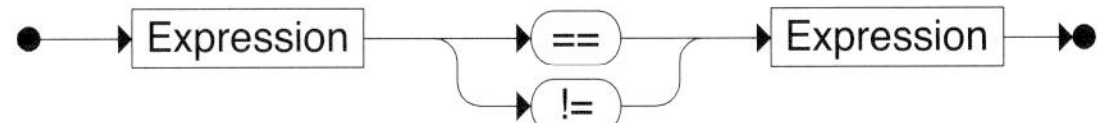

Relational Expression

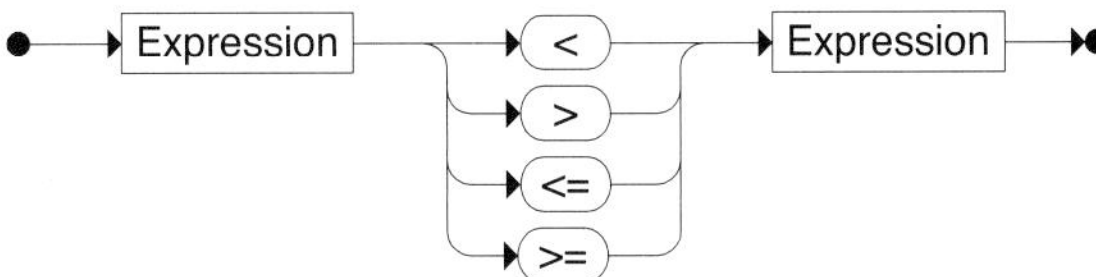

Logical Expression

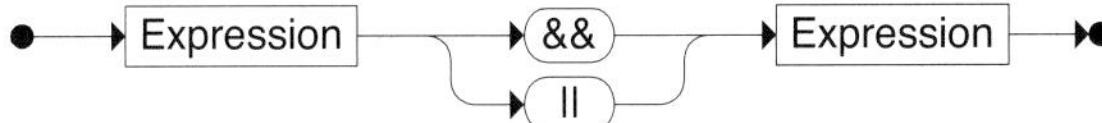

Bitwise Expression

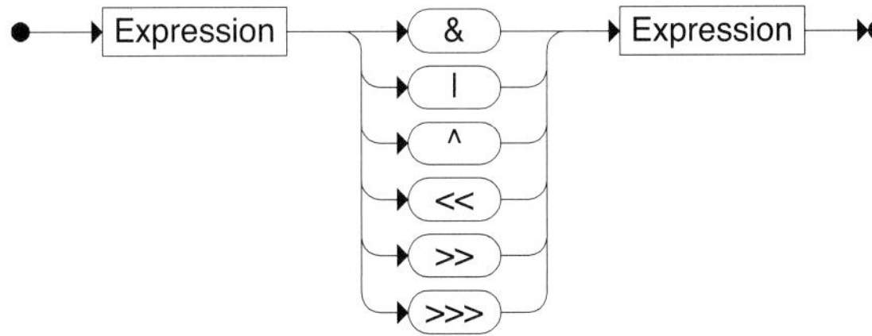

Conditional Expression

Instance Expression

Cast Expression

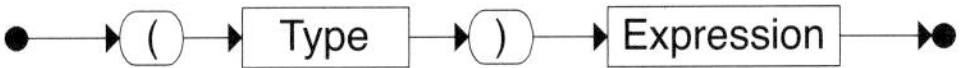

Unary Expression

Prefix Expression
Postfix Expression
+
-
!
~
Expression

Prefix Expression

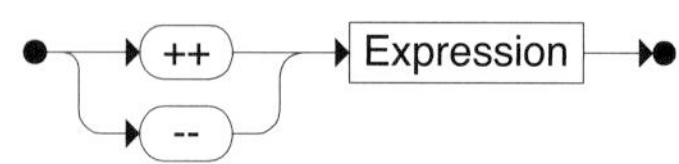

Postfix Expression

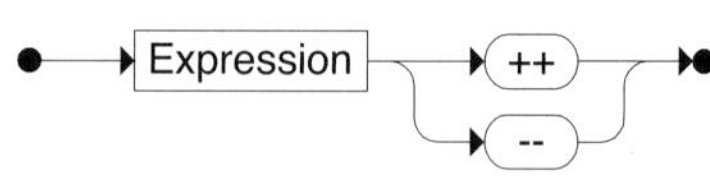

Literal

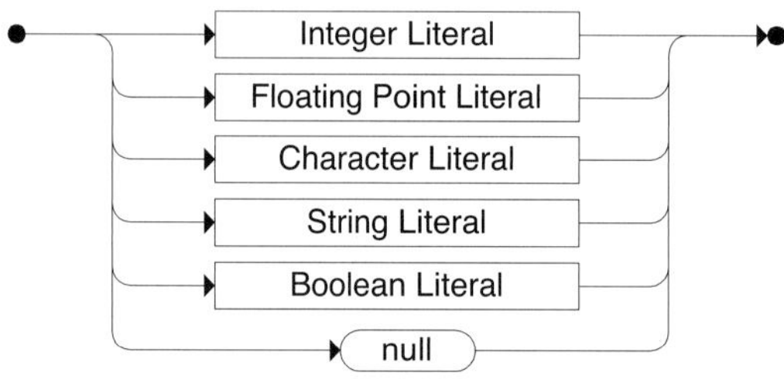

Integer Literal

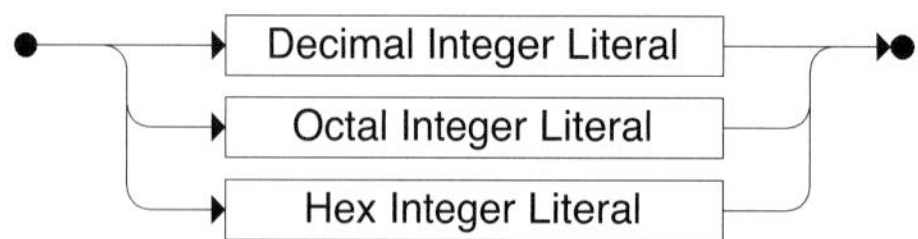

Decimal Integer Literal

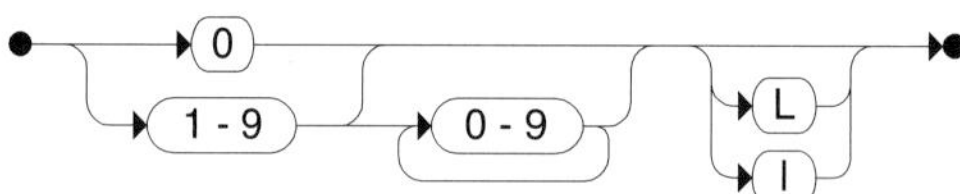

Octal Integer Literal

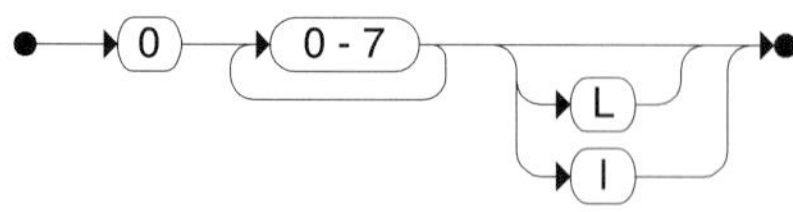

Hex Digit

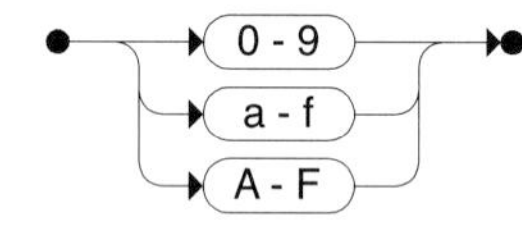

Hex Integer Literal

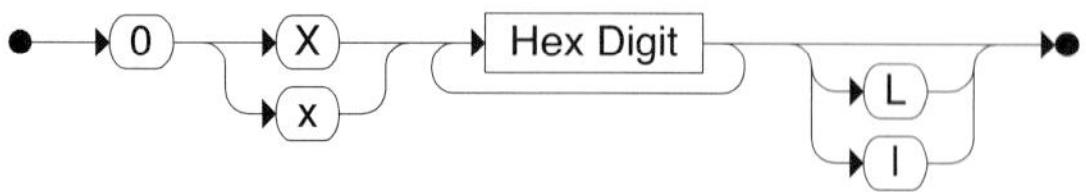

Floating Point Literal

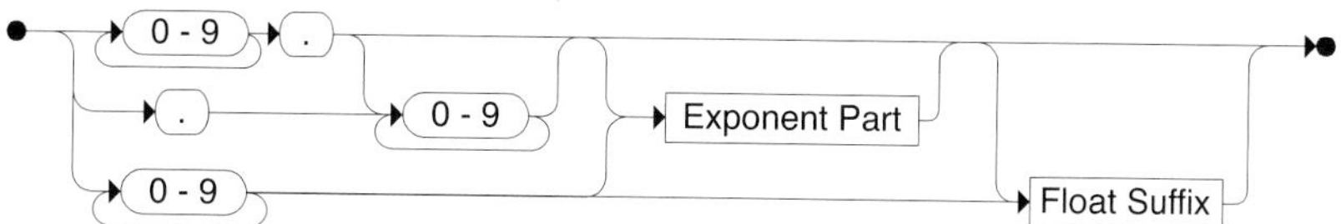

Exponent Part

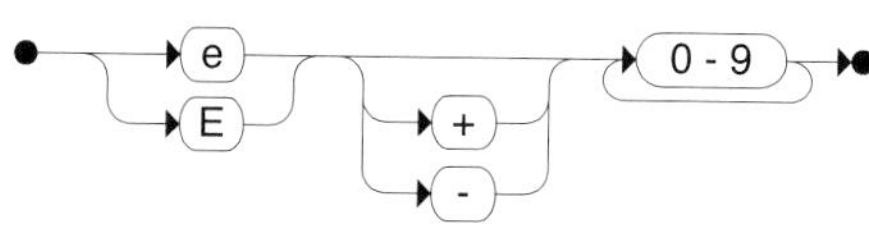

Float Suffix

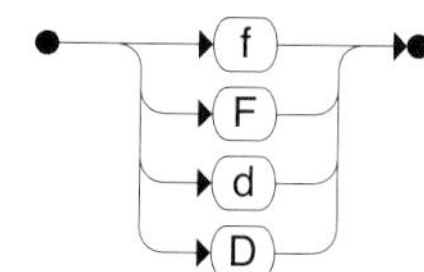

Character Literal

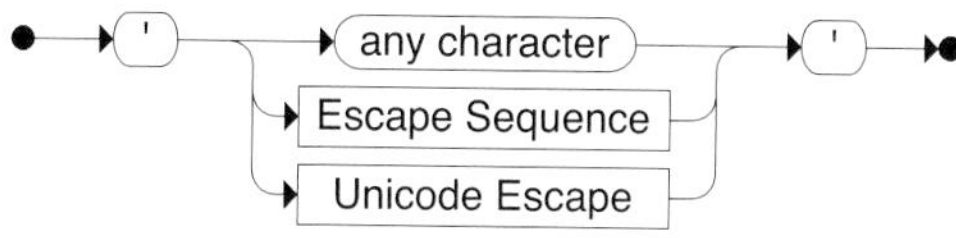

Boolean Literal

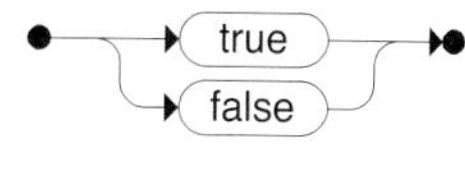

String Literal

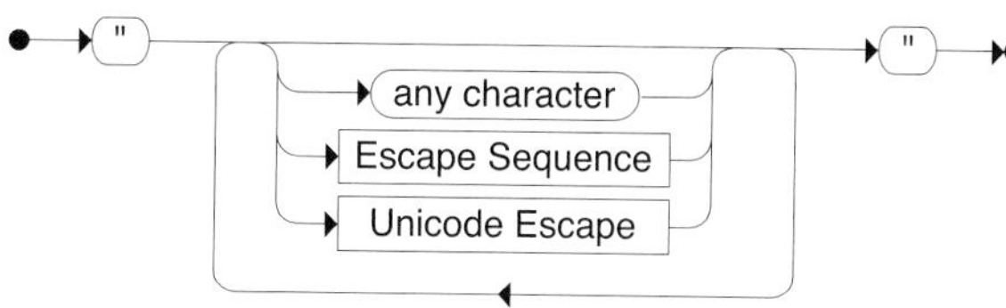

Escape Sequence

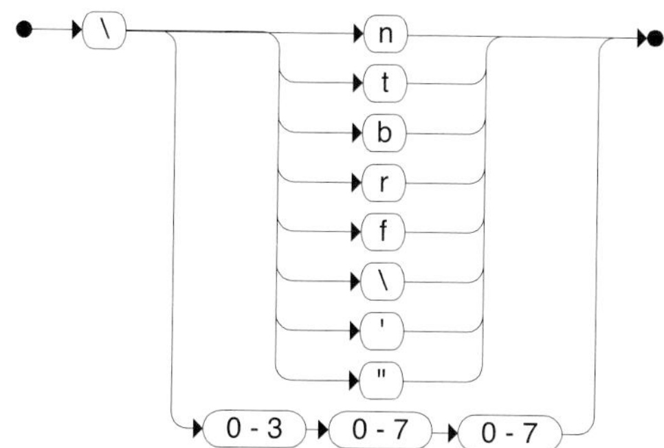

Identifier

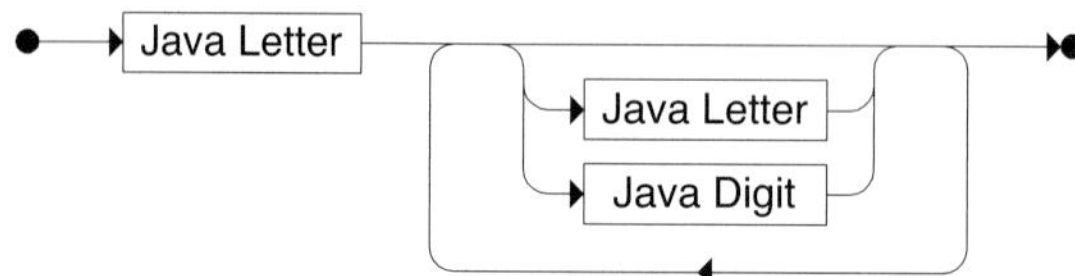

Java Letter

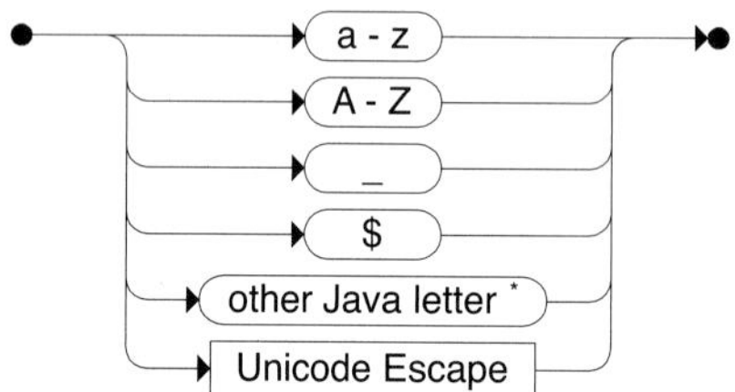

* The "other Java letter" category includes letters from many languages other than English.

Java Digit

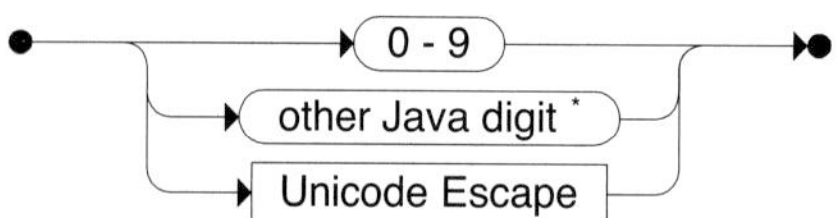

* The "other Java digit" category includes additional digits defined in Unicode.

Unicode Escape*

* In some contexts, the character represented by a Unicode Escape is restricted.

Index

Symbols

A

D

T

Sun Microsystems, Inc. Binary Code License Agreement for the JAVA 2 PLATFORM STANDARD EDITION DEVELOPMENT KIT 5.0

SUN MICROSYSTEMS, INC. ("SUN") IS WILLING TO LICENSE THE SOFTWARE IDENTIFIED BELOW TO YOU ONLY UPON THE CONDITION THAT YOU ACCEPT ALL OF THE TERMS CONTAINED IN THIS BINARY CODE LICENSE AGREEMENT AND SUPPLEMENTAL LICENSE TERMS (COLLECTIVELY "AGREEMENT"). PLEASE READ THE AGREEMENT CAREFULLY. BY DOWNLOADING OR INSTALLING THIS SOFTWARE, YOU ACCEPT THE TERMS OF THE AGREEMENT. INDICATE ACCEPTANCE BY SELECTING THE "ACCEPT" BUTTON AT THE BOTTOM OF THE AGREEMENT. IF YOU ARE NOT WILLING TO BE BOUND BY ALL THE TERMS, SELECT THE "DECLINE" BUTTON AT THE BOTTOM OF THE AGREEMENT AND THE DOWNLOAD OR INSTALL PROCESS WILL NOT CONTINUE.

1. DEFINITIONS. "Software" means the identified above in binary form, any other machine readable materials (including, but not limited to, libraries, source files, header files, and data files), any updates or error corrections provided by Sun, and any user manuals, programming guides and other documentation provided to you by Sun under this Agreement. "Programs" mean Java applets and applications intended to run on the Java 2 Platform Standard Edition (J2SE platform) platform on Java-enabled general purpose desktop computers and servers.

2. LICENSE TO USE. Subject to the terms and conditions of this Agreement, including, but not limited to the Java Technology Restrictions of the Supplemental License Terms, Sun grants you a non-exclusive, non-transferable, limited license without license fees to reproduce and use internally Software complete and unmodified for the sole purpose of running Programs. Additional licenses for developers and/or publishers are granted in the Supplemental License Terms.

3. RESTRICTIONS. Software is confidential and copyrighted. Title to Software and all associated intellectual property rights is retained by Sun and/or its licensors. Unless enforcement is prohibited by applicable law, you may not modify, decompile, or reverse engineer Software. You acknowledge that Licensed Software is not designed or intended for use in the design, construction, operation or maintenance of any nuclear facility. Sun Microsystems, Inc. disclaims any express or implied warranty of fitness for such uses. No right, title or interest in or to any trademark, service mark, logo or trade name of Sun or its licensors is granted under this Agreement. Additional restrictions for developers and/or publishers licenses are set forth in the Supplemental License Terms.

4. LIMITED WARRANTY. Sun warrants to you that for a period of ninety (90) days from the date of purchase, as evidenced by a copy of the receipt, the media on which Software is furnished (if any) will be free of defects in materials and workmanship under normal use. Except for the foregoing, Software is provided "AS IS". Your exclusive remedy and Sun's entire liability under this limited warranty will be at Sun's option to replace Software media or refund the fee paid for Software. Any implied warranties on the Software are limited to 90 days. Some states do not allow limitations on duration of an implied warranty, so the above may not apply to you. This limited warranty gives you specific legal rights. You may have others, which vary from state to state.

5. DISCLAIMER OF WARRANTY. UNLESS SPECIFIED IN THIS AGREEMENT, ALL EXPRESS OR IMPLIED CONDITIONS, REPRESENTATIONS AND WARRANTIES, INCLUDING ANY IMPLIED WARRANTY OF MERCHANTABILITY, FITNESS FOR A PARTICULAR PURPOSE OR NON-INFRINGEMENT ARE DISCLAIMED, EXCEPT TO THE EXTENT THAT THESE DISCLAIMERS ARE HELD TO BE LEGALLY INVALID.

6. LIMITATION OF LIABILITY. TO THE EXTENT NOT PROHIBITED BY LAW, IN NO EVENT WILL SUN OR ITS LICENSORS BE LIABLE FOR ANY LOST REVENUE, PROFIT OR DATA, OR FOR SPECIAL, INDIRECT, CONSEQUENTIAL, INCIDENTAL OR PUNITIVE DAMAGES, HOWEVER CAUSED REGARDLESS OF THE THEORY OF LIABILITY, ARISING OUT OF OR RELATED TO THE USE OF OR INABILITY TO USE SOFTWARE, EVEN IF SUN HAS BEEN ADVISED OF THE POSSIBILITY OF SUCH DAMAGES. In no event will Sun's liability to you, whether in contract, tort (including negligence), or otherwise, exceed the amount paid by you for Software under this Agreement. The foregoing limitations will apply even if the above stated warranty fails of its essential purpose. Some states do not allow the exclusion of incidental or consequential damages, so some of the terms above may not be applicable to you.

7. TERMINATION. This Agreement is effective until terminated. You may terminate this Agreement at any time by destroying all copies of Software. This Agreement will terminate immediately without notice from Sun if you fail to comply with any provision of this Agreement. Either party may terminate this Agreement immediately should any Software become, or in either party's opinion be likely to become, the subject of a claim of infringement of any intellectual property right. Upon Termination, you must destroy all copies of Software.

8. EXPORT REGULATIONS. All Software and technical data delivered under this Agreement are subject to US export control laws and may be subject to export or import regulations in other countries. You agree to comply strictly with all such laws and regulations and acknowledge that you have the responsibility to obtain such licenses to export, re-export, or import as may be required after delivery to you.

9. TRADEMARKS AND LOGOS. You acknowledge and agree as between you and Sun that Sun owns the SUN, SOLARIS, JAVA, JINI, FORTE, and iPLANET trademarks and all SUN, SOLARIS, JAVA, JINI, FORTE, and iPLANET-related trademarks, service marks, logos and other brand designations ("Sun Marks"), and you agree to comply with the Sun Trademark and Logo Usage Requirements currently located at http://www.sun.com/policies/trademarks. Any use you make of the Sun Marks inures to Sun's benefit.

10. U.S. GOVERNMENT RESTRICTED RIGHTS. If Software is being acquired by or on behalf of the U.S. Government or by a U.S. Government prime contractor or subcontractor (at any tier), then the Government's rights in Software and accompanying documentation will be only as set forth in this Agreement; this is in accordance with 48 CFR 227.7201 through 227.7202-4 (for Department of Defense (DOD) acquisitions) and with 48 CFR 2.101 and 12.212 (for non-DOD acquisitions).

11. GOVERNING LAW. Any action related to this Agreement will be governed by California law and controlling U.S. federal law. No choice of law rules of any jurisdiction will apply.

12. SEVERABILITY. If any provision of this Agreement is held to be unenforceable, this Agreement will remain in effect with the provision omitted, unless omission would frustrate the intent of the parties, in which case this Agreement will immediately terminate.

13. INTEGRATION. This Agreement is the entire agreement between you and Sun relating to its subject matter. It supersedes all prior or contemporaneous oral or written communications, proposals, representations and warranties and prevails over any conflicting or additional terms of any quote, order, acknowledgment, or other communication between the parties relating to its subject matter during the term of this Agreement. No modification of this Agreement will be binding, unless in writing and signed by an authorized representative of each party.

SUPPLEMENTAL LICENSE TERMS

These Supplemental License Terms add to or modify the terms of the Binary Code License Agreement. Capitalized terms not defined in these Supplemental Terms shall have the same meanings ascribed to them in the Binary Code License Agreement . These Supplemental Terms shall supersede any inconsistent or conflicting terms in the Binary Code License Agreement, or in any license contained within the Software.

A. Software Internal Use and Development License Grant. Subject to the terms and conditions of this Agreement and restrictions and exceptions set forth in the Software "README" file, including, but not limited to the Java Technology Restrictions of these Supplemental Terms, Sun grants you a non-exclusive, non-transferable, limited license without fees to reproduce internally and use internally the Software complete and unmodified for the purpose of designing, developing, and testing your Programs.

B. License to Distribute Software. Subject to the terms and conditions of this Agreement and restrictions and exceptions set forth in the Software README file, including, but not limited to the Java Technology Restrictions of these Supplemental Terms, Sun grants you a non-exclusive, non-transferable, limited license without fees to reproduce and distribute the Software, provided that (i) you distribute the Software complete and unmodified and only bundled as part of, and for the sole purpose of running, your Programs, (ii) the Programs add significant and primary functionality to the Software, (iii) you do not distribute additional software intended to replace any component(s) of the Software, (iv) you do not remove or alter any proprietary legends or notices contained in the Software, (v) you only distribute the Software subject to a license agreement that protects Sun's interests consistent with the terms contained in this Agreement, and (vi) you agree to defend and indemnify Sun and its licensors from and against any damages, costs, liabilities, settlement amounts and/or expenses (including attorneys' fees) incurred in connection with any claim, lawsuit or action by any third party that arises or results from the use or distribution of any and all Programs and/or Software.

C. License to Distribute Redistributables. Subject to the terms and conditions of this Agreement and restrictions and exceptions set forth in the Software README file, including but not limited to the Java Technology Restrictions of these Supplemental Terms, Sun grants you a non-exclusive, non-transferable, limited license without fees to reproduce and distribute those files specifically identified as redistributable in the Software "README" file ("Redistributables") provided that: (i) you distribute the Redistributables complete and unmodified, and only bundled as part of Programs, (ii) the Programs add significant and primary functionality to the Redistributables, (iii) you do not distribute additional software intended to supersede any component(s) of the Redistributables (unless otherwise specified in the applicable README file), (iv) you do not remove or alter any proprietary legends or notices contained in or on the Redistributables, (v) you only distribute the Redistributables pursuant to a license agreement that protects Sun's interests consistent with the terms contained in the Agreement, (vi) you agree to defend and indemnify Sun and its licensors from and against any damages, costs, liabilities, settlement amounts and/or expenses (including attorneys' fees) incurred in connection with any claim, lawsuit or action by any third party that arises or results from the use or distribution of any and all Programs and/or Software.

D. Java Technology Restrictions. You may not create, modify, or change the behavior of, or authorize your licensees to create, modify, or change the behavior of, classes, interfaces, or subpackages that are in any way identified as "java", "javax", "sun" or similar convention as specified by Sun in any naming convention designation.

E. Distribution by Publishers. This section pertains to your distribution of the Software with your printed book or magazine (as those terms are commonly used in the industry) relating to Java technology ("Publication"). Subject to and conditioned upon your compliance with the restrictions and obligations contained in the Agreement, in addition to the license granted in Paragraph 1 above, Sun hereby grants to you a non-exclusive, nontransferable limited right to reproduce complete and unmodified copies of the Software on electronic media (the "Media") for the sole purpose of inclusion and distribution with your Publication(s), subject to the following terms: (i) You may not distribute the Software on a stand-alone basis; it must be distributed with your Publication(s); (ii) You are responsible for downloading the Software from the applicable Sun web site; (iii) You must refer to the Software as Java™ 2 Platform Standard Edition Development Kit 5.0; (iv) The Software must be reproduced in its entirety and without any modification whatsoever (including, without limitation, the Binary Code License and Supplemental License Terms accompanying the Software and proprietary rights notices contained in the Software); (v) The Media label shall include the following information: Copyright 2004, Sun Microsystems, Inc. All rights reserved. Use is subject to license terms. Sun, Sun Microsystems, the Sun logo, Solaris, Java, the Java Coffee Cup logo, J2SE , and all trademarks and logos based on Java are trademarks or registered trademarks of Sun Microsystems, Inc. in the U.S. and other countries. This information must be placed on the Media label in such a manner as to only apply to the Sun Software; (vi) You must clearly identify the Software as Sun's product on the Media holder or Media label, and you may not state or imply that Sun is responsible for any third-party software contained on the Media; (vii) You may not include any third party software on the Media which is intended to be a replacement or substitute for the Software; (viii) You shall indemnify Sun for all damages arising from your failure to comply with the requirements of this Agreement. In addition, you shall defend, at your expense, any and all claims brought against Sun by third parties, and shall pay all damages awarded by a court of competent jurisdiction, or such settlement amount negotiated by you, arising out of or in connection with your use, reproduction or distribution of the Software and/or the Publication. Your obligation to provide indemnification under this section shall arise provided that Sun: (i) provides you prompt notice of the claim; (ii) gives you sole control of the defense and settlement of the claim; (iii) provides you, at your expense, with all available information, assistance and authority to defend; and (iv) has not compromised or settled such claim without your prior written consent; and (ix) You shall provide Sun with a written notice for each Publication; such notice shall include the following information: (1) title of Publication, (2) author(s), (3) date of Publication, and (4) ISBN or ISSN numbers. Such notice shall be sent to Sun Microsystems, Inc., 4150 Network Circle, M/S USCA12-110, Santa Clara, California 95054, U.S.A , Attention: Contracts Administration.

F. Source Code. Software may contain source code that, unless expressly licensed for other purposes, is provided solely for reference purposes pursuant to the terms of this Agreement. Source code may not be redistributed unless expressly provided for in this Agreement.

G. Third Party Code. Additional copyright notices and license terms applicable to portions of the Software are set forth in the THIRDPARTYLICENSEREADME.txt file. In addition to any terms and conditions of any third party opensource/freeware license identified in the THIRDPARTYLICENSEREADME.txt file, the disclaimer of warranty and limitation of liability provisions in paragraphs 5 and 6 of the Binary Code License Agreement shall apply to all Software in this distribution.

For inquiries please contact: Sun Microsystems, Inc., 4150 Network Circle, Santa Clara, California 95054, U.S.A.

(LFI#141623/Form ID#011801)

Sun Microsystems, Inc. Binary Code License Agreement

for the JAVA SE DEVELOPMENT KIT (JDK), VERSION 6

SUN MICROSYSTEMS, INC. ("SUN") IS WILLING TO LICENSE THE SOFTWARE IDENTIFIED BELOW TO YOU ONLY UPON THE CONDITION THAT YOU ACCEPT ALL OF THE TERMS CONTAINED IN THIS BINARY CODE LICENSE AGREEMENT AND SUPPLEMENTAL LICENSE TERMS (COLLECTIVELY "AGREEMENT"). PLEASE READ THE AGREEMENT CAREFULLY. BY DOWNLOADING OR INSTALLING THIS SOFTWARE, YOU ACCEPT THE TERMS OF THE AGREEMENT. INDICATE ACCEPTANCE BY SELECTING THE "ACCEPT" BUTTON AT THE BOTTOM OF THE AGREEMENT. IF YOU ARE NOT WILLING TO BE BOUND BY ALL THE TERMS, SELECT THE "DECLINE" BUTTON AT THE BOTTOM OF THE AGREEMENT AND THE DOWNLOAD OR INSTALL PROCESS WILL NOT CONTINUE.

1. DEFINITIONS. "Software" means the identified above in binary form, any other machine readable materials (including, but not limited to, libraries, source files, header files, and data files), any updates or error corrections provided by Sun, and any user manuals, programming guides and other documentation provided to you by Sun under this Agreement. "Programs" mean Java applets and applications intended to run on the Java Platform, Standard Edition (Java SE) on Java-enabled general purpose desktop computers and servers.

2. LICENSE TO USE. Subject to the terms and conditions of this Agreement, including, but not limited to the Java Technology Restrictions of the Supplemental License Terms, Sun grants you a non-exclusive, non-transferable, limited license without license fees to reproduce and use internally Software complete and unmodified for the sole purpose of running Programs. Additional licenses for developers and/or publishers are granted in the Supplemental License Terms.

3. RESTRICTIONS. Software is confidential and copyrighted. Title to Software and all associated intellectual property rights is retained by Sun and/or its licensors. Unless enforcement is prohibited by applicable law, you may not modify, decompile, or reverse engineer Software. You acknowledge that Licensed Software is not designed or intended for use in the design, construction, operation or maintenance of any nuclear facility. Sun Microsystems, Inc. disclaims any express or implied warranty of fitness for such uses. No right, title or interest in or to any trademark, service mark, logo or trade name of Sun or its licensors is granted under this Agreement. Additional restrictions for developers and/or publishers licenses are set forth in the Supplemental License Terms.

4. LIMITED WARRANTY. Sun warrants to you that for a period of ninety (90) days from the date of purchase, as evidenced by a copy of the receipt, the media on which Software is furnished (if any) will be free of defects in materials and workmanship under normal use. Except for the foregoing, Software is provided "AS IS". Your exclusive remedy and Sun's entire liability under this limited warranty will be at Sun's option to replace Software media or refund the fee paid for Software. Any implied warranties on the Software are limited to 90 days. Some states do not allow limitations on duration of an implied warranty, so the above may not apply to you. This limited warranty gives you specific legal rights. You may have others, which vary from state to state.

5. DISCLAIMER OF WARRANTY. UNLESS SPECIFIED IN THIS AGREEMENT, ALL EXPRESS OR IMPLIED CONDITIONS, REPRESENTATIONS AND WARRANTIES, INCLUDING ANY IMPLIED WARRANTY OF MERCHANTABILITY, FITNESS FOR A PARTICULAR PURPOSE OR NON-INFRINGEMENT ARE DISCLAIMED, EXCEPT TO THE EXTENT THAT THESE DISCLAIMERS ARE HELD TO BE LEGALLY INVALID.

6. LIMITATION OF LIABILITY. TO THE EXTENT NOT PROHIBITED BY LAW, IN NO EVENT WILL SUN OR ITS LICENSORS BE LIABLE FOR ANY LOST REVENUE, PROFIT OR DATA, OR FOR SPECIAL, INDIRECT, CONSEQUENTIAL, INCIDENTAL OR PUNITIVE DAMAGES, HOWEVER CAUSED REGARDLESS OF THE THEORY OF LIABILITY, ARISING OUT OF OR RELATED TO THE USE OF OR INABILITY TO USE SOFTWARE, EVEN IF SUN HAS BEEN ADVISED OF THE POSSIBILITY OF SUCH DAMAGES. In no event will Sun's liability to you, whether in contract, tort (including negligence), or otherwise, exceed the amount paid by you for Software under this Agreement. The foregoing limitations will apply even if the above stated warranty fails of its essential purpose. Some states do not allow the exclusion of incidental or consequential damages, so some of the terms above may not be applicable to you.

7. TERMINATION. This Agreement is effective until terminated. You may terminate this Agreement at any time by destroying all copies of Software. This Agreement will terminate immediately without notice from Sun if you fail to comply with any provision of this Agreement. Either party may terminate this Agreement immediately should any Software become, or in either party's opinion be likely to become, the subject of a claim of infringement of any intellectual property right. Upon Termination, you must destroy all copies of Software.

8. EXPORT REGULATIONS. All Software and technical data delivered under this Agreement are subject to US export control laws and may be subject to export or import regulations in other countries. You agree to comply strictly with all such laws and regulations and acknowledge that you have the responsibility to obtain such licenses to export, re-export, or import as may be required after delivery to you.

9. TRADEMARKS AND LOGOS. You acknowledge and agree as between you and Sun that Sun owns the SUN, SOLARIS, JAVA, JINI, FORTE, and iPLANET trademarks and all SUN, SOLARIS, JAVA, JINI, FORTE, and iPLANET-related trademarks, service marks, logos and other brand designations ("Sun Marks"), and you agree to comply with the Sun Trademark and Logo Usage Requirements currently located at http://www.sun.com/policies/trademarks. Any use you make of the Sun Marks inures to Sun's benefit.

10. U.S. GOVERNMENT RESTRICTED RIGHTS. If Software is being acquired by or on behalf of the U.S. Government or by a U.S. Government prime contractor or subcontractor (at any tier), then the Government's rights in Software and accompanying documentation will be only as set forth in this Agreement; this is in accordance with 48 CFR 227.7201 through 227.7202-4 (for Department of Defense (DOD) acquisitions) and with 48 CFR 2.101 and 12.212 (for non-DOD acquisitions).

11. GOVERNING LAW. Any action related to this Agreement will be governed by California law and controlling U.S. federal law. No choice of law rules of any jurisdiction will apply.

12. SEVERABILITY. If any provision of this Agreement is held to be unenforceable, this Agreement will remain in effect with the provision omitted, unless omission would frustrate the intent of the parties, in which case this Agreement will immediately terminate.

13. INTEGRATION. This Agreement is the entire agreement between you and Sun relating to its subject matter. It supersedes all prior or contemporaneous oral or written communications, proposals, representations and warranties and prevails over any conflicting or additional terms of any quote, order, acknowledgment, or other communication between the parties relating to its subject matter during the term of this Agreement. No modification of this Agreement will be binding, unless in writing and signed by an authorized representative of each party.

SUPPLEMENTAL LICENSE TERMS

These Supplemental License Terms add to or modify the terms of the Binary Code License Agreement. Capitalized terms not defined in these Supplemental Terms shall have the same meanings ascribed to them in the Binary Code License Agreement . These Supplemental Terms shall supersede any inconsistent or conflicting terms in the Binary Code License Agreement, or in any license contained within the Software.

A. Software Internal Use and Development License Grant. Subject to the terms and conditions of this Agreement and restrictions and exceptions set forth in the Software "README" file incorporated herein by reference, including, but not limited to the Java Technology Restrictions of these Supplemental Terms, Sun grants you a non-exclusive, non-transferable, limited license without fees to reproduce internally and use internally the Software complete and unmodified for the purpose of designing, developing, and testing your Programs.

B. License to Distribute Software. Subject to the terms and conditions of this Agreement and restrictions and exceptions set forth in the Software README file, including, but not limited to the Java Technology Restrictions of these Supplemental Terms, Sun grants you a non-exclusive, non-transferable, limited license without fees to reproduce and distribute the Software, provided that (i) you distribute the Software complete and unmodified and only bundled as part of, and for the sole purpose of running, your Programs, (ii) the Programs add significant and primary functionality to the Software, (iii) you do not distribute additional software intended to replace any component(s) of the Software, (iv) you do not remove or alter any proprietary legends or notices contained in the Software, (v) you only distribute the Software subject to a license agreement that protects Sun's interests consistent with the terms contained in this Agreement, and (vi) you agree to defend and indemnify Sun and its licensors from and against any damages, costs, liabilities, settlement amounts and/or expenses (including attorneys' fees) incurred in connection with any claim, lawsuit or action by any third party that arises or results from the use or distribution of any and all Programs and/or Software.

C. License to Distribute Redistributables. Subject to the terms and conditions of this Agreement and restrictions and exceptions set forth in the Software README file, including but not limited to the Java Technology Restrictions of these Supplemental Terms, Sun grants you a non-exclusive, non-transferable, limited license without fees to reproduce and distribute those files specifically identified as redistributable in the Software "README" file ("Redistributables") provided that: (i) you distribute the Redistributables complete and unmodified, and only bundled as part of Programs, (ii) the Programs add significant and primary functionality to the Redistributables, (iii) you do not distribute additional software intended to supersede any component(s) of the Redistributables (unless otherwise specified in the applicable README file), (iv) you do not remove or alter any proprietary legends or notices contained in or on the Redistributables, (v) you only distribute the Redistributables pursuant to a license agreement that protects Sun's interests consistent with the terms contained in the Agreement, (vi) you agree to defend and indemnify Sun and its licensors from and against any damages, costs, liabilities, settlement amounts and/or expenses (including attorneys' fees) incurred in connection with any claim, lawsuit or action by any third party that arises or results from the use or distribution of any and all Programs and/or Software.

D. Java Technology Restrictions. You may not create, modify, or change the behavior of, or authorize your licensees to create, modify, or change the behavior of, classes, interfaces, or subpackages that are in any way identified as "java", "javax", "sun" or similar convention as specified by Sun in any naming convention designation.

E. Distribution by Publishers. This section pertains to your distribution of the Software with your printed boo or magazine (as those terms are commonly used in the industry) relating to Java technology ("Publication"). Subject to and conditioned upon your compliance with the restrictions and obligations contained in the

Agreement, in addition to the license granted in Paragraph 1 above, Sun hereby grants to you a non-exclusive, nontransferable limited right to reproduce complete and unmodified copies of the Software on electronic media (the "Media") for the sole purpose of inclusion and distribution with your Publication(s), subject to the following terms: (i) You may not distribute the Software on a stand-alone basis; it must be distributed with your Publication(s); (ii) You are responsible for downloading the Software from the applicable Sun web site; (iii) You must refer to the Software as JavaTM SE Development Kit 6; (iv) The Software must be reproduced in its entirety and without any modification whatsoever (including, without limitation, the Binary Code License and Supplemental License Terms accompanying the Software and proprietary rights notices contained in the Software); (v) The Media label shall include the following information: Copyright 2006, Sun Microsystems, Inc. All rights reserved. Use is subject to license terms. Sun, Sun Microsystems, the Sun logo, Solaris, Java, the Java Coffee Cup logo, J2SE, and all trademarks and logos based on Java are trademarks or registered trademarks of Sun Microsystems, Inc. in the U.S. and other countries. This information must be placed on the Media label in such a manner as to only apply to the Sun Software; (vi) You must clearly identify the Software as Sun's product on the Media holder or Media label, and you may not state or imply that Sun is responsible for any third-party software contained on the Media; (vii) You may not include any third party software on the Media which is intended to be a replacement or substitute for the Software; (viii) You shall indemnify Sun for all damages arising from your failure to comply with the requirements of this Agreement. In addition, you shall defend, at your expense, any and all claims brought against Sun by third parties, and shall pay all damages awarded by a court of competent jurisdiction, or such settlement amount negotiated by you, arising out of or in connection with your use, reproduction or distribution of the Software and/or the Publication. Your obligation to provide indemnification under this section shall arise provided that Sun: (a) provides you prompt notice of the claim; (b) gives you sole control of the defense and settlement of the claim; (c) provides you, at your expense, with all available information, assistance and authority to defend; and (d) has not compromised or settled such claim without your prior written consent; and (ix) You shall provide Sun with a written notice for each Publication; such notice shall include the following information: (1) title of Publication, (2) author(s), (3) date of Publication, and (4) ISBN or ISSN numbers. Such notice shall be sent to Sun Microsystems, Inc., 4150 Network Circle, M/S USCA12-110, Santa Clara, California 95054, U.S.A , Attention: Contracts Administration.

F. Source Code. Software may contain source code that, unless expressly licensed for other purposes, is provided solely for reference purposes pursuant to the terms of this Agreement. Source code may not be redistributed unless expressly provided for in this Agreement.

G. Third Party Code. Additional copyright notices and license terms applicable to portions of the Software are set forth in the THIRDPARTYLICENSEREADME.txt file. In addition to any terms and conditions of any third party opensource/freeware license identified in the THIRDPARTYLICENSEREADME.txt file, the disclaimer of arranty and limitation of liability provisions in paragraphs 5 and 6 of the Binary Code License Agreement ll apply to all Software in this distribution.

rmination for Infringement. Either party may terminate this Agreement immediately should any Software or in either party's opinion be likely to become, the subject of a claim of infringement of any al property right.

n and Auto-Update. The Software's installation and auto-update processes transmit a limited a to Sun (or its service provider) about those specific processes to help Sun understand and Sun does not associate the data with personally identifiable information. You can find more t the data Sun collects at http://java.com/data/.

ontact: Sun Microsystems, Inc., 4150 Network Circle, Santa Clara, California 95054, U.S.A.